NORTH COUNTRY

NORTH COUNTRY

THE MAKING OF MINNESOTA

MARY LETHERT WINGERD

ILLUSTRATIONS COMPILED AND ANNOTATED BY
KIRSTEN DELEGARD

PUBLISHED IN COOPERATION WITH

THE OFFICE OF THE PRESIDENT,
UNIVERSITY OF MINNESOTA

AND

ST. CLOUD STATE UNIVERSITY

University of Minnesota Press
Minneapolis
London

Original maps were created by Philip Schwartzberg,
Meridian Mapping, Minneapolis

Published by the University of Minnesota Press
111 Third Avenue South, Suite 290
Minneapolis, MN 55401-2520
http://www.upress.umn.edu

Library of Congress Cataloging-in-Publication Data
Wingerd, Mary Lethert.
North country : the making of Minnesota / Mary Lethert Wingerd ;
illustrations compiled and annotated by Kirsten Delegard.
p.   cm.
Includes bibliographical references and index.
ISBN 978-0-8166-4868-9 (hardcover : alk. paper)
1. Minnesota—History—To 1858. 2. Frontier and pioneer life—Minnesota.
3. Borderlands—Minnesota—History. I. Delegard, Kirsten. II. Title.
F606.W56 2010
977.6'01—dc22
2009054169

Printed in Canada on acid-free paper

21   20   19   18   17   10   9   8   7   6   5   4

THE MINNESOTA HISTORY PROJECT

Ann M. Pflaum
Project Director

Hyman Berman
Senior Advisor

Kirsten Delegard
Researcher

Douglas Armato
Director, University of Minnesota Press

Todd Orjala
Senior Acquisitions Editor,
University of Minnesota Press

————◆————

The University of Minnesota Press gratefully acknowledges financial assistance
for the publication of this book from the following donors:

Russell M. and Elizabeth M. Bennett

Conley Brooks Sr. and Marney Brooks

The Edward and Markell C. Brooks Family
Fund of the Minneapolis Foundation

Curtis L. Carlson Family Foundation
(Dr. Glen D. Nelson and Marilyn Carlson
Nelson; Edwin C. "Skip" and Barbara Gage)

Cleveland Cliffs Foundation

Edward Dayton Family Fund
(Edward N. and Sherry Ann Dayton)

John W. and Arlene Dayton

Mary Lee Dayton

Robert J. and Joan Dayton

Hubbard Broadcasting Foundation
(Stanley S. and Karen Hubbard)

A. J. Huss Foundation
(John and Ruth Huss)

Lucy Rosenberry Jones Charitable Trust
(Lucy Jones)

Longview Foundation (Ella P. Crosby)

W. Duncan and Nivin S. MacMillan

The Ted and Dr. Roberta Mann Foundation
(Donald E. Benson and Roberta Mann
Benson)

Marbrook Foundation
(Conley Brooks Jr., Executive Director)

Meadowood Foundation
(Douglas J. and Wendy Dayton)

Oakleaf Foundation (Julia W. Dayton)

Stephen R. and Ann M. Pflaum

The Southways Foundation
(George S. and Sally Pillsbury)

Philip and Joanne W. Von Blon

WEM Foundation
(Whitney and Betty MacMillan)

D. M. (Michael) and Penny Winton

Wood-Rill Foundation
(Bruce B. and Ruth Stricker Dayton)

C. Angus and Margaret V. B. Wurtele

For James Brewer Stewart
teacher, mentor, friend

Contents

Prologue

———•❧•———

TRUE NORTH

From the Land of Sky Blue Waters
From the land of pines, lofty balsams . . .
Hᴀᴍᴍ's Bᴇᴇʀ ᴊɪɴɢʟᴇ

When I was ten years old, my grandmother took me on an unforgettable vaca-
tion. In St. Paul we boarded the Empire Builder, then the jewel of the Great
Northern Railway, sped across the plains of North Dakota, and disembarked
two days later in what seemed a magically different world. We stepped from
the train right onto the rolling lawns of Montana's Glacier Park Lodge, an imposing log edifice with the majesty of the Rocky Mountains as its backdrop.

The memory is as vivid today as if I were there yesterday. We were met by a
party of stately Blackfoot Indians, dressed in full ceremonial garb, and I was
certain that for the first time I had entered Indian country. Of course, my introduction to "real Indians" was a romanticized version crafted for the tourist trade. Nonetheless, despite my childishly imperfect understanding, I knew
that Indians were central to the story of this place. Its history seemed a world
away from what I knew of my home state of Minnesota.

Minnesota certainly had no shortage of Indian imagery. Countless businesses prominently featured Indian figures in their logos and advertising campaigns, from the lissome maiden who graced Land O'Lakes butter boxes to
the cartoon Indian princess Minnegasco Minnie, who sported a gas flame for
a head feather. Every schoolchild of my generation knew by heart the Hamm's
Beer jingle, featuring woodland creatures frolicking to the beat of a tom-tom:
"From the Land of Sky Blue Wa-a-ters, from the land of pines, lofty balsams,
comes the beer refreshing, Hamm's, the beer refreshing. Ha-a-a-mm's."

To be sure, another, more dignified depiction of Indians held sway as well,
but one no more grounded in history than the Hamm's bear or Minnegasco

Minnie. In statuary and pageant, communities throughout the state paid homage to the mythical "noble savage," who sprang from the imaginations of eighteenth- and nineteenth-century writers such as James Fenimore Cooper and Henry Wadsworth Longfellow. In the popular imagination, if the likes of Hiawatha or Minnehaha had ever roamed the woods and prairies of Minnesota, it was long before the real stuff of state history began. The state seal codified this harmonious passing of the torch in its depiction of an Indian peacefully riding into the setting sun, observed by an industrious farmer leaning into his plow.

All this Indian imagery notwithstanding, for most Minnesotans, adults as well as children, Native people were no more a part of the making of Minnesota than dancing bears and squirrels hawking beer or the apocryphal folktales of Paul Bunyan and Babe the Blue Ox. We might hold powwows at summer camps like Lakamaga, Ojiketa, or Widjiwagan, cheer on local teams called the Warriors or the Braves with their Indian mascots, fish on Lakes Winnibigoshish or Minnetonka, or even live in towns named Mankato, Shakopee, or Wabasha. Yet the actual shared history of Indians, Europeans, and Americans that shaped this region for more than two hundred years was largely absent from popular consciousness, despite the fact that the state map was littered with Indian names and in the mid-twentieth century more than twelve thousand people of Dakota and Ojibwe ancestry called Minnesota home.

I traveled to Glacier National Park in the summer of 1958, the same year Minnesota celebrated its state centennial. The landmark event was constantly in the news. Programs about state history flooded classrooms, and every summer weekend featured at least one community pageant honoring its place in Minnesota's saga of progress. As a special tribute to the generation of women who braved the frontier, a thirty-six-foot-tall gold-painted statue representing the "pioneer mother," schoolbook tucked under her arm, was unveiled at the state fair in August.[1] The crown jewel of the yearlong celebration was an official Centennial Train that traveled to every corner of the state, a "rolling museum of Minnesota's past, present, and future." Tellingly, the thirty-page booklet that accompanied the museum on wheels made only passing mention of supposedly long gone Native people, "quelled" by courageous settlers who faced down unspecified "frontier savagery."[2] As told in the centennial narrative, the history of Mini Sota Makoce (literally, the place where the Dakota dwell) centered squarely on those sturdy pioneers and immigrants who hewed prosperous farms and cities from an apparently unpeopled wilderness. Despite the constant centennial ballyhoo, I had learned next to nothing about the centrality of Native people in the history of my home state.

The themes of progress that the pageantry celebrated and advertisers promoted could not help but make us proud of our North Star State, with its ten thousand lakes, progressive politics, renowned educational system, innovative businesses, unsullied natural resources, and enviable quality of life. All of this was true—but it was not the entire story. The heritage we honored that centennial year illuminated for the world a distinct regional identity that set us apart from other states and, at the same time, situated Minnesota in the larger American story. But heritage does not suffice as history. As scholar David Lowenthal points out, heritage is crafted to affirm what we wish to be true about ourselves, whereas history strives (albeit imperfectly) to discover the truth about the past.[3] History, of course, is far more complex and problematic than heritage. History must come to terms with injustice and tragedy as well as achievement, asking hard questions that heritage, steeped in nostalgia, tends to obscure. None of this served the objectives of the centennial planners.

Thus, in 1958 advocates of history rather than heritage found no voice in the public forum. In retrospect, this is not surprising. The cold war was at its height and America believed it was in a life-and-death struggle with Communism for the hearts and minds of people throughout the world. Any slight criticism of the American way was regarded as tantamount to disloyalty. To include the history of Native people in the state narrative would raise troubling and unresolved questions about race and inequality in mid-twentieth-century America. It would also significantly complicate the tale of unbroken achievement that was the centennial celebration's theme.

Indians had actually been written out of the state saga decades earlier. The first generation of treaty makers, land speculators, politicians, and boosters had consciously rewritten the story of their acquisition of Minnesota, selectively crafting a chronicle of development that supported a dual agenda: to justify the new order they imposed on the land and the people who had called it home and to reassure potential residents that Minnesota was a safe and civilized place to put down roots and prosper. Subsequent generations thus came to believe as "history" this impoverished version that did more to obscure than reveal events of the past. The centennial script only carried forward an already embedded narrative, grounded in the moral certainty of manifest destiny, the quintessential American story.

Admittedly, popular history gave a nod to the fur trade and the era of European adventurers, but it was colored by an aura of legend—peopled by jaunty voyageurs, courageous explorers, regal Indian chiefs, and lovelorn Indian braves and princesses—romantic figures who had disappeared long before the "real" history of American progress began. To avoid confronting the trail of coerced treaties and broken promises that purchased the timberlands and farmsteads so central to Minnesota's subsequent prosperity, the state saga expunged much of the richness of the region's past as well. Few centennial celebrants had any idea that the state they held so dear (to paraphrase the official anthem) was built on the ruins of an earlier society, a multivocal cultural and economic meeting ground created by the fur trade that thrived in the north country long before the boundaries of a state called Minnesota were drawn onto the continental map.

Popular recollection of Minnesota's political history was equally truncated, victim of a remembered past that stretched no farther back than statehood. Statehood itself, though the arbitrary starting point, was a mere prologue to

Minnesota's shining moment of national importance: the valorous role the young state played in the Civil War just three years after admission to the Union. Ironically, popular absorption in every minute detail of the fighting on southern battlefields was equaled only by the lack of interest in the concurrent conflict fought on its home ground—the 1862 U.S.–Dakota War, what might truly be termed Minnesota's civil war—that resulted in the exile of the Dakota people from the state. As for the two hundred years of imperial wars and sovereign treaties that culminated in that tragic event, only a cohort of academics, working away in dusty archives, granted them attention in the story of Minnesota's past.

Much has changed in the fifty years since that one-dimensional centennial frenzy of self-congratulation. As Americans, we are no longer unwilling to acknowledge injustices or mistakes of the past as we strive toward that "more perfect Union" of our democratic ideal. Two generations of exceptional scholarship have taken us far down that road to a more nuanced understanding of our complicated, and not always pretty, history. But state history, let alone the national story, has yet to receive a comprehensive reconsideration that takes this new scholarship fully into account. This volume is a first attempt to craft such an integrated narrative of Minnesota's origins. Bringing together the work of numerous scholars, it proposes a new history to supplant old and incomplete presumptions.

The history of Native people is long and complex, stretching beyond and independent of their encounter with Europeans. A fully articulated narrative of that past is beyond the scope of this work, as are the origins of the Europeans who made their way to this region. My focus is the meeting and melding of Indian and European cultures that began haltingly to take shape in the Upper Mississippi and Lake Superior regions at the midpoint of the seventeenth century. I term this country a borderland, not in the sense of geographical or national borders, since such distinctions were largely meaningless to those who lived in the region for much of the era under consideration, but rather to describe a place where disparate peoples met, interdependence fostered cooperation and cultural exchange, and social and racial distinctions blurred among Dakotas, Ojibwes, and their European neighbors.

A word about Indian names is necessary here. Europeans, who left the written record of this era, called the Dakota people "Sioux," derived from the Ottawa word *Nadouessioux,* meaning "snake" or "enemy"—clearly not what the people called themselves. As French and British explorers struggled to sort out the various Indian tribes, they then applied that term freely to all who shared the common "Siouan" language group. But the Siouan-speaking people of the Upper Mississippi called themselves "Dakotah," as did most of those who came to live in the region. Also, Europeans generally called the Ojibwe people

"Chippewa," a mangled version of how the name "Ojibwe" sounded to ears unfamiliar with the language. Today the Ojibwes are also known as Anishinaabeg, which translates as "the people." In this book I use the names Ojibwe and Dakota, as the people generally called themselves at the time.

The problem of names is further complicated with people of mixed Indian and Euro-American ancestry. Throughout the Great Lakes region and Canada, from the time of first contact, intermarriage was common between Indian women and French traders and voyageurs. Over generations these mixed-ancestry people, known as Métis, developed an identifiable culture that was different from either European or Indian ways, though it incorporated elements of both. Other people of mixed ancestry, children of British, American, or French fathers and Indian mothers, moved with ease between their Indian and white kin, sometimes living as whites, other times as Indians. At home in both cultures, they played an essential role in the borderland as cultural brokers and interpreters. Historians most commonly identify these people as "mixed blood." The distinction between Métis and mixed blood is a fine one, based on culture rather than bloodline, and is imprecise at best, though people of European–Dakota ancestry would almost always be described as mixed blood rather than Métis.

The world of the borderland that unfolds in these pages was complex indeed and, as is evident, presents descriptive challenges for historians since it defied reified Euro-American taxonomies of race and status. As might be imagined, it was nearly incomprehensible to newcomers to the region. Confounded by this racial and cultural indeterminism, they often declared that whites and Indians seemed equally uncivilized and alien. Nonetheless, if they intended to stay, they soon accommodated themselves to the customs and practices of the country.

Such fluid borderland societies flourished for brief periods all across North America as Native and European people first encountered one another. But generally, settlement and the quest for land soon ended the era of intercultural cooperation. What makes the Minnesota region unique is that, because of its geographical inaccessibility, this multicultural meeting ground endured for two centuries, far longer than in any other part of the country. It was a profoundly local world, where national loyalties had little relevance. At the same time, from the first day that Europeans stepped on the shore of Lake Superior or paddled up the Mississippi River, international contests for empire reverberated in unseen ways on the lives of those who came to call the region home. Though claims of European or American sovereignty carried no real authority until at least the 1830s, existing only as imaginary lines on maps drawn by distant cartographers, from the days of first encounter, politics and capitalism played an invisible but powerful role in shaping the region's destiny.

The fur trade was the economic raison d'être that undergirded this society, bringing together Dakota, French, Ojibwe, British, American, and a scattering of other tribes and nationalities in what began as a mutually beneficial partnership. The cultural linchpin that held such disparate people together, even once the economic foundation of the trade began to founder, was kinship, especially marriage between European men and Indian women. By 1830 six generations of intermarriage had produced an intricate web of relationships, with people of mixed ancestry acting as an essential bridge between their white and Indian kin. Everyone adopted at least some cultural elements of what had become a European/Indian amalgam.

Indians soon came to rely on woolen blankets, iron kettles, and other manufactured goods that eased the rigors of their daily life; transplants from Europe or the East quickly discarded hard-soled shoes for much superior leather moccasins, donned deerskin leggings, and, of necessity, depended on wild rice and pemmican as staples of their diet. Everyone traveled by dogsled in winter and by canoe the rest of the year, the only practical means of transportation in a country ribboned with waterways and devoid of roads. Most important, both traders and Indians adhered to a code of reciprocity that demanded they assist one another when in need, acknowledging their mutual dependence in the harsh and unforgiving landscape of fur trade country.

Deep in the center of the continent, far from land speculators or settlement pressure, this intercultural fur trade society flourished, shifting only gradually, over generations, from reciprocity to exploitation. By the nineteenth century, events that seemed a universe away from the Upper Mississippi borderland had begun to impinge on the quality of social relations there. The economic underpinnings of the trade, captive to the vacillations of international capital and markets, were in serious decline, and hard-pressed traders increasingly discarded long-respected customs of generosity with Indian hunters for more exploitive practices. Still, old obligations of kinship, though degraded, carried some influence until the 1850s, when swarms of speculators and settlers finally descended on the region. In no time, land and timber replaced pelts as the region's most desirable resources. These newcomers had no need or desire to forge relationships with Native people, whose hold on the land merely impeded their aims. Armed with beliefs of racial superiority as well as axes and ploughs, and backed by the might of the U.S. government, they soon clamored for Indian removal.

Many Indians, confronted by a seemingly unstoppable deluge of settlers, attempted to adapt to and accommodate the new world order that had overtaken them while still maintaining their core traditional values. Some of the old fur trade fraternity resisted such a wholesale remaking of their world and stubbornly adhered to old customs of mutual obligation, but it was a losing battle. The most prominent agents of the trade—men like Henry Sibley and Henry Rice—joined the march of "progress," used their influence to advance a series of land cessions, and enriched themselves and their friends in the process. In just twelve short years, the onslaught of settlers and speculators had transformed the region; the rich, multicultural world of the borderland was eradicated; and history, as written by the winners, began.

The U.S.–Dakota War of 1862 and its aftermath mark the forceful closure of this era of cultural mingling, a sharp divide between the familiar Minnesota story of settlement and the neglected history of the multicultural borderland that preceded it. The final chapters of this transformation are unsettling, even tragic, and painful to acknowledge. But it is tragic as well to have forgotten such a vibrant part of our past and the lessons of coexistence it reveals. The social relations that thrived and then were eventually wiped out not only suggest roads not taken but also may help us reflect on new, more inclusive ways of thinking about America and the world, as well as Minnesota, in the future.

To conjure the canvas of this world of the north country, try first to imagine forests alive with game, the trees so dense that a man on horseback could find no way through; lakes and rivers, teeming with fish, the primary pathways of travel; and prairies replete with buffalo. In 1650 this was the domain of the Dakotas, the lords of the Upper Mississippi. Here the story begins.

Chapter 1

———•◦•———

THE FORTUNATE LAND

My father's grandfather said that before the earth was made there was water everywhere; no land was to be seen. The Great Power (Waka-taka) made the earth and then made man and woman. From them the Dakota were born. There was no white man on the earth. . . . The Great Power then made all those animals that have fur and swim in the water. These we were to eat. He then made the wild animals that live on the land, causing them to be fit for food. This was the beginning of everything.

    WILSON D. WALLIS, "Beliefs and Tales of the Canadian Dakota," *Journal of American Folklore*

Dakota Country

The Dakota Sioux were indeed a fortunate people.[1] For generations beyond remembering, they had made their home on the lands that would become Minnesota. The domain of the Dakota people and their Lakota cousins encompassed a territory that stretched from western Wisconsin to the Missouri River. Though Europeans would describe them as a tribe or nation, the Siouan people did not think of themselves in such nationalistic terms, nor were they subject to any kind of unified governance. Extended kinship was the organizing principle that bound them with ties of mutual obligation. Still, the very name *Dakota* translates as "allies," and when threatened they often joined forces in numbers that kept interlopers from infringing on their territory.[2]

    The confederation of Siouan people was made up of seven ancestral political units called council fires.[3] The western tribes—the Yanktons, Yanktonais, and Tetons, known as the Lakota Sioux—long held possession of the prairies of the Red River valley, where the buffalo was a primary source of sustenance. Over time, as the bison herds migrated westward, the Lakotas gradually followed, a movement that accelerated rapidly once they acquired horses and firearms in

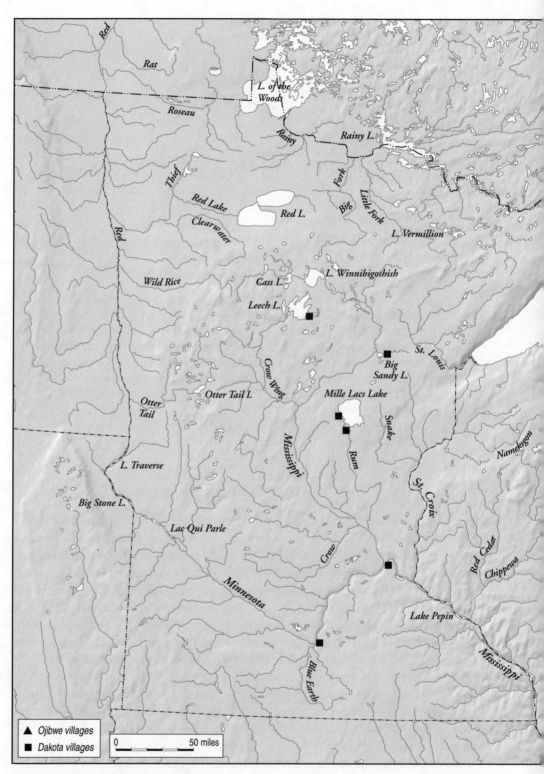

Dakota and Ojibwe villages, ca. 1700.

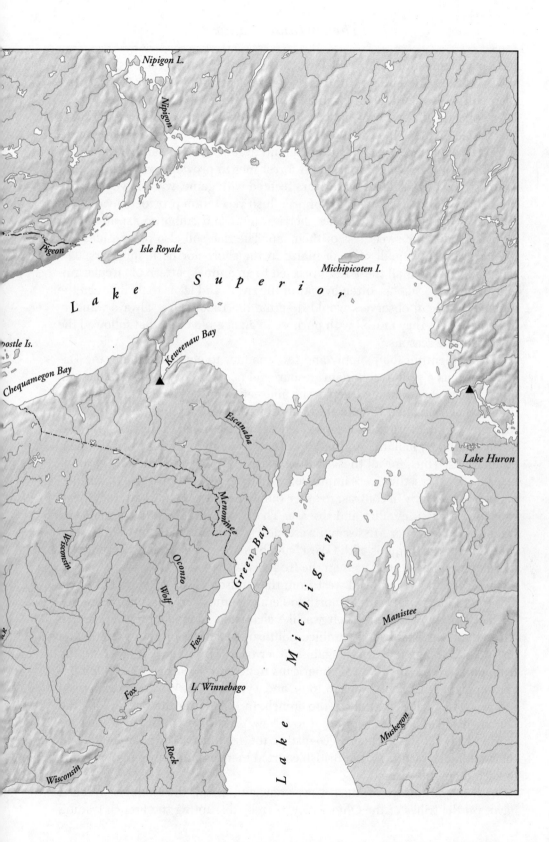

Nipigon L.

Nipigon

Pigeon

Isle Royale

Michipicoten I.

L a k e   S u p e r i o r

ostle Is.

Chequamegon Bay

Keweenaw Bay

Escanaba

Lake Huron

Menominee

Oconto

Wisconsin

Wolf

Fox

Green Bay

L a k e   M i c h i g a n

Manistee

Fox

L. Winnebago

Rock

Muskegon

Wisconsin

the early eighteenth century. Before 1750 some bands had established themselves as nomadic buffalo hunters as far west as the Missouri River, where their culture would flourish for more than a century.[4]

In contrast, the eastern Dakotas, whom Europeans frequently referred to as the Santee Sioux—Mdewakantons, Wahpekutes, Sissetons, and Wahpetons— were a woodland people and stayed behind in the bountiful land of the Upper Mississippi River, where prairie and forest met to provide a rich array of resources. The forests, lakes, and rivers teemed with game, waterfowl, and fish; herds of buffalo still roamed the prairie; lush vegetation provided a variety of foodstuffs that included wild rice, berries, nuts, and edible roots; and sugar maples yielded the sweetness of their sap. The rich soil also proved ideal for the cultivation of small plots of maize in the short northern summers. The seasonal harvest of all these resources led to an annual pattern of circular migration for the Dakotas, often by way of the rivers and lakes that ribboned the region. European observers would describe the Dakotas as "always wandering," but in fact they moved with purpose in an age-old cycle that followed the rhythm of the seasons.[5]

With a plentiful food supply and few enemies to challenge them, the Dakotas lived as a proud, confident, resourceful people. They also were blessed, unknowingly, by isolation. Deep in the midsection of the North American continent, they remained remote from sustained European contact until late in the seventeenth century. As a consequence, they were spared the worst ravages of the smallpox, malaria, and measles that decimated so many other Indian populations. Thus, for all these reasons, when Europeans eventually encountered the Dakotas, they were impressed with the "tall, vigorous, gifted, warlike" people, particularly in contrast to other Indian peoples already battered by European-instigated conflict and disease. The approximately 38,000 unbowed Dakotas of the Upper Mississippi were clearly a formidable force. The Jesuits called them "the Iroquois of the West," and by some estimations they were even more brave and courageous than the Iroquois.[6]

The Iroquois, who ranged west from the Hudson River valley to Lake Erie and from Lake Ontario in the north to Pennsylvania, were certainly fearsome, but not simply because of their warlike character. Alone among the eastern tribes they had established a unified political confederation that gave them a distinct advantage in warfare against other tribes. Even more important, the Iroquois were the first Native Americans to acquire firearms. The Dutch began supplying them with guns in 1639, and a year later 2,000 Iroquois massed to war against tribes friendly to the French. In 1664, after the British took the Dutch village of New Amsterdam (now New York City), they turned their attention fully on the French. Recognizing the Iroquois as invaluable allies in their colonial adventures, the British courted them assiduously and took pains to keep them fully armed.[7]

With the advantage of musket over bow and arrow, the Iroquois wreaked havoc on the tribes of the Ohio Valley, thereby disrupting the French trading network. While the embattled tribes never fully abandoned their home territories, a number of bands of Algonquian-speaking peoples—including Fox, Mascoutens, Ottawas, Ojibwes, Potawatomis, and Kickapoos, along with Hurons, Petuns, and many others—retreated to the west of Lake Michigan into present-day Illinois and Wisconsin and north to Lake Superior. There the refugees stopped, as though they had reached a wall. Though "neither fences nor maps delineated the boundaries [between Indian tribes], the lines were no less real for being immaterial."[8] Despite a shortage of game and constant friction among the various tribes, they seldom crossed into Dakota country, other than for occasional brief forays. When the French asked the Algonquins to describe the power of this unknown tribe, they explained simply, "They are men."[9]

Geographical isolation clearly had its advantages, but it also had troubling and potentially dangerous drawbacks. Without doubt, the Dakotas were well aware of Europeans and the goods they had to offer long before the Europeans "discovered" Minnesota. Networks of trade and communication among Native people crisscrossed the continent from one end to the other. What appeared as uncharted wilderness to European explorers was familiar territory to Native North Americans.[10] By 1600 European goods had been circulating among Native tribes for nearly three-quarters of a century. The Dakota tribes had heard rumors about the white strangers and their valuable gifts—iron pots, knives, blankets—and especially guns. A small number of these desirable trade goods had come into their hands through Ojibwe or Ottawa middlemen, who also possessed terrifying new weaponry.[11] In 1640 Jesuit missionaries established a mission at the juncture of Lakes Huron and Superior. Sault Ste. Marie, as the place came to be called, became a multitribal magnet as a trading center. Within easy reach of the Dakotas, Indian traders periodically made contact. But without direct European trading relationships, the Dakotas had no reliable way to ensure guns or powder for themselves. As the tribes who crowded western Wisconsin acquired increasing numbers of firearms, Dakota advantages in traditional warfare were seriously threatened.[12] Thus, when French adventurers eventually appeared in the Upper Mississippi River valley, the Dakotas had no reason to be either shocked or frightened. They had no illusion that these were superior beings sent by the Great Spirit, though they were deeply impressed by their wondrous technology. Eager to acquire all that the Europeans had to offer, the Dakotas were predisposed to greet them with courtesy, curiosity, and even relief, anticipating only good things to come.[13]

To the Grand Lac and the Great River

Rumors about the Dakotas and the riches of the continent's uncharted interior had long fueled the imagination of French explorers and traders. In 1535, under a royal commission from Francis I, Jacques Cartier ascended the St. Lawrence River to the site of what would become the city of Montreal, but concerted efforts at colonial expansion did not take off until 1603, when the

European craze for beaver hats convinced a group of French merchants that they could make a killing in the North American fur trade. After securing a monopoly from the crown on the anticipated trade, they capitalized the Company of New France and prepared to rake in the profits from their venture in furs. Samuel de Champlain, a military veteran and the royal geographer, was recruited to head the operation on the ground. He was directed to chart French explorations, ensure that the lands they "discovered" would be claimed for France, and, most important, establish a profitable trading relationship with Native people.[14]

Champlain devoted thirty-two years to this task in pursuit of dual goals: to fulfill the mandate of his merchant employers but also to discover a continental route to the Orient, which he knew would be well rewarded by the king. Over the course of his years in New France (now Canada), Champlain could count many accomplishments: He charted vast territories of the Northeast and four of the Great Lakes; founded the city of Quebec; created amicable trading relationships with the Huron and Ottawa; and established Montreal as a profitable French trading mart, though the flow of furs and goods was regularly interrupted by hostile Iroquois incursions armed by Dutch and English competitors. Yet Champlain never relinquished his dream of opening a route to the China trade and offered financial support and encouragement to explorers willing to penetrate the interior. With no idea that thousands of miles lay between Montreal and the Pacific, he was repeatedly inspired by Indian accounts of a "grand lac" far to the west and a great river that flowed to the sea. Surely this must be the route to China.[15]

Champlain did not live to test his theory, but five years after his death in 1635, the Jesuit missionaries Charles Raymbault and Isaac Jogues reached Sault Ste. Marie—in search of souls rather than trade routes—and saw for the first time the grandeur of Lake Superior. They also heard tales from local Ottawas and Ojibwes of the great tribe of Dakotas who dwelled on the great river just eighteen days from their mission. This long-awaited discovery did not, however, initiate further official expeditions into the interior. By the 1640s the Company of New France was in dire financial straits. Iroquois offensives had slowed the flow of pelts into Montreal to a trickle, European creditors were hounding the company for payment on trade goods advanced, and unlicensed traders, known as coureurs de bois, were siphoning off what Indian trade was left, bypassing Montreal for Dutch and English posts. The beleaguered company had neither the will nor the means to underwrite further expeditions to the west.[16]

The coureurs de bois were essential, if undocumented, players in shaping the history of Minnesota. Official histories credit Pierre Esprit Radisson and his brother-in-law, Medard Choart des Groseilliers, as the first whites to enter the future state of Minnesota sometime between 1659 and 1660. However, it is almost certain that illicit French traders had paved the way years earlier. They left no record of their travels or their numbers since, as historian William Folwell noted, "it was their interest to conceal rather than to advertise the regions in which they drove their trade." Their names are unrecorded, but some 200 illegal traders are estimated to have worked the Northwest before Radisson and Groseilliers set out on their historic travels.[17]

While the question of who made first contact in Minnesota country cannot be ascertained, the *quality* of contact is far more important to the course of history. Most of the independent traders were of peasant farmer origin. Some had paid their transport to North America as *engagés,* indentured servants who were bound for three years to labor in the French colony, often hauling goods and pelts through the woods and waters of the north. Others came from the ranks of highly skilled but ill-paid woodsmen, the voyageurs who provided the hard manual labor and navigational expertise that drove the brigades of canoes into the interior. They saw opportunity in Montreal's declining trade. If the Indians wouldn't come to Montreal, they reasoned, they would take the trade to the Indians. Experienced in forest survival, familiar with the terrain and waterways, and conversant in Indian customs and language, the voyageurs were well equipped for the task. Most married Indian wives and lived at least part of the year in the villages of their adopted native kin. While the explorers, whose names are inscribed in history books and who are memorialized in the names of towns, counties, and even a global hotel chain, came in search of celebrity and wealth, the coureurs de bois had more modest goals. They sought independence from overbearing employers and meant to make a permanent life in the lands of their Native American trading partners.[18]

As for the Dakotas, at last they had access to the exotic trade goods that would ease the burdens of their daily life—iron kettles, knives, woven cloth and blankets. (It is unlikely that the traders could offer guns since the price of musketry would have been prohibitive for these small-scale, unlicensed entrepreneurs.)[19] The mutual benefits that Indians and whites reaped from this relationship set the parameters of a cultural meeting ground. The offspring of French Canadian fathers and Indian mothers, a creole people known as Métis, would become the central cultural brokers in shaping Indian-white relationships in the Upper Great Lakes region for nearly a century.

Meanwhile, the drama of European exploration recommenced in the 1650s with another pair of illegal adventurers, the brothers-in-law Radisson and Groseilliers. Arriving in New France as boys, neither had financial resources (though both claimed minor aristocratic titles that may well have been self-invented). They quickly became fast friends and, like so many others in the French colony, hatched a scheme to make their fortune: an unlicensed expedition into Superior country. Groseilliers had already tried his hand at trading in 1654 and had returned to Quebec triumphantly with fifty canoes loaded with furs. Radisson was enthusiastic to join him on a second expedition. When they could not secure a trading license, in 1659 they set out in secret and made their way as far as present-day western Wisconsin. While wintering there with the Ottawas, the young buccaneers seized an opportunity to rise out of the ranks of common smugglers. From the Indians they learned that the legendary Dakotas were not many days distant and determined to be the first Europeans to make contact with them. Accompanied by twenty-three canoes of friendly Indians, who, according to Radisson, kept them company "in hopes to gett knives from us, which they love better than we serve God," they set out to find the Dakotas. Following the shore of Lake Superior, they entered Dakota country, making theirs the first recorded expedition by whites into the land that would become Minnesota.[20]

In one respect, Radisson and Groseilliers fit the profile of the coureurs de bois: both were deemed smugglers by colonial authorities. In other, more important ways, however, they were quite different. Unlike the plebian traders, these two were driven by dreams of glory and wealth and had no intention of making a life in the interior. Their eyes were set on Europe, not on Indian country, as Radisson's tale of their encounter with the Dakotas attests.[21]

The young Frenchmen were no doubt at first surprised by the "great ceremoneys" and feasting, the deference and "great favor and token of friendshippe," that the Dakotas showered upon them in return for the kettles, hatchets, knives, and other assorted trade goods the explorers presented to them. In their minds, "preoccupied with problems of personal honour and social place," they were treated like European nobility and happily accepted the overtures as a sign of their newly elevated status. In Radisson's words, "We are Cesars, being no body to contradict us." What they failed to understand was that, rather than bowing to innate European superiority, the Indians were engaged in an intricate ritual of diplomatic courtesy. The exchange of gifts was more than a simple trade. By Dakota custom, it signified the creation of bonds that would establish a long-term trading partnership and alliance. Most particularly, as the Indians urgently emphasized, they needed "a thunder," which the Frenchmen well understood meant guns and powder.[22]

Dakota diplomacy, however, did not yield the desired result. Despite hollow promises to return again soon, Radisson and Groseilliers had no intention of setting themselves up as simple traders. Instead, they considered their adventure in Dakota country merely a stepping-stone to European fame and riches. With the optimism of youth, they eagerly departed for Montreal, expecting to be lionized when they arrived, loaded down with illegally obtained furs and news of the new lands and people they had seen. To their dismay, instead their pelts were confiscated and they were taken into custody for illicit trading.[23]

Still, the brothers-in-law managed to turn the trip to profit. Once he extricated himself from the colonial authorities, Radisson quickly penned an account of their expeditions (taking all the credit for himself as well as shamelessly embellishing and inventing facts, including an imaginary trip to Hudson's Bay). Then the pair took their tale to England, where they found a more receptive audience. Wealthy merchants, aristocrats, and even the king feted the explorers and eagerly devoured their account of untold riches in furs awaiting in the north. The prospect of unparalleled profit fired the imagination of English investors and led to the founding of the Hudson's Bay Company in 1670. Thus, for Radisson and Groseilliers their exploits in North America were instrumental to achieving a goal that was firmly fixed in Europe. The route to celebrity and success came not from trading endeavors themselves but from the way that information, stories, and self-promotion could be used to win them accolades in European capitals.[24]

The story of Indian-white encounter in Minnesota country is shaped by two social narratives. The more familiar, of course, is that represented by Radisson and Groseilliers, a chronicle constructed for public consumption by and for Europeans. In this first narrative, Native people appeared as exotic objects of curiosity, savages to be civilized by European contact. The other story takes place on what Richard White calls "the Middle Ground," a borderland of cultural exchange rather than conquest.[25] Its drama is the stuff of daily life and the actors' names are most often lost or ignored. Their version of Minnesota history was written not on paper but in the acting out of their lives on the land they shared. They sometimes fought or cheated one another; often shared meals, possessions, and knowledge; exchanged ideas; intermarried; and learned to live together with some degree of understanding. In White's words, "Indians and whites of widely different social class and status had, for a variety of reasons, to rely on each other in order to achieve quite specific ends."[26] Their interaction shaped a hybrid culture that was neither purely Indian nor purely European. Rather, it was a new world, specific to the northern borderland.

Enter the Ojibwes

Unlike the Dakotas, the Ojibwe people (or Anishinaabeg), whom Europeans generally called Chippewas, had a trading history with Europeans that dated back to the 1620s.[27] The Ojibwes were part of an extended linguistic family of Algonquin-speaking peoples, who, though they identified themselves as autonomous political units, also honored commonalities that both composed tribal identity and made for fluid intertribal relations as well. Related by intermarriage, language, and cultural practices, they formed a loose web of kinship connections that stretched from the Atlantic to the Great Lakes and north into present-day Canada. Many of the bands that coalesced to become the Great Lakes Ojibwes had originally made their homes near the Atlantic Coast, where they first interacted with French traders. When threatened by the gun-toting Iroquois and their English allies in the 1640s, the Ojibwes drew on existing family connections to resettle among their western kin. Scholars in the past identified this as a refugee movement, but recent research asserts that, though the geographic locales changed, the relocation was a continuation of patterns

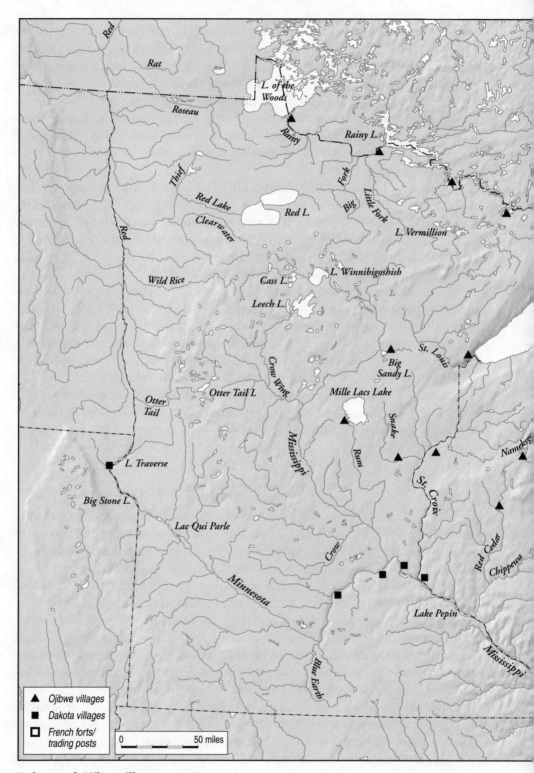

Dakota and Ojibwe villages, ca. 1768.

Red

Rat

Roseau

L. of the Woods

Rainy L.

Thief

Red Lake

Red L.

Fork

Big

Little Fork

L. Vermillion

Clearwater

Red

Wild Rice

Cass L.

L. Winnibigoshish

Leech L.

Crow Wing

St. Louis

Big Sandy L.

Otter Tail L

Mille Lacs Lake

Snake

Namekgg

Otter Tail

Mississippi

Rum

Red Cedar

Chippewa

L. Traverse

St. Croix

Big Stone L.

Lac Qui Parle

Crow

Lake Pepin

Minnesota

Mississippi

Blue Earth

▲ Ojibwe villages
■ Dakota villages
□ French forts/
trading posts

0   50 miles

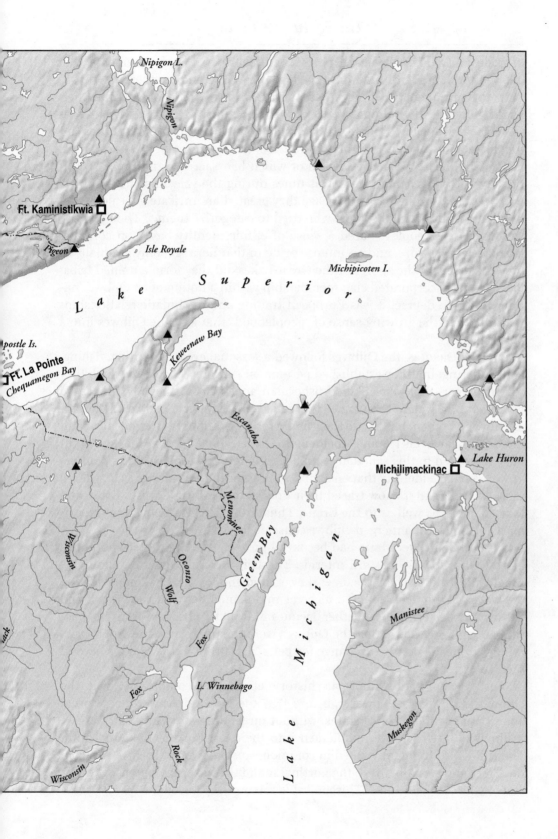

Nipigon L.

Nipigon

Ft. Kaministikwia □

Pigeon ▲

Isle Royale

Michipicoten I.

L a k e   S u p e r i o r

postle Is.

Ft. La Pointe

Chequamegon Bay

Keweenaw Bay

Escanaba

Lake Huron

Michilimackinac □

Wisconsin

Menominee

Oconto

Green Bay

Wolf

L a k e   M i c h i g a n

Manistee

Fox

Muskegon

Fox

L. Winnebago

Rock

Wisconsin

of "widespread but seasonally expected, politically negotiated movements" that allowed for fluid identities to form between one tribe and another.[28]

In the seventeenth century, these "proto-Ojibwes" did not organize their world either in the nationalistic terms or by the firm territorial boundaries by which Europeans ordered their existence. Rather they functioned as autonomous kinship clans or "totems," represented by animals such as the loon, crane, wolf, bear, and marten, each of which had sacred significance. Traditionally, the clans came together at times during the year in shared cultural practices, and through intermarriage they created an intricate genealogy that bewildered European observers who tried to categorize them.[29] Though these various Native peoples shared a sense of ethnic identity based on common language and culture, and an intense pride in that heritage, only gradually as they coalesced on the shores of the Great Lakes did they form a unified tribal identity that incorporated clan membership within a notion of an Ojibwe "nation." To some degree, it was European trading and diplomatic relationships that catalyzed the growing sense of "peoplehood" that knit the Ojibwes into a political entity.[30]

Like the Dakotas, the Ojibwes followed a seasonal cycle of hunting, fishing, and gathering, but they established permanent summer villages to which they returned year after year. Skilled fishermen and women, they always settled near bodies of water. The Crane clan, called the Saulters ("people of the rapids") by the French, had made their home for generations at present-day Sault Ste. Marie, far from Iroquois incursions. Displaced clans from the east naturally gravitated to this sanctuary and began to identify themselves as Saulters as well, a village identity that encompassed rather than displaced a clan-based sense of self. Saulters now traced their lineage to the Bear, Catfish, Loon, and Marten clans, as well as to the Crane. Thus, Sault Ste. Marie became the primary birthplace of a merged Ojibwe consciousness.[31]

By 1660 Sault Ste. Marie had become a bustling trading center and jumping-off place for the western interior. The Ojibwes, renowned for the lightweight and swift birch bark canoes they crafted and for their skill in navigating the waterways, quickly found a niche as middlemen between the French and the distant western tribes. Father Jacques Marquette observed from his mission at Sault Ste. Marie that the Ojibwes were "instinctive businessmen," carrying European goods to exchange for pelts "at a profit to the nations beyond the Sault."[32]

Most accounts of Minnesota history emphasize conflict between the Ojibwes and Dakotas; however, before 1737 the two nations were more often allies than enemies. The Dakotas, without direct access to European traders, willingly allowed Ojibwe middlemen into their territory to trade and hunt. The tribes also frequently allied in common cause to protect themselves from the Crees and Assiniboins to the northwest and the Fox, Mascoutens, and Miamis to the south and east. This amicable relationship paved the way for some amalgamated Ojibwe bands to migrate to the south shore of Lake Superior at the edge of Dakota country. By 1680 a growing population was straining the resources of the region around Sault Ste. Marie and game had become scarce, causing many Ojibwes to expand their seasonal migration farther west along the south shore of Lake Superior.[33] The Dakotas raised no objection when the Ojibwes established themselves at Chequamegon Bay in present-day northern Wisconsin. On what is now called Madeline Island at the entrance to the bay, an Ojibwe settlement flourished, and soon La Pointe, as it came to be known, became a permanent, sedentary village. Ojibwe elders described the Chequamegon era as "a golden age." The region abounded with beaver, otter, marten, fox, and mink; fish and game were plentiful; and the Ojibwes played an essential role as fur trade intermediaries. Chequamegon quickly became the geographical center of trade for the Lake Superior region. By the mid-1660s it had become a marketplace that drew Ottawas, Potawatomis, Kickapoos, Crees, and even a few Dakotas, as well as French and Ojibwes, to trade, hunt, garden, and fish in peace. It was a time of unparalleled abundance.[34]

Still, quarrels among the tribes periodically erupted, often over trapping or hunting rights, frequently over issues of honor, revenge, or the quest for personal power. Whatever the cause, when the tribes were disputing rather than trapping, it disrupted the flow of pelts, which created hardship for everyone involved in the trade, Indians and French alike. Indians missed the European goods and weapons that had become important innovations in easing the rigors of daily life. For the French traders, an entire year's profits could easily disappear. Thus, Frenchmen on the ground worked hard to mediate among the warring factions, which required an understanding of and respect for Native culture. This economic and cultural interdependence was the essential underpinning of the emerging fur trade's political economy.

The Politics of Kinship

The European concept of the nation-state had no parallel among Native Americans, though Europeans, and later Americans, would persistently categorize the tribes in those terms. Instead, tribal identity was formed through bonds of kinship. In the Indian world, those who were not kin were by definition enemies. Thus, the politics of alliance or entente fundamentally relied on the creation of real or fictive kinship ties. Adoption was one common practice that extended the kinship network; elaborate rituals of gift exchange were another, less permanent method. But intermarriage was far and away the most common and effective means to create alliances and bonds of obligation. Thus, in both Ojibwe and Dakota society, women played centrally important economic, social, and political roles.[35]

Many Europeans and Americans misread the place of women in Indian society because of cultural practices that were alien to their worldview.

Acculturated to a different, though equally gendered, division of labor, Europeans often described Indian women as overworked, exploited drudges and Indian men as lazy loafers. In reality, in a society that sustained itself by hunting and gathering, the constant labor of both men and women was essential to feeding and protecting the community. Women were responsible for gathering, growing, and preparing food, scraping pelts, sewing, weaving, and myriad other demanding tasks; the search for game and pelts required the men to undertake frequent and arduous hunting and trapping expeditions in addition to protecting the band from enemy attacks. All members of the community, men and women, were accorded respect for their skills and contributions.[36]

Politically, though women seldom participated in formal diplomatic parlays, they were essential players, not merely marital pawns exchanged to cement alliances between tribes. Wives exerted continuing influence as mediators between newly allied families and their extended kin. They were honored for the role they played and often as they aged became revered for their wisdom and supposed spiritual power. Quite naturally, as Native people set about establishing trading relationships with European traders, they expanded the custom of intertribal marriage to include the strange new tribe of whites bearing gifts.[37]

At first contact, explorers and missionaries were startled when they were offered Native women and interpreted the gesture as a sign of Indian promiscuity rather than the honor of proposed kinship. Nor did they understand the obligations such a union was meant to imply. Because they could not read the customs that attended Indian marriage, they believed they were being offered casual sex rather than a "true" marriage.[38] The traders who followed them, however, of necessity quickly learned the customs of their potential trading partners and fully grasped the economic and social significance of intermarriage. Almost to a man, they courted Indian wives and married *à la façon du pays*, "in the custom of the country." Some traders took these unions lightly, but they did so at their economic peril. Nearly all those who achieved long-term success maintained close ties with Indian kin networks. Some, no doubt, married for purely economic and political reasons and, when they left the region, abandoned their wives and offspring without a backward glance. Many, however, especially the laboring-class voyageurs, made marriages of the heart as well as pragmatism that endured for decades or for life. As historian Daniel Richter notes, these ties, whether wrought from affection, convenience, or necessity, "functioned much like rungs of a ladder. They both connected two parallel worlds and kept them from crashing together in a catastrophic collapse."[39] Indian-white unions and the children they produced created the cultural milieu that kept a delicate political and social balance in equilibrium. When trading networks tentatively began to extend their reach toward the Dakota people in the 1660s, these cultural brokers were poised to play a pivotal role.

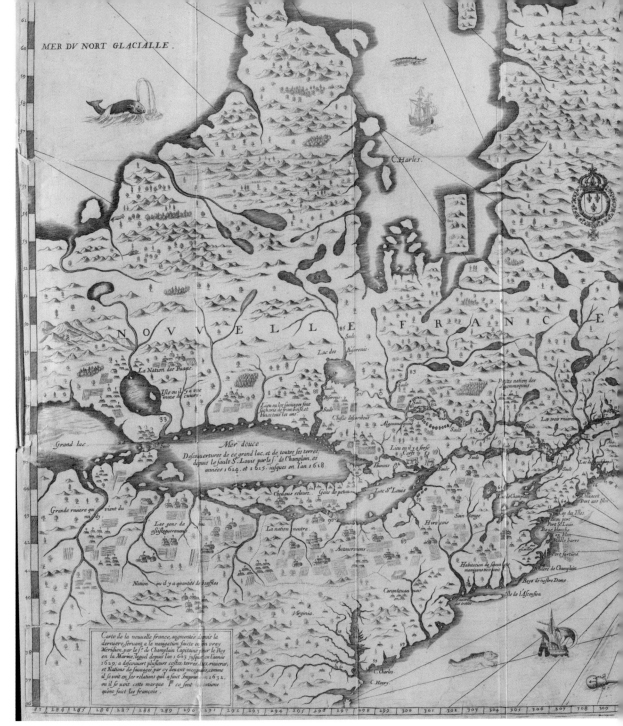

Plate 1. Samuel de Champlain, *Carte de la Nouvelle-France*, 1632. James Ford Bell Library, University of Minnesota.

The region that became Minnesota was first presented to the wider world in the form of maps, which were created to satisfy the intense curiosity of Europeans about a part of the world very few would ever have the chance to visit in person. This 1632 map was published near the end of Samuel de Champlain's career as an artist, cartographer, explorer, and administrator (he was appointed governor of New France in 1625). Motivated in part by a desire to find a water passage to Asia, Champlain began his investigation of North American geography in 1603 and continued to map the human and physical landscape of the region until his death three decades later. Champlain gleaned knowledge from his travels on the St. Lawrence River and the Great Lakes, but his most important sources were the Native Americans he interviewed and the coureurs de bois and Catholic missionaries he sent out to gather additional intelligence about the region west of Quebec. This map shows Lake Huron, which Champlain called Mer Douce, and the eastern tip of Lake Superior, which he dubbed Grand Lac. Lake Michigan does not appear. It is notable for its relatively accurate latitude measurements.[1]

Plate 2. Nicolas Sanson d'Abbeville, *Amerique septentrionale* (Paris: Pierre Mariette, 1650). James Ford Bell Library, University of Minnesota.

French cartographer Nicolas Sanson created the earliest printed map that showed the Great Lakes in recognizable form. Assembled entirely from reports of Jesuit explorers, the map represents the sum total of European cartographic knowledge about this region. It is the first map to show all five Great Lakes and to name Lake Superior and Lake Ontario, but at the same time it illuminates how little was known about the region by Europeans. While it outlines the eastern shores of Lake Superior, the western half of the lake bleeds into a large blank spot on the map. Minnesota was terra incognito, yet that did not stop mapmakers from claiming it as part of New France, since it had been visited by French explorers. Sanson's map provided a bird's-eye view of the region rather than a detailed guide for prospective explorers, who were still largely dependent on the willingness of local Native Americans to share their knowledge of the best routes into the North American interior.[2]

PLATE 2

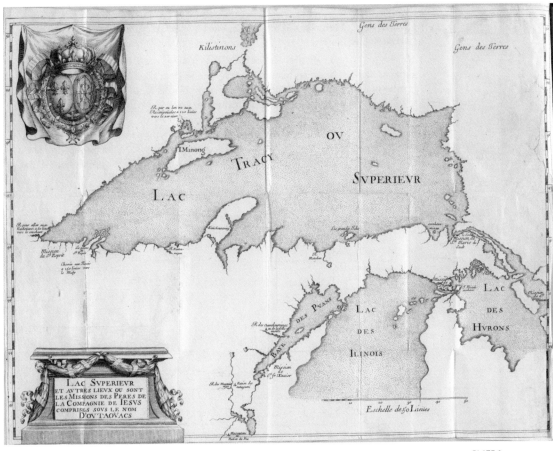

PLATE 3

Plate 3. Claude Dablon, Lac Superieur et autres lieux ou sont les missions des peres de la Compagnie de Jesus comprises sous le nom d'Outaouacs (Paris: Sebastien Mabre-Cramoisy, 1673). James Ford Bell Library, University of Minnesota.

This 1672 map of the Great Lakes was created by two Jesuit missionaries determined to share their firsthand knowledge of this region. Claude Dablon and Claude Allouez navigated the lake in a birch bark canoe with the help of two Indian guides. This experience allowed them to craft this relatively accurate picture of Lake Superior. By the mid-seventeenth century, missionaries like Dablon and Allouez had become the most reliable source of information about New France for interested Europeans. Unlike fur traders, who were too busy to commit their adventures to paper, missionaries wrote diligently about their experiences with the land and people of North America. Between 1632 and 1673, missionaries' accounts were published annually in *Jesuit Relations,* sales of which helped to support the missions. Interested readers must have eagerly awaited these descriptions of New France, which one Jesuit described as the gateway to "a land which on the side of the west, as far as China, is full of Nations more populous than the Huron." The text that accompanied this map explained how Lake Superior — with its clear waters and abundant fish — attracted people from twelve to fifteen Native American nations who met by its shores to fish and trade. Allouez dubbed the body of water "Lac Tracy," after the Marquis de Tracy who had defeated the Iroquois. But he also labeled the lake "superior" to delineate its position to the north of Lakes Illinois and Huron.[3]

Plate 4. Louis Hennepin, *Carte de la Nouvelle France et de la Louisiane*, detail (Paris: Sebastien Hure, 1683). Minnesota Historical Society.

This map illustrated Father Hennepin's *Description de la Louisiane*, one of his very popular books about his travels in New France during the seventeenth century. Hennepin's limited geographical knowledge is obvious to modern viewers. He places the Falls of St. Anthony at the same latitude as Lake Superior's western end, chops off the southern Mississippi River before it flows into the Gulf of Mexico, and splits the great river into two tributaries at its northern end. Hennepin, who explored the Upper Mississippi River in 1680, won renown for taking literary licenses that compromised the credibility but not the popularity of his Minnesota travel accounts among European audiences.[4]

PLATE 4

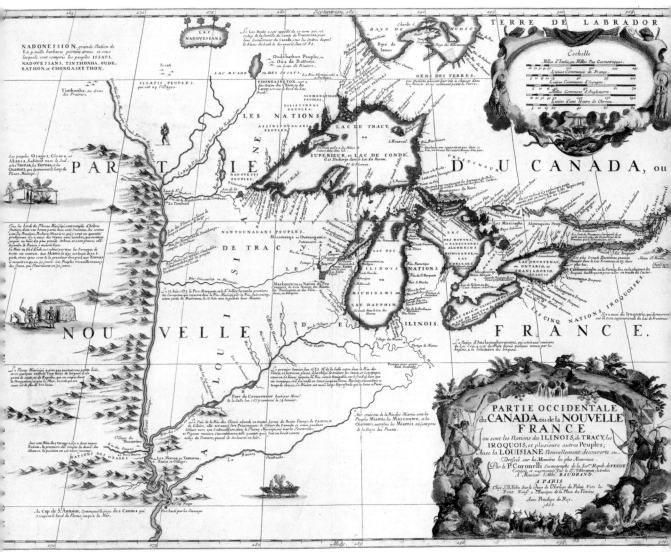

PLATE 5

Plate 5. Vincenzo Coronelli, *Partie occidentale du Canada ou de la Nouvelle France* (Paris: J. B. Nolin, 1688). James Ford Bell Library, University of Minnesota.

This beautiful map by Venetian Franciscan Vincenzo Coronelli demonstrates how reports from missionaries, explorers, and fur traders working in North America quickly shifted the frontier of geographical comprehension west over the course of the seventeenth century. As royal geographer to the French king, Coronelli reviewed all the seventeenth-century reports from the field before creating this overview of New France. The location and size of the Great Lakes are shown quite accurately in Coronelli's map, which also gives great prominence to an imperfect rendition of the Mississippi River. The map shows the river stopping short at a seemingly random spot in the northwest; it drains south only to the present-day location of St. Louis. A range of mountains towers over the west bank of the river while the land to the east is depicted as a flat plain. The map also features a collection of comments about the landscape, the locations of various Native American tribes, and the routes of various explorers, as well as images of Indians going about their daily activities, including making boats and roasting fish over open fires.[5]

PLATE 6

**Plate 6. Dog-like beavers from François du Creux, *Historiae Canadensis,
seu Nouae-Franciae libri decem, ad annum vsque Christi MDCLVI* (Parisiis:
Sebastianum Cramoisy, et Sebast. Mabre-Cramoisy . . . , 1664), 52. James Ford
Bell Library, University of Minnesota.**

This engraving shows a dam being built by beavers that strongly resemble dogs or
small sheep. In the seventeenth century, few viewers would have had an understanding of how beavers actually appeared in nature since the animals were virtually extinct
in Europe. Fortune-seeking Europeans crossed the ocean in search of North America's
largest rodent, whose barbed underfur made their pelts highly attractive to European
hatmakers. Visitors also admired the social habits of beavers — especially their dam-
building activities — which inspired comparisons to larger domestic animals and even
humans.

Authors like François Du Creux, a Jesuit scholar residing in Paris who wrote the
text that accompanied this engraving, were forced to rely on secondhand descriptions of the natural world of New France. Du Creux never visited the region, relying

on the annual *Jesuit Relations* as well as interviews with returning missionaries to fuel his powerful descriptions of the north country for a fascinated European public. Du Creux's narrative was driven by his desire to save souls and record the successes of missionaries to New France. His text demonstrates how difficult it was to distinguish between spiritual, commercial, and political missions in the seventeenth and eighteen centuries. The sometimes contradictory desires to develop the fur trade, convert Native Americans to Christianity, and establish imperial claims on new territory converged both texts and expeditions to the region around the Great Lakes.[6]

Plate 7. "A Beaver Pool" from Louis Armand de Lom d'Arce, Baron de Lahontan, *New Voyages to North-America* (London: H. Bonwicke, T. Goodwin, M. Wotton, B. Tooke, and S. Manship, 1703), 2:59. James Ford Bell Library, University of Minnesota.

This surreal engraving shows a stream that has been pooled by a beaver dam. At the center of the pool is a schematic view of a beaver lodge labeled "a Beaver kennel." The rest of the pool is dotted with images of beavers at work felling trees and

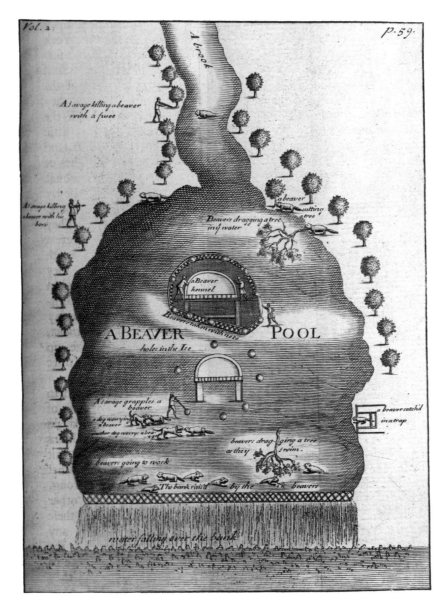

PLATE 7

strengthening their dam. Around the periphery are Indian figures engaged in hunting beavers using traps, dogs, bludgeons, nets through holes in the ice, and guns, as well as bows and arrows. This visual dissection of the lives and deaths of North American beavers reflects the keen commercial interest of Europeans in these animals. One estimate is that ten million beavers inhabited North America before the arrival of Europeans. This number quickly plummeted as their pelts became the raw material in a new global commercial endeavor.

This image accompanied an immensely popular travelogue written by Louis Armand, Baron de Lahontan, a French aristocrat who journeyed to Canada as part of the French military. He spent his time in the region exploring, traveling extensively in the area that became Minnesota. After his return to Europe he wrote his memoir, which was largely fiction, much like Hennepin's popular chronicle. Most significant was his invention of the "Longue River" — filled with crocodiles — that stretched from the Mississippi River to a range of mountains in the west. While his description of a water route to the Pacific drew excited readers to his account, it significantly distorted geographical understandings of the region. For the next one hundred years, respected cartographers incorporated the Baron de Lahontan's river in their maps.[7]

Plate 8. Bison from Louis Hennepin, *A New Discovery of a Vast Country in America, Extending above Four Thousand Miles, between New France and New Mexico* **(London: M. Bentley, J. Tonson, H. Bonwick, T. Goodwin, and S. Manship, 1698). James Ford Bell Library, University of Minnesota.**

Like the beaver, the American bison was one of the exotic animals of North America that produced intense curiosity among Europeans. This image of a bison — one of the first visual representations of this iconic North American beast — was published in Louis Hennepin's account of his travels in this region. One of the most popular authors of his time, Hennepin wrote vivid tales of the country surrounding the Mississippi River. His descriptions of the flora, fauna, and Indian lifeways of the region that would become Minnesota fascinated eighteenth-century readers, who had extremely limited understandings of North America. The jumble of palms, conifers,

PLATE 8

and deciduous trees in the background of this image would not have been jarring for viewers of this period, who had little context for judging either the veracity of Hennepin's spare images or his fanciful text. While Hennepin is still given credit as the first European to record a visit to St. Anthony Falls, most of the other claims of his text have been dismissed as fictitious by historians. Hennepin's writings were controversial even in his own time, but the absence of factual grounding did little to detract from their popularity.

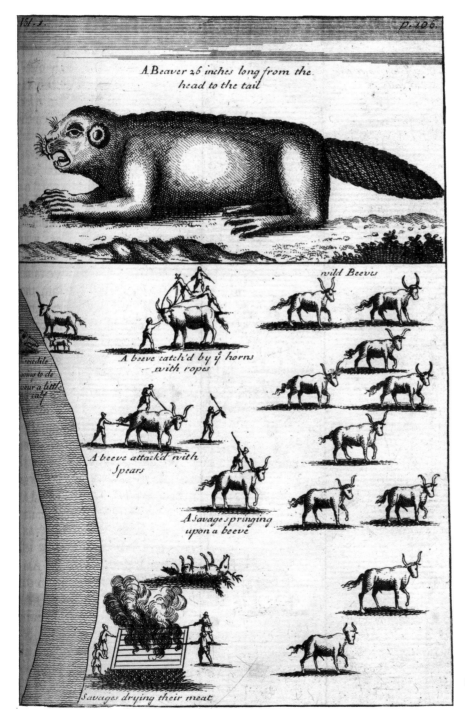

PLATE 9

Plate 9. A beaver and wild beeves from Louis Armand de Lom d'Arce, Baron de Lahontan, *New Voyages to North-America* **(London: H. Bonwicke, T. Goodwin, M. Wotton, B. Tooke, and S. Manship, 1703), 1:106. James Ford Bell Library, University of Minnesota.**

A vicious-looking beaver and a herd of bovine-type creatures fill this page from the Baron de Lahontan's *New Voyages to North-America*. This account garnered at least some of its popular appeal through its attempts to describe in detail the exotic world of the Great Lakes for a fascinated European public. Lahontan's fanciful narrative explored the habits and appearances of the animals he encountered during his North American sojourn, explaining that a "beaver has two lays of hair, one is long and of a shining black color with a grain as big as that of man's hair; the other is fine and smooth and in winter fifteen lines long. In a word, the last is the finest down in the world." The "wild Beeves" shown here may have been intended to be bison; the engraving depicts the various ways they were hunted by the people the author called "savages." Or they may have been figments of Lahontan's imagination, much like the crocodile lurking in the river running along the far left side of the page. Perhaps this river was intended to be Lahontan's "Longue River," a crocodile-infested waterway he asserted could serve as a water route to the Pacific Ocean.[8]

Plate 10. "Dresses of the 17th Cent." from Joseph Strutt, *A Complete View of the Dress and Habits of the People of England: From the Establishment of the Saxons in Britain to the Present Time* **(London: J. Nichols, 1796–99), vol. 1, plate 143. Special Collections and Rare Books, University of Minnesota.**

PLATE 10

The early exploration of the region that became Minnesota was driven largely by the European popularity of beaver hats, as pictured here. This image depicts the cavalier hat that first became fashionable in the mid-seventeenth century, thanks to the military triumphs of the Swedish military, whose cavaliers wore these large, brimmed hats. The French nobility's embrace of the cavalier's sartorial style left European hatmakers scrambling to find more beaver fur, the only material suitable for felting into the type of large brim shown here. The short, soft, barbed undercoat of beaver fur, "beaver wool," was ideal. In the hands of an experienced hatmaker this "fur felt" could be rendered supple and brushed into a glossy sheen. The resulting hat was waterproof, a critical benefit in a rainy climate before the invention of umbrellas. It was also durable: the widest brimmed hats could retain their shape through years of hard wear. The only problem was that beaver pelts were in short supply. Beavers had been hunted virtually to extinction in Europe. Early reports of large beaver populations in North America fired the imaginations of fortune hunters, who pushed into the interior of North America to collect the pelts so prized by hatmakers. The result was a new industry that ultimately integrated the once remote Great Lakes region into a global capitalist market.[9]

Plate 11. "Modifications of the Beaver Hat" from Horace T. Martin, *Castorologia, or the History and Traditions of the Canadian Beaver* (Montreal: W. Drysdale, 1892), 125. Minnesota Historical Society.

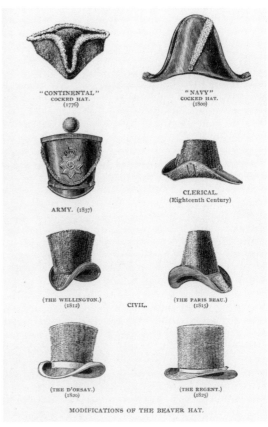

MODIFICATIONS OF THE BEAVER HAT.

PLATE 11

The North American fur trade allowed the beaver hat to remain a critical social marker for European gentlemen for more than two hundred years. While beaver hats were practical additions to any wardrobe, they also provided at least a patina of gentility to wearers, who distinguished themselves from those who covered their heads with wool or woven caps. Men doffed and donned hats to show their social status; to refuse to remove a hat in the presence of a social superior was an act of defiance and insubordination. This image shows some of the varieties of beaver hats worn during the eighteenth and nineteenth centuries. The loose fur of the beaver's undercoat could be pressed and steamed into any shape, giving wide latitude for hatmakers' creativity. The width of the brims and the height of the crowns on beaver hats waxed and waned over the years but remained a ubiquitous part of a gentlemen's wardrobe until the 1840s, when the advent of inexpensive silk top hats finally toppled the beaver hat from its place of preeminence in European men's fashion.[10]

Plate 12. "At the Portage: Hudson's Bay Company's Employés on their Annual Expedition" from George Monro Grant, ed., *Picturesque Canada: The Country As It Was and Is* (New York: Belden Brothers, 1882), facing page 241.

In the late seventeenth century, white explorers began to visit Minnesota and to trade with the state's inhabitants directly. Once large quantities of furs from the region began to show up in Montreal, entrepreneurs began to imagine the rewards of journeying to the middle of the continent to trade with Indians. The result was a new chapter of the fur trade, no longer predicated on the assumption that Indians would travel to white settlements like Montreal. Traders instead began to paddle into the heart of the continent, using canoes to transport goods and supplies between Montreal and wilderness trading posts. In this image, voyageurs are pictured unloading a canoe at a remote trading post. The cargo in the canoes — either furs or trade goods — was organized into the standard-sized packages shown here. Each "piece" weighed ninety pounds. Pieces were carefully distributed among the flotilla of canoes so that each group of paddlers was responsible for an equal load.

The fur trade was organized around a class hierarchy that clearly delineated the duties of the traders, or *bourgeois*, from the voyageurs. The voyageurs did the physical labor of the trade. This scene depicts them working under the direction of a man who is presumably a trader. Portages required each voyageur to carry at least two pieces on his back. Notice how one of the men pictured here supported his piece with a tumpline, or portage collar, that was secured across his forehead.[11]

Starting in the eighteenth century, men involved in the fur trade spent most of their time in the backcountry; most married Native American women and created

PLATE 12

mixed-race families that were vital to their prosperity and survival. This engraving shows an Indian woman with her children observing the men, who presumably include her husband. This scene could have taken place during either the eighteenth or the nineteenth century in Minnesota.

Plate 13. Beaver from Denis Diderot, ed., *Encyclopédie, ou dictionnaire raisonné des sciences, des arts et des métiers: Recueil de planches.* . . . (Paris: Briasson, 1751–65). Special Collections and Rare Books, University of Minnesota.

Early explorers were amateur naturalists who developed elaborate theories about the beaver. They admired the animal's industry and habits, asserting that its dam building demonstrated a grasp of advanced engineering and architectural concepts. Baron de Lahontan Louis Armand asserted that "these Animals join together in a Society consisting of an Hundred, and they seem to talk and reason with one another by certain bemoaning and inarticulate Sounds. . . . They consult among themselves about what Things they must do to maintain their Cottages, their Banks, and their Lakes, and about every Thing that concerns the Preservation of their Commonwealth." European images of beavers became more realistic, as this drawing from Diderot's eighteenth-century French encyclopedia shows. More than a century after some of the first images of North American beavers reached Europe, the habits and character of these animals continued to intrigue readers who understood that beavers provided the raw materials for an important global industry.[12]

PLATE 13

Plate 14. Parisien furriery from Denis Diderot, ed., *Encyclopédie, ou dictionnaire raisonné des sciences, des arts et des métiers: Recueil de planches. . . .* **(Paris: Briasson, 1751–65). Special Collections and Rare Books, University of Minnesota.**

Furs collected in the backcountry were shipped to Europe, where they were graded and resold at auction in London, Paris, or Moscow. Once they reached the workshops of skilled European artisans, they were transformed into fine felt hats, trimmings for coats or mittens, and muffs. This engraving shows a fashionable storefront, where luxurious clothing was displayed to entice rich customers. Rows of fur muffs line the walls. A fur-trimmed cape hangs on the right, where it can catch the eye of well-heeled shoppers. Pelts are suspended from the rafters. While a wealthy couple examines a variety of fur muffs at the counter, one of the shop's artisans works off to the side, beating the insects out of a yet unprocessed fur. This shop did not feature the beaver hats that first set off the rush to befriend the Indians of the Great Lakes. But the scene shows how a dependable supply of furs shaped the face of European fashion, making stylish furriers like this one a fixture in the lives of the European elite.[13]

PLATE 14

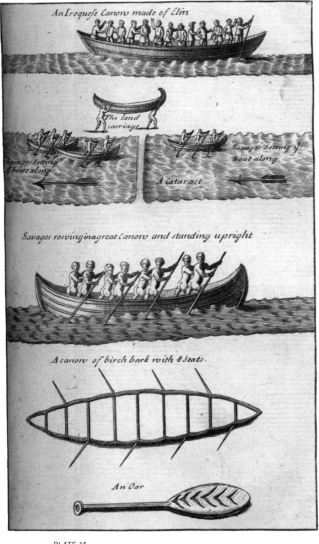

An Iroquese Canow made of Elm

The land carriage

Savages setting
ye boats along

Savages setting
ye boat along

A Cataract

Savages rowing in a great Canow and standing upright

A canow of birch bark with 8 Seats

An Oar

PLATE 15

Plate 15. Canoes and paddle from Louis Armand de Lom d'Arce, Baron de Lahontan, *New Voyages to North-America*, 2nd ed. (London: printed for J. and J. Bonwicke, R. Wilkin, S. Birt, T. Ward, E. Wicksteed, and J. Osborn, 1735), 1:27. James Ford Bell Library, University of Minnesota.

This panel of images depicting canoes being piloted by crowds of Native Americans was published as part of Lahontan's 1703 travelogue. After traveling extensively around the Great Lakes, he returned to Europe to write a hugely popular memoir that was equal parts ethnography, natural history, theological commentary, and fantasy. Like most early European visitors to the Great Lakes, Lahontan recognized that the canoe was the key to all travel and exploration in the region. A more reputable explorer had explained a century earlier that "in the canoes of the savages one can go without restraint, and quickly, everywhere, in the small as well as large rivers." Samuel Champlain asserted that "by using canoes as the savages do, it would be possible to see all there is, good and bad, in a year or two."

For newcomers to North America, this craft was completely unfamiliar. Elegantly constructed out of dugout trees and animal skin or birch bark wrapped around a wooden frame, canoes were marvels of utility and design. They were sturdy enough to haul heavy cargo and significant numbers of people, agile enough to navigate shallow and serpentine waterways, and light enough to be carried over frequent portages by one or two people. Without canoes, it would have been impossible to overcome the logistical challenges of the fur trade, which demanded the transport of furs and goods over long distances.

Europeans quickly realized that these exotic objects of curiosity were in fact essential tools. Anyone venturing into the interior had to acquire a canoe, either from a Native American builder or a skilled newcomer to the region. White newcomers

who mastered the art of canoe building adapted native design to the needs of modern global commerce, using the same principles to construct larger canoes capable of hauling more cargo. For almost two centuries the fur trade was dependent on two kinds of canoes: the huge Montreal canoe *(canot du maître)* and the smaller north canoe *(canot du nord)*, which was used on trips to interior trading posts.

The canoe, in many ways, served as the foundation for a multicultural society grounded in economic exchanges and intermarriage between indigenous women and European men. The canoe was only one of the instruments for survival in this landscape that newcomers incorporated into the hybrid society they built, which melded the customs and legends of their place of birth with the traditions and mythologies of their adopted home.[14]

Plate 16. John Halkett, *Canot du maître* carrying two officers, 1822. Hudson's Bay Company Archives, Archives of Manitoba.

This image shows a large Montreal canoe laden down with gear and two officers of the Hudson's Bay Company. A reified class structure organized the fur trade, which limited authority and significant financial rewards to a select number of men with the proper ethnic backgrounds, class positions, and family ties. This sketch clearly delineates the gentlemen from the workers, who are holding paddles. The *bourgeois* — who might have been high-ranking partners in the Hudson's Bay Company — broadcast their distinguished social position with their glossy beaver top hats. Their wool-capped compatriots were charged not only with paddling this massive canoe but also carrying the pieces, portaging the canoe, and guiding the expedition to its destination. These arduous and challenging tasks were divided among the crew according to another pecking order. The clerks occupied the top of this labor hierarchy, followed by the guides, then the men at each end of the canoe (the foresmen and steersmen, or *bouts*), and finally the middle paddlers, who had the monotonous and demanding job of paddling all day. The men pictured here would have been described as *mangeurs de lard,* or pork eaters, seasonally employed summer workers who transported goods across the Great Lakes. In the cosmology of fur trade culture, they were seen as inferior to the more experienced northmen, or *hommes du nord,* the men who wintered in the interior, paddling and portaging the smaller north canoes through the north backcountry on trading expeditions.

The canoe pictured here was made from birch bark wrapped around a wooden frame, sewn together by spruce roots, and then sealed with gum from spruce or pine trees. Montreal canoes were the largest canoe used in the fur trade — about thirty-six feet long and six feet wide — and were reserved for the one- to two-month journey from Montreal through the Great Lakes. While this sketch shows fourteen voyageurs in action, these kinds of boats usually employed crews of eight to ten men. One canoe could hold up to four tons of cargo, a load that typically included sixty pieces wrapped in water-repellant canvas, nine hundred pounds of food, forty pounds of personal baggage for each man in the boat, and a variety of other equipment for making camps

PLATE 16

PLATE 17

and keeping the boat in good repair. Poles were laid on the bottom of the canoes to keep the pieces from damaging the outer shell, which was quite fragile. In fact, great care had to be taken when landing and portaging these canoes to avoid ruptures and tears. All voyageurs had to master the skill of canoe repair, which demanded significant time on every journey.[15]

Plate 17. Frances Anne Hopkins, *Voyageurs at Dawn*, 1871. Library and Archives of Canada.

In the short months that waterways were open, voyageurs enjoyed few moments of the type of leisure pictured here. Voyageurs had astonishing physical endurance and were expected to sit in canoes for days on end, routinely paddling for eighteen hours a day and sometimes all night long. The men slept in the open or under the canoes, awakening from their short slumbers at the guide's call of "lève, lève." A typical day began well before dawn; brigades embarked between 3 a.m. and 6 a.m. Once afloat, the men sang to keep themselves awake and to synchronize their paddling. After several hours they paused for breakfast. Since every journey was a race against the calendar, the men had no time to hunt or fish along the way. Meals thus were monotonous affairs of easily transportable fare like rice, cornmeal, and salt pork, made palatable by generous rations of alcohol. West of Grand Portage, paddlers also consumed large quantities of pemmican, a nutritious and portable food made from dried buffalo meat mixed with fat and wild berries. Intervals of hard paddling were broken up by regular pauses for pipes, breaks known as *pipeés*. This painting by Frances Anne Hopkins depicts an early morning breakfast; one member of the crew appears to be still asleep. The wife of a high-ranking Hudson's Bay Company official, Hopkins enjoyed accompanying her husband on canoe journeys to the interior and is renowned for her vivid portrayals of voyageur life. This scene is no exception and features the ubiquitous tools of the trade arrayed on a beach: a porridge kettle, a long-handled frying pan, an ax, a trunk, a hamper, and multiple paddles. Although she created this image in the late nineteenth century, this scene could easily have transpired earlier in the century around Lake Superior, before the collapse of the fur trade in present-day Minnesota.[16]

For France and Glory

Meanwhile, far across the Atlantic Ocean, the European powers continued their quest for "ownership" of North America. In 1663, tantalized by explorers' tales of riches yet unmined and fed up with the failures of the Company of New France, Louis XIV declared the French colony a royal province. He then dispatched civil administrators and a small garrison to put the colony back on a profitable track. But it was the establishment of the Hudson's Bay Company in 1670, signaling a direct British challenge to French interests, that inspired a new sense of urgency to claim the Northwest interior. Almost immediately, New France's intendant, Jean Talon, launched a flurry of expeditions west to map and claim the lands for the French Empire.[40] As he reported to the king, "Since my arrival I have dispatched persons of resolution who promise to penetrate further than has ever been done. . . . They are to take possession, display the King's arms and draw up *process verbaux* to serve as titles."[41]

The tales of these explorers have become the stuff of legend, the triumphal march of European conquest. But a close look at the record offers a somewhat different perspective. Take, for example, the expedition in 1671 of Simon François Daumont, Sieur de St. Lusson. On the orders of Talon, St. Lusson was to assemble a council of all the Indian nations in the western region to inform them that they were now under the rule of France. The voyageur Nicholas Perrot was sent ahead to invite the chiefs to council (since St. Lusson himself could not have found the villages, let alone communicated with the chiefs). On the appointed day, representatives from some fourteen Algonquian-speaking bands, including the Ojibwes who would soon migrate into Minnesota country, gathered at Sault Ste. Marie for the ceremony. St. Lusson and his lieutenants, in their best formal attire, raised the French flag and proclaimed Louis XIV sovereign of "Lakes Huron and Superior . . . and all other Countries, rivers, lakes and tributaries, contiguous and adjacent thereto, as well discovered as to be discovered . . . bounded on one side by the Northern and Western Seas and on the other side by the South Sea." With a flourish, the official papers were signed and witnessed, formal documentation that nine-tenths of North America now belonged to France.[42]

This performance of imperial arrogance had multiple interpretations and effects. St. Lusson could report back to Quebec and to his king that he had successfully claimed the North American interior for France, an achievement that was sure to bring him status and acclaim. On this slim justification, France would redraw the boundaries of the continent, setting off arguments and even wars among the imperial contestants for America. But on the ground, on the shores of Lake Michigan, this "grand council" carried quite a different meaning.[43]

No one present that day seriously believed that the meager contingent of strangers had taken possession of Indian lands. Even St. Lusson, as he looked out on the crowd of chiefs and their retinues—a mere fraction of the forces they represented—must have recognized the audacity of his proclamation. The military presence in all of New France numbered scarcely 1,000 men, its entire population barely 3,000 souls. Clearly, they lacked the means to challenge even one of the tribes. In fact, throughout their tenure in North America, the French were acutely aware that their presence was possible only because the Indians tolerated it. Moreover, their commercial success was entirely dependent on good relations with their Indian partners.[44] In European capitals the French might squabble with the English and Spanish over claim to the continent, but everyone present that day on the shores of Lake Michigan knew full well that they were standing in Indian country.

Yet this ritual did have meaning for the Indian attendees, just as it did for the Dakotas who had met with Radisson. It was a means to establish important fictive ties of kinship, a pledge of alliance that obligated the French to support them in intertribal wars, particularly against the Iroquois, as well as to cement valued trading relationships. It is essential to keep in mind that in the Indian worldview, trade was framed as an exchange of gifts rather than as a simple commercial transaction. It had a symbolic value that exceeded even its material worth. One traded only with friends, and friendship, as long as it remained intact, bestowed the rights and obligation of extended kin. In the eyes of the Indian guests who put great store in the importance of ritual, the highly stylized performance orchestrated by St. Lusson gave added weight to the pledges of French benevolence. When the French, in their imperial hubris, described themselves as "fathers," the Indians interpreted the metaphor as one of obligation rather than domination—a father's obligation to care for his children. In the most practical and urgent terms, the Indians demanded and received from their "father" the firearms and military assistance to protect themselves from their enemies, the Iroquois to the east and the Dakotas to the west.[45]

Despite that in their minds the French now "owned" Minnesota country, the land and its people largely remained shrouded in mystery to the colonial government in Quebec. They had found the Grand Lac but the great river that ran to the sea was still uncharted. Fearing that the English or Spanish might discover the riverine route to the Orient, in 1673 the Comte de Frontenac, governor general of New France, commissioned explorers Louis Joliet and the Jesuit Jacques Marquette to find and reaffirm French claims to the waterway. The whereabouts of the river was no secret to the Indian people. Friendly Native guides led the way and hardy voyageurs, paddling from Green Bay via the Fox and Wisconsin rivers, carried the two gift-laden explorers to its banks, near present-day Prairie du Chien, Wisconsin. Choosing to follow the current south rather than paddle upriver, the disappointed adventurers eventually realized that they were not on their way to China. Nonetheless, they had found a second pathway into Dakota country. The gateways to the mysterious interior were open at last: a northern route by way of Lake Superior and an arduous but achievable paddle up the river called Mechassipi.[46]

French trade with the eastern tribes was increasingly challenged by British traders, who offered more and better-quality goods and more attractive prices for Indian peltries. Thus, the French were eager to make alliance with new trading partners, more isolated from the lure of British competitors. But before they could launch a major expedition into the Upper Mississippi River valley, the impatient Dakotas took matters into their own hands. By the 1670s, the borders of Dakota territory were no longer secure. All the neighboring tribes to the east had acquired a supply of firearms that changed the balance of power, and despite the Dakotas' daunting reputation as warriors they were constantly fighting off incursions. Thus, in 1674 a contingent of Dakota diplomats made the trek to Sault Ste. Marie to parlay with the Saulters, an important Ojibwe band. This first attempt at peace negotiations fell apart in mayhem when a visiting Cree murdered one of the Dakota ambassadors, but six years later the Ojibwes, anxious to expand their hunting rights, reinitiated diplomatic relations.[47]

As the Ojibwe delegation was preparing to head west to meet the Dakotas, Daniel Greysolon, Sieur du Luth, arrived at Sault Ste. Marie. Fresh from a recent campaign against the Iroquois and eager to improve his prospects, Du Luth had been engaged by a group of Quebec and Montreal merchants to find new trading partners in the west. With seven voyageur and Indian companions, he set off via the Lake Superior route to find the Dakotas. When he learned that the Ojibwes were about to embark on a similar mission, he asked to accompany them. Following the lakeshore, the party first encountered a Dakota village near the present-day site of Duluth. They were then led south to "a great village of the Sioux" on the shores of Lake Mille Lacs.[48]

Historical accounts traditionally have emphasized the heroic leadership of Du Luth on this journey, which is not surprising since the sources stem from his reports and memoir. The fact that he tagged along on an Ojibwe diplomatic mission was conveniently omitted from his narrative. In Du Luth's account, he "urge(d) the fierce Sioux to keep peace with the Chippewa [Ojibwe]," succeeding, it would seem, by simple force of his personality. He secured the friendship of the Dakotas and, like Radisson and Groseilliers before him, raised the arms of the king, reaffirming that all of the western interior was now a possession of France.[49]

In reality, the Ojibwes and Dakotas were in charge of the events that transpired at that historic council. They effected an alliance that benefited both sides. The Dakotas were eager to participate in trade, especially anxious to acquire firearms; the Ojibwes gained hunting rights in Dakota territory; and the two agreed to ally against the aggressions of the Fox and Mascoutens, who were harrying both peoples. They smoked the calumet together, the traditional ceremony signifying peace, and finally, creating the most compelling of kinship ties, Dakota warriors married Ojibwe women—a pact that carried more authority and social enforcement than any written treaty.[50]

This is not to say that Du Luth was merely a bystander at the event. He represented the source of long-anticipated European goods and his presence carried great import, but perhaps in ways he did not fully understand. By bringing Du Luth to the Dakotas, the Ojibwes offered a powerful show of good faith, a willingness to bring their western brothers into the trading network. The Dakotas gladly accepted this overture, welcomed Du Luth to their council fire, accepted his gifts and professions of friendship with alacrity, and indulged with good humor the rest of the foreign rituals and flag waving that seemed so important to the strange European.

Some miscommunication was inevitable in the meeting of these two very different cultures, despite a genuine effort on both sides to understand one another. The Dakotas ardently desired to establish friendly relations with the French and the French knew well that their presence in the interior was utterly dependent on the goodwill of the Indians.[51] But since only one side left written records of the encounter, and those records were colored sometimes by self-interest, sometimes by failures of memory, and almost always by an imperfect understanding of Indian culture, European misperceptions have become reified as undisputed fact. Thus, it is not surprising that the history of the era was written as one of conquest rather than negotiation. However, with a reconstructed view of the world as it looked through Indian eyes, historical "facts" often bear some reinterpretation. Du Luth's dramatic rescue of French explorers Michel Accault, Antoine Auguelle, and Father Louis Hennepin is one such event.[52]

In the same year that Du Luth entered Dakota country by way of Lake Superior, René-Robert Cavelier, Sieur de la Salle, another impecunious, petty aristocrat turned explorer, was pushing west by way of a more southern route. In February 1680 the expedition had reached the mouth of the Illinois River, where it spilled into the Mississippi. With other destinations in mind for himself, La Salle dispatched a small party to follow the beckoning river north into the uncharted lands of the Dakota people. Command of the mission was entrusted to Michel Accault, an experienced voyageur who, with Antoine Auguelle and Father Louis Hennepin, gamely set off into the unknown. For two brutal months the three explorers battled the current, winter winds, and floating ice. In early April they finally met a flotilla of thirty-three canoes carrying some 120 Mdewakanton Dakota warriors heading downriver in search of hostile Miamis. The Frenchmen must have been a sorry sight by this time, and the Dakotas insisted that they join their party, either as guests or captives.

At this point in the narrative, some cultural confusion seems to have come into play. The two groups could communicate only "by means of signs and marks in the sand," and the Frenchmen, understandably intimidated by the army of Dakotas painted for war, may well have feared for their lives. However, it is far more likely the Indians had only friendly intentions toward these long-awaited ambassadors of the fur trade. With the frightened explorers in tow, they abandoned their expedition south and made haste with their "guests" to the chief Dakota village at Mille Lacs.[53]

In the two months the Frenchmen spent with the Dakotas they were treated more like honored guests than prisoners. Father Hennepin related that he was given a robe of beaver skins dressed with porcupine quills and "treated to a steam bath, [then] rubbed with wildcat oil." Even more tellingly, he was adopted by a chief who then offered to provide him with a wife—the classic rites for creating bonds of kinship. Presumably, Accault and Auguelle were treated in a similar fashion, though they left no account of their experiences. The three men participated in the annual buffalo hunt, and Auguelle and Hennepin left the band to freely travel down the Mississippi in search of supplies that had been promised by La Salle. On this journey they first saw the great falls that Hennepin christened St. Anthony. Rather than attempting to escape downriver, the two men later rejoined the hunting party. A strange captivity account indeed.[54]

Still, it is possible that the Dakotas considered the explorers both captives and adopted kinsmen. Indian peoples frequently took captives into their families to take the place of slain warriors. In this case, however, it is equally plausible that hospitality and especially adoption were intended primarily as a means to create the bonds that would promote both an alliance and long-term trading relationship with the French.[55]

Though the status of the explorers remains open to speculation, the heroic account of their "rescue" demands a critical reexamination. According to Du Luth, who was once again in Dakota country near the mouth of the St. Croix, he learned that three white men had been seen with Indian hunters. William Folwell, dean of early Minnesota historians, writes that Du Luth suspected they were either English or Spaniards trespassing in the French domain. Other historians assert that Du Luth was outraged because the Dakotas had broken their pledge of friendship and taken French hostages. Whatever his motivation, the alarmed Du Luth, taking only three companions, rushed down the Mississippi to meet the returning Dakota hunting party. Finding Accault, Auguelle, and Hennepin among them, the "indignant Duluth [according to his account] took Hennepin and his companions under his protection . . . forced the Sioux to return to their Mille Lacs village . . . and gave them a tongue lashing." He then demanded the release of the captives from the chastened Indians. All in all, a highly suspect tale.[56] Even Du Luth's contemporaries scoffed at his self-aggrandizing accounts of his adventures. In La Salle's scornful estimation, "he will not fail to exaggerate everything. It is his character. . . . He speaks more in keeping with what he wishes than what he knows."[57]

The chronology of events, criticism by contemporaries, and simple common sense all cast doubt on Du Luth's version of the story. Had he attempted to threaten or upbraid a contingent of more than 200 warriors or insulted them in any way, he would likely have signed his death warrant. By his own admission, after finding the presumed captives, they all returned together to the Mille Lacs village, where Du Luth remained for more than a month in apparently congenial circumstances. When the Frenchmen eventually made ready to leave, the Indians helped them prepare for the journey, even providing a map to guide their course. Promising to "come again to trade," they paddled off into the sunset—a decidedly undramatic rescue.[58]

Yet, despite the ambiguity of its facts, the heroic version of this rescue tale became incorporated into the canon of early Minnesota history. Father Hennepin almost immediately returned to France to capitalize on his adventures in Indian country. Within a year, he published an account of his exploits, *A Description of Louisiana,* and became an instant celebrity. Playing to the European fascination with the exotic, he took considerable dramatic license in describing his experiences and emphasized the strangeness of the Indians he encountered (as did most other explorers' chronicles). The book became a best seller, translated into several languages, the first published account of the land that would become Minnesota.[59] Oddly enough, he made no mention of Du Luth's so-called rescue. Still, over time, based on Du Luth's report of the events, the story increasingly came to resemble the common trope of captivity narratives that first enthralled eighteenth- and nineteenth-century audiences and then later became part of the formula of the twentieth-century western. The complexities of cultural interaction were lost in a national myth of "taming" the frontier that reduced Native Americans to alien savages who stood in the way of civilization. This version of the national saga so informed the consciousness of American culture that no room was left for alternative interpretations, even when, as in the case of Father Hennepin, the historical record called events into question.[60]

A Different World

At the end of the seventeenth century, cultural understandings were evolving in the Upper Mississippi River valley that were quite different from the frontier tales that have informed popular history. At long last, the French colonial government, with its eastern trade reduced to shambles by British competition and unlicensed traders roaming in the west, made a concerted effort to open official trade with the Dakotas. In 1685 Nicholas Perrot, a trader with twenty years' experience in the Great Lakes region, was commissioned commandant of the west and directed to establish a post in Dakota country. The Dakotas eagerly flocked to the fort he established on the eastern shore of the Mississippi River's Lake Pepin, where they finally were able to acquire guns in substantial numbers. Ironically, even as Perrot armed the Dakotas, he labored to effect peace between them and the tribes who were harrying them from the east—the Fox, Mascoutens, and Kickapoos. But despite his experience in

Indian country, Perrot had underestimated the difficulty of maintaining trade with the contesting tribes. As Gary Clayton Anderson notes, "The Dakotas obviously could not understand how Perrot could establish ties with them and then exchange presents, the symbols of alliance, with their enemies." According to their custom, the French had betrayed them.[61]

Throughout the short history of Fort St. Antoine, as Perrot had christened the rough-hewn outpost, intertribal quarrels and jealousy frequently disrupted trading relations. Frustrated in his attempts at diplomacy, Perrot tried to mandate peace by invoking the power of French sovereignty. In 1689 he repeated yet again the ritual of claiming the "Western Nations of the Upper Mississippi" for the French crown, adding for good measure possession of "the countries and rivers inhabited by the said Tribes and of which they [the Dakotas] are proprietors."[62] However, with his garrison of fewer than a dozen men, Perrot's imperial might was even less commanding than his diplomatic prowess. As he later complained, the western Indians held "the arrogant notion that the French cannot get along without them and that we could not maintain ourselves in the colony without the assistance that they give us."[63]

Every European who ventured into Indian country experienced the same, unsettling truth of that "arrogant notion." Those who would succeed in the trade soon learned to adapt their profit-making tactics to accommodate Indian custom and desires. More than any Frenchman of his time, Pierre Le Sueur mastered this art of cultural exchange. Raised in New France, Le Sueur had some firsthand knowledge of Native peoples from his youth, and tales of returning traders and explorers had probably inspired the young Canadian to seek his fortune in the West. Once among the Indians, he immersed himself in their world. After spending five years with the Ojibwes at Sault Ste. Marie, Le Sueur first appeared in Minnesota's historical record in 1683, writing in his memoir, "It is by the River of the Ousconsins that I came for the first time to the Mississippi in 1683, on my way to Sioux country, where I lived seven years at various times." He was with Perrot at Fort St. Antoine in 1689 and spent the next decade in the Upper Mississippi valley among the Dakotas and Ojibwes. A student of Indian ways, he left a meticulous record of his observations in his journal. By 1693 he was well enough versed in Native protocol to be sent to Chequamegon Bay to keep the peace between the Ojibwes and Dakotas. Two years later he was back on the Mississippi, establishing a trading post on Prairie Island (near the present-day city of Red Wing), an endeavor that apparently met with more success than did the post at Fort St. Antoine. When Le Sueur returned to Montreal with the furs collected in his first season, a Dakota chief accompanied him to press Le Sueur's petition for a permanent trading license with the Dakotas, promising the allegiance of twenty-two villages of his nation.[64]

When authorities in Montreal refused to grant his request, Le Sueur was undeterred. Buoyed by his demonstrated success in the trade (as well as some useful political connections), he boldly set off for France to make his case directly to the king. Unfortunately, a change in colonial policy dashed his hopes. All trade with the Dakotas was to be abandoned, ironically due to the very bounty in pelts that it promised. The European market was glutted, prices dropping precipitously, and in the classic logic of supply and demand, the French government determined to create a scarcity in furs to drive up the prices. In addition, the royal coffers had been drained by a war with England, fought on both European and eastern North American soil (King William's War, 1689–1697). The crown had no appetite to stretch its already thin resources deeper into the continent.[65]

The ever resourceful Le Sueur then tried a new approach. He managed to wheedle a license to mine for copper, thanks to wholly unfounded assurances that he had located a rich seam in what is today southern Minnesota. Despite the astute assessment of one French official that "the only mines that he seeks in those regions are mines of beaver skins," Le Sueur soon had a mining license in hand. Confident in his ability to parlay with the Dakotas, in 1700 he returned to the Upper Mississippi, unfazed by "various reports and warnings of danger awaiting him from hostile natives." Establishing his party of twenty men at the mouth of the Blue Earth River, where it flowed into the Minnesota, he immediately set about renewing his alliance with the Indians, pledges of mutual friendship sealed by gifts of guns, tobacco, pipes, and other desirables—and commenced trading for furs.[66]

Despite the official trade embargo, Le Sueur soon discovered that he was not alone among the Dakotas. France had no military presence to back up its edicts and the coureurs de bois continued their small-scale trade without fear of reprisal, finding a ready market for their furs among the British to the east; seven of the unlicensed traders boldly appeared one day at Fort L'Huillier, Le Sueur's "mining" outpost. Le Sueur could hardly object since he was engaged in equally illegal operations.[67]

Friendly Dakotas flocked to the post. They had been stockpiling pelts, awaiting a trader's return, and on one occasion alone they brought in more than 4,600 beaver skins to trade. Still, they urged Le Sueur, in the name of kinship, to relocate closer to their villages.[68] The present location, they complained, was dangerously near enemy tribes. Le Sueur was in a quandary. To keep up the pretext of his mining expedition, he was compelled to remain where he was, yet he understood that the obligations of adoptive kinship could not be ignored. The Mdewakanton chief Sacred Born introduced a compromise solution: "Behold thy children, thy brethren, thy sisters, it is for thee to see whether thou wishest them to live or die. They will live if thou givest them powder and ball." Which is exactly what he did, providing to his "brothers" a generous stock of arms along with other tokens of regard and promises of alliance. The Dakotas were now fully armed, thanks to amicable trading relationships with the Ojibwes and to the compelling obligations of custom that the French did not dare ignore. As a result, by 1700 the Dakotas were "a match for all aggressors."[69]

As this instance of negotiation illustrates, by the turn of the eighteenth century the French and Dakotas were developing a language of reciprocity that mediated cultural differences. In short, they had worked out a way of dealing with each other that was neither entirely Indian nor entirely European. This borderland culture was newly evolving in Dakota country, but it replicated an established pattern of Indian–French relationships. The French had long employed a policy of careful diplomacy with Indian trading partners. Force was not an option with a skeletal military presence and insignificant colonial population; in 1650 fewer than 700 people lived in all of New France. Government representatives to the tribes were charged to learn Indian languages and customs. Native complaints against traders or officials were taken seriously and could bring about the offender's immediate recall. Moreover, the Indians were the indispensable workers of the trade, with the skills and knowledge to harvest the furs. The colonial government fully recognized that its economic enterprise could succeed only by vigilantly tending to Indian custom and expectations.[70] As long as both sides reaped benefits from the relationship, each had a vested interest in making it work. Thus, the viability of the system depended on a balance of power. Le Sueur was well schooled in the fine points of Indian diplomacy, as his negotiations with the Dakotas attest. In the exchange, the Dakotas acquired the European goods they desired and, most important, the weaponry to fend off aggressors. Le Sueur, after a season of successful trading (and a couple of weeks of perfunctory digging), loaded his canoes with a small fortune in peltry—along with a boatload of worthless blue clay to keep up the mining charade—and set off on the long journey back to France.[71] Both sides considered it a bargain well made.

[23]

Chapter 2

CULTURAL CROSSROADS

Those with whom we mingle do not become French, our people become Indian.
    MARQUIS DE DENONVILLE, 1685

As the eighteenth century dawned, the Upper Mississippi and the western
Great Lakes were beyond the edge of European empires. Though geographers
in London, Paris, and Madrid might redraw their maps of North America to
reflect the spoils of European wars, in reality the Dakotas and Ojibwes were
the masters of the land that would become Minnesota. Europeans who ventured into Indian country to reap the riches of its furs trod carefully on this
alien soil. Their small parties of adventurers had no real power in the midst of
thousands of Native people; moreover, they were weeks, if not months, away
from their provisioning points. Survival itself, let alone success, depended on
the goodwill of Indian trading partners. Thus, of necessity, traders schooled
themselves in Native customs and, living among the Indians, adopted many
of their ways.

The north country was not a site of conquest. Rather, it had become a meeting ground of civilizations, a place where geographic and cultural borders were
blurred and unfixed. The mutually beneficial exchange of furs for European
goods required a cultural exchange as well, a process of interaction that left
no one—Indian or European—unchanged. Similar cultural meeting grounds
emerged, at least for a time, all along the North American frontier, but the
hybrid society of the Upper Great Lakes, sustained by the fur trade, developed more fully and lasted longer than anywhere else on the North American
continent.[1]

The frontier, by its very definition, was a temporary and moving locale. At every point where Europeans pushed inland, border cultures evolved, then were overwhelmed by the pressures of white settlement, backed by the political and military power of empire. The Missouri River valley, Rio Grande basin, Spanish Florida, and Ohio Valley, to name only a few regions, all experienced at least some brief period when European interlopers met and mingled with Indian peoples on relatively symbiotic terms. But as settlers moved in and individual ownership made land a premier commodity, Indians became an obstacle to be removed, a policy justified by the creation of racial and cultural hierarchies that have informed American history throughout most of the twentieth century.[2]

In the Upper Mississippi River valley, however, the borderland endured for nearly two centuries. Deep in the northwestern interior, legendary for its harsh climate and dangerous Native people, the region did not attract settlers until well into the nineteenth century. Neither the French nor the British who succeeded them wished to encourage settlement. Their economic interest was fixed solely on extracting furs. An influx of farmers would only drive the forest creatures, as well as the trade's Indian labor force, out of the region. Moreover, as Europeans knew from Indian wars in the east, land-hungry settlers would irrevocably destabilize the relationship between traders and Indians.

For diplomatic purposes, French officials struggled to sort the confusing array of Indian bands into nations that conformed to European territorial understandings. They created maps that carved Indian country into fixed tribal fiefdoms and tried to identify leaders of each "national" unit with whom they could parlay. But the organization of Indian society by kinship, which blurred tribal boundaries, and the seasonal movement of bands across vast stretches of land made such a project meaningless.[3] As a result, the French often blundered in their ambassadorial efforts. Nonetheless, within the limits of their understanding they employed diplomatic protocols in all matters connected with the trade. They were careful to receive permission from local bands before setting up trading posts and prohibited whites from infringing on Native trapping rights. Despite all the ceremonial proclamations that claimed the region for France, the French made no attempt to act on their supposed title to the land. Territorial dominion applied only in reference to their European rivals. The French were determined to keep the British out, but they had neither the military might nor the will to challenge Indian sovereignty. The fur trade, which to outsiders seemed unfettered by the boundaries of civilization, actually depended on a well-established code of conduct. As long as it served both Indian and white interests, the borderland remained intact. The functioning of this delicate system depended on personal relationships, the face-to-face negotiations between Indians and traders. Yet the intimate encounters of the borderland were regularly rocked by distant clashes of empire. The fortunes of the Great Lakes fur trade were deeply entwined in larger contests for power.[4]

Imperial Gamesmanship

The French had no ambitions to settle the Upper Great Lakes, but they were determined to keep the British from tapping the wealth of the region, which they feared would upset the balance of power in Europe. Ironically, though a fortune in furs flowed out of the region, profits were discouragingly small both

for the Montreal merchants and the crown. Unlicensed traders seemed to be everywhere, diverting a good portion of the trade to rival English markets at Hudson's Bay and Albany, and the colonial government was hard-pressed to keep the loyalty of its Indian allies. The French had made bonds of kinship with the tribes and, according to Native custom, kinship demanded generosity, regardless of fluctuations in incomprehensible distant markets. Meeting those expected obligations was a costly enterprise. The ever-growing distribution of guns and gifts ate steadily into profits, but the French, reckoning that the cost of losing their Indian allies would be greater still, had no choice but to keep the goods flowing.[5]

Between 1702 and 1763 France and England engaged in a series of wars, fought both in Europe and on the colonial frontier, punctuated by relatively brief interludes of peace. In North America, as they squared off in Queen Anne's War (1702–1713), King George's War (1744–1748), and the French and Indian War (1754–1763), both the French and the British relied on Indians as their primary fighting force. Though the bloody battles took place far to the east of the Upper Mississippi—along the New York and New England frontiers, the length of the Allegheny Mountains, and in the Ohio Valley—the distant clash of empires reverberated throughout the northern borderland.[6]

In 1696, to control the flow of pelts into the saturated European market, France had ordered traders to withdraw from the west, just as the Dakotas finally had established direct trading ties. But only two years later war with England was impending and the French crown reversed its policy. Despite the stagnant market in furs, an expansionist plan was put in place to win the loyalty of the western tribes and hem in the English colonies. However, with the outbreak of Queen Anne's War in 1702, western policy changed yet again as the French pulled back from the west to concentrate their efforts on protecting their eastern interests. To the frustration of the Dakotas, direct trade with the French would stagnate for another decade.[7]

After 1701 the fur trade itself became only incidental to imperial political aims, most urgently the need to halt the English march across North America. Nonetheless, the strategies put in place had multiple effects in the western interior. The on-again, off-again presence of French trading partners weakened the loyalty of the Dakotas, who found the French to be unreliable "brothers." Thus, they had no compunction about trading with coureurs de bois, either French or English, when the opportunity arose. And trading prospects began to broaden after 1701 when, despite protests from merchants in Montreal, the French developed two new strategic outposts to protect their imperial interests: Detroit, to guard access to the Great Lakes, and the colony of Louisiana, to forestall English control of the Mississippi River. As the Montreal merchants had feared, both settlements created avenues of trade that would ultimately divert the flow of furs away from Montreal and weaken Dakota reliance on the vagaries of the government of New France.[8]

Both the French and English were dependent on Indian allies as their primary military force in North America. The French kept fewer than 1,000 troops posted in all of New France, which required them to tend Indian loyalties with careful diplomacy, lavish presents, and premium prices for furs. Though the cost of goods escalated in wartime, they could not afford to pass those increases on to their Indian customers. As a result, the trade often operated at a loss, another cost of waging war. However, deep in the interior, isolated from sustained English influence, Indian loyalties were of less concern to France and the colonial government mandated cost-cutting measures. Thus, the Dakotas found trading opportunities limited, goods hard to come by, and prices high.[9]

In the short term, the most important consequence of French policy in the Upper Mississippi region was a strengthening of the entente between the Dakotas and Ojibwes. When French traders disappeared, the Ojibwes reassumed the role of key middlemen in carrying European goods to their neighbors. Writing in the early 1700s, trader Nicholas Perrot noted, "They have for neighbors and friends the Sioux, on whose lands they hunt when they wish."[10] Trapping rights, however, belonged exclusively to the Dakotas, and when periodic local conflicts broke the peace between the tribes in this era they were usually caused by infringements on trapping prerogatives or disputes between individuals. These were minor upheavals, however, and for the most part the Ojibwe–Dakota alliance held fast against surrounding tribes.[11]

With the cost of extended warfare draining the royal treasuries, in 1713 the French and English put down their arms and hammered out a treaty that resituated the strategic importance of Minnesota country. The treaty gave the English the right to trade in the western interior, a concession that the French fully intended to thwart in practice. Consequently, courting the Dakotas and Ojibwes began again in earnest. The governor of New France lost no time in licensing traders and authorizing the establishment of posts in the west. Traders leaped at the opportunity. Again the fur trade functioned as a means to a political end. By bringing goods to the western Indians, France hoped to hold the allegiance of the tribes against the English. Accordingly, the first priority was to reoccupy the posts on the Great Lakes, where the English Hudson's Bay Company might extend its reach. By 1720 the Lake Superior posts of Kaministiquia and Chequamegon were again bustling with activity. Michilimackinac, located in the straits between Lakes Huron and Michigan, became the central exchange point for a global trading network. At Michilimackinac, goods obtained from Europe, Asia, and the colonies were parceled out to the posts on the frontier and pelts collected from the interior were graded, weighed, and exported to Montreal, Europe, and as far as China. Each spring more than one hundred provision-laden canoes voyaged from Montreal to Michilimackinac and returned with a year's harvest of furs. The market for pelts had rebounded and fortunes beckoned adventurers into the west.[12]

Unfortunately for the French, their previous abandonment of the west had injured their credibility as trading partners. The Ojibwes, who had a long history as French trading partners, had not been entirely deserted during the war. Moreover, the Ojibwes had not yet become dependent on European products for their survival and well-being. Thus, while fewer goods and weaponry made their way to the western Great Lakes, the scarcity had been inconvenient but not disastrous. In fact, the disappearance of French traders had yielded some benefit. Though trade had diminished, by sharing the scarce commodities with their Dakota neighbors, they had strengthened their position as middlemen.[13] All of these considerations helped assuage Ojibwe resentments against the French.

The Dakotas, however, were less easily wooed. Too many times Frenchmen had come with gifts and pledges of friendship and then failed to return, leaving their Dakota "brothers" without the weapons to challenge their better-armed enemies. As the French would discover, the Dakotas had turned to other available sources for goods—Ojibwe middlemen and the unlicensed coureurs de bois. When licensed French traders returned, they found that the Dakotas were willing to barter, but with increasing access to other commercial partners the Indians intended to set the terms. Further destabilizing the French monopoly, the Dakotas had made peace with the Fox tribe of the Wisconsin River area. The Fox then established a thriving trade, carrying English goods to the Dakotas. Intent on keeping French traders from interfering with their customers, they barred the Mississippi route into Minnesota. The French retaliated in what became essentially a trade war, turned to a rare use of force, and set out to exterminate the Fox. The Fox wars, which continued intermittently until 1734, made travel up the Mississippi a perilous enterprise.[14]

In 1727 the French managed to secure a temporary truce with the Fox, allowing a trade expedition backed by Montreal merchants to finally enter Dakota territory from the south. The party of thirty—a few French officers, two Jesuit missionaries, the rest traders and *engagés*—had high hopes as they set to building Fort Beauharnois on the western shore of Lake Pepin, near present-day Old Frontenac.[15] They had acquired an official three-year monopoly on the Dakota trade and expected the Indians to flock to them with furs as they had in the past. But times had changed. The French had been absent for years and the Dakotas had access to trade goods through Fox middlemen. Though a band of several hundred Dakotas made camp nearby, warily watching construction of the fort, they soon disappeared and only a few returned to trade. The Jesuits were equally disappointed. Confident that the Dakotas would welcome Christianity along with kettles, axes, and knives, they opened the Mission of St. Michael the Archangel, the first Christian mission in Minnesota. But it attracted no potential converts. In fact, for the most part the Dakotas seemed distinctly suspicious of French overtures. Adding to the list of troubles as the months wore on, game was scarce, the Mississippi flooded the fort in the spring, the Dakotas were increasingly aloof, and word came that the Fox had broken the truce with the French in the south. Abjectly discouraged and fearing for their lives, eleven members of the party, including the post commander, fled south after less than a year. The rest struggled on until 1729 when the fort was abandoned.[16]

The tale of Fort Beauharnois illustrates the practical reality of French–Indian relations. The French needed the Indians more than the Indians needed the French. As the western tribes had demonstrated during Queen Anne's War, European goods—though desirable—were not necessities. In fact, a general scarcity of guns and powder tended to promote peace among the tribes. Moreover, the French were never able to enforce their official trade monopoly. With only a skeletal military presence, they were powerless to stop the ever-growing number of unlicensed traders. By the 1720s hundreds of coureurs de bois roamed the West, coming north from New Orleans as well as through the Great Lakes. All these factors weakened French influence among the tribes. And France could not hold its possessions in North America without Native allies. This gave the Indians tremendous leverage. The Dakotas were no longer captive to the French market. If prices rose, they could refuse to trade. If the French betrayed their expected obligations, they could expect retribution.[17]

With the British colonial presence expanding at an alarming rate along the eastern seaboard, the French were in an unenviable position, "in a continual mismatch between claims to power and funds [and manpower] to back the claims." By the mid-eighteenth century the population of New France barely exceeded 70,000, while the thirteen British colonies counted more than 1.5 million inhabitants. Decades of war had depleted the royal treasury, and the revenues from the fur trade were outweighed by the costs of maintaining Indian alliances; but the trade, though it operated at a loss, was essential to keeping those alliances intact—on terms that were agreeable to the Indians. The Indians never considered themselves subjects of the French and the French lacked the military might to treat them as such. Whatever influence they exerted relied on serving the Indians' interests. Royal expenditures for gifts ranged between 20,000 and 60,000 livres per year, and diplomatic relations had to be handled with great sensitivity.[18] As one official confided to his superior, "I grant you these nations would have become far more useful to the colony had we been able to subdue them . . . [but] we have found the task to be an impossible one; nor are there signs that it will become less so. Kindly apprise me of any means you should conceive of for securing such obedience."[19]

Obedience was an unattainable dream. Even cooperation required constant tending and profuse generosity. As Richard White writes, it was "an odd imperialism where mediation succeeded and force failed, where colonizers gave gifts to the colonized and patriarchal metaphors were the heart of politics."[20] To hold on to their far-flung territories, the French needed to maintain alliances with multiple Indian nations, yet intertribal wars made the task a constant balancing act. Mediating intertribal conflicts by necessity became essential and expensive elements of colonial policy. As an example, in 1741 at Chequamegon, conducting peace negotiations between the Dakotas and the Ojibwes cost the crown 2,304 livres in presents to the tribal representatives.[21]

Diplomacy was indeed expensive, but trading with warring tribes could be lethal. Weapons, shot, and powder were essential trade goods, yet the tribes understandably considered arming their enemies a betrayal and were quick to retaliate. In 1735, a Dakota war party killed two Frenchmen who had been trading with an enemy tribe, then appeared at a post on Lake Pepin (near old Fort Beauharnois), brandishing the traders' scalps as a warning. After several such intimidating incidents, the post commandant asked Dakota chief Sacred Born why they insulted their French brothers. The chief replied succinctly that the act was done "with reflection and design."[22]

War Zone

The priorities of empire had turned colonial politics into a chronic financial drain as well as a diplomatic nightmare, so it is not surprising that by the 1730s France began to take a renewed interest in finding a route to the Western Sea. The lure of the China trade, along with the prospect of less contentious Native trading partners, attracted enthusiasm from both royal officials and Montreal merchants. In 1731, a brigade of canoes left Montreal on what would be France's last great expedition of discovery in North America. The leader of the venture was a native Canadian and former post commandant, Pierre Gaultier de Varennes, Sieur de la Vérendrye. Heading a party of fifty that included three of his sons, and supplied with a trading monopoly granted by the crown, the financial backing of a consortium of merchants, and a birch bark map that supposedly led to the Pacific, La Vérendrye confidently headed west.[23]

The map was drawn by Auchagah, the Cree guide who accompanied the expedition. A few years earlier Auchagah had fired La Vérendrye's imagination with tales of a northern passage to the salt sea. Conveniently, since the Crees were anxious to establish trading relationships with the French and arm themselves against the Dakotas, his map led the explorers directly through Cree territory. Whether by happy coincidence or more likely by design, Auchagah

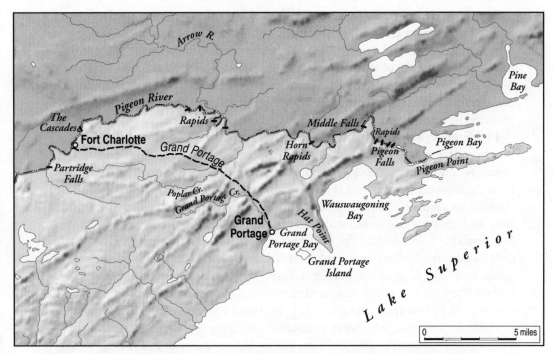

The Grand Portage, the overland route connecting Lake Superior to the interior waterways.

succeeded in bringing the French to his people. The route took the explorers far north of earlier expeditions and required an arduous nine-mile portage from Lake Superior, but it had one great advantage: it avoided Dakota territory, where diplomatic relations were decidedly tense. The Crees, on the other hand, eagerly invited the French to their lands, as did their allies, the Assiniboins, northern Ojibwes, and Cree-Ojibwes, who had fused into merged bands northwest of Lake Superior.[24]

Though Montreal merchants funded the expedition, La Vérendrye had little interest in business and an unfortunate lack of political savvy. His passion was exploration and he doggedly pursued his dream of a northwest passage until his death in 1749, eventually reaching the upper Missouri River. In the course of his travels La Vérendrye pioneered the route that would later become the main conduit for trade in the Canadian Northwest. But even more than his geographical discoveries, the missteps he made in the 1730s along what is now the Canada–U.S. border made its mark on the course of Minnesota history.

The initial portage the expedition followed from Lake Superior to the Pigeon River was so daunting that it nearly caused a mutiny. La Vérendrye wrote of the "Grand Portage," "All our people in dismay at the length of the portage . . . loudly demanded that I should turn back." Somehow he managed to persuade them to carry on, and by the following summer—nearly a year after leaving

Montreal—they had reached Rainy Lake, where the party was met by fifty canoes of welcoming Crees. Pushing farther northwest to Lake of the Woods, La Vérendrye established Fort St. Charles at the lake's Northwest Angle inlet, the northernmost point of what is now Minnesota—a primitive outpost that would be the home base for his later expeditions west. Ironically, Fort St. Charles, the most remote of all the French forts in the region, was the most enduring, remaining in operation until the end of the French regime.[25]

[32]

La Vérendrye was delighted by the warm reception he received from the northern tribes and quickly developed a close, sympathetic relationship with them. When the Crees proposed adopting his son Jean-Baptiste into the tribe, he was honored to consent. He also understood that adoptive kinship would strengthen trading allegiances to the French over English traders at Hudson's Bay. As he was quick to point out to his Indian friends, when they dealt with the English, "you have to do as if you were their enemies; they give you no credit." As proof of his friendship, La Vérendrye liberally dispensed "bullets, guns, butcher's knives, daggers, gunflints, awls, tobacco, etc." But even as he armed the Crees, Assiniboins, and northern Ojibwes, he was uncomfortably aware that the weapons he provided enabled them to wage frequent attacks against the Dakotas, who were established trading partners of the French. La Vérendrye's solution to the problem was ill conceived at best. Writing to Quebec, he urged the government to reestablish a post on the Mississippi in hopes of pacifying the Dakotas. The result was that at the same time the French were urging the tribes to make peace, they ensured that both sides received a steady flow of arms.[26]

Matters came to a head in 1734. Following a Dakota raid, the Crees and Assiniboins were planning a retaliatory attack and asked that their adopted son, Jean-Baptiste Vérendrye, join their war party. The elder La Vérendrye was caught in a bind. Far too involved in tribal disputes, he had sung the war song and wept for the dead of the Crees. If he refused to send his son with them, he feared the Indians would "take the French for cowards" and consider him a hypocrite. Reluctantly he agreed.[27]

This was an enormous error in judgment. Though the French had certainly participated in indigenous warfare alongside their Indian allies, no Frenchman had taken up arms against an established trading partner. The Dakotas had maintained peaceful, if troubled, relations with the French for many years and the carefully cultivated ties of fictive kinship made La Vérendrye's actions a monumental betrayal. Already angered by what they considered French double-dealing with their enemies, the Dakotas vowed to take their vengeance. In June 1736 a Dakota war party that included a few southern Ojibwe allies tracked down and murdered young Vérendrye and twenty-three fellow Frenchmen at Lake of the Woods. Jean-Baptiste's body was "scored with knife cuts, a stake thrust into his side," and to make certain that the French understood the message they meant to send, the Indians decapitated the victims, wrapped their heads in beaver skins, and positioned them as if in a council circle. All this signified that the French had brought the attack on themselves.[28]

The event had far-reaching consequences. The Dakota attack was motivated as much by politics as by revenge. They had no intention to go to war against the French. Rather, the purpose of the attack was to enforce the implied obligations of their alliance and frighten the Frenchmen into abandoning arms trade with the Crees and Assiniboins. However, the fearsome Dakotas may have overplayed their hand. The French, admitting they were powerless to impose control, pulled all their traders and missionaries out of Dakota territory. Then, at the urging of Jean-Baptiste's father, who was hungry for vengeance, the colonial government sponsored the Crees, Assiniboins, and Ojibwes in a full-scale war against the Dakotas, supplying advisers and a few troops as well as "guns, powder, ball, and knives" to Native combatants.[29]

Indian Wars

French efforts to expand their scope of influence destabilized intertribal relationships in multiple ways. They had played a dangerous game—"arms dealers in a war zone"—and set off a chain of violence. The newly armed Crees and Assiniboins challenged the Dakotas and Lakota Sioux along their northern border. The southern Ojibwes, caught between the two sides, made alliance with the northern Ojibwes, Crees, and Assiniboins, ending nearly one hundred years of peaceful relations with their Dakota neighbors.[30]

Though French commercial interests invariably suffered when hostilities broke out between Indian tribes—trapping and hunting for the market came to a virtual standstill in wartime—by establishing posts on the Mississippi the French had unwittingly helped destroy the Ojibwe-Dakota entente. The posts offered a convenient alternative to distant Chequamegon Bay, the center of the Ojibwe trading network, and allowed the Dakotas to cut out the middlemen. No longer dependent on the Ojibwes for trade goods, the Dakotas became increasingly unwilling to tolerate Ojibwe presence on their lands.[31]

At the same time, the Ojibwes desperately needed to expand their territory. Their population had grown significantly, both from natural increase and inmigration of clans fleeing conflicts in the east. Game was disappearing fast and they needed to claim new hunting grounds or starve. Moreover, the Ojibwes had long been a commercial nation; trading ties with the French had become an established part of their livelihood. They could not afford to alienate their commercial partners by allying themselves with the hostile Dakotas. Thus, the Indian war that would be fought sporadically across Minnesota for the following century—one of the longest wars in American history—was intrinsically tied to European imperial politics and an international market economy.[32]

Because the Ojibwes eventually came to claim the contested territory of northern Minnesota, history has portrayed them as victors who drove the

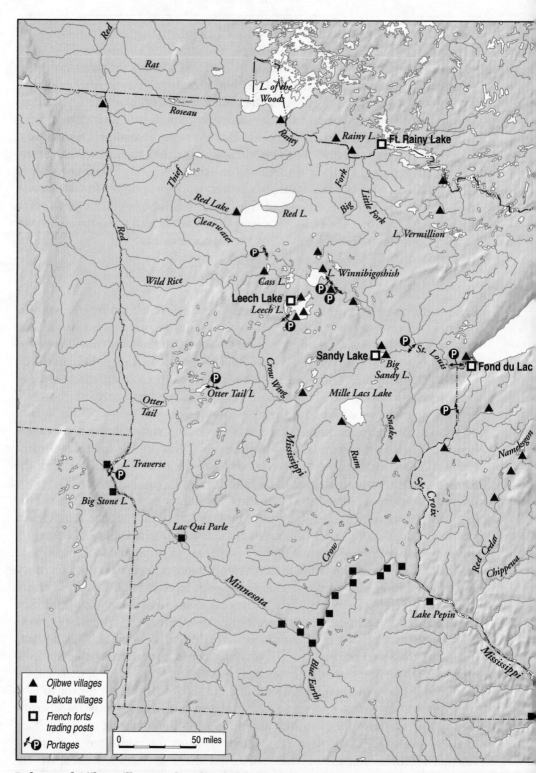

Dakota and Ojibwe villages and trading hubs, ca. 1800.

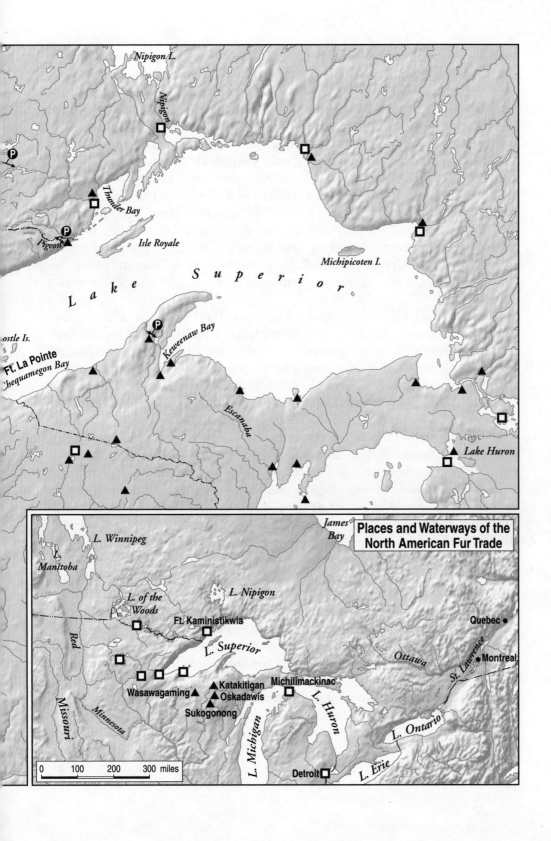

Nipigon L.

Nipigon

P

Thunder Bay

P

Pigeon

Isle Royale

Michipicoten I.

L a k e   S u p e r i o r

P

Keweenaw Bay

ostle Is.

Ft. La Pointe

Chequamegon Bay

Escanaba

Lake Huron

Places and Waterways of the North American Fur Trade

James Bay

L. Winnipeg

L. Manitoba

L. of the Woods

L. Nipigon

Ft. Kaministikwia

Quebec •

Red

Montreal •

L. Superior

Ottawa

St. Lawrence

Wasawagaming

Katakitigan

Michilimackinac

Oskadawis

Sukogonong

Missouri

Minnesota

L. Michigan

L. Huron

L. Ontario

Detroit

L. Erie

0   100   200   300 miles

[36]

Dakotas from the land. However, the course of the Ojibwe–Dakota wars was determined by complicated circumstances that cannot be defined in simple terms of victory or defeat.[33] At the outset of the war the Dakotas were in a perilous position. Adding to the Ojibwes, Crees, and Assiniboins lined up against them—not to mention the French—were hostile Ottawa and Potowatomi bands along their border (who held long-standing grudges against the Dakotas). Of the other neighboring tribes, only the Fox, far to the southeast of the contested territory, were Dakota friends. Still, the Dakotas soon demonstrated that their legendary reputation as warriors was well earned. The Ojibwes drew first blood, attacking the Dakotas at Lake Pepin, but the Dakota counterattack was so fierce that the Ojibwes were forced to abandon their villages and retreat to safer ground nearer to their French allies. They joined northern Ojibwe villages at Grand Portage, Rainy Lake, Lake Vermilion, and along the Vermilion River, a region that has remained home to Ojibwe peoples to the present day.[34]

The Crees and Assiniboins attacked northern Dakota villages at Red Lake, Lake Winnibigosh, Cass Lake, and Leech Lake, a multipronged assault that presaged disaster for the outgunned Dakotas. However, the Crees and Assiniboins soon found themselves facing a far more deadly enemy. A smallpox epidemic exploded in their villages in 1736, just as the war was getting under way. The death toll was catastrophic, wiping out entire bands. Suddenly the Ojibwes found themselves standing alone against the Dakotas.[35]

Though the tribes remained in a state of war, little territory changed hands over the next five years. Unlike Europeans, warring Native Americans did not carry on sustained campaigns over long periods. Instead they preferred brief attacks that minimized loss of life separated by lengthy lulls devoted to the necessary business of feeding their families. Thus, until some time in 1740–41, hostilities were confined to small-scale sorties that did not substantively redraw tribal boundaries. By 1740, however, demographic, ecological, and commercial changes gave the Ojibwes a new advantage.[36]

Ojibwe population in the lakes region was on the rise, whereas the Dakota presence there had been declining for decades. The Dakotas, whose culture was based on seasonal migration, had been on the move well before hostilities broke out in 1736. Some bands migrated south into the richer lands of the Lower Mississippi River valley, probably drawn by French trading posts as well as the search for game. Others followed the buffalo, which had for unknown reasons begun a westward migration. Buffalo had been an important part of the diverse Dakota economy for generations, and by 1700 the introduction of guns and horses had made the massive animals easy prey, as well as an ideal source of sustenance.[37] The buffalo provided a bountiful supply of fresh meat that also could be dried into pemmican to carry villages through the scarcity of winter. From the hides people made clothing, robes, and even the coverings for their dwellings. Only tenuously tied to the European commercial network, the Dakotas had never devoted their full attention to hunting for trade. When trading opportunities faded, they quickly returned to hunting for subsistence rather than the market, increasing their reliance on the buffalo. As the buffalo moved out of reach of hunting parties in the lakes region, Dakota villages followed. According to a French census taken in 1736, only scattered bands of Dakotas with perhaps 300 warriors remained in the woodlands north and east of Mille Lacs.[38]

Given the circumstances, it seems that issues of honor and tradition more than necessity compelled the Dakotas to defend the contested territory. But there came a point when the cost in lives and quality of life outweighed the resolve to defend their besieged villages in the lake country. In the early 1740s a massive force of Ojibwes attacked a major Dakota stronghold at Sandy Lake, west of Lake Superior. After a bloody three-day battle, the Dakotas were forced to abandon the village, marking a turning point in the conflict. Though the tribes traded offensives—punctuated by sustained periods of détente—for more than another decade, by 1760 Ojibwe bands occupied the lands around Leech and the Red lakes, the St. Croix and Crow Wing rivers, and the headwaters of the Mississippi and had gained firm control of northern Minnesota. The Dakotas of the lakes region gradually migrated south and west to the buffalo-rich plains west of the Mississippi, following the pattern of their Lakota relations already established on the plains.[39]

Ironically, the French, after setting the war in motion, almost immediately changed course yet again. The government in Montreal soon realized that creating enemies of the Dakotas served neither their political nor commercial objectives, and thus by 1740 they were attempting once again to reestablish friendly relations and broker peace among the tribes. Of course, reopening trade meant that again they were arming both sides of the ongoing conflict, ensuring that the bloodshed would continue. The Dakotas, who needed a steady supply of guns and ammunition, accepted the French overtures and were even persuaded to send representatives to a general council of tribes convened in Montreal in 1742.[40] The peace agreement that came out of the council had some success, though little credit was due to French colonial policy. Quite the contrary: the outbreak of King George's War (1744–48) brought trade with the western tribes once again to a virtual standstill. As a result, both the arms and commercial incentives for waging intertribal war dwindled. In 1750 the French resumed trading at Lake Pepin, but only three years later the final conflict between the French and British in North America erupted and shortly thereafter the post was once more abandoned. Finally, in 1760 Montreal fell to the British and their Indian allies. The French and Indian War was over. In the Treaty of Paris, worked out in 1763, the French ceded their North American possessions (with the exception of New Orleans) to England. New France was dead, and according to the newly redrawn European map of North America, Indian country east of the Mississippi now belonged to the British crown.[41]

Local Politics

Unquestionably, the social and economic world of fur traders and Indians was influenced by European imperial politics, but it is equally true that the international fur trade and the power that went along with it were fundamentally dependent on local, face-to-face relationships. Somewhat surprisingly, despite a colonial policy that was inconsistent and fraught with problems, the French reaped healthy profits from the Lake Superior and Upper Mississippi regions in the unsettled last decades of their regime. The Lake Superior trade flourished throughout the 1740s, thanks to the Ojibwes, who remained steady partners. The Dakota trade, despite its fitful stops and starts, proved profitable as well. In the few years that the Lake Pepin post was occupied, it cleared more than 150,000 francs annually.[42]

Meanwhile, French–Indian relationships in other regions were sinking to an all-time low. Civil and military authorities in Montreal and Paris, with no personal experience on the frontier, tried to impose orders on their Native American allies that they could not hope to enforce. In addition, with a treasury depleted by years of warfare, they cut back on gifts and raised the price of goods. Wherever these breaches of custom were carried out, they eroded the loyalties of Indian trading partners. In contrast, on the Upper Mississippi River and the northern lakes, far from meddling government officials, local custom prevailed. French and Indian relations restabilized and commercial ventures prospered. After La Vérendrye was removed in 1744, subsequent post commandants in the north made few missteps in their dealings with the northern Indians. Schooled in the customs required for French–Ojibwe cooperation, they tended the bond with "kind offices and liberality in dealing." Though they sometimes complained privately that the Indians were "unsettled and very impertinent" with a "want of subordination," French authorities understood the need to court their goodwill. In return, the Ojibwes brought in a wealth of beaver and other valuable pelts and even fought alongside the French at Quebec in 1759.[43]

Dakota–French relations were a considerably more complicated matter. After a quarter century of what the Indians perceived as broken promises and betrayals, they were skeptical of French intentions. Still, they needed the guns and powder the French could provide. In 1750, when Montreal determined to reopen a post on the Mississippi, the governor tapped Paul Marin to take charge of the delicate negotiations. Marin was supremely suited to regain the trust of the Dakotas. A native French Canadian, he had spent a lifetime in the western trade and had a keen understanding of Dakota culture. According to Gary Clayton Anderson, "He fostered kinship ties with every important Dakota leader; gaining the trust of these people as no European had done since Le Sueur." Marin arrived at Lake Pepin in a brigade loaded with gifts, including weaponry. Most important, though, he understood that both the Dakotas and Ojibwes were anxious to make peace. The constant warfare threatened the survival of entire villages. It disrupted the necessary tasks of hunting and gathering food for the people and also was killing off a generation of young men. Dakota chiefs at the council in Montreal had asked for the traders to return and help "give them sense" in effecting a truce with their neighbors. As for the Ojibwes, a French observer wrote that they feared if the war continued "they would expose themselves to die by hunger the next winter." Marin had been working for a decade to broker peace between the tribes and was well versed in the culture of Indian diplomacy. He also knew that the success of his post on the Mississippi depended on his ability to parlay with both sides in good faith.[44]

Understanding the centrality of kinship ties, Marin arranged to have his son Joseph appointed commander at the Madeline Island village of La Pointe, in Ojibwe country. Joseph had lived in Indian country from the age of thirteen and shared his father's understanding of Indian ways. Though no record remains, it is most probable that both father and son entered into marriage with Dakota and Ojibwe women, since such unions were nearly ubiquitous among long-term traders.[45] But whether through marriage or adoption, it is clear that the Marins forged ties of kinship that connected them to both the Dakotas and Ojibwes. They worked tirelessly to promote peace between the tribes, using the trust they had earned as kinsmen, along with diplomatic acumen and lavish gifts, to bring the parties together. Their efforts proved successful where all other attempts had failed. As honest brokers, they won the respect and loyalty of the tribes, who frequently turned to them to keep minor disputes from reescalating into full-scale war.[46] The peace agreement remained more or less intact throughout the Marins' tenure in the north country. Unfortunately, the French and British were less successful at keeping peace among themselves. The rumblings of war began in 1753 along the Ohio frontier, and both father and son were ordered to report for duty in the east. The Mississippi post was abandoned in 1854; two years later, with France marshaling all its colonial resources to defend Quebec, the French left the Lake Superior posts as well. This time they would not return.[47]

The map of Minnesota is dotted with places that still bear French names— Mille Lacs, Lac qui Parle, Traverse des Sioux, Grand Marais, and dozens more—the only physical reminder of more than one hundred years of the French and Indian encounter. French explorers and entrepreneurs pioneered trading routes and fueled the European imagination about the riches of North America's interior but they planted no permanent settlements in Minnesota; their trading posts crumbled away and were forgotten—until rediscovered by archaeologists many generations later. Nonetheless, the legacy of this era was profound. The interdependence, and cultural accommodation it demanded, between the French and Indians created a new social space—a hybrid culture that would shape Indian–white relations in the region for the next one hundred years.

À la Façon du Pays

The French described the union of Europeans and Indian women, joined without benefit of Christian clergy, as "according to the custom of the country"— *à la façon du pays.* The term itself was an implicit acknowledgment that the North American interior, what they called the *pays d'en haut,* was a different world with rules of conduct all its own. Commercial endeavors were fundamentally tied to a social process based on family, friendship, and obligation. Intermarriage was the cultural linchpin of the economic system.

Unlike the British and Americans who followed them, the French had few prejudices regarding intermarriage. In fact, for a time the colonial authorities, urged by Jesuit missionaries, encouraged Christian intermarriage, hoping to convert the Indians and also perhaps to gain some control over the unmanageable traders. Civil and military officials had discovered, to their dismay, that the isolation of the wilderness bred a troublesome independence that led French subjects to throw off the constraints of European society—so-called civilization—as well as play fast and loose with colonial laws and orders. As intendant Jean Talon complained, they were men "without Christianity, without sacraments, without religion, without priests, without magistrates, sole masters of their own actions and of the application of their wills."[48]

Most men in the trade did indeed marry Native women—some in Catholic ceremony and the majority by Indian custom—but the effect was not quite what the church and civil authorities had hoped. Instead of bringing the Indian nations and men of the trade closer into the orbit of French authority, marriage enmeshed the trading fraternity deeper within the Indian world. Some degree of cultural mingling was ubiquitous regardless of class, as demonstrated by Paul and Joseph Marin, who epitomized the cultural fluidity of officers and pedigreed traders by the end of the French regime. But despite decades spent in the interior that made them uncomfortable with European ways, the two men were also decorated officers of the crown who kept a sense of separateness and "social distinctness" from Indian society as well.[49]

Among the lower ranks of the trade, the cultural blending was more fully internalized. While the *bourgeois* (as the district heads were known) and their clerks usually intended eventually to return to Montreal, if not to Europe, the canoe men and *engagés* were committed to the frontier for life. Peasants by background and poorly paid, they had no dreams of accumulating wealth; their only capital consisted of the wilderness skills they had learned from the Indians. Few left the trade until driven out by age or the breakdown of their strength. Most could neither read nor write, but they were fluent in Indian languages and could read the terrain of the forests and rivers with an unerring eye. Life in the backcountry offered them a freedom that would have been impossible in any other venue. Not surprisingly, the laborers of the trade embraced

Indian culture with enthusiasm. They married Indian women and between expeditions often lived in the villages of their wives' families.

Even more deeply immersed in Indian ways were the coureurs de bois. Considered outlaws by French authorities, they married into Indian families and lived among their wives' kinsmen. Periodically they showed up at French outposts to trade their furs and let off some steam. In the interior, enforcement of colonial law was problematic to say the least and the illicit traders came and went, apparently with little fear of legal consequences. Contemporary descriptions and historians agree that the coureurs de bois became "a unique blend of French and Indian, wearing Indian dress, traveling like the Indians, eating the same sort of food, speaking their languages, making war in the Indian manner, living off the land and enduring privations with the fortitude of the Indian," and marrying into Indian families. Increasingly, as the French came to realize, life in the wilderness was forging a new identity that was distinctively "Canadian"—and strikingly different from their own. While they approved of the Canadians' bravery, skills, and willingness to endure the extreme hardships of the frontier, as the governor general wrote in the 1680s, these Canadians were "ungovernable." "I cannot emphasize enough . . . the attraction that this Indian way of life has for them."[50] The missionaries found them equally ungovernable and heedless of church law. As one priest complained, "Those who should have aided and served us in the education and conversion of these peoples by their good examples were the very ones who hindered us and destroyed the good which we went to establish." Since intermarriage was not accomplishing what they had hoped, and instead the "godless" traders appeared to be a corrupting influence, the missionaries importuned French officials to outlaw fraternization between whites and Indians. French officials, though they weren't about to obstruct the friendly relationships that were necessary to the trade, began to frown on intermarriage but were powerless to reverse what had become common custom. By the turn of the eighteenth century the colonial governor bemoaned the practice: "Bad should never be mixed with good. . . . All the Frenchmen who have married savages have been licentious, lazy and intolerably independent." Their children "incorporated the worst character traits of both races and were a constant source of trouble."[51]

What the governor, from a Eurocentric perspective, described as vices instead reflected a different set of cultural values. The traders were indeed "intolerably independent." Severed by distance from colonial influence, they did not think of themselves in nationalistic terms or as subjects of the crown and bowed to French authority only when they could not avoid it. The French were continually frustrated in their attempts to bring order to the trade. Most often, officials could not even track the illicit traders down "because everyone associated covers up for them." Even those legally employed in the trade only selectively obeyed the law. As one officer stationed at Michilimackinac complained in 1702, "It is very fine and Honourable for me, Monsieur, to be charged with your orders but it is also very vexatious to have only ink and paper as a means to enforce them." Like their Indian kinsmen, the independent traders did not recognize France as their master. When the news of King George's War reached the coureurs de bois at Michilimackinac, they quickly headed west to live with the Dakotas rather than become embroiled in a conflict that was meaningless to them.[52]

[42] What the French deemed laziness—a label that was almost universally thrown at Native peoples—in actuality stemmed from a nonmaterialist value system that was incomprehensible to Europeans. The French—and the British and Americans who followed them—tried their best to enmesh the Indians in an acquisitive culture of consumption, which would then impel them to put all their energies into hunting for the trade. However, to the continuing frustration of the Europeans, the Indians refused to embrace the profit-making ethos that was central to the European mindset. While Indians put great store in the presents that their trading partners pressed upon them, the exchange of gifts mattered as much for their symbolic values of respect and kinship as for their intrinsic worth. Despite the array of trade goods available, they hunted for the market only to fulfill their immediate needs. When those needs were met, they turned their attention to other priorities of life. The voyageurs and coureurs de bois who spent their lives in the backcountry demonstrated an equal disregard for asset accumulation, which French officials considered a character flaw. One officer likened them to pirates, writing, "They Lavish, Eat, Drink, and Play all away as long as the Goods hold out; and when these are gone, they e'en sell their . . . cloaths. This done, they are forc'd to go upon a New Voyage for Subsistence."[53]

Finally, both missionaries and officials were appalled by what they viewed as promiscuity between Indian women and men in the trade. In their minds, the only legitimate form of marriage was blessed by the church, monogamous, and a union for life. Though officials tacitly sanctioned unchurched unions with Indian women because they cemented important economic relationships, most of them failed to understand the cultural practices that shaped Indian marriage customs.[54]

Among both the Algonquian and Siouan peoples (as well as most other Indian groups), women had nearly as much freedom in choosing their marital partners as did men. Parents typically arranged the match but daughters usually were free to refuse a proposed bridegroom. The marriage bond remained intact only as long as both parties were contented with the arrangement and either husband or wife could choose to divorce without stigma. Thus, according to Native custom, it did not necessarily constitute abandonment when traders moved on to new territory or returned east and left their Indian wives behind. Since married couples generally remained in the village of the wife's family, it would not be surprising for women to choose to remain with their kin and marry again. Polygamy, though not the norm, was also an accepted practice. Recurring warfare left most villages with a shortage of young men and polygamy provided a practical means for the community to absorb an excess of females into a limited number of households. Therefore, as perceived by Indian people, it was not out of bounds for traders to have more than one wife simultaneously.[55]

Though some voyageur-traders undoubtedly engaged in casual liaisons (especially as the trade degraded in the British and American era), the majority of Euro–Indian unions appear to have been true marriages, according to Indian custom. Many endured for decades or even lifetimes. Outside the backcountry, however, Europeans and especially missionaries regarded such marriages as sinful or, at the very least, "uncivilized" breaches of the social order. Nonetheless, the practice of intermarriage *à la façon du pays* was so widespread—and important to the trade—that critics were powerless to challenge its legitimacy. The best the missionaries could strive for was to urge couples to have their marriages blessed by the church after the fact.[56]

While ties of affection no doubt existed between many of these marriage partners, it is important to remember that the ideal of romantic love as a basis for marriage was a product of the nineteenth century. In earlier times, European marriages typically were intended to fulfill economic or political needs. The upper class cemented political alliances through marriage while for common folk marriage was most often an economic partnership that sustained the family economy. Similar considerations came into play in French and Indian marriages. Traders enhanced their status by marrying into prominent Indian families and Indian women who wed traders became important cultural ambassadors between their people and European trading partners, which gave them prestige among their kin.[57]

Among the lower ranks of the trade, wives were critical economic partners. In the Minnesota region most intermarriage took place between French men and Ojibwe women who possessed skills that were invaluable for both subsistence and for trade. Not only did the women cook, sew, and attend to all the chores of daily life, they also contributed significantly to the trade itself. They tanned the hides and helped build and repair the canoes that carried the furs to market and, equally important, they produced products for the trade themselves. The French grew almost none of their own food and, far from any agricultural settlement, were dependent on the Indians to keep them from starving. Ojibwe women fished; harvested wild rice; planted corn, squash, and pumpkins; and managed the sugar-making process—all of which had value as items of trade as well as food for their families. They also produced the shirts, moccasins, and robes that were essential for European survival in the backcountry. And some wives traded directly along with their husbands or took over when spouses either died or became ill or separated from them.[58]

In the fur trade, economic transactions were inseparable from the social relationships that bridged cultural difference. In multiple ways intermarriage was fundamentally important in constructing the system and keeping it functioning. As the trade matured, generations of mixed-blood children grew to adulthood in this fluid environment between European and Indian worlds. They created a unique identity, indigenous to a particular time and place where racial categories blurred and cultures merged.

[44]

Gens Libre

When France surrendered its North American territories to the British in 1763, it left a legacy of nearly two hundred years of interaction with Native American peoples. By the time the French had begun to penetrate the Minnesota region at the end of the seventeenth century, patterns of intermarriage were well established and mixed-blood interpreters, guides, and *engagés* were in demand for the expeditions of trade and discovery that advanced into the Upper Mississippi and lakes regions. These Métis acted as cultural as well as geographic pathfinders, helping transform strangers into friends and allies. Natives of the north country who moved easily between the European and Indian worlds, they became the essential cultural middlemen of the fur trade. Some Métis were sent by their fathers to Montreal or Quebec for schooling; they could figure sums, read and write in French, and eventually established themselves as clerks or traders. Some lived most of their lives among their mother's people. All moved fluidly between cultures but belonged fully to neither. Over time, a distinct syncretic culture emerged that was identifiably Métis. It was rooted in loyalties forged by kinship connections and face-to-face relationships rather than nationhood. For good reason they called themselves *gens libre*—the free people.[59]

The French left behind no towns or enduring settlements, but the contours of French and Indian relations would make a lasting imprint on the subsequent history of Minnesota and all of the western Great Lakes region. Those who followed would have to negotiate the established culture of this Indian–European meeting ground.

Chapter 3

———◆◆◆———

GEOGRAPHIES OF DOMINION

Hail to the chief: who his buffalo's back straddles,
When in his own country, far, far, from this fort;
Whose brave young canoe-men, here hold up their paddles,
In hopes, that the whizzing balls, may give them sport.
Hail to great Wapashaw!
He comes, beat drums, the Sioux chief comes.

   Arent Schuyler DePeyster,
   British Commandant, Fort Michilimackinac, 1779

A new class of men, of far different temperaments, whose chief object
was to amass fortunes, now made their appearance among the Ojibways. . . . To some degree the Indian ceased to find that true kindness,
sympathy, charity, and respect for his sacred beliefs and rites, which
he had always experienced from his French traders.

   William Warren, Ojibwe historian, ca. 1851

Distant Rumblings

Seventeen sixty-three was a trying year for trade in the north country. Beaver
were abundant and Indians eager to exchange their pelts for needed goods
and provisions. But French posts sat abandoned and trade goods were in short
supply. Coureurs de bois continued to ply the waterways, but they had little
to offer in exchange for the furs they desired. As a result, trade stagnated and
dissatisfied Indians turned away from market hunting and concentrated on
sustaining themselves through traditional seasonal rounds of hunting, fishing,
and gathering.

   Once again, imperial clashes had made themselves felt in the far distant
North American interior. The disruption in the fur trade could be traced directly to the Treaty of Paris. Signed in February, the treaty officially ended the

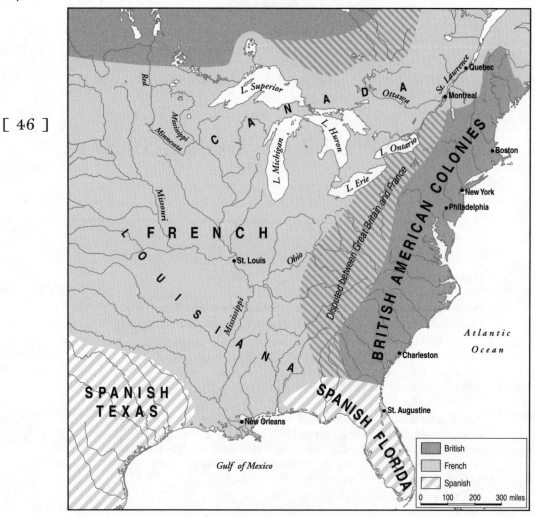

European imperial claims before the 1763 Treaty of Paris.

French and Indian War, with France giving up all of its North American possessions, except New Orleans, to England. The reshuffling of colonial dominion was further complicated when the French revealed that in the previous
year they had secretly ceded Louisiana territory to Spain, thus keeping it out
of British hands. According to European mapmakers, the Minnesota region
was now divided between two new imperial powers: east of the Mississippi
the lands belonged to Great Britain, and from the west bank of the river on-
ward into yet unmapped distant regions Spain held sovereign rule. This paper
transfer of European dominion, of course, was meaningless in terms of actual
power in the north country. Neither nation was in a position to challenge Native sovereignty there. No one in the Upper Mississippi River valley or in the
lakes region to the north doubted that they resided in Indian country. Still, as

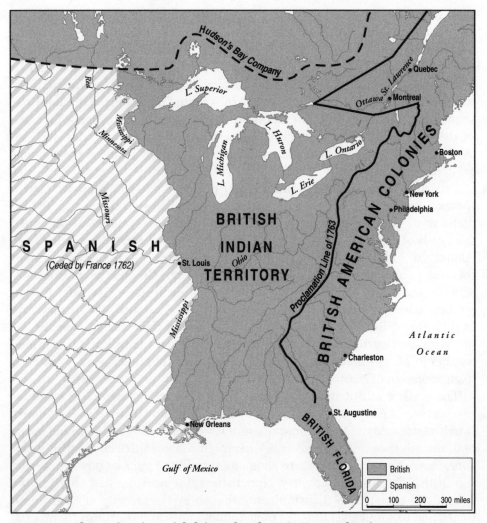

European and American imperial claims after the 1763 Treaty of Paris.

events played out, European politics and the clashes they set off on the eastern part of the continent generated a series of separate yet related resentments and upheavals that rolled across North America to the Great Lakes, the Mississippi, and beyond, ultimately destabilizing the delicate balance of power and fluid culture of the northern borderland.

Spain, engrossed in extracting the wealth of Mexico, made no effort to establish itself on the Upper Mississippi and never attempted to extend its reach beyond St. Louis. British ambitions were another story. Already involved in the fur trade at Hudson's Bay and Albany, New York, the British had long-term plans to expand their commercial interests into the Lake Superior and Upper Mississippi region. In the short term, however, they had their hands full in the Ohio Valley. The British had proved far less adept than the French in their relations with Native people. Though traders in the interior understood the nuances of Indian diplomacy, at a policy level the British were blinded by imperial arrogance. Once they eliminated the threat of French competition, they approached the tribes as conquered subjects rather than partners and allies. General Thomas Gage expressed the official stance when he observed, "All America in the hands of a single power robs them [the Indians] of their Consequence, presents, & pay." Intent on recouping some of the expense incurred in the war, the British cut back on gifts, raised the price of goods, haggled over payment for provisions and services, and generally insulted the customs crafted over a century of trade.[1]

Officials with experience in Indian country were dismayed and pleaded with their superiors to reconsider their high-handed policies. As they knew, the Indians would not bend easily to British will. Sir William Johnson reminded the Lords of Trade, "The Six Nations, Western Indians &c. having never been conquered, Either by the English or French, nor subject to the Laws, consider themselves as a free people." His colleague George Croghan concurred, describing the tribes collectively as "a people who will never Consider Consequences when they think their Liberty likely to be invaded, tho' it may End in their Ruin." But British policy makers, flush with their recent conquest, ignored all such warnings until simmering Native resentments burst into armed conflict in May—only three short months after Britain had formally crowned itself sovereign of North America.[2]

The massive multitribal Indian uprising known as Pontiac's War raged for two years from Niagara to the trading center of Michilimackinac, where Ojibwe warriors stormed the British fort and sent its troops fleeing to Montreal. In the end, though the confederated tribes captured nine of thirteen English garrisons, they were unable to secure adequate supplies of guns or powder to evict the British from Indian country. Nonetheless, the uprising had changed the calculus of power. The British, deeply shaken by the ferocity of their opponents, had to admit the failure of their Indian policy and the limits of imperial power. Acknowledging Indian sovereignty, they tried to pattern a new diplomatic strategy based on that of the French, both to quell Indian hostilities and to reestablish commercial alliances essential to reviving the fur trade.[3]

Unfortunately for the British, unlike the French, the policy had to serve two populations with mutually incompatible goals. Even as officials struggled to win the trust and allegiance of Native people, colonial settlers in the backcountry who boldly declared themselves "Indian haters" undercut their efforts. Pushing ever farther into Indian lands, settlers clamored for Indian removal. A frustrated William Johnson declared the settlers to be an ignorant, prejudiced, and ungovernable lot who "ill treat, Rob and frequently murder the Indians," making it impossible to keep peace along the frontier. The only way to protect the trade and avoid costly military expeditions was to halt the advance of settlement. Even before Pontiac's War erupted, in 1763 the crown published a proclamation declaring all lands west of the Appalachians closed to white settlement. But until the British confronted the power of the united tribes, little effort had been made at enforcement.[4]

Despite heightened British resolve in the wake of the uprising, enforcement of the proclamation proved nearly impossible. The tide of settlers continued to cross the Appalachians, undeterred by a mere "paper barrier." As one observer noted, "Not even a second Chinese wall, unless guarded by a million soldiers, could prevent the settlement of the Lands on the Ohio." Understandably, the Indian nations drew little distinction between the British and their colonial subjects and regarded the inflow of settlers as a promise betrayed, which weakened even further an already shaky trading entente.[5]

The Proclamation of 1763 had a much more measurable effect on land speculators. Settlers might take their chances on establishing farms without obtaining legal ownership, but speculators, in the game for profit, could not sell land without title. Land speculation, as old as the British colonies, had made many a fortune among colonial elites. Numerous prominent Virginians, including George Washington and Thomas Jefferson, were deeply invested in Ohio Valley lands, which the proclamation had, in essence, stripped of their worth. For southerners like Washington and Jefferson, British land policy ignited the indignation that, in little more than a decade, would bring on the American Revolution.[6]

For the northern colonies, the burning issue was taxation, which also had its roots in "Indian problems." Some version of Indian war in North America, along with European conflicts, had been draining the British treasury since 1689. The Seven Years' War (called the French and Indian War on the North American front) alone had nearly doubled England's national debt. Though the colonial conflicts most often had served larger imperial aims, Parliament, casting about for desperately needed revenue, determined that it was high time that the colonies paid a share of the burden for protecting their borders. Thus, it implemented unprecedented policies of taxation that outraged the northern colonies and brought stirrings of rebellion to that region. The first of these taxes, the Stamp Act, was imposed in 1765, just as Pontiac's War, which Parliament sourly noted was a purely colonial conflict, was coming to a close. Clearly, British fumbling on the western frontier was inadvertently setting the colonies on the path to revolution.[7]

All this occurred many miles from the Upper Mississippi. Pontiac's War had spread no farther west than Michilimackinac and did not enlist the Dakotas or Lake Superior Ojibwes as participants. Even news of events in the East took weeks or months to make its way to the interior, if it reached the people there at all. Remote from the heart of the conflicts, relationships between Indians and Europeans remained peaceful, if uneasy. Still, distant tensions made themselves felt in ways that were indirect but ultimately would prove profound.

The immediate effects only slightly disturbed the rhythms of life. Coureurs de bois could carry furs to Montreal by the northern route, bypassing upheavals to the east, but they found it nearly impossible to provision themselves there for the following season. For the Indians, this dearth of trade goods was an annoyance and inconvenience but not a disaster. The Indians, not yet dependent on European wares, retained the knowledge and traditional skills to sustain themselves until traders returned. As an unintentional benefit, the temporary shift away from market hunting allowed wildlife populations to rebound throughout the region. When trader Peter Pond ascended the "River St. Peter" (today's Minnesota River) in 1773, he recorded, "We Lived as well as hart Could wish [on an] abundans of annamels"—buffalo, deer, raccoons, geese, and ducks in countless numbers, as well as the much-desired beaver.[8]

[50]

Ties of kinship between Indians and French traders remained undisturbed. Other than officers, aristocrats, and civil officials, few French left North America in the wake of the British victory. Canada, albeit now under English rule, had become their homeland. The French Canadians and Métis who made their livelihood in the interior and intermarried with Native peoples were even more disconnected from European loyalties. Their identity was embedded in the social relations of the borderland and there they would stay, making do with their Indian relations until the trade revived. However, when the trade returned, they would find the rules of the game had substantially changed.[9]

Into the West

To the British, looking across Lake Michigan from Michilimackinac, the West was a foreign land shrouded in mystery, with tantalizing prospects of wealth and adventure. Fortunes in furs were surely waiting there as was the elusive route to the Pacific and the China trade. Robert Rogers, hero of the French and Indian War and now commandant at Michilimackinac, was eager to push into the West. He had heard dozens of stories from voyageurs and Indians about water routes in the interior that might lead to the Western Sea and was convinced that he could find the fabled Northwest Passage. To his frustration, however, the government not only declined to finance his proposed expedition, it also banned trade beyond Michilimackinac, blocking both avenues of potential profit. But the enterprising Rogers found a way around both official roadblocks. In 1766 he managed to scrape together the funds to send out a small expedition under the command of James Tute, a fellow veteran of the French and Indian War. The expedition, as Rogers planned it, had a dual purpose. Trading ventures into the West might be forbidden, but no law kept the Indians from bringing furs to Michilimackinac. Under the guise of explorers, Tute and veteran fur trader Charles Goddard, his second in command, could legally travel to Prairie du Chien (in present-day Wisconsin) and spend the winter there persuading the Indians to come to Michilimackinac. Then, in the spring, the explorers would begin their quest in earnest for the Northwest Passage. At this point, they would join with the third member of their party, an unemployed fifty-six-year-old Massachusetts mapmaker named Jonathan Carver.[10]

The middle-aged Carver was an unlikely adventurer and, after accepting Rogers's proposal in Boston, quite likely was surprised, if not dismayed, when he arrived at Michilimackinac and learned the details of his mission. To make the most of his slim resources, Rogers was sending Carver on his own, along with a single voyageur and a Mohawk guide, into Dakota country. He was to spend the winter making friends with the Indians and persuade them to travel to Michilimackinac to trade. Then, in the spring, Carver would join the others and serve as surveyor on the expedition west. Perhaps he took the assignment on with enthusiasm—or, after journeying all the way to Michilimackinac, he may have had no choice but to go forward. In any case, with his two companions Carver began the grueling trip by the Mississippi route into Dakota country. The Indians greeted him with hospitality and he wintered with them near St. Anthony Falls. In the spring he met up with the other members of the expedition as planned and they made their way north to Grand Portage to collect supplies that Rogers had promised to deliver there. But no provisions had arrived, and after three weeks of waiting the disgruntled adventurers, as Carver later wrote, "universally agreed to return to Michilimackinac and give over our intended expedition."[11]

As a voyage of discovery, the journey had been a bust. The party followed established routes that were well documented by the French and mapped no new territory. Carver himself was a minor figure in the expedition. The crusty trader Peter Pond later scoffed, "This was the Exstent of his travels, his Hole toure; I with One Canew Well mand Could make in Six weekes."[12] Yet Jonathan Carver won a place in Minnesota history as the most famous explorer of his era. He managed to turn the failed expedition quite literally into gold.

Apparently, by the time he returned to Michilimackinac, Carver had had enough of the wilderness. He returned to the East and, after a brief reunion with his wife and children, set sail for England. Once in London, he started a second family, though still legally married, and made a career of his so-called exploration of the west. His fame derived from a self-aggrandizing version of his north country adventure titled *Travels of Jonathan Carver through the Interior Parts of North America in the Years 1766, 1767, and 1768,* in which he was the sole hero of the tale. The first travel book about the region by an English author, it became an immediate sensation and was translated into many languages. The power of the press ensured Carver's place in history, while his uncelebrated companions slipped into obscurity. Though he was guilty of exaggeration, distortion, and a significant amount of plagiarism (not to mention a poor sense of geography for a mapmaker), Carver did provide a rare glimpse into the world of the Dakotas in this era. His vivid and somewhat fanciful prose also portrayed the land in glowing terms that would have done credit to any nineteenth-century booster. The Minnesota River valley was "a most delightful country, abounding with all the necessaries of life. . . . Every part is filled with trees bending under their loads of fruits, such as plums, grapes, and apples . . . [with] amazing quantities of maples, that would produce sugar sufficient for any number of inhabitants." Though Minnesota was still generations away from Euro-American settlement, Carver did his part to plant the seed that an eden was waiting in the west.[13]

Return of the Trade

[52]

Long before settlers looked toward the Upper Mississippi, traders once again stamped their mark on the land. Even as Rogers's emissaries were urging the western Indians to visit Michilimackinac, in 1767 the government gave in to pressure from commercial interests and lifted its trading restrictions. In its place a loose system of licensing was implemented. By merely posting a small bond any British subject could obtain a license to enter the trade, which essentially opened the door for all comers. Within a few years traders returned to the Northwest in numbers that far exceeded their earlier presence in the region.[14]

Official British reluctance to venture beyond their established posts had been a direct consequence of the fierce resistance they had met in Pontiac's War. In the West they were particularly distrustful of the Ojibwes. Staunch partners of the French, the western Ojibwes had supported the uprising and their eastern relatives had stormed Fort Michilimackinac itself. Despite the ban on western trade, however, a few favored traders had wheedled permission to enter the Upper Mississippi, and the reports they brought back of friendly Dakotas, anxious to trade, soon persuaded revenue-hungry officials to reopen the gateway to the West. If the Ojibwes interfered with the trade, one Dakota chief assured a British lieutenant, the Dakotas would "put them off from the face of the earth." The lieutenant was duly impressed, describing the Dakotas as "certainly the greatest Nation of Indians ever yet found."[15]

Unlike the Ojibwes and most of the other tribes in the region, the Dakotas had no particular animus toward the British. For them, the French had seemed unreliable partners at best and double-dealing enemies as often as not. The British were likely to be no worse. However, their experience with the French had ensured that even as the Dakotas established trading relations, they would maintain a healthy skepticism about British intentions. The Ojibwes, on the other hand, were more than skeptical; they were unabashedly unreceptive to British overtures. As Minnehwehna, chief of the Michilimackinac Ojibwes, warned trader Alexander Henry, "Englishman, although you have conquered the French, you have not yet conquered us! We are not your slaves. . . . Your king has never sent us any presents, nor entered into any treaty with us, wherefore he and we are still at war." Only after the British sent ambassadors to offer gifts and ask for peace with the Ojibwes did the tribes grant them the "liberty to trade as formerly."[16]

But trade with the British quickly diverged from accustomed patterns. French traders had operated under a system of government monopolies. The crown granted certain traders exclusive rights to a particular territory and essentially functioned as a partner in the enterprise. Though the French had never been able to fully enforce the monopolies, undermined by the elusive coureurs de bois, the system still relied on complex understandings worked out between French and Indian leaders on behalf of their respective peoples. The relationship was forged through diplomatic and military ties as well as commercial exchange. When the British took over the trade, they reorganized it to conform to emerging ideas of modern capitalism. The government's goal was to secure the greatest profit at the least cost to the crown. Free trade and competition seemed much more attractive than costly government involvement. Thus, after only a short period of limited licensing, in 1767 they lifted all restrictions and opened the trade to anyone who could scare up the capital to take the plunge.[17]

The result was a free-for-all. Traders flooded into the region, some small operators, others backed by mercantile capital in Montreal, New York, or London. Laissez-faire capitalism fundamentally transformed the trade. Complex diplomatic and military obligations forged at the tribal level gave way to negotiations between individuals. Traders functioned more like storekeepers who competed among themselves for Indian customers. In the short term, competition enhanced Indian bargaining power. Goods were more easily obtainable than ever before, with traders taking their wares throughout the region. Vying for customer loyalty, they engaged in cutthroat competition, offering abundant gifts and a wide array of goods at attractive prices to lure the Indians to bring in their furs. As an additional means to tie individual Indians to their post, traders freely offered credits, advancing goods in the fall on the promise that Indians would repay the debt with furs in the spring. Though the French had also provided credit, for their purposes profit had been secondary to maintaining military alliances. Thus, as part of diplomatic negotiations among equals, debts were frequently ignored or written off. The English credit system was something quite different, a purely economic relationship that shifted the roles to those of creditor and debtor. From the perspective of the traders, they were buying Indian labor and most wintered at their posts to make sure there was no slackening of effort. "When we are on the spot to winter with them," one Montreal merchant explained, "we have always an Opportunity of knowing their dispositions, pressing them to exert their Diligence." Once the credit relationship was established, traders then felt free to mark up goods many times over their cost. Egregious price inflation protected them against some inevitable default on the advances and kept Indian customers in their debt. It also signified a not-so-subtle shift in established social relations.[18]

The arrival of rampant capitalism shook the very underpinnings of borderland culture, but it also required traders to observe at least some of the etiquette of trade relationships. British entrepreneurs, on the whole, were ill equipped for a venture into the West. Few would-be traders had either the necessary language skills, familiarity with Native culture, or the wilderness expertise to succeed on their own. Experienced French Canadian and Métis voyageurs were vital to the success of their gamble. Former coureurs de bois and other veteran backwoodsmen found their talents in high demand.[19]

A few, like Jean Baptiste Cadotte (or Cadot), set up independently and parlayed their knowledge of the people and geography of the region into a prosperous enterprise. Though uneducated and illiterate, Cadotte used his wilderness skills and familiarity with Indian language and customs to build a thriving fur trade business that made him and his sons men of prominence in the Lake Superior region. Like Cadotte, who teamed up with trader Alexander Henry, most French Canadian entrepreneurs either partnered with or were employed by British traders, the Canadians providing the skills, the British the political leverage and capital. However, for every Jean Baptiste Cadotte there were a thousand nameless Canadian and Métis laborers. Surviving records suggest that by 1777 perhaps 5,000 voyageurs were working in the interior.[20]

New Taxonomies of Race and Class

French influence infused the trade. The common commercial language was a French–Indian patois and the working vocabulary of the trade itself was composed of French terms. In fact, English was seldom heard in the north country before the 1790s. Most important, the web of intermarriage that connected the French and Indians sustained the cultural meeting ground so crucial to the trade. However, neither the British nor the Americans who followed them fully entered into that hybrid culture. Confident in presumptions of inherent Anglo superiority and established hierarchies of race and class, as they took control of the trade the British increasingly viewed the people of the borderland as their natural inferiors.[21]

Though it would be a gross overstatement to claim that French officials had regarded Indians as their equals, their condescension derived from cultural rather than racial differences. To the French, Indians were *sauvages* who, once they embraced Christianity and European culture, had the potential to become full citizens. Colonial policy initially encouraged intermarriage as a means to Europeanize the tribes. Only when they realized that social mingling changed the Europeans as much if not more than the Indians did French officials attempt to discourage intermarriage. More important, in the harsh environment of the interior itself a curious transformation had taken place: The French and Indians lived together in a relatively egalitarian fashion, ate the same foods, dressed similarly, and suffered the same hardships. As generations of mixed-blood children came of age and entered the trade, racial differences blurred even further. On the level of daily interaction, a unique hybrid culture had emerged. British officials frequently commented on the understandings that underlay the French and Indian trading system. "They were bred up together like Children in that Country," wrote George Croghan, "& the French have always adopted the Indians Customs & Manners, Treated them Civily & supplied their wants generously." Another observer declared that the French had "adopted the very Principles and Ideas of the Indians and differ from them only a Little in color."[22]

The British arrived in the north country with a radically different set of cultural and racial presumptions. Their worldview was grounded in a rigid British class system and in the broader politics of empire, which defined subject people as inherently inferior. Many also were veterans of the recent Indian wars and had absorbed the anti-Indian prejudices of British colonials. Colonials who entered the trade added fuel to racialist tendencies. While intermarriage remained common in the lower ranks of the trade, especially among voyageurs and traders who wintered in the interior, the British never melded with Native culture as the French had done. In fact, though they used the rhetoric of diplomacy and trade that had served the French so well, they looked down upon those who crossed the boundaries of class and race that separated traders from their "inferiors." In 1772 stiff-backed British trader Matthew Cocking wrote critically of the Canadian "pedlar" François Le Blanc, "As to command I do not find he keeps any [of] the Common Fellows [from] coming into his apartment and talking with him almost like one of themselves. The Natives I observed had free liberty to come in when they liked."[23]

For more than a decade, necessity kept British class and racial bias to a disgruntled murmur, seldom expressed overtly. In private correspondence, Indians were "thieves" and French Canadians not much better, but for the moment their goodwill was indispensable. The unregulated competition of the 1760s and 1770s created an environment of interdependency where power was fairly equally dispersed. The British supplied the capital, the Canadians and Métis the skills, and the Indians the indispensable labor. By the 1780s, however, wealthy capitalists in Montreal were working to monopolize the trade. The emergence of the North West Company in 1784 marked the beginning of the end of this delicate balance and would profoundly change the region's social geography.

Native Conflicts and Connections

In the interim, after a decade of relative calm between the Dakotas and Ojibwes, the return of traders set off a new round of hostilities. After the French had abandoned the West in the 1750s, the incentive and the means for waging war had gone with them. Without a market for their furs, the tribes no longer felt pressed to expand their hunting grounds. Moreover, without a steady source of resupply, guns and ammunition became precious commodities, necessary to secure food for the community and not to be wasted on warfare. Finally, an

[55]

outbreak of smallpox had struck both the Dakotas and Ojibwes in 1750. With their populations already reduced by disease, they could ill afford to lose more young men in battle.[24]

By 1765 the calculus had changed once more. Market hunting was again a priority, which spurred a drive for territorial expansion; supplies of guns and ammunition were again accessible; and a new generation of warriors had come of age to avenge old grievances. Conditions were ripe for war. Trader Alexander Henry reported an army of 1,500 Ojibwes gathering at La Pointe on Madeline Island for an assault against the Dakotas in 1765. The lake region Dakotas were equally bellicose. Though the majority of the bands had migrated south and west, those remaining wanted revenge for past insults and attacks. And so the war was on. Various bands traded offensives in the north country for about three years, with major battles at St. Croix Falls, Crow Wing, Sandy and Rainy lakes, and countless skirmishes along disputed borders. In the final outcome, the Ojibwes, fighting in the heart of their territory, had more at stake than the Dakotas, for whom the lands had less strategic importance. The Dakotas eventually gave up their northern settlements at Leech and Red lakes, which allowed Ojibwes to control the entire Minnesota lakes region. By the war's end in 1768, no Dakota villages remained east of the Mississippi above St. Anthony Falls. The bands had moved west, staking claim to the headwaters of the Minnesota and Red rivers, Big Stone Lake, Lake Traverse, the Crow Wing River, Lac qui Parle, and west to the Missouri. Only the Mdewakantons stayed in the woodlands east of the Mississippi. The other bands transitioned seasonally between woodland and plains. The loss of their northern territories apparently did not cause significant hardship. When explorer Jonathan Carver met the Dakotas in 1766—in the midst of the war—he described them as "merry sociable people, full of mirth and good humor. They spend whole nights in feasting and dancing."[25]

The border between the tribes remained largely unchanged until 1862. Though the border zone was never entirely quiet, no further large-scale wars over territory occurred. Raiding parties breached the border zone with a fair amount of regularity, but they were most often set off by personal feuds or young warriors eager to prove their bravery. For the most part, the Dakotas and Ojibwes observed a guarded détente, neither quite friends nor enemies. Personal connections helped maintain the uneasy peace. For generations intermarriage and adoption between the tribes had been established practice, and even in the midst of the most heated conflicts ties of kinship often mediated all-out hostilities. Many Ojibwe and Dakota leaders, such as Ojibwe chiefs Flat Mouth and White Fisher and Dakota chief Wabasha, were of mixed heritage. Blood ties such as these were considered sacred and often complicated wartime considerations.[26] Ojibwe historian William Warren told of an encounter in the border region that illuminates the complex nature of Ojibwe–Dakota relations:

[56]

[The Ojibwe] camp was fired on by a party of Dakota warriors. At the second volley, one of his men being wounded, Ma-mong-e-se-da [also known as Big Foot] grasping his gun sallied out, and pronouncing his name loudly in the Dakota tongue, he asked if Wabasha, his brother, was among the assailants. The firing ceased immediately, and after a short pause of silence, a tall figure ornamented with a war dress, his head covered with eagle's plumes, stepped forward from the ranks of the Dakotas and presented his hand. It proved to be his half brother Wabasha, and inviting him and his warriors into his lodge, Ma-mong-e-se-da entertained them in the style of a chief.[27]

By the end of the eighteenth century the social terrain of the north country was spun from an intricate web of kinship relationships. For example, following the same family, Nancy Sayer, the wife of John Sayer, a trader who ran a post on the Snake River in 1804–5, was a full-blood Ojibwe also known as Obemau-unoqua. She was the daughter of the celebrated chief Ma-mong-e-se-da and thus the niece of the Dakota chief Wabasha. The Sayers' children, Henry, John Charles, and Guillaume, with blood ties to all these disparate groups, personified the complex identity that shaped the northern borderland.[28]

The "Wild West"

The "equal opportunity" of free trade was short-lived. With so many traders vying for a limited harvest of furs, they did not hesitate to use any means to get a jump on their competitors. They stole furs, sabotaged canoes, spread lies, and sometimes resorted to murder to gain the advantage. The region had no official governance. Supposedly, traders were subject to British law, but no courts or magistrates were in place to put law into practice. Justice, such as it was, was meted out on the spot with fist, knife, or gun, with little fear of consequences. Peter Pond was one of many traders who took the law into his own hands. In his memoir he complacently recalled a dispute in which he and a rival trader "Discharged Pistels in which the Pore fellow was unfortennt. I then Came Doan the Cuntrey & Declard the fact But thare was none to Prosacute me." The merchant financiers who had celebrated unfettered competition soon complained that the chaos it had wrought would bring about "manifest ruin" and "destruction of the trade."[29]

In the short term, the Indians benefited from this competitive frenzy. Even the credit system worked to their advantage for a while, ensuring that they could meet their needs over the harsh winter months. Moreover, with their furs in great demand, they could insist that traders honor the customs of generosity and gift giving. While the Ojibwes and Dakotas took reciprocal obligations seriously and generally honored their part of the credit bargain, they drew a distinction between articles of trade (household goods, cloth, blankets, guns, and powder) and items that had symbolic value as tokens of regard and metaphorical kinship (food, tobacco, and alcohol). With these items, generosity was expected whether the hunt had been bountiful or poor. They unfailingly shared their food supplies with the traders even in times of scarcity and expected an equal openhandedness in return, especially in regard to alcohol. If traders failed to live up to these obligations of kinship, it was seen as a sign of disrespect and all other obligations were nullified.[30]

Alcohol quickly became the pernicious glue that held trading relationships intact. Merchant financiers first urged traders to entice the Indians with an array of consumer goods and "Excite a desire in them to have the commodities of Europe." But, to the puzzlement of materialist Europeans, Native people had no taste for excessive acquisitions. Seasonally on the move between hunting grounds, Indians chose their belongings for utility and portability. Moreover, in Native culture, an accumulation of goods conveyed no accompanying status. Instead, individuals gained stature through generosity rather than acquisition. By material standards, chiefs were often among the poorest men in their village.[31]

Thus, the desire for material goods was limited. And the Indians provided most of the food, not only for themselves but for the traders as well. Alcohol was the one commodity for which there seemed to be a limitless demand. Not surprisingly, from the time the French first introduced it, the Indians found alcohol to have almost magical qualities. It eased weary bones and warmed the chill away; it staved off hunger pangs in times of scarcity; and it had the capacity to transport one into a closer connection with the spirit world.

Much has been made of the Indians' passion for drink, but it is important to note that in the eighteenth and early nineteenth centuries a steady consumption of alcohol was ubiquitous among whites as well. According to historian Peter Mancall, American colonials consumed far more alcohol than Indians. He estimates that in 1770 America, per capita consumption of distilled spirits was about 3.7 gallons per year and on the rise. By the 1820s it had reached 5 gallons per person. On the frontier, it is safe to assume that consumption levels were well above the average. Rum was a priority item in recruiting crews for a trading brigade. Men considered it a part of their pay and simply would not sign on unless they were assured a steady supply of alcohol. Traders' journals are rife with accounts of "drunken frolics." John Sayer noted in his diary that he "was prevented from departing untill the Afternoon my Men being all Drunk." Traders, voyageurs, and Indians all craved alcohol as a welcome relief from the unforgiving hardships they faced each day.[32]

Where whites and Indians differed was in their cultural and pragmatic disposition toward stockpiling. Indians had few means to store food and thus were accustomed to eating as much as possible while it was available, knowing that starving times lay ahead. They approached alcohol in a similar fashion, drinking until the keg was empty. But for Native people, alcohol meant more than intoxication. Like tobacco, it had a mesmerizing influence that assumed a spiritual significance. It became centrally important to kinship ceremonies and mourning rituals. Intoxication seemed to help people make contact with their departed friends and family members. By the late-eighteenth century, the addictive qualities of alcohol, along with its ceremonial importance, had made it the most valuable commodity in the trade. In fact, traders considered it impossible to carry on business without it.[33]

A New Order

As the trade pushed into the Upper Great Lakes and beyond, Grand Portage emerged as the preeminent trade emporium of the west. Strategically located on Lake Superior, the post lay at the end of a nine-mile portage from the Pigeon River, the crucial point of connection between Montreal and the interior—the same difficult portage that had nearly caused a mutiny against La Vérendrye fifty years before. Now, as the insatiable quest for more and better furs drove traders ever farther west and north, Grand Portage replaced Michilimackinac as the most remote and important provisioning post in the trade. By 1778 more than 40,000 pounds of goods and furs made their way in and out of the region by way of Grand Portage, a village of sorts had sprung up on the spot, and some 500 people passed through during the season. According to one trader, it was "a pent-up hornets' nest of conflicting factions in rival forts." The Northwest had become thoroughly saturated with competing traders desperate to turn a profit in a limited market. More and more they turned to unscrupulous practices to wrest Indian customers from their competitors. Virtual rivers of alcohol flowed into the region and, as described by Alexander Henry, "the traders [were] in a state of extreme hostility, each pursuing his interests in such a manner as might most injure his neighbor."[34]

The merchants and financiers in Montreal who capitalized the trade viewed all this untrammeled competition with alarm; it was eating into everyone's profits. The solution they worked out was to consolidate their interests. Then, they reasoned, with the power of combined capital they could squeeze out small competitors and bring order (and much increased profit) to the trade. In short, they intended to create a monopoly. But this version of monopoly was no throwback to the royal system employed by the French. It was created through a merger of private interests who could harness enormous amounts of capital to dominate the market. What they envisioned became in fact the prototype for the monopoly capitalism that would transform America a century later.[35]

Ironically, about the same time that the Montreal merchants were beginning to move toward consolidation, the first shots of the American Revolution were fired in Massachusetts. The wheels had been set in motion that would eventually evict the British from much of the region they were strategizing to control. As a further irony, British mandates, supposedly designed to protect the territory of the fur trade from future settlement and bring some semblance of law to the region—both initiatives ardently desired by the merchants—had added fuel to the fires of rebellion.

The Calculations of War

In 1774 Parliament passed the Quebec Act, which incorporated the formerly unorganized Northwest—a territory that stretched west to the Mississippi and south to the northern banks of the Ohio—into the Province of Quebec. The act reaffirmed that settlement in the region was forbidden and placed it under the authority of the governor of Quebec. The decree primarily was intended to control the northern Ohio Valley and had no practical effect on the Upper Mississippi or lakes region. Settlement was an unlikely prospect so deep in the interior; as for legal authority, no military or civil officials were posted west of Quebec itself to enforce the law. However, the act had a stirring effect on the already restive colonies in the East. The British had found it impossible to enforce the Proclamation of 1763 and an intensive lobbying campaign by prominent Virginia land speculators had won a partial repeal in 1769. The Quebec Act threw speculators once again into a panic over the value of their land holdings. Settlers, already moving into the northern Ohio Valley, were also up in arms. And agitators for rebellion in New England declared that this was yet another in the series of Parliament's "intolerable acts" that infringed on colonial liberties.[36]

A provision of the act also dissolved Quebec's representative legislature, replacing it with a governor and council appointed by the king. Liberty-loving colonials had high hopes that this outrage on Canadian rights would bring Quebec into the growing confederation of rebellious colonies. However, as a strategy to maintain Canada's loyalty, Parliament had also included official protection for the Catholic Church, the faith of most Canadians. With what one historian terms "incredible stupidity," the Continental Congress added this "establishment of Popery" to its list of grievances against the crown, which drove a wedge between the Catholic, French-descended Canadians and the other colonies. Nor did the land-hungry expansionism of the lower colonies serve the interests of the Canadian economy, which was almost entirely dependent on the fur trade. Thus in the end, differences in religion, culture, and economy created a barrier that outweighed common interests and Canada did not join the rebellion. Nonetheless, in the volatile months leading up to the war, the optimistic prediction that they might make common cause bolstered revolutionary enthusiasm.[37]

By any measure of interests, the future state of Minnesota resembled Canada far more than any of the American colonies. As the Indians knew from the eastern tribes, colonial settlers had an insatiable appetite for expansionism. From the time they arrived in North America, the Americans had invaded Indian hunting grounds, claimed their lands, and were clearly bent on displacement rather than coexistence. As far as the Indians were concerned, the British had many shortcomings but the Americans were decidedly worse. American expansionism also presented a deadly threat to the fur trade, as ominous to the traders as to the Indians. In terms of religion, Catholicism was the only form of Christianity that had any standing in the region. While most Indians held fast to their traditional spirituality, Jesuit missionaries had planted Catholicism among a small but growing cohort, especially among the Ojibwes. It was also the nominal faith of the French Canadians and Métis who constituted the vast majority of non-Indians in the region, creating yet another French and Indian cultural bond. The overt anti-Catholicism of revolutionary rhetoric would win no friends in the Northwest.[38]

When the revolution erupted in 1775, only faint reverberations were felt in the Northwest. No troops faced off in either present-day Wisconsin or Minnesota. Any discernable loyalties were decidedly with the British, but for most of the north country's Indians and traders, the ebb and flow of the course of the war seemed largely irrelevant and a world away from their daily lives. However, as in all the previous wars on the continent, the revolution did constrain the movement of goods and furs, forcing a shift in trading routes—a geographical reorientation that would also create new hierarchies of power.

Before the war broke out, the Dakota trade had blossomed. Traders venturing into the interior had favored the Mississippi route and, like Peter Pond, soon found the Dakotas hospitable and willing partners with an abundance of furs to trade. But once hostilities commenced, travel up the river became a risky enterprise. As a result, the center of commerce shifted north to Lake Superior, which increased the Ojibwe share of the trade and made Grand Portage, for the moment, the most important post of the era. The war also inevitably created shortages that made provisioning expeditions a more difficult task. Persistent supply problems created added urgency among a small group of wealthy and influential Montreal merchants to consolidate their efforts, moving them closer to an eventual monopoly of the trade. The war had become an invisible lever that was shifting power away from independent traders and, more disastrously, from the Indians themselves.[39]

Germs of War

For the Indians of the Northwest, the most devastating effect of the war derived from an invisible killer: smallpox. The formation of the Continental army brought together thousands of young men who had no acquired immunity to the disease, setting off a pandemic that swept across the continent over a six-year period. Smallpox killed far more American patriots than did British musket balls.

Before this time, Indians in the Minnesota region had experienced several outbreaks of the disease, but it had never spread so widely and with so much virulence. Only infrequently did Europeans carry the virus to Indian trading partners in the interior. The reason for this was starkly simple: By the eighteenth century smallpox had become endemic in the cities of Europe. It was the rare French or Englishman who grew to adulthood without surviving a bout of the disease. Those it did not kill became immune to future attacks. Since the virus spread only from human to human, without an infected host or his recently tainted belongings the disease had no means of transmission.[40]

The only protection from smallpox was either isolation or acquired immunity—either from natural infection or by means of inoculation, a procedure that intentionally implanted the live virus in an incision.[41] By the 1750s inoculation was widely practiced in France and became an accepted procedure in Canada as well, which may explain why Canadians seldom brought the disease among the Indians. The American colonies, however, presented a different case. Immunity was not nearly so widespread. Population density was much lower than in Europe and the lack of transportation networks tended to keep the disease locally confined, allowing years to pass between outbreaks. In addition, public opinion weighed in against inoculation, fearing the introduction of infection into communities. Many towns, especially in New England, legally banned the practice. Thus, whole generations of Americans came of age without exposure to the disease. The war gathered thousands of these susceptible individuals from throughout the colonies into crowded military camps. They were like tinder waiting for a match to strike.[42]

In the early years of the war, smallpox was England's most important ally. While British troops were largely immune to the disease, it spread through the Continental army with horrific efficiency. In the fall of 1776 smallpox literally destroyed the American troops during the siege of Quebec. Soldiers fell like dominoes to the deadly virus. Reinforcements only provided additional fuel for the disease, since it needed new, susceptible hosts to sustain itself. By spring the British easily routed the sick and dying army, and soldiers who were incubating the virus took it back to their home communities and to the rest of the army.[43]

Epidemics quickly broke out in Pennsylvania and Connecticut and within months smallpox had begun its deadly march westward. Indians transmitted it from tribe to tribe through their trading networks. By the winter of 1777 the virus had reached Michilimackinac. Locked in for the winter, with no new source of human transmitters, the disease temporarily burned itself out. But the epidemic had too many sources, too many avenues of transmission to be stopped for long. The isolation of the interior slowed the spread of the disease, but by 1780 it reached the Lake Superior and Upper Mississippi regions. As historian Elizabeth Fenn notes, "*Variola*, it seemed, had unwittingly become an article of trade."[44]

The Minnesota region was caught in a pincer movement. In addition to the advancing threat from the East, smallpox was moving in from the Southwest as well. In 1779 the disease had reached Mexico City. By December nearly 50,000 residents were infected and a full-blown epidemic was under way. Soon the disease was marching through the Spanish territories along Indian trading routes to the western plains, wreaking devastation among the western tribes. The death toll among the Mandans, Hidatsas, and Arikaras, the masters of the northern plains, reached at least 68 percent, driving them eventually to near extinction. On a raiding expedition to the Missouri River, Ojibwe braves found a village abandoned and strewn with the dead. They then unwittingly carried the disease home, spreading it among themselves from Rainy Lake to Grand Portage, then south to Leech and Sandy lakes.[45]

The Ojibwes most likely had a higher level of immunity than the tribes to the west, acquired in surviving the outbreak of the 1750s. Nonetheless, the devastation, as described by trader Alexander Henry, was immense: "This great extent of country was formerly very populous, but [now] the aggregate of its inhabitants does not exceed three hundred warriors; and among the few whom I saw, it appeared to me that the widows were more numerous than the men." Trader Jean Baptiste Cadotte morosely wrote in 1782, "All the Indians from Fond du Lac, Rainy Lake, Sandy Lake and the surrounding places are dead from smallpox." According to Ojibwe history, between 1,500 and 2,000 people died in one year alone. The village of Sandy Lake, a major Ojibwe settlement, "became reduced to but seven wigwams."[46]

Such profound depopulation put the very life of the bands in jeopardy. Their collective survival depended on the labors of everyone working together to provide food, protection, and shelter. With their numbers decimated by disease, the prospect of starvation stalked the survivors. Grief and desperation also undermined the social structure of communities. As historian Carolyn Gilman writes:

> It would be hard to overstate the effect of the epidemic on Indian society. Craft techniques died with the artisans; with the elders went medicine, knowledge, tribal history, religious traditions, stories, and songs. The political structure faltered when clan leaders died. People left without families had no one to protect them, and in the decades following, reports of domestic violence and murder became more common.[47]

The Dakotas fared somewhat better. Sensing the contagious nature of disease, Native people employed isolation techniques as much as possible, mainly with regard to outsiders. Historians speculate that the Sioux nation, with its nomadic lifestyle, was better able to contain transmission of the virus than tribes like the Arikaras, Hidatsas, and Mandans, who lived in densely populated agricultural villages. The consequent decimation of those western tribes removed all obstacles to Sioux dominance on the plains. But the Dakota Sioux, fully enmeshed in a vast international trading network that carried disease as well as goods and furs, were more vulnerable than the western Sioux of the plains. While the overall Sioux population in 1780 is estimated at approximately 25,000, the combined population of the Minnesota Dakota bands by 1786 was probably no more than 4,200 persons. Clearly, smallpox had taken many lives. Still, with access to both woodland resources and plains hunting grounds, Dakota villages, though weakened and under stress, managed to rebound.[48]

In 1781, the American victory at Yorktown marked the last battle in the War for Independence. As the British surrendered their arms in Virginia, smallpox was rampaging throughout the northern borderland. In this remote part of the new United States, the ravages of disease were its most tangible connection to the monumental contest just concluded. Decades would pass before the new republic exerted any control over the region. Yet the smallpox pandemic, begun in the ranks of the Continental army thousands of miles to the east, set a chain of events in motion that would profoundly shape the subsequent history of Minnesota and its people.

Monopoly and Power

The war gave birth to a republic founded on a system of democratic principles. It also catalyzed a new era in the organization of the fur trade, one significantly less democratic. Beginning in 1775, wartime shortages created headaches for independent traders. With goods in scarce supply, they were hard-pressed to provision their ventures into the interior. Montreal merchants seized the opportunity to take control of the trade and began experimenting with different versions of consolidation. They put together several temporary partnerships over the course of the war and perfected the arrangement in 1784 with the founding of the North West Company.

A loosely organized cartel, the North West Company was a partnership based on shares, divided among the Montreal merchants and the most successful traders in the interior, known as the wintering partners. This arrangement turned competing entrepreneurs into the heads of specific geographical "departments" with direct access to investment capital and marketing agents for their furs. The partners became part of an efficient, vertically integrated machine that soon produced annual returns averaging £200,000 sterling. Small, independent operators had little chance of survival against the might of consolidated capital. The company established a fleet of sailing ships to provision Grand Portage and could ensure its partners an uninterrupted supply of high-quality goods at a lower cost than independents could meet. They also could determine what price furs would bring on the Montreal market—to the advantage of their associates. The independents seemed to have but two choices: join the partnership if invited or become employees of the firm.[49]

The interior relations of the company were complex. Because the partners included wintering traders as well as merchants, power was divided between Montreal and the backcountry. As part of the agreement, only men who had "risen through the ranks" were eligible to buy or be granted shares in the company. This common experience on the ground created a culture among the so-called Nor'Westers that was more like an exclusive club than anything resembling modern corporate culture. However, coming up through the ranks was a somewhat exclusive privilege itself, limited by class, race, and family ties.[50]

The powerful influence of the North West Company imposed a rigid division of labor that transformed the fluid egalitarianism of the fur trade world. French Canadians greatly outnumbered Anglo Canadians and were essential to the functioning of the trade, but positions of authority were reserved almost entirely for those of British descent. A reified caste system evolved that reinforced the authority of the British minority and confined most French and Métis to permanently subordinate roles. Future partners, or *bourgeois,* came up from the ranks of company clerks, or *commis,* a position that was filled (with few exceptions) from the British trading fraternity. French Canadians and Métis voyageurs were the essential workers of the trade, an ethnic niche they had filled for generations. They might rise to the position of guide or interpreter but only a few rose higher within the company. Moreover, independent trading was an increasingly limited option, smothered by the might of the Nor'Westers. The voyageurs also were captive customers to the company store, their only source for clothing or equipment. They paid a premium price for goods, which tended to keep them in a state of perpetual debt. The company estimated that in 1791 some 900 men owed between ten and fifteen years' wages on their accounts. In sum, the French Canadians had been relegated permanently to a subordinate laboring class.[51]

This had a profound effect on the traditional social relations of the trade. Whereas the French and Indians had worked together and freely mingled in multiple ways that bridged class and racial differences, the British took pains to emphasize the social hierarchy. The *bourgeois* and clerks did no manual labor, never lifting a paddle or a pack. Even in their clothing they emphasized social distance, donning frock coats and beaver hats, hardly practical apparel for the backcountry. Social and cultural distance bred disdain for the "thoughtless" French Canadians, "by nature more strong and more wicked than the Savages and as ignorant."[52]

When the wintering brigades and Montreal merchants congregated at Grand Portage for the great summer rendezvous and annual company meeting, it seemed at first glance to be a rollicking multiethnic celebration, with "music and dancing, revelry and feasting." In truth, however, the participants sorted themselves into discrete encampments. The partners and clerks carried on inside the post with "festive balls" and banquets prepared by cooks brought in from Montreal. The voyageurs made rough camps outside the post and entertained themselves with their own music, dancing, and gambling. No banquets were prepared for the laborers of the trade; they made do with their standard daily ration of boiled hominy pudding. Even among the voyageurs caste came into play. The *hivernants,* those who wintered in the backcountry, looked down on the "pork eaters," the *mangeurs du lard,* who transported goods between Montreal and Grand Portage but had no experience in the interior. The pork eaters, so named because they couldn't stomach the hominy diet unless mixed with pork fat, made separate camp from the more elite *hivernants* and fights frequently broke out between them.[53]

Indian encampments formed yet other separate enclaves near the post but still apart from it. Grand Portage was part of Ojibwe territory, with an established village that included a "grand lodge" where the band held ceremonies and gatherings. Crees, Assiniboins, and other Indian trading partners also sometimes attended the rendezvous and carried on their own festivities within their separate camps.[54] Grand Portage, the "great gathering place," brought all these groups—traders, voyageurs, Indians—together, but proximity did little to mediate social or cultural differences. Rather, the rendezvous made more starkly apparent the hierarchies of race, class, tribe, and ethnicity that the company fostered, eroding the common bonds that bridged social and cultural differences.

Social stratification also created fault lines in the upper ranks of the company, which by the 1780s had become dominated by Highland Scots. Between 1760 and 1780, 77 of the 128 men who had importance in the trade were either Highland Scots–born or of Scottish descent. Over the course of the Revolutionary War, Scots loyalists involved in the trade in New York and other parts of the colonies relocated to Montreal, where the economic and political climate was more in line with their self-interests. This migration augmented the pool of Scottish capital that fueled the trade from Montreal. But more than business calculation or political preference drew the colonial merchants to Canada. The Scots-American emigrants followed family connections north. The Scottish fur trade brotherhood was fundamentally structured by ties of kinship. Highlanders were as clannish as any Indian tribe, their loyalties shaped more by family ties than by nation or even ethnicity. Highlanders, like Native Americans, tended to divide the world into family and outsiders. Out of necessity, when the North West Company formed, it took "outsiders" into the partnership. (Connecticut-born Peter Pond, one of the region's most experienced and successful traders, was a founding partner.) But once the firm had established its grip on the trade, the managing partners brought in more and more relatives from Scotland to fill the upper ranks. Soon it became clear that upward mobility was reserved for those tied by blood or marriage to the men already in positions of power.[55]

The man who held the reins of the company was Simon McTavish. A brilliant and ruthless businessman, the Highland-born Albany merchant had left the colonies for Montreal in 1776. Once settled in Canada, McTavish became the principal architect of the North West Company and, with his partner Joseph Frobisher, soon owned more than half the shares of the company. Like the Highland chieftains of his native Scotland, McTavish firmly believed that positions of trust should be kept within family lines. Before long, the upper echelons of the company were filled with McTavish nephews and cousins, Frasers, McGillivrays, McDonalds, and other Highlanders connected to Clan Tavish by birth or marriage. Scots who lacked the essential family ties, let alone enterprising French Canadians or Yankees, faced a roadblock to advancement.[56]

The limits to advancement frustrated a number of the wintering partners. They also resented that, as power centralized in Montreal, their influence in company decisions declined. Increasingly, the summer rendezvous at Grand Portage became the scene of stormy partners' meetings that pitted the winterers against the agents from Montreal, what McTavish dourly described as "a Dish of Grande Portage politicks." In 1799 discontent came to a head. A group of disgruntled winterers, led by Alexander Mackenzie, broke from the North West ranks and created a partnership of the remaining small operations that struggled against the North West juggernaut. The XY Company, as they called themselves, determined to challenge North West's control of the region, setting off another round of fierce competition.[57]

Power Games

Once again, traders vied for Indian loyalties, but Native people no longer had the bargaining might they once held. The independence of the Ojibwes, Crees, and Assiniboins, who were the chief trading partners in the Lake Superior region, had been seriously compromised by the smallpox epidemic of the 1780s. With so many of their people lost to the disease, too few remained to hunt and take care of their villages' needs without outside assistance. Disease had been the breaking point that created dependence on the trading economy. More and more of their energies had to be devoted to hunting for market, putting ever greater demands on the resources of the region. Overhunting created a scarcity of game for food as well as for the desperately needed peltries. Starving times became more common, with people sometimes reduced to eating woolen blankets and boiled leather moccasins. Hunger forced Indians to rely on credits from traders to get them through seasons of want. The balance of power that had shaped the mutually beneficial relationships of the trade had shifted in favor of the traders and they made the most of their advantage. North West partner Duncan McGillivray laid out official policy in the starkest of terms. Their goal was to make the Indians "dependent; and consequently industrious & subordinate."[58]

The battle between the XY and North West company traders returned some negotiating leverage to the Indians, but Native people's growing dependence on the trade limited their range of options. In addition, the weakened relationships that bound Europeans and Indians had degraded the obligations of kinship and made exploitation an all too common practice. The social distance that Anglo-Canadians kept between themselves and the Indians changed the organization of the trade in subtle but important ways. The companies extended their reach throughout the region by establishing a network of sub-sidiary "jackknife posts," small stations manned by between one and six men. The winterers lived near but not among the Indians themselves. They made frequent trips *en derouine* (short visits to Indian villages), but the purpose of their visits was supervision rather than socializing. They meant to oversee their investment, making sure the Indians were diligently working to repay the credits they had received. Though the traders often were forced to use some measure of diplomacy in their dealings, privately they described Indians as "beggarly," lazy, and insolent. When they thought they had the upper hand, they did not hesitate to show their contempt. Trader George Nelson admitted, "We are often obliged to say (& do) give me your skins if you don't I'll take them & perhaps beat you in the bargain." Domination had replaced coopera-tion as the underlying principle of the trade.[59]

The winterers continued the custom of marrying Indian women *à la façon du pays,* but the quality and commitments of the relationship had changed. Some, like the trader John Sayer, treated the union as a legitimate and long-term marriage, but even in these circumstances the women resided at the posts with their husbands rather than among their kin and increasingly ad-opted anglicized ways. Tellingly, Sayer's wife, Obemau-unoqua, became known as Nancy and her children were called Henry, John Charles, and Guillaume. Many traders also showed a growing preference for Métis women who shared more cultural traits with themselves. Still other Anglo-Canadians were more cavalier about their relationships with Native women. Increasingly, they re-garded the traditional gift giving that was part of the marriage ritual as merely a business transaction and the relationship one of expedience. Traders' jour-nals make frequent reference to "buying" women or accepting them as pay-ment for credit or debts. Clearly, the bonds of kinship that had formerly char-acterized fur trade society were fast degrading.[60]

No holds were barred in the intercompany war for control of the trade out of Grand Portage. In hopes of luring Indian customers, the traders again flooded the region with alcohol, which further destabilized social relations at every level. The ruthless Duncan McGillivray knew exactly what he was doing. "When a nation become addicted to drinking," he wrote, "it affords a strong presumption that they will soon become excellent hunters." By 1803 the two trading companies were annually shipping more than 20,000 gallons of spir-its to Grand Portage. When smooth talk and liquor did not suffice to gain their ends, the competing interests regularly turned to trickery, intimidation, and violence. The traders did not hesitate to take pelts by force if other means failed. Alexander Henry described how, when he encountered an Ojibwe hunt-ing party in 1804, he "fought several battles with the Women to get their Furs from them," which he found "most disagreeable" but unfortunately necessary. The borderland had devolved into chaos.[61]

Chaos was bad for business. The XY and North West companies faced off in opposing forts at Grand Portage, and the situation was even more out of control in the backcountry. One trader described the region as being "in a ferment of murder and robbery so that men were not in safety to stir out." Another declared that they were "determined to fight, & kill, if driven too it." Finally, after warring with one another for some seven years, in 1804 pragmatism trumped personal vendetta. The companies declared a truce and agreed to a merger. The new North West Company, more powerful than ever, held unchallenged control of the region—at least until the Americans began to stir.[62]

[69]

On the Mississippi

Meanwhile, in Dakota territory the political landscape evolved somewhat differently. North West Company agents only occasionally advanced beyond Ojibwe lands into the Mississippi River valley. But scores of other British (and a few American) traders made the trek from Michilimackinac, down the Fox and Wisconsin rivers to the Mississippi, and then north up the great waterway to the Dakota people. In fact, when the trade revived in the 1770s the friendly Dakotas and the bounty of furs they had to offer attracted far more traders than did the lakes region. The Dakota trade engendered the same sort of unregulated competition as did the trade to the north; however, no one company could effect a monopoly in the region. Instead, successful independent traders combined into a variety of partnerships. With less capitalization than the North West Company could bring to bear and a looser organizational style, these partnerships brought some order to the trade but did not eliminate competition.[63]

Competition enhanced Dakota bargaining power. Perhaps even more important, the smallpox epidemic, while it unquestionably injured the viability of the bands, did not have the destructive effect among the Dakotas that it wrought among the Ojibwes. The Dakotas also had free access to the resource-rich western plains, the domain of their Lakota kinsmen. All in all, they were well positioned to protect their interests in trade negotiations.

The balance of power between Indians and competing traders reinforced the culture of mutual obligation and the value of kinship bonds. While the powerful Nor'Westers established rigid hierarchies of class and race that eroded connections that had distinguished fur trade society for generations, such relationships remained integral elements of the Dakota trading realm. French traders, with a long history in the region, maintained their status and success in the so-called British era. Intermarriage was a critical key to this accomplishment. They built solid trading relationships through kinship ties to Dakota bands, established through their Indian wives—ties that carried obligation as well as benefits. British traders who went among the Dakotas quickly learned to follow the example set by the French and Indians. By the 1790s a dense web of family ties knit the traders to one another and to their Dakota trading partners. Joseph Renville, Jean Baptiste Faribault, Joseph Rolette, James Aird, Archibald John Campbell—virtually every trader who became important in the region—wed Dakota women *à la façon du pays*. Almost invariably, they treated the relationship and its obligations seriously. The children born from these unions often married one another and became important figures in the trade themselves. In the years ahead, this "mixed blood" generation also would become key brokers between the Dakotas and American expansionists.[64]

While intermarriage unquestionably offered commercial and diplomatic benefits to the traders—who most often wooed sisters or daughters of important Dakota leaders—the intensity of kinship ties appears to have upheld a level of esteem between Europeans and Indians that was degrading to the north. From the top ranks down, evidence suggests that intermarriage continued to signify a culture of respect. Well-born Scot Robert Dickson, one of the most important figures in the trade, established kinship with the Indians through his marriage to Toto-win, sister of the Yanktonai chief Red Thunder. From the time of his marriage around 1797 until his death in 1823, Dickson remained committed to Toto-win and their children. He also maintained close relationships with Red Thunder and other Indian leaders as a trusted kinsman.[65]

The life story of Philander Prescott, a young clerk on the Minnesota River in the 1820s, provides added evidence that intermarriage based on more than commercial calculations endured well into the nineteenth century. Prescott touchingly writes of his youthful courtship of the Dakota girl who became his wife and recalls how he missed her when he had to travel into the backcountry without her. His recollections leave no doubt that neither his marriage nor the kinship obligations that went with it were born out of mere expedience:

> It was ten days before I could get my wife, as she was then timid. At last, through much entreaty of the parents, she came for to be my wife or companion as long as I chose to live with her. Little did I think at the time I should live with her until old age. . . . The old chief lived in his tent near us all winter. I fed and clothed them all winter.[66]

To a significant degree, traders treated the Dakotas with respect as a simple acknowledgment of their power. Montreal merchants considered the tribe "warlike and uncontrollable" and to ignore the role of power in shaping social relations would be a mistake. But evidence also suggests that pragmatic circumstances had the effect of fostering genuine esteem. For example, in his reminiscences of a council held at Michilimackinac, Peter Pond took pains to counter the common stereotypes of the drunken Indian. In his words, "Thay Dined to Geather in Harmoney and finished the Day in Drinking Moterately—Smokeing to Gather Singing & Briteing the Chane of frindShip in a Verey Deasant way." They sang a "fue songs and went to Rest in a Verey Sevel Manner."[67] In Dakota country, at least, it seems the intimate world of intertwined cultures was holding.

Borders and the Borderland

Throughout most of the British era of Minnesota history, the territory that the British and Anglo-Canadians freely roamed and fought over technically belonged to the infant United States of America, at least in the eyes of Euro-Americans. West of the Mississippi, Spain was the theoretical sovereign, though no Spanish expedition had ever made its way so far north. In 1783 the Treaty of Paris had ceded Grand Portage and all the lands to its south to the Americans—two years before the North West Company was established. Nonetheless, for several reasons the British and Anglo-Canadians felt comfortable ignoring new international boundaries. Most immediately, the weak union of states had neither the means nor the will to defend its northern border. It took a year of wrangling simply to convince the individual states to cede their western land claims to the new federal government. Moreover, the international boundary itself was a matter of dispute.[68]

Treaty participants had designated as the boundary a line drawn through the Great Lakes to the source of the Mississippi, but where that line actually fell was a point of confusion. No one at the council table in Paris had the foggiest notion about the actual geography of the lands they were dividing, nor had any European pinpointed the source of the Mississippi. Out of ignorance, the British ceded to the Americans their most important fur trade posts—Niagara, Detroit, and Michilimackinac, as well as the key position at Grand Portage. Still, as long as the border remained unsurveyed and the weak American republic was unable to enforce its sovereignty, for all intents and purposes British traders considered themselves still on British soil. (The Spanish possessions west of the Mississippi were unquestionably open to all comers.) The forts on the Great Lakes continued to fly the union jack without challenge from the Americans, who had their hands full trying to draft a constitution.[69]

Most Europeans doubted that the American republic would survive for long and thus initially did not take boundary issues very seriously. However, other, more urgent matters, primarily regarding commerce and seizure of American ships, brought Britain and the United States to the bargaining table once more in 1794. As part of the compromise agreement worked out by presidential envoy John Jay, Britain agreed to evacuate its American garrisons by 1796. Parliament considered this concession to be of small importance, but to the Great Lakes fur traders Jay's Treaty had serious implications. The treaty also troubled the dormant Spaniards, who feared that British and American interests

[72]

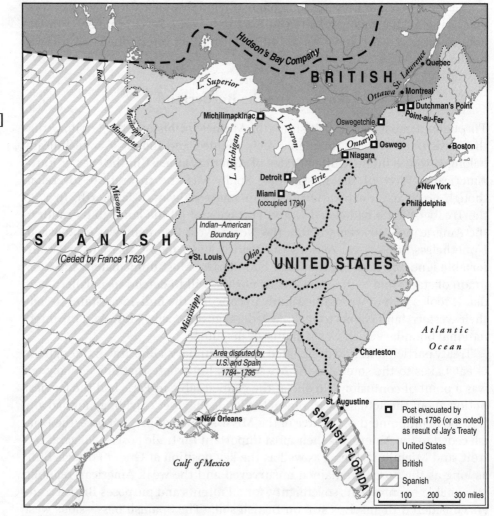

European and American imperial claims, 1795.

might unite against them. As a strategy to create a protective buffer for their resource-rich Mexican territories, Spain retroceded Louisiana to the French in 1800. The chess game of European politics again imposed new borders on the borderland.[70]

The redrawn map of North America did not affect the daily rhythms of life in fur trade country. Few people in the backcountry had strong allegiances to one nation-state or another and governmental claims lacked any means of enforcement. However, not even the Indians felt as immune from Euro-American high politics as they had in the past. They regarded the Americans as advancing enemies who would try to strip away Indian lands as they had in the Ohio Valley. As for the traders, while at the moment they could ignore borders with impunity, they worried that if the Americans managed to assert their sovereignty, issues of licensing, tariffs, or even seizure of their posts could spell financial disaster for the trade. They were dismayed to see British troops replaced by American soldiers along the Great Lakes, and though the North West Company defiantly flew the British flag over its posts in the American Northwest for another twenty years, the company began to take precautionary moves. The partners engaged trader–surveyor David Thompson as the Grand Portage post astronomer to ascertain where the boundary line actually ran. With that confidential information in hand, in 1803 the Nor'Westers abandoned Grand Portage, burned the post buildings to the ground, and established a new headquarters, christened Fort William, on the Kaministikquia River, well north of the 49th parallel.[71]

That same year, on the Fourth of July, President Thomas Jefferson made a stupendous announcement. The United States had purchased all of Louisiana territory from France. Two years earlier, Jefferson had instructed Robert Livingston, his minister to France, to attempt negotiation for the sale of New Orleans, which would give the United States a strategic port on the Mississippi. Much to Livingston's shock, the emperor Napoleon—currently at war with England and in need of funds—offered to sell the entire territory at the bargain price of $15 million. Once again, European wars of empire had reverberated

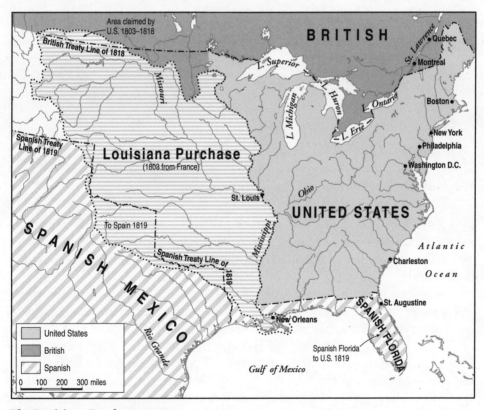

The Louisiana Purchase, 1803.

in North America and all of present-day Minnesota had suddenly become officially part of the United States.[72]

No one in the government knew exactly what they had purchased, since no maps existed of most of the territory. Still, from the outset Jefferson envisioned a country of yeoman farmers spreading across the plains, a scenario that would spell the end of the fur trade economy and the social world it had engendered. Standing at Grand Portage or paddling up the Mississippi in 1803, it would have been impossible to imagine the changes that lay just decades ahead. As the future state of Minnesota entered the nineteenth century, it bore almost no resemblance to the settled parts of the nation. Socially, politically, and culturally, Minnesota remained a foreign land.

Chapter 4

SHIFTING GROUND

> The traders and their clerks were then the aristocracy of the country;
> and, to a Yankee at first sight, presented a singular state of society.
> To see gentlemen selecting wives of the nut-brown natives, and rais-
> ing children of mixed blood, the traders and clerks living in as much
> luxury as the resources of the country would admit . . . all this to an
> American was a novel mode of living, and appeared to be hard fare.
>
> JAMES H. LOCKWOOD, "Early Times and Events in Wisconsin,"
> in *Second Annual Report and Collections of the State Historical
> Society of Wisconsin, for the Year 1855*

American Adventure

On a bright late September morning in 1805, U.S. Army lieutenant Zebulon
Pike rounded a bend of the Upper Mississippi in Minnesota country and recorded his first glimpse of the future site of St. Paul. As the oarsmen propelled
Pike's party of two dozen men up the river, the vista must have been glorious,
a riot of autumn glowing from the sandstone bluffs against an azure sky.[1] But
the twenty-six-year-old lieutenant wasted little ink in his journal on the scenery. He was a man on a mission.

Far to the west, Lewis and Clark's famed Expedition of Discovery was about
to reach the Pacific Coast. Two years earlier, President Jefferson had sent the
explorers to map and assess the unknown lands secured by the Louisiana Purchase. At first glance, Pike's expedition appears to have had similar aims, but
a closer look reveals that its priorities were quite different. Pike's orders came
not from the president but from James Wilkinson, commanding general of
the U.S. Army and the new governor of Louisiana Territory. In residence at
St. Louis, Wilkinson (who would prove to be one of the most corrupt political figures of the nineteenth century) likely had established connections with

wealthy St. Louis fur trade financier Pierre Chouteau, whose family firm was deeply involved in the Mississippi trade. Chouteau was incensed that the unregulated state of the western trade allowed British traders to siphon profits that should rightly go to American concerns—most specifically to Chouteau and Company. Scotsman and former British general Robert Dickson was a particular thorn in Chouteau's side. Working the region between the Upper Mississippi and the James River (in present-day South Dakota), Dickson's group of traders alone annually brought out between £40,000 and £50,000 in furs. Chouteau peppered Washington officials with complaints and warnings that the British were a pernicious influence on the Indians, "who are easy to seduce." Jay's Treaty, claimed Chouteau, provided unfair advantages to non-Americans, and everyone in the trade knew as well that the Nor'Westers and the raft of British independents ignored the duties they were required to pay on goods that crossed the border.[2]

Chouteau had good reason for his complaints. Jay's Treaty had called for the evacuation of British garrisons, but it allowed British and Canadian traders to carry on within U.S. borders under a liberal licensing system. For all practical purposes, the British remained in possession of the Northwest. In fact, when Indiana Territory was established in 1800 (which included the future states of Indiana, Illinois, Michigan, Wisconsin, and Minnesota east of the Mississippi) there were so few Americans in the region that British citizens had to be appointed to fill many of the administrative posts. Understandably, Chouteau and his fellow American traders were anxious to eliminate such entrenched competitors.[3]

To the financier's frustration, Washington failed to respond to his concerns, but Louisiana's territorial governor appears to have been more receptive. Pike's mission, as spelled out by Wilkinson, was directly intended to shore up the American position in the trade. It was a daunting set of orders. The young lieutenant was to gather intelligence about the scope and value of British trade in the region; establish friendly relations with the Dakotas and Ojibwes, "spar[ing] no pains to conciliate the Indians and attach them to the United States"; scout out suitable sites for military and trading posts; negotiate permission from the Indians to build on those sites; and, in addition to all this, locate the source of the Mississippi.[4]

Finding the river's headwaters had significance that far exceeded scientific or geographic curiosity. When negotiators at the Treaty of Paris had drawn the international boundary they had only the vaguest notions about the territory they were carving up. They agreed on a line "drawn through the four Great Lakes and the Rainy River waterway . . . and thence to the source of the Mississippi." But since no European had identified just where the river began, the boundary itself was uncertain. Before the Americans could assert sovereignty over the northern trade, they needed to clarify the extent of their territory.[5]

Pike intended to follow the river to its origin, but first he had other matters to attend to. Wilkinson had charged him to secure permission from the Indians to build military and trading posts at the confluence of the Mississippi and St. Peter (Minnesota) rivers and, a few miles farther upstream, at St. Anthony Falls—probably based on the recommendation of his fur trading advisers. Consequently, the party made camp on an island where the rivers met (now known as Pike Island) and prepared to hold the first official council meeting between the United States and the Dakota people. Pike's interpreter, Joseph Renville, was the key figure in this historic event. Renville, a Dakota mixed blood of presumed French heritage, had been born just downriver in the Mdewakanton village of Kaposia and educated in Canada. As kinsman to the Dakotas and the most proficient Dakota language interpreter in the region, Renville had the contacts to identify and persuade the important Dakota leaders to attend the council.[6]

On the morning of September 23, the inexperienced lieutenant faced seven of the most powerful Mdewakanton chiefs—Little Crow, Fearless One, Grand Partisan, Standing Moose, Shakopee, Broken Arm, Walking Buffalo, and Red Wing—along with some 200 of their warriors. It must have been a daunting sight. No doubt young Pike was thankful and relieved to discover that the Dakotas were pleased to see him. To the Indians the arrival of the Americans represented another trading opportunity—and competition always worked to their advantage. They had no reason to suspect American intentions, particularly since their kinsman Renville was among the party. Thus, negotiations for what the Americans considered the first land cession in Minnesota went off smoothly.[7]

This treaty, however, was quite different from those that later stripped the Indians of their land. While it granted the United States the sovereignty to establish posts on a tract between the rivers and the falls for an eventual payment of $2,000—what Pike described as "100,000 acres for a song"—it also guaranteed the Dakotas the right to "pass, repass, hunt or make other uses of the said districts as they have formerly done." From the perspective of the Indians, for whom land was not a commodity to be bought and sold and who defined territorial sovereignty as use rights, they had given nothing away. To the contrary, they viewed an American post on their land as a positive, the reliable source of trade goods that they had long been seeking. Pike reported to Wilkinson that the eager Dakotas "had bound me up to many assurances that the post shall be established."[8]

Pike concluded the council by passing out traditional gifts of tobacco and goods and urging the Dakotas to live in peace with their Ojibwe neighbors. He also took the opportunity to warn them against the Canadians, "bad birds" who incited the Ojibwes against them. Finally, buoyed by his apparent oratorical success, he notified the Indians that the Great Father in Washington wished them to give up the use of alcohol. Evidently the Indians let him know this request exceeded the limits of their goodwill since, in an abrupt about-face, the young lieutenant then immediately dispensed sixty gallons of whiskey, which brought the council to a harmonious close.[9]

As Pike prepared to continue his ascent of the Mississippi, he had no way of knowing the hardships that lay ahead. Unfamiliar with the rigors of a northern winter, he was unprepared for the freezing conditions and the snow and ice that soon barred his way. The expedition stalled about 100 miles upriver at the site of Little Falls, where it was forced to make a winter camp. Nonetheless, Pike was determined to press on with his mission and in the middle of January continued north with a small party of men. After days of struggling through three feet of snow, the half-frozen party was rescued from sure catastrophe by North West Company traders who welcomed them to the comforts of their post at Sandy Lake. A few days' recuperation with the traders revived the intrepid explorer's spirits and he set out again to complete his mission. But by February 1, when he and a single companion staggered into the North West post at Leech Lake, he was ready to give up the quest. Leech Lake, Pike declared, was the source of the Mississippi.[10]

Lieutenant Pike was in an awkward position. As the official emissary of the American government, he was expected to enforce U.S. sovereignty over the British traders. Yet he was uncomfortably aware of how pathetic his company seemed in contrast to the competence and comfort of the Nor'Westers. He and his men had survived only through their hospitality. Adding to his chagrin, the Ojibwes, draped with British medals, were clearly unimpressed by the power of the United States, and the Union Jack brazenly flew above the posts that sheltered him. Pike attempted to resolve the dilemma through a face-saving exchange of letters with the North West post's director. The British, Pike wrote, must pay duties on the goods they imported and be regulated by American law. Furthermore, they must cease flying the British flag on American soil. The canny Nor'Wester amicably agreed to all the terms and made no objection when Pike ceremonially had the flag shot down from above the post. Both men knew this was an empty gesture. After paying lip service to American authority and bidding Pike and his party farewell (with British trader Robert Dickson as a guide), the Nor'Westers no doubt ignored the unenforceable directives and hoisted the flag once again to its appointed place.[11]

To his credit, Pike made every effort to complete his assignment despite what he described as "as many hardships as almost any party of Americans ever experienced by cold and hunger." But the harsh winter conditions only made starker the true source of his problem. Lacking any real presence on the ground, American authority was an illusion in the north country.[12]

On his way downriver, Pike stopped once again at the island that would later bear his name, still hoping to broker a peace between the Dakotas and Ojibwes and convince a Dakota delegation to return with him to St. Louis. The Dakota chiefs received him cordially, but for some reason that Pike could not explain, the "interpreters were not capable of making themselves

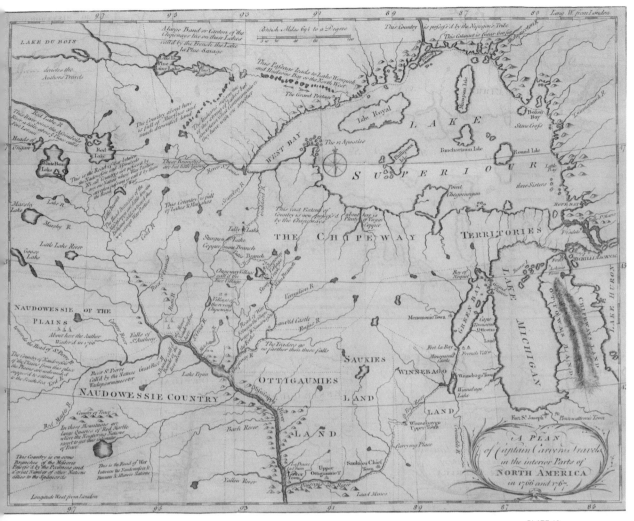

PLATE 18

Plate 18. Jonathan Carver, "A Plan of Captain Carver's Travels in the Interior Parts of North America in 1766 and 1767," from *Travels through the Interior Parts of North-America, in the Years 1766, 1767, and 1768* (London, 1778). James Ford Bell Library, University of Minnesota.

This is the first map that allows viewers to get a glimpse of the future state of Minnesota. Jonathan Carver's map accurately delineates some of the important bodies of water that would come to define the state, including the string of northern lakes that connect Lake Superior to the interior and the tributaries flowing into the Mississippi River from the east. Carver was an explorer, writer, and self-educated mapmaker who decided to teach himself surveying in order to plot the lands that were transferred from French to British control in the 1763 Peace of Paris. He joined an expedition organized by Major Robert Rogers, traveling the area he depicted on this map between 1766 and 1768. The map is dotted with observations about the human geography, history, and natural features of the land that became Minnesota. He notes traders' routes, the location of Indian villages, and the sites of past wars. He also makes hopeful annotations about possible routes to the Pacific Coast, one of the reasons Rogers's expedition was launched. The map was published as part of Carver's book, which made him famous before his death in 1780.[17]

PLATE 19

Plate 19. John Melish, *Map of the United States: With the Contiguous British and Spanish Possessions* (Philadelphia: J. Melish, 1819). Minnesota Historical Society.

Residents of the region that became Minnesota probably evinced little interest in the political upheavals of the American Revolution, but the new nation that emerged from this conflict would quickly begin to leave its imprint on this still remote part of the world. American visions for the north country were articulated in this map by John Melish, a Scottish-born mapmaker who set up shop in Philadelphia in 1811 and helped to make the city the national center of the map publishing business. While the vast majority of this land was owned and controlled by its original indigenous inhabitants in 1818, Melish represents the region as if it were already integrated into an American national empire that stretched from the Atlantic to the Pacific Oceans. "The map so constructed," Melish wrote in 1816, "shows at a glance the whole extent of the United States territory from sea to sea; and in tracing the probable expansion of the human race from east to west, the mind finds an agreeable resting place on its western limits. The view is complete, and leaves nothing to be wished for." The map and the nationalist vision that inspired it would have seemed remote and perhaps even irrelevant to people on the ground in Minnesota, where lives were ruled by kinship relationships, the exigencies of survival, and the rhythms of the backcountry fur trade. Few people in the region would ever have the chance to see the document and the accompanying book by Melish, which would have been inaccessible to all but the wealthiest and most literate urban dwellers. But this vision of an American continental empire drove efforts to establish an American military presence in the region, thus opening the door for more permanent settlement that would ultimately displace the multicultural society supported by the fur trade. This map also delineates how the section of Minnesota east of the Mississippi River had already been claimed in 1787 as part of the Northwest Territory, a large area encompassing what eventually became six states: Ohio, Indiana, Illinois, Michigan, Wisconsin, and Minnesota. By 1818, only the area that would become Minnesota and Wisconsin remained as part of the Northwest Territory, a political jurisdiction that did little to shape life in the region, which still remained under the control of its Native American inhabitants and their white trading partners.[18]

Plate 20. Peter Rindisbacher, *Indian Women in Tent*, 1830. U.S. Department of the Army, United States Military Academy, West Point Museum.

This painting from the Red River region provides an intimate glimpse into the fur trade culture that had become well-established in the north country by the beginning of the nineteenth century. It is the first rendering of an interior of a Plains Indian tent and was created by Peter Rindisbacher, a young Swiss-born artist who came to the region in 1821 as part of a settlement effort championed by the Earl of Selkirk. The young Rindisbacher quickly established a reputation for himself as an entirely new kind of painter who produced detailed ethnographic images of Indian life.[19]

PLATE 20

Rindisbacher's work illuminates how Native Americans were hardly suspended in some kind of aboriginal timelessness. By the time the artist reached the region, life had been transformed through the cultural contact and trade that had flourished since the first half of the eighteenth century. The painting depicts a domestic fireside scene, presumably an extended family sitting at their hearth smoking traditional pipes. Only two members of the group are garbed in leather clothing; the rest are wearing garments crafted from the trademark red and blue "stroud cloth," the vibrantly colored woolen cloth manufactured explicitly for the Indian trade and brought to the region by fur traders. On the left side of the painting a man sits with his arm draped affectionately around a woman in a blue dress. Attired in European-style clothing, he was probably some kind of trader who had formed a domestic partnership with the woman he was embracing. The young boy kneeling by the fire might have been their son. They are seated under a gun and horn for gunpowder, items acquired through trade. The gun hangs alongside a more traditional bow. Both weapons were undoubtedly employed to obtain furs like the ones hanging from the tent poles on the left; these pelts were the currency that paid for the cloth, the gun, and the bucket on the right side of the painting.

When Rindisbacher reached his new home, manufactured goods had become necessities of life for the indigenous people he encountered, transforming survival strategies for once isolated inhabitants. But the fur trade should not be understood as simply the imposition of a European economic system on a once self-sufficient group of people. The culture of the fur trade was grounded in pragmatic exchange. Native people were eager to acquire cloth, for instance, once they realized that it was more comfortable and practical than leather for apparel. Traders marveled at the utility of snowshoes, dog sleds, moccasins, and fur-lined mittens, which provided far more protection to vulnerable digits than leather or woolen gloves. Newcomers embraced Indian practices as enthusiastically as their partners in trade welcomed manufactured goods. Survival in the region depended on a willingness to adopt the tools best suited for life in the cold and isolated backcountry. So while the more traditionally garbed man on the right side of this painting may have altered his hunting strategies to accommodate the use of powerful firearms, the trader on the left side of the domestic circle would have had to master the use of canoes and snowshoes. Women in this world served as skillful emissaries between the two cultures, making domestic alliances that served as the foundation for economic and cultural exchanges. The fur trade was grounded in cultural encounters that exposed both Indians and whites to new tools; both groups used these tools to perform familiar jobs but also to craft a new way of life. These discrete exchanges blossomed into a hybrid culture that distinguished life in the region from communities in eastern North America or Europe until the middle of the nineteenth century.[20]

Plate 21. William Richards, *A Man and His Wife Returning with a Load of Partridges from Their Tent*, 1804–11. Archives of Manitoba, Hudson's Bay Company Archives.

This watercolor by William Richards provides another rare view of the domestic side of early nineteenth-century fur trade culture, featuring a couple living near Hudson Bay at the beginning of the nineteenth century. Painter William Richards was a native of northern Canada, the son of a Hudson's Bay Company father and a Native American mother. The couple pictured was probably joined in the same kind of *mariage à la façon du pays* that had united Richards's own parents. These marriages were cultural, economic, and domestic partnerships; they formed the base of the mixed-race society that dominated the region until the mid-nineteenth century. Native American women married traders to secure a reliable stream of trade goods for their families; their husbands benefited in myriad ways from their wives' skills

PLATE 21

and connections. Wives guided their husbands through cultural and linguistic challenges, provided their husbands with a steady supply of furs from their male kin, and
most important, ensured their husbands' survival in the harsh climate of the north.
Among Native American groups in this region, women were the ones responsible for
cooking the meals, making the moccasins, netting the snowshoes, and dressing the
pelts so coveted by the fur trade industry. As these tasks were all unfamiliar to male
traders, a female partner was needed if a fur trader wanted to stay alive and perhaps
even prosper. Families like these depended on tools made on two continents. In this
painting, the man totes a gun and an ax, both of which would have been industrially
manufactured and imported into the backcountry. The woman wraps herself against
the cold with two overlapping trade blankets that are adorned with imported ribbons.
Their journey would have been impossible without their dog and baggage sled, a type
of winter conveyance devised by the region's indigenous inhabitants.[21]

Plate 22. Peter Rindisbacher, *A Halfcast with His Wife and Child*, 1825. Winnipeg Art Gallery.

When Peter Rindisbacher's family joined the already established group of Scottish settlers in the Red River valley in 1821, they may have been surprised to find the colony
in conflict with another group of people who contested the newcomers' right to cultivate the land. Adjacent to the floundering Selkirk colony was an entrenched Métis
settlement. While neighboring Indians accommodated the new settlers and even
provided food that allowed the struggling colonists to survive, the Métis resisted what
they came to see as an occupation. The Métis — or "halfcasts," as they were commonly
called in the early nineteenth century — were the mixed-race descendants of French

PLATE 22

Canadians and Native Americans who settled north and west of the Great Lakes starting in the middle of the eighteenth century. Closely allied with area fur traders, they sustained their families by provisioning fur trade posts with meat. Neither white nor Indian, belonging neither to tribal villages nor European-style communities, the Métis were a distinct ethnic group that had forged its identity in the crucible of cultural interchanges, economic exchanges, and environmental challenges that made this region unique. They distinguished themselves, in part, through their colorful and distinctive apparel, which Rindisbacher records in meticulous detail in this painting of a Métis family. Note the father's woven sash or *ceinture fléchée*, the most distinctive item of the Métis costume, which was renowned for combining European materials and Indian designs in innovative and often flamboyant ways. The father carries a gun while the son sports a bow and arrow; these accessories hint at the Métis' formidable reputation as hunters.

This family portrait helps to illuminate why cultural contact was not immediately devastating for Indian groups. Economic and social exchange between Europeans and Indians produced mutual benefits as well as new societies based on reciprocal exchange rather than colonial domination. This Métis family is depicted at a moment of hope for the north country, before rigid American racial hierarchies marginalized racially hybrid communities. The Métis vigorously opposed the establishment of the Selkirk colony, which they believed would settle the land in such a way that game would be driven away. Métis resentment simmered after watching surveyors lay out farms on land they believed to be theirs; they were goaded into violence against the settlers by representatives of the North West Company, which viewed the Selkirk colony as a threat to its existence.

This portrait by Rindisbacher gives no hint of this tension. Young Peter seemed to have had the ability to transcend cultural boundaries and existing hostilities in order to portray the entire range of people who inhabited the Red River valley at the beginning of the nineteenth century.[22]

Plate 23. Peter Rindisbacher, *Chippewa Mode of Travelling in Winter*, ca. 1823. U.S. Department of the Army, United States Military Academy, West Point Museum.

Peter Rindisbacher was only fifteen years old when he began observing the different groups of Indians who passed through the Selkirk settlement. The curious Swiss teenager combined an eye for detail with a bold willingness to make anyone his subject, creating a new style of painting that featured ethnographic studies of individual Indians, a genre that would be popularized by more well-known artists like Seth Eastman and George Catlin. Neither of these artists would match Rindisbacher for his details and his personal engagement with his subjects, whose lively and dignified faces gaze boldly at viewers. Rindisbacher's paintings are laden with none of the assumptions about aboriginal savagery and racial extinction that would burden later works of this type. While many well-known artists fashioned their scenes from memory or imagination, Rindisbacher's paintings were done from direct observation. As a result they serve as priceless historical records of Native American life in the Red River valley at the beginning of the nineteenth century, before the ascendance of white agricultural settlement. In this painting, Rindisbacher shows how Ojibwe families used dogs, toboggans, and snowshoes to travel during the winter hunting season. The pelts captured in cold weather were more luxuriant and thus more valuable than those collected during warmer months. Indians were heavily dependent on game at this time of year, when other sources of subsistence were unavailable.[23]

PLATE 23

PLATE 24

Plate 24. Peter Rindisbacher, *Hunting the Buffaloe,* 1830. Amon Carter Museum.

Rindisbacher's depictions of the buffalo hunt became some of his most acclaimed work in his short lifetime. All of the artists who came to the region after Rindisbacher attempted to emulate his novel treatment of the buffalo hunt, a scene that became the iconic representation of the American West. Thomas Loraine McKenney selected a Rindisbacher portrayal of a buffalo hunt as the frontispiece for the second volume of *History of the Indian Tribes of North America,* intended to be an official record of the continent's rapidly "vanishing" peoples. This kind of artistic rendering of a Native American buffalo hunt continued to be highly sought after by collectors and publishers for the rest of the nineteenth century. While those who viewed Rindisbacher's early images from the Plains predicted a bright future for the young Swiss artist, his untimely death at age 28 meant that he had little time to establish a lasting reputation. Rindisbacher may have pioneered new ways of portraying the North American West, but he remains little known to modern audiences.[24]

Plate 25. Peter Rindisbacher, *Chippewa Mode of Travelling in the Spring and Summer,* 1830. U.S. Department of the Army, United States Military Academy, West Point Museum.

Rindisbacher's depiction of an Ojibwe family shows, again, how even the most traditional of the region's Indians had incorporated trade goods into their subsistence lifestyles by 1830. The father in this painting carries both a gun and an ax, manufactured goods most certainly obtained from traders. This entire family is garbed in red and blue trade cloth, fashioned into garments of Indian rather than European design. Their cloth leggings, however, are paired with leather moccasins, the footwear of choice for all inhabitants of this region. The young boy carries a traditional bow. For early nineteenth-century Indians in this region, dogs were the most desirable beasts of burden. They could be harnessed to travois, as shown here, or to sleds in the winter. These small pack animals were preferable to horses, which required too much hard-to-obtain food over the long winter months and could not skitter across deep snow. In this subsistence culture, horses rarely lasted more than one season, as they were

PLATE 25

frequently eaten for their meat during the most difficult of the winter months, when starvation always threatened. Since the mother carried a canoe paddle along with the remainder of her family's belongings, the group may have been headed to a nearby waterway, where a birch bark canoe could provide a speedier conveyance.

Plate 26. Dakota puckered moccasins, collected by Nathan Sturges Jarvis, 1833–36. Nathan Sturges Jarvis Collection of Eastern Plains Art, Brooklyn Museum of Art.

This is a dress version of the universal footwear worn in the Minnesota territory in the early nineteenth century. The elaborate decorations on these moccasins suggests that they were crafted for special occasions; they may have been worn a couple of times before being acquired by Nathan Jarvis, the Army surgeon at Fort Snelling from 1833–36.

PLATE 26

Like many other Army officers posted in Indian country, Jarvis entertained himself during his time at the fort by collecting what he and other amateur ethnographers called Indian "curiosities": arrows, quivers, bows, tomahawks, pipes, baskets, moccasins, leggings, shirts, headdresses. Jarvis accepted these Indian-made objects in exchange for medical services rendered to both traders and Indians in the area, carefully preserving and documenting his collection, which he ultimately donated to the New York Historical Society. Yet Jarvis evinced scant interest or affection for the people who made these items. Only forty-seven days after arriving at his post on the Mississippi River, Jarvis complained that Indians "begin to lose their novelty with me, and any further notice to what I have already given would be tiresome both to you & me."[25]

An early agent of American empire in the region, Jarvis shared the widespread conviction that collecting Indian artifacts was a way of memorializing people and lifeways that would soon be extinct. Jarvis might have seen his moccasins as relics from a quickly vanishing aboriginal lifestyle, but in the 1830s moccasins were still everyday apparel for everyone in the region, in much the same way that canoes were the watercraft of choice. Indian families never abandoned their time-tested footwear in favor of heavy European-style boots. In fact, moccasins in all their forms were quickly adopted by newcomers, who quickly discovered the impracticality of hard-soled shoes in the terrain of the north country. Moccasins protected feet, allowing their wearers to walk over swampy or snowy ground without falling into deep holes; moccasins permitted toes to move, thus keeping feet warmer than regular boots; and they dried quickly, wicking moisture away from feet. In cold weather or for long journeys they could be stuffed with scraps from blankets, wool, and dried grass.

Indian women could make a simple pair in one day but might take up to five days to create an elaborate set for a special young man. The ability to craft moccasins was one of many skills that made Indian women attractive partners for white traders working in the backcountry. As game shortages, tightening credit, and epidemics made life more difficult for many Indians in the 1830s, some women spent increasing amounts of time crafting moccasins for the market. Indian handiwork had become a fashionable collectors' item, and some traders developed a side business in moccasins and pouches, which were shipped downriver to markets like St. Louis or sold to local Army officers and adventurous tourists who made their way up the Mississippi. Jarvis himself purchased at least ten pairs of moccasins for his personal collection.[26]

Plate 27. Joseph E. Heckle, *Topographical Sketch of Fort St. Anthony at the Confluence of the Rivers Mississippi and St. Peters,* **detail, 1823. Minnesota Historical Society.**

This view of Fort Snelling was drawn in 1823 by Sergeant Joseph E. Heckle, the quartermaster sergeant at the fort. The map was annotated by Major Josiah H. Vose, who had overseen the construction of the American military's first winter quarters on the bank of the Minnesota River in 1819 and would later serve as the post's commandant. In his marginal notes, Vose describes the building of Fort Snelling in 1823, providing details about its construction as well as the environs of the fort, including the officers' gardens, the roads leading to the fort, and the boats that plied the adjacent rivers.

The American military first moved to establish a post at this site in the spring of 1819 when Lieutenant Colonel Henry Leavenworth got instructions to move his Fifth Infantry regiment from Detroit to the juncture of the Minnesota and Mississippi Rivers, land originally acquired by Zebulon Pike in 1805. The arduous journey to the site of the new military outpost left many of Leavenworth's soldiers seriously ill; backbreaking portages, extreme heat, poor drinking water, and ravenous mosquitoes prompted one of its members to conclude that the north country was "not fit for either man or beast to live in."[27]

American soldiers and their dependents endured several years of misery before they settled into the military quarters drawn by Heckle and described by Vose in 1823. Cantonment New Hope was first established on the banks of the Minnesota River in the fall of 1819. This log stockade provided minimal protection from the harsh winter that followed. One of the season's early storms tore the roof from one of the hastily erected cabins. Ice blocked boats from bringing a fresh supply of food, leaving the camp to subsist on "rusty" pork and bread. "The mercury is 10 below zero and the ink freezes in my pen while I write. . . .The dysentery yet rages," Leavenworth wrote at Christmas in 1819.[28] By the time spring finally arrived in 1820, thirty soldiers from the original expedition had died.

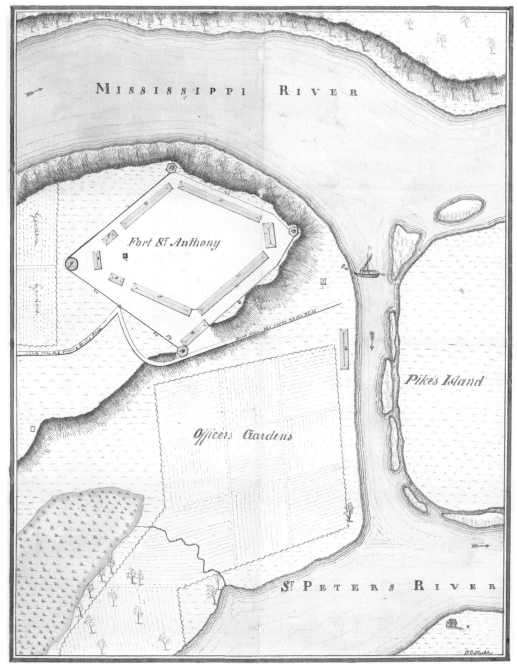

MISSISSIPPI RIVER

Fort St Anthony

Officers Gardens

Pike's Island

St PETERS RIVER

PLATE 27

Leavenworth moved his camp to higher ground in the summer of 1820. He was then relieved of his command by Colonel Josiah Snelling, who directed the construction of the permanent barracks on the site shown by this topographical sketch. Troops spent the winter of 1822–23 in what was then known as Fort St. Anthony. It was renamed Fort Snelling in 1825 to honor Josiah Snelling's herculean efforts to construct a stone fortress in what the American military viewed as a remote wilderness.[29]

PLATE 28

Plate 28. George Catlin, *Fort Snelling, United States, Garrison at the Mouth of the St. Peter's River,* 1851–53. Gilcrease Museum.

George Catlin observed this view of Fort Snelling during his 1835 visit to the Upper Mississippi, when he spent a month studying the Dakotas and Ojibwes around the military outpost and discussing federal Indian policies with agent Lawrence Taliaferro and fort surgeon Nathan Jarvis. This painting shows how the fort was situated at the confluence of the Mississippi and Minnesota rivers and demonstrates how visitors and supplies arrived at the fort from the rivers below its walls. Catlin's visit to Fort Snelling proved pivotal to his development as a chronicler of Native American life. Note the Indian encampment of the river flats below the fort. Catlin deemed the surrounding Indians uncorrupted enough to serve as interesting artistic subjects while being perfectly amenable to white advances, accepting payment from Catlin for staging dances and ball play that he immortalized in his Indian gallery. The fort provided scenes that inspired the painter to work furiously, each day presenting him with the opportunity to produce multiple portraits and sceneries. Fort Snelling Indian agent Taliaferro served as Catlin's willing tutor in Indian policy, shaping the artist's understanding of Native American life and currying his antipathy toward the fur trade. Catlin lionized Taliaferro in his *Letters and Notes,* singling him out as the only "public servant on these frontiers, who has performed the duties of his office, strictly and faithfully, as well as kindly, for fifteen years."[30] Fur traders like Henry Sibley would come to dismiss Catlin during his rise to national prominence, castigating the painter as an ungrateful eastern romantic whose scant experience in the backcountry left him ill-equipped to interpret Native American life for the rest of the world.

Plate 29. George Catlin, *Sioux Village, Lake Calhoun, near Fort Snelling*, 1835–36. Smithsonian American Art Museum.

One of the most important settlements within close proximity to Fort Snelling in the 1830s was Eatonville, or Cloudman's village, an agricultural experiment sponsored by Indian agent Lawrence Taliaferro. Major trails and myriad social connections joined the two outposts, making it easy for George Catlin to paint this image of the Indian village during his visit to Fort Snelling in 1835. The settlement — which was located on the banks of Lake Calhoun — was part of Taliaferro's efforts to change the lifeways of Minnesota Indians, encouraging them to give up hunting in favor of European-style agriculture. In 1828, Taliaferro convinced a group of families to establish this hamlet and hired Philander Prescott to work as a farmer in the settlement, which he named in honor of Secretary of War John H. Eaton. With support from Dakota leader Cloudman, who endorsed this experiment, Prescott plowed the prairie, demonstrating new farming techniques to Indians accustomed to cultivating small fields or gardens with hoes. The community flourished, attracting new residents eager to share in its bumper harvests and eventually welcoming two missionaries, Gideon and Samuel Pond. Taliaferro would have undoubtedly shared his pride in the agricultural experiment with the curious eastern painter, who developed enormous respect for the Minnesota Indian agent during his stay at Fort Snelling. The village prospered until 1839, when intensified fighting between the Dakota and the Ojibwe made villagers vulnerable to attack and forced them to flee to the Minnesota River Valley.

PLATE 29

Plate 30. Stephen Return Riggs, *Dakota Tawoonspe, Wowapi [Dakota Lessons]* **(Louisville, Kentucky: Morton & Griswold, 1850), 6. Minnesota Historical Society.**

Protestant missionaries associated with the American Board of Commissioners for Foreign Missions saw education as the key to their efforts to Christianize Minnesota Indians in the first half of the nineteenth century. Pictured here is a page from one of missionary Stephen Riggs's elementary readers, which pairs a winter scene with some basic text in Dakota featuring phrases like "I see a small dog" and "very deep snow" and "good sleigh." The snowy scene resembles an English country village more than a Minnesota prairie hamlet; this juxtaposition of Dakota text with an unfamiliar scene must have been jarring to Dakota readers struggling to master the written word. This strange synthesis highlights the often contradictory aims of the missionaries, who conducted their schools in Dakota in order to imbue Indian children with conventional American values. Missionaries urged the Dakota to reject traditional spiritual practices, sever ties with the fur trade, ignore kinship obligations that were not church sanctioned, and trade hunting for a life of settled agriculture. The destruction of Indian culture, they asserted, was the only way to save Indian people.

Gideon and Samuel Pond pioneered the work of creating a written alphabet for Dakota and began assembling a dictionary that had grown to three thousand words by 1839. This compilation provided the foundation for the later publications of Stephen Riggs, a missionary remembered for his translation of the Old and New Testaments into Dakota and his 1852 *Grammar and Dictionary of the Dakota Language.* Riggs also published a series of readers like the one pictured here. Riggs used these publications to argue that Dakota speakers should be granted full citizenship when he participated in a suit brought on behalf of nine Dakota men in 1861. Speaking Dakota, Riggs asserted to the court, did not preclude civilized behavior since the language "had been reduced to a system and was capable of use in the printed books, in writing, and for all other practical purposes." The judge hearing the citizenship case disagreed.

6   DAKOTA TAWOONSPE.

Canwiyusdohe akan yankapi.

Wa xbe rinca.	Icimani yapi.
Canwapa wanica.	Xuktanka nacapcapapi.
Canwiyusdohe waxte.	Xunka cistina wan
Icapsinte wan hanska	wanmdaka.
	Wa kin kokipe xni.

PLATE 30

wan-ye'-ca	wa-re'-ca
wa-pa-mna	wa-to-ha
wa-sku-ya	wa-to-pa

PLATE 31

The court concluded that "Sioux was a barbarous language" and did not have sufficient vocabulary to allow its speakers to understand "our system of government."[31]

Riggs's proficiency in Dakota made him a central figure during the military trials
that followed the U.S.–Dakota War, when he spent weeks extracting confessions and
surreptitiously compiling evidence against hundreds of captured Indians suspected of
having a role in the killings. His ignominious role in the exile of the Dakota from Minnesota, however, has never erased the value of his scholarly work in Dakota linguistics.
Riggs's dictionary and grammar books remain seminal books in Dakota and have
served as important tools for advocates of Dakota cultural preservation in the 150
years since the U.S.–Dakota War.

Plate 31. Peter Rindisbacher, *Winter Fishing on Ice of Assynoibain and Red River,* 1821. Library and Archives of Canada.

By the time Peter Rindisbacher's family arrived in the Red River region in 1821,
winter's cold had already arrived. Because of devastating crop losses during the
previous summer, starvation loomed over the entire colony, sending new arrivals
scrambling to devise a survival strategy for the coming winter. Peter's family was part
of a group that shared quarters with more established colonists in Fort Douglas, the
Selkirk colony's seat of government. These settlers subsisted on roots, rations of wheat
given them by the fur company, meat that was provided by Indians, and finally by fish
that was caught through the thick river ice. One month after his arrival, Peter created
this superficially cheerful scene of settlers, Indians, and their dogs on the river below
Fort Gibraltar, an old fur post being rebuilt by the Hudson's Bay Company. The bright
sunshine and seemingly festive air of the eclectic company belies the desperation of
the situation that forced these new settlers to master ice fishing. A few months later
the colonists received a visit from George Simpson, the Hudson's Bay Company governor, who was appalled by the conditions he observed: "How they have spun out the
Winter and Spring is unexplicable; Horses, Dogs, Bears, Buffalo in short whatever
came in their way was devoured"[32]

PLATE 32

Plate 32. Peter Rindisbacher, *Colonists on the Red River in North America*, 1822. Library and Archives of Canada.

This drawing provides a rare glimpse into the domestic life of the Selkirk settlers, who were the first to attempt to create a European-style agricultural colony in the region that became Minnesota. The Rindisbachers remained in the Red River colony until 1826, when massive spring flooding washed away the entire community. Settlers rebuilt, only to have their newly planted fields of barley and potatoes eaten by grubworms in a single night. This last calamity was the final straw for the Rindisbachers, who joined hundreds of other Selkirk colonists who fled south to the American military outpost that became known as Fort Snelling, the newly established American military garrison at the confluence of the Minnesota and Mississippi Rivers. The fort's soldiers provided temporary shelter to the settlers; most continued on their way out of Minnesota to join communities in Illinois and Indiana. A few were allowed to squat on the military reservation in exchange for providing food and goods to the fort as small-scale farmers, petty traders, or artisans. These refugees ultimately helped to form the nucleus of the haphazard settlement that was to become St. Paul.[33]

understood"—a peculiar circumstance, considering that Joseph Renville and Robert Dickson, both fluent Dakota speakers, acted as interpreters. Perhaps Dickson and Renville, who had good reason to minimize Dakota contact with the Americans, intentionally muddled the communication. Or maybe the chiefs feigned confusion to avoid an outright denial of Pike's requests. In either case, the lieutenant was unable to persuade any Dakota dignitaries to accompany him to St. Louis.[13]

All in all, Pike's expedition displayed a weak show of American power. Still, the British traders did not take its appearance on the Mississippi lightly. They knew it was only a matter of time before the Americans returned with more force and hoped that, before it was too late, England would rouse itself to retake the northern territories.

[79]

Another War in the Borderland

Relations between the United States and Britain were already tense. England, once again embroiled in war with France, was interfering with American neutrality on the seas, stopping ships, impounding cargoes, and impressing sailors. Congress was outraged by the insult to the young nation's sovereignty as well as the debilitating effect on its commerce. In retaliation, in 1807 the United States cut off all trade with Great Britain, which created serious problems for British fur traders.[14] With Michilimackinac closed to international commerce, all goods and provisions had to be smuggled into the interior. As relations between England and the United States continued to deteriorate, North West Company moguls in Montreal agitated for war and promised to "furnish to the government both naval and military cooperation." With their men and resources, they assured the Canadian governor, they could stopper U.S. commerce on the Great Lakes and reclaim the region for the crown.[15]

In preparing for the likelihood of war, Canadian officials and fur traders alike knew that, as in every previous contest on the frontier, Native American allies would be essential as a critical fighting force. Holding their loyalty would be the key to success. Beginning in 1807, British officials, including Canada's governor, thus sent out confidential directives to traders in the interior, urging them to stir up the Indians against the Americans. For the fur traders, of course, this was nothing new. They had long derided the weakness of the Americans on the one hand and on the other warned the Indians about American designs to occupy Native lands. With newly imposed trade restrictions threatening their livelihood, the traders raised the tenor of their warnings. To buttress their words and demonstrate the contrasting power and goodwill of the British, the Nor'Westers dispensed gifts among the Indians with an open hand. In the winter of 1811–12 Robert Dickson distributed nearly £2,000 in merchandise to the Dakotas, who were suffering from a particularly desolate winter.[16]

It is important to note that Dickson was motivated by more than self-interest. He had lived among the Dakotas for most of his adult life and was kin to them through marriage. His ties to the Dakotas were emotionally compelling as well as economic. Such relationships of kinship and trust forged between long-time traders like Dickson and Indian people were perhaps the most important factor in winning the tribes of the Upper Mississippi to the British cause. Gift-giving ratified these connections and carried a symbolic value as important as its material worth. Moreover, Dakota contact with the Americans had brought them no benefits. Despite Pike's promises in 1805, no post had been established, no trade commenced. Instead, as the traders informed them, the Americans were holding up the goods the Indians needed to survive. Thus, by the time the War of 1812 was declared, Dickson could report that he already had 300 Indians ready to march, including the great Mdewakanton Dakota chiefs Wabasha and Little Crow (Wakinyatanka). Throughout the west, Dakota support for the British was nearly unanimous. Of all the important leaders, only Red Wing, who had presciently dreamed of an American victory, vacillated in his loyalties.[17]

All along the frontier, Indians aligned against the Americans. At the outbreak of the war confidential correspondence from Prairie du Chien portrayed a grim situation: "I must tell you every thing is against you Americans, all nations in general have given their word to the English." But broad Indian support for the British sprang from a variety of motives, all grounded in local circumstance. On the settlement frontier—Indiana, Illinois, Ohio, Kentucky, and Tennessee—the tribes were in a life-and-death struggle to save their lands. Theirs was an Indian war. But in Michigan, Wisconsin, and the Upper Mississippi River Valley, support for the British was a multicultural alliance. The fur trade companies advanced the possibility of a permanent Indian nation to act as a buffer between Canada and the United States—and to keep settlers out of the region. Everyone involved in the trade would benefit. British traders, French Canadians, Métis, and Native people all had a stake in the outcome and fought together to protect a common way of life.[18]

In the Lake Superior region, the Ojibwes kept aloof from the fight. Settlers were not encroaching on their lands and they had little reason to trust the words of the British. The North West Company had used its monopoly power for more than a decade to exploit its Ojibwe partners, betraying the longstanding culture of mutual obligation. As a result, the Ojibwes, unlike the Dakotas, had come to resent the British traders they were dependent upon. Thus, with few exceptions, the Ojibwes refused to go to war. When asked to take up arms, Flat Mouth, chief of the Pillager band, expressed a general sentiment in his response. "When I go to war against my enemies," he said, "I do not call on the whites to join my warriors. The white people have quarreled among themselves, and I do not wish to meddle in their quarrels." On this part of the fur trade frontier, the bonds of trust and kinship had irretrievably eroded.

According to Ojibwe historian William Warren, those few who did fight with the British did so mainly "through coercion."[19]

Even without the support of the Ojibwes, the traders and other Indians constituted a compelling force under Dickson's command. Many of the North West Company's leading agents were commissioned as officers in the British army, including prominent mixed-blood Joseph Renville, and Wabasha and Little Crow were both named generals of the Indian forces. Though no engagements took place on Minnesota soil, they all had a stake in the war's outcome and their soldiers fought with skill and cunning. They captured Fort Michilimackinac and Fort Dearborn at Detroit, and after a brief American occupation of Prairie du Chien they took back that strategic post as well. Throughout the course of the war they won and held all the Northwest, never allowing American forces to pass north of Prairie du Chien on the Mississippi. Even with supplies and ammunition running low, according to the commander at Michilimackinac, the Indians remained "all staunch." Though enthusiasm waned as the war dragged on, and many Dakotas returned home, fearing that in their absence the Ojibwes would overrun their villages, none defected to the Americans.[20]

[81]

On the fur trade frontier, the British were clearly victorious. However, in the larger scheme of the war, the Northwest was only a minor front. When after two years of fighting the hostilities concluded in a stalemate, all their victories counted for naught. The fur companies lobbied hard for a peace agreement that would cede the territory north of the Ohio back to Great Britain. Failing that, they argued that at the very least it should be made a permanent Indian reserve, closed to future settlement. But when the terms of the Treaty of Ghent were published in 1815, the Canadians were shocked to learn that they had won nothing at all. The boundaries remained unchanged. The traders were outraged. The commander at Michilimackinac wrote, "Our Negociators as usual have been egregiously duped: As usual, they have shown themselves profoundly ignorant of the concerns of this part of the Empire."[21] The Indians felt deeply betrayed. Dakota allies had traveled far from their homes to fight alongside the British and been promised an Indian nation; they had won every battle and were left empty-handed. When the British tried to appease them with gifts, Little Crow spoke from the heart of the Dakota people:

> After we have fought for you, endured many hardships, lost some of our people, and awakened the vengeance of our powerful neighbors, you make a peace for yourselves and leave us to obtain such terms as we can! You no longer need our services, and offer us these goods as a compensation for having deserted us. But no! We will not take them; we hold them and yourselves in equal contempt![22]

For a number of years following the war, British traders illicitly continued to work the Minnesota region, especially near the border, but they had lost the loyalty of the Dakotas forever. When Wabasha and Little Crow next encountered the Americans at Prairie du Chien in 1818, they ceremoniously handed over their British flags and medals, cheered the American president, and denounced the British king, making the best of a bad situation. Their primary interest was still to establish a stable trading relationship. Whether the Union Jack or the Stars and Stripes flew over the desired post was irrelevant to them. Thus, a year later, when the Americans again came calling on the Upper Mississippi, they received a most hospitable welcome. The Dakotas had no way to know that this expedition would mark the beginning of the end of their world.[23]

The Americans Make Their Mark

In 1819 the Americans reappeared in Dakota country. Finally they were ready to build the post at the confluence of the Mississippi and St. Peter rivers that Pike had promised in 1805. The Dakotas were expecting them. An advance party had preceded the full contingent of soldiers to tardily fulfill the payment pledged to the Mdewakanton chiefs by Lieutenant Pike nearly fifteen years earlier. The $2,000 that Congress had allocated to compensate the bands for the strip of land along the Mississippi was distributed in the form of "gifts" along with promises of the benefits and protection from their enemies the fort would provide.[24]

The Dakotas greeted the long-awaited arrival of a permanent American post with friendly hospitality, though to most of the 200 soldiers—raw eastern recruits without experience on the frontier—the Indians must have seemed a fearsome sight. Adding to their unease, the journey up the Mississippi had taken the soldiers through dangerous territory where hostile Sac, Fox, and Winnebago bands were battling to hold back settlers from taking their lands. On the Upper Mississippi, however, no white settlers clamored for land. In fact, the only whites in the region were traders, who must have seemed to the soldiers to share more traits with the Indians than with themselves.[25]

The military objective in Minnesota was not to protect whites from the Indians but rather to win Indian allegiance away from British traders and keep the Dakotas and Ojibwes from warring among themselves, which had a damaging effect on the trade. Most important, their mission was to guard against British poachers and stop the flow of furs from American territory to Montreal. The United States had defended its sovereignty in the War of 1812, and President James Monroe and Secretary of War John C. Calhoun agreed that the time had come for the young nation to assert itself. In 1817 Monroe barred non-Americans from trading on U.S. soil and Calhoun initiated a plan to construct garrisons along the frontier to enforce the policy. The post eventually named Fort Snelling was designated as the farthest northwestern sentinel. Strategically located at the mouth of the St. Peter (at a site known as Mendota, the Dakota word for "entry"), the garrison could control passage in and out of the fur trade interior via the Mississippi route.[26]

This was indeed a blow to British companies that worked the Dakota trade and to high-profile British traders like Robert Dickson, the most prominent figure in the western trade and famous—or infamous—for his military exploits in the late war. But for most traders, who considered themselves no more British than American, the new regulation merely required a meaningless formality. Most men in the Dakota trade were of French Canadian ancestry, with deep ties of kinship to the Dakotas. Their loyalties were locally circumscribed. Thus, Joe Rolette, Joseph Renville, Jean Baptiste Faribault, Alexis Bailly, Louis Provençalle, and Joseph La Framboise, along with nearly every other British subject in the trade, promptly applied for American citizenship and continued business as usual. Indian agent Lawrence Taliaferro, who carried on a running battle with the traders, had no illusion that this change in citizenship reflected any new allegiance to the United States. In his estimation, the ungovernable traders were loyal only to themselves: "Mississippi demi-civilized Canadian mongrel English American citizens"—a description quite close to the mark.[27]

New Partners, New Rivals

The belated assertion of American authority caused no immediate change in the day-to-day relations between the Dakotas and the agents, traders, and *engagés* of the trade, though the profits of their labors flowed now to St. Louis and New York rather than Montreal and London. John Jacob Astor, a German immigrant with a genius for business, had been working for years to take control of the American fur territory. With the new muscle provided by the U.S. military, Astor's American Fur Company, which he had begun to put together in 1808, at last had the support it needed to wrest the trade from the British. Astor schemed relentlessly to effect a monopoly. He soon became the dominant player in the trade but monopoly eluded him, especially in Minnesota country. Among the Dakotas, American Fur competed with a host of smaller operations and independents, which, for a time, sustained a balance of power between Indians and traders, holding any plans for exploitation at bay.[28]

Farther north in Ojibwe territory, new competition from American traders had real, immediate benefits. The North West Company monopoly had stripped the Ojibwes of much of their bargaining power. Nonetheless, though they had no voice in shaping company policy, many of the French and Scots–Canadian winterers, knit by kinship to the Indian people, did not fully discard the obligations of family connection. In 1821 the Ojibwes lost even this slender advantage when the Hudson's Bay Company absorbed the North West Company. Unfettered by any personal relationships with the Indians, Hudson's Bay officers mandated a merciless policy. "However repugnant it may be to our feelings," wrote the head of the company's Northern Department, "I am convinced they must be ruled with a rod of iron, to bring and to keep them in a proper state of submission."[29]

Fortunately, this ruthless strategy proved unenforceable in the border region. The Hudson's Bay Company soon discovered it faced stiff competition from agents of the American Fur Company as well as independent trader John Johnston. The British, with their posts confined to the Canadian side of the international border, could no longer follow the Indians to their hunting grounds. Instead they had to persuade the hunters to carry the pelts to them, across the imaginary line. Rather than use the draconian practices the company recommended, its agents were forced to court Indian patronage in a bidding war with American Fur, offering cut-rate prices on goods, generous gifts, and veritable oceans of alcohol to demonstrate their goodwill. Astor, in turn, directed his agents to undercut British prices, even if it meant taking a loss. At first, the blood ties that bound Johnston and his chief associates, Joseph Cadotte and Paul and Bazil Beaulieu, to the Ojibwes enabled them to hold their own against the warring giants of the trade, but Johnston's outfit simply couldn't match the prices of its capital-rich competitors, who were driving him into bankruptcy. Consequently, the need to provide for their families eventually caused most Indians to turn away from their extended kin, however reluctantly. Within a few years Johnston and his men had become employees of American Fur.[30]

The arrival of the Americans meant that for the first time in decades the Ojibwes found themselves with bargaining leverage. They commanded a premium price not only for their furs, but also for their wild rice, the essential food staple of the border trade—and nearly all of it grew on the American side of the border. Traders often survived the winter on a diet of rice gruel alone. The companies were willing to pay nearly any price to keep the grain and other Indian-supplied foodstuffs out of the opposition's hands, hoping to starve them out of the region. Trader Philander Prescott recalled, "The custom in this country [was to] starve out, ruin out, and drive out every opposition, either by fair or foul means, that they possibly can." The Ojibwes played this situation to their advantage with shrewd intelligence. Company agents, who prided themselves on their own sharp bargaining, regarded negotiations in a different light when the Indians had the advantage. "They cheat, lie and steal," wrote one disgruntled clerk. "It is a pity such Indians should have a trader."[31]

The petty traders, mainly French Canadians and Métis, bore the brunt of this international trade war. As one trader described his plight to Prescott in 1822, "The whole trade [at his post] was worth only about $2,000 a year and it hardly paid for the trouble and expense, but as he was in the trade he did not know what to do for a living except to follow up the trade." He also claimed, "There was no game about where [he] lived and they seldom ever had meat. Once in a while they got a little grease from the Indians, but had to pay a great price for it." The Ojibwes, despite their trading advantage, also suffered from want in the north country. While the trade war improved their bargaining position, the resources of the region had been sadly depleted, which increased their dependence on manufactured goods and purchased provisions. Hard bargaining was driven by desperation as well as by guile. The land could barely support the tribe's population (which had grown to at least 30,000) and game for food, let alone pelts, was distressingly hard to find. Scarcity forced the Indians to focus their energies almost entirely on market hunting until the region was nearly barren of game. One trader described it simply as a desert.[32]

By 1833 Ramsay Crooks, who directed American Fur's field operations, had persuaded Astor that the value of the border trade was not worth the cost of competition. In a secret agreement devised with Hudson's Bay, Astor agreed to pull his agents out of the border region for an annual cash compensation of £300—a turn of events that made hard times even more difficult for the northern Ojibwes. The combination of depleted resources and the return of monopoly exploitation in the border region drove people into Minnesota's lakes region to the south, from Fond du Lac to Mille Lacs, where furs were more abundant and American traders had established posts. But as more tribal members migrated southward, those resources were taxed to the limit as well, which inexorably forced hunters into the border zone that separated the Ojibwes from the Dakotas.[33]

Border Wars

Reports from Minnesota country suggested that the Ojibwes and Dakotas were in a constant state of war in the presettlement era, a perception that helped delay land-hungry migrants from casting their eyes to the north. Certainly, the Americans were no more successful than the British or the French in mediating tribal hostilities. In his first seven years as Indian agent at Fort Snelling, Lawrence Taliaferro convened no fewer than ten peace conferences between the Dakotas and Ojibwes, none of which had any measurable effect on intertribal relations. However, what the Americans deemed "war" was in reality never a full-scale conflict between the tribes. Rather, the confrontations that broke out on a regular basis were more accurately local skirmishes between discrete individuals and villages set off by personal insults, rogue banditry, youthful bravado, or competition for hunting rights in the border zone between the tribes. The missionary Samuel Pond understood that the frequent instances of localized violence among the Indians were no more savage than in any other society. They fought "not because they were Indians but because they were like other men." Only rarely did these clashes result in more than a few casualties on either side.[34]

For the most part, the tribes were inclined more toward peace than warfare that diverted time and resources from the critical tasks that sustained them

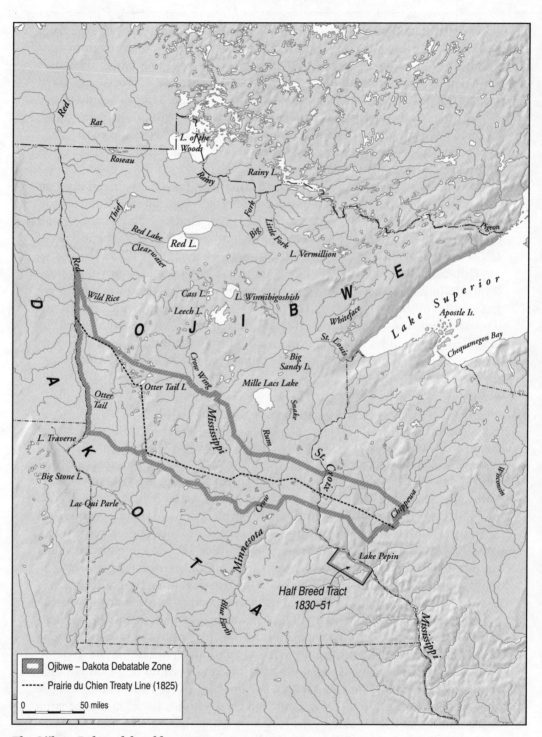

The Ojibwe–Dakota debatable zone.

from season to season. Rather than face off with one another, villages tended to avoid close contact. As evidence, the buffer zone that separated the tribes was virtually unpopulated. Ironically, this "contested" or "debatable" zone roughly followed the diagonal belt of hardwood forest that separated the prairie from the pine forest and provided exceptionally rich habitat for game. Because neither the Ojibwes nor Dakotas were eager to establish villages within reach of their enemies, animal populations flourished there. Meanwhile, in more populated areas game was rapidly disappearing.[35]

Basic need and hard economic facts forced the tribes into competition in the contested zone. The trade had come to operate almost entirely on a credit system. Traders were everywhere, providing goods, guns, and ammunition on credit, then pressing the Indians to bring in increasing numbers of furs to repay their debt. This necessarily resulted in intensive market hunting, which escalated a downward cycle toward dependency. Overhunting rapidly depleted nearby game, which forced the Indians to undertake longer and less fruitful hunting trips. With their energies increasingly devoted to collecting pelts, they had to rely heavily on purchased goods to support the necessities of life and equip themselves for the hunt. Paying for those provisions required even more furs, which became harder and harder to secure. A winter when the snow was too deep or when no snow fell at all could be equally devastating to the hunt, bringing whole villages to the brink of starvation. In these years especially, hunters were inevitably drawn to venture into the buffer zone.[36]

Most of the recorded hostilities occurred within this narrow strip of land that stretched some 340 miles from the Chippewa River in present-day Wisconsin to Otter Tail Lake and the Red River of western Minnesota. Pure necessity drove the tribes to risk the dangers of hunting in the buffer zone, along with prodding from traders anxious to make a profitable season. Taliaferro blamed the traders for "pushing" the Indians into confrontation. In his estimation, the hostilities were "one of the fruits of the Indian trade in the north." Major Stephen Long, who led a scientific expedition through Minnesota in 1823, noted both the abundance of game and the dangers that faced hunters in the "debatable land, which both Chippewas [Ojibwe] and Dacota claim, and upon which both frequently hunt, but always in a state of preparation for hostilities." They never entered the region unless "prepared for war."[37]

War, however, was too strong a word. No significant territory changed hands and casualties were few. For decades, the Americans labored to make peace between the tribes by establishing a fixed boundary line between them. But the treaty makers failed to understand the politics that made such a division unfeasible. Border skirmishes, as the Indians attempted to explain, were a necessary show of strength. They maintained a balance of power and protected the status quo. Little Crow laid out the logic of limited hostilities to Indian agent Thomas Forsyth:

He remarked that a peace could easily be made, but said that it is better for us to carry on the war in the way we do, than to make peace, because, he added, we lose a man or two in the course of a year, and we kill as many of the enemy during the same time; and if we were to make peace, the Chippewas would overrun all the country. . . . Why then, said he, should we give up such an extensive country to another nation to save the lives of a man or two annually?[38]

[88]

Relations between the tribes were always complex—seldom either uniformly hostile or peaceful. While conflicts erupted in one locality, at the same time friendly interchange went on in others. The tribes continued to intermarry and unions of mixed-blood children complicated family ties even further. Dakotas and Ojibwes sometimes hunted and feasted together, played lacrosse, exchanged gifts, and engaged in trade. Hostilities were locally circumscribed and ebbed and flowed from year to year, usually intensifying in periods of scarcity. Both tribes were growing in population and, as ethnologist Harold Hickerson notes, "although the causes for war were always expressed in terms of grievance and retaliation, one sees that the land could not, given the conditions of trade and technology of the time, support in comfort as many Chippewa and Dakota as were in the region." Conflict was almost inevitable.[39]

Whatever the cause or nature of intertribal disputes, they posed almost no danger to whites in the region. In fact, the Indians took pains to avoid injuring whites in their forays.[40] For example, in 1839 two young Ojibwe braves ambushed and killed a respected Dakota near Fort Snelling, which caused his enraged kinsmen to launch an unusually wide-scale revenge attack. A war party of 100 Mdewakanton Dakotas from Kaposia caught up with a group of Ojibwes at Stillwater, but scouting out the encampment, they discovered that trader William Aitkin had joined the Ojibwes. Rather than attack immediately, the Dakotas waited until Aitkin had left, then swooped down to exact harsh retribution, leaving twenty-one Ojibwes dead and another twenty-nine wounded. Little Crow later told Agent Taliaferro, "We might have killed every soul of the Chippewas, had there been no white people along."[41]

Indian-white relations were in a constant state of tension, but Indians only rarely resorted to physical violence against whites. According to Taliaferro, during the twenty-one years he served as agent to the Dakotas, not a single white person was killed by their hand. Instead both Dakotas and Ojibwes expressed displeasure with whites in less direct ways, often by slaughtering livestock or horses, frequently in the offending party's presence. This served as an effective but not lethal message. In the 1830s missionaries reported numerous livestock killed at Lake Traverse and Lac qui Parle to the west and Fond du Lac to the northeast. Traders, wrote one observer, "are unable to obtain any redress and perhaps even dare not reprove those [Dakota] who have done it." Ojibwes used similar tactics against a surveying expedition in 1835, dispatched to mark a fixed border between the tribes. Neither the Ojibwes nor Dakotas were happy with the proposed boundary line. The surveying party, which had reached the Sauk River in Ojibwe country, found its mules stabbed early one morning. This so unnerved the soldiers who accompanied them that they soon abandoned the surveyors and headed back to Fort Snelling. Philander Prescott, who had hired on as interpreter for the expedition, noted also that "the Indians destroyed all the [surveyors'] landmarks they could find." Without resorting to violence against the party, the Indians had made their point, thus ending what Prescott deemed "another expedition that was of no benefit to the government or the Indians."[42]

The feeble military presence at Fort Snelling had little influence in holding Indian attacks at bay—never more than 200 soldiers versus thousands of Dakotas and Ojibwes. Rather, the Indians chose their tactics shrewdly. The trade had become essential to their survival. The last thing they wanted was to drive traders from the region. Thus, they used just enough force to assert their rights in an increasingly unequal economic relationship and yet avoid outright hostilities. On those rare occasions when attacks against traders occurred, it may have been because of their undefined status as either Indian or white. In 1833 veteran trader Jean Baptiste Faribault was stabbed, though not fatally, by a Dakota man in a dispute over credit for provisions. Faribault was related to the Mdewakantons through marriage and had lived among the Dakotas for decades. Though newcomers to the fur trade frontier would classify the assault as an Indian attack on a white man, Faribault's assailant—and perhaps the trader himself—might regard it as a personal squabble between tribal kin rather than a racial dispute.[43]

The stories that made their way east in the 1820s and 1830s evoked images of a dangerous land, filled with warring savages who lay in wait for unsuspecting future settlers. Adding credence to the tales, reports of hostile Indians poured out of Wisconsin and Iowa, where the Sacs, Fox, and Winnebagos were engaged in a last-ditch struggle against an invasion of settlers. Soldiers on their way to Fort Snelling in 1820 found settlements along the route rife with stories of scalpings and shootings in the vicinity. Even Fort Crawford at Prairie du Chien was preparing for attack.[44] Of course, the situation on the Upper Mississippi was quite different. Nonetheless, as long as the fur trade remained profitable, traders were quite content to promote this erroneous impression to the outside world. For the present, Minnesota country was Indian territory and settlement was prohibited. The traders hoped to keep it that way.

The Politics of Culture

In 1820 Minnesota country was still a world unto itself, with a culture that was foreign to the settled parts of the United States. Scarcely a soul in the region was not related to the Dakotas or Ojibwes—or sometimes to both—either by birth or through marriage. After generations of intermarriage a single individual could conceivably trace a lineage that included Scots, French, American, Dakota, and Ojibwe forebears among his extended relations. English was scarcely spoken; French was the lingua franca of the region. Traders adopted some Indian forms of dress—moccasins, coats made of skins, buffalo robes—and Indians made clothing of woolen cloth and incorporated manufactured goods as essential parts of their way of life.[45] Identities were fluid and contingent and the line between white and Indian was often unclear, determined in large part on how individuals chose to represent themselves. In this intimate world, relationships rather than national allegiances or race were the foundation of the social order. Within a decade, this familiar way of life would be well on its way to extinction.

In 1819, when the first American troops arrived at the future site of Fort Snelling, they seemed unlikely agents of cultural change. Dispatched to construct the fort at the mouth of the St. Peter, they set up a cantonment near the site as a staging ground. "New Hope," as the camp was optimistically named, proved to be a poor prediction for the experiences that awaited them that first year. Ill prepared for the winter's isolation, the troops ran short of provisions and were decimated by scurvy. Philander Prescott, who arrived the following spring, found conditions dismal: "They had been out of groceries for a month or more and the scurvy had got amongst the troops, and there had already died about fifty men before I got there, and several died after I arrived. Their rations was nothing but rusty pork and bread." It seems the commanding officer, Colonel Henry Leavenworth, was as disheartened as his men. Under his command, the troops made little headway on the project throughout the summer. Finally, in August 1820, Leavenworth was relieved by Colonel Josiah Snelling, who got construction back on track, erecting a sawmill at St. Anthony Falls and "infus[ing] system and energy among men and officers." In 1824, with the fort at last completed, the war department recognized Snelling's accomplishment by naming the post in his honor.[46]

The imposing fortification that rose on the bluffs above the Mississippi and Minnesota rivers suggested far more power than the military actually wielded. In fact, they were forbidden to intervene in tribal disputes. The garrison's mission was to act as a "civilizing" force, to win hearts and minds rather than impose order by force. In practical terms, this left the common soldiers with almost nothing to do, especially over the long winters. Generally speaking, they were a motley lot. The army filled the ranks of frontier posts with the dregs of the service, "convicts, chronic deserters, and other desperadoes." The soldiers filled their days with card playing, drinking, and quarreling. Provisions often ran low, but the commandant made up for it with generous daily rations of whiskey. According to one female resident at the fort, "Sometimes it seemed that about all they had was whiskey." She recalled that "intemperance, among both officers and men, at that time, was an almost universal thing, and produced deplorable effects." Even the redoubtable Colonel Snelling was known to indulge in frequent "convivial spells" to buck up his morale. Maintaining any semblance of discipline among men he described as "convicts and refuse and foreigners" was a constant struggle. "Whiskey is their God," he wrote, "and mutiny their watchword." These denizens of Fort Snelling were unlikely to spread "civilization" among the "savage" tribes.[47]

However, inside the walls of the fort other forces of cultural change were at work that would ultimately make a more lasting mark. Fort Snelling's officers, nearly all of whom were married, brought wives and families to this farthest post on the frontier. The ladies, undaunted by the alien environment, were determined to replicate as best they could the lifestyle they had left behind. To Barbara Ann Schadecker, a starry-eyed Swiss girl who spent several years at Fort Snelling, the ladies were "of the best families . . . endowed with beauty and many accomplishments," paragons of "wealth and good taste . . . who would have shone in any circle." Compared to the rough conditions of Barbara Ann's experience, "society at the Fort at that period was of the most select and aristocratic."[48]

In reality, the ladies may not have been quite as wealthy and aristocratic as they seemed to Schadecker, but they were indeed thoroughly respectable and wedded to conventional mores. They set themselves to the task of countering not only the unsavory habits of the soldiers, but also the alien culture of borderland society. They made their homes a haven of civilization, with furnishings, china, decorative items, and even a piano laboriously hauled up the river. They established Sunday services and arranged tea parties, receptions, balls, and theatricals to break the monotony of life at the fort. They studied French with a veteran of Napoleon's army and oversaw the proper education of their children. By 1823 Colonel Snelling had engaged a Harvard-educated tutor to provide officers' children with a classical education that included the rudiments of Greek and Latin.[49]

Fort society was sharply divided by class. Despite the close quarters and frontier conditions, officers, most of them graduates of West Point, socialized only among themselves, even in their most ungentlemanly pursuits. Any enlisted man with an ambition of moving up in rank recognized that drinking tea, attending Sunday services, and paying courtesies to the ladies of the fort (rather than courting Native girls) was the surest route to promotion and social mobility. Joseph Brown, who became a prominent trader, land speculator, and politician, began his career in 1820 as a sixteen-year-old penniless private at Fort Snelling. With little formal education but an abundance of savvy and charm, Brown became a favorite of the commandant and his wife. He was a star pupil in the Sunday school class, performed in the theatricals, studied the manners of a gentleman, and even claimed to have taught himself Greek and Latin. As a personal attendant to the Snelling family, he managed to make useful connections and avoid onerous work details. Brown's most auspicious accomplishment in the military was the wooing and winning of Helen Dickson, the mixed-blood daughter of the famous British trader, Robert Dickson. All evidence suggests that Brown's pursuit of Helen was driven by ambition more than affection. Her family considered the lowly soldier a poor match, but once the marriage was made Brown had ensured his entrée to a position in the trade. The moment his term of enlistment was up, he made the leap from soldier to trading entrepreneur.[50]

New Men, New Rules

Joe Brown represented a new type of man who was beginning to appear on the frontier. In generations past, the most successful traders were those who integrated themselves most fully into the ways of Native people. Formal education and gentlemanly airs were of little use in the woods and waters of the north. Louis Provençalle, whom the Dakotas called Le Blanc, was an example of the older breed who relied on native intelligence, personal relationships, and bargaining savvy. Unschooled and illiterate, Provençalle had nonetheless made a success of his post at Traverse des Sioux by winning the trust of the Sisseton Dakotas, who were usually antagonistic toward traders. He kept his books with a unique system of pictographs that served his purposes well and also allowed his Indian customers to see for themselves the standing of their accounts—something most traders preferred not to share.[51]

But by the 1820s the rules of the trade were changing and a younger generation of agents began to overshadow men like Louis Provençalle. Astor's hard-headed American Fur Company kept its balance sheet with a very sharp pen. Under the British system traders had operated on shares. In other words, a winterer's return for the season was calculated as a percentage of how the company as a whole had fared that year. The American system was different. American Fur, which became the model for the trade, shifted the risk to smaller units called "outfits" that ranged in size from a single trader to a major regional division. The parent company provisioned the outfits on credit in return for an exclusivity agreement that bound the traders to buy from and sell their furs only to the American Fur Company. If the season's pelts failed to cover the advance, the debt fell wholly on the traders. If bad luck or poor management drove the trader out of business, all his assets were forfeit to the company, including any outstanding Indian debts.[52]

The company was always in the position of first creditor. Nevertheless, bankruptcy was never good for business. In essence, the company functioned much like an investment banker and sought out good credit risks that would produce a return on its investment and introduce sound business principles into the unpredictable nature of the trade. Old hands like Provençalle, who had established relationships with the tribes, were too valuable to replace, but Ramsay Crooks, the company's director in the field, was looking for other qualities in newcomers to the trade. Men like Hercules Dousman at Prairie du Chien exemplified the modern businessman the trade now required. Described by his friend Henry Sibley as "a man of sound and cultivated judgment and of great executive ability" who managed merchandise "amounting in the aggregate to hundreds of thousands of dollars annually," Dousman demonstrated "the business tact and energy requisite to bring order out of confusion." Agents in this new era had to maintain good relations with military and civil officials as well as with Native people. They needed to demonstrate business sense and book-keeping skills along with boldness and adaptability to wilderness conditions. Education and good character, the qualities of a gentleman, factored heavily into who would be deemed creditworthy and receive the company's backing. It was no wonder Joe Brown devoted so much energy to self-improvement.[53]

Henry Hastings Sibley was an ideal candidate to become an important "new man" of the trade. Born and raised in Detroit, Sibley was no stranger to the cosmopolitan nature of fur trade society. In the 1820s Detroit and Michilimackinac retained their place as the two most vital points of exchange for the trade. Detroit was a hive of activity, sending provisions west and forwarding furs to New York and Montreal. Voyageurs and Indians thronged the town's streets along with Yankee strivers fixed on building Michigan's territorial capital into a full-fledged city. Young Henry grew to manhood in this multilingual, multicultural environment. He was also a member of the Yankee elite. Sibley's father, Solomon, was a pillar of the community who had made his mark in law and politics, eventually becoming chief justice of the Michigan Territorial Supreme Court. Solomon Sibley's son was well educated, with two years' training in the law, politically connected, and a gentleman through and through. But the adventurous Henry was not ready to settle down to a dull career in the law, and in 1828, despite family misgivings, at the age of nineteen he signed on with the American Fur Company to seek adventure and romance on the frontier.[54]

Five tedious years as a company clerk at Sault Ste. Marie and Michilimackinac had nearly cured Sibley of his romantic notions when Ramsay Crooks, who had kept his eye on the promising young man, made him an offer too tempting to refuse. Crooks proposed to make Sibley a junior partner with Hercules Dousman and Joe Rolette, who together made a formidable team. The gentlemanly Dousman, with his executive skills, and Rolette, a wily, roughshod veteran of the trade with the wisdom of experience, would handle operations from Prairie du Chien; Sibley would be posted to Mendota and have independent management of the Western Outfit, which encompassed the Dakota trade north of Lake Pepin and throughout the St. Peter (Minnesota) River valley. To the twenty-four-year-old Sibley, it seemed the opportunity of a lifetime. He signed a six-year contract, fully expecting to fulfill his dreams of adventure, make a sizable fortune, then return in glory to Detroit. He never imagined that events would conspire to keep him in Minnesota for the rest of his days.[55]

When Sibley arrived at Fort Snelling in November 1834, one of the first contacts he made was with Indian agent Lawrence Taliaferro. President James

[94]

Lawrence Taliaferro, ca. 1830. Courtesy of the Minnesota Historical Society.

Monroe had personally appointed Taliaferro as part of the original expedition-
ary force ordered into Minnesota country. Though he carried the honorary
title of major, Taliaferro was a civilian appointee, dispatched to keep the peace
between the tribes, protect them from exploitation by the traders, and win
their allegiance to the United States. Taliaferro was a study in contradictions.
A Virginia patrician, he valued his integrity and honor above all else, and unlike the stereotypical Indian agent, he could not be bribed or corrupted by the
lure of personal gain. Contemporary accounts agree that for twenty years he

worked unstintingly to protect Indian interests and "was cordially hated by all who could neither bribe nor frighten him to connive at lawbreaking to the harm of the Indians." However, Taliaferro also was a slaveholder, with a sense of paternalism and race consciousness bred into his bones. He regarded Indians as inherently inferior, "children" who lacked the ability to make decisions for themselves. He never doubted that his natural superiority as a white man and a gentleman granted him the duty and the right to look out for their interests as he determined was best. This was a radical departure from the rough egalitarianism that had characterized earlier interactions between whites and Indians.[56]

Throughout his long tenure at Fort Snelling, Taliaferro was at war with the fur traders. He accused them—with some good reason—of exploiting the Indians, though Native people consistently demonstrated the judgment, if not the power, to protect their interests. Crusty veteran Joe Rolette insisted that the Indians were too smart to be fooled. "I have been trying to cheat them for years," he declared, "and I have never once succeeded." For all his faults, Rolette had a grudging respect for the Indians that the paternalistic Indian agent, despite his good intentions, was lacking. Taliaferro was particularly determined to halt the flow of alcohol that lubricated the trade. In 1826, backed by policy makers in Washington, he tried to ban whiskey altogether from the Indian trade. This set well with neither traders nor Indians. Taliaferro, who issued the licenses required to trade in the region, was no doubt "the most important and influential civil official on the upper Mississippi." Nonetheless, he found enforcement of his edict an impossible task. Occasionally he managed to confiscate an illegal shipment of whiskey, but it was like trying to empty the ocean with a teacup. Traders easily evaded inspection of their packs. In the rare event that they were caught with alcohol, they claimed it was for the use of their men, who were exempted from the ban (since the *engagés* would not sign on without guaranteed daily rations of whiskey). The soldiers at the fort were equally fond of drink and considered it small compensation for the hardships of the frontier; for many, their chief recreation was drunkenness. Thus, Taliaferro could count on little sympathy from military authorities to enforce his temperance crusade.[57]

The frustrated major despised the traders for their extralegal activities and disregard for his authority. But his opinion of them may also have been colored by deep-seated discomfort with "these Mississippi, demi-civilized Candian mongrel English American citizens" who defied racial classification. It must have been difficult for the Virginia-born Taliaferro, whose culture was ordered by a clear racial hierarchy that made miscegenation a crime, to come to terms with the acknowledged mixed ancestry of the trading fraternity. Men like Jack Frazer, a "fine, intellectual-looking man" with a British father and a mother who was the mixed-blood sister of Mdewakanton chief Wacouta, fit no simple racial definition. Frazer spent his first thirty years living as a Dakota, then assumed the dress and pursuits of a white trader. Was Frazer a white man or an Indian? Even Jean Baptiste Faribault, after decades spent in the wilderness with a Dakota wife and a flock of mixed-blood children, must have seemed as much Indian as white, despite the pure French blood that flowed in his veins.[58]

As the most powerful enterprise in the region, the American Fur Company was the most frequent target of Taliaferro's wrath. And no one angered the major more than trader Alexis Bailly. Taliaferro was well aware that Bailly flagrantly smuggled whiskey into the region, contravening the major's orders. The son of a French Canadian father and mixed-blood mother, Bailly may have exacerbated the major's dislike by his suspect background and "uncivilized" lifestyle. At any rate, their frequent run-ins caused expensive legal complications for the company. Failing after repeated attempts to get Taliaferro removed, Ramsay Crooks took another route to resolve the problem. He determined to replace Bailly with someone more compatible with the major. The impeccably credentialed Henry Sibley perfectly fit the bill.[59]

A Multiplicity of Interests

The men who entered the fur trade in the 1820s and 1830s differed from the older generation in more than manners and education. Attuned to the profit-making schemes that were transforming the settlement frontier south and east of Minnesota country, from the outset they had their eyes on ventures beyond the trade. Before 1837 no part of present-day Minnesota was open to settlement, but anyone with a shred of sense knew that legal obstacle was destined soon to be swept aside. The fur trade economy itself was headed toward collapse, not so much because of overhunting or decline in demand, but because the credit edifice that sustained it was increasingly riddled with uncollectible debt. A bad year when animals were inexplicably scarce or weather hampered the hunt created problems throughout the system; several bad years in a row shook the credit pyramid to its foundation. Even if the year's pelts did not erase the Indians' current debt, they had to have provisions and ammunition to hunt the following season. Thus, Indians were in debt to petty traders, traders owed agents, agents owed the company, and even Astor's vast resources were taxed to keep the system afloat. The astute financier recognized that the system was unsustainable. He retired from the business in 1834, just when young Henry Sibley was beginning his career at Mendota, leaving the great firm to limp along another decade before finally succumbing to bankruptcy. Throughout the 1830s more furs were extracted from the Upper Mississippi than ever—in 1836 Sibley's Western Outfit shipped more than 293,000 furs, skins, and buffalo robes from Mendota to Prairie du Chien—yet traders' books were filled with red ink more often than black.[60]

Petty traders took the hardest blows. Conditions in Ojibwe country were particularly bleak. At a post near Mille Lacs in 1824, a veteran French Canadian trader, whose daughter was married to American Fur Company agent

William Aitkin, lived in an impoverished state despite his family connection to one of the "big men" of the trade. He declared they had to "live poor, as the trade would not afford any great expense. . . . They only got flour about once a week; as for pork, they never thought of such a thing." On the Snake River, William Johnston reported equally dire conditions. His family was subsisting primarily on a diet of wild rice: "There was no game where [he] lived, and they seldom ever had meat." Born into the trade, Johnston knew no other way of life. He said, "The whole trade was worth only about two thousand dollars a year and it hardly paid for the trouble and expense, but as he was in the trade he did not know what to do for a living except to follow the trade." The traders' dilemma created even greater hardship for the Indians, who complained, "Their old traders were so very hard on them they could hardly live. They could not get ammunition enough to kill game to live on." Without ammunition or adequate sustenance, hunting for market was nearly impossible, guaranteeing another poor season for everyone involved.[61]

Young men starting out in the business in the 1820s, like Philander Prescott, who recorded the conditions in Minnesota's lakes region, had a hard road ahead. Year after year, Prescott took up posts in Ojibwe or Dakota country that, after his debts were paid, inevitably left him with little or nothing to show for the year's effort. But unlike the old traders, Prescott was able to take on a variety of supplemental jobs to keep his family fed. At various times he worked as a storekeeper, guide, interpreter, builder, and as a farmer paid by Taliaferro to teach the Indians agricultural practices. What is significant about Prescott's endeavors is that at the same time they allowed him to continue as a trader, they all promoted changes that, either directly or indirectly, were inimical to the trade. He helped surveyors mark the boundary between Dakota and Ojibwe territory, which became an important tool for the land cession treaties in the years ahead; by teaching Indians to farm, he was discouraging the traditional hunting culture that was essential to the trade. He even spent a season on the St. Croix River holding down a town site claim (the future city of Prescott, Wisconsin) for a group of Fort Snelling speculators. The golden rule of the fur trade for nearly two hundred years had been to oppose settlement, but by the late 1820s the only way most traders could make a go of it from year to year was to take part in the economic and cultural projects that foreshadowed the trade's demise.[62]

Farther up the economic ladder, shrewd businessmen like Hercules Dousman and Joe Rolette at Prairie du Chien and Joe Brown in Minnesota country had concluded that the time had come to hedge their bets. They continued to work the trade but profits were ever more uncertain, and they were more than ready to diversify when opportunity presented itself. No one was more attuned to the main chance than Joe Rolette. His hand seemed to be in every enterprise, earning him the appellation "King Rolette"—not necessarily a compliment. Even his partners secretly referred to the sharp old trader as "Don José." Rolette had bought up most of the real estate in Prairie du Chien; at one

[98]

Joseph Rolette in an early daguerreotype, ca. 1841. Courtesy of the Minnesota Historical Society.

time he paid seven-eighths of the town's property taxes. He also pastured hogs and sheep, owned several farms, and built and operated a sawmill. By 1828 he was in Ojibwe country, illegally cutting and rafting timber on the Black and Chippewa rivers to feed his mill and build the towns that were marching westward.[63]

The entrepreneurial Brown, a quick learner, took his cue from Rolette and let no opportunity to turn a profit slip by. By 1833 he had a number of ventures under way. He put a crew to work illegally harvesting pine on the St. Croix River. Another crew spent the winter fishing and brought in nearly 2,000 pounds of sturgeon that Brown sold to Alexis Bailly. He also established a post at Oliver's Grove (present-day Hastings), a strategic location where traders often landed their whiskey barrels to avoid Fort Snelling authorities. In addition to his trading activities—both legitimate and extralegal—Brown established a full-fledged farm at the post. Homesteading in Indian territory was illegal, but under cover of his trading license Brown ran a dairying operation, kept pigs and chickens, and sowed crops of grain, vegetables, and hay—all of which found a ready local market.[64]

[99]

None of this went unnoticed by the Indians. The Ojibwes frequently complained about the thieves who cut down their trees, but no military force was available to police the activities along the rivers. The Dakotas also were disturbed by incursions on tribal lands. Little Crow (Wakinyatanka), chief of the Mdewakanton band at Kaposia, protested strongly to Taliaferro:

> There is a white man at the Olive Grove near St. Croix [Joe Brown] who has a farm and his cattle are running over our lands and scaring off what deer we were in the habit of hunting and also fencing in our old encamping grounds where [we] always place our lodges to fish for our families. We wish him removed as his house is of no use to the trade.[65]

Taliaferro responded to Little Crow's complaint by revoking Brown's license to trade at Oliver's Grove and forcing him to move. But he had no power to influence the economic calculus that was beginning to value land over furs.

Little Crow clearly understood the threat that was looming just over the horizon as American settlers marched into Wisconsin Territory. Four years earlier he had been part of a Dakota delegation that attended a council at Prairie du Chien, along with members of the Sac, Otoe, Iowa, and Omaha tribes. Ostensibly the council was convened to create a buffer zone to separate the Dakotas and Iowas from the hostile Sacs and Fox. To achieve this, the tribes assented to a complicated transaction in which the Dakotas and Sacs each agreed to sell the American government a twenty-mile strip along their border that would become, in effect, a "no-man's land." As compensation, they were promised a small annuity, a $500 annual education fund, and a conveniently located blacksmith shop. The Iowa relinquished considerably more territory (which would soon be open to settlement) in return for a "permanent home" on lands purchased from the Otoe and Omaha in present-day western Iowa and Nebraska. As part of the pact, the tribes also each conveyed a tract of land to their mixed-blood relatives—a so-called "half-breed tract."[66]

What motivated the Dakotas, who were only minimally involved in the land exchange, is not entirely clear. Some sources claim that traders secretly brokered the deal with the government as compensation for bringing the tribes to the council. Since all of the traders had mixed-blood family connections, the tract would provide a way for them to secure land for themselves, either for homesteading or, more likely, for future speculation. Others point to Taliaferro's influence with the chiefs. The agent, who constantly promoted the virtues of farming to the Indians, hoped that mixed bloods would turn the tract into farmsteads—a model for their full-blood kin to emulate. But, quite certainly, farmsteads were not what the chiefs envisioned. More likely, they viewed the tract as a gift to formally acknowledge and afford protection to their mixed-blood kin. Or perhaps it was simply a point of honor, the Dakotas wishing to appear no less generous than the other tribes. In the politically charged atmosphere of the council negotiations, most probably all of these factors came into play.[67]

[100]

Whatever the intention, cabins soon sprouted on the land. The tract was to be held collectively, but profit-minded traders like Alexis Bailly and Joe Brown (on behalf of his mixed-blood children) immediately began to lobby for it to be divided into individually owned parcels. In the end, the question became legally moot since Congress never ratified the treaty, but events in Washington had little effect on local perceptions. As far as the people involved were concerned, the agreement was already law. Though mixed-blood families showed little interest in farming, a few sold their interest in the land to whites, who moved onto the tract. It was a small incursion but a disturbing portent of the wave of settlers and speculators to come.[68] Thus, Little Crow had good reason to be alarmed when Joe Brown began to look more like a farmer than a trader.

Chapter 5

HIGHWAY TO THE NORTH

PLEASURE EXCURSION
FROM DUBUQUE TO ST. PETERS AND
THE FALLS OF ST. ANTHONY

The War Eagle is a new and Splendid Boat . . . Capt. Harris intends
to make a pleasure excursion in reality, and will stop at all places of
curiosity or amusement as long as the passengers may desire. A Band
of Music will be on Board. Strangers and Travelers will have a fine opportunity of visiting one of the most beautiful and romantic countries
in the world.

HANDBILL, 1845

"Grand Adventures"

The barriers of distance and daunting geography that had protected the interdependent world of the fur trade were crumbling fast. The first steamboat
had churned up the Mississippi to Fort Snelling in 1823. The stern-wheeler
Virginia made the trip from St. Louis in an astonishing twenty days. The appearance of this belching monster at first terrified the Indians and probably
did more to impress them with the Americans' power than any mustering of
troops had accomplished. Residents of the fort, on the other hand, were ec-
static over this tangible link to civilization. Suddenly, technology had transformed the journey of more than 200 miles between Prairie du Chien and Fort
Snelling from an arduous trek by oar, paddle, and pole to a relatively comfortable journey that could be completed in days rather than weeks. Steamboats
eased the problems and reduced the cost of provisioning the fort and trading
posts and made it possible to import the trappings of civilization, like pianos,
into the north country.[1]

Most important, steamboats carried passengers. Before the *Virginia*'s
maiden voyage up the river, visitors to the fort had been a rare occurrence,

limited to official business of one sort or another. Lewis Cass, governor of Michigan Territory (which included all of Minnesota east of the Mississippi), had passed through in 1820 as part of a survey of the western reaches of the territory. Cass's party traveled in the time-honored fashion of the watery interior. A flotilla of canoes carried forty-two men and provisions by the lakes route to Fond du Lac, then laboriously to the Mississippi over numerous portages, "swampy grounds—and rocky precipices—dark forests of hemlock and pine," with the travelers often sinking in mud to their hips. As one member of the expedition related, "It is impossible to describe the fatigues." Three years later another government expedition brought geologist Major Stephen Long to the fort on a scientific mission to assess the St. Peter and Red River regions. Long made the trip from Prairie du Chien by horseback, a grueling eight-day ride over rough, roadless terrain. Neither form of transportation recommended itself to the casual tourist.[2]

In the 1820s much of Minnesota country remained largely inaccessible, unmapped and unknown to all but those who lived there. The source of the Mississippi was still officially in question, which made it impossible to determine the exact location of the Canadian border. Both Cass and Long searched for the headwaters without success. Cass, deceived by low water, stopped short of Lake Itasca and misidentified Upper Red Cedar Lake as the source (rechristened Cass Lake in the governor's honor). Henry Schoolcraft, a mineralogist and member of the governor's expedition, doubted Cass's conclusion but discretely kept his thoughts to himself until 1831, when he returned to follow his suspicions. Unlike the earlier explorers, Schoolcraft, now Indian agent at Sault Ste. Marie and kin to the Ojibwes through marriage, had a close relationship with the Indians, and thus they were willing to share with him their intimate knowledge of the terrain. The Ojibwe guide Ozawindib (also known as Yellow Head) agreed to show Schoolcraft where the river began. He drew the maps, gathered the small canoes necessary to reach the source above Cass Lake, and guided the party on a two-day trek that ended with a six-mile portage. When the party at last stood on the shore of Lake Itasca, they had finally reached the "transparent body of water" that gave birth to the Mississippi. Thanks to Ozawindib, Schoolcraft had finally solved the puzzle of the great river.[3]

Expeditions like these were costly to mount and entailed months of planning and many more months of travel under arduous conditions. Not surprisingly, they were undertaken only rarely. Even a simple provisioning trip was daunting, and neither military nor trading expeditions encouraged the added burden of inexperienced commercial passengers. Thus Minnesota country had remained a tantalizing mystery, known only by legend and literature, to most people beyond its borders.

The steamboat opened the north country to a new variety of travelers. The first season brought only two visits by the *Virginia*, but within a decade an average of twenty-five boats docked at Fort Snelling each season. Ten years later the number had nearly doubled. Fort residents impatiently waited each spring for the ice to break up on the river, signaling the imminent return of steamboat traffic. Along with provisions and news from the East, the boats carried an eclectic variety of visitors to break the monotony of winter's isolation. Scientists, speculators, artists, tourists, curiosity seekers, and visiting relatives from the East all were greeted with delight.[4]

Perhaps the most colorful visitor to steam into fort society was the first. Giacomo Constantino Beltrami bounded off the *Virginia* in 1823, ready for adventure. A wealthy Italian émigré, Beltrami was enraptured by everything he had seen along the journey. Wooded islands "appeared like the most enchanting gardens"; the hills were "veiled with magical effect in the transparent mist of the horizon"; "verdant meadows" rose alongside "limpid streams." Fascinated by the Indians, he admired their ferocity and skill with weapons as well as the "perfect equality" of their community. The curious tourist even managed to secure a medicine bag and a scalp as dubious souvenirs.[5]

Beltrami fancied himself an explorer in the vein of his countrymen, Marco Polo and Columbus. His destiny, so he believed, was to discover the elusive source of the Mississippi. One observer described him as a "hero worshipper, with but one hero, and that himself." Nonetheless, the fort's small circle of gentility was utterly charmed to have the aristocratic, if peculiar, European in their midst. Indian agent Lawrence Taliaferro considered him "a man of talent" and provisioned him for his quest, despite the Italian's lack of any wilderness experience. Beltrami's ensuing adventures in the north country suggest he had far more nerve than sense. Abandoned by his guides somewhere on Red Lake River, he made it back alive only after a fortuitous encounter with some friendly Ojibwes and a French Métis. Still, the romantic gentleman was pleased with his accomplishment, convinced (in error) that he had indeed located the Mississippi's headwaters. The subsequent account he published of his adventures in Minnesota added more fuel to the growing interest in the mysterious north.[6]

Other travelers who followed Beltrami, though less flamboyant, made a more significant impact. Scientists began an orderly and thorough assessment of the topography and resources of the region. The pioneering work of Long and Schoolcraft was followed in 1835 by English geologist George Featherstonehaugh, who made a preliminary geological survey of the Minnesota River valley for the U.S. government. The next year Joseph Nicollet, an erudite French astronomer and cartographer, arrived at Fort Snelling, intrigued by Featherstonehaugh's findings. Over the following four years Nicollet made an intensive study of the geology and resources of Minnesota's terrain and created detailed topographical maps. This flurry of scientific study marked a profound change in the meanings ascribed to the land. Though Nicollet himself was devoted to pure science, his work would enable the government and private speculators to map out and assess the value of the land based on what could be extracted from it. It marked the beginning of the commodification of land into real estate, the necessary first step to enable a shift to private property and settlement. Tellingly, Pierre Chouteau and Company, which had become the supplier for Sibley's Western Outfit, provided support for Nicollet's expeditions. By the mid-1830s, the fur trade financiers had read the trend of the future and begun to envision new paths for profit making.[7]

With their education and fine manners, Nicollet and Featherstonehaugh also added to the culture of "civilization" that was slowly crowding out the egalitarian society of the fur trade. In this version of civilization, there was no room for the racial indeterminism that bridged Indian and European cultures in traditional fur trade society. In the eyes of the newcomers, Indians were either savages to be scorned and feared or exotic primitives to be studied and perhaps appreciated for their colorful customs. Either perspective was accompanied by a certainty that the Indian was destined for extinction. It was only a matter of time. Just as American settlement had rolled westward across the continent from the Atlantic, the God-given mission of manifest destiny made it the right and the duty of Euro-Americans to conquer the West and make this "barren" land fruitful.

Even those who most admired Indian culture regarded it as alien to themselves. They might live among the tribes for weeks or months but did not consider themselves connected in any way to the society that sheltered them. Instead, they played the role, in modern terms, of participant–observer. Amateur ethnographers, they studied and recorded Indian culture for a Euro-American audience. Nicollet, ever the humane, inquiring scientist, wrote with great appreciation for Indians he encountered and meticulously recorded their languages, customs, and social structure. At the same time, his scientific survey of their lands served the very forces that threatened their existence.[8]

The artist George Catlin steamed up the river in 1835 to record on canvas the noble faces and landscape of Indian peoples before they were overrun by what he called "the splendid juggernaut rolling on." "Thus far have I strolled . . . for the purpose of reaching *classic ground*," he proclaimed. "This place is great (not in history, for there is none of it, but) in traditions and stories, of which this Western world is full and rich." History, in Catlin's mind, was made by Europeans. Full of romantic preconceptions about Native people, the artist viewed the Indians not as independent societies with complicated pasts and legal rights but as objectified exotics, part of a timeless landscape about to be transformed by "history." Significantly, at that time neither the Dakotas nor the Ojibwes had ceded any lands in Minnesota country and settlement was prohibited. Yet Catlin had no doubt that the "grand and irresistible march of civilization" would soon obliterate the noble "primitives" he portrayed. Ironically, Catlin's work, which he claimed was dedicated to "rescuing from oblivion the looks and customs of the vanishing races of native man in America," fueled the forces marching west. Returning to New York, he opened a gallery with his paintings and Indian "artifacts," toured the country to share his art and self-proclaimed expertise on Native culture, and wrote glowingly about the beauty of the land and the soon-to-be "vanished" Indian. All this added to growing interest in the north country and pressure to open the gates to settlement.[9]

Catlin also urged the public to make a "fashionable tour" to see the "amazement and wonder" of the Upper Mississippi for themselves before it was too late. "Wait not," he said, "but make it while the subject is new, and capable of producing the greatest degree of pleasure." Steamboat travel, he proclaimed, had made the Upper Mississippi's Indian country "so easily accessible to the world, and the only part of it to which *ladies* can have access." Catlin's recommendation helped popularize an already budding tourist trade. By the mid-1830s steamboats regularly carried passengers along with cargo and promoted the nineteenth century's version of adventure travel. "See the red man as he actually lived," touted the packet operators. Scarcely a week passed without visitors to Fort Snelling, the northern terminus of the tour. By the late 1830s the fashionable tour had become so popular that excursion boats devoted solely to passengers, equipped with "commodious" staterooms, washstands, and other amenities, were a fairly common sight on the river.[10]

Most of the travelers were men, and many of them had more than a pleasure tour on their minds. Intrigued by rumors of the riches of the region, politicians, businessmen, and scores of men on the make were eager to assess the profit-making potential at the end of the steamboat line. They were not disappointed. Forests of pine and hardwood stretched north to the Canadian border, larger than the entire state of Maine, and the plains rolling west seemed ideally suited for the turn of the plow. A quick visit to St. Anthony Falls alone was enough to make many an aspiring capitalist enthusiastic. The cascade that thundered over the limestone ledge unleashed visions of mill wheels and steam-powered engines in the not-too-distant future.[11]

The officers and ladies at Fort Snelling were happy to entertain the cultured visitors and show off their version of frontier society. They escorted parties to nearby St. Anthony and Minnehaha Falls, and hosted tea parties and soirées. When Alexander Hamilton's eighty-year-old widow, Elizabeth Schuyler Hamilton, made the tour in 1837, fort society gave her a royal reception. "A carpet had been spread, an armchair ready to receive her, the troops were under arms," and a "fine band" played as the lady and her party passed between two double rows of soldiers.[12]

The local aristocracy was a bit rough around the edges but no less attuned to the niceties of polite society than their esteemed visitors. Travelers who crossed the St. Peter River to call at the "fine stone house" of American Fur's chief agent, Henry Hastings Sibley, were impressed not only by Sibley's gracious manner and aristocratic bearing, but also by his book-lined study and the general air of civilization that he managed to create at his wilderness post. The fact that at least a few Dakotas were almost always camped nearby only highlighted the contrast between the "savages" and the charming "Squire of Mendota," as Sibley was (only half in jest) coming to be known. The fort's most distinguished guests—Featherstonehaugh, Catlin, and Nicollet, for example—all gravitated to Sibley's hospitality. Nicollet spent the entire winter of 1837 as Sibley's guest. The two men whiled away long winter evenings discussing their shared interests and became fast friends. Sibley described Nicollet as a kindred spirit and helped the scientist secure backing from fur trade financiers for his future expeditions. The following year Nicollet wrote to Sibley, his "dear friend," that "my heart beats with joy" at the prospect of box[ing] and sing[ing] with you again."[13]

Such extended visits were, however, the exception. Most travelers spent only a few hours or a day at the fort and what they really wanted was to experience the local color, to observe the "Indians in their primitive state." The gentlemen and ladies of the fort and the Squire of Mendota did their best to see that the tourists were not disappointed. Agent Taliaferro and Sibley urged both the Dakotas and Ojibwes to come to the fort, show their skill at lacrosse, and perform traditional dances for the visitors. No doubt Taliaferro and Sibley made the case to the Indians that the strangers wished to attend the performances as a sign of respect. The visitors, however, viewed Native people as entertainment who provided "a fine and wild scene of dances, amusements, &c." George Catlin, the supposed champion of indigenous people, was untroubled by the cultural condescension that permeated these encounters. The Indians, he wrote, "seem to take pleasure in 'showing off' in these scenes, to the amusement of the many fashionable visitors, both ladies and gentlemen." Like his fellow white Americans, Catlin never questioned the cultural superiority of his race.[14]

Mission Impossible

Among the travelers who made their way to Fort Snelling in the 1830s were a hardy few who had neither profit nor entertainment on their minds. They believed they were on a quest to do God's work. In 1834 two young lay missionaries, Gideon and Samuel Pond, appeared at the fort, the first of many fervent Protestant men and women who would step off the edge of civilization to take the word of Christ into the wilderness. They were part of a Protestant missionary impulse that grew out of the Second Great Awakening, a wave of pietism that swept across the country in the first half of the nineteenth century. An essential element of the movement's religiosity was the conviction that Christians were called to save the souls of pagans throughout the world. Missionary societies dispatched workers to the Far East, Africa, and Hawaii as well as to the "foreign" territories within the United States. Indeed, to the missionaries who accepted an assignment in Minnesota country, the world they entered must have seemed only slightly less alien than China. They came with no knowledge of Indian language or culture, armed only with their Bibles and the heartfelt belief that God would bless their endeavors.[15]

The missionaries imbued their work with a sense of national as well as religious purpose. The basic tenet of Protestant faith was acceptance and understanding of the Bible, which they believed required literacy and "an intellect above that of the savage to comprehend." Thus, to understand the word of God, Native people must be transformed from savagery to civilization—meaning, of course, that they must conform to the superior values of American society. The doctrines of manifest destiny and Christian evangelization were thus inextricably intertwined. Writing in 1846, missionary Stephen Riggs made explicit the coupling of religion and American expansionism: "*As tribes and nations the Indians must perish and live only as men!* With this impression of the tendency of God's purposes as they are being developed year after year, I would labor to prepare them to fall in with *Christian civilization* that is destined to cover the earth."[16]

When missionaries arrived at Fort Snelling, they found an enthusiastic ally in Agent Taliaferro, who was determined to persuade the Dakotas to take up farming as their primary occupation. Taliaferro believed that an agricultural lifestyle would address several pressing issues that threatened Dakota survival. Game was becoming increasingly scarce and several severe winters in the 1820s had caused severe hardship among the tribes. Without adequate resources to alleviate their suffering, Taliaferro had "been compelled to be the witness of scenes the most unpleasant." Necessity then drove the Dakotas into the game-rich buffer zone, causing an upsurge in confrontations with equally stressed Ojibwes. Farming, Taliaferro asserted, would provide a more reliable food source and promote peace between the tribes. It also would break the Indians' relationship with the traders, who, the agent was convinced, were a pernicious influence, plying the Indians with contraband whiskey to keep them dependent on hunting for market. Most important, farming—in the style of white settlers—would "conduct his charges along the road to civilization." It would teach them the values of hard work, sobriety, and enterprise, wean them from their "improvident" lifestyle, and eventually replace their collectivist worldview with an appreciation for the superiority of economic individualism and private property. Neither Taliaferro nor the missionaries who worked to transform the Indians' way of life questioned their deeply held assumption that the only "civilized" man must look exactly like themselves.[17]

The missionaries, with rare exceptions, were sincere in the belief that they were bringing material as well as spiritual salvation to the Native people. They believed, along with most nineteenth-century Americans, that the existing world of the Indian was destined for extinction. The only way to save them was to remake them in the white man's image. Moreover, what the missionaries offered, they devoutly believed, was entrée to a far superior culture. As one evangelist wrote, "In the school and in the field, as well as in the kitchen, our aim was to teach the Indians to live like white people." Secure in the cultural imperialism inherent in American Protestantism, the missionaries unself-consciously attacked every aspect of Native culture. Not surprisingly, after decades of dedicated commitment, they would have few converts to show for their efforts.[18]

From the 1830s through the 1850s various Protestant denominations sent workers "into the wilderness" of Minnesota country. Some showed a stunning lack of understanding of Indian language and culture. Methodist Alfred Brunson, who established a mission near Fort Snelling at Kaposia in 1836, had no knowledge of the Dakota language, nor did he make any effort to learn, believing it to be a waste of time. After all, he declared, "English would finally become the universal speech of the savages"—a bold assertion in a country where English was rarely spoken outside the fort stockade. In consequence, classes and services at the mission were conducted only in English and elicited little interest from their intended audience. Brunson also complained that "the Indians do not know how to work." In his mind, hunting was simply sport, an indication of Indian laziness. Intentionally blind to Dakota lifeways, Brunson blamed his mission's failure on shortcomings of the Indian character.[19]

Edmund Ely, working among the Ojibwes at Fond du Lac in the 1830s, had similar difficulties. Though, unlike Brunson, he made a close study of Ojibwe religion and culture, his problems were similarly grounded in the conviction that his own cultural belief system was superior in every way. According to Ojibwe historian Rebecca Kugel, "Ely continually violated Ojibwa values, norms, and deeply held beliefs." He transgressed the central Ojibwe values of communalism and generosity, attempting to impose a model of "thrift, hard bargaining, and individual accumulation of surplus wealth." Refusing to share his supplies with those in need, he considered the Indians to be not only improvident but also insolent and ungrateful. He even threatened "to *scare* every child . . . whom [he] should take in [his] garden stealing." The deeply offended Ojibwes accused the missionary of greed and stinginess. If this was Christianity, they wanted no part of it. By 1838 relations between Ely and his potential converts had deteriorated so badly that he closed the mission and moved on in search of more appreciative "savages."[20]

Cultural disdain for Indian values was common among Protestant missionaries, which crippled their evangelizing endeavors. Years later, Presbyterian minister Edward Duffield Neill explained away the failure of "civilizing" efforts, declaring that the "savages . . . have nothing that corresponds to civilized government," no legal system nor any work ethic. The root of the problem, he believed, was the collectivist ethos that neither recognized private property nor rewarded accumulation of surplus. There was simply no incentive, he believed, for hard work. The Reverend William Boutwell, working among the Ojibwes at Leech Lake in the 1830s, recommended a stringent mission policy that would "instruct them in the principles of political economy":[21]

> At present there is among them nothing like personal rights, or individual property, any further than traps, guns, and kettles are concerned. They possess all things in

common. If an Indian has anything to eat, his neighbours are all allowed to share it with him. *While therefore, a mission extends the hand of charity in the means of instruction, and occasionally an article of clothing, and perhaps some aid in procuring the means of subsistence, it should be only to such individuals as will themselves use the means so far as they possess them.*[22]

Boutwell believed that fostering individualism and accountability "might operate as a stimulus with them to cultivate and fix a value upon corn, rice, etc. . . . rather than squander it in feasts and feeding such as are too indolent to make a garden themselves." Instead, the Indians more often regarded Christianity as pinched and mean, antithetical to the communal values they held most dear.[23]

Not every missionary was such a cultural bumbler. Dr. Thomas Williamson, who led a group of five men and women to establish a mission station at Lac qui Parle in 1835, and Stephen Riggs, who joined the mission two years later, assiduously studied the Dakota language. Nonetheless, their avowed purpose was also to "civilize" the Indians and their mission an outpost of colonial expansion. They used their language skills to make the written word of the gospels accessible to the "heathens" they hoped to lead down the path to salvation. They established a school that, though conducted in the Dakota language, still promoted conventional Protestant values, and they tirelessly worked to turn Dakota hunters into farmers.[24]

Ironically, the most culturally sensitive of the missionary cohort were the unordained pair who were first to reach Fort Snelling. Samuel and Gideon Pond, who came without official church backing, had experienced a calling to missionary service during a Congregational revival they attended in their home state of Connecticut. The brothers, in their early twenties, arrived at the fort with $300 in their pockets and an openness and cultural curiosity that was rare among missionaries to Indian country. They immersed themselves in Dakota language and culture, lived closely with the Indians, and accompanied them to their hunting grounds. As a result, the Ponds recognized that rather than "indolent fellows who never did anything," Dakota men showed admirable "industry and enterprise." In later years, they spoke of the Dakotas with great appreciation. But writing from the distance of the 1880s, Samuel Pond also rejected the stereotype of the vanished noble savage that was then in vogue: "Romantic and sentimental writers may amuse themselves, and may deceive the simple, by such fabulous descriptions of the Indian character; but the real Dakota never sat for the picture, and would not feel flattered by it." Samuel and Gideon Pond, who spent twenty years among the Dakotas, instead saw the Indians as whole human beings, "men like other men," with "the same diversity among them as among white people."[25]

The Pond brothers were not entirely free of bias, especially when it came to religion. To their minds, Protestant Christianity was the only true faith; on that they were unbending. Still, they approached cultural interaction with a level of acceptance that was unique among their fellow Protestants. Stephen

Riggs noted Gideon's unusual degree of interest in Dakota ways: "Mr. Pond had long been yearning to see inside of an Indian, if only for half an hour, that he might know how an Indian felt, and by what motives he could be moved." Though the Ponds, despite their efforts, achieved few lasting conversions, they succeeded where others failed in finding a common cultural ground where Indian and missionary met as respectful equals.[26]

[110]

Gideon Pond with his wife, Agnes, ca. 1854. Courtesy of the Minnesota Historical Society.

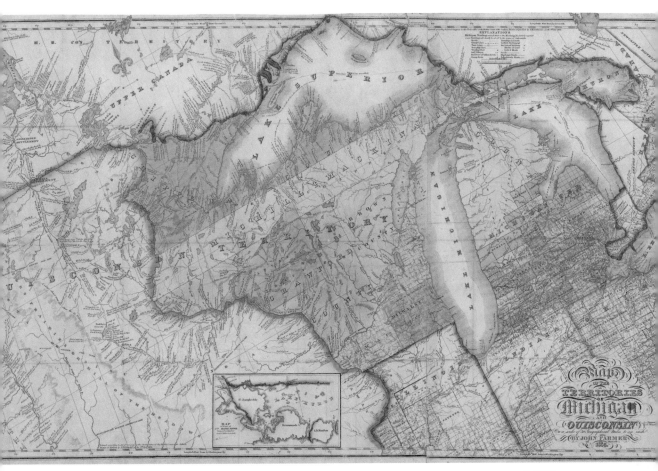

PLATE 33

Plate 33. John Farmer, *Map of the Territories of Michigan and Ouisconsin*, detail (New York: J. H. Colton & Co., 1835). Minnesota Historical Society.

This map shows Minnesota when it was part of Michigan territory, which extended west to the Missouri River. The caption told readers to expect statehood for Michigan shortly, at which point the territory's western lands would be "set off as Ouisconsin." This map records the routes of explorers Major Stephen H. Long and Henry Schoolcraft, the Indian agent and ethnographer who trekked through the Lake Superior region. Despite the fact that the map was intended to encourage white development of the region, it also provides viewers with a remarkable level of detail about Native American inhabitants, labeling the territories of different bands, locating villages, and pinpointing the locations of Indian agencies and trading posts. The Mississippi River provides a clear demarcation line on this map, which distinguishes the territory to the west of this river as still closed to settlement.[34]

Plate 34. James Otto Lewis, *Chippeway Squaws*, 1826, from *The Aboriginal Port-Folio: A Collection of Portraits of the Most Celebrated Chiefs of the North American Indians* (Philadelphia: J. O. Lewis, 1835–[1836]). Minnesota Historical Society.

This portrait of Ojibwe women with their babies was part of a sustained effort that began in the 1820s to create a pictorial record of Indian life. Detroit artist James Otto Lewis created this triptych based on his observations as part of the official delegation attending a council with the Ojibwe at Fond du Lac near the western end of Lake Superior in 1826.

PLATE 34

Thomas McKenney, the head of the new Office of Indian Affairs, asked Lewis to accompany the treaty delegation in the interest of recording the lifeways and costumes of Indians in their natural environment. While McKenney supported documentation of Indian life, he was no high-minded advocate of Indians. He echoed many of the most common prejudices of his day, decrying the "disgusting habits" of Indians and their "state of helpless ignorance and imbecility."[35] As a result, images produced by Lewis and sponsored by McKenney remain tainted by their problematic origins, having been conceived in contempt for their subjects. This attitude is underlined by the title *Chippeway Squaws;* the derogatory term "squaw" reflects the context in which this image was conceived. While this image can be read more as a manifestation of American expansion than as a meticulous Indian ethnography, it is part of a series that is frequently reprinted, largely because early nineteenth-century images of Native Americans are so rare.

This print reveals as much about the artist's cultural preoccupations as the lives of the women portrayed. Lewis attempts to document both the costumes and the child-rearing practices of Ojibwe women in this crudely rendered portrait, where the subjects are shown preoccupied with their maternal duties. Whites in the north country were entirely dependent on Native American women, who were the critical cultural intermediaries in the fur trade. Women were the ones who provided new residents of the region with the food, clothing, and moccasins they needed for daily survival; they also were responsible for processing pelts and interpreting both language and social customs. Newcomers to the region were typically most fascinated by Indian women's responsibility for tasks they deemed more appropriate for men. The gendered division of labor practiced by Indians appalled and intrigued observers who concluded that the excessive burdens borne by women demonstrated Native American cultural inferiority.

In 1835, Lewis issued a compilation of his portraits under the title of *Aboriginal Port-Folio*, which provides little evidence of artistic mastery. These paintings were, however, the product of direct observation and would provide the raw material for an entire generation of artists to follow. Lewis was the first artist after Peter Rindisbacher to go to the Indians and paint them in the field. His subjects were adopted by more accomplished artists like Charles Bird King and Henry Inman, who used Lewis's work rather than living subjects as the basis for their own depictions of Native Americans.[36]

Plate 35. Ojibwe cradleboard, ca. 1835. Peabody Essex Museum.

This photograph features a beautiful example of a cradleboard, the innovative baby care device also featured in Lewis's portrait of Ojibwe women at Fond du Lac. Cradleboards, or *dikinaaganan*, have been favorite subjects for artists seeking to document Indian life. Newcomers to the region were intrigued by these often beautifully adorned cradles that allowed mothers to care for their babies while also attending to their other chores. Most cradleboards were far simpler than the one pictured here; mothers usually wrapped a blanket around a stiff wooden board that had a bumper affixed to its top that protected the baby's head. Women could prop the boards next to them while they worked, which allowed them to talk to their babies while also ensuring their safety; mothers could also strap the boards to their backs while they gardened, paddled, chopped wood, or even boiled maple syrup. Women often attached small toys to the bumper rail to entertain the growing child, who was confined to the cradleboard throughout the first year of life.

PLATE 35

The origins of this elaborate *dikinaaganan* illuminate the intercultural mixing that defined life in Minnesota through the first half of the nineteenth century. The carrier pictured here was probably owned by Mrs. Hester (Crooks) Boutwell (b. 1817), the child of a *mariage à la façon du pays* of the influential fur trader Ramsay Crooks and Abanoku, an Ojibwe woman. Hester was educated at the Mackinac mission school, joined the church at La Pointe, on Madeline Island, and then taught at the Yellow Lake mission until 1834 when she married Protestant missionary and Dartmouth graduate William T. Boutwell, a white newcomer to the territory. When her first child, Elizabeth, was born in 1835, her Indian friends and family probably honored her with the gift of this baby carrier. The Boutwells had nine children together before Hester died at the age of thirty-six in Stillwater, Minnesota.[37]

PLATE 36

Plate 36. James Otto Lewis, *Chippewa Lodge of Poles, Covered with Birch Bark,* **ca. 1826. Smithsonian Institution National Anthropological Archives.**

James Otto Lewis made this drawing of an Ojibwe "lodge of poles" in his capacity as the artist assigned to the treaty negotiations conducted at Fond du Lac near the western end of Lake Superior in 1826. Like cradleboards, wigwams *(wiigiwaam)* were another subject of intense fascination for observers of Indian life like Lewis. The house pictured here could have been constructed in less than a day. Women did the lion's share of work, first creating a framework of raw wood saplings, which they bound together with wood fibers. Nine or ten rolls of birch bark were stretched around the exterior of the frame in overlapping layers. When the time came for the family to move — which happened several times each year — the covering was rolled up and carried along to the next site; the frame was left behind.

Ojibwe households needed to be highly mobile since families relied on a system of seasonal food gathering. Fishing gave way to hunting, which was supplanted by maple sugaring, which in turn was succeeded by nut and berry gathering, while the harvest of corn and wild rice dominated the autumn months. Families moved to the area best suited for each of these activities. Treaty cessions greatly curtailed the ability of all Indians in the north country to roam freely over the landscape in search of food. By the mid-nineteenth century, some Ojibwe had chosen to live in more permanent dwellings, at least for the coldest months of the year, but even at the beginning of the twentieth century a significant number of families still practiced the ancient craft of *wiigiwaam* construction. Families would move for the summer months into these birch bark houses, which had the advantage of being cooler and cleaner than rough log cabins.[38]

Plate 37. William Fisk, *George Catlin,* **1849. National Portrait Gallery, Smithsonian Institution.**

This 1849 portrait by William Fisk shows painter George Catlin garbed in a buckskin shirt, proudly displaying this souvenir of the time he spent in the American West documenting life among different Native American groups. Catlin posed for his portrait in London, where he had taken his gallery of Indian portraits to be admired by European audiences. The shirt pictured here may have originated in Minnesota, which made a deep impression on Catlin during his visit in 1835. Catlin's sojourn at Fort Snelling gave him the opportunity to observe a variety of Indian groups in the area while befriending Army surgeon Nathan Sturges Jarvis and Indian agent Lawrence Taliaferro. Both Taliaferro and Jarvis were collectors of Indian apparel like this shirt, which became popular souvenirs of visits to the backcountry. None of these men would have been likely to wear such a shirt while they were resident in Indian country. But men like Catlin, intent on establishing their credentials as "frontiermen," did not hesitate to costume themselves in Indian-produced garments once they returned to St. Louis, New York, or Europe. The skin shirt became a complex and multifaceted icon of the region, elevated to that status at a moment when this section of the continent was roiling over struggles to determine its social, political, and cultural destiny.

PLATE 37

Plate 38. Red River Métis or Yanktonai-Métis shirt, collected by Nathan Sturges Jarvis, 1833–36. Nathan Sturges Jarvis Collection of Eastern Plains Art, Brooklyn Museum of Art.

This buckskin shirt was collected between 1833 and 1836 by Fort Snelling Army surgeon Nathan Sturges Jarvis, who amassed a considerable collection of Indian-made objects during his time on the Mississippi. Skin shirts like this were greatly prized by collectors like Jarvis, who probably viewed them as artifacts from an isolated culture perched on the cusp of extinction. This exotic prize was hardly an archaic remnant of an ancient and unchanging society; it incorporates Hudson's Bay blue trade beads and is accented with red trade cloth as well as the artistic traditions of several different bands of Indians. It is the product of the intense intercultural exchange and economic transformations that defined life in this region in the early nineteenth century.[39]

Jarvis focused on assembling articles he viewed as authentic to share with admirers in

PLATE 38

the East, oblivious to the fact that Indians had adjusted their apparel once they had a guaranteed supply of manufactured goods from traders. Residents of the region around Fort Snelling were making their clothing from commercially manufactured thread and trade cloth — especially blue and red wool stroud — by the 1830s. Using cloth for apparel allowed women to devote more time to other tasks, including preparing skins for the market. And cloth was more comfortable than leather when wet. To amass his collection of skin shirts, Jarvis had to look northwest of Fort Snelling, to the cultural entrepôt of the Red River valley, where Yanktonai Sioux mixed and married and traded with Cree, Ojibwe, and Métis people. More women in this area still wore clothing crafted from animal skin, and they were renowned for their skill in fashioning garments that reflected the region's mélange of cultural influences.[40]

Plate 39. Joseph Rolette, ca. 1860. Minnesota Historical Society.

This early photograph of Joseph Rolette Jr. shows the legendary trader in a blanket coat, with a classic Métis tobacco or shot pouch secured around his waist with a woven sash. The pouch he is wearing probably originated in the Red River valley, which became renowned for the beautiful ornamental handiwork of its women, who drew on a rich blend of European, Ojibwe, Cree, and Dakota cultural traditions. Much like the extended families in the region that bound together people with diverse cultural identities, this handiwork serves as a physical legacy of the cultural fusion that had defined life in the region for the previous century.[41]

Rolette represented the Pembina Métis in the Minnesota territorial legislature and has been memorialized as a colorful trickster who "stole" the 1857 bill that would have moved the state capital to the newly created town of St. Peter. Rolette was a

PLATE 39

sophisticated political and economic operator rather than the "jolly half breed" of state legends. Rolette's ancestry was in fact almost entirely French Canadian and British. The son of a successful trader, Rolette was educated at a private school in New York City. After completing his education, the trader moved to Pembina in the 1840s. Eventually he married a Métis woman, whose family ties undoubtedly helped him broker trade and political deals between St. Paul and Pembina. His portrait illuminates the cultural politics of mid-nineteenth-century Minnesota. His Métis costume — particularly the shot pouch — proclaimed his allegiance to the "old" Minnesota cultural, economic, and political system that was quickly being supplanted by the newcomers pouring into the territory in the 1850s. Rolette was undoubtedly trying to project a certain cultural exoticism by wearing a shot pouch; the clothing of this hybrid culture served to distinguish those familiar with the customs and challenges of frontier life on the northern borderlands from new arrivals who were eager to integrate Minnesota into the economy and political structure of the continental United States. This portrait served as the basis for the later oil painting of Rolette completed posthumously in 1890.[42]

Plate 40. Dakota or Ojibwe man's pouch, ca. 1800–1810. Minneapolis Institute of Arts.

PLATE 40

This shot pouch dates from an earlier period than the example of Métis artistry featured in Rolette's portrait. One of two remaining objects from the collection of Major Lawrence Taliaferro, the Indian agent at Fort Snelling from 1819 to 1839, this pouch is the work of a Dakota or Ojibwe artisan who combined established styles of leather quillwork with new techniques of loom beading. While most contemporary pouches were fashioned from plain leather, this pouch features quillwork and beading that foreshadows the more decorative bandolier bags worn after the Civil War in Minnesota. Taliaferro received many such items as gifts from the Indian people living around the military outpost. Sadly, most of his collection was destroyed in a later fire.

For the first half of the nineteenth century, shot pouches like these were part of the standard outfit of all men who lived in Minnesota. They were used to carry gun accessories or fire-making tools like flint, steel, and touchwood. While these utility pouches were usually spare, the relatively elaborate decorations on Taliaferro's bag suggest it was not intended for everyday use. It was likely crafted as a gift to be presented on a ceremonial occasion, such as a treaty negotiation. The fate of shot pouches illuminates how quickly life changed in the region. Technological advances and cultural transformations reduced these once essential accessories to tourist trinkets by 1854, when British traveler Laurence Oliphant observed that Indian traders in St. Paul had established a brisk business in selling "overhauled moccasins embroidered with porcupine quills; tobacco-pouches ornamented with beads; tomahawks, pipes, and all the appurtenances of Indian life which these men pick up from Sioux or Chippeway warriors, and sell as curiosities."[43]

PLATE 41

Plate 41. J. Ayers, *Map of the Settled Part of Wisconsin Territory Compiled from the Latest Authorities*, detail, from William Randolph Smith, *Observations on the Wisconsin Territory* (Philadelphia: E. L. Carey & A. Hart, 1838). Minnesota Historical Society.

In this 1838 map, the area that became Minnesota is shown as part of Wisconsin territory. The map was published as part of a larger guide written by William R. Smith, a new arrival to the area intent on encouraging settlement in Wisconsin. While Ayers's depiction of Minnesota geography is not entirely accurate, his map illuminates the proximity of white settlement to Native American territory in Minnesota. The line of white settlement in Wisconsin portended the demise of the geographic isolation that had insulated the region's mixed-race culture and economy.[44]

Plate 42. H. L. Hime, Ojibwe tents on the banks of the Red River, near the middle settlement, September–October 1858. Library and Archives of Canada.

This image of Ojibwe tents is one of the earliest surviving photographs of an outdoor scene from this region. It features a *bajishka'ogaan* — a type of dwelling known among the Dakota as a tipi — a framework of spruce poles covered by birch bark. Photographer H. L. Hime captured this scene as part of his larger efforts on behalf of the 1858 Hind expedition, mounted by the Canadian government to document the geology, natural history, topography, and meteorology of the region to the west of Lake Winnipeg and the Red River.

Taken more than thirty years after Peter Rindisbacher worked in the same area, this photograph shows how visitors continued to be fascinated by Indian lifeways. While Rindisbacher seemed to find residents of the Red River valley amenable to his artistic endeavors, Hime complained that the Indians he encountered refused to allow their photographs to be taken. As a result we do not know whether these structures were inhabited. By the time Hime visited the region, the Red River Ojibwe had more reason to be wary of white strangers than in the early years of the Selkirk settlement. They must have been feeling the same pressures from white encroachment that had impoverished their relatives to the south and east; recent land cessions had undermined the system of seasonal food gathering that had supported Ojibwe people throughout Minnesota. They were forced to cede their land in 1863.

Hime was perhaps the first photographer to master the use of collodion wet-plate photography in a wilderness setting. First introduced in England in 1851, this process involved creating glass-plate negatives that had to be exposed and developed before they dried. It required cumbersome equipment and long exposure times. The technical demands of photography made it ill-suited as an illustration medium for this kind of expedition, whose leaders were determined to cover long distances each day. Hime's lenses were also better suited for studio portraits than landscapes. Hime created his best images — including this one — during the autumn months spent by the expedition at Red River, where the skilled photographer had the time necessary to await favorable weather, carefully set up his equipment, and take his exposures without rushing. Hime's photographs of this settlement were published in 1860 to illustrate the narrative of the Hind expedition, offering readers in Canada and Great Britain the chance to view the northern borderlands through an entirely new medium.[45]

PLATE 42

PLATE 43

Plate 43. Eastman Johnson, *Canoe of Indians*, 1856–57. St. Louis County Historical Society.

Henry Wadsworth Longfellow's 1855 romantic poem, *The Song of Hiawatha*, probably helped to inspire this painting done by well-known artist Eastman Johnson. Johnson spent 1856–57 living in a rough cabin on the shores of Lake Superior, where he mastered the art of paddling a canoe. The artist painted portraits of local Ojibwe as well as the settlement of Grand Portage, which was no longer the trading center it had been in the eighteenth century.

The literary legend of Hiawatha was already starting to obscure the reality of Ojibwe lives and culture in the 1850s. Johnson's rich landscapes and romantic portraits provide no indication of how poverty and dispossession were roiling Ojibwe communities across the state. Irregular annuity payments were one of many problems facing the Ojibwe, who were also struggling with hunger, intensified epidemics, growing alcohol abuse, and the rise of an increasingly militant warrior class determined to challenge white power, with violence if necessary.[46]

The classic birch bark canoe pictured here was the most important mode of transportation for the Ojibwe and most other residents of the region until the mid-nineteenth century. At the zenith of the fur trade, travelers to the interior traded for kettles, cloth, knives, beads, gunpowder, weapons, and blankets for canoes made by the Ojibwe, who built frames that they covered with birch bark and sealed with spruce resin. Canoes and canoe making remained favorite subjects for white artists and photographers, who recognized the enormous skill involved in handcrafting these vessels that had defined life in this region for centuries. Ojibwe canoe builders continued to practice their craft through the end of the nineteenth century despite the increasingly desperate conditions of their existence.

Plate 44. Robert O. Sweeny, *Interior of Bark House*, n.d., Minnesota Historical Society.

This view shows the interior of a pole-frame bark house that would have been shared by several Dakota families. The sketch was completed by Robert Sweeny, a talented artist and pharmacist who settled in St. Paul in 1852 and immediately devoted himself to creating a pictorial record of his adopted home. Sweeny's sketch suggests a familiarity with his subjects that could not have been gained in a single visit. His simple drawing provides an intimate glimpse into the seemingly commodious dwelling, which featured interior platforms that could be used for smoking, sleeping, and handiwork while the evening's meal bubbled on the central hearth.

PLATE 44

Plate 45. Seth Eastman, *Dakota Village*, 1851–57, in Henry Rowe Schoolcraft, *Historical and Statistical Information respecting the History, Condition and Prospects of the Indian Tribes of the United States*, vol. 2 (Philadelphia: Lippincott, Grambo, 1851–57). James Ford Bell Library, University of Minnesota.

This engraving is taken from a government publication meant to serve as an encyclopedic resource on Indian culture. Eastman spent five years working on the illustrations for the Schoolcraft volumes, which were meant to illustrate the everyday life and customs of Indians across North America for both Washington policy makers and the general public. Eastman was one of the most influential Indian artists of his time, and his depictions of life in the region that became Minnesota influenced a whole generation of nineteenth-century artists. While Eastman was a sympathetic chronicler of Indian life in Minnesota, he worked from a firm belief in white superiority. As a result, his images cannot be regarded as transparent windows on Indian life. These ethnographic portraits are framed by white assumptions about manifest destiny that shape their composition and tenor.

PLATE 45

This close-up view of a Dakota community probably depicts Medicine Bottle's village, a small Mdewakanton hamlet created by a group that splintered away from the larger Kaposia village. Villages like these — the summer residences of the Dakota — were usually located close to rivers or lakes. Several families shared each of these ridged-roof houses. These structures — which were framed with poles and covered with bark — featured low platforms inside that provided places for sitting, eating, and sleeping. See Plate 44 for an interior view of this kind of dwelling. When the weather allowed, villagers sat and worked and socialized on mats and benches under the attached scaffolds, which provided shade and a cool place to sleep as well as a place to dry corn and furs.[47]

PLATE 46

Plate 46. Johann Baptist Wengler, *Kaposia, Wigwams of the Sioux Indians*, 1851. Oberösterreichischen Landesmuseen (Upper Austrian State Museums).

In the 1850s, the Indian village of Kaposia attracted many visitors intent on observing the region's indigenous inhabitants. The village was originally located at the junction of the St. Croix and Mississippi rivers, but in 1838 it was moved to what is now South St. Paul. Its close proximity to St. Paul made it easily accessible for mid-nineteenth-century artists who were determined to record scenes of Indian life before these people "vanished" in the wake of white settlement. Austrian artist Johann Baptist Wengler, who spent the summer of 1851 in Minnesota, made this sketch, which shows tipis adjacent to bark lodges. Most residents spent the summer months in bark lodges, reserving tipis for hunting expeditions and the winter months. Tipis had the advantage of being portable, allowing Dakota families to seek the additional shelter of the woods in the winter where they had protection from inclement weather as well as proximity to the game that provided their subsistence through the coldest months of the year. Constructed from animal skins stretched over a conical framework of poles, tipis were comfortable even in the coldest weather as long as they were properly heated with a good fire.[48]

Plate 47. Seth Eastman, *Little Crow's Village on the Mississippi*, 1846–48. Minnesota Historical Society.

Kaposia was also known as Little Crow's village. The Indian leader was born in this village in 1810, when it was still located at the junction of the St. Croix and Mississippi rivers. Seth Eastman painted this image in the 1840s, after the village had been moved to what is now South St. Paul.

Nine years after Little Crow's birth, the U.S. Army established what would become Fort Snelling near the village. The military outpost became a hub for traders, government agents, tourists, and Indians who converged on the site to trade, influence government policy, and socialize. This proximity benefited Kaposia in the short term but ultimately made its residents economically dependent on white traders and government officials. Little Crow's father and grandfather forged close ties with American agents, especially Lawrence Taliaferro. By the time Eastman created this image of the village, Kaposia had also become home to a missionary, whose house and garden can be seen on the left side of the image. The people of Kaposia traditionally returned to this site each spring to plant corn, an endeavor that assumed increasing importance in the 1840s and 1850s at the urging of missionaries and government agents. Kaposia was also the site of a famous cemetery, which is pictured on the hill above the village. The scaffolds used by the Dakota to bury their dead created a memorable scene for

visitors and newcomers to the region, most of whom passed Kaposia on their way up the Mississippi River to Fort Snelling and the growing towns of St. Anthony and St. Paul. The village remained in existence until its residents were moved to the Dakota reservation along the Minnesota River.[49]

Plate 48. Seth Eastman, *The Tanner*, 1848. Rockwell Museum of Western Art.

This oil painting shows a woman tanning a hide while her baby sleeps in a cradle-board. A bark house of a Dakota summer village serves as a backdrop to her labors; a group of men sit smoking a pipe under the house scaffold. While the fur trade is usually represented as a thoroughly male world, this image highlights the pivotal role played by Indian women in this economy.

PLATE 48

The transactions of the fur trade occurred between groups of men: Indian hunters, white traders, and government agents. But it was women who cemented these cross-cultural relationships, brokering economic networks by creating kinship ties through marriage to white traders. It was also women like the one pictured here who did the essential work of preparing the pelts so that they could be transported to eastern markets. Indian tanners stretched skins on the type of frame shown here, removed the tissue and flesh, and then used a mixture of animal brains and plant matter to make the hides supple. This painting reflects Eastman's sympathetic superiority toward Native Americans; he pities the tanner, portraying her as a victim of Indian "savagery." His heroine looks harried by her workload, torn between the tedious task of tanning and her desire to tend her infant. While the men of her village lounge in the background, she performs a task most white observers of the time would have deemed more suitable for men. White observers perceived Indian women's overwhelming workload to be evidence of what the artist's wife called their "degraded state." The writer Mary Eastman complained that Dakota women's "work is never done . . . She tans the skins of which coats, moccasins, and leggings are to be made for the family; she has to scrape it and prepare it while other cares are pressing upon her. When her child is born, she has no opportunities for rest or quiet."[50] Most white observers viewed the gendered division of labor within Native American groups to have significant bearing on the moral questions surrounding the displacement of Indians. In *The Homes of the New World: Impressions of America*, Swedish writer Fredrika Bremer asserted "that cruel race which scalps children and old people, and which degrades women to beasts of burden, may as well move off into the wilderness, and leave room for a nobler race. There is, in reality, only a higher justice in it."[51]

Plate 49. Seth Eastman, *Gathering Wild Rice*, 1851–57, in Henry Rowe Schoolcraft, *Historical and Statistical Information respecting the History, Condition and Prospects of the Indian Tribes of the United States*, vol. 6 (Philadelphia: Lippincott, Grambo, 1851–57). James Ford Bell Library, University of Minnesota.

This engraving depicts women harvesting wild rice, one of the most important staples of a north country diet through the nineteenth century. While the harvest of wild rice is usually associated with Ojibwe people today, the Dakota and the Menominee ("wild rice people") were also heavily dependent on the plant that was also called marsh rye or wild oats. Wild rice was harvested in late August and early September, traditionally by women, who paddled their canoes among the rice plants and knocked the grains off the plants into the boat with small sticks or hooks. After the rice was brought to shore, it was dumped into iron kettles, which were suspended over fires until the hulls were parched. Parching loosened the hulls, which were removed by putting the rice in a pit lined with clean deerskin and tramping on it. After being tossed in the air to winnow it from its hulls, the rice was bundled into bags for winter consumption. People who lived along the rivers and lakes of eastern and northern Minnesota traded sacks of wild rice to Yanktonai and Sisseton tribes for buffalo meat and robes as well as to fur traders for manufactured goods. Thus, wild rice was an important source of nourishment for everyone who lived in the region, even those far from the marshy wetlands where the rice plants were most prevalent.[52]

PLATE 49

PLATE 50

Plate 50. Seth Eastman, *Indian Sugar Camp*, ca. 1845. Seth Eastman, LLC.

This watercolor shows Indian women at work in a maple sugaring camp. In the mid-nineteenth century, when Eastman observed this scene, Native American women were the main producers of maple syrup and maple sugar, which were important dietary supplements for everyone who lived in the region. The lodges in the background of this scene suggest that this particular group is Ojibwe, though Dakota women also produced maple sugar. Maple sugaring became an established rite of spring with the advent of the fur trade, which brought thousands of newcomers to the region who were accustomed to having sweetener for their food. Maple sugar was thus produced not only for the subsistence of the Indians themselves but also as a trading commodity.

With the first thaw of the spring, men set off to hunt muskrats, whose pelts were another important commodity for Indians who had become dependent on American trade goods. At the same time, women and children moved to a sugar bush, where they set up a temporary village and worked through the entire month of April to produce maple sugar. While Indian women probably did some maple sugaring before the fur trade became firmly established in the region, the introduction of metal kettles and implements allowed them to undertake the large-scale production pictured here. Without these tools it would have been almost impossible to collect and boil such vast amounts of sap, which they worked into sugar and ultimately stored for later sale and use in birch bark containers. A family could produce up to five or six hundred pounds of sugar in a good year, which would provide enough for their own consumption plus plenty to trade. The maple sugar was consumed locally, where it was "profusely eaten by all of every age," according to Schoolcraft. An important seasoning for all kinds of food, maple sugar was also eaten plain; its widespread consumption led to enormous problems with tooth decay.[53]

PLATE 51

Plate 51. Seth Eastman, *Guarding the Corn Fields*, 1850. Seth Eastman, LLC.

The cultivation of corn became a point of conflict between indigenous Minnesotans and white newcomers, especially missionaries and government agents who believed that the region's agricultural potential was being squandered by Indian men too indolent to work in the fields. Indians in the region largely resisted the pressure to change their gendered division of labor. Women hung on to their responsibility for agriculture and their traditional farming methods, planting corn patches on small mounds rather than in large fields of rows. As the corn ripened, women used scaffolds like the one pictured here as a platform from which they could repel the flocks of hungry blackbirds that preyed on the ripening corn. Missionary and ethnographer Samuel Pond described how women and children "kept off the blackbirds of which two species were abundant, one wholly black, the other red-winged. A peculiar cry, heard only on such occasions, announced the arrival of a flock of birds, and being joined in by all the watchers, was continued until the birds withdrew." Harvested corn was dried on these same kinds of scaffolds and then could be stored for up to three years, although these stores rarely lasted that long because this type of small-scale cultivation failed to produce large surpluses. Corn was viewed by most Indians as a small supplement to the game, fish, berries, and wild rice that formed the bulk of their diet.[54]

Agent Taliaferro must have recognized the exceptional character of the brothers. He entrusted them to establish a mission at his prized agricultural experiment, located near the village of Cloud Man, on Lake Calhoun in present-day Minneapolis. After surviving two particularly harsh winters in a row, in 1829 Cloud Man had agreed to try farming in the way of the white man. Taliaferro, envisioning a future for the Indians as yeoman farmers, paternalistically claimed naming rights to the village, christening it "Eatonville"—a good, solid Yankee name—and hired Philander Prescott to plow up some land and teach the Indians proper farming practices. By the time the Ponds arrived in 1834, the experiment had yielded some success, producing small crops of corn, potatoes, and a variety of vegetables, though how much the Dakotas participated in the effort is debatable.[27]

Christianizing the Indians was clearly the next step toward civilization. Taliaferro had high hopes for the Ponds; however, rather than dive into missionary activity, the brothers spent the first year familiarizing themselves with Dakota language and culture. Then, to their frustration, Jedediah Stevens, an ordained minister, arrived to claim oversight of the mission. The overbearing Stevens quickly demoted the Ponds to the role of manual laborers and ignored the connections they were so carefully building. Where Samuel Pond had viewed Cloud Man as "a man of superior discernment and of great prudence and foresight," Stevens regarded the Indians with disdain, as "ragged, half-starved, indolent beings." The Pond brothers, seething with frustration, soon moved on and, to Stevens's dismay, so did the Indians. Clashes with the Ojibwes who frequented Fort Snelling had made Cloud Man's village vulnerable to attack. Wisely, the chief and his people abandoned the site—and the unpopular Reverend Stevens—without a backward glance for their fields and fences. Eatonville—Taliaferro's model community—silently disappeared.[28]

Stung by Stevens's condescension, Samuel Pond returned east to study for ordination as a bona fide minister. Gideon accepted an invitation from Thomas Williamson to join the mission community at Lac qui Parle, where his knowledge of Dakota language and culture was more appreciated. Of the many Protestant mission stations that came and went over the years, only Lac qui Parle could claim a measure of success, at least for a time. The station endured for almost twenty years and the missionary cohort there put great effort into learning the Dakota language. Thanks to the Ponds, who had created a Dakota alphabet that incorporated sounds unfamiliar to the Euro-American tongue, they also were able to teach reading and writing in Dakota and translate parts of the Bible and other religious writings into the Indians' native language. No missionary in Minnesota country put more sustained dedication into the evangelizing effort than the group at Lac qui Parle. Nonetheless, what success they achieved was due almost entirely to the influence of Joseph Renville rather than their persuasive powers.[29]

Renville was a remarkable figure. The Dakota–French mixed-blood trader had an incomparable ability to navigate between the world of whites and Indians. As an interpreter and guide, he earned the respect of Zebulon Pike, Stephen Long, Joseph Nicollet, and other emissaries from the East. Nicollet, betraying his cultural bias, declared that Renville "daily becomes more and more noteworthy for principles of which one did not believe the Indians capable." Military officials and Agent Taliaferro appreciated Renville for his "civilized" behavior and influence with the western tribes. And Henry Sibley and other fur trade agents valued his trading savvy and the profits they reaped from his skills. Renville's influence was so great among the western tribes that he was able to set the terms of his relationship with Sibley and his superiors.[30]

Educated in Canada and at least nominally a Catholic, Renville could converse in French and English as well as Dakota. Though his features favored his Indian heritage, still he was able to shift his identity with chameleonlike ease. Among the Dakotas, he represented himself as a full-blooded Indian; in dealing with whites, he used his French background to advantage. Renville's courtesy and polish surprised many whites, who considered mixed-blood people as barbaric as their full-blooded Indian kin. Even the haughty Englishman George Featherstonehaugh, who found little to like in Minnesota country, grudgingly observed that Renville possessed "a little touch of French manners." Alexander Huggins, who was part of Williamson's missionary group, was so startled by the gracious manners of "Mr. Renville, the old gentleman," when first they met that he made note in his diary that "the knifes and forks were placed round a large Table and the plates all set by Mr. Renville, who cut meat and put on all our plates, then helped himself last." Coffee served by a "French man" topped off the meal. Mr. Huggins was impressed.[31]

While Renville had the skills and savoir faire to interact effectively with whites, what distinguished him from other traders was his desire and ability to bend the forces of change to serve his extended kin as well as himself. His value system was grounded in the Dakota tradition of the collective rather than in the acquisitive individualism of his European forebears. Samuel Pond, looking back on an acquaintance of many years, summed up his character well: "Mr. Renville," Pond declared, "was certainly a man of superior natural abilities, and he had many admirers; but the most prominent traits of his character were such as belonged rather to a Dakota than to a white man."[32]

By backcountry standards, Renville was a wealthy man. Two hundred miles west of Fort Snelling he had established a virtual fiefdom at Lac qui Parle. Protected by a personal militia of young braves, Fort Renville, as the post was commonly known, was far more than a typical trader's station. Renville grazed one hundred cattle, more than two dozen horses, and a substantial flock of sheep; he also had begun to engage in small-scale agriculture. But unlike Joe Brown or any other enterprising trader, Renville shared the wealth with an open hand. He gave goods on credit to any hunter who asked, regardless of past performance or previous debts. He generously shared provisions and food with everyone in the band, holding nothing back, and was known widely for his hospitality to visitors. Samuel Pond recalled, "He gave much to the poor, many of whom were always with him." Another contemporary recalled, "An Indian never left his house hungry, and they delighted to do him honor." In classic Indian tradition, Renville accrued power by giving away material possessions rather than through personal accumulation. As a result, his influence was unsurpassed, from the St. Peter to the Missouri rivers. As the nineteenth century moved toward its midpoint, Lac qui Parle may have been one of the last bastions where customs of reciprocity between traders and Indians endured.[33]

When the Reverend Dr. Williamson and his party—Williamson's wife, Jane, Jane's sister, Sarah Poage (who would later marry Gideon Pond), Alexander and Lydia Huggins, and several children—arrived at Fort Snelling, they hoped to establish themselves at Lake Calhoun, where the Ponds had made a good beginning and which was within easy reach of the fort, a comforting link to civilization. Unfortunately, Jedediah Stevens, who arrived two weeks later, brandishing papers from the American Board of Commissioners for Foreign Missions, which sponsored both groups, insisted on prior claim to the site. At this point, Joseph Renville, who happened to be at the fort, stepped in to offer the Williamson group a place at Lac qui Parle. Lacking other options, the missionaries gratefully accepted his invitation and commenced an exhausting seventeen-day journey to their new home. Though the stalwart missionaries did not record any regrets at the time, the trip to Lac qui Parle was enough to make more timid souls flee back to civilization. First traveling by mackinaw boat up the St. Peter to Traverse des Sioux, they were beset by swarms of mosquitoes, and then jouncing in carts across the trackless prairie, they frequently became mired in chest-deep mud holes. It must have seemed like a journey to the end of the world. Upon reaching their destination, Williamson described Lac qui Parle in a letter as "this country where the mosquitoes in summer and the cold winds near all the rest of the year render comfortable meditation . . . for the most part out of the question."[34]

The missionaries were willing to suffer to bring God's word to the heathen, but the hospitable Renville was more interested in other talents they had to offer. Williamson was a physician as well as a minister, the women were teachers, and Huggins an experienced farmer. As a man who understood well the changes that were soon to overwhelm his people, Renville intended to prepare and protect them as well as possible. If that meant accommodating Christian evangelism, he considered it a reasonable price to pay. He wanted his family and kin to learn to read and write. A Bible served as well for a text as a primer, so Renville willingly assisted the missionaries in translating religious texts into the Dakota language. As for farming, though Dakota men continued to resist what in their culture was "women's work," Huggins and the others

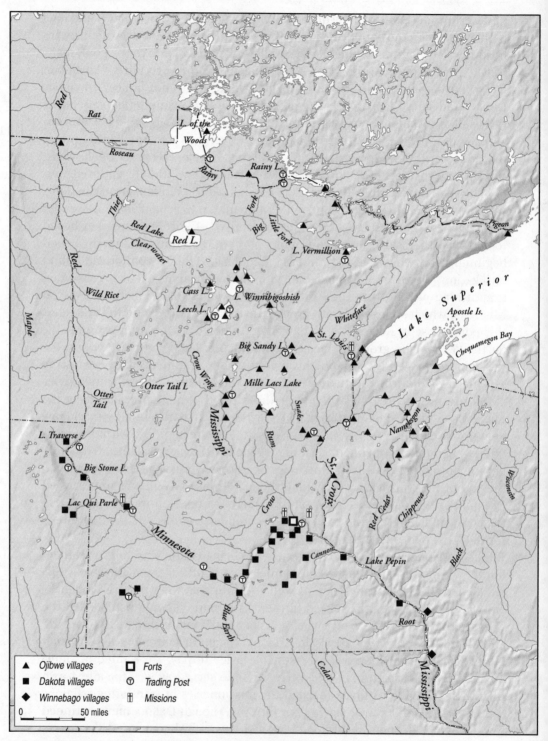

Dakota, Ojibwe, and Winnebago villages and trading hubs, ca. 1830.

plowed, sowed, hauled manure, chopped wood, ground corn, and performed myriad other tasks on their behalf. All in all, it seems to have been a bargain well made.[35]

Renville left no written account of his intentions, but the proof is evident in the success and failures of the mission project. Churchgoers and school attendees almost all belonged to Renville's extended family, membership in the church generally hovering at less than two dozen congregants, most of them women and children. The first Dakota man at Lac qui Parle was not baptized until 1841. Occasionally attendance at services would swell to sixty or seventy, but that may have been due to the feasting that followed more than religious inclination. Meanwhile, Williamson vaccinated the people against smallpox and treated a wide range of illnesses; Renville's family and any others who were so inclined had schooling available to them, his daughters eventually becoming teachers themselves; and Alexander Huggins and other lay missionaries who joined him over the years worked like Trojans in the fields. Renville himself became an elder in the church, but the role seems to have had more to do with asserting his authority than religious conviction. Indeed, it was Renville's influence that assured even the limited success the missionaries achieved. Whenever preaching diverged from the trader's interests, he and his family boycotted the services until the missionaries revised their position. They had little choice in the matter since when Renville stayed away the rest of the congregants did as well. After his death in 1846, church attendance dropped precipitously and the missionaries faced growing hostility from the band. Members of the mission community began abandoning the station one by one, until finally it officially closed in 1854.[36]

Even before Renville died, the evangelists were wearing out their welcome. Renville himself had displayed growing impatience with the missionaries, who despite their knowledge of Dakota language seemed incapable of understanding the Indians' internal values. Not only did they constantly inveigh against "the folly and wickedness of [the Indians'] idolatrous system," the missionaries preached against warfare, pressed them to change their way of dressing, take up farming rather than hunting, and even insisted that baptized males cut their hair. Renville began to talk of the need for a Catholic priest, which confirmed growing suspicion among the missionaries that, though he paid lip service to their version of Christianity, he was a Catholic at heart.[37]

Saints and Spirits

In the minds of Protestant missionaries, Catholicism was only one degree removed from heathenism. In the 1830s and 1840s, anti-Catholicism was rampant in the United States. A growing influx of poor Catholic immigrants, primarily Irish, created anxieties among the Protestant majority, who feared that their inferior character and alien faith threatened both the democratic principles of the republic and the Protestant values on which it was founded. Thus, the Minnesota missionaries must have been dismayed to discover that the great majority of the Christians they encountered beyond the walls of Fort Snelling considered themselves to be Catholic—though a priest had not been seen in the region for more than one hundred years. Catholicism had been the faith of the original French voyageurs and was still embraced, after a fashion, by their descendants. Moreover, a cleric or two had accompanied nearly every French expedition into the Upper Mississippi River valley, leaving a Catholic imprint on the land itself in the names they imposed upon its features—St. Peter, St. Croix, St. Anthony, and dozens more. The Catholic footprint was everywhere. Though the early clerical adventurers had spent little time on conversion efforts as they passed through the region, the Jesuits did establish missionary beachheads at Michilimackinac and Sault Ste. Marie, where the faith took hold and was informally carried west along the trading networks.[38]

The Catholicism of the north country was a unique frontier version of the faith, one that blended Native and Christian spirituality into a compatible hybrid. The very elements of Catholicism that Protestants found so unsettling—mysterious ritual, veneration of relics, the pantheon of saints—gave it a certain legitimacy in the eyes of Native people, who could identify parallels with their own religious systems. The emphasis of community over individual and the fictive kinships created through godfathers and godmothers reinforced rather than challenged a worldview where kinship was the ordering principle. Moreover, the Jesuits had consciously shaped their teaching of the faith to conform to Native understandings of spirituality. In the eighteenth century, Father Jacques Marquette had freely admitted that he made no effort to obstruct Ojibwe reverence for "imaginary spirits," considering such beliefs to be harmless. Writing in 1858, Presbyterian minister and historian Edward Duffield Neill declared that Marquette had "made a fatal mistake as a minister of Christianity." It was simply not possible to serve both "God and Manitou." In Neill's estimation, the difficulties that Protestant missionaries confronted in the nineteenth century were due in no small part to Catholic heresies practiced more than a century earlier.[39]

In fact, the syncretic nature of Catholicism was what enabled it to survive for more than one hundred years in a region where priests only rarely made an appearance. When the French turned over North America to the British in 1763, most of the clergy, lacking support from the new Anglican authorities, retreated to the Catholic stronghold of Montreal. Nonetheless, Catholic practices continued, largely due to Indian and Métis women who kept the faith alive and acted as its chief interpreters. The Catholicism they practiced became an integral part of the cultural fabric that knit traders, Indians, and Métis into a coherent society.[40]

As evidence, some version of Catholicism survived at Grand Portage for nearly a century without benefit of clergy. In 1838, when news reached the

Ojibwes living there that a "black robe" was en route to their village, at least some band members rejoiced. When Slovenian missionary Francis Xavier Pierz arrived at the remote spot, he found that the Indians, "under the direction of Mrs. Pierre Cotte, the wife of the resident fur trader," had built a temporary chapel in his honor. While Madame Cotte was preparing for the priest's arrival, her husband, a devout Catholic himself, was assiduously working to undermine Edmund Ely's already troubled mission at Fond du Lac. Pierre Cotte's efforts and Ely's constant missteps with the Ojibwes soon caused the Protestant mission to collapse, but Father Pierz served his Catholic congregation (about evenly split between Ojibwes and Métis) in apparent harmony until recalled by his bishop in 1840. As a testament to Pierz's success, the Grand Portage congregants petitioned the bishop to send them a permanent replacement for their priest. But clergy qualified and willing to serve on the frontier were in short supply and the bishop was forced to deny their request. Nonetheless, when Pierz returned for a brief visit in 1847, he discovered the congregation keeping up its religious practices despite the absence of a priest.[41]

Catholic missionaries faced a problem quite different than that confronted by the Protestants. While Protestants struggled to win a handful of converts, the Catholics lacked the manpower to serve an already existing flock that was scattered throughout the Upper Mississippi. In 1839, when Matthias Loras, bishop of Dubuque, made his first trip up the river to assess the far reaches of his newly formed diocese, he was astonished to discover the number of Catholics awaiting a priest. Loras reported, "Our arrival was a cause of great joy to the Catholics, who had never before seen a Priest or Bishop in these remote regions." At St. Peter's (Mendota), the bishop counted 185 Catholics—traders, soldiers, farmers on the reserve, voyageurs—and nearly all the surnames were French, augmented by a few Irish and Scots and a substantial number of Indian wives, designated in his records only as "Sioux" or "Chippewa." During their brief visit Loras and his assistant, Father Anthony Pelamourgues, performed fifty-six baptisms, administered the sacraments of Holy Communion and confirmation to another forty-one, and blessed four marriages. The bishop found the women especially eager for the sacraments. "I have many of them under instruction who are married to Canadians and Irishmen," he wrote, "and am preparing them to receive, on Sunday next, the sacrament of the Eucharist and confirmation."[42]

The needs of the flock at St. Peter's must have exhausted Bishop Loras, leaving him little time to worry about converting Indians. But on his trip downriver, he stopped at a number of Dakota villages, which stirred his missionary zeal. The Indians he met "had nearly forgotten the doctrines of Christianity preached to their ancestors by the Recollects and Jesuits two hundred years before. Still they were clamoring for *black robes* as if they had been abandoned only the day before." Even more troubling, Protestant missionaries were already among the Indians, "doing no good." Loras became determined to send a priest to work among the tribes to counter Protestantism as much as paganism. "The greatest difficulty," he confided, "is from the Protestants, who will redouble their efforts to throw every obstacle in our way."[43]

In numbers and resources, the Protestants had a great advantage. The evangelical fervor wrought by the Great Awakening moved both ministers and laypeople to serve God in the mission field. Those who could not serve themselves contributed generously to mission societies that assisted their brave co-religionists. In contrast, the Catholic Church throughout the United States was struggling with a general shortage of native-born clergy to serve a rapidly growing population of working-class Catholic immigrants. Bishop Loras had to recruit seminarians from his native France to serve his far-flung diocese and rely on foreign mission societies to fund his efforts. As a result, he was able to dispatch only two young, newly ordained French priests to the Minnesota mission field. In 1841 Father Lucien Galtier set off for St. Peter, charged to minister to the white and Métis population in the region around Fort Snelling. Father Augustin Ravoux received the more daunting assignment, sent alone to bring the Catholic gospel to the vast nation of the Dakotas.[44]

Out of necessity, Father Ravoux became an itinerant missionary rather than one with a fixed station in the style of the Protestants. His travels carried him as far west as the Missouri as well as up and down the St. Peter and Mississippi rivers. Because he usually stayed no more than a month or two in a single locale, he made no attempt to introduce agriculture or other changes to the Indian way of life. Proficient in Dakota, he created a catechism and translated simple prayers and hymns but relied primarily on homely preaching rather than biblical translation as the backbone of his teaching. Alone and with few resources, he depended on the hospitality of the Indians, living among them and sharing their way of life. As might be expected, he encountered less resistance than did his Protestant contemporaries. During several months Ravoux spent at Traverse des Sioux, Lake Traverse, and Lac qui Parle in 1842, word of his popularity alarmed the Protestant missionaries at Lac qui Parle, who noted "the diminution in our Sabbath assemblies" wherever the priest appeared. With their standing among the Dakotas already fading, Thomas Williamson anxiously wrote to Samuel Pond, "Caution any whom you may employ and all our members who may go there (to Lac Travers) to keep aloof from the priest and have nothing to do with him."[45]

Despite Protestant anxieties, after three years in the field Father Ravoux admitted "the progress of religion among the Indians is not very consoling. . . . Conversions are rare." His most sustained missionary effort was at Little Prairie (present-day Chaska), where Jean Baptiste Faribault helped him establish a base. Living in the most meager conditions, his clothing in tatters, Ravoux doubted his effectiveness. Still, when he was recalled to St. Peter in 1845 to replace Father Galtier, he had baptized seventy-six Dakotas and Métis at Little

Reverend Augustin Ravoux photographed by Charles Alfred Zimmerman around 1870. Courtesy of the Minnesota Historical Society.

Prairie alone—a record that far outdistanced even the most successful Protestant mission.[46]

Ravoux's relative success was due in part simply to circumstances that made any attempt at cultural change unfeasible. Partly it was due to assistance from Catholic traders like Jean Baptiste Faribault, Louis Provençalle, and even Joseph Renville, who used their influence to ease Ravoux's acceptance among the Dakotas. Many Dakotas were already acquainted with Catholicism, comfortable with the syncretic version that had evolved without clerical supervision. Though relatively few ascribed to the faith, it seemed far less alien than the Protestant version of Christianity. Finally, some credit certainly was due to Ravoux's personality and style, which was more like that of the Pond brothers than of other, more culturally insensitive and inflexible missionaries. He insisted that the Indians "in many ways . . . were not inferior to the whites." The Natives followed a code of morals, "loved their children and mourned their dead . . . believed in a Great Spirit" and an afterlife. Like all men, some were honorable, some were rogues. For Ravoux, it was their common humanity rather than cultural difference that was the defining characteristic. His perspective derived from and reinforced the hybrid culture of the north country. Sadly, it reflected values that were rapidly losing their persuasive power.[47]

By the time missionaries first appeared in Minnesota country, the commonalities that had shaped the culture of the fur trade frontier were increasingly challenged. Two centuries of geographic isolation had allowed a hybrid culture to develop that bridged the world of the Indian and the European. While the fur trade from the beginning was part of an international market system, the internal social relations that undergirded the trade had operated as a world apart. But as the nineteenth century advanced, new pressures emerged to unbalance both the culture and the economic system that was its foundation. Soldiers, speculators, scientists, tourists, and missionaries, along with traders caught between the old order and the new, all acted as agents of the changes that were beginning to make themselves felt. Reduced to starkest terms, land would soon become more valuable than furs. The salient question was, who would own the land and how would they acquire it?

Chapter 6

—◆—

A WORLD UNRAVELING

I have spent the flower of my life in the Indian country, in the hope of obtaining a competency. . . .
I am fatigued almost to death by the vexation & trouble inseparable from the trade with the Indians.
HENRY HASTINGS SIBLEY, 1840

Red River Roots

On a July afternoon in 1836 Alexander Huggins spied an unexpected sight on the horizon. "There was 70 carts came here from Red River," he wrote in his diary, "& there was fifty souls in the Caravan, a great part of them were Scotch Presbyterians." The lay missionary/farmer, part of the delegation led by Thomas Williamson, had been settled less than a week at Lac qui Parle. After braving the journey across the featureless prairie the small party of missionaries must have felt alone and adrift in an alien world. The last thing they expected was a visit from English-speaking Europeans, especially coming from the wild north country rather than the settled territory to the east. The missionaries had little knowledge of the Red River colony north of the U.S. border or the steady trickle of disillusioned settlers who each year made their way south to the Mississippi. Nor could they know that the oxcart route between Fort Snelling and the Red River colony had been in steady use for more than twenty years.[1]

Remarkably, long before land fever lured hopeful farmers from Illinois, Ohio, and points east, the first incursion of settlers into Minnesota country came out of the trackless north, thanks to a somewhat impractical, aristocratic philanthropist armed with a controlling interest in the Hudson's Bay Company. Lord Thomas Douglas, fifth Earl of Selkirk, had founded the Red River colony in 1811, nearly a decade before the Americans established an official

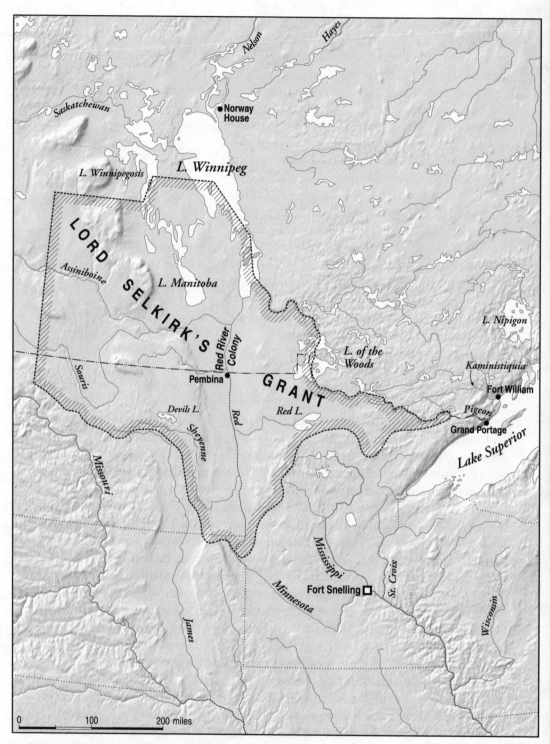

Red River Colony and territory claimed by Lord Selkirk.

presence at Fort Snelling. The idealistic earl believed he had a plan that would reduce costs for the company and also bring relief to Scots Highlanders uprooted by the enclosure movement and Irish tenants suffering under absentee rule. He proposed to establish an agricultural colony that could supply the company with cheap, locally grown agricultural products, livestock, and an available pool of workers. The resettled tenants would benefit as well, with a fresh start on farms provided by the earl. Lord Selkirk's plan met strong opposition among some company directors who were firm in their belief that "colonization was at all times unfavorable to the fur trade." Nonetheless, Selkirk wielded enough influence to prevail and the Hudson's Bay Company conveyed to him an estate of some 116,000 square miles, roughly encompassing the province of Manitoba and northern parts of present-day North Dakota and Minnesota. Selkirk called his new possession Assiniboia.[2]

[123]

Unfortunately, the earl had no personal experience with conditions in Assiniboia. He had never traveled west of Montreal. His knowledge of the Northwest was colored equally by optimism and "stirring tales" of adventure gleaned from men in the fur trade. Touting the region's fertile soil and "a Climate far more temperate than the Shores of the Atlantic," he was confident that "the Colonists may, with a moderate exertion of industry, be certain of a comfortable subsistence, & they may also raise some valuable objects of exportation."[3] His hapless settlers soon faced a harsher reality.

Only weeks after the first contingent of would-be farmers arrived at the forks of the Red and Assiniboine rivers in the autumn of 1811, they found themselves facing the most severe winter recorded in twenty years. Shelter was inadequate and provisions in short supply. Even worse, they faced continual harassment from the North West Company, which was willing to go to any lengths to keep settlers out of its trading preserve. The Red River valley marked the southernmost extreme of the Hudson's Bay trading network, where it nibbled at the long-standing dominance of the Nor'Westers. As Selkirk had vigorously argued, a settlement there could provide a valuable nearby source of resupply for Hudson's Bay traders that would outweigh its disadvantages. However, the border country was the heart of the North West Company's empire and neither farmers nor Hudson's Bay agents would go unchallenged. North West Company principals worked in London to throw political roadblocks in the way of Selkirk's venture; they dispatched agents into the countryside to dissuade potential colonists and also sent off a flurry of missives to their representatives in North America, warning that "the Hudson's Bay Company . . . by their grant to Lord Selkirk . . . are striking at the very root of . . . [the] fur trade. In short, no means should be left untried to thwart Selkirk's schemes." North West traders took up the charge with a will, buying up and hoarding all available foodstuffs and inciting the local Métis with warnings that the settlers would drive the buffalo from their hunting grounds. The Nor'Westers were determined to expel the settlers from the region by fair means or foul.[4]

Hudson's Bay officials in North America also opposed the settlement scheme that infringed on the fur trade terrain. They dragged their heels in assisting the colonists and slyly obstructed Selkirk's orders by claiming shortages of food and supplies. With so many forces lined up against its success, the project was in danger of collapsing before it had fairly begun. Selkirk, to his credit, never abandoned the floundering immigrants. Until his death in 1820, he poured in money and supplies, brought in additional contingents of settlers, and worked to strengthen ties with American traders, who were also enemies of the Nor'Westers. Robert Dickson, Joseph Renville, Joe Rolette, Alexis Bailly, and Michael Dousman (father of Sibley's partner Hercules) all played a role at one time or another in keeping the colony functioning. Nonetheless, only the most determined colonists endured. Surrounded by hostile traders and plagued by grasshopper infestations, floods, blizzards, crop failures, and the daily hardships of wresting a living in the unforgiving northern climate, many settlers wanted only to escape.[5]

Return by the way they had come was unthinkable. The stranded colonists had neither the skills nor the means to make their way back across 700 trackless miles to Hudson's Bay and then across the Atlantic to their homelands. Their only option was to resettle in the United States. Every spring brought forth a ragtag caravan of settlers fleeing south. The first band of emigrants left Red River in 1812, straggling through unsettled Minnesota country in a months-long journey to find more hospitable homes in Missouri, Illinois, or Indiana. Once Fort Snelling was established in 1820, it provided a welcome temporary haven. Between 1821 and 1835, 489 refugees from Selkirk's colony arrived at the fort, and they continued to come in the following years. Still, by the 1830s, in spite of the daunting obstacles, the colony had achieved a fairly stable footing—which only created a different sort of problem. The farmers discovered that in years when nature favored them, the market was their foe. Hundreds of miles from the nearest American settlements, they had no buyers for their grains or livestock. Trapped in a subsistence economy, disheartened settlers continued to abandon the colony. By 1840, 200 more had sought shelter at Fort Snelling, including the 50 who surprised Huggins and his fellow missionaries at Lac qui Parle in 1836.[6]

After a brief respite, most of the refugees continued southward out of Indian territory, but a few families, either too dispirited to go on or attracted by the promise of the Upper Mississippi, petitioned to stay. In the 1820s most of the refugees were francophone Swiss, "captivated and seduced" by Selkirk's most recent recruiting effort, which had targeted artisans and tradesmen rather than farmers—an attempt to broaden the skill base of the colony. According to one regretful immigrant, the "poor Switzers" were "totally unsuited to the wilderness into which they were going." Indeed. With occupations such as watchmaker, jeweler, peddler, and pastry chef, the new arrivals had little hope of success. Barbara Ann Schadecker's father had hoped to set up shop as a weaver, but where was he to get the wool? Horrified by the contrast between the glowing promises of Selkirk's agents and the reality of their new home, five families in the first contingent of Swiss émigrés took one look at conditions in the settlement and set off immediately for the United States. When they reached Fort Snelling, the post commandant, sympathetic to the immigrants' plight and attuned to the services they could provide the fort, granted their plea to settle unofficially on the military reserve, where they engaged in small-scale farming, worked as artisans, or set themselves up as petty traders. In the ensuing years the exodus from Red River continued. In 1826 alone, after spring floods unleashed the river in a devastating flood, 243 mostly Swiss colonists packed up and headed south.[7]

After five months of hard traveling by oxcart and boat to reach Fort Snelling, it is understandable that some families chose to end their journey there. They put down permanent roots and eventually became part of the haphazard, nameless settlement that was to become St. Paul. Familiar names in the city's roster of pioneers—Benjamin and Pierre Gervais, Joseph Rondo (Rondeaux), and Abraham Perry (Perret)—they were the first families without ties to the fur trade to breach the settlement frontier. Ironically, while traders and Indians kept a wary eye on the East as American expansionism rolled toward them, the first tangible challenge to their world slipped in from the north. Sheer desperation rather than dreams of manifest destiny drove the first stirrings of Minnesota's new order.[8]

A People Apart

By the 1830s, though Minnesota was still officially closed to settlement, isolated agricultural outposts were beginning to dot the landscape. Native people continued to resist government and missionary efforts to shift them from hunters to farmers, but on the Fort Snelling reserve, in the half-breed tract along Lake Pepin, and at posts of entrepreneurial traders like Joe Brown, immigrants, Euro-Americans, and some mixed-blood people were beginning to put the plow to the land. At Mendota a prototype frontier community also was emerging to serve the needs of soldiers and squatters as well as the trade. Fur trade agents like Henry Sibley, with an eye on the future, looked for income-producing schemes to augment and eventually replace trading revenues. With white customers now at hand, agents became Yankee storekeepers as well as provisioners for the trade. Change was in the air.

In the border region another sort of permanent settlement was coalescing. At Pembina on the Canadian border, a Métis community had taken hold that resembled neither a typical American town nor an Indian village.[9] Though through the 1840s Métis and mixed-blood people still fulfilled an important role as cultural brokers, the fluidity of their racial identity was diminishing. For generations cultural attributes—dress, social rank, and lifestyle—had organized the members of fur trade society. Mixed-blood people were often categorized in specific terms such as *bois brulé, gens libre,* or *Canadien,* but these characterizations referred to occupation and lifestyle rather than racial genealogy and could just as easily apply to full-blooded French voyageurs. But by the 1820s pseudoscientific race theory began to put an emphasis on "blood" as racial determinants. Historian Jacqueline Peterson notes that in the Great Lakes region "following the War of 1812, terms such as *half-breed, métis* and *métif* began to appear with increasingly *[sic]* frequency in the travel literature, carrying with them the pejorative baggage of social inferiority or degeneracy." Race prejudice intensified in tandem with the arrival of newcomers who were not part of the interdependent web of the fur trade. To them, mixed-blood people were "a miserable race of men," "a spurious breed," "as motley a group of creatures . . . as the world ever beheld." The hardening of racial categories moved west with settlement. Due to Minnesota's isolation, the old social order based on kinship and culture endured longer there than in any other part of the frontier. However, when the troops arrived at the mouth of the St. Peter in 1819, they planted the seeds of a new racialism that would soon take hold. When Protestant missionaries followed in their wake, they also carried cultural presumptions along with their Bibles. Indians and "Indianlike" mixed-blood people seemed equally alien, savages in need of the "gospel of soap" as well as the word of Christ. Despite (or perhaps because of) the Catholic faith of many mixed bloods, in the reports Protestant missionaries sent back to their sponsors they included mixed-blood people in their discouragingly slim tally of "savage" conversions.[10]

[126]

At the same time, a sense of ethnic or racial distinctiveness was developing among Minnesota's Métis and mixed-blood peoples themselves. For more than one hundred years, gender-specific intermarriage patterns had sustained their identity as a people "in-between." Métis sons generally married Indian women or other Métis, whereas daughters took either white or Métis husbands—customs that reinforced their families' economic and cultural niche as brokers of the fur trade economy and worked against their assimilation as either white or Indian. A distinctive hybrid culture grew out of this recurring marital mingling as families who shared similar values and customs were drawn to settle near one another.[11]

Thus, a combination of imposed racial categorization and evolving ethnic self-consciousness fostered the growth of identifiably Métis towns and villages near trading stations throughout the Great Lakes region. Michilimackinac, Green Bay (or La Baye), and Prairie du Chien all were peopled primarily by Métis, settlements that borrowed from both Indian and European cultural traditions. They all shared certain characteristics that set them apart: a rambling design unfettered by the niceties of "private property"; roughshod but permanent housing, what disdainful Euro-Americans referred to as "rude huts"; common fields and pastures with freely roaming horses and livestock; and small, subsistence garden patches rather than any sustained attempt at market agriculture. Primarily hunters, traders, and woodsmen who practiced a subsistence-barter economy, the residents of Métis towns and villages showed little interest in diversifying their occupations. Euro-Americans, who could imagine no alternative to the ideology of profit and maximum resource extraction, made no secret of their contempt for these peculiar Indianlike people. In the estimation of Major Stephen Long, who visited Prairie du Chien in 1817, the people there, "principally of French and Indian extraction," were "degenerating . . . instead of improving."[12]

Though few Métis left a record of their opinions about American interlopers, the fact that they established communities apart from both whites and Indians gives testament to a growing sense of peoplehood. In Minnesota country, the most stable and significant Métis community grew up at Pembina, which at various times was the site of trading posts established by both the North West and Hudson's Bay companies as well as the American Fur Company. The Pembina Métis were uniquely positioned in the border trade. They considered themselves *gens libre*, free people bound to neither Great Britain nor the United States. They scoffed at attempts to regulate their trade along the uncertain international border, much to the consternation of the competing fur trade companies, which were in no position to control Métis trading prerogatives. Nor'Westers commonly referred to the Métis as the "New Nation," an explicit acknowledgment of their independent and separate status. George Simpson, governor of Hudson's Bay Territory, complained that the Métis could claim to be "either American or British subjects as suits their purpose, being natives of the soil." Once the border was firmly established in 1823, they continued to cross the undefended line with impunity. In fact, a corps of free traders quickly developed that seemed to include "every white man, half-breed, and Indian in the Red River District." In the minds of all concerned, what the companies termed smuggling was simply their customary birthright.[13]

The Pembina Métis made their living solely by trapping and by the annual buffalo hunt, which was a highly organized operation that involved the entire community. The buffalo was vital to their trading economy, both for its skins and for the meat that they pounded into pemmican, an essential part of the fur trader's diet. During hunting season the village appeared nearly abandoned, but it was a permanent settlement nonetheless. At the completion of the hunt, the people—some 350 by 1823—returned to Pembina, their carts loaded with a year's supply of hides and meat, drawn home to their log dwellings, Catholic church, and school. American visitors considered both the settlement and its inhabitants to be "a very low rank in the scale of civilization," but they had to admit that Pembina had at least some characteristics of a "real" town.[14]

To the fur trade companies Pembina was a smugglers' den. To American outsiders it was an uncivilized shantytown. But the settlers of Lord Selkirk's colony viewed Pembina and its residents in a different light. For them, Pembina was a refuge of safety and hospitality. Farther north in the heart of Selkirk's colony, North West Company agents incited Métis to harass and attack the settlers under command of traders, who convinced them that the colonizers intended to destroy their way of life. But at Pembina the immigrants were met with generosity and kindness from people "faithful to the tradition of mutual aid" that was an integral part of their culture. Indeed, the colonists would not have survived their first few winters without the buffalo meat, wild berries, and prairie turnips supplied them by friendly Métis. The Métis also guided the caravans of refugees safely to the Mississippi, "carry[ing] out their promises faithfully and, indeed, with a large measure of thoughtfulness. Throughout the trip they showed themselves to be really mild, generous, and trustworthy." Grateful Red River settlers described the Pembina Métis in the most glowing terms as "naturally humble, benevolent, kind, and sociable."[15]

[128]

The fortunes of Pembina rose and fell with the vicissitudes of the fur trade, but the Métis, with "a lingering fondness for the place of their birth," did not abandon the settlement on the banks of the Red River. By the late 1840s more than 1,100 men and women called Pembina home. Second only to the infant city of St. Paul in population, the often maligned residents of Pembina would become pivotal players in the coming game of territorial politics.[16]

Desperate Measures

Henry Sibley had arrived on the Mississippi in 1834 with plans for a brief adventure, a quick fortune, and a triumphal return to civilization. But he soon learned what traders in the region already knew well: making a profitable living in the traditional fur business was no longer an easy proposition. Veterans like Joe Rolette and Alexis Bailly had easily overcome their aversion to settlers when they realized that commerce with Selkirk's colony could augment their bottom line. Promised provisions from Hudson's Bay arrived only sporadically or not at all at the colony, forcing desperate settlers to turn to American sources of supply. In 1820 the folks at Prairie du Chien had been surprised by the arrival of agents from Red River, who had made the grueling trek to purchase desperately needed provisions and seed grains. Shrewd agents there immediately recognized a promising market for goods and livestock. Rolette offered to deliver cattle to the colony at $100 a head, a price that proved too rich even for Selkirk's purse, but in the following years Rolette, Bailly, Michael Dousman, and a number of other American traders all made profitable cattle drives to Red River. Thus, the first diversification of commerce in Minnesota country grew on a north-south axis rather than with eastern markets. Within a few years, the ever-entrepreneurial Joe Brown also had his eye on commerce with the Métis community at Pembina. "At this time," he noted, "there is no other place for those people to get their necessaries, nor had [there] been for several years, this has caused that compy [Hudson's Bay] to change its conduct towards those people, and they are discontented and would jump sky high at the chance of throwing off the yoke."[17]

By the 1820s the fur trade economy in Minnesota country was already evolving into an ad hoc mixture of barter, credit, and cash exchange, with cash-poor traders scrambling to find additional sources of income. The establishment of Fort Snelling brought much needed new streams of income into the region, opportunities for traders to pick up temporary government jobs as interpreters, guides, or farming instructors for generally indifferent Indians. More lucratively, savvy operators like Sibley used their political connections to secure government contracts that provided reliable income to shore up their otherwise unpredictable annual returns. Sibley struck a deal to manage the sutler's store at Fort Snelling for 50 percent of the profits, which accorded him a near monopoly in providing goods to soldiers, civilians, and nearby Indians. He also secured the government mail contract, another political plum and reliable source of cash. By the 1830s the federal government was becoming an increasingly important prop to the region's economy.[18]

Even more alluring were the pine forests of the St. Croix watershed. For years both longtime traders and freebooters had been illegally harvesting timber on Indian lands. But their operations were necessarily small scale and precarious, always at risk of eviction or arrest by the military or, more dangerous still, confrontation with the Indians whose lands they were stripping. By the 1830s more respectable players in the fur trade were vying for a stake in the game, attempting to bypass federal prohibitions against logging on Indian lands by negotiating timber leases directly with the tribes. But not even prominent American Fur Company agents like Henry Sibley, William Aitkin, or Lyman Warren were able to wheedle government sanction for large-scale ventures. Frustration mounted as the market for timber grew exponentially each year. Word around Fort Snelling in 1836 was that "pine boards are now selling at Galena, St. Louis, and the intermediate towns at Sixty dollars per thousand feet! And one-twentieth part of the demand cannot be supplied." Inevitably, the government felt growing pressure from politically connected potential investors and would-be lumber barons to provide them legal access to the pineries of the north. Alexis Bailly expressed a common sentiment of the westerners when he somewhat disingenuously bemoaned, "Is it to be expected that a population like that of the valley of the Mississippi above St. Louis to suffer for want of Lumber because a few miserable Indians hold the country?" Though the interested parties were far more concerned with turning timber into gold than with town builders "suffering" from a lumber shortage, a general consensus was growing that the time had come for the United States to take rightful ownership of the pinelands and put them to "useful" purpose. Thus, the whipsaw rather than the plow carried manifest destiny into Minnesota country.[19]

At first, politicians in Washington were reluctant to sanction treaty negotiations for territory in the western Wisconsin–eastern Minnesota region. Plenty of unclaimed land was already available for western settlement, making further expansion at that time an unnecessary expense. Moreover, reports suggested that the territory in question was not particularly promising for agriculture. The pressure for treaty making instead emanated from multiple voices in Indian country, groups with widely different stakes in the outcome. Along with outside speculators hungry to claim the timberlands, fur traders, reformers, mixed-blood people, and even many Ojibwes and Dakotas were eager to work out a land exchange.[20]

[130]

In 1836 Indian agent Lawrence Taliaferro led the charge to begin treaty negotiations. Whatever his shortcomings or cultural blindness might have been, Major Taliaferro was steadfast in his determination to serve Indian interests. His unswerving belief that only a shift from hunting to agriculture could stave off disaster for the Indians grew with each passing year. He despised the traders who, in his estimation, used contraband whiskey as a tool to exploit and degrade Native people. Moreover, the eastern bands could barely eke out a living on lands that had been nearly stripped of game for either pelts or food. The Mdewakantons along the Mississippi were in the greatest need. By the 1830s the scarcity of game had reduced the once proud warriors to a state of near dependency. In 1835 even the respected chief Wakinyatanka (Little Crow) had come to the agent, asking for a "plough and a yoke of oxen and a man to assist in opening a farm." Times were desperate indeed. The annuities received from the 1830 treaty, small as they were, provided some relief for the suffering people, and Taliaferro frequently used his own funds to supply much-needed meat and flour. According to Taliaferro's plan, in return for their lands east of the Mississippi, where only one Mdewakanton village remained, the tribe would receive a substantial payment and annuities that would free them from dependence on the traders and help them transform themselves into farmers. In addition, most of the volatile clashes between the Dakotas and Ojibwes occurred in and around the contested zone between the Mississippi and St. Croix rivers. The proposed treaty would eliminate that battlefield and hopefully effect more peaceful relations between the tribes.[21]

Serendipitously for Taliaferro's case, in 1836 Wisconsin Territory was organized, with the Missouri River as its western boundary. Henry Dodge, the freshly appointed territorial governor, also became superintendent of Indian Affairs for the region and Taliaferro's immediate superior. Dodge was eager to eliminate Indians from the eastern part of the territory in order to accelerate settlement. To bolster his case, he made the plea to officials in Washington that a land-cession treaty was also a humanitarian imperative. Freebooting timber cutters were illegally clearing Ojibwe and Dakota land, depriving the Indians of just compensation. By taking possession of the pinelands, the government would right this egregious injustice to the tribes.[22]

Protestant missionaries added their voices in support of a treaty. Like Taliaferro, they considered themselves advocates for Native people and shared his commitment to saving them by remaking them in the white man's image. The missionaries also looked forward to an education allotment, as was included in the 1830 treaty, that would help support their efforts to establish and maintain mission schools. Though the missionaries may not have carried much direct weight among politicians, their advocacy and that of their home congregations added moral legitimacy and public support for claims that the treaties represented a humane Indian policy.[23]

Taliaferro had expected the American Fur Company and its traders to marshal their considerable resources to oppose the treaty. Two hundred years of experience had proved the axiom that settlement killed the trade. But even without settlers, the trade in Minnesota country was bleeding a slow death. Ramsay Crooks and his American Fur Company agents on the Mississippi were quick to realize that a properly crafted treaty could be their financial salvation. The key, as modeled in treaties enacted with other tribes, was to include compensation for Indian debts in the payment provisions. Since credits rolled over from year to year, a treaty payout was a once-in-a-lifetime opportunity to clear paper debts that stretched back over a generation. When a financial panic in May 1837 brought the nation's banking system to the brink of collapse, the price for furs dropped precipitously, adding to the urgency that drove traders to shed their former distaste for settlement schemes. As Hercules Dousman grimly noted, without treaty payments "we were gone coons." Thus, an unlikely alliance of traders, reformers, and politicians joined forces to press for treaty negotiations to begin.[24]

As for the Ojibwes and Dakotas, who were the most important players in the game, a significant number of tribal members, including key influential chiefs, considered cession of a small part of their lands a reasonable, if not ideal, solution to the problems that beset them. Enmeshed in the credit system, they had learned the power that hard cash carried. Traders no longer honored the old obligations of the trade. As losses mounted, some traders even tried to repossess guns, kettles, knives, and other necessities from Indians who failed to cover their debts at the end of the season. Increasingly, traders granted credit selectively, only to those they deemed "good risks." The elderly or less able were left to fend for themselves, a nearly impossible task in the depleted lands east of the Mississippi. Even the best hunters had to scour the woodlands to bring in pelts, which caused frequent and wearying clashes between the tribes. As one Mdewakanton sadly told Taliaferro in 1836, "It seems that everything is changed for the worse."[25]

Though in Indian culture land was not a commodity to be bought and sold, Native people clearly understood the monetary value that white men extracted from their lands and resources and how that money, which was rightfully theirs, could alleviate the suffering of the tribes. While the Indians endured shortages of food and necessary goods, a growing cohort of rogue timber cutters made illegal profits from Native pinelands. Incensed chiefs frequently petitioned Taliaferro and Ojibwe agent Henry Schoolcraft, demanding compensation for the theft. The Ojibwe chief Iaubus (Little Buck) complained to Schoolcraft in 1834 that Joe Brown and his men were cutting timber "without asking our permission, nor have we received any remuneration whatever in lieu of those logs." Dakota spokesmen made similar claims on Taliaferro. Out of necessity then, while Indians maintained an internal culture of mutual obligation and collectivism, in dealing with whites they adapted to the harder rules of monetary exchange. They understood that money had become the currency of power.[26]

The Tangled Road to Land Cession

By the summer of 1837 Congress could no longer ignore the clamor from the West and agents were authorized to negotiate the first major land cession in the Upper Mississippi River valley. Looking back on the sorry history of broken promises and disastrous consequences of U.S. Indian policy, sympathetic chroniclers have often portrayed Indians simply as dupes or victims, exploited by both the government and unscrupulous traders. However, as noted historian Gary Clayton Anderson argues, in 1837 "there is no reason to believe Dakota leaders felt they had lost control of their political destiny." Nor could they predict the consequences of what seemed at the time to be a rational decision. As the government's representative, Major Taliaferro had repeatedly proved a trustworthy advocate, and as much as the trading culture had become debased, the trade itself was still the essential prop for Indian livelihoods. Most Dakotas also retained some faith in the personal relationships forged with their traders and favored repayment of outstanding debts. As they saw it, the fortunes of the Indians and traders were intertwined since they "lived by their traders," most of whom they regarded as kin by birth or marriage. Many petty traders were of mixed Indian and European parentage, which further blurred the line between Indian and trader interests.[27]

The Ojibwes, with a skepticism born of experience, may have required more persuasion or perhaps dissembling. But they too were dependent on the trade and very likely were strongly influenced by Métis traders who were members of their families. When 1,200 Ojibwes congregated at Fort Snelling on July 29 to work out the land cession, it may have seemed a rational, if unpalatable, solution to their problems. On the other hand, many of the participants at the council had no stake whatever in the outcome. The government had made no distinction among the many bands scattered throughout the vast Ojibwe realm; those who signed the treaty included representatives from as far west as Red and Leech lakes who had no authority to speak for the eastern bands. According to at least one source, many representatives from the lands in question did not even arrive at Fort Snelling until after the negotiations were completed and thus had no voice in the disposition of their homelands. Nonetheless, on behalf of the "Chippewa Nation," the assembled chiefs agreed to the cession of sixty million acres of timberland in present-day western Wisconsin and eastern Minnesota. In return, they were to receive $700,000 in goods and annuities to be distributed over twenty years, along with blacksmith shops, farm implements, and a school fund if they desired one. In addition, $100,000 was to be distributed among their mixed-blood relatives—"half-breeds," in the language of the treaty—and a whopping $70,000 was designated to pay Ojibwe debts to traders.[28]

Accounts of the event suggest that more than a little fraud and chicanery accompanied the negotiations, along with the dubious credentials of some of the treaty participants. Hercules Dousman and "another Sioux trader" rushed in at the last moment to present some blatantly specious claims, and wily William Aitkin, head of the Northern Outfit based at Fond du Lac, walked away with $28,000. Lyman Warren, arriving from Leech Lake with a large band of Pillager supporters (described by Henry Sibley as "howling red devils"), managed to force insertion of a claim for $25,000 into the treaty, despite Taliaferro's threat to shoot him on the spot. Chief Hole-in-the-Day, an elder of the Gull Lake Ojibwes, urged the agent to fire, but at the insistence of territorial governor Henry Dodge, cooler heads prevailed and the treaty was somehow concluded.[29]

Despite such dubious machinations, the Ojibwes won a provision that was rare among the hundreds of treaties enacted between the U.S. government and Indian tribes and set a precedent for future treaties with the tribe. Though the government acquired legal title to the lands, the Ojibwes retained "the privilege of hunting, fishing, and gathering the wild rice, upon the lands, the rivers, and the lakes included in the territory ceded." In other words, they did not face removal. Though these rights could be withdrawn at "the pleasure of the President," for the immediate future at least, they had wrested a compromise they could live with.[30]

Agent Taliaferro was far less sanguine about the treaty's outcome. Outraged by what he regarded as "plain fraud traded on the helpless Indians" by his old enemies, the traders, he was determined that the upcoming treaty with the Dakotas should be free of their pernicious influence. Unlike conditions at the Ojibwe treaty, only Mdewakantons, the band with claim to the land east of the river, were to be party to the Dakota negotiations, and traders in the region were already hard at work wooing their support for repayment of traders' uncollected credits.[31] As the Ojibwe negotiations had shown, Fort Snelling was far too vulnerable to meddling traders and mixed bloods. Indeed, Hercules Dousman urged Sibley to "leave no *stone unturned* to get something handsome for us." Sibley took his partner's advice to heart. Recognizing Taliaferro as his greatest obstacle, he had enlisted Ramsay Crooks, the head of American Fur, to lobby his contacts in Washington to prevent the major's appointment as a treaty commissioner. Somewhat surprisingly, Taliaferro not only survived the campaign against him, he secured permission to hold the treaty negotiations in Washington. On August 18, before the traders knew what was happening and with the assistance of several mixed-blood assistants, the major covertly assembled a delegation of twenty-one Mdewakanton chiefs and subchiefs and spirited them away by steamboat. In an almost comic scenario, nearly a dozen traders, including Sibley, Bailly, and Brown, frantically took off down the river after them in a race to Washington City.[32]

Ostensibly, the trip to Washington had a twofold purpose: to hold a peace parlay between the Dakotas and their perennial enemies, the Sacs and Fox, and to negotiate cession of the delta between the St. Croix and Mississippi rivers, fixing the Mississippi as a permanent boundary between the Dakotas and white settlers. However, when Sac and Fox representatives failed to appear, negotiations for the land cession began at once. Though some sources insist that the Dakotas were lured to the capital under false pretenses, intending only to take part in a peace treaty, evidence strongly suggests that they had decided, however reluctantly, to part with at least some of their lands before they left Fort Snelling. As treaty negotiations briefly faltered over the terms of the agreement, the subchief Okapota stood and asserted that his people "did not come to Washington to go home empty."[33]

The Dakotas were quite aware of the value of the land they were ceding and initially set a price on it of $1.6 million, but desperate conditions at home limited their negotiating leverage when the government balked at their proposal. They were determined to bring relief to their kin, though as Chief Iron Cloud admitted, he was "uneasy about giving up these lands as you would not give us our price" and worried that the people at home would not be satisfied. When the treaty was signed on September 29, 1837, the Mdewakantons gave up "all their land, east of the Mississippi river, and all their islands in the said river" for a complicated formula of compensation that created a $300,000 trust fund that would pay out no less than an annual 5 percent annuity (about $15,000) in perpetuity. The band also was to receive an annual distribution of $25,000 in food, goods, farm equipment, and services for twenty years, as well as immediate delivery of $10,000 in agricultural tools and livestock. In addition, $110,000 was allocated for mixed-blood "relatives and friends of the chiefs and the braves," who were ineligible to receive annuity payments. Finally, over Taliaferro's objections, $90,000 was designated to pay debts to the traders—a seemingly exorbitant sum, yet a little more than a third of the debts that they had claimed.[34]

Ironically, though traders had long ago given up negotiating collective trading arrangements with villages and bands and dealt with the Indians on an individual basis, when it came time to balance the accounts, debt repayment became the burden of the entire tribe—a patently unjust formula. Clearly traders had intended to wring as much as possible from the Indians' settlement, yet tellingly the chiefs themselves had insisted that the treaty add $10,000 to the traders' share, as well as $20,000 to the mixed-blood payment. Apparently, at least from the Indians' perspective, old loyalties and intertwined self-interests had not yet been entirely severed.[35]

Cascading Consequences

The land cessions, painful as they were, left the Dakotas and Ojibwes in a generally optimistic frame of mind. The terms of the treaties seemed to promise both immediate relief and long-term security. But neither tribe was prepared for the speed at which events moved once the treaties were signed. The ink was barely dry on the Ojibwe treaty before timber speculators began converging on Fort Snelling and soon literally hundreds of small operators ranged up and down the St. Croix River, ignoring the fact that the treaties had yet to be ratified. Squatters from the reserve also began moving across the river, claiming choice pieces of Dakota land, building cabins, and planting crops. Little Crow complained to Taliaferro that he wanted them ordered away: "These things seem hasty on their part. They might at least wait until the news of our treaty is fully known." Steamboat traffic boomed the following spring, passengers eagerly hanging over the rails to get a look at what the newly opened lands had to offer. The only things that didn't come up the river that season were the provisions and monies promised to the Indians and the traders.[36]

In the midst of an economic depression, Congress was reluctant to approve what seemed extravagant treaty expenditures for lands so far beyond the boundaries of civilization. The debate dragged on for nearly a year before the treaties were finally ratified in June 1838, and more months ticked by before any funds or supplies were disbursed. The traders, on the brink of financial ruin, were beside themselves. Not only were they desperately short of cash, but many Indians, expecting their annuities and supplies, had refused to hunt for the market that winter. Hercules Dousman fumed to Sibley that the Mdewakantons "say it is not necessary to work for the traders any more as they will now have plenty to live on independent of the traders' goods." Instead, as fall turned to winter without word from Washington, the eastern Ojibwes and Dakotas once again faced near starvation. Tension between whites and the disillusioned Indians escalated to an unprecedented level. The Indians slaughtered cattle and livestock, both for food and revenge, and imminent violence was in the air. With only fifty men in the garrison at Fort Snelling, the military would be helpless to keep order if hostilities broke out. In June 1839 a despairing Taliaferro begged Washington for relief: "Give me something satisfactory by which the feelings of the Indians may be calmed. . . . What mortal man could do—has been done, and will continue to be done to keep my *miserable and starving people* quiet until we hear from you." And still the weeks passed without relief. When a steamboat appeared in July on the St. Croix (the first to navigate that river), expectant Ojibwes gathered near present-day Stillwater,

Minnesota, to collect their annuities. Instead the boat brought workmen and equipment to construct the first commercial sawmill in the St. Croix valley—a cruel irony for the waiting Indians.[37]

Finally in October steamboats loaded with goods and food began to arrive at Fort Snelling, but the goods were a peculiar and disappointing assortment. Unable to supply enough guns, blankets, and kettles to complete the $10,000 requisition, St. Louis provisioners had filled out the order with a bizarre array of items that were useless to the Indians—fine cloth, handkerchiefs, even castanets—charged to their account at "scandalous prices."[38] Some 1,100 Ojibwes waiting at Stillwater did not receive their shipment until November. According to a lumberman who was present, the late disbursement created a tragic debacle:

> While there receiving it the river and the lake froze up, and a deep snow came on; thus all their supplies, including one hundred barrels of flour, twenty-five of pork, kegs of tobacco, bales of blankets, guns and ammunition, casks of Mexican dollars, etc., all were sacrificed except what they could carry off on their backs through the snow hundreds of miles away. Their fleet of birch canoes they destroyed before leaving, lest the Sioux might have the satisfaction of doing the same after they left.
>
> Many of the old as well as the young died from overeating, they being nearly starved. Thus their first payment became a curse rather than a blessing to them, for their supplies soon gave out, the season for hunting was past, they were away from home and had no means of getting there except by wading through the deep snow.[39]

The Indians were justifiably angry about the delays and quality of the goods they received, and the Dakotas were even more incensed to discover that no annuity payments would be forthcoming until the following year when sufficient interest had accrued on their $300,000 trust fund—a financial detail that the treaty commissioners had failed to discuss with them. The traders and mixed bloods, however, faced no similar delay. When the treaty monies finally arrived, their immediate troubles were over—though most of the funds ended up in the coffers of the American Fur Company to satisfy the traders' outstanding debts. Still, with what was left and with the payments made to their mixed-blood children, most must have been quite satisfied with the outcome. Joe Brown netted a tidy $3,000 and promptly quit the trade to settle on Grey Cloud Island (near present-day Cottage Grove) and dive into more lucrative pursuits—as storekeeper, farmer, timberman, town site speculator, and whiskey seller. From Brown's perspective, and that of other Euro-Americans in Minnesota country, the treaties spelled boundless opportunity.[40]

The traders added to their windfall through another, even more lucrative treaty. No sooner had the Dakota chiefs departed Washington than a contingent of Winnebagos arrived in the capital city, invited to negotiate yet another land cession. The Winnebagos, natives of present-day Wisconsin, had pushed back against encroaching settlement for more than twenty years and were considered a dangerous impediment to the growth of the new territory. Governor Dodge had thus made their removal a priority.

Effecting removal of the Winnebagos proved particularly difficult since they functioned primarily as small, autonomous villages dispersed widely throughout the territory and they seldom acted with tribal solidarity. The government had already signed a treaty with tribal representatives in 1832 but soon discovered that very few of the more than forty villages considered themselves bound by its provisions. The treaty itself had been stunningly ill conceived. The Winnebagos were to give up their traditional homeland and resettle in the "neutral zone," the very lands that the Dakotas, Fox, and Sacs had ceded to the government in 1830 to create a buffer between the warring tribes. Since conflicts among the tribes were most often precipitated by a contest over scarce resources, it seems unimaginable that government policy makers did not foresee that adding another population to the region would only replace one set of combatants with another. That is, in fact, what happened. The few Winnebagos who moved to the so-called neutral zone confronted enemies on every side and soon migrated back to their original lands.[41]

[137]

The Treaty of 1837 was a second try to relocate the tribe to the same inhospitable region, with more generous annuities, provisions, and services to act as an incentive to agreement. The treaty, which ceded all Winnebago rights to territory east of the Mississippi, even grudgingly allowed the Indians limited hunting rights on their former lands. However, the same problem stymied compliance. Unable to identify leaders who could speak for all the scattered villages, government negotiators gave treaty-making authority to "paper chiefs" of their own choosing who wielded little influence outside their own villages. Consequently, most Winnebagos ignored the treaty and continued, at least for a few more years, to live and hunt on their Wisconsin lands.[42]

The great beneficiaries of the Winnebago treaty were indisputably the traders, who had perfected their claims for "lost credits" to an art. The 1832 treaty had stipulated a total of slightly less than $2,000 to cover debts to traders, "acknowledged [by the Indians] to be justly due." Five years later, the 1837 treaty allocated $200,000 to pay claims that had been submitted—$40,000 more than the Ojibwe and Dakota debts combined. The traders were jubilant. With anticipated payments from the treaties, Henry Sibley hoped to close out his partnership with American Fur and return to Detroit, solvent if not wealthy. He wrote optimistically to his father, "I think it probable now that I shall leave this country next year, if I can arrange my affairs satisfactorily." However, government payouts to the traders had become a public scandal and Congress held up the Winnebago distributions for several years, keeping Sibley and his fellow traders from reaping the immediate profits they expected. Hercules

Dousman, still impatiently waiting for payment on the Winnebago treaty in 1840, complained, "Times have never been so hard on this river since it was settled." Still, in the meantime schemes abounded to wring often fraudulent profit from the treaties in other ways. The Winnebago treaty had designated $100,000 for mixed-blood relations. As the months rolled into years without the promised payment, avid speculators bought up anticipated mixed-blood claims for a quarter of their value. The Dakota treaty yielded similar opportunities for profit. One particularly bold profiteer even managed to secure a contract for $5,000 to remove a few Dakotas from one side of the Mississippi to the other.[43]

Agent Taliaferro viewed these events with profound dismay. The treaties had achieved none of the benefits he had anticipated. Instead, it seemed all his plans had been thwarted by unintended consequences engineered by unscrupulous men who made a "mock fulfillment" of the treaties. He felt personally compromised by the government's delay and incompetence in fulfilling its promises to the Indians, a delay that put their very lives in danger. Moreover, for the first time since he had arrived in Indian country, Taliaferro felt his life was at risk as well. Many Dakotas and Ojibwes had lost faith in the agent, holding him personally responsible for their plight—a bitter pill for the major, who prided himself on his honor and integrity above all else. He found it nearly impossible to hire the promised blacksmiths, teachers, and farmers at the unrealistically low salaries the government specified, especially now that the traders had no shortage of cash. He had succeeded in breaking the old interdependency between the Indians and their traders, but the traders, not the Indians, had reaped the benefits. Instead of the intertribal peace he had imagined, conflicts between Dakotas and Ojibwes escalated as the restive Indians milled about near Fort Snelling, waiting for annuities and provisions with their tempers rising. Whiskey fueled the volatile mix. With the east side of the river no longer under military rule, grog shops boldly sprouted like mushrooms on its banks, right under the impotent Indian agent's nose.[44]

The treaties had effectively unfettered the ceded lands from any enforceable government authority. Deep in the western wilds of Wisconsin Territory, the nearest civil authorities were hundreds of miles to the southeast. All restrictions were lifted and the result was a free-for-all. In this new "white man's country" a man could stake a claim, trade without a license, sell whiskey or anything else at whatever price he could command, and strip the timber at will. As old-timers and newcomers jostled to get the jump on one another, no law restrained them. The Upper Mississippi had never been so wild or lawless. Profoundly discouraged by the transformation the treaties had wrought, in 1839 Taliaferro resigned his post, writing, "I have the *sad consolation* of leaving after *twenty seven years* the public service as *poor* as when I first entered—*the only evidence of my integrity.*" With Taliaferro's departure, the Indians lost their most reliable and well-meaning advocate.[45]

The Indian Trade

The sudden infusion of government money into the region transformed both the economy and the relationships that had defined the world of the fur trade. From 1837 forward, Indian annuities rather than furs became the region's most sought-after extractable resource. The traders/storekeepers continued to extend credit to Indian customers, but increasingly repayment was preferred in the form of dollars rather than pelts. Even the terminology of the trade reflected a fundamental change. In local parlance it had become the "Indian trade" rather than the fur trade. As historian Rhoda Gilman notes, furs had become "only an incidental by-product."[46]

At first, annuities had seemed a boon to the Indians. In the tradition of mutual reciprocity, they had shared their lands with their "father" in Washington and in return he promised to care for the people's needs. A poor hunting season—increasingly common in the game-depleted Upper Mississippi River region—would no longer force hardship and starvation on hard-pressed villages. However, annuities created a new sort of dependence—on the good faith and competence of the federal government, both of which frequently proved lacking. The old fur trade relationships had undeniably come to advantage the traders, but the well-being of the Indians had still been essential to the functioning of the trade. Starving Indians could not hunt, nor could they bring in pelts without guns, ammunition, and traps. Thus traders, for their own self-interest if not for other reasons, had grudgingly continued to advance credit for provisions and supplies. In contrast, once the Indians had signed away their land, they had no bargaining power with faceless government agencies and could only hope that treaty obligations would be fulfilled.[47]

The first substantial land cessions transformed the Upper Mississippi from a fur trade frontier to one focused on development. With each passing year, Indian labor would become increasingly irrelevant; however, for another two decades Indians themselves remained central to the developing region's economy. Treaty payments and annuities, and the salaried positions that went with them, became the primary source of money flowing into the region. Traders and avaricious newcomers alike set their sights on extracting as much of the Indians' money as their inventive schemes could bring in. They gladly provided credit, marking up goods to many times their actual value, and they plied the Indians with whiskey to impair their judgment about the "bargains" they were making. Creditors made certain to be on hand to collect their debts when annuity payments were distributed—and they invariably made out handsomely. After an Ojibwe payment in 1838 at La Pointe, Ramsay Crooks estimated that "between their debts, and goods they bought here," American Fur walked away with "about $3,500 out of the $4,700 they received from the government." At a Winnebago payment in 1843 Hercules Dousman related that "I got $18,000 out of the $36,000 that was paid, but the Inds have at least $8,000 in their hands yet"—clearly an incentive for further finagling. As late as 1850, when removal had become the commonplace solution for the "Indian problem" throughout the Great Lakes region, Minnesota politicians lobbied to resettle Ojibwes and Winnebagos from Wisconsin *into* Minnesota Territory. As former fur trader Henry Rice confided to Alexander Ramsey, Minnesota's territorial governor, the Indians "should receive their annuities on the Mississippi River, say at or near Sandy Lake. . . . Minnesota would reap the benefit whereas now their annuities pass via Detroit and not one dollar do our inhabitants get altho' we are subject to all the annoyance given by those Indians."[48]

Some veteran traders exploited their former Indian trading partners with unscrupulous delight. Others, like Hazen Mooers, quit the business in disgust. A native New Yorker, Mooers had traded with the Dakotas for more than twenty years and raised a mixed-blood family at Lake Traverse with his Sisseton Dakota wife, Grey Cloud Woman. Long after other traders had turned away from old customs of generosity and reciprocity, Mooers, like his friend Joseph Renville, had continued to give credit with a generous hand. Refusing to comply with his employer's demand that he restrict his openhanded policies, he had been fired from his position with American Fur in 1834. For the next several years Mooers carried on as an independent trader, but the rampant avarice that followed the treaties drove him to give up the trade altogether. Settling his family on Grey Cloud Island (named in honor of his wife), Mooers took up farming and continued to follow customs of generosity with his Indian kin. According to missionary Samuel Pond, Mooers "had too many Indian visitors, who shared with him the products of his farm, so that he did not succeed as a farmer"—at least by Pond's standards. Nonetheless, he had a high regard for Mooers's character and observed that those who knew him "could hardly help regretting that it should have been his lot to spend so much of his life among savages." Apparently Hazen Mooers did not share those regrets, since he continued to live among the Dakotas until he died at the age of seventy in 1858.[49]

Other traders found themselves caught between competing demands and desires. Even those who wanted to preserve the fur trade in its traditional form could not deny that the years following the 1837 treaties were exceptionally bleak. A series of harsh winters and scarce game, combined with Indians' reluctance to hunt for the market, drove traders ever deeper into debt. Adding to their troubles, the market for furs was extremely weak. The humble muskrat, which had become the staple of the Mississippi trade, was selling for just ten cents per pelt. In 1842 the credit edifice that sustained the American Fur Company finally collapsed and the once mighty combine fell into bankruptcy. Despite his recent windfall at the Winnebago annuity payment, Hercules Dousman despondently declared, "My earnings of 18 years I can consider lost & I am used up root & branch."[50]

Even before the company's demise, Henry Sibley's hope to make a profitable exit from the trade was receding from his grasp. Bound by contract and debt to his partners and the company, he wrote in discouragement to a friend, "I have spent the flower of my life in the Indian country, in the hope of obtaining a competency. . . . I am fatigued almost to death by the vexation & trouble inseparable from the trade with the Indians." Like his friend Taliaferro, Sibley put a high value on his integrity and honor as a gentleman; but unlike the Indian agent, Sibley had to choose between fair dealing with the Indians he called "friend" and his personal interests. In the end, Sibley cast his lot with his fellow traders and soon became the most prominent figure in Minnesota's quest to become a territory and then a state. But bedeviled by the knowledge that his actions were at odds with his image of himself as an honorable man, Sibley tried to advocate for Indian rights even as he participated in the very treaties and schemes that spelled their disaster—an impossible compromise. Looking back in the 1880s, Sibley described the traders (and himself) in a most positive light: "[The trader] was regarded by the savages among whom he was thrown, as their superior, their counselor, and their friend. When sickness prevailed in their families, he prescribed for them, when hungry he fed them, and *in all things he identified himself with their interests* and became virtually their leader." However, in the years when the world of the borderland was unraveling, Henry Sibley knew well that his interests diverged from those of Native people and that he was participating in their exploitation. Standing between the past and the future, he was a man with what his biographer describes as a "divided heart" and unspoken regrets that he would carry for a lifetime.[51]

[141]

A Road Not Taken

For a brief time in 1841, Sibley believed a solution to his moral conundrum was at hand. For more than twenty years reformers had been advocating the creation of a permanent all-Indian territory that, once it had achieved the desired level of "civilization," might eventually be granted statehood. With the election of William Henry Harrison to the presidency in 1840, the political winds at last shifted to favor the reformers' utopian proposal. Two important Harrison appointees, Secretary of War John Bell and Wisconsin territorial governor James Doty, were strong advocates for the plan, which would have effected a virtual revolution in U.S. Indian policy. Bell and Doty immediately set to work to craft a treaty that would make all the Dakota lands in present-day Minnesota a permanent home for the northwestern tribes. As they envisioned it, the Indian territory would eventually have a constitutional government with a legislative body, elected by thoroughly assimilated Indian citizens.[52]

The plan seemed to have much to recommend it and garnered many advocates in the West. Newspapers in Wisconsin and Iowa territories, both eager to remove Indians beyond their settlement frontier, enthusiastically supported the proposed Indian territory. Fortuitously, the small white population in Minnesota country was more than happy to take in additional Indian bands and thereby capture the increased Indian trade that would come with new treaty annuities. Since white settlers had so far shown little interest in the region—put off by the common belief that winters were too long and the growing season too short to profitably sustain agriculture—the Indian trade seemed their best bet to turn a profit. Like Oklahoma Territory, which had been "permanently" allocated to the tribes of the Southwest, Minnesota seemed to have few prospects for profitable development, which made it the ideal locale, as one candid chronicler wrote, "into which to dump all the odds and ends of Indian tribes still left east of the Mississippi."[53]

The fur trade fraternity eagerly promoted the scheme, with Ramsay Crooks, his American Fur Company sinking under massive debt, its most ardent proponent. A permanent Indian territory, closed to white settlement, would function as a fur trade preserve and, more immediately, debt repayments vital to staving off impending bankruptcy were sure to be included in the treaty. Crooks had been forced to sell off the Western Outfit to Pierre Chouteau and Company the year before, but the partnership—Rolette, Dousman, and Sibley—still owed him significant sums. He anticipated $150,000 in trader payments from the treaty. The Western Outfit's partners were equally fervent in promoting the plan. Dousman wrote Sibley to do everything possible to ensure that the treaty negotiations went smoothly, urging him to "have the interpreters and Indians as much under your thumb as you can."[54]

Henry Sibley viewed his role more delicately. In his mind, the proposed treaty benefited the Dakotas as well as offering a way out of his financial difficulties. It proposed seven new Indian settlements and sweeping federal investment in schools, doctors, blacksmiths, livestock, seed, tools, roads, and other necessities for creating an agricultural society. Most important, those Indians who chose the farmer's assimilationist path would become eligible for U. S. citizenship. As Sibley wrote to Ramsay Crooks, it seemed the best of all worlds, "better calculated for securing the interests of the Indians and of the people in the country than those of any treaty which has been made with the north-western Indians." Governor Doty also intended to recommend Sibley as governor for the new territory, which no doubt added to the trader's enthusiasm.[55]

As for the Dakotas themselves, most were understandably amenable. This was a radical departure from all earlier treaties. True, they would have to share some part of their lands with other tribes, but in return for relinquishing only a small buffer zone to remain unoccupied by either Indians or whites (supposed protection from the "degradation" induced by white contact), the Dakotas were assured permanent exclusion of settlers from the proposed territory. In addition, as compensation for opening their lands to other northwestern tribes, they would receive a payment of $1.3 million in annuities and assistance. Those who chose assimilation had the promise of eventual equality as

PLATE 52

Plate 52. Seth Eastman, *Indian Burial Ground*, 1851–57, in Henry Rowe Schoolcraft, *Historical and Statistical Information respecting the History, Condition and Prospects of the Indian Tribes of the United States*, vol. 2 (Philadelphia: Lippincott, Grambo, 1851–57). James Ford Bell Library, University of Minnesota.

Newcomers to the region were intrigued by the Indian practice of burying their dead on raised scaffolds. These cemeteries were usually situated on elevated ground, making them easily visible to travelers curious about Native American lifeways. The location of the scaffolds shown in this painting may have been on Barn Bluff at Red Wing.

This haunting and spare image spoke to white curiosity about unfamiliar Indian rituals. Eastman's drawing can also been seen as an artist's memorial for a culture he thought was doomed. Eastman shared the conviction of his wife and many other Americans that the "hunting grounds of a few savages will soon become the haunts of densely peopled, civilized settlements."[55] The art and writing of both Seth and Mary Eastman aimed to curry sympathy for government policies that would "civilize" Indians by converting them to Christianity and agriculture, the only path to salvation they could imagine for Native Americans facing the pressure of white westward expansion. Many visitors to the region viewed the scaffolded graves as portents. "A coffin beneath an autumnal tree," Fredrika Bremer wrote, "was the first token which I perceived of this poor decaying people."[56]

PLATE 53

Plate 53. Seth Eastman, *Feeding the Dead*, 1869. U.S. House of Representatives.

Seth Eastman completed this oil painting depicting Dakota death rituals from the distance of the post–Civil War East Coast, after white settlement and Dakota removal banished these kinds of ceremonies from Minnesota. But in the 1840s, when Eastman was stationed at Fort Snelling, newcomers to the region could still observe scenes like this one. Instead of trying to bury bodies in the frozen earth, Indians elevated the corpses of the recently deceased onto platforms to protect them from scavenging animals. This painting shows how bodies were frequently placed in coffinlike boxes — an increasingly common practice over the course of the nineteenth century — and then wrapped in some kind of cloth or flag. In this case, the box was wrapped in scarlet and the scaffold was hung with a small kettle and a medicine bag to ward off evil spirits. The kettle contained food meant to ease the journey to the spirit world. Relatives visited the bodies of loved ones for many months, providing food, drink, and conversation meant to nourish the traveling soul.[57]

Plate 54. Seth Eastman, *Indians Travelling*, 1851–57, in Henry Rowe Schoolcraft, *Historical and Statistical Information respecting the History, Condition and Prospects of the Indian Tribes of the United States,* vol. 2 (Philadelphia: Lippincott, Grambo, 1851–57). James Ford Bell Library, University of Minnesota.

Minnesota Indians made only limited use of horses, which set them apart from western neighbors, who had a more fully articulated horse culture. Horses demanded care and food that was difficult to procure in lean winter months of this harsh northern climate. However, those families who could afford horses had a tremendous advantage in their seasonal migrations, when travois like the ones pictured here could be

PLATE 54

fastened to a horse's back. Families attached tipi covers, household implements, and even children in their cradleboards to the travois, which was crafted from attached poles that dragged behind the horse. Women walked behind the pack animals and carried on their backs any remaining goods, which were balanced by a strap that ran across the forehead. If there was an extra horse in the family, men would ride along with the pack horses.

Eastman's image — prepared for the Schoolcraft ethnographic volumes — cannot be read as a pure reflection of mid-nineteenth-century Native American life. The scene was composed to emphasize what Eastman saw as the barbaric distribution of work in Indian families. The artist's wife, Mary Eastman, asserted that Indian women bore "the burdens of the family. Should her husband wish it, she must travel all day with a heavy weight on her back; and at night when they stop, her hands must prepare the food for her family before she retires to rest."[58] This perspective of this scene also served as a dark portent, communicating what Eastman saw as the ultimate fate of Native Americans in North America. Members of this family have their backs to the viewer, which renders them anonymous. They appear to be in an inevitable and un-ending march to the west.

Plate 55. Seth Eastman, design for Minnesota territorial seal, 1849. Minnesota Historical Society.

When Minnesota became a territory in 1849, Henry Sibley asked Seth Eastman to design a territorial seal. The result was this watercolor, which showed a farmer in the foreground set against a backdrop of a riding Indian and the Falls of St. Anthony. When Minnesota became a state, the legislature initially discarded Eastman's scene in favor of a design submitted by Robert O. Sweeny. Governor Henry Sibley overrode the wishes of the legislature and retained Eastman's image as the Great State Seal,

PLATE 55

although he substituted the French phrase "L'étoile du Nord" (the north star) for the territorial motto "Quo sursum velo videre." For the 1858 state seal, Sibley also modified Eastman's original watercolor to have the Indian riding into the west and the plowman moving east. This reflected widely held assumptions about the fate of Native Americans in the new Minnesota.[59]

Plate 56. John Mix Stanley, *Camp of Red River Hunters*, 1853. Glenbow Museum.

Métis hunters based in Pembina greatly expanded the scale of buffalo hunts on the western plains in the 1840s in response to escalating demand for the hides of these iconic animals. By this time, the fur trade was no longer focused on beaver pelts, as inexpensive silk top hats had begun replacing beaver hats in popularity. The business practices of the trade were shifting as well. The old system of extending credit to Indian hunters had given way to a new world shaped by global market capitalism in which Métis hunting parties like the one pictured in this chromolithograph by John Mix Stanley became the primary suppliers of furs and buffalo hides to the market, which had its commercial center in St. Paul.

The *gens libre* — as the Métis liked to call themselves — considered themselves a new nation distinct from both whites and Indians. They lived by trapping and hunting, traveling to the north and the west of Pembina in search of mink, weasel, marten, and muskrats as well as the buffalo. Highly skilled horsemen, they perfected a system for hunting that made it possible to kill thousands of buffalo in a single day. The typical expedition — as pictured here — would include one thousand men, women, and children traveling in a brigade of carts. These expeditions maintained a military discipline, arranging their tents and carts in a tight circle that provided protection both

PLATE 56

from animal and human foes. Once in the hunting ground, "the captain reconnoiters the plain, and as soon as a herd of buffalo is discovered, assigns to each lieutenant his place in the hunt," a writer for *Harper's New Monthly Magazine* explained. As many as four hundred men would advance, "first at a slow trot, then at a gallop, then at full speed. As their speed increases, the earth trembles; but when the herd perceive their enemy, and begin to paw the ground and make off, the sound and shock are like an earthquake. . . . Each man has his mouth full of balls, and loads and fires at full gallop. As he seldom pulls a trigger until his gun is within a few feet of the mark, he hardly ever misses."[60] The end result was mass carnage. According to another observer, "The wake of the hunters is marked by mounds of dead buffalo, and the torn and trampled plain is deluged with blood.[61]

The hunters used their carts to transport the carcasses to the camp, where the women were responsible for skinning the hides, drying the meat for pemmican, and manufacturing tallow. Mass quantities of meat went unused. The industrial scale of these hunting operations alarmed Plains-dwelling Indians who were dependent on the buffalo for their subsistence and feared that intensive and wasteful hunting practices would quickly depopulate the region of game. They responded by attacking the Pembina hunters in an effort to drive them out of the hunting grounds they hoped to preserve for their own use.

PLATE 57

Plate 57. Robert O. Sweeny, *Pembinese Team*, ca. 1858. Minnesota Historical Society.

The furs collected by the Pembina Métis were transported to St. Paul in this type of cart, made entirely of wood and pulled by oxen. This same type of cart had been used by the refugees of the Selkirk settlement who fled to Fort Snelling in the 1820s; until the advent of the railroad, this was the most practical way of transporting people and goods overland in the region during the summer.

The distance between Pembina and St. Paul was about five hundred miles; the journey by oxcart took about thirty to forty days. Traders

PLATE 58

sold their buffalo tongues, buffalo robes, pemmican, and furs upon arrival. Then they rested their teams for several weeks, camping on the outskirts of the city. A favorite site was Larpenteur's Lake, a body of water situated between the present-day streets of Dale, St. Albans, Carroll, and Marshall.[62] Artist Robert Sweeny might have sketched the team shown at this rendezvous.

Plate 58. Oxcart train at Third and Washington, St. Paul, 1858. Minnesota Historical Society.

Oxcart trains from the north were critical to the economic development of the state's urban center along the Mississippi River. Pembina traders made St. Paul into a commercial hub, hauling enough pelts south to make the city into one of the largest fur markets in the country. Furs became cash, which was spent filling the carts with enough groceries, tobacco, textiles, clothing, and other manufactured goods to last a year. The Red River cart trade grew throughout the 1850s at the same time that the population and economy of the city expanded exponentially. The town's population diversified to include an increasingly large number of residents who were unfamiliar with the multicultural mélange of Minnesota's old fur trade culture. Even as they laid the bedrock for the economic expansion of St. Paul, these traders from the north were increasingly perceived as foreign in an Americanizing St. Paul.

Traders came to be regarded as exotic envoys from another world. One woman remembers how she was transfixed by the long procession of Red River carts during her early months in the region, when more established residents had told her to listen for the "squeaking of two-wheeled wooden carts."[63] Their drivers appeared barely "civilized" to new residents like Philadelphia native Robert Sweeny, who marveled at "their dark, coarse blue coats, glittering with a savage profusion of enormous buttons of polished brass; their long, waving sashes of the brightest red, and jaunty little caps, half Tartar and half French; even their loose trowsers of English corduroy or some dark woolen stuff, if not of elk or bison skin, down to the quaint and dingy moccasins."

PLATE 59

Their ensembles evoked "the wild, wondrous, and romantic" for this easterner. Sweeny was fascinated by his inability to assign racial classifications to the men from Pembina, whose complexions proclaimed "the intermingling of the Caucasian with the blood of the aborigines." This eclectic ancestry had produced a community that included "the dusky Indian with his arrowy raven hair, up through all the intervening tints of dingy browns, to the ruddy cheek and blue eyes of the fair-haired Gael." Sweeny displayed little awareness of the culturally cosmopolitan history of the region when he observed that "within the circle of their camp is heard a strange mélange of languages, as diverse as their parentage."[64]

Plate 59. Joel Emmons Whitney, view of St. Paul, 1851. Minnesota Historical Society.

St. Paul was still a frontier town when this early daguerreotype was made by Joel Whitney in 1851. The new territorial capital boasted only a few log houses of the cheapest construction, no regular roads, and many "strolling Indians," according to Alexander Ramsey, the first territorial governor.[65] The year before this image was created St. Paul had a population of 1,294 living in 384 dwellings. Over the course of the 1850s, the international trade in furs from the north helped to transform the community into a thriving metropolis. The fur trade created lines of communication that positioned St. Paul to grow into a commercial center after other industries eclipsed the cart trade in importance. By 1857, some 10,000 people resided in the territorial capital.

Plate 60. Sidney E. Morse and Samuel Breese, *Iowa and Wisconsin, Chiefly from the Map of J. N. Nicollet* (New York: Harper & Brothers, 1844). Minnesota Historical Society.

This map shows how the political boundaries of the region had rapidly evolved during the first decades of the nineteenth century. The area that would become Minnesota

PLATE 60

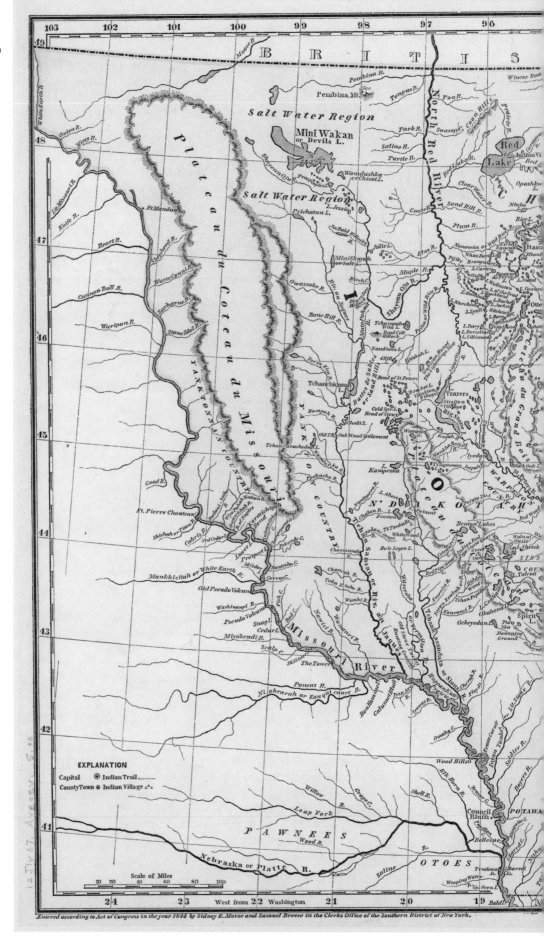

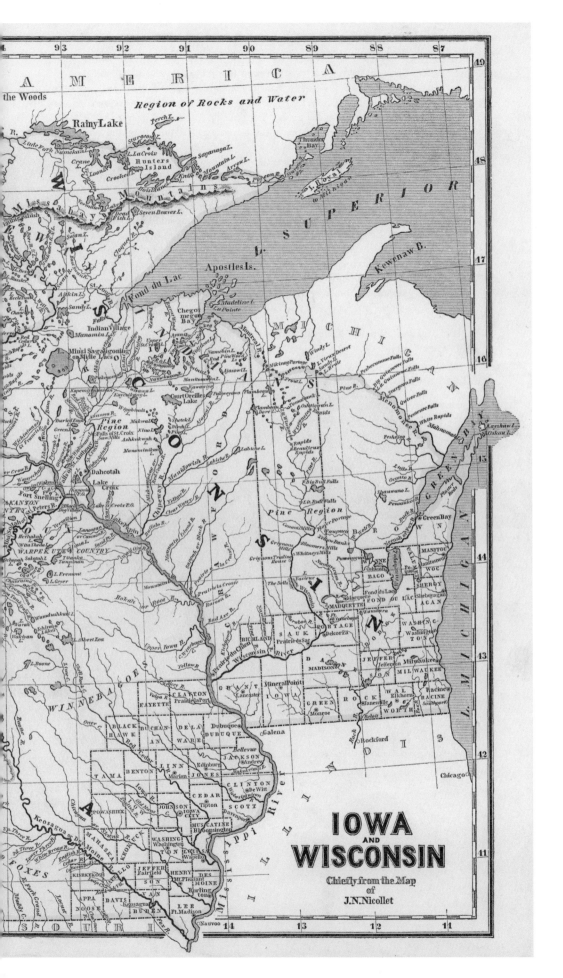

IOWA
AND
WISCONSIN

Chiefly from the Map
of
J.N. Nicollet

was divided between the territories of Wisconsin and Iowa. Iowa had become a territory in 1838, and some of its residents envisioned a future state that encompassed the Falls of St. Anthony and Fort Snelling. Under the leadership of Illinois representative Stephen Douglas, Congress drew the northern border for Iowa at its current location, hoping to carve another free state out of the region that had once been the Northwest Territory. Iowa was incorporated as a state in 1846, three years before Minnesota earned recognition as a freestanding territory.[66]

The area of the map detailing the future Minnesota emphasizes natural geography over human settlement, reflecting the fact that the 1840 census recorded only 351 non-Indians living in the St. Croix–Mississippi Triangle and 458 in the Lake Superior region. But mapmakers Morse and Breese had plenty of information about the region's geographic features, thanks to the meticulous survey of the Upper Mississippi Basin done by French cartographer and geographer Joseph Nicollet. The map also hints at the overwhelming changes about to engulf the region. County boundaries had been platted to the south and east, illuminating how white settlement was about to converge on Minnesota, binding the once isolated region into the political, social, and economic networks of the continental United States.

Plate 61. Frank Blackwell Mayer, *Indians of the Plains, Sisseton Dakota*, 1899. Goucher College.

On July 4, 1851, these Sisseton Indians rode into a tent city that had sprung up at Traverse des Sioux, an old trading post and mission station near present-day St. Peter. Their arrival was heralded by American treaty commissioners, who were eager to start

PLATE 61

Indians of the plains; Sisseton Dakota.

negotiations to buy the Dakota-held territory west of the Mississippi. This land purchase was the highest priority of territorial leaders like Governor Alexander Ramsey, who was one of the men who ultimately negotiated the cession with the Sisseton and Wahpeton bands. The difficult winters of the late 1840s had made Dakota leaders willing to consider a deal that would trade some land for annuities that would ensure basic subsistence for their people. It took a year for fur traders to woo Dakota leaders to the negotiation table, and the Dakota continued to assert their independence during the talks. The Indians portrayed in this painting kept the impatient commissioners waiting to start discussions, signaling that they were in no hurry to sell their land, despite past hardships.

Frank Blackwell Mayer was a young Baltimore artist who attached himself to the military and traveled to Minnesota in the summer of 1851, attracted by the prospect of thousands of Indians converging on the Minnesota River Valley. During this hot and buggy month, Mayer sketched a vivid pictorial record of the treaty negotiations, which he envisioned as one of the last opportunities to observe the native inhabitants of this region before they were overwhelmed by white settlement. Mayer used these sketches as the basis for this later painting.[67]

Plate 62. Frank Blackwell Mayer, *Sioux Evening Meal, Traverse des Sioux, July 20, 1851*, 1851. Newberry Library.

Treaty commissioners tried to entice the largest possible number of Dakota to the negotiations at Traverse des Sioux with unlimited food, a strong draw for people who had been starving since the region's game had disappeared. Upon landing at the treaty camp, commissioners gave an ox to a butcher "who divided it, surrounded by eager eyed Indians, evidently much in want of food," according to Frank Mayer, the Baltimore artist who accompanied the government officials up the river to the council site.[68] During the weeks of negotiations, treaty commissioners distributed government rations of pork and beef to everyone in attendance. Commissioners viewed this feasting as an effort by the Dakota to exploit government generosity; the Dakota perceived

PLATE 62

Sioux Evening meal — Traverse des Sioux — July 20. 1851.

Ball-play, Traverse des Sioux, July 1851.

PLATE 63

the provision of food as an essential part of basic hospitality. Plentiful food gave the Dakota the opportunity to engage in the lengthy deliberation that was essential to any important group decision, a process dismissed by government envoys as childish equivocation.

Plate 63. Frank Blackwell Mayer, *Ball-play, Traverse des Sioux, July 1851*, 1898. Goucher College.

The lacrosse games played by both men and women provided some of the most dazzling moments during the protracted treaty negotiations at Traverse des Sioux. Lacrosse was a sport familiar to Indians all over eastern North America. While haggling over the terms of the land cession at Traverse des Sioux, ballplayers from Kaposia challenged the local Dakota to a match that transfixed the entire camp. This painting does little justice to the visual excitement of the match. Artist Frank Blackwell Mayer waxed eloquent in his description of the players painting their bodies, donning ornamented breechcloths, and adorning themselves with "feathers & crests" before throwing themselves into the fray, "their bodies turning with serpentine ease & deerlike swiftness." He compared the players to "so many Mercuries, the brilliant colors of dress & paint, & the flashing armlets & diadems, & varied position leading the eye thro' an exciting & luxuriant chase."[69] While Mayer recognized the beauty and the skill demanded by the game, he had little sense of its diplomatic purpose. The Dakota used elaborate performances of ball playing, horsemanship, dance, and music to assert their position as a powerful nation that could not be forced into a disadvantageous agreement by domineering treaty commissioners.

PLATE 64

Plate 64. Ball stick. Collected in Minnesota by Giacomo Costantino Beltrami, 1823. Museo Civico di Scienze Naturali "E. Caffi," Bergamo, Italy.

This was the type of crooked stick used by the lacrosse players at Traverse des Sioux and elsewhere in eastern North America, where the game was played by all kinds of different Indian groups. Lacrosse sticks have nets at one end, which players use to catch and scoop a small leather ball. The object is to drive the ball over a goal line. The game and the sticks it requires were unfamiliar to nineteenth-century visitors like Mayer or Italian Giacomo Costantino Beltrami, one of the first tourists in the region. After arriving on the steamboat *Virginia* in 1823, Beltrami waxed poetic about the Indians he encountered and acquired several objects, including this stick, as souvenirs of his visit. These same kinds of sticks were still being used three decades later, when players at Traverse des Sioux mounted a display of their athletic prowess for the watching commissioners, traders, journalists, artists, and other denizens of the temporary treaty camp.

Plate 65. Frank Blackwell Mayer, *Encampment, Traverse des Sioux*, 1851. Rare Books Division, New York Public Library, Astor, Lenox and Tilden Foundations.

The treaty negotiated at Traverse des Sioux would ultimately destroy the delicate racial, political, and economic balance established by the fur trade society. Mayer's sketches from the treaty camp — which brought together all of the constituencies of this old order — provide the last glimpse from a world that would soon disappear. In the tents and tipis set up to overlook St. Peter's River in the summer of 1851, dragoons mixed with voyageurs; white soldiers befriended Indians; Métis and mixed-race Indians mediated the myriad cultural differences that surfaced during the heated debates over land cessions. Clothes proclaimed the cultural allegiances of their wearers. The sashes and caps of the voyageurs declared their intention to defend the world of the *gens libre* while Indians garbed themselves in a spectrum of costumes that broadcast their commitment to traditional lifeways or white accommodation. Mayer was both exhilarated and disoriented by his foray into this polyglot society where he "heard

PLATE 65

French & Indian spoken almost exclusively" and he faced "the countenances of for-eign appearance, French, Indian and half breed." Fur trade society rewarded people capable of crossing cultural boundaries; this ability would be regarded with suspicion in the Minnesota that emerged after the Traverse des Sioux agreement. The "foreign land" experienced by Mayer would be engulfed by a flood of American settlers to the region. The large American flag he sketched flying over the "camp and grave yard" served as a portent for a new political and social hierarchy grounded on the premise of Indian inferiority and the Anglo right to rule. The racially mixed people who had been at the center of "old" Minnesota soon found themselves struggling on the periphery of this racially stratified new world. [70]

Plate 66. Frank Blackwell Mayer, *Traverse des Sioux Camp*, 1851. Newberry Library.

The atmosphere in the treaty negotiation camp — which quickly swelled to two thou-sand people — was relaxed as commissioners waited for all the necessary parties of Indians to arrive. Between meals, campers lounged in their tents, reading and visiting with other residents of the impromptu community. Indians performed ball plays and dances. Other entertainment included "talks by the camp fire of frontier & Indian subjects"; the "wild, monotonous music" of Indians; and "canadian boat songs, or the

PLATE 66

national airs of old France with spirit by melodious voices" by traders and voyageurs of "French descent," according to artist and observer Frank Blackwell Mayer.[71] This sketch by Mayer captures a moment in one of these camp days. An enclave of white-style tents is foregrounded by two people who appear to be sharing an Indian-style pipe.

Plate 67. Frank Blackwell Mayer, *Signing of the Treaty of Traverse des Sioux*, 1851. Rare Books Division, New York Public Library, Astor, Lenox and Tilden Foundations.

The festive atmosphere in the Traverse des Sioux camp grew somber when discussions of land cessions actually began on July 18. Frank Blackwell Mayer made this sketch during the intense last days of the negotiations. Commissioners sat under the American flag, on the right side of this sketch. They were faced by Indian leaders, who were seated on a semicircle of benches. The space between the two parties was occupied by interpreters. Alexander Ramsey asked the assembled Dakota for all of their land in present-day Iowa and Minnesota. The Indians were stunned by the size of this request. Anguished discussions followed. None of the assembled Indians had expected that they would be asked to give up their entire homeland. Yet the need for annuities combined with a conviction that white settlement was unstoppable, regardless of their legal claim to the land, made acceptance of the terms inevitable.

Under the arbor of young trees depicted in this sketch, the Sisseton and Wahpeton Indians signed the treaty ceding their homeland on July 23, 1851. All of their lands in what is now Minnesota, Iowa, and the Dakotas were transferred to the U.S. government. This agreement encompassed some of the richest agricultural lands in North America. A large cash sum, which was promised to the Indians to "settle their affairs" and tide them over while they moved to their new reservation, went largely to traders like Henry Sibley, who viewed this payment as a settling of past debts. Sibley had been instrumental in bringing his long-term trading partners to the negotiations. Like many of his colleagues, he had family ties to the Dakota; traders typically had kin among the Dakota or were themselves mixed-race.

PLATE 67

Plate 68. Frank Blackwell Mayer, *Night on Keelboat*, 1851. Rare Books Division, New York Public Library, Astor, Lenox and Tilden Foundations.

The July 24 journey back to St. Paul was merry for the treaty party. Immediately after the agreement was signed, the tents that had housed the commissioners, traders, and observers like artist Frank Mayer were dismantled. The baggage was packed with great speed by those happy to escape the hot and buggy treaty camp. "With three good cheers," the keelboat pictured here was "pushed into the stream."[72] The boat carried fifty jubilant people — including the commissioners and traders — downstream, where officials planned to negotiate a second treaty with the Mdewakanton and Wahpekute bands. The boatmen smoked and sang to stay awake through the twenty-four-hour race back to Fort Snelling. "The greatest variety of voyageur songs inspirited the oarsmen, who were unremitting in their labours," Mayer recorded. "They were determined to be awake themselves, and permitted no one to be otherwise, for, at the end of every song, they varied the monotony of the chorus with an Indian yell which fully succeeded in destroying the slumber which we were seeking on the deck, wrapped in our buffalo robes."[73] The boat reached Fort Snelling at noon on July 25, and the commissioners disembarked, eager to negotiate the final agreement with the Dakota.

American citizens; those who hewed to traditional ways were promised the right to their lands in perpetuity. Skeptics may have been persuaded by the counsel of their mixed-blood kinsmen Renville, Faribault, La Framboise, and Bailly, who, along with the trusted Sibley, all had a financial stake in the outcome. According to Doty, the traders provided "indispensable aid" and expected to be compensated for their efforts. In addition, the governor spent $12,000 in gifts and food to win the Indians' assent. As a consequence, on July 31, 1841, at Traverse des Sioux, after only a brief parlay, the Wahpeton, Sisseton, and Wahpekute bands agreed to the treaty, despite the absence of several major chiefs, including Sleepy Eyes and Burning Earth. Four days later at Mendota, the scenario repeated itself. Mdewakanton leaders signed a similar agreement, though the respected chiefs Wabasha and Wacouta refused to attend. Despite their absence, Doty declared the treaty concluded, leaving Sibley with orders to somehow secure the missing chiefs' agreement. As the final piece of the massive land purchase, Doty negotiated cession of the half-breed tract along Lake Pepin, a neat disposition of the estimated 2,000 mixed-blood people who, in Doty's estimation, "float[ed] between savage and civilized life." Posting the terms of the treaty to Secretary Bell in Washington, Doty crowed that he had obtained some 35 million acres for less than $2 million, a tract that stretched from the Mississippi on the east to the Couteau des Prairies and from the neutral ground on the south to the Crow Wing River—a bargain indeed.[56]

Treaty proponents hoped for a speedy ratification. Nearly all the traders had been offered government jobs as well as the prospect of recouping outstanding Indian debts. Two-thirds of the Wisconsin legislature sent a petition to Washington endorsing the treaty, which they expected to stimulate their economy as well as resolve the troublesome "Indian problem." Despite the stated intention that the purchased lands would be "devoted to Indian occupation forever," the general belief was that the "buffer zone" would soon be open to white settlement. Secretary Bell flatly stated to Congress that the southern and eastern part of the acquired lands would be made available for sale at many times its purchase price. Speculators queued up to be at the ready. Vermont-born Winnebago trader Henry Rice, soon to be a major player in Minnesota politics, wrote to Sibley that he planned "to make the St. Peters my future home . . . destined to become the center of a great state. . . . I mean to be in on the ground and invest at every opportunity." The only opposition in the west seemed to come from the Sac, Fox, and Winnebago tribes who, when belatedly consulted, unequivocally refused removal to the new Indian territory—an impediment that was largely ignored by everyone else concerned.[57]

In Washington, however, the treaties faced an unexpected uphill battle. The sudden death of President Harrison only a month after his inauguration dashed the political fortunes of his appointees, Secretary Bell and Governor Doty among them. Animosity quickly grew between John Tyler, Harrison's successor, and his inherited cabinet, who resigned en masse before the treaties could be considered by Congress. With the departure of Secretary Bell, the chief advocate of Indian policy reform, opponents led by powerful Missouri senator Thomas Hart Benton railed against the "unjustifiable & reprehensible" provisions of the treaties. Benton was particularly incensed by the Indian "civilization policy." A dismayed Ramsay Crooks dispatched Sibley to Washington to lead the lobbying effort for ratification, reminding him that the future status of the Western Outfit "depends very much" on the outcome. The debate dragged on for months. Finally, on August 29, 1842, despite Sibley's best efforts and the not inconsiderable influence of Crooks and fellow fur trade mogul Pierre Chouteau, the U.S. Senate overwhelmingly rejected ratification by a vote of 26 to 2. In the end, whatever benefits the treaty may have included could not overcome biases of race and culture. The fervor of expansionism demanded that white settlement should march unopposed across the continent. There was no room in the American imagination for an Indian state that might someday gain equal entry to the body politic.[58]

[144]

As imperfect as Doty's treaty undeniably was, grounded in cultural imperialism and riddled with special interests, it made an attempt to eventually incorporate Native people into the national fabric. Culture rather than "blood" would be the ultimate test for citizenship. Subsequent treaties would make no such concessions. With race as the guiding principle, they were designed to cleanse Indians from the expanding settlement frontier. As prominent Minnesota booster James Goodhue would assert in the following decade, "Thousands upon thousands, in and out of Minnesota . . . are anxiously and impatiently waiting for [an expected treaty] and for the opening of the magnificent country, which is spread out west of us like a beautiful map—a country full of game and heavy timber, and delightful prairies and rich bottom lands—its resources of natural wealth not only not exhausted, but as yet scarcely seen." As for the Native people who held claim to those lands: "The[ir] civilization . . . is utterly hopeless; and the welfare of the Indians requires their speedy removal from a neighborhood which makes them daily more dependent, and in which they learn the vices, but attain to none of the virtues of civilized life." Goodhue's words exemplify the sentiments that drove a single-minded political strategy of dispossession, removal, and confinement.[59]

Broken Ties

The politics of race that shaped the development of the West in the nineteenth century infused the most intimate details of daily life. For two centuries white and Indian partnerships had sustained the fur trade, held together by marriage between traders and Indian women. Family formation had made the women full partners in the enterprise. They acted as diplomatic ambassadors and cultural mediators and they performed essential labor for the family and the trade. All of this accrued considerable prestige and autonomy for traders' wives, joined in enduring "country marriages."[60]

Still, it had never been uncommon for men who quit the trade to leave their wives and mixed-blood children behind, who would then return to the care of their Indian kin. By European standards, which defined the nuclear, individual family as the basic unit of society, such behavior constituted abandonment. However, most Native American societies defined the family unit in broader terms that incorporated parents, siblings, and extended kin. When Indian women married white men, they brought them into this circle of kinship. If the husbands departed, their leaving did not affect the primary relationships and support system that constituted family. Thus most women, given the choice, preferred to remain near their parents and kin. For instance, in 1814 Grey Cloud Woman, the Dakota mixed-blood daughter of Mar-pi-ya-ro-to-win and the British trader James Aird, left her trader husband when he proposed to take her and their children to a post far from her family at Prairie du Chien. Only after her father's death some years later did she agree to marry Hazen Mooers and move with him to a trading station on the St. Peter's River, along with her children and widowed mother.[61]

[145]

But with the advent of the Americans—soldiers, officials, and a new breed of gentleman traders, more interested in western development than incorporating themselves into the existing social order—the intimate relationships between men and women and the families that grew out of them became qualitatively different. The newcomers viewed Indian women as inherently inferior and desired them primarily as sexual objects or servants rather than as partners. While in the past, nuclear families had frequently dissolved when traders left the region, in this new era intermarriage itself grew increasingly untenable, leaving Indian women often exploited and then abandoned.

When the American military first arrived at Fort Snelling, soldiers, officers, civil officials, and their wives introduced a hardened racial taxonomy to the borderland that ultimately proved fatal to its existing hybrid culture. The ubiquitous Indian–white intermarriages that were the underpinning of fur trade society offended the newcomers' cultural sensibilities, both because most couples were joined *à la façon du pays*, without the sanction of Christian clergy, and because they publicly legitimized unions between whites and so-called savages.[62]

Men on the frontier were no less eager to seek female companionship among Indian women than they had ever been, but the arrival of even a few white women on the scene precipitated a profound shift in the social status of interracial relationships. At first the change was barely apparent. Veterans of the trade—men like Robert Dickson, Hazen Mooers, and Joe Rolette, who wielded far more influence than the military in fur trade country—had enduring relationships with their Indian or mixed-blood wives and extended Indian kin and proudly introduced their mixed-blood children to the newcomers.

The officers, officials, and their wives were in no position to pass public judgment on the mores of such influential figures and their families. They confined their distaste to private correspondence among themselves, often referring to the wives and daughters in denigrating terms—"dusky maidens" who were in need of the "gospel of soap." Agent Taliaferro, who had behaved with perfect courtesy and respect while at his post, later scornfully referred to Totowin, Robert Dickson's Yanktonai wife, as "the Colonel's esteemed lady (an old squaw)."[63]

[146]

White women in particular held fast to their cultural ideals, the touchstone to the familiar world they had left behind. These middle-class wives of officers, government officials, and missionaries were shaped by the nineteenth-century "cult of true womanhood," a racially specific ideal that defined woman's role as "pious, pure, domestic, and submissive," confined to the private sphere of household and family. The interracial partnership between traders and their wives—who paddled canoes, hauled packs, bartered goods, and involved themselves in every aspect of their husbands' enterprises—seemed to transgress all that middle-class white culture deemed womanly and proper. Consequently, most often the ladies disdained to mingle with Indian and mixed-blood wives. For instance, as Sarah Doty, wife of then territorial judge James Doty, reluctantly set up housekeeping in Prairie du Chien in 1823, she stayed aloof from the largely Métis community's social affairs. She was not "at ease" in the home of Joe Rolette, its most prominent citizen, and Joe's wife, Jane, a "gay, spirited, and beautiful" Métis woman, "did not appeal to the conventionally reared Sarah." Her evident distaste for the people of Prairie du Chien, and snub of Jane Rolette in particular, created prickly relations between her husband and Joe Rolette. Judge Doty, trying to assuage his wife's offended sensibilities and bring some semblance of civilized order to the region, made matters worse by mandating that all couples must produce certificates of marriage or face prosecution for fornication or adultery. The result was a wave of antagonism against the judge, who insulted their honor and dared to meddle in the residents' private affairs. The unpopular Doty soon relocated permanently to Green Bay, where he trod more carefully among the local customs.[64]

The authorities at Fort Snelling made no similar attempts to reform existing marriage customs. In the 1820s the fur trade and its agents still carried far more economic and cultural weight in the region than the American government. Savvy entrants into the trade continued to follow the example of veteran traders, forming families with Indian women, both to cement trading connections and in response to personal attraction. Young Philander Prescott ardently courted Spirit-in-the-Moon and honored his bond with her, their nine children, and her Mdewakanton family throughout his lifetime. But after fourteen years together Prescott felt compelled to legitimate his union with Spirit-in-the-Moon in a formal church ceremony conducted by Samuel Pond. The wedding may have been prompted by Prescott's newly revived religiosity or perhaps it seemed a necessary nod to changing conventions. In either case, it reaffirmed what had long been a genuine marriage.[65]

In another case, Joe Brown legally married three mixed-blood wives. Evidence suggests that his first two marriages—to Robert Dickson's daughter Helen and subsequently to Margaret McCoy, the Anglo-Ojibwe daughter of another trader—were unions born more of expedience than affection. Nonetheless, he acknowledged each woman as his legitimate wife and secured a divorce before moving on.[66] Brown's contemporaries roundly criticized him for his faithless ways, "a gay deceiver amongst the Indian fair," but in Indian culture divorce was an accepted practice that carried no shame.[67] Brown's third marriage, to Susan Frénière, granddaughter of old Chief Red Wing, was indisputably a marriage of the heart as well as a means to connect the trader with several important Dakota bands. Brown fell head over heels in love with the beautiful fifteen-year-old Susan. Long after intermarriage had ceased to be acceptable in polite society and despite his deep involvement in territorial and state politics, Brown never wavered in his commitment to Susan and their eleven children. After Brown's death in 1870, his contemporary Joseph Wheelock eulogized that "if he had not been dragged down by the slipshod half-vagabond associations and habits of his frontier life, from the high career for which he was formed, he would have been one of the foremost men of his day." Clearly, Brown's mixed-blood marriage had its political costs. Wheelock's assessment vividly testifies how profoundly cultural values had changed in one man's lifetime.[68]

Henry Sibley faced no such criticisms in later life. As one of the new generation of gentlemen agents dispatched to the West in the 1830s, he never seriously considered adding an Indian wife to the distinguished Sibley family tree, however much it might help his trading operation. As he wrote jestingly to a friend in Detroit, "We cannot boast of any but copper-colored beauties . . . and I have half a mind sometimes to take one to wife (as I would not meet with a refusal!) were it not that a certain Mrs. Sibley in your neighborhood might strenuously object to having a red daughter in law, be she never so pretty." While clerking for American Fur at Michilimackinac, Sibley and his fellows had freely taken their pleasure with Indian women, but only rarely did one enter into a committed relationship. The same was true at other bustling posts. Henry Schoolcraft's younger brother James reported from Sault Ste. Marie, "If the census were rightly taken, there is now 10 children in Embryo whose legitimacy may be doubted."[69]

Once Sibley had taken up his position at Mendota, however, his behavior was more circumspect, due perhaps to the watchful eyes of the officers' wives as well as his own self-conscious sense of the dignity of his position. Still, though he wrote in his autobiography that "I had no intention of taking to myself an

Indian maiden for a wife," he entered into a liaison with Red Blanket Woman, the daughter of Mdewakanton headman Bad Hail, who bore him a daughter in 1841. Sibley did not try to hide the paternity of his daughter Helen, but neither she nor her mother ever lived in his imposing home, where two years later he brought Sarah Jane Steele as a more appropriate bride.[70]

In the evolving racialism of the 1820s and 1830s, the small Anglo community at Fort Snelling considered such temporary "indiscretions" more respectable than an enduring intermarriage, whether *à la façon du pays* or sanctioned by clergy. It was perfectly acceptable for unmarried officers, or those whose wives were absent, to take up with Indian women as expedient companions. When missionary Stephen Riggs arrived at the fort in 1837, he was shocked: "Until my location here, I was not aware that it was so exceedingly common for officers in the army to have two wives or more—but one, of course, legally so. . . . There were but two officers who were not known to have an Indian woman, if not half-Indian children." Even Lawrence Taliaferro, who prided himself on protecting the Indians from exploitation by the traders, saw no hypocrisy in entering into what was clearly intended as a temporary arrangement with The Day Sets, daughter of Taliaferro's friend, Cloud Man. Their union produced a daughter, Mary, born the same year that Taliaferro married Eliza Dillon and brought her to Fort Snelling.[71]

Taliaferro and other Anglo fathers did not hesitate to acknowledge their mixed-blood offspring. Taliaferro readily explained to a visiting general that his daughter, Mary, was cousin to three other mixed-blood granddaughters of Cloud Man, each with a different set of parents.[72] But none of Cloud Man's daughters formed families with the white fathers of their children. Like Helen Sibley, the children either lived with their mothers' kin or were placed in foster situations with respectable white or mixed-blood families. While the ladies of fort society apparently overlooked their husbands' extramarital adventures, albeit with gritted teeth, they drew the line at accepting mixed-blood stepchildren into their homes.[73]

Sibley and Taliaferro took seriously their responsibilities to the children they had fathered, at least in terms of sustenance and education. True to their belief that only assimilation could save the Indian, they monitored their daughters' upbringing from a distance to make sure they did not take on the customs or traits of their Dakota kin. Sibley kept a discreet eye on Helen, who lived with a family just across the river in the infant town of St. Paul. He even paid for her to attend boarding school in the East for several years to school her in gentile refinements. Taliaferro, who left Mary behind when he resigned his post as Indian agent, feared that by living with her mother's people she would become too much like an Indian. Before he left the region, he arranged for her to join the household of Samuel Pond, where she would learn proper "habit and instruction in household matters." But, he cautioned Pond, "the indolent habits and aversion to light labours will have to be gotten over with these Half-Breeds by flattering their vanity—small rewards, etc." Despite the fact that Mary was his daughter, Taliaferro's words reveal that he regarded her still as fundamentally different from himself.[74]

Usually the major chose his words more carefully, at least in public settings, and he generally acted circumspectly toward the Indians and customs of the country. However, his writings often betrayed the racial condescension that simmered beneath his surface courtesies. As he revealed in his autobiography, what was termed marriage in fur trade country was, in Taliaferro's estimation, nothing but a sham. The women were simply commodities, "purchas[ed] from their parents" by licentious traders. After naming all the men licensed to trade in the region, he went on to say, "Most of these traders, and many of their hands, had the use of Indian women as long as it suited their convenience, and children were born to them." In this group he included Philander Prescott, Hazen Mooers, Jean Baptiste Faribault, Joseph Renville, and a number of others who were well known to maintain long and stable marriages. Taliaferro's portrayal described more accurately the slaveholding culture that had formed his own worldview. Perhaps in looking back, he ascribed the values that shaped his identity to a society that he never truly understood.[75]

[149]

Men like Sibley and Taliaferro, who considered themselves pillars of integrity, salved their consciences by taking at least some responsibility for their mixed-blood children. Many others had far fewer scruples. Soldiers at the fort were notorious for their exploitation of Indian women. Taliaferro related that "orders had to be issued by the respective commanding officers of the post excluding *Indian ladies* from daily and nightly visits to their friends in the Fort." In his opinion, the soldiers had taken on these reprehensible practices "after the fashion of the traders," who, to Taliaferro, were the root of all the prevailing evils. But in reality, the soldiers, unfettered by customs of the trade or personal relationships with Native people, carried exploitation to unprecedented extremes. Missionary Stephen Riggs declared in disgust that "once, in my childhood's simplicity, I regarded the army and its discipline as a school for gentlemanly manners, but now it seems a sink of iniquity, a school of vice."[76]

Since the first encounter between Indians and white men, marriage had been the primary means of creating and defining relationships. Even when the unions themselves were dissolved, the kinship connections they had created continued to be honored. Thus, when the new Americans on the frontier casually abused marriage customs and stripped such unions of their meaning, they undermined the foundation of the social order. At first the Dakotas encouraged relationships between their daughters and influential newcomers, expecting the unions to create bonds of obligation as they had in the past. Red Blanket Woman's Dakota relatives believed her brief relationship with Sibley obliged him to assist them in their needs long after he had ended the arrangement. And Cloud Man, who trod a more assimilationist path than most of his contemporaries, seems to have encouraged his daughters to form relationships with Anglo partners. Cloud Man and Keiyah (Philander Prescott's father-in-law), the headmen of Eatonville, Taliaferro's model agricultural village, secured important support for their people through their sons-in-law—though the stronger tie with petty trader Prescott reaped less benefit for the village than the more tenuous connection with the powerful Taliaferro.[77]

[150]

Despite the benefits that accrued to the village, a growing pattern of exploitation was painfully in evidence. The unusual number of women and children at Eatonville suggests that it served as a handy repository for dependents abandoned by soldiers at the nearby fort. The soldiers, like a typical army of occupation, exploited the Indians' impoverished circumstances to prey upon vulnerable young women, who were driven to trading sexual favors for necessities of life. Such sexual barter represented a crude perversion of the traditional Dakota custom of bride purchase. In Dakota society, a suitor was expected to offer payment for a bride—much like the European dowry custom, only in reverse. As missionary Samuel Pond explained, "It was as disreputable for a young woman to become the wife of one who had not purchased her, as it is with us for a woman to cohabit with a man without the ceremony of marriage. . . . Women did not consider it disgraceful to be bought and sold. The higher the price paid for them, the better they were pleased, for the payment of a great price proved that they were esteemed valuable." However, esteem played no role in the transactions at Fort Snelling. The soldiers treated the women as common prostitutes, purchased for a day for a bit of desperately needed clothes or food for their families. As year by year the Indians were forced deeper into dependency, the customs of exploitation became more widespread. Dakota chiefs frequently spoke out in protest but no longer had the power to enforce a code of behavior. Mdewakanton chief Big Eagle wrote sorrowfully in his memoir, "The white men abused the native women . . . and disgraced them." Where once the union of white men and Indian women had symbolized friendship and mutual regard, in the new racialized social order on the settlement frontier, contact with white men brought only shame and resentment to Indian women and their kin.[78]

The pace of change in these years was breathtaking. At the same time that treaty making hacked away at Indian lands and the reorganization of the fur trade eroded Native people's economic viability, a newly hardened racial ideology undermined existing social relations at their most intimate core. The first land cession treaties in Minnesota country were negotiated in 1837. A mere twenty-one years later, when Minnesota entered the Union as the thirty-second state, the borderland culture born in the fur trade had been thoroughly supplanted by a society shaped by white settlers. Native people soon would have no place in this new social and economic order.

Chapter 7

DRAWING BOUNDARIES

We are now near the dividing line of civilized and savage life. We can look across the river and see Indians on their own soil. Their canoes are seen gliding across the Mississippi to and fro between savage and civilized territory. They are met hourly in the streets.

E. S. SEYMOUR, *Sketches of Minnesota, the New England of the West,* 1849

Reimagining the Terrain

When "Doty's treaties" died on the Senate floor in 1842, all prospects for a west that would incorporate Native people into the American polity died as well. Once the proposal for an Indian state was resoundingly rejected, no white man in the West doubted that the entire region, soon to be known as Minnesota, was destined for white settlement and eventual statehood. People were already pouring into Wisconsin and Iowa territories and the march of westward expansion seemed unstoppable. Nonetheless, in 1843 few signs of this transformation were apparent in Minnesota country. The 1840 territorial census had counted only 351 non-Indians living in the St. Croix–Mississippi River triangle and 458 in the Lake Superior region—and most of those assuredly were partly of Indian heritage. The only communities of more than a few whites were rough outposts near Fort Snelling—Mendota, St. Paul, St. Anthony— and a few sparsely settled logging settlements along the St. Croix. Pembina, on the Canadian border, could hardly be included since its Métis population considered themselves "free people," neither white nor Indian and unattached to either the United States or Great Britain. Still, territorial boosters like Joe Brown envisioned a vastly different landscape in the near future.[1]

The winter of 1843 found Brown, his French-Dakota wife, Susan, and their three children setting up housekeeping on the Sheyenne River, west of present-day Fargo, North Dakota. The ever-resourceful Brown had once again taken up the business of the fur trade, drawing on Susan's kinship connections with the western Dakota bands. The Senate's rejection of Doty's treaties had forced Brown and his contemporaries to put their development schemes for the St. Croix–Mississippi region on hold, at least for a time. Until another, more acceptable treaty could be hammered together, they would have to resort to other means to put food on the table. Fortunately, the American market for buffalo hides was booming. Bison had disappeared east of the Mississippi, the last one sighted in 1832, but great herds roamed not far to the west. In 1840 a single day's hunt on the Sheyenne brought in 2,000 hides.[2]

[152]

Unfortunately for the American Fur Company, the demand for hides had come too late to avoid financial catastrophe. When Hercules Dousman learned that the treaties had failed, he bitterly observed, "Here is death to the great *Panacea* which was to cure all the lame *Ducks* and give the wherewith to so many to be joyful. It is no use to cry we have to swallow it as bitter a Pill as it may be—we shall have to work harder & spend less." But neither hard work nor frugality could save the company. Without the urgently needed treaty payments to cancel its mountain of debt, the once mighty firm toppled into bankruptcy. The company's competitors who had squirmed under its thumb wasted no tears on its misfortune. "The Great American Fur Company . . . has exploded," wrote one delighted rival. "Disappeared, overwhelmed with the most miserable bankruptcy. . . . They have met their just desert." Suddenly, with the giant slain, a clear field had opened for independent traders like Brown, who flocked to Lake Traverse, Lac qui Parle, and points west to establish trade with the western tribes.[3]

With the new vigor that infused the trade, it may have seemed on the surface that the old order had reestablished itself, but nothing could have been further from the truth. In the minds of forward-thinking traders, the quest for pelts and hides was a dying operation, a stopgap measure to tide them over as they went about the business of diversifying their interests. Shrewd entrepreneurs like Dousman, Brown, and Henry Sibley were busily investing in steamboats, timber, sawmills, and land, both as individuals and on behalf of the companies that employed them.[4]

Despite his relocation to the westernmost edge of the trading network, Brown kept his finger on the pulse of territorial politics to the east. During each of the four years he spent on the Sheyenne, he made frequent trips to Mendota and even to the Wisconsin territorial capital at Madison, a 1,200-mile round-trip trek. He was so eager to keep abreast of political developments (and protect his interests) that not even the gales of winter could keep him at home. In March 1843 he strapped on snowshoes and set off alone and on foot to tend to business in Madison. As he crossed the snow-covered terrain and tramped to the St. Peter's River, the land looked much as it had when Pierre Le Sueur had traded there in 1700. But in his mind's eye, Brown reimagined the undulating prairie, marshlands, and stands of hardwood as a landscape of future town sites and agricultural acreage, knit with a network of roads that would carry bountiful harvests to eastern markets. Similarly, when newly arrived Henry Rice paddled up the Crow Wing River to trade with the Ojibwes in 1847, he mentally translated the towering pines into board feet of lumber to be harvested.

In the Lake Superior region, officials and speculators scarcely noticed the spectacularly rugged terrain. Their attention was focused on what might lie below the ground. Precious seams of copper had already been discovered in Michigan's Upper Peninsula, and quite likely the western part of the lake region hid similar treasures. The same year that the Senate had rejected Doty's proposed Indian state, it cheerfully ratified a treaty wrung from the Lake Superior Ojibwes that ceded all their lands east of Fond du Lac and north of the 1837 treaty line. As in 1837, the primary interest in 1842 was in resource extraction rather than the land itself, which was considered unfit for agriculture. This was fortunate, since the Ojibwes had no intention of abandoning their lands. Robert Stuart, acting superintendent of Indian Affairs for the region, assured the Ojibwes that they would not be required to move in the foreseeable future. Since the land was undesirable for settlement, it "would not probably be wanted during your lifetime." As Stuart magnanimously explained, "You are to have the privilege of living on your lands to hunt & fish, till your father requires you to remove, you understand he does not want the land now, it is only the minerals he wants." According to Stuart, the Great Father in Washington knew the Indians were poor and offered to purchase their land only to help them. But in spite of Stuart's assurances, he had been privately instructed to prepare the groundwork for future relocation. The territory in question was located in present-day Wisconsin, but the Mississippi, Fond du Lac, and Sandy Lake Ojibwes were to be included in the negotiations and subsequent annuity payments. That way, the unceded land west of Lake Superior would become "common property," and the bands who lived there would have to take in the Wisconsin Ojibwes when the government chose to relocate them.[5]

With the assistance of traders and interpreters who were trusted and tied by kinship to the Ojibwes, Stuart managed to persuade most of the assembled chiefs to sign away the desired territory—some seven million acres for about four cents an acre. Based on their previous experience with government promises, the chiefs were not easily convinced. Wabijeshi (Marten), the head chief at Lac Courte Oreilles (in north-central Wisconsin), reiterated the conditions of the treaty before he signed to be sure there was no mistake, "that we should remain on the land, as long as we are peaceable. We have no objections to the white man's working the mines, and the timber and making farms, but we reserve the Birch bark and cedar for the canoes, the Rice and the Sugar tree and the privilege of hunting without being disturbed by the whites." Another chief who remained unconvinced considered the treaty "a lying, cheating concern, the whole of it." Others, though they put their hand to the pen, were equally dubious. But times were hard and the annuities and goods promised by the Treaty of 1842, along with the assurance that the Indians would continue to have free use of the ceded lands for fifty or even a hundred years, overcame their resistance to the offer. Once signed, the treaty opened the door to waiting prospectors, who hustled into the region. By 1845 forty-eight separate mining companies had filed mineral permits on the ceded lands.[6]

Anyone who resisted the juggernaut of "progress" did so at his peril. Lyman Warren, a twenty-five-year veteran of the trade who worked out of La Pointe, learned firsthand the cost of standing even slightly in the way of the oncoming tide. Once a successful and respected agent of American Fur and a partner in lumbering ventures with Henry Sibley and William Aitkin, Warren had fallen on hard times. Though he had famously finagled $25,000 in credits into the 1837 Ojibwe treaty, the company had taken every penny. As a further blow, the following year, Ramsay Crooks fired him from his post for alleged mismanagement. Then, forced to sell his lumbering interests to cover his debts, Warren was reduced to working as a government farmer for an Ojibwe band on the Chippewa River, his meager salary stretched to the limit supporting a family of fifteen, including the orphaned children of his brother. Understandably, Warren leaped at the offer to assist in the 1842 Ojibwe treaty negotiations, hoping to win a more lucrative government appointment.[7]

However, as the talks proceeded, Warren seemed to show a bit too much concern for Indian interests, a natural consequence of his family ties. Married to French-Ojibwe Marie Cadotte, Warren had spent most of his adult life at La Pointe, forging close connections with his wife's Indian kin as well as with the Cadotte household, the most prominent mixed-blood trading family in the region. La Pointe was a last bastion of the old fur trade society, where Indian and European cultures comfortably coexisted and combined. Marie Cadotte Warren never learned to speak English and her children were raised to respect both their Indian and Euro-American heritage, spending their childhood among their Indian kin, then shipped East to their father's relatives for the polish of a more formal, Euro-American education. Lyman Warren took his family responsibilities seriously, and evidence suggests that his sense of obligation included, at least to some degree, his extended Indian kin, who would be affected by the terms of the treaty he was helping to broker. Thus, it was natural that he shared the Indians' unease and felt a responsibility to watch out for their interests. Though it seems that Warren faithfully carried out his duties during the negotiations and the treaty was signed, it appeared to Superintendent Stuart that the trader was more concerned with the interests of his Ojibwe relatives and mixed-blood children than in easing the course of the negotiations. A few months later Stuart retaliated for this perceived disloyalty by summarily firing Warren from his post as government farmer. Stripped of the only means of supporting his family, Warren sank into a deep depression from which he never recovered. His son William described his father as "hopelessly insane, mainly through the troubles, losses and persecution . . . heaped on his poor head."[8]

As Lyman Warren's case illustrates, by the 1840s powerful economic and government interests were making their influence felt in myriad ways that affected the economic condition and social relations of everyone who lived in Minnesota country. White men could either wholeheartedly get on the bandwagon of progress or suffer the consequences of clinging to an outmoded way of life. Indians could only strategize to hold off the usurpation of their homelands as long as possible.

Race for Riches

The American ideology of free market capitalism fueled the ambitious plans of individuals to acquire and remake Minnesota country. But none of the schemes could have succeeded without the power of the government at its side. A legal infrastructure enforced by civil and military authority was necessary to legitimate claims and protect investments. In Indian country, boundaries had always been somewhat inexact, unless marked by the course of a river. As long as private ownership of land was not at issue, precise demarcation had been an unnecessary nicety. With the first land cession in 1837, however, this abruptly changed. As men scrambled to acquire their individual pieces of what had become "acreage" and "real estate," boundary lines became the stuff of legal disputes, fisticuffs, and even an occasional murder. Terms like "preemption" and "proving up" (which meant making some visible mark of ownership on the property) soon became part of the lexicon of daily conversation. Claimants hustled to the federal land office at Prairie du Chien and later St. Croix Falls, where they legally recorded ownership of their little piece of Minnesota country.[9]

As part of the United States, Minnesota did not evolve as an organic process, growing naturally into a territory and then a state as settlers made their way up the Mississippi. Political machinations and speculative ventures shaped its development every step of the way. Even its capital city was born as the consequence of a complicated power game involving private interests and government power. In 1837, with preparations for the first major land cession treaties under way, the War Department belatedly decided to clarify the exact parameters of the military reserve that Zebulon Pike had negotiated from the Dakota people in 1805. Since the reserve had been somewhat vaguely described in the treaty, the secretary of war left it up to Fort Snelling's new commandant, Major Joseph Plympton, to conduct a survey and submit a map "mark[ing] over" what in his opinion "will be necessary to be reserved" for the military's interests. By fiat, then, Plympton's map would define the boundary of the reserve, regardless of what the Dakotas had agreed to in 1805. This proposed

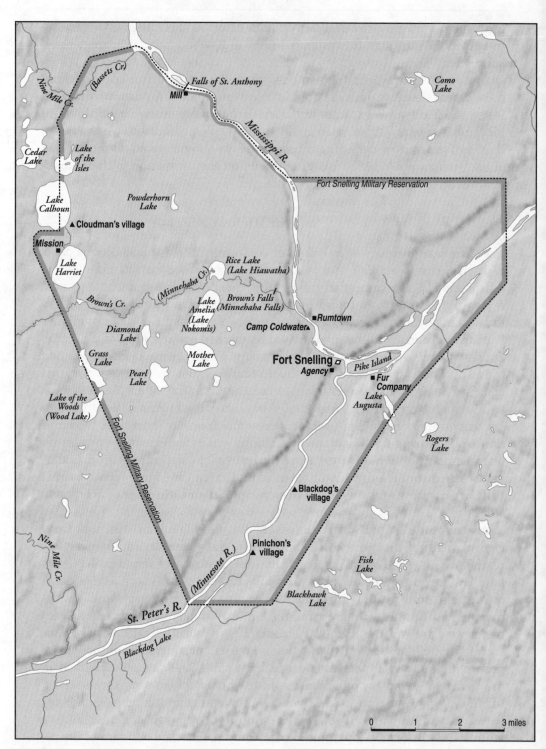

Fort Snelling military reservation, 1839.

redrawing of the reserve set off a wave of anxiety among the people who had settled on the west side of the river. A series of post commandants had allowed and even encouraged squatters to make homes on the reserve, since their live-stock and gardens served as a reliable source of food for the garrison. By 1837 the original little contingent of Red River emigrants and itinerant fur trade personnel had grown to a substantial cohort of 157 persons "in no way con-nected with the military." With good reason they feared that they were about to be evicted, since they could make no legal claim on the land. Plympton had already demonstrated that the "era of good feeling" was about to come to an end, having complained about civilians chopping down firewood and timber needed for the fort, keeping cattle that broke down fences and trampled gov-ernment gardens, and illegally selling whiskey to the garrison's soldiers. Some of the settlers had a great deal to lose. Abraham Perret (Perry), for instance, who had settled near the fort in 1827, had built up a substantial farm with the help of his wife, Mary Ann, who contributed to the family's income with a thriving practice as midwife to the ladies of the fort. A "great cattle raiser," Perret at one time was said to have "owned more cattle than all the rest of the inhabitants of what is now Minnesota," excluding Joseph Renville.[10]

In addition to settlers like Perret, the entire hamlet of Mendota, which counted twenty-six residents, was technically within the reserve. As a licensed fur trader, Henry Sibley, the "Squire of Mendota," was not in danger of evic-tion, but he had a substantial investment in additional buildings and livestock that could very well be at risk. Even worse, his store at the settlement might lose its entire non-Indian customer base. Thus, he and Fort Snelling sutler Samuel Stambaugh, who partnered with Sibley in their mercantile ventures, were firmly on the side of their customers. Using all their rhetorical skills, Stambaugh and Sibley penned a memorial to President Martin Van Buren on behalf of the unlettered Canadians, mixed bloods, and Red River refugees who were their neighbors. Every male settler on the west side of the river signed the petition, asking that they be allowed to take legal title of their lands. Or at the very least, if they were forced to leave, they asked that "a reasonable and just allowance be made us in the treaty for our improvements" since "all the labor of years is invested in their present habitations" and they "have no other homes." No reply to their petition was received.[11]

Some of the settlers doggedly held on until they were forcibly removed from their homesteads three years later, in 1840. Others did not wait to have their fate determined and moved across the river, a stone's throw from the fort, as soon as the 1837 treaty was signed, hoping to snap up the best parcels of land. The Mdewakantons, who had as yet received no compensation for the ceded territory, considered this incursion highly premature and insisted the settlers leave, killing several head of their cattle to punctuate the point. As Dakota spokesman Big Thunder vigorously complained to Agent Lawrence Taliaferro, until the treaty was ratified and the promised payment in hand, white men had no right to build cabins on Indian land. The poor settlers were caught between the power of the U.S. Army, which wanted them to vacate the west side of the river, and irate Indians, who considered the east side still their domain. The squatters nervously clung to their east river claims, apparently believing they stood a better chance to hold off the Indians until the treaty was ratified than to challenge Major Plympton, who in their experience "ruled supreme."[12]

[158]

As the settlers had suspected, the commandant was indeed intent on evicting all civilians from the west side of the river. However, no one had anticipated that the newly mapped reserve would also include substantial land on the eastern shore, which everyone had assumed would be open for settlement. Thus, when the new boundaries of the reserve were published in 1838, along with Plympton's order forbidding "all persons not attached to the military from erecting any buildings or fences, or cutting timber" on government lands, the dismayed settlers were shocked to discover they were once again about to be evicted.[13]

Major Plympton had boldly argued that a twenty-mile radius around the fort carved from both public and Indian lands on either side of the river was "absolutely necessary to furnish the daily wants of this garrison." Even more important, he averred, was the need to insulate soldiers from the civilians who clustered near the fort, most of whom, according to him, were lowlife whiskey sellers. Fort surgeon John Emerson concurred, reporting "the most beastly scenes of intoxication among the soldiers of this garrison and the Indians in its vicinity," all due to "citizens who are pouring in on us . . . who live by robbing the men of the garrison of health, comfort, and every cent they possess."

The alcohol problem among the soldiers was indisputable. It seemed there was nothing they would not risk to quench their thirst. As one fort resident recalled, they drowned in the river, fell off the bluffs, and passed out in the snow, losing hands and feet to frostbite and sometimes freezing to death. A few who lay in an unconscious stupor were even eaten by wolves. They carried on in "uproarious sprees" that the commandant was helpless to control. One night alone, forty-seven men were confined to the guardhouse. As for the Indians, according to Presbyterian minister and pioneer historian Edward Duffield Neill, the commonly held opinion of the Dakotas was that they were simply a "nation of drunkards"—a stereotype that apparently did not apply to the American military. Nonetheless, Plympton asserted that both groups were in need of protection from unscrupulous purveyors of demon rum. Such evidence easily convinced the secretary of war to approve the major's survey proposal.[14]

Still, a closer examination of the politics in play suggests that "nefarious" whiskey traffickers played only a small role in accounting for the peculiarly configured Fort Snelling reserve. On the west side of the river (which was already closed to white settlers), the reserve boundary followed Basset's Creek, well above St. Anthony Falls, which gave the military control of the falls' mill power. However, the eastern boundary took a peculiar detour. From the falls it followed the west bank of the river south for approximately three miles, leaving the water power site open to development. Then, just below the point where rapids produced by the falls made the river unnavigable, the line abruptly veered east to take in both banks of the Mississippi for some five miles below the fort. Every possible steamboat landing within fifteen miles of St. Anthony was thus inside the military reserve, as were all landings for five miles up the St. Peter's River.

[159]

Evidently, the men at the fort had more than military priorities on their minds. Major Plympton, his fellow officers, and Dr. Emerson all were deep into land speculation. Plympton had planned to lay claim to the site of the falls as soon as the 1837 treaty was ratified, but Franklin Steele, a young timber speculator with "potent political connections," got the jump on the overconfident major and foiled his scheme. With advance notice that the treaty had been ratified, Steele raced to the falls in the dead of night to take possession of the most valuable section of land on the Upper Mississippi. When Plympton arrived the next morning, he discovered that he had been trumped. Disappointed but undaunted, the major and his confreres from the fort (including Dr. Emerson) quickly grabbed up other claims near the falls. By drawing the reserve to take in all the steamboat landings for fifteen miles downriver, the Fort Snelling speculators intended to eliminate competition for the wealth of the pinelands. To further guard against competition, Plympton suggested to the War Department that it might be prudent to consider an even larger reserve. If the limits "could be extended even further into the country on the east side of the river," he suggested, "it would, no doubt, add to the quiet of this command." Dr. Emerson even went so far as to propose that the reserve should extend east all the way to the St. Croix River.[15]

The problems of resource depletion and rampant whiskey selling that Plympton described to his superiors convinced officials in Washington to approve the submitted boundaries—though they declined to extend jurisdiction to the St. Croix. But no one around Mendota doubted that the Fort Snelling group had acted purely in their own self-interest. The uproar of indignation was immediate. Joe Brown, who was running an extremely profitable grog shop within shouting distance of the fort on the east bank of the river, was predictably incensed—and astute in his assessment: "Any man who will examine that tract east of the Mississippi asked for as a reserve will see that it does not contain any timber of consequence, all the best timber being already cut by the troops; and as for the sale of spirits, it is useless to suppose the distance of two, three or five miles will prevent soldiers from getting it when so inclined." Brown's frustration grew out of more than the loss of a grog shop; he had been confident that an important town would grow up near the confluence of the Mississippi and the St. Peter rivers (a spot inauspiciously known as Rumtown), and he had claimed some of the site's choicest real estate—which suddenly had become worthless.[16]

Samuel Stambaugh and Franklin Steele, though they both held claims at the falls, also joined in the chorus of protest. While the Fort Snelling group shortsightedly focused on immediate gain, with no intention of remaining permanently in the region, Steele and Stambaugh, along with Joe Brown and Henry Sibley, were speculators on a grander, long-term scale. They envisioned Minnesota's future as a territory and then a state. Both Steele and Stambaugh intended to set up sawmilling operations. With the northern pinelands as a seemingly inexhaustible resource, they meant to make their fortunes supplying the lumber that would build the booming towns and farmsteads they imagined rising along the Mississippi. But how, Stambaugh asked in a letter to the secretary of war, was this new country to attract visitors, let alone settlers, when boats could not dock anywhere near the falls? Where would they build houses or hotels? And how could settlers feel safe in this untamed place when miles of forest would necessarily separate them from the soldiers who were supposedly there to protect them? It seemed the government was foolishly stripping Minnesota's nascent boosters of every tool for development. At the urging of the reliably persuasive Joe Brown, the Wisconsin territorial legislature joined the protest, formally objecting to what it deemed an illegal seizure of its public lands. But Wisconsin legislators, lacking the political standing of a state, had little influence in Washington, and voices from Minnesota country, at the territory's barely populated western edge, had even less.[17]

[160]

None of these calculations were meaningful to the displaced settlers, who had neither profit making nor city building on their minds. Most were descendants of French Canadian *habitants*, many were mixed blood, and all had been part of the borderland culture for decades. For them, property simply meant the place they called home. Understandably, the Red River refugees, unwilling to be uprooted yet again, tended to cling more tenaciously to their plots than did the veterans of the fur trade. The little colony that had reestablished itself on the east side of the river—Abraham Perret, Joseph Rondo, Benjamin and Pierre Gervais, and a few other Red River families—stubbornly refused to abandon their homesteads until 1840, when soldiers bodily ejected them from the newly defined reserve, destroying all the cabins and outbuildings to ensure the settlers would not return. Without wealth or political influence, they were the collateral damage in a contest not of their making.[18]

Making St. Paul

Hardship was no stranger to the former Fort Snelling squatters, and they soon reconstituted a small community of sorts, just below the military boundary line. In less than a decade this informal settlement would grow to become Minnesota's capital city. Once described more elegantly as the Grand Marais, the sandy landing place that sloped gradually upward to the bluffs soon came to be called Pig's Eye, in honor of its first resident, a disreputable one-eyed voyageur-turned-whiskey trader named Pierre "Pig's Eye" Parrant. Along with most of the other fur trade veterans, Parrant had taken eviction from the reserve largely in his stride. When the new fort commandant had made it hot for Parrant's surreptitious whiskey trade on the west side of the river, he equably moved the operation to the other bank, supposedly out of the military's jurisdiction. When the expanded dimensions of the reserve forced him out of business again, he paddled downstream to the first feasible docking point and set up shop once more, with no apparent disruption in his trade. Other former voyageurs, traders, harried settlers, and even a few discharged soldiers soon followed in his wake, making Pig's Eye a bona fide, if ramshackle, point on the map.[19]

[161]

These first residents of what was to become St. Paul had no ambitions for city building. Indeed, if they alone had shaped the course of settlement, Pig's Eye probably would have looked much like the Métis outposts that characterized Prairie du Chien or Green Bay decades earlier. Most had no desire to store up more wealth than they needed to sustain their current lifestyle, nor were they interested in setting up businesses or claiming vast tracts of land for resale. They valued, instead, a community shaped by mutual support and conviviality. Ex-voyageur Vital Guerin, "feeling lonesome, and, wanting a neighbor," gladly gave half his claim to Pierre Gervais, whose cabin had been burned by the soldiers. Those who were more footloose or without families traded property rights with abandon. Another former petty trader, Donald McDonald, gave up his well-located claim for a "barrel of whiskey and two Indian guns." In fact, land claims became a sort of quasi-currency, traded, gambled, or given away from one hand to another with bewildering rapidity. With thousands of miles available for the taking, whiskey was a far more valuable commodity; a gallon sold for as much as $80. Land claims were commonly traded for a horse, a wagon, a gallon of whiskey, or a gun, or to settle gambling debts of $10 or $20.[20]

But Pig's Eye also soon drew the interest of a class of speculators who had decidedly different priorities. Shrewd fur trade agents like Henry Rice, Henry Sibley, and Norman Kittson foresaw a big future for the little hamlet and were more than happy to snap up as many claims as they could get their hands on. With all the land between Pig's Eye and St. Anthony Falls closed to settlement, they knew for certain that they were investing in a land developer's gold mine. The ramshackle outpost of Pig's Eye—which, thanks to Major Plympton, had become the practical head of navigation for the Mississippi—was destined to become the trading entrepôt of the north and they intended to make the most of it.[21]

In 1841, the settlement, which by then counted some fifteen, mostly Catholic families, welcomed its first priest, Father Lucien Galtier. Vital Guerin and Benjamin Gervais happily donated land to build the Chapel of St. Paul on a bluff above the landing, and when Father Galtier proposed that "St. Paul" might be a more dignified name than Pig's Eye for the infant town, its residents—both Catholic and Protestant—enthusiastically endorsed the suggestion. For the French Catholics, it was a way to honor their faith; for the city-building Anglo Protestants, it was a first step in converting the polyglot, disreputable outpost into an urban citadel.[22]

Other eager entrepreneurs soon made their way up the river from all parts of the settled United States to establish themselves as storekeepers in St. Paul, hoping primarily to profit from the Indian trade and invest their profits in land speculation. Before long, steamboats began stopping at St. Paul's Landing on their way to Fort Snelling. Almost immediately, the accidental town site overtook Mendota as the center of commercial operations for the region. Henry Sibley saw his dreams for the future of Mendota fading away, along with the value of his post and its surrounding lands. Neither legitimate entrepreneurs nor shady operators cared to navigate the government oversight or licensing requirements that limited trade there on the west side of the river. Settlement at the falls also languished, cut off from river access to trade and transportation routes by fifteen miles of restricted territory. Steele and Stambaugh had been proved right in opposing Plympton's plan, and the major must have seethed to see his land values stagnate while the "den of whiskey sellers" at St. Paul made money hand over fist. Steele was unable to get his sawmill up and running until 1847, but even had he produced a supply of lumber there was no way to get it to markets downriver—or even to St. Paul, where builders laboriously hewed planks by hand to house a growing trickle of new residents. As an unintended consequence of government intervention, Mendota, located ideally where the St. Peter River joined the Mississippi, and St. Anthony, with its invaluable water power waiting to be tapped, were blocked from development while St. Paul was fast becoming the premier destination for new investors in Minnesota country.[23]

Transition Time

The story of the frontier has been written as a tale of western expansion, but the artery that nourished Minnesota's development ran along a north-south line, with settlement a minor factor until *after* Minnesota became a territory in 1849. In the preterritorial era, the region's economic life was dependent on two interrelated sources: the Indian trade and a reconfigured form of the fur trade in which pelts and buffalo hides flowed to St. Paul from the north.

By the 1840s, most of the fur-bearing animals that were pursued for trade had become scarce in much of what is now Minnesota, hunted to near extinction by an Indian population of perhaps 25,000 that had come to depend on market hunting as their primary source of subsistence.[24] However, in the border region and north into British territory, mink, weasel, and marten were easily trapped, and muskrat, the staple of the Upper Mississippi trade, were abundant. Even more valuable were the great herds of buffalo that roamed the Red River valley and the plains to the west. Accounts from the 1840s note that bison, which had migrated west for a number of years, had returned to the region around Lac qui Parle and Lake Traverse. Farther north, the haul was even richer. The free traders of the border region ignored the international boundary at will, and much to the frustration of the Hudson's Bay Company, increasingly carried their furs and hides south to the American market, where competition drove prices well above what the British monopoly was willing to pay. Using wooden carts uniquely fashioned to withstand the grinding journey across the roadless prairie, in the 1830s Métis hunters began trekking south to the Mississippi with pelts, hides, cattle, and horses, where Henry Sibley was more than happy to buy what they had to sell. The first contingent arrived at Mendota in 1835; by 1839 more than forty carts made their way to Fort Snelling in a single season. Sibley, struggling to turn a profit, ached to take full advantage of the rich border trade, but he was stymied by the noncompete agreement that had been privately worked out between the principals of the American Fur and Hudson's Bay companies. When Ramsay Crooks sold Sibley's Western Outfit to Pierre Chouteau and Company in 1842, Sibley, unshackled at last, immediately began making plans to position himself on the border.[25]

In 1837, Sibley had closed his outlying posts west of Lac qui Parle. The Sisseton, Wahpeton, and Yankton Dakotas, proud and independent still, refused to bow to traders' authority and gave Sibley's agents no end of trouble. With the nation in a depression and the market for furs bottoming out, Sibley took the advice of his partner, Hercules Dousman, to "burn all of the buildings, fences, etc. immediately and withdraw everything from there. . . . Besides punishing the dogs, no new post can pay the expense at the present rate of furs." Five years later, the situation had changed. Sibley had hoped to extricate himself from the trade as the governor of Doty's proposed new Indian state. With that dream dashed, the fur market rebounding, and buffalo hides in high demand, his best avenue for financial rescue was to once again court the western bands and push north into the border region to trade with the Métis. The man he tapped to head this operation was Norman Kittson, a young Anglo-Canadian who had already proven himself in a trading partnership with Franklin Steele.[26]

Kittson lost no time in hustling to Pembina, where he ingratiated himself with a salesman's charm and a bulging purse, paying cash for furs, hides, and pemmican at rates that were 25 percent over what Hudson's Bay Company was offering. Within a year Pembina had become a magnet for Métis hunters from both sides of the border, and every punitive measure that Hudson's Bay officials put in place to stopper the rampant smuggling only drove the fiercely independent Red River Métis into Kittson's waiting arms. Kittson reported with glee to Sibley, "We have created quite a censation in our favor in their [Hudson's Bay Company] colony, which is working strongly against them." The population at Pembina was burgeoning—by 1850 the territorial census would count more than 1,000 residents in Pembina County, almost 19 percent of the territory's population—and Kittson was fast becoming known as the "king of the border."[27]

The border post was so successful that soon it required all of Kittson's attention, and another agent had to be enlisted to manage the other western stations. Kittson organized brigades of Red River carts, loaded with pelts and hides, and made the thirty- to forty-five-day journey to the Mississippi. At first, half a dozen carts pulled by oxen or shaggy ponies could carry the load, but by the end of the decade, trains of more than two hundred carts, carrying some $20,000 worth of furs, set off southward across the plains. Once the furs were unloaded, Kittson's carts returned to Pembina laden with a dazzling array of goods—everything from blankets and cookstoves to oysters and champagne—destined not only for Pembina and the free traders, but also, ironically, for British soldiers who patrolled the boundary and even for the men of the Hudson's Bay Company.[28]

Kittson's trains generally unloaded and resupplied at Traverse des Sioux (where Henry Sibley was, not coincidentally, engaged in plans for future town site development). The furs and hides were then ferried downriver to the Mississippi. Other cart trains made up of independent Métis traders and their families headed directly for St. Paul with the products of their annual hunt. In 1844 Sibley opened a retail outlet there and three years later established a permanent St. Paul Outfit to handle the Red River trade. These routes carved from Pembina, famed as the Red River Trails, were Minnesota's first roads, and all roads led ultimately to St. Paul. The little town had become the vital nexus that connected the wealth of the North to eastern markets and forwarded the goods and provisions shipped from the East to the northern frontier.[29]

The fur trade was alive and well, but it scarcely resembled the old way of doing business. The system of providing credit to Indian hunters in return for pelts and hides was rapidly falling out of favor. Traders and merchants continued to advance credit to the Indians, but they wanted repayment in cash from annuity payments rather than in furs harvested by Indian labor. Métis trappers and hunters had become the backbone of the trade, but they too were part of a cash economy. Rather than depend on a limited stock of goods provided and priced by traders in the backcountry, they preferred to be paid in dollars, which allowed them to shop and bargain as they pleased among the merchants at St. Paul and storekeepers at Pembina. Competition from independent merchants reduced the margin Sibley could extract from his provisioning operation and significantly cut into his profits from the Red River trade. But for the bustling little outpost of St. Paul, competition was a tonic that generated unlimited optimism and drove its economic engine. No fool, Henry Sibley recognized that his days as the squire of Mendota were numbered. Writing to a friend in 1847, he observed, "It needs no prophet to forsee that things

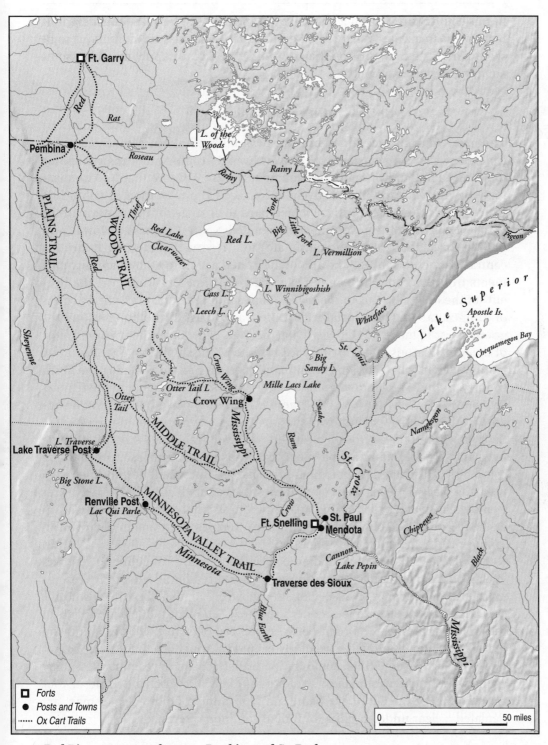

Red River cart routes between Pembina and St. Paul.

in this country are now in a transit state, and that the fur trade must ere long be brought to a close. What I shall do then, if my life be spared, remains to be seen; perhaps I may turn politician or office seeker, or apply myself to some equally mean occupation."[30]

Culture Clashes

The untrammeled race for riches that was taking hold in Minnesota country created new tensions and paradoxes. Even as Euro-Americans clambered to acquire land and promote development toward a future that had no place for Native Americans, they actively encouraged the relocation of tribes into the region. In 1847 Henry Rice lobbied hard to arrange for the removal of the Winnebagos from the government-designated Neutral Ground in Iowa (now desired for settlement by the new state) to a reservation at Long Prairie, in central Minnesota. In 1849 he also orchestrated a shift in Ojibwe annuity payments from La Pointe to Sandy Lake, where "Minnesota would get the benefit" of the cash paid out to the tribes. That same year, one of the first actions of Minnesota's new territorial legislature was to pass a resolution asking the government to move all Ojibwes living on lands ceded in earlier treaties (most of them in Wisconsin) to territory west of the Mississippi, above St. Paul. The truth was that, whatever long-term plans boosters had for civilizing the north country, in the 1840s Indian annuities were the essential anchor of the region's economy. As late as 1850, the *Minnesota Pioneer* reported, "One would suppose by the promises about town, that the Indian payment would square every debt in Minnesota, but the 'debt of Nature.' Every reply to a dun is, 'after the payment.'" Between annuity payments cash was in such short supply that furs commonly substituted as a medium of exchange. But when the annuities were paid, the price of goods went up in local stores and whiskey flowed like water to more easily persuade the Indians to purchase what traders and storekeepers had to offer. The rest of the year Indians were less welcome in the town, an "annoyance" to be grudgingly tolerated.[31]

Adding more bands to an Indian population already struggling to glean its livelihood from a diminishing resource base ensured for all a drift into resentment and dependency. It also fomented hostility among the tribes, who increasingly infringed on one another's territory. The late 1830s had witnessed the worst clashes yet recorded between the Dakotas and Ojibwes, and skirmishes both small and large regularly erupted throughout the next decade.[32] However, at the same time, some Indian leaders began to redefine the enemy as the white man, who lied and exploited Indians of every tribe. Hole-in-the-Day II, chief of the Gull Lake band and a prominent Ojibwe spokesman, articulated a clear understanding of Indian common interests:

> I do not hate the Sioux; I love them, as I do every one of the continent who has a red skin. Of course, as I go to St. Paul very often, I frequently meet the Sioux and also the

Winnebagoes. I shake hands with them, and, reminding them that the Indian once owned the continent, ask them where they are now. I tell them this every time I see them, that, when they fight, they punish themselves and not the whites.[33]

Nonetheless, despite his own advice, Hole-in-the-Day continued to lead sorties against Dakota foes. Honor and respect in Indian culture demanded that vengeance be exacted for lives taken by one's enemies. To break with that tradition would have cost the chief his standing among his people. Thus, so long as a single act of violence was unavenged between the tribes, no lasting alliance could hold and the cycle of small-scale hostilities continued.

Frequent conflict also broke out in this era between Dakota bands and Métis of the north. While mixed-blood people in general had maintained kinship relations with both their Indian and white relatives and often moved back and forth between the two cultures with chameleonlike ease, the borderland Métis had developed a distinct identity. The *gens libre,* as they were often called, considered themselves a "new nation," set apart from both whites and Indians by culture, lifestyle, and dress. They even designed a flag that declared their independent status. They had adopted the horse culture of the plains and had perfected a highly efficient technique for hunting buffalo that operated with the discipline of a military operation. A typical hunting expedition would include upwards of 1,000 people—men, women, and children—traveling in a brigade of more than 1,000 carts, which would return weeks later loaded to the brim with hides and dried meat. Since, unlike the Indians, the Métis did not rely on the buffalo for housing, clothes, or other essentials of life, they hunted it mainly for hides and pemmican that could be sold to purchase foodstuffs and manufactured goods. The more buffalo they killed, the better they could maintain the independent lifestyle that they valued.[34]

The Métis of the northern border were primarily of mixed Cree, Ojibwe, and French ancestry and thus friction with Dakota and Lakota buffalo hunters—mainly Sissetons, Wahpetons, and Yanktons—might have been expected. But bands of western Ojibwes and Crees also viewed such wholesale slaughter of their most important resource with alarm. The buffalo meant independence to the Indians as well, but for them it was crucial that the herds carried on from year to year. They remembered the hardships they had experienced in years when the buffalo inexplicably disappeared and knew that the great shaggy beast ensured their self-sufficiency and protected them from the dependence on annuities that had overtaken their relatives to the east.[35]

Norman Kittson's arrival at Pembina brought reliable access to the American market, which would pay top dollar for as many hides as the *gens libre* had to sell. Predictably, they hunted with ever more vigor, ranging south as far as Lake Traverse and Lac qui Parle. Just as predictably, Indians and Métis clashed on the hunting grounds. In 1844 Indian agent Amos Bruce reported to the War Department that "the halfbreeds come to hunt in large bands, well armed and in too much force to fear the Indians; and as to the threatened interference of our Government, they laugh at the idea." Tensions ran high all along the Couteau des Prairies and the traders were worried. One skirmish with a party of Sissetons in 1844 left eight warriors dead at Métis hands. Joe Brown, who that season was trading independently with the Sissetons, reported that the Indians had promised to kill every half-breed they saw. And, Brown warned, "it would be erroneous to suppose that the Sioux would make distinction between halfbreeds living as whites and the pure white man." Sure enough, when a group of Sissetons encountered a party of cattle drovers from Missouri who had wandered northwest after losing their way to Fort Snelling, the Indians mistook them for Métis and swooped down on them. Only one member of the party survived.[36]

This almost unprecedented attack on white men prompted the commandant at Fort Snelling to send a detachment of troops to apprehend the murderers, but the expedition turned into a farce, the Indians not cowed in the least by the military's tepid show of force. The western bands, still haughtily independent, "bowed to no man." Nonetheless, neither did they desire to cut off trading relations, which supplied them with guns, ammunition, traps, and an array of manufactured goods. Consequently, when Brown nimbly used his persuasive skills (and a wagonload of gifts) to broker a solution, he found the Indians receptive to his overtures. For the good of the band, the perpetrators agreed to turn themselves in, assured that they would be imprisoned only briefly, then released to their people unharmed. In return, the fort commandant promised to roust the Métis hunters from the Indians' lands. With this agreement reached, in a formal ceremony accompanied by an enormous entourage of Sissetons and Yanktons dressed in their finest garb and headdresses, the warriors Sullen Face and Forked Horn gave themselves up at Brown's post. In essence, what had been worked out was a diplomatic charade, designed to save face for all concerned.[37]

Unfortunately, the careful diplomacy went awry. The prisoners escaped from the Dubuque jail where they had been taken and Sullen Face died on the journey home. As news spread from camp to camp along the Coteau, anger surged among the Indians, who believed they had been betrayed. Brown, who had brokered the delicate arrangement, was genuinely remorseful—and also in fear for his life. As the Indians viewed it, he informed Agent Bruce, "by my advice [Sullen Face] had gone below; if he had remained with his band he would not have incurred the hardships that caused his death; his wife would not have been a widow, or his children orphans! I was the cause of his death; through my instrumentality alone was he cut off in the flower of his age, and through me alone were his friends deploring the loss of one of their bravest comrades!" While reasonable men might agree that Brown was not to blame, he assured the Indian agent that the accusations "become strong and convincing when uttered by a band of wild Sissetons at the door of the only white man within fifty miles of them." Somehow Brown was able to cool the Indians' anger, probably through the offices of his wife, Susan, who was their kinswoman, as well as by a very expensive outlay of gifts in reparation for their loss.[38]

The conflicts over the buffalo represented a larger clash between the old world of the fur trade and a new order driven by market capitalism. The era was rapidly passing when individuals could make a life that incorporated elements of both. The Métis buffalo hunters, who prided themselves as owing allegiance to no outside authority, were no exception. Fulfilling the promise made to the western Dakotas, in the summer of 1845 a military expedition was dispatched to warn the Métis back to Canada. This was the first time the Americans had shown the slightest sign of interfering with their trade, and it made the hunters exceedingly anxious. If they were prevented from running the buffalo, it would threaten their entire way of life. In the past, the Métis had contended that, as native-born people, they "were entitled to the same privileges as those enjoyed by the Indians," but their interests had clearly diverged from those of Native people. With the plains tribes now their avowed enemies and the military threatening to cut off access to American markets, the *gens libre* chose a new course and petitioned for the right to become American citizens, whether they lived below or above the border. The American government dealt with this unusual request—which was resubmitted numerous times between 1844 and 1849—by ignoring it, thereby judiciously avoiding an international incident with the British. (But neither did it make any attempt to stop the flow of valuable pelts and hides from above the border.) With their petitions unanswered, a great many Canadian Métis resolved the dilemma by migrating to Pembina, the "smugglers' rendezvous" in American territory. The best way to preserve the way of life they cherished—one that blended elements of both white and Indian culture—was to take on, at least for legal purposes, the identity of white Americans.[39]

[169]

As Henry Sibley had asserted, Minnesota country was indeed in a "transit state" in the 1840s. While traders tried to maintain traditional trading relationships with the nontreaty Indians in the west, their connection with "annuity Indians" had devolved into schemes to part them from their government payments. Métis and other free traders had taken the Indians' place as the chief suppliers of furs and hides, a system that relied on cash transactions rather than credit based on personal relationships. Though Sibley and his fellows tried to keep both systems functioning, they were increasingly at odds with one another, as Joe Brown and Norman Kittson could attest. The Sissetons warned Kittson that if he carried supplies to Pembina, which aided their enemies, then he was their enemy as well. No one took these threats lightly. When Kittson was late in returning to Pembina in 1844, rumors flew throughout Red River that he had been killed by a Dakota war party. The cart route that followed the St. Peter south to Mendota had become so dangerous by mid-decade that the

Red River brigades laboriously carved new trails through Ojibwe territory to avoid the hostile western Dakotas. These new routes, called the Woods Trail and the Middle Trail, bypassed Mendota altogether and headed directly into the commercial hub that was St. Paul.[40]

Native Adaptations

The transformation of the fur trade economy touched everyone in Minnesota country, Indians and whites alike. Native people were quick to grasp the importance of money as a measure of power and demonstrated frequently that they were as able as any white man to set a dollar value on their lands and resources. By the 1830s, the Ojibwes along the St. Croix River had developed a keen understanding that white men were converting Indian timber into cash. In 1837, before any treaty was made, forty-nine Ojibwe chiefs and headmen signed a private contract with Sibley, Lyman Warren, and William Aitkin that sold them logging rights along the St. Croix and Snake rivers.[41] Other, less scrupulous timber cruisers invaded Ojibwe and Dakota pinelands without permission, and the Indians lodged numerous formal protests with agents Henry Schoolcraft and Lawrence Taliaferro, demanding payment from the renegade logging crews. In 1834 Chief Little Buck of the Folles Avoines band complained to Ojibwe agent Schoolcraft that his people had not "received any remuneration whatever in lieu of those logs" taken by Joe Brown and his crew on the St. Croix. The problem, as the Indians saw it, was not so much that loggers were stripping the pinelands, but that they failed to pay for the resources they extracted.[42] Increasingly enmeshed in a cash economy, Native people had begun to view their land as a means of producing income as well as sustenance.

As cart trains became a regular feature on the trails from Red River to Mendota, the western Dakota people began demanding tribute for the right to cross their lands. By the 1840s these same bands had put a monetary value on wood, water, and pasturage as well. Indian "ingratitude" at Lake Traverse and Lac qui Parle stunned missionary Stephen Riggs. Despite all the missionaries had done to promote the Indians' physical and spiritual welfare, he related, "all this was, in their estimation, no compensation for the field we planted, and the fuel we used, and the grass we cut, and the water we drank. They were worth a thousand dollars a year!" Furthermore, some Dakota parents even tried to exact payment for sending their children to the mission school.[43]

Clearly, as development and resource extraction moved into Minnesota country, Indians understood and adapted to the new conditions of the marketplace. Money had become as essential to sustaining their collective culture as furs had been in the past. But their ability to secure compensation for their resources was limited by dependence on the traders for key necessities of life. The Indians commonly expressed their displeasure by killing cattle or horses, but overt confrontations were rare, since everyone knew that violence would either drive the traders away or bring threats of retaliation by the military.

Thus, the Indians' primary recourse was to complain to the authorities, with generally unsatisfying results.

All this paved the way to land cessions as the one sure way to secure a reliable source of income for the tribes. When Mdewakanton negotiators went to Washington in 1837, they set a price of $1.6 million for the St. Croix–Mississippi delta, demonstrating that they were aware of the value of the forestlands they were ceding. But, as in most treaty negotiations, they were bargaining from a position of weakness and were unable to exact their price. Simply put, the Indians needed immediate relief for their people and were forced to accept what the government was willing to offer—a package of annuities and provisions paid out over decades rather than a lump sum transaction, along with farm equipment and school funds designated to replace rather than sustain their traditional way of life.[44]

Native people seldom, if ever, received fair compensation for their land, but they used their limited leverage to wring as much from the government as possible. They usually insisted on some form of cash payment to mixed-blood relations, partly perhaps as a way to increase the immediate dispersal of hard money. Repayment of debts owed to traders was a more controversial provision. While most treaty participants supported such payments, others raised objections that derived from their new understanding of the monetary value of their land and resources. In the 1837 negotiations, Flat Mouth, chief of the Ojibwe Pillager band, insisted that traders owed the Indians for food and wood they had taken from Ojibwe lands. "And they talk to us about paying our debts?" he protested. In 1842 White Crow of the Lac du Flambeau Ojibwes raised similar objections, insisting that the traders "ought to pay us back instead of bringing us in debt."[45] Though such arguments did not prevail, they demonstrate that Indians in Minnesota country had developed an understanding of market values that was quite different from their old relationship with the land.

Once the treaties were in place, tribal leaders kept a close account of where, when, and how the promised payments were dispersed and did their best to hold the government to account. When annuities failed to arrive or came up short of the owed amounts, the leaders were quick to protest to the authorities. Often they discovered that the government at will subtracted costs from their payments that had never been discussed: reparations for slaughtered cattle and horses, costs for relocating the tribes, even the "gifts" that had been part of the treaty ritual. The injustice of such underhanded accounting incensed the Indians, but once the treaties were signed, they had little means to force compliance, which led to growing distrust and resentment. They soon realized that the only leverage they wielded was their buying power—which, ironically, depended on the fidelity of the same American government that was playing them false.

Evidence abounds that the Ojibwes and Dakotas were not locked into a static premarket culture, impervious to the changing conditions around them. Rather, they were continually strategizing to adapt themselves to a new economy in ways that would enable them to survive with their core cultural values intact. Some Indians, and many mixed bloods, convinced that survival depended on conforming to the Euro-American model, went even further down the assimilationist path. They cut their hair, donned white man's clothing, and put their hand to the plow. They framed up farmhouses and converted to Christianity, at least in outward practice. Some even took English names. Inevitably, clashes arose within the tribes between those who held fast to traditional ways and the "cut hairs" who tried to accommodate themselves to an ever more powerful cultural imperialism. When Big Thunder, chief of the Mdewakanton Kaposia band (known as Little Crow III), lay dying in 1845, he counseled his son and chosen successor, Taoyateduta, to accept the inevitable and lead his people in accommodation to the ways of Euro-Americans.[46] Taoyateduta, who assumed the title of Little Crow IV, took his father's words to heart and invited missionary Thomas Williamson to open a school at Kaposia. The young chief had spent a decade at Lac qui Parle with the Renvilles, who were extended kin. He attended the mission school there and became adept at arithmetic and computation as well as reading and writing. Little Crow was eager for his people to acquire these same skills to hold their own against white exploitation, but opposition to the missionary and his school proved so intense that Little Crow was forced to withdraw his support or face losing his leadership position.[47]

While the people of Kaposia vehemently resisted cultural accommodation, they were more than willing to become commercial actors in the new economy. From his youth, Little Crow, along with his Anglo-Dakota friend Jack Frazer, had demonstrated entrepreneurial leanings, trading alcohol with the western tribes for horses and furs. Schooled by his Renville relatives, he soon discovered, as his biographer notes, "that being a capitalist rather than an exploited hunter provided a better opportunity for making a living." As chief of the Kaposia band, Little Crow transformed nearly the entire population of his village into traders, competing with Sibley and his peers for buffalo robes and furs. The white traders, dismayed at this reversal of roles, tried to patrol the rivers to stop the unlicensed Indian traders and even enlisted the military to halt the growing competition. But nothing could stop the Indian entrepreneurs, who knew the terrain far better than any pursuer. A growing cohort of Native traders soon included braves from all the Mdewakanton villages. In 1847 Joseph La Framboise reported from Traverse des Sioux that a single Mdewakanton trader had acquired 130 buffalo robes. Clearly, the purpose of this trade was to turn a profit rather than to directly acquire necessities of life—a very different trading position from decades past. Nonetheless, though they competed with white traders in the market, Indian traders had not embraced the tenets of acquisitive individualism that were central to the capitalist ethos: the profits they sought were meant to sustain the collective village, not to store up individual wealth. Only the means to the end had changed.[48]

Dakota and Ojibwe women also were deep into commercial enterprises. They had long functioned as go-betweens who carried liquor from traders to their villages. With whiskey now easily accessible on the east side of the Mississippi, women stepped up their role as whiskey traders in Indian country. They also peddled sugar, wild rice, pumpkins, corn, squash, and other agricultural products to traders and the military. With virtually no food produced for market by whites in Minnesota country in the 1840s and fresh produce in high demand, Native women entrepreneurs could set premium prices on their small surplus harvests. Their enterprises, like those of their male relatives, served the village as a whole and enhanced their status as caretakers of their people.[49]

[173]

Thus, in multiple ways Native people participated in the developing cash economy, demonstrating skills of adaptation that belied claims among whites that they could not accommodate themselves to "civilization" or that they must fully assimilate to Euro-American ways or die out. Though Indians rejected assimilation into the dominant white culture, they showed a social, economic, and cultural flexibility, a selective acculturation that enabled them to sustain traditional values in an evolving capitalist economy—at least for a time. However, a multicultural society had no place in the American manifesto of empire, and as territorial ambitions moved forward Indian removal became an integral part of the agenda.

Free Soil and Territorial Schemes

In the half century following the birth of the United States, maps of the new nation became outdated almost before they were published. Cartographers made a steady income redrawing the nation's continually changing legal contours. Before Minnesota Territory was created in 1849 it fell under the jurisdiction of no fewer than eight legal entities. Before the Louisiana Purchase was made in 1803, the land west of the Mississippi was claimed first by Spain, then briefly receded to France before President Thomas Jefferson snatched up the bargain of the century. The lands west of the Ohio River and east of the Mississippi had been originally organized in 1787 as the Northwest Territory, which eventually became the states of Ohio, Indiana, Illinois, Michigan, Wisconsin, and part of Minnesota. As each state was carved out, the remaining territory was renamed and reconfigured with new political and legal bodies. Thus, at least as far as the U.S. government was concerned, the governors of Indiana, Illinois, Michigan, and Wisconsin Territories, one after another, oversaw the governance of at least part of Minnesota (with the lands west of the Mississippi part of Iowa Territory between 1836 and 1846) as settlement marched west. However, in terms of real authority, for decades the land that would become Minnesota remained Dakota and Ojibwe country, and American control of the region existed only on the frequently revised territorial maps. After 1820, federal troops stationed at Fort Snelling created at least a feeble presence, but for the most part the fur traders had free rein and British influence exerted more persuasive power than American law, especially in the border region.[50]

Civil authority was almost entirely absent from Minnesota country until it became part of Wisconsin Territory in 1836. Even then, the nearest circuit court was in Prairie du Chien and the seat of government at far distant Madison. The single justice of the peace on Minnesota soil was none other than Joseph R. Brown. The same popular man of many talents served as Minnesota country's sole elected representative to the Wisconsin territorial legislature. As long as Minnesota remained Indian territory, closed to settlement, this arrangement suited the fur trade population quite well, especially those associated with the American Fur Company, which exerted at least as much power as the military in the region. However, once development schemes began to supersede interest in furs, everyone with a stake in the game, including Representative Brown, was infected with the fever to make Minnesota a territory in its own right.[51]

This was no simple process. Nearly half a century of territorial permutations were driven by more than a natural westward flow of migration and population increase. Each new state became part of a complicated chess game to determine the balance of power between the North and South. The interests of the two regions had been at odds since the nation's founding—the North seeking to develop a commercial and manufacturing economy and the South committed to large-scale agriculture, dependent on slave labor—differences that widened exponentially during the market revolution of the early nineteenth century. Legislators quarreled bitterly over a raft of economic development issues—monetary and banking policy, infrastructural improvements, and especially the implementation of protective tariffs. Northern legislators clamored for high taxes on imported goods to protect emerging American manufacturers, a policy that southern congressmen vehemently opposed. Tariffs, the southerners insisted, drove up the price of goods for their constituents and, more important, dangerously undermined the cotton export trade. With regional interests so fundamentally in opposition, only a sectional balance in the Congress could force compromise solutions on these key issues and keep one region from imposing its priorities to the detriment of the other. Thus, the configuration of western expansion was of critical importance.[52]

Of course, from the earliest days of the republic, the issue of slavery had been at the heart of sectional conflict. However, it was slavery's impact on political and economic power, rather than its inherent immorality, that drove the debate—though the argument was usually framed in moralistic terms. The constitution had unintentionally made slavery a tool of political power. As the framers had worked to craft a document that all the disparate colonies would accept, they had to allay southern concerns that the more populous North would trample Southern interests. The constitutional solution to the (white)

[174]

population differential was to declare that, for purposes of apportionment, each slave would count as three-fifths of a person. As a result, by 1820, the South had seventeen more representatives in Congress than it would have had if only whites were counted. Slaves themselves, quite obviously, had no political voice, and since southern elites virtually dictated the politics of their states, as the slave population grew (accounting for one-third of the South's population in 1860), a small cohort of southern landed gentry—about 1 percent of the nation's population and 5 percent of the South's—wielded enormous political influence. Only a small group of radical abolitionists dreamed of—or even desired—an end to slavery where it already existed, but the northern states were united in their determination to block what they called the "slave power" from increasing its already formidable "aristocratic" and "anti-egalitarian" influence in national affairs.[53]

Each new state that joined the Union thus became part of a delicate political balancing act on either side of the Mason-Dixon line: Indiana entered with Mississippi, Illinois with Alabama. But when Missouri applied for statehood in 1820 as a slave state, a ferocious debate arose on the Senate floor since Missouri's northern boundary extended well into "free soil" territory. The compromise that was finally worked out admitted Maine as a free state to balance Missouri and also outlawed slavery in all of Louisiana Territory north of Missouri's southern boundary. The Missouri Compromise, as it was called, temporarily averted a sectional crisis, but politicians on both sides of the debate kept a careful eye on the progress of future expansion.[54]

The Old Northwest (what remained of the Northwest Territory) was key to political calculations. The Northwest Ordinance had banned slavery from the territory and also limited its eventual division into between three and five states, each requiring a minimum of 60,000 free inhabitants (excluding Indians) for admission to the Union. The free soil political bloc had a large stake in seeing that five rather than three states were created—and those as soon as practicably possible. This national contest for political power would have an enormous impact on the fortunes of sparsely settled Minnesota country.[55]

When Iowans applied for statehood in 1846, they proposed a northern boundary that would take in St. Anthony and the Fort Snelling area, hoping to acquire what already was expected to become a trading and industrial center. But Congress, under the foresighted leadership of Illinois representative Stephen Douglas, instead drew Iowa's northern boundary at its present location, holding back the region that seemed the Upper Mississippi's best hope for population growth. Two years later the Wisconsin territorial legislature lobbied hard to include the rich pinelands of the St. Croix–Mississippi delta within the new state of Wisconsin, but their plan was scotched as well and they had to settle for a boundary line at the St. Croix River.[56]

Wisconsin was the fifth state created out of the Northwest Territory. Logically, as Wisconsin legislators insisted, it should have included the remainder of the territory, between the St. Croix and Mississippi rivers. But now-Senator Douglas and his allies had larger political aims. With Texas admitted to the Union as a slave state and sectional tensions at a boil, they were anxious to add another free state. Unfortunately, the prospects for the immediate development of Minnesota were not particularly bright. Few settlers had ventured to the region since common wisdom considered the country "too far north and too cold to raise either corn or wheat." One pioneer Minnesotan had been warned before heading up the Mississippi, "You can't live there . . . unless you burrow in snow huts as the Esquimaux do." Moreover, everything west of the Mississippi was still designated Indian Territory, closed to white settlement. Any ambition to make a state from this "howling wilderness" in the foreseeable future would be hopeless unless it included St. Paul, St. Anthony, and the St. Croix River valley, the only places that had any measurable white population at all.[57]

Anticipating Wisconsin's imminent statehood, in 1846 the forward-looking Douglas had marshaled legislation through Congress to allow the formation of a sixth state from the remnant of the Northwest Territory excluded from Wisconsin. Once that hurdle was out of the way, Douglas promptly introduced a bill to organize the "Territory of Minasota." However, even the most ardent free-soil northern senators scoffed at the idea that "Minasota" could claim anywhere near the 5,000 free adult males required for legal territorial status. Senator William Woodbridge of Michigan insisted the population was "not one-tenth that number." The following year Douglas doggedly reintroduced the bill, which failed a second time.[58]

The senator's half-completed plan left Minnesota in a peculiar predicament. Wisconsin's western boundary had been pushed back to the St. Croix River but no new territory had been created. The result was that the St. Croix–Mississippi triangle—the only part of the region open to settlement and development—was left "a no-man's land without law or government, and its people without corporate existence"—an untenable state of affairs for the budding capitalists in the St. Croix and Mississippi River valleys.[59]

Minnesota—A Territory at Last

Anglo-American residents of St. Paul and lumbermen along the St. Croix had vigorously protested their inclusion in the new state of Wisconsin, which would have relegated them to a minor role at its sparsely settled, far western edge. They had bigger dreams for themselves as the center of a new territorial government, with the jobs, patronage, and influence that went along with it. Territorial status was also sure to lure both new residents and outside investment. An infusion of capital from eastern financiers had finally enabled Franklin Steele to get his sawmill up and running at St. Anthony, which encouraged territorial boosters to no end. As one reporter commented, "Westerners rejoiced at the prospect of a vast outlay of capital in their midst and anticipated 'big things' from the Boston folk." But no one had anticipated that Congress would leave them in a legal and governmental vacuum—a state that would surely put a damper on their grand designs for Minnesota's future.[60]

The would-be "Minnesotans" immediately began making plans to rectify the situation. Joe Brown, Henry Sibley, Henry Rice, and their lieutenants had already been working to legalize all the region's far-flung British and Canadian inhabitants by securing their declarations of intent to become American citizens. The uncertain status of mixed-blood people was, for the moment, ignored. As long as they displayed any semblance of European dress, those who were willing were counted as white. Even so, reaching the threshold of 5,000 free adult males was a stretch. As for the region's legal status, local political strategists agreed to proceed as though Wisconsin Territory still existed, now a mere sliver between the St. Croix and Mississippi. As Henry Sibley would later argue before Congress, surely it "could not have intended to disfranchise and outlaw some thousands of citizens, whose petitions were before that body asking not to be included in the state of Wisconsin, but to remain under the existing territorial government. They surely did not ask to be left without the protection or denied the benefits of law."[61]

Sibley immediately emerged as the foremost spokesman for Minnesota country. With his patrician manner, political and financial connections, and the loyalty of most of the area's French-speaking people, he was the natural choice to represent the hoped-for territory's interests. His old partner, Hercules Dousman, who had extricated himself from the trade in 1846, sourly advised Sibley that his Dakota trade would be better served in unorganized Indian country. A new territorial government would only crowd out and shackle trader prerogatives. But Sibley, with a growing taste for high political office and a belief that "the fur trade must ere long be brought to a close," had set his sights in a different direction.[62]

Sibley may have been the face of Minnesota statecraft, but Joe Brown indisputably was the political genius that carried the project forward. Described by a contemporary as "one of the shrewdest politicians and most extraordinary men the Northwest has ever produced," Brown was Henry Sibley's "chief counselor and manager." The two veterans of the trade had similar interests and investments in Minnesota's future. And Brown, schooled in the hardscrabble dealings of Wisconsin territorial politics, had no compunctions about bending the legalities a bit to advance the cause—which allowed Sibley to ostensibly remain above the fray.[63]

Throughout the spring of 1848, the question of how to achieve territorial status fueled spirited political gatherings in St. Paul and Stillwater. Intent on securing official status for Sibley to take "Wisconsin Territory's" interests to Washington, in August Brown orchestrated an informal "convention" in Stillwater. The sixty-one self-appointed "delegates" were composed almost entirely of a complement of Anglo merchants, traders, sawmillers, and lumbermen, with a few lawyers thrown in for good measure. The meeting had scarcely begun before Brown whipped out an already-prepared petition to the president, requesting the formation of a new territory for the disfranchised Minnesotans. Sibley then magnanimously offered to take the petition to Washington and put the case before Congress at his own expense.[64]

Not everyone at the meeting was anxious to put the fate of Minnesota into Henry Sibley's hands. Some newcomers to the region resented his haughty demeanor, presumed status as "first citizen," and the patron-client relationship he enjoyed with the French-speaking majority. Others suspected he would protect "fur company interests" above all else. Such rumblings induced Henry Rice, Sibley's new business partner—in Minnesota just a year and a man of boundless ambition—to quietly sound out his chances to supplant Sibley as the endorsed representative. But Brown had timed the meeting brilliantly to discourage opposition to his man.[65]

Federal surveyors had recently completed a partial survey of lands west of the St. Croix and the first public land sale was scheduled to take place at St. Croix Falls on August 28, two days after the Stillwater convention. Brown had proposed the convention date supposedly to make it convenient for those attending the land sales. It was a masterful move. The upcoming sale certainly added a sense of urgency to the Stillwater proceedings, a reminder that they all were technically squatters until they acquired legal deeds to their claims. No one's property rights were secure while they were adrift in this legal no-man's land. Most important, Brown knew that St. Paul's majority French-speaking population was particularly fearful that sharp-dealing Anglo speculators were poised to cheat them out of their property. To protect their interests, they had asked the trusted Sibley to represent them at the sale. Thus, Sibley arrived at Stillwater accompanied by a body of "fierce" francophone St. Paulites, who were armed with large sticks they intended to use against anyone who challenged Sibley's bids at the forthcoming sale. The unlettered settlers, though they did not participate in the convention, no doubt factored into its outcome. Even those who grumbled about Sibley's baronial manner had to admit his unmatched influence among the "semicivilized" general population. And so, the convention unanimously endorsed Henry Sibley as their candidate to take the people's case to Washington. As one disgruntled participant complained, "The whole plan was concocted before [Sibley] crossed the Mississippi river, as he brought about 30 Frenchmen who are entirely under his control." Brown's calculations had gone precisely according to plan.[66]

Only the formality of general election was required to confirm Sibley as the official delegate of the fictive Wisconsin Territory. But to everyone's surprise, Henry Rice, unable to restrain his ambition, threw his hat into the ring. The contest that commenced was wild and rife with political irony. Neither candidate resided east of the Mississippi and thus were not even residents of Wisconsin Territory, which itself no longer legally existed. In addition, at least a third of the potential voters were mixed-blood people, whose status as Indian or white shifted with the political winds. In the name of political expediency, no one questioned or even commented on the rather glaring irregularities of Minnesota's first electoral campaign. But the politicking itself was considerably less restrained. Supporters on both sides engaged in energetic smear campaigns and unabashed vote buying. On election day, they dispensed rivers of free whiskey to entice voters' allegiance. While Sibley loftily abjured this bare knuckle campaigning, Brown carried on the fight in his behalf. When the votes were tallied, Rice had taken St. Anthony Falls. As one candid Sibley supporter regretfully reported, "We should have done better but they commenced buying votes in the morning." Elsewhere Rice was not so fortunate. The brash newcomer proved no match for the combination of Sibley's influence and Brown's political acumen. The final count resoundingly proved Sibley the people's choice, with 236 votes to Rice's 122. Of course, the greatest irony of Minnesota's first electoral contest was one that never crossed voters' minds—that a mere 357 individuals should determine the future of a territory home to more than 30,000 Indian people.[67]

[179]

By his own later admission, Henry Sibley had doubted that Congress would recognize his standing as the delegate of what he knew was a fictional territory. However, much to his surprise, his credentials were approved and he was seated in the House. No doubt the urbane and eloquent Sibley cut an impressive figure, but his success in pleading Minnesota's case derived more from national imperatives than from his persuasive powers. Since the previous year, the congressional contingent of Conscience Whigs, Free Soilers, and other antislavery factions had increased in number. Sectional animosity shaped every floor debate, and the antislavery bloc was eager to promote development of Minnesota as a future free state. In the charged climate of sectional partisanship, it was in their interest to accept the "benign fiction" of Wisconsin Territory and seat its earnest delegate. Moreover, when Stephen Douglas reintroduced the territorial bill, the slim antislavery majority now readily accepted his assurance that somewhere between 8,000 and 10,000 non-Indian individuals made their home within Minnesota's proposed boundaries. As Sibley lobbied for passage of the bill, Douglas advised him at every turn, brokering the deals behind the scene that finally, on the last day of the session, steered the bill to passage. On March 3, 1849, Minnesota Territory, with St. Paul as its capital, came into being—166,000 square miles that stretched from the St. Croix River on the east to the Missouri on the west and from the Iowa border to the British possessions in the north.[68]

Meanwhile, the Upper Mississippi, locked into "the severest winter known in the Northwest for many years," was cut off from the outside world. A first-person account describes the anxiety that gripped people in St. Paul as they awaited word from Washington, river traffic held up by the ice that "still held its iron grasp on Lake Pepin." Finally, on the stormy night of April 9, a steamboat whistle pierced the air:

In an instant the welcome news flashed like electricity throughout the town, and, regardless of the pelting rain, the raging wind, and the pealing thunder, almost the entire male population rushed to the landing. . . . At length the news was known, and one glad shout resounding through the boat, taken up on shore, and echoed from our beetling bluffs and rolling hills, proclaimed that *the bill for the organization of Minnesota Territory* had become a law![69]

[180]

Henry Sibley returned home a hero. His rival, Henry Rice, who also had spent the winter in Washington, supposedly on "private business," shouldered in for a share of the limelight, spreading word that he had thrown "his earnest efforts and personal influence in the scale also, being personally acquainted with a number of members [of Congress]." Sibley must have silently burned at Rice's hubris, adding fuel to the antagonism that would characterize a lifelong political rivalry between the two men. However, neither Sibley nor Rice, both Democrats, could look for any immediate political spoils. Sibley had imagined himself governor of the territory since James Doty had first dangled the appointment before him in 1842. But territorial appointments were the prerogative of the president, and as luck would have it, in the presidential election the previous fall Whig Zachary Taylor had defeated Democrat Lewis Cass, whom Sibley had known for years. Sibley and Rice both were ruefully aware that no patronage appointments would be coming to Minnesota Democrats.[70]

In fact, only two of the key territorial appointments went to Minnesotans, both from the St. Croix valley where transplanted New England Whigs predominated. The most prestigious appointments, in time-honored fashion, were dispensed as patronage to party faithful from Ohio, Tennessee, Pennsylvania, and Kentucky, who had worked to elect President Taylor. Though such appointments generally were considered political plums, a post in the wilds of Minnesota was not necessarily the most desirable of prospects. Two candidates politely declined the governorship before Alexander Ramsey of Pennsylvania accepted.[71] As the new officials of Minnesota Territory stepped onto the levee and got their first look at St. Paul, they may have experienced a moment's regret for the honor they had received. Governor Ramsey recalled his first impression of "but a few small log houses, no regular roads, plenty of trees and underbrush, running streams, strolling Indians, and but few human white beings, and these partook of all the characteristics of frontier life."[72]

In addition to the inauspicious surroundings, the new officials had to adjust to the unique contours of Minnesota's political economy. Pioneer historian J. Fletcher Williams (looking back from the 1870s, when mixed-blood ancestry had taken on a highly negative cast) asserted that when the territory was established, the bona fide "white" population, contrary to Senator Douglas's optimistic estimate, "could not have been more than 1,000 persons." Territorial status ignited an immediate surge in that population, as a steady stream of men on the make steamed up to St. Paul, eager to check out opportunities in the new territory. Seventy new buildings went up in the month of May, and by the middle of June St. Paul proudly exhibited 142 buildings (if one counted sheds and shanties), along with no fewer than twelve attorneys. But even so, when the first territorial census was taken that month "after many hundreds of immigrants had arrived," the non-Indian population of the entire territory totaled only 4,680 persons—many, if not most, partly of Indian ancestry. Seven hundred of the total lived along the Missouri in the present-day Dakotas and 367 were soldiers, who were not permanent residents at all. Of the 637 counted at Pembina, in Williams's opinion only a few were actually white. Moreover, all but a tiny fraction of the vast territory was unceded land, the domain of the Dakotas, Ojibwes, and the western plains tribes. Agriculture, the cornerstone of settlement, was almost nonexistent, with nearly all foodstuffs imported by steamboat from downriver. Newspaperman John Phillips Owens, on the ground in 1849, quickly discerned that the economy was fueled by a single source: "Beyond a few mercantile establishments suited in capacity to the limited domestic trade of the time, the business was almost exclusively confined to the Indian trade, which was carried on to the extent of millions. . . . The Indian trade was the great business of the country."[73]

The task to steer this "uncivilized" frontier to statehood was a daunting one, but Alexander Ramsey took on the challenge with energy and enthusiasm. Orphaned at the age of ten, Ramsey was no son of privilege. He had risen up the ranks through years of toil in the political trenches. When appointed governor of Minnesota Territory at the age of thirty-four, he considered it the chance of a lifetime. "Bluff Alec," as he was sometimes called, put all his political acumen to work to learn about and promote Minnesota. No doubt Henry Sibley was pleased to take the young governor under his wing and school him in the intricacies of local politics and the Indian trade. Ramsey and his family stayed with Sibley at his fine stone home in Mendota until a suitable governor's residence was readied in St. Paul, commencing a friendship and political alliance that endured despite their differences in party and social background.[74]

Ramsey was a quick study. He maintained cordial relations with the prominent traders, Democrats all, recognizing that their influence with the Indians made them crucial allies in his plans for Minnesota's future. He had a keen understanding that the territory's immediate needs demanded a two-pronged Indian policy that was at least superficially contradictory. On the one hand, it was critically important to open the land west of the Mississippi to settlement to bring more people into the territory, which meant removal of the Dakota people; at the same time, the more treaty Indians who lived within Minnesota's borders, the better it was for the territory's current economic health. The cooperation of the traders was essential on both fronts.

Most immediately, annuity payments spelled prosperity or ruin for the economy. Not only did Indians themselves buy goods with the cash they received, but also the payments and other government expenditures produced a multiplier effect that worked its way through the entire economy. As succinctly described by scholar Bruce White:

Businessmen who contracted with the government or who dealt directly with Indian people used their money to invest in real estate, to build buildings and houses, to buy, sell, and hire. Each person they paid spread the money around to others, helping to create a Minnesota economy, though little long-term benefit accrued to Indian people themselves.[75]

[182]

As superintendent of Indian Affairs for the territory as well as its governor, Ramsey had considerable influence to wield in this regard, and by the time the first session of the territorial legislature was called to order in 1849, he

Alexander Ramsey in a daguerreotype image made around 1844. Courtesy of the Minnesota Historical Society.

demonstrated full command of the complex, if temporary, role that Indians played in Minnesota's infant economy. The governor vigorously urged the assembly to ask for removal of all the Ojibwes living on lands ceded in the 1837 and 1842 treaties, a proposal they enthusiastically took up. The supposed purpose for removal was to "ensure the security and tranquility of the white settlements in an extensive and valuable district of this Territory." In reality, however, the vast majority of these Indians resided in Wisconsin. The true goal of the petition was to bring them *into* Minnesota, confined to territory west of the Mississippi, out of reach of Wisconsin traders. That way, annuity payments would flow to St. Paul rather than east to Detroit through Wisconsin. Though removal supporters vociferously claimed that the Ojibwes were guilty of "misbehavior" and "depredations" against whites, a scouring of the sources unearths only a handful of specific incidents. In fact, even as the legislature crafted its petition for removal, Indian agent Jonathan Fletcher reported that he found the Ojibwes "peaceable, temperate, and industrious."

In contrast, claims against the Winnebagos were common. Miserably unhappy on their heavily wooded Minnesota reservation, hemmed in on all sides by hostile tribes, the Winnebagos could neither hunt nor grow their traditional crops to sustain themselves. Dispirited and resentful, they frequently drowned their sorrows in alcohol peddled by ever-present whiskey sellers anxious to part them from their annuity monies. They also expressed their discontent by frequently harassing whites—stealing, killing cattle, and behaving in a generally threatening manner. Yet no voice was raised suggesting that they should be "removed." Whatever problems the Winnebagos caused were considered a necessary annoyance, repaid by the rich annuity payments that fed the Minnesota economy.[76]

The Dakotas west of the Mississippi were a different matter. Only the Mdewakantons received annuity payments from the Treaty of 1837. The rest of the tribe, since they had not participated in any land cessions, had no annuities to give them value in the "new" Minnesota. On the contrary, they were, by their very existence, a barrier to progress. Big development plans for the territory were stymied as long as growth was confined to the measly St. Croix–Mississippi triangle. Frustratingly, most of the 166,000 square miles of Minnesota Territory was Dakota land and thereby closed to development schemes. As for the fur trade as it had once existed, all forward-looking men agreed that it was a dead letter, an economic relic fast on its way to extinction. The buffalo migrated farther west each year, and the St. Peter River traders were eager for a treaty to erase their load of Indian debts. Everyone agreed: the Indians had to go.

Henry Sibley, who had the greatest investment in the Dakota trade, was an enthusiastic treaty proponent. He had been trying to extricate himself from the business for years and looked to a Dakota land cession as the means to finally recoup his losses and retire from the trade. In 1849, after his triumphal return from Washington, Sibley's political star was at its zenith. In the territory's first legitimate election in August, not even Henry Rice was rash enough to challenge him. Unopposed, Sibley garnered every vote and the grateful populace returned him to the capital as Minnesota's first congressional delegate. Understandably, he envisioned a brighter future for himself in politics and business than as a trader sinking deeper into debt each year. Whatever their other differences might be, Sibley, Rice, and every other territorial booster agreed that Minnesota's future—and their personal prosperity—depended on gaining control of the "Suland," as the newspapers had begun calling the land west of the Mississippi. That the Dakotas showed no interest in selling their lands was considered only a temporary obstacle.[77]

[184]

"Bluff Alec" Ramsey led the charge with a will, buoyed by the incessant drumbeat of "the one predominant and absorbing interest of the white people of the territory": to acquire the Dakota lands. "I soon imbibed this feeling," he wrote, "and lent myself with all my energies to bring about a purchase of the country in question." On September 4, 1849, three months after first setting foot on Minnesota soil, the governor stood before the legislature to lay out his agenda for the territory. They needed federal money to build roads and establish a regular mail service, as well as a stringent law restricting the sale of alcohol to the Indians. The Ojibwes must be removed from the ceded lands. But the overriding priority was acquisition of the Suland, that "extensive, rich and salubrious region . . . equal, in soil, to any portion of the valley of the Mississippi; and in healthfulness . . . probably superior to any part of the American Continent . . . rich in minerals . . . watered by the finest rivers . . . bespangled with lakes in every direction . . . wooded hilltops, luxuriant natural meadows, and abundance of the purest water." Ramsey ended his stirring speech with a pledge to "do right, to do justice, to live in harmony with all, and to use whatever power I incidentally possess, entirely for the true and abiding weal of Minnesota." The legislators must have risen in a body to cheer the governor's inspiring address. His words were clearly heartfelt and without intended irony. Despite the facts that Indians were centrally important to the territory's economy; that they owned about nine-tenths of the land; and that more than 85 percent of the territory's population were Dakota, Ojibwe, or Winnebago people, their interests did not factor into the "true and abiding weal" of the territory that Ramsey pledged to serve in justice and harmony. Quite simply, Indians were no part of the future Minnesota he imagined.[78]

Chapter 8

CIVILIZED PURSUITS

Give way, give way, young warrior
Thou and thy steed give way—
Rest not, though lingers on the hills
The red sun's parting ray.
The rocky bluff and prairie land
The white man claims them now,
The symbols of his course are here,
The rifle, axe, and plough.

    MARY EASTMAN, 1849

There is one thing more which our great father can do, that is, gather
us all together on the prairie and surround us with soldiers and shoot
us down.

    WABASHA, Mdewakanton chief, 1852

Suland Strategies

On June 29, 1851, as the first streaks of early morning light dappled the deck
of the steamboat *Excelsior*, Governor Alexander Ramsey, territorial delegate
Henry Sibley, and a parade of prominent officials, handpicked unofficial aides,
newspapermen, and observers prepared to depart Fort Snelling for Traverse
des Sioux. It had taken two years of careful planning and positioning, but at
last they were ready to effect the coup that would make Minnesota's future.
They were on their way to extract the Suland from the Dakotas. Missionary
Gideon Pond, long known as a friend of the Indians, had not been invited to
join the party. Noting the "very early hour" of the *Excelsior*'s departure and the
"class of persons on board," Pond reluctantly admitted to "painful suspicions"
about the conduct of the forthcoming treaty negotiations.[1]

The purpose of the expedition was no secret. People in St. Paul had talked of nothing else for months, impatiently pressing for treaty negotiations to begin. The previous year chartered steamers had begun carrying fashionable St. Paulites up the St. Peter River (now more commonly called the Minnesota) into Indian country to dine, dance, and explore the "uninhabited" western lands. Thrilled by the prospects for development as much as by the "beautiful, charming, delightful, enchanting, enrapturing, overwhelmingly lovely" landscapes they passed, the tourists unanimously agreed "these lands ought and must be ours." As for the current inhabitants, the travelers scarcely noted them. In their eyes American expansionism was an ordained right that imperiously swept aside Native impediments in its path. Schoolteacher Harriet Bishop, who traveled in the first junket up the Minnesota, described the Indians she saw as "filthy inmates" of primitive lodges and, even more tellingly, asserted later that "no sign of human life appeared" along the steamer's route.[2]

More savvy expansionists knew better than to ignore the more than 20,000 Dakotas who held rightful ownership of the lands they coveted. Alexander Ramsey, in the first flush of gubernatorial zeal, had tried to convene a treaty council at Mendota in the autumn of 1849. But he soon discovered that the Dakotas were not easily wooed by an unknown stranger, regardless of his official position. To Ramsey's embarrassment, after pressing Washington for immediate permission to negotiate a treaty, he had to report that only a few Indians deigned to attend the council. "Most . . . had left for their fall hunt," he lamely explained. Others stayed away due to "other [unnamed] causes of difficulty."[3]

The "difficulties" were significant, both embedded in government policy and on the ground in Minnesota. Most crucially, Ramsey did not have the backing of the all-important traders. Congress had agreed to pay only a paltry 2½ cents per acre, most of which was to be in the form of "useful goods," provisions, livestock, and farm implements, with only a minimal cash payout. Sibley cautioned Ramsey that the Indians would never accept such meager terms—a warning that derived at least as much from self-interest as from concern for his Dakota friends. Sibley, who prided himself on his unbending integrity, was a frequent critic of the government's "wretched" Indian policy, which in his estimation treated the Indians "as a damned race." But he also had a personal stake in the terms of the land sale. Commerce with the Indians had become the backbone of the trade and the bulk of government payments would find its way directly into traders' pockets. A generous, more just settlement, with a liberal disbursement of hard money, so Sibley could tell himself, would benefit Indians and traders alike; thus, he made no move to promote Ramsey's initiative. In fact, according to missionary Stephen Riggs, Sibley's traders in the west urged the Sissetons and Wahpetons to stay away from the council meeting, suggesting to the chiefs that the governor intended to depose them from their leadership positions.[4]

An act of Congress, passed in 1847, posed an even bigger stumbling block. Trader payments, which had become a national scandal, were to be expressly excluded from all future treaties. Sibley, who had more influence among the Dakotas than any white man in the territory, bluntly informed the governor that no treaty could be concluded if the Indians were not "allowed" to pay their just debts. In other words, unless he and Ramsey worked out a way to compensate the traders, he would withhold his support in bringing the chiefs to the table.[5]

Just how crucial that support was to the negotiations quickly became apparent to the governor. The few Mdewakanton leaders who attended the council came only to present a list of grievances (which, Ramsey may have noted, was penned in Sibley's hand). First among their complaints, Mdewakanton spokesman Chief Wabasha informed the governor, was that promises made in the 1837 treaty remained unfulfilled. Specifically, the Indians demanded immediate distribution of some $50,000 held in an "education fund." Until their grievances were satisfied, they would not discuss further land cessions. Rather than open a perilous discussion about broken promises, Ramsey wisely passed out an array of gifts to the Indians, ended the council, and retired to regroup—and enlist Henry Sibley's support.[6]

Apparently, over the winter the governor and Sibley had come to an understanding. Ramsey endorsed raising the price offered from 2½ to 10 cents per acre (most of which would make its way into St. Paul's economy), and as later events would demonstrate, the two men had hatched a clever plan to ensure that the traders would be paid. Satisfied with the agreement, Sibley went to work. He directed his traders to court the Indians' goodwill by returning to past practices of openhanded credit and liberal gift giving, even if it meant taking short-term losses. The veteran traders, nearly all kin to the Dakotas either by blood or marriage, were happy to oblige in easing the hardships that beset their Indian relatives. These kinship relations would prove centrally important in the months to come. The following year, prominent mixed-blood traders Gabriel and Joseph Renville and the Faribault brothers would play a key role in bringing the Dakotas to the council table.[7]

Most mixed-blood people were in favor of a treaty. Well aware that the tide of settlement was now unstoppable, they hoped to win favorable terms for their Indian kin in the sale of their lands. Moreover, most of them were affiliated with the trade themselves and held handfuls of currently uncollectible Indian debts. They also expected to receive cash payments, as they had in past treaties. As a final sweetener, Sibley assured them he was working to include the sale of the half-breed tract along Lake Pepin in the treaty package, land that mixed bloods had been deeded communally in 1830 but had no rights to sell. Given all these expected benefits, it is not surprising that mixed bloods promoted the treaty to their full-blood kin.[8]

Sibley also took pains to win support from the missionaries, who wielded considerable influence among some Dakotas who were beginning to adapt themselves to Euro-American ways. Though the missionaries tended to blame the traders for all the Indians' ills, they made an exception for the gentlemanly

Sibley, who seemed to share their cultural values more than the rest of the rough-hewn backwoods fraternity. Moreover, Sibley was known as a critic of the way previous treaties had "betrayed and deceived" the Indians. Even as he paved the way for an unprecedented land grab, he spoke out in Congress against the policy of "utter extermination" that his government had practiced. "Minnesota," he vowed, "shall at least be freed from any responsibility on that score." Stephen Riggs and Thomas Williamson thus regarded Sibley approvingly as a kindred spirit who shared their Christian concerns and were easily enlisted as treaty advocates. The treaty also neatly supported their plan for "saving" the Indians. Only recently, they had jointly published an "Outline of a Plan for Civilizing the Dakota." The agenda it set out called for the abolishment of the "community property system" and the need to "restrict" and "confine" the Indians to "persuade" them to give up hunting and gathering for a more "worthwhile" agricultural lifestyle. In other words, since proselytizing and persuasion had failed, they hoped to force the Indians into farming by limiting their access to land, which would make it impossible to sustain themselves by hunting. Once civilized and under the close supervision of the missionaries, the former savages would more readily embrace Christian principles. The proposed massive land cession would clearly advance the plan they had conceived.[9]

As the various treaty promoters worked among the tribes over the subsequent months, the Dakotas themselves were not of a single mind. In the west, the Sissetons and Wahpetons were in dire straits. A succession of bad winters had repeatedly brought the bands to the brink of starvation, forcing them to eat their "horses, dogs, and even the skins covering their tepees." In 1850, massive autumn prairie fires had raged from the Minnesota River valley to the James River in present-day South Dakota, driving the buffalo west to the Missouri. Trader Martin McLeod, writing from his post on the Minnesota River, reported that the desperate Sissetons and Wahpetons were anxious for a treaty and would sell "a large portion of their country if liberally dealt with." Their Mdewakanton relatives had clearly benefited from their small land cession in 1837. The $10,000 per year that the band received in annuities cushioned them from the worst of the deprivations experienced by the other Dakota bands. To be sure, most of the money was funneled directly to traders and St. Paul merchants, but it assured that the Mdewakantons had access to credit, even if the terms were hard and prices for goods unconscionably high. Many Sissetons and Wahpetons were thus willing to sell a portion of their lands to secure reliable income to sustain themselves, especially since the plains stretched to their west as far as a man could ride in a week, the domain of their Lakota kin.[10]

The Mdewakantons and Wahpekutes who peopled the Mississippi and Cannon River valleys were more problematic. Mdewakantons in particular were reluctant to treat for additional land cessions. They already received annuity payments and had personal experience with the unreliability of government promises. They also resented that the bulk of their payments were disbursed in the form of goods, provisions, and agricultural implements over which they had no control. Moreover, they were a woodland people and had no desire to relocate on the plains, as they had already demonstrated in 1849. Writing from Lake Traverse, McLeod advised Sibley to treat first with the upper bands (Sissetons and Wahpetons), who were so desperate for relief "they would sign almost anything." Once those lands were ceded, the lower bands (Mdewakantons and Wahpekutes) would be encircled by white settlement and would have no choice but to negotiate.[11]

Taking McLeod's advice, the treaty strategizers determined to hold two councils, first with the Sissetons and Wahpetons at Traverse des Sioux, followed by a second council with the Mdewakantons and Wahpekutes at Mendota. Sibley was confident that he had prepared the ground for a smooth operation. He could assure his creditor, Pierre Chouteau in St. Louis, that his debts would soon be cleared, confidently boasting, "The Indians are all prepared to make a treaty when we tell them to do so, and such a one as I may dictate. . . . I think I may safely promise you that no treaty can be made without our claims being first secured."[12]

When the *Excelsior* put to shore at Traverse des Sioux on June 29, the official party was disappointed to find only a handful of missionaries and a small band of local Sissetons awaiting them—"and no news that the Indians of the upper bands are on their way here to the treaty." The resident Indians were planting corn, which suggested that they were not anticipating vacating their land any time soon. Nonetheless, Ramsey, Commissioner of Indian Affairs Luke Lea, and the rest of the "interested parties" confidently set up tents and marquees, began distributing food, and prepared to wait. As St. Paul newspaperman James Goodhue brightly noted, in fishing for Indians "Uncle Sam baits the Sioux with bullocks." Indeed, for the hungry Indians, even those who opposed treaty making, the lure of abundant feasting was irresistible. Soon groups of Sissetons and Wahpetons began arriving in a slow but steady stream, joining Mdewakanton "observers" who cheerfully took part in the prepared bounty. Goodhue reported ebulliently to his readers in St. Paul, "The way they take the bait is amazing," and for "every crack of the rifle that brings down a bullock for a Dahcota feast, there is sacrificed at least a township of their territory."[13]

Lea and Ramsey optimistically had hoped the treaty could be negotiated in a matter of days. But the Indians had no incentive to hurry the proceedings. Decision making among the Dakotas traditionally was reached by consensus that resulted from lengthy democratic deliberation and they refused to begin negotiations until the bands to the west had arrived. Nor were they eager to end the feasting, games, drumming, and contests that filled the days while they waited. Perhaps most important, while the Indians no doubt knew that some sort of land cession was inevitable, they intended to assert their position as a still powerful nation who must be courted for their favor. Dressed in their finest apparel and displaying their skills at riding, shooting, gamesmanship, and ceremonial singing and dancing, the Dakotas meant to present themselves as equal, if not superior, to any white person present. As one chief placidly informed the commissioners, "If our Great Father wants to buy our land, we will talk with him about it at a proper time. Our Great Father has several cattle left yet. There is no hurry."[14]

Meanwhile, it rained. Day after day, drenched and miserable, the official party suffered "buffalo-gnats and musketoes here among the savages for a month, sleeping out of doors and feeding upon tough beef and pilot-bread." But the traders wisely counseled patience, and as the days passed a virtual city of teepees gradually took shape at the Traverse. Martin McLeod arrived with a contingent from Lac qui Parle, Stephen Riggs shepherded another from Lake Traverse, Joseph La Framboise came in with Sisseton kin and friends from the west, and many hundreds more came on their own. By midmonth the congregation of Dakotas had grown to more than 2,000 and the commissioners feared that they would soon run out of provisions.[15] The vista of the treaty grounds was stunningly transformed. Described euphorically by Goodhue to his readers:

> Behold, yonder, upon the sleeping hillside, the glorious flag of our country, every wave of which sends a pulsation of pride through American hearts under its protection, a few tents and marquees of a little handful of men, constituting the commission, unguarded by sentinel or musket, amid hundreds of savages, lodging everywhere in their sugar-loaf shaped tepees of skin, along the brow of terrace beyond terrace, and rising ridge beyond rising ridge, far in the back-ground, the tepees showing their sharp outline against the blue sky in the rear.[16]

Very soon, Goodhue rhapsodized, a greater transformation would take place in the Suland, making it "the home of thriving husbandmen, and the birth-place of magic villages and cities, enlivened by steamboats, and railroad cars, and the clatter of manufactories, and the bustling activity of commerce." The time had come for treaty making to begin.[17]

Three weeks of rain, heat, and insects had dampened the high spirits and goodwill that the commissioners and their entourage had brought to the council. In his first dispatches, Goodhue had described the assembled Indians as a noble people, writing, "In our intercourse with them, fairness, justice, and honor, these people possess such qualities to a degree that seems astonishing, in those whose only book is creation, and whose only God is nature." Two weeks later, when it appeared the Indians were not about to sign away their country without a murmur of dissent, the newsman's opinion had soured considerably. "The poetry of the Indian character and life is all in the imaginations of those who have never seen them," he fumed. "They are the most idle, filthy, lewd, and cowardly vagabonds possible, not at all better or unlike any other race of savages." Goodhue wanted nothing more than to get back to St. Paul and civilization.[18]

Commissioners Ramsey and Lea were equally eager to depart. They felt they had wasted enough time catering to Indian sensibilities and intended to get the treaty signed and delivered without further delay. In the opening council session, convened on July 18, Ramsey immediately got down to business, informing the assembled chiefs and headmen that the Great Father in Washington was distressed that his "red children" were suffering and wanted to help them by purchasing "the country which you possess here which is of comparatively little value to you." He asked for all their land in present-day Minnesota and Iowa, reserving for the Indians as a new "permanent and common home" only a one-hundred-mile stretch, ten miles wide, along either side of the Minnesota River from Yellow Medicine Creek to Lake Traverse. "Collected together" in one location, he assured the Dakotas, they would be "happier and more comfortable, and every year growing better and richer." The governor then quickly moved on to lay out the package of annuities, goods, provisions, improvements, and farming assistance that had typified earlier treaties—a total value of just over $1.5 million for what was regarded as "twenty-one millions of acres of the finest land in the world." The irony of the moment was inescapable. Less than a decade earlier, on that very spot, many of the same Dakota leaders gathered at Traverse des Sioux in 1851 had signed a treaty that would have created a permanent Indian state. Now they were being asked to leave those same lands forever. The Indians, stunned by the dimensions of the proposed land purchase, sat in silence. Ramsey advised them to go home, think it over, and return in the morning with their answer.[19]

The Indians spent the night in heated discussion. Though most of those present had desired a treaty, they had not expected to be asked for their entire homeland. Some wanted to reject the treaty; others, with an educated understanding of land values, wanted to set a price of $6 million. But tribal elders sorrowfully knew that they had little negotiating room. As historian Rhoda Gilman writes, "Scarcely anyone was too naïve to see that the elaborate drama at the treaty table was a mask for naked conquest. If no treaty were signed, white men would swarm into the land anyway, and should the Dakota try to drive them out, some pretext would be found to send in troops."[20]

Reaching no consensus after hours of debate, the chiefs and headmen hoped to delay the proceedings. When the council convened the following morning, to Ramsey and Lea's frustration the chiefs refused to speak. Finally, Orphan (sometimes called the Star), a chief of the Lake Traverse Sisseton, announced that he wished to wait until his young men arrived from the west. Ramsey, discarding all pretence of diplomacy, retorted, "We have now been here three long weeks doing nothing. . . . You who are here are men and chiefs, and you should just take hold of this business like men and arrange it at once." Sisseton chief Sleepy Eyes, cut to the quick, responded, "Your coming and asking me for my country makes me sad; and your saying I am not able to do anything with my country makes me still more sad. Those who are coming behind are my near relatives, and I expected certainly to see them here." With that he arose and left the council, followed by his men.[21]

Ramsey was incensed. He ordered no further rations be issued and notified the Indians that unless they agreed to treat by evening, the commissioners would strike their tents and depart the next day. Faced with the naked reality of their need and the limits of their options, within hours the chiefs capitulated. Sleepy Eyes apologized for the "misunderstanding": "No offence or disrespect was intended. We only wanted more time to consider." The next day negotiations commenced in earnest, with Sibley and his traders and Stephen Riggs constantly shuttling among the bands to urge their acceptance of the terms. Two days later, on July 23, the chiefs put their hand to the pen and signed away their lands. It was not a happy occasion. Though Commissioner Lea pronounced that "nothing but our kind feelings to the Sioux people would have induced us to make a treaty so favorable to them," the Indians were not deceived. Sleepy Eyes, before signing, stated that the commissioners had taken advantage of their "difficult circumstances" to offer less than the land was worth. He wanted a copy of the treaty to be kept with the Indians "that we may be looking at it and know whether you are telling us the truth or not." Orphan noted that he wanted the treaty to "remain unchanged and not to go to Washington to be altered." Wahpeton chief Big Curly Head perhaps said it best: "You think it a great deal of money to give for this land, but you must well understand that the money will all go back to the whites again, and the country will also remain theirs."[22]

Even as the chief was speaking, treaty payments were transferring into the hands of the traders, thanks to a clever provision designed to take care of traders' claims. Though the treaty did not specifically compensate them, a special cash sum of $305,000, called "hand money," was allotted to assist the bands in establishing their new homes on the reservation, provide for their mixed-blood relations, and allow the chiefs in open council to "settle their affairs"—which, of course, meant pay their debts to the traders. Sibley and his friends had prepared a paper that pledged the chiefs to repay their bands' debts and provide gift money to mixed-blood relatives. At the treaty-signing ceremony, each signator, after making his mark, was directed, either by a trader or mixed blood or by missionary Stephen Riggs, to a nearby upended barrel, where Joe Brown waited with another pen. The prepared "traders' paper" that the Indians were then handed to sign was not explained. Some understood the nature of the document but many thought it was another copy of the treaty, though in later testimony the traders swore it had been previously agreed upon. Indian subagent Nathaniel McLean, suspecting that the Indians did not understand what they were signing, requested that the paper be read and explained in open council. The commissioners, indebted to the traders and anxious to end the tiresome proceedings, brushed him off. The result was a masterful coup for the debt-ridden traders, clearing accounts that stretched back to 1819. Henry Sibley, true to form, stayed aloof during the signing ceremony. Though he was the architect of the plan, he could rely on his friends and associates to see it through. Nearly every veteran of the Dakota trade appeared on the list of creditors for substantial sums, which in large part would go to pay off their own debts to Sibley—who made direct claims of $144,984. His efforts on behalf of the treaty had been well worthwhile. When the claims were tallied and adjusted, $210,000 went to the traders and $40,000 to mixed-blood payments, leaving a mere $60,000 for the more than 15,000 Wahpetons and Sissetons to establish and sustain themselves for a year on the narrow strip of land that was to be their home.[23]

For the treaty party from St. Paul, the journey home was a merry one. The men cheerfully piled onto a waiting keelboat and swung into the current of the Minnesota "with three hearty cheers." Not surprisingly, few Indians came down to the landing to wish them bon voyage. No matter. The hours quickly passed with song, toasts, and congratulations all around. Some of the jovial passengers even tried their hands at the oars. In less than twenty-four hours they docked at Mendota, eager to finish the business with the lower bands. With the western lands now in their possession, they expected no difficulties from the encircled Mdewakantons and Wahpekutes who were awaiting them there.[24]

However, when the treaty council at Mendota commenced on July 29, the commissioners soon discovered that the small band of Wahpekutes deferred to the Mdewakantons, and the Mdewakantons would prove hard bargainers. Living in closer proximity to white settlers than the other tribes and schooled by experience with earlier treaties, they knew both the value of their land as real estate and the dubious worth of government promises. One contingent, mainly young braves led by Chief Wabasha, wanted no part of any further land cessions. Another group, mostly those who had taken up farming and were accommodating themselves to living among whites, were in favor of trading land for annuity payments. Others were undecided. But no one was satisfied with the terms that were offered—with provisions similar to the Traverse des Sioux treaty and a narrow reservation proposed along the Minnesota River, just below the upper bands. "For their good," Ramsey advised, they should "pass away from the [Mississippi] river and go farther west" since now "you would not only have the whites along the river in front but all around you." Wabasha retorted that until they received the money owing from the 1837 treaty, they had no interest in opening further discussions. Anticipating this demand, first advanced in 1849, Henry Sibley had borrowed $30,000 from Chouteau and Company to cover what the Indians were owed, and the commissioners tried to use it to leverage agreement to the treaty. They promised that as soon as the treaty was signed, the funds would be handed over. The ploy did not succeed with the wary Mdewakantons. Little Crow IV (Taoyateduta), who emerged in the council as a shrewd and sophisticated negotiator, declared, "We will talk of nothing else but that money if it is until next spring. That lies in the way of the treaty."25

Over the next few days, the traders and commissioners worked on the Indians with a combination of persuasion and veiled threats of force. But the Mdewakantons remained adamant until the $30,000 was finally handed over—a small victory for the Indians and a boon for the merchants of St. Paul, where most of the money was immediately spent on guns, horses, provisions, and whiskey. The *Minnesota Pioneer* gleefully reported the surge in business: "Indians all over town with double-eagles, and Third Street especially was converted into a temporary horse bazaar."26

Then the negotiations began in earnest. A high point near the Minnesota River, known as Pilot Knob, had been chosen as the council site. From the vantage there, the Indians could observe the settlements across the river growing visibly larger by the day. Despite their internal disagreements, they all knew in their hearts that they could not hold off the tide of white invaders. But neither were they willing to passively accept the government's terms. They scoffed at the $800,000 offered for their land, forcing the commissioners to boost the offered package of cash, goods, and services to $1,410,000, nearly equal to what had been agreed to at Traverse des Sioux for a much larger tract of land. They also demanded that the reservation boundary extend farther southeast into the woodlands along the lower Minnesota. Both Wabasha and Little Crow argued that their people were "used to the woods and do not like the prairies." Grudgingly, the commissioners agreed to extend the reservation a bit, though not as far as the valuable hardwood forest.27 Finally, the Mdewakantons made a stand to gain control over shaping their future. Addressing the commissioners, Wabasha demonstrated a keen understanding of the connection between cash and tribal autonomy:

> In the treaty I have heard read, you have mentioned farmers and schools, physicians, traders, and half-breeds. To all these I am opposed. You see these chiefs sitting around. They and others who are dead went to Washington and made a treaty, in which the same things were said; but we have not been benefited by them, and I want them struck out of this one—we want nothing but cash turned over to us for our lands.28

This was an argument that the Indians had no chance of winning. After days of wrangling, the treaty was signed on August 5. In the end, the Mdewakantons had wrested the best terms possible, considering the disadvantages under which they labored. As Commissioner Lea ominously had pointed out, their "Great Father" could, if he wished, "come with 100,000 men and drive you off to the Rocky Mountains." The Indians had to settle for annuities, goods, and services rather than a cash payment. Neither the Mendota nor the Traverse des

Sioux treaty would disburse any of the principal from the land sale in the form of cash directly to the bands to use at their discretion. Instead, the funds were to be held in trust by the government, the Indians receiving only the interest, in the form of annuities, over a period of fifty years. Though the commissioners harangued them during the negotiations to make decisions like "chiefs and men—not women and children," the Euro-Americans persisted in treating

Little Crow sketched by Frank Blackwell Mayer in 1851 at Traverse des Sioux. Courtesy of Edward E. Ayer Collection, The Newberry Library, Chicago.

them as children. One after another, in later testimony, they insisted that the Indians could not be trusted to handle their own money. Moreover, reformers like Riggs counted on the noncash provisions to assist in their "civilization" agenda, "making men" of the Dakotas. The farming communities that the treaty was designed to create would, according to Ramsey, "render labor respectable . . . enlighten their ignorance . . . conquor [sic] their prejudices." Most important, if the hand money were turned over to the chiefs, the traders expected to have much more difficulty in collecting their debts. No one but the Indians would benefit from a purely cash sale.[29]

[196]

Spoils to the Victor

The treaties set off a frenzy of celebration in St. Paul. In the *Pioneer*, editor James Goodhue achieved new heights of triumphal boosterism, envisioning "the red savages with their tipis, their horses, and their famished dogs, fading, vanishing, dissolving away, and in their place a thousand farms and white cottages and waving wheat fields . . . cities crowned with spires and railroads with trains of cars." Settlers and speculators scrambled in a mad dash to check out and claim the newly ceded lands. In Sibley's words, "People [were] almost crazy to get claims on the west of the Mississippi." Legally they had no right to trespass in Dakota country until the treaties were ratified, but that technicality seemed to deter no one. Governor Ramsey, buoyed by his success with the Dakotas, set off almost immediately for Pembina to treat with the Ojibwes for the Red River valley in the north. Successfully employing his now proven tactics of inducement and coercion, he soon had another land cession of five million acres in hand. Meanwhile, Sibley departed for Washington to make sure that ratification of the treaties proceeded smoothly through the Congress.[30]

As far as the jubilant Minnesotans were concerned, the virtue of the treaties was self-evident, making ratification a mere formality. But Sibley, already schooled in national politics, was less confident. He knew that Minnesota was a pawn in a much larger game. The pro-slavery bloc had nothing to gain in advancing Minnesota's march to statehood and, sure enough, a battle over ratification soon took shape in the Senate. Sibley needed all his powerful Free Soil allies, as well as a proficient hired lobbyist, to push the treaties through. Finally, after four months of debate, arm twisting, and quite likely a liberal dose of bribery (with the funds later deducted from the Indians' payment), the Dakota treaties were approved by the narrowest of margins. But the apparent victory was not all that it seemed.[31]

Sibley advised Ramsey with regret that the Pembina treaty had not survived, "offered up as a conciliatory sacrifice" to save the Dakota treaties. For the time being at least, the Red River valley would remain in Ojibwe hands. Much more problematic, though, were certain amendments attached to the Dakota treaties by their opponents. Unable to quash ratification altogether, the southern senators cleverly revised the terms in ways that they were confident the Indians would not accept, then added the stipulation that the Indians must assent to the changes in writing. The key amendments eliminated the reservation lands along the Minnesota River, effectively sending the Dako-

president would later designate. ... ould never agree to such terms. ... tract at Lake Pepin, which they ... st the revised agreement. Satis-... ath, they voted to ratify, fully ex-...

anticipate trouble from the Indi-... e bands. When the Sissetons and ... traders' paper they had signed, ... it, and the other chiefs protested ... all the promised hand money to ... oley's traders but also kin to the ... claring that the Indians had been ... e chiefs and headmen of the up-... to protest that their signatures ... y were willing to pay their just ... claims and disburse the funds ... responded that the traders' pa-... matter "entirely between them-... o control.[33]

fall that Sibley had engineered, ... est. Shortly after the council at ... er arrived there to set up a post. ... Ewing brothers, who ran a trad-... d followed the Winnebagos into ... he Dakota trade. Sweetser soon ... bands, providing a sympathetic ... lispensed with an open hand. In ... f the discontented chiefs. When ... omplaint, they entrusted Sweet-... laims. Sweetser then hustled off ... to W... and put the ratification process in jeop...

Also stirring up trouble behind the scenes was Henry Rice. It must have galled the ambitious Rice, who had no trade with the Dakotas, to see Sibley reap many thousands in profit from the treaties while Rice was consigned to the sidelines. The simmering rivalry between the two men had bubbled over into a full-blown feud two years earlier when a messy dispute had abruptly ended their business partnership and stained Rice's reputation. Sibley had become disturbed by the scale of Rice's real estate speculation and, what seemed to Sibley, a propensity for shady business dealings. Suspecting Rice of using company funds to finance his personal ventures, he urged Pierre Chouteau to send someone to audit his partner's accounts. When an examination of Rice's books turned up gross irregularities, it resulted in an injunction against him that shocked his St. Paul neighbors. Though the matter was resolved without a lawsuit, Rice was publicly embarrassed and harbored deep resentments against his former partner. Given the opportunity, Rice probably was eager to diminish Sibley's profits and, if possible, discredit his integrity in the process.[35]

The personal feud between Rice and Sibley, Minnesota's most prominent Democrats, effectively split the party into two warring factions that would shape the course of state politics for decades to come. Statewide, Sibley's stature was incontestable, but Rice was the darling of St. Paul. He had concentrated most of his speculative ventures on the rough-hewn capital and become its most ardent booster. He and his new bride, Matilda, had set up housekeeping in St. Paul in 1850, where he continued to acquire land and built a hotel and several warehouses. He also freely donated land for civic improvements and, employing his legendary charm, soon became St. Paul's preeminent citizen—undoubtedly to Sibley's chagrin. In 1849, when Ramsey had first attempted to treat for the Suland, Rice had cautioned him to wait two years until St. Paul was on a firmer footing. If the treaty were made prematurely, he warned, Mendota would overtake the little town and Henry Sibley would dominate civic affairs as "the man." By 1851, St. Paul was well established and Rice himself was "the man." Still, Sibley's coup with the treaties must have made Rice seethe. However, with all his friends anxious for the land acquisition to succeed, he had to work discreetly to subvert the trader payments without endangering his stature as a public figure. Sweetser and the Ewings may have provided the necessary cover.[36]

Thus, a tangle of political, economic, and personal interests complicated the road to ratification. With sectional conflict shaping the course of national politics and Indian discontents and trader intrigue roiling the waters on the local front, it is no wonder that Sibley found it rough going in Washington. Complaining to Ramsey, he declared, "I have had more vexation & hard labor, mingled with no little mortification this past winter & spring, in pushing forward these treaties, than any consideration would induce me to undergo again." No doubt the image-conscious Sibley was mortified by Sweetser's accusations of fraud, though the Senate showed little interest in examining the Dakotas' claims—additional evidence that Indian rights never factored into the debate over the treaties. In the end, the final version had very little to do with any priorities in Minnesota and everything to do with the ongoing national power struggle. Nonetheless, the pro-slavery politicians in Washington, as they made their calculations, could not know that events in Minnesota had outpaced their strategies and would carry the treaties through, despite their untenable amendments.[37]

When news of the amended treaty reached the Indians, they were understandably outraged. Wabasha, who had opposed the treaty from the outset, declared, "There is one thing more which our great father can do, that is, gather us all together on the prairie and surround us with soldiers and shoot us down." All the bands initially rejected the outrageously revised terms, but Wabasha's despairing assessment reflected what most of the tribal statesmen understood all too well: In fact, if not by law, they had already been dispossessed of their land.[38]

Settlers and speculators, not waiting for official word that the land was theirs for the taking, had already scrambled across the Mississippi by the hundreds, if not thousands. The Dakotas lodged vehement protests against this illegal invasion, but neither military nor civil officials made a move to intervene. In fact, Henry Sibley advised Governor Ramsey from Washington to "let the people go on to the purchased country in the thousands if they will." A large population already in place would make it difficult for southern senators to oppose ratification, especially in the face of Sibley's grim warning that failure to ratify would likely set off a ferocious Indian war. Ramsey himself was delighted at the pace of development, reporting that "some half dozen embryo towns" had already established themselves west of the Mississippi. The fledgling town of Le Sueur alone counted more than 100 residents. The Indians recognized that there was no way now to push the settlers back. Their numbers were too great and the government tacitly supported their illegal claims. In addition, with whites overrunning Dakota hunting grounds and driving away what little game remained, the Indians knew they had to have annuities to make it through the coming winter. But neither could they survive as a people without the promised reservation, where they could reestablish their communities. The treaty commissioners had touted the benefits that would be showered on the new reservations—schools, medical care, mills, roads, blacksmiths, farming assistance, etc. What was to become of those promises now? And where, the angry Indians asked, were they expected to go?[39]

The Mdewakantons presented the most immediate problem, since the majority of the squatters had crowded onto their lands and tensions between settlers and Indians were rising by the day. Fewer settlers had made their way into the territory of the upper bands, but anger flared there with a white heat as well. The Sissetons and Wahpetons, who believed they had been duped and cheated at Traverse des Sioux, were firmly opposed to "signing any more papers." Adding to the growing controversy, the missionaries were beginning to voice a new opposition. They had supported the treaties precisely because they would "contain" the Indians on reservations where they could more easily be schooled in a "civilized" Christian lifestyle. Denied a reservation, the Indians would scatter to the winds, making the missionaries' task more difficult than ever.[40]

With dissatisfaction ominously endangering the treaties, Ramsey was desperate to get the land cession ratified before all his hard work and plans came to naught. He knew he had to resolve the reservation issue and petitioned the president to allow the Indians to occupy temporarily—perhaps for twenty years—the lands that originally had been marked out for the reservation. He was so anxious to seal the treaties that he offered the proposal to the Dakotas without waiting for the president's reply. But the damage had been done. All trust had been broken between the Dakotas and those who had brokered the treaties. Despite that all the bands were in dire need of annuities and supplies—the previous winter had been exceptionally harsh—not even Sibley's assurances could move the chiefs to affix their mark on the suspect document.[41]

Enter Henry Rice. Quite likely Rice was enjoying every moment of Sibley's discomfiture. Already renowned for his powers of persuasion with the Winnebagos and Ojibwes, Rice boasted that for $10,000 *he* could convince the Indians to sign the treaty. Hercules Dousman, who had a significant financial stake in the proceedings, took Rice up on his offer on behalf of the traders and counseled Sibley to swallow his pride and work with his rival. Since Rice had no earlier relationship with the Dakotas and thus no profit to be gained from the treaty, he had the best chance of gaining their trust. Reluctantly, Sibley acquiesced, though he left it to one of his traders to communicate with Rice. Governor Ramsey enthusiastically supported the plan, pledging to cover the cost of gifts and expenses, in addition to the $10,000 the traders would pay for Rice's services. A month later, as good as his boast, Rice had obtained the necessary signatures on both the Mendota and Traverse des Sioux amended treaties.[42]

Just how he accomplished this masterstroke has never been fully determined, since he kept no record of his negotiations. Certainly, with winter coming on, the Indians were in a poor bargaining position. Expecting to receive their annuities and perhaps move over the summer, they had planted no corn or other garden crops, nor were their prospects for the hunt very hopeful. But they had faced many lean winters before. Rice also courted their friendship with lavish gifts and feasts. Philander Prescott, who served as Rice's interpreter, commented that the chiefs had been fed "like gluttons." But a few good meals would hardly be enough to make them sign away their homeland. A number of Indians claimed Rice had done much more. He led them to believe that the reservation was to be theirs forever. Furthermore, he persuaded the Sissetons and Wahpetons to revoke Sweetser's power of attorney and assign it instead to Ramsey. Assured that this new document "broke all former papers," as the Indians understood it the paper they signed not only revoked Sweetser's power of attorney, it also "unmade" the traders' paper they had signed at Traverse des Sioux. They were soon to discover their error.[43]

While it is not possible to prove that Henry Rice intentionally deceived the Dakotas, his record of business dealings, both with Native people and Anglo associates, makes the suspicion at least plausible. While Henry Sibley, despite a penchant for self-interest and self-deception, drew the line at outright fraud,

Rice evinced no similar scruples. In any case, he must have been pleased to finally squeeze some profit out of the treaties, especially the $10,000 charged to Sibley and his traders. He also presented a bill for fees and expenses (which included "gifts" to the Indians) that totaled $5,713, all of which was deducted from the Indians' subsistence and removal fund.[44]

[201]

Henry Mower Rice in a photograph attributed to Mathew Brady, 1863. Courtesy of the Minnesota Historical Society.

Once the Indians had signed the treaty, they lost any negotiating leverage they had held, as they learned when it came time to disburse the treaty monies. The Mdewakantons and Wahpekutes each had been assigned $90,000 in hand money to clear their debts, cover relocation costs, and provide gifts to their mixed-blood relations. The Wahpekutes turned over the entire amount to their trader, Alexander Faribault, a kinsman who had continued to honor the customs of generosity and reciprocity. The Mdewakantons, in contrast, insisted on examining the traders' account books for accuracy and determining for themselves who and how much should be paid. When Ramsey lectured the chiefs on their obligation to pay their "just" debts "as white men do" and threatened to take the money back to Washington, Wabasha scornfully told him to go ahead and do so. However, Ramsey also refused to hand out the annuities due under the 1837 treaty until the matter at hand was settled. The winds of November were already whipping up their icy blasts and the Indians desperately needed provisions. In practiced fashion, Ramsey and Sibley worked in tandem, using incentives to soften the brutal edges of coercion. Sibley, as a "friend" to the Indians, promised gifts of horses and guns if they would sign the disbursal document; Ramsey handed over $20,000 in gold to the chiefs for them to distribute to their mixed-blood kin and promised to release the son of Bad Hail, who was incarcerated in the Fort Snelling stockade. With these slight face-saving concessions and their lands already occupied by white settlers, the chiefs reluctantly acquiesced and signed their remaining hand money over to the traders. As one Mdewakanton summed up the final outcome, "We have sold our lands and paid our debts and are now poor."[45]

The payment at Traverse des Sioux was even more contentious. The upper bands had far fewer settlers trespassing on their lands, and the Sissetons and Wahpetons also believed that they had revoked the traders' paper. When Ramsey informed them that they must honor their obligations to the traders, a contingent led by Sisseton chief Red Iron demanded to examine the accounts. Red Iron was no hotheaded radical. He was a farmer and "friend of the missionaries." Too civilized perhaps for Ramsey's purposes, Red Iron understood quite well the way credit and debt was resolved in white society. According to the interpreter, Alexander Campbell:

> The Indian chiefs demanded their money in their own hands, when Governor Ramsey replied that they ought to pay their honest debts as white men do. Red Iron then sprang up and took the governor by the hand and said, that was what they wanted to do; that he wanted the books of the traders laid on the table, and if they wanted them to pay their debts like white people, they would do so; that he would pay the debts for those who were living, but not for those who had been dead long ago.[46]

Ramsey would not consider Red Iron's proposal; the traders' paper must be honored as it stood. Nor was he willing to examine a revised debt schedule that the Indians presented, based on what they believed they owed. The governor's debts, quite clearly, were to the traders, especially to his good friend, Henry Sibley. Negotiations were at an impasse. Some of the Indians appeared willing to accede to the governor's terms, their immediate need for annuities and assistance overcoming their sense of injustice, but many of the most influential men, including those educated by the missionaries—Cloud Man, Running Walker, and Lorenzo Lawrence, to name a few—stood staunchly with Red Iron. When reason failed, Red Iron turned to a show of power at the head of a cohort of young braves. Instead of coming to council, they raced through the campsite on horseback, shouting and brandishing weapons. The intimidated governor, fearing that he was losing control of the situation, dispensed with persuasion in favor of force. He sent for troops from Fort Snelling, arrested Red Iron, and deposed him from his position as a chief. Unable to win agreement from the remaining chiefs to honor the traders' paper, Ramsey simply replaced those who dissented with new chiefs of his choosing. Then, with the necessary documents duly signed, the governor returned to St. Paul and proceeded to turn over $250,000 in hand money to the traders and mixed bloods—most of it going to Sibley, Dousman, McLeod, and Ramsay Crooks, who was long retired from the trade.[47]

Ramsey's great project to open Minnesota had ended in a sorry spectacle of deceit, coercion, and promises broken almost before they were recorded. After the traders and mixed bloods were paid and the costs of "gifts," food, travel, and miscellaneous "expenses" in Washington deducted, nothing was left of the subsistence funds to assist the bands in moving to the reservation, let alone to help them establish their villages and provide food for the coming year—as had been promised. None of this bothered the white citizens of Minnesota Territory, who viewed the treaties as an unmitigated triumph. But many of those who participated in acquiring the Suland were more ambivalent about their achievement. In his memoir *Forty Years with the Sioux*, Stephen Riggs, who had worked as hard as anyone to push the treaties through, mentioned only in passing that he had been present at Traverse des Sioux, focusing instead on the exceptionally wet weather that fateful summer of 1851. Martin McLeod acknowledged even at the time that the Indians had been done "a great wrong and injustice," which may help explain his actions that fall—easing his conscience with a combination of whiskey and churchgoing. Henry Sibley, though he wrote volubly about his early experiences among the Dakotas, published no account of his key role in securing what Minnesotans hailed as the most important Indian treaties ever concluded.[48]

Hercules Dousman gloomily predicted, "The Sioux treaty will hang like a curse over our heads the balance of our lives." He was at least partly correct. Shortly after the treaty monies had been disbursed, Madison Sweetser and Daniel Robertson, editor of the *Minnesota Democrat*, leveled charges of fraud against Ramsey, based on how the Indians' debts had been handled. But the allegations did not spring from indignation on behalf of the Indians. Rather, they were motivated by schemes of personal and political gain. Sweetser hoped either to be rewarded by the Indians if he succeeded in making their case or (more probably) to extract a payment from the traders to "desist from any further attempts to interfere." Either outcome was equally agreeable to him. Robertson, on his part, had lofty political ambitions. A new Democratic president had been elected in November and the governorship of the territory was up for grabs. President-elect Franklin Pierce would soon name a Democrat to replace the Whig-appointed Ramsey, and Robertson aspired to be that man. Thus, it was in Robertson's interest to discredit Sibley, the most prominent Democrat in Minnesota and most likely gubernatorial appointee. Technically, charges had been leveled against Ramsey only, but they clearly implicated Sibley as his coconspirator. Sibley, stiff-necked and ever protective of his reputation, vigorously appealed to the Senate for an investigation to clear his and Ramsey's names.[49]

In July 1853 investigatory hearings convened in St. Paul. A two-man commission heard testimony from fifty-seven witnesses, including sixteen Dakotas. The proceedings provided lively gossip for the local populace into October, but in the end the commission found no evidence of fraud. However, the testimony collected did raise questions about Ramsey's judgment in enforcing the traders' papers. The commissioners concluded that he had violated the treaty and broken implied promises to the Indians. By association, the findings cast a cloud on Sibley's integrity as well. Nonetheless, when the report was forwarded to the Senate, the findings were waved aside. The Senate declared instead that Ramsey's conduct "was not only free from blame, but highly commendable and meritorious."[50]

Tellingly, in making Ramsey's case his counsel had focused on Indian character rather than the legality of his actions. One witness after another was asked: Could Indians be relied upon to tell the truth? How would they be expected to handle large sums of money? Were they likely to honor their debts? Since nearly every non-Indian witness either directly or indirectly benefited from the treaties, it is not surprising that they confirmed that the Indians would have squandered the money, would not have paid their debts, and were inveterate liars when it suited them. None of this, even if true (which it patently was not), was pertinent to the charges that treaty payments had been illegally withheld and diverted. Such questions would be deemed irrelevant in a financial transaction between white men, but in this case Indians as a race were on trial. Thus, the outcome of the investigation turned not on possible misappropriation of funds but on the confirmation of Indians' racial inferiority and the Anglo right to rule.[51]

A New Social Order

In 1852 St. Paul was a cosmopolitan kaleidoscope, bewildering to new arrivals in its diversity of language, dress, and custom. On its muddy streets, politicians in frock coats jostled with French-Indian settlers, Yankee speculators and merchants, Red River Métis, Indians, a spattering of German and Irish immigrants, a few African Americans, and a French priest or two. Bonneted ladies clad in respectable Victorian garb exchanged greetings with mixed-blood housewives and suspiciously eyed the Native women they encountered. Four newly arrived Sisters of St. Joseph, gliding along serenely in their black habits, added to the exotic air of the town. A babel of tongues—French, German, Ojibwe, and Dakota—vied with English in local conversation, with a French patois the lingua franca of the community. Seminarian Daniel Fisher had come to Minnesota from New York, fired by a desire to convert the Indians. Instead he found himself assigned to St. Paul, "teaching the Catholic school— my mission is among the dirty little ragged Canadian and Irish boys." The disappointed cleric confided in a letter, "The Catholics are very poor here—and what is worse very irreligious and indifferent—they are Half Breeds, Canadians and Irish. The Yankees have all the influence, the wealth and the power, although they are not near as numerous as the others." Indeed, the wealth and political power of the territorial capital was almost entirely in the hands of Anglo politicians, speculators, and former fur traders. As they plotted out a course for growing the settlement into a city and driving the territory toward statehood, they were determined to transform this polyglot community into a proper "American" town and make their fortunes in the process.[52]

As early as 1847, a few eager reformers expressed concern about the "uncivilized" character of the town. Missionary Thomas Williamson, who, at the invitation of Little Crow, was evangelizing at nearby Kaposia, considered St. Paulites to be more in need of redemption than the Indians he was serving. In his estimation, the populace was "entirely ignorant of God" (the presence of a Catholic priest more a danger than a means to salvation). Reverend Williamson sent off an urgent appeal to famed reformer Catherine Beecher, pleading for a female teacher/missionary to serve this benighted community.[53] Harriet Bishop, a thirty-year-old spinster studying under Beecher at the New York State Normal School, answered the call.[54]

Bishop was the first of what would become a significant cohort of reform-minded Anglo women to settle in St. Paul. Williamson had specified that St. Paul required a teacher who was "entirely free from prejudice on account of color, for among her scholars she might find not only English, French, and Swiss, but Sioux and Chippewas, with some claiming kindred with the African stock." Bishop, however, proved the antithesis of that description. In her book *Floral Home*, published in 1857, she scornfully described non-Anglo St. Paulites as motley, ignorant, and deluded. By her standards, she was "the only professing Christian resident in St. Paul." Apparently Catholics did not qualify.[55]

She saved her most vituperative comments for the Indians, whose customs she made no effort to understand. "Their habits," she wrote, "are disgustingly filthy, and their dress, if such it may be called, extremely unchaste." In her telling, Indian stoicism became "listless apathy." As a race, Indians were treacherous, lazy, and "embedded in moral pollution." In short, she informed her readers, the romantic perception of the Indian as noble and manly had no basis in fact. Even those Indians who accommodated themselves to the white man's customs came in for derision, "aping the whites sufficiently to wear a dress coat." When the Dakota Hock-e-wash-ta attended a service at First Baptist Church and politely shook hands with the congregants, Bishop described the scene as simply "ludicrous."[56]

[206]

Harriet Bishop depicted in an engraving by J. S. Buttre, ca. 1860. Courtesy of the Minnesota Historical Society.

PLATE 69

Plate 69. J. H. Young, *Map of Minnesota Territory,* **1853 (Philadelphia: Cowperthwait, Desilver & Butler, 1854). Minnesota Historical Society.**

By emphasizing the vast expanse of land opened up for settlement, this map proclaimed that a new era had dawned in Minnesota with the cession of the Dakota lands. The map's legend explained that the agreements reached at Traverse des Sioux and Mendota covered "about 54,100 square miles or 35 million acres; comprising a region fully equal in extent to the States of Pennsylvania and New Jersey." Minnesota's days as a frontier territory were clearly numbered. The map was designed both to entice new residents and to illuminate the changes to the region since it had gained official territorial status. The map clearly delineates the growth of population around St. Paul and Fort Snelling, enumerating the proliferating towns in what would become the state's most populous corner. The new status of the state's Indians was also recorded. Both the Long Prairie reservation of the Winnebago and the Dakota reservation are marked on the map; a decade later both would be gone. The Dakota reservation was the strip of land along the Minnesota River that was promised to the Indians who signed away their homeland in 1851. It was removed from Dakota control in the aftermath of the U.S.–Dakota War. Indian advocates believed that the Dakota would benefit from being concentrated into a farming community within the boundaries indicated on the map. In this 1853 rendering, Minnesota territory still flows seamlessly into present-day North and South Dakota. The western boundaries of the future state would not be firmly established until 1858.[74]

PLATE 70

Plate 70. Franz Hölzlhuber, *Land Surveyors in the State of Minnesota*, 1859. Glenbow Museum.

An Austrian artist traveling through Minnesota in 1859 came across these men laying out a new town in one of the state's forests. The crew was cutting trees and dynamiting stumps while several surveyors determined where to run the new town's streets.[75] Town sites like this were plotted all over Minnesota as soon as the Dakota agreed to land cessions in 1851. In fact, fortune seekers had poured into Indian country before the ink on the treaties was dry. Squatting gave new settlers priority claim to choice pieces of land, which could be sold after they had been surveyed. To the dismay of the Indians still awaiting congressional approval for the land sale, whites felt entitled to take possession of Dakota lands before the law allowed, convinced that prime acreage was being "wasted" by nomadic hunters unwilling to exploit its full commercial and agricultural potential. Some of these new settlers were legitimate home seekers, intent on acquiring a permanent home or farm, but many of these newcomers were speculators who hoped to acquire tracts for town sites they could plat and subdivide into individual lots for resale at great profit. Over the course of the 1850s, millions of acres of public land were sold in the Minnesota Territory only to be resold multiple times by people intent on making a quick profit.

By 1853, speculators had claimed "every eligible site for a town on the Mississippi from the Iowa line to St. Anthony."[76] While the national depression of 1857 greatly curtailed this kind of real estate development, 860 new town sites were plotted between 1853 and 1859. Some of these ventures developed into substantial communities, but the majority only existed on paper.[77] Two million new residents would have been needed to fill all these new town lots; while the population of the state reached 155,000 by 1860, only 16,000 of those residents lived in the state's towns.[78]

PLATE 71

Plate 71. Benjamin Franklin Upton, first real estate office in Minneapolis, 1856. Minnesota Historical Society.

This picture was taken at the peak of the real estate boom of the 1850s. It shows the first real estate office in Minneapolis; its proprietors, Simon P. Snyder and William K. Macfarlane, are two of the six gentlemen lounging outside of this modest structure. Situated in the heart of what would become the business district of Minneapolis, Snyder and Macfarlane's headquarters were somewhat removed from the commercial action of this period, which was centered on St. Paul. A steady stream of steamboats delivered new residents to the levee in the territory capital, where they were met by "town-site speculators" who "thronged the curbstones," according to historian William Folwell.[79] Snyder and Macfarlane were able to profit handsomely from the speculative fever of their time, making money by reselling land plots to eager homesteaders and fortune seekers.[80] Until the crash of 1857, "fortunes seemed to be dropping from the skies, and those who would not reach and gather them were but stupids and sluggards. Every man who had credit or could obtain it invested in property which ever continued to rise in value," according to Folwell.[81]

Plate 72. Julius Berndt, *Ansicht von New Ulm*, Minnesota, 1860 (Cincinnati: Nägele, Gerstenbauer & Co., 1860). Minnesota Historical Society.

The lands newly opened for settlement in Minnesota attracted thousands of immigrants from Germany, who were the largest group of foreign-born residents in the new state's 1860 census. These new residents had been attracted by the territory's cheap land. German immigration societies mounted promotional efforts like this poster, which showcased New Ulm, a community designed to embody modern ideas of efficiency and order. In stark contrast to more organic communities like St. Paul, the streets were wide and the blocks were regular in this planned town.

This panoramic view of New Ulm was drawn by Julius Berndt, a surveyor and architect from Silesia who settled in New Ulm and later became known for his efforts

Ansicht von New Ulm, Minnesota, 1860.

Souvenir des „Minneapolis Freie Presse-Herold."

PLATE 72

to promote German heritage in Minnesota. Berndt showed the houses spaced widely to emphasize that the German-speaking community still had plenty of room for new arrivals. A row of hills in this drawing served to shield the community from unwanted outside influences. He documented the existence of the infrastructure essential for future prosperity: a windmill and a well-developed boat levee. Multiple steamboats ply the river in front of the town to show how the community was well situated next to an easily navigable river.

Foregrounding the tidy town is a camp of romanticized Native Americans performing domestic chores. In Berndt's imagined landscape, the Indians were situated a safe distance from the new German community, a construction that completely obscured the escalating tensions between the Dakota and the new German-speaking arrivals. The two groups regarded each other with suspicion and hostility. German-speaking settlers tended to cluster in insular communities, which did little to accommodate or assist the Dakota who were angry to discover that their new neighbors did not share their values of reciprocity. The Germans regarded the Dakota as beggars; the Dakota saw the Germans as selfish encroachers on Indian land. These tensions exploded into violence during the U.S.–Dakota War, when German settlers became the targets of Indian violence. Most of the buildings shown in this promotional poster were burned by angry Indians only two years after Berndt created it.[82]

Plate 73. Joel Emmons Whitney, Charles D. Elfelt's store and Whitney's Gallery, Third and Cedar streets, St. Paul, 1852. Minnesota Historical Society.

Joel Whitney — one of the earliest photographers in Minnesota — established his studio above Charles D. Elfelt's clothing store in 1851. Boasting that he constructed his new gallery with special lighting "expressly for taking Daguerreotypes," Whitney initially advertised a range of services but asserted a special affinity for preserving "likenesses of sick or deceased persons."[83] From these humble beginnings, Whitney's business blossomed into a three-story art depot in the heart of St. Paul's embryonic commercial district.

Whitney's Gallery exhibited and sold photographs as well as other kinds of art. Even modest photographers' studios served as public spaces during these years; galleries tried to lure people off the street by showcasing portraits of news-making personalities. In 1861, for instance, curious St. Paulites could have visited Whitney's establishment to see portraits of Governor Alexander Ramsey, Joseph R. Brown, Senator Henry M. Rice, educator and historian Edward D. Neill, and Senator Morton Wilkinson. After satisfying their curiosity about the visages of public figures, customers were then encouraged to spend additional time enjoying the art collection that Whitney had assembled for sale on the first floor. They could browse among the photographs, statuary, chromolithographs, paintings, engravings, stereoscopic images, and card pictures for the right item to give as a gift or enhance their own parlors.[84]

Visitors to Whitney's Gallery who wanted to have their portraits done registered at the reception desk before climbing to the "sitting room" on the second floor. They might have lingered in the dressing rooms, experimenting with different looks and costumes. Ultimately they would have been ushered into the "operating room" on the third floor, which was equipped with a variety of cameras suitable for "taking any size picture, from a card picture up to almost life size," according to a newspaper account from 1866.[85]

Whitney — who was deaf — learned the craft of daguerreotype photography from Alexander Hesler, a well-known photographer based in Galena and Chicago. Whitney used this technique to illustrate the scenery of the region for a national audience; territorial booster William Le Duc brought Whitney's daguerreotypes to New York in the spring of 1853, where he set up an exhibit at the World's Fair that was designed to attract additional settlers to the young territory. Daguerreotypes are small images imprinted on silver-coated metallic plates that are difficult both to display and to reproduce. Whitney became recognized for his mastery of this medium, but soon recognized its limitations and began offering his patrons photographic images in 1855. This allowed him to expand his gallery by making it possible to create innumerable copies of the same image. Whitney had a gift for selecting the right images for mass reproduction, assembling a body of photographs to sell that documented the growing city of St. Paul, the territory's natural wonders, the faces of prominent Minnesotans, and the costumes and faces of a range of Dakota and Ojibwe Indians, who were carefully posed to meet white expectations.

PLATE 73

Commercially produced photographs, like those produced by Whitney, satisfied many desires in mid-nineteenth-century America. They were employed as a tool in territorial boosterism and were distributed to excite curiosity about the region, whose leaders were keen to continue attracting new settlers. They provided an additional perspective on current events, since newspapers and magazines could only use lithographs and engravings to illustrate their pages. Minnesotans bought Whitney's photographic images for their own albums and to send to faraway friends and relatives. Whitney's marketing acumen distinguished him from more skilled competitors; he earned the respect of well-known photographers like Benjamin Upton, who allowed Whitney to package and distribute his work. The entrepreneur knew how to stage, select, and market images to make them broadly appealing to a public still excited by the novelty of photography.[86]

Plate 74. Johann Baptist Wengler, *Sioux Indians*, 1851. Oberösterreichischen Landesmuseen (Upper Austrian State Museums).

In addition to serving as a gateway for prospective settlers, St. Paul also drew curious tourists who were eager to encounter Native Americans without inconveniencing themselves with an arduous overland trek. The economic and political hub for the region was perceived to be a community "near the dividing line of civilized and savage life," in the words of one 1849 visitor.[87] Tourists did not have to leave the city to "see Indians on their own soil. Their canoes are seen gliding across the Mississippi, to and fro between savage and civilized territory. They are met hourly in the streets."[88] Regional promoter Edward Duffield Neill boasted that "Saint Paul is quite thronged with parties of Ojibway, Winnebago, and Dacota braves."[89]

Austrian artist Johann Baptist Wengler was one of these ethnographic tourists. Wengler had left Vienna determined to see the American West and its indigenous inhabitants in 1850. He ultimately spent six weeks around St. Paul in the summer of 1851. At some point during his visit Wengler encountered this small group of Dakota. The man's showy costume may have attracted the artist's attention; the elaborate lance and headpiece indicate that he was probably garbed for some ceremonial occasion. His companions are probably his wives and child; the women are more prosaically attired in trade cloth. All the adults are shod in moccasins, the universal footwear for all inhabitants of the region before the north country was fully integrated into the United States.

PLATE 74

Plate 75. Johann Baptist Wengler, *Sioux Indian*, 1851. Oberösterreichischen Landesmuseen (Upper Austrian State Museums).

The sight of a Dakota man carrying a Northwest gun (the type of gun supplied by the fur trade companies) and smoking a traditional pipe would have been unremarkable to St. Paul residents at the beginning of the 1850s, when artist Johann Wengler made this watercolor sketch during his visit to the city. Sporting both a pouch and a powder horn on his back, the striding man appears lost in contemplation as he navigated streets where Dakota, Ojibwe, and Winnebago Indians jostled Métis from Red River, French Canadian voyageurs, Yankee speculators, Anglo housewives, new immigrants from Germany, and the occasional African-American inhabitant. Newcomers to St. Paul seemed to delight in the sensation that they had arrived in a "foreign" land inhabited by an eclectic populace. Alexander Ramsey reminisced fondly about the street scene he encountered in his new posting as territorial governor, remembering how "the blankets and painted faces of Indians, and the red sashes and moccasins of French voyageurs and half-breeds" overshadowed "the less picturesque costume of the Anglo-American race."[90] The fact that Ramsey was waxing nostalgic about this "motley humanity" in 1853 indicates perhaps how quickly the city was changing. But in the immediate aftermath of the Dakota land cession treaties of 1851, Indians like the one pictured here would have mixed freely in the territorial capital with the office seekers, speculators, and travelers who were hustling to make their fame and fortune now that restrictions on American settlement had virtually disappeared in the region. The bearded artist-adventurer who painted this watercolor would have himself been a colorful addition to the diverse street life of the town; he drew stares for his ragged clothing and arsenal of weapons, which included a double-barreled rifle, a revolver, and a Bowie knife.[91]

PLATE 75

Plate 76. Joel Emmons Whitney, scalp of an Ojibwe man killed by Fort Snelling soldiers, 1853. Minnesota Historical Society.

This image of an Ojibwe scalp is one of the earliest surviving daguerreotypes made in the new territory of Minnesota. The picture was created by St. Paul entrepreneur and daguerreotyper Joel Whitney, who proved to be a master at marketing images featuring Indians. Sometime after 1860, Whitney refashioned this daguerreotype image into a carte de visite, or trading-card-sized photo, that was reproduced for wide distribution.[92]

The scalp pictured here was taken from an Ojibwe killed in the spring of 1853 by Fort Snelling soldiers. This slaying was justified as punishment for another crime. The man was blamed for a murder on April 27, when a Dakota woman was shot in the trading house of the American Fur Company on Third and Jackson Street in the middle of St. Paul. White denizens of St. Paul were outraged that the Ojibwe would pursue their traditional foes through the streets of St. Paul and fire their weapons through the windows of a crowded store. Governor Ramsey dispatched dragoons from

Fort Snelling to apprehend those responsible for the attack. The pursued Ojibwes responded to this chase with "an insolent spirit," in the words of one historian, which prompted the soldiers to shoot the man they deemed responsible for the St. Paul killing. His scalp was brought back to St. Paul as a trophy.[93]

Since the beginning of white settlement in the 1820s and 1830s, new arrivals to the north country were preoccupied with stories of scalping. The practice of taking scalps was a marker of savagery, in the minds of white outsiders, who believed that this tradition distinguished Indian warriors as sadistic primitives. While these tales may have filled soldiers on their way to Fort Snelling with trepidation, they fascinated early tourists like Giacomo Constantino Beltrami, who collected a scalp as a souvenir during his visit to Minnesota. Beltrami's choice of a keepsake illuminates how scalps became more than talismans of Indian savagery; they became icons of the entire territory, coming to signify its liminal status "near the dividing line of civilized and savage life," a description that Anglo-American settlers embraced with enthusiasm.[94]

PLATE 76

This daguerreotype fed this mythic image of the region, reinforcing popular assumptions about Minnesota and its Indian inhabitants. It resonated with both a local and national audience, serving as the basis for one of the views of St. Paul featured in an article published in Philadelphia's *Graham's Magazine* in 1855. It is reproduced here to highlight how myths are communicated through images; over the hundred years that followed the article in *Graham's Magazine*, these types of mass-produced images effectively obscured the complicated reality of Indian life and culture. While Whitney presented the Ojibwe scalp as an authentic Indian artifact, the publication of this image in a national publication demonstrates the ascendance of American military power in the region rather than the persistence of Indian traditional practices.

The image also indicates the sea change in racial ideology that was about to transform every aspect of life in the territory. White newcomers to the region had traditionally embraced Indian practices and tools as matter of survival. By the 1850s, however, it was no longer necessary to adopt Indian neighbors as trading partners, companions, and kin. Eastern transplants like Whitney brought with them a rigid racial hierarchy, which conditioned them to regard Indians through cultural stereotypes. While earlier immigrants had married into Indian families and donned moccasins made by their kin, later arrivals like Whitney developed completely different types of relationships with the original inhabitants of the region. Whitney made his fortune by creating images that commodified Indian culture and traditions, reinforcing popular assumptions of Indian "savagery."

Plate 77. Hole-in-the-Day (Po-go-nay-ke-shick), ca. 1855. Minnesota Historical Society.

Photographer Joel Whitney sold a large inventory of Indian portraits at his St. Paul art depot. This early daguerreotype of Hole-in-the-Day, who was known in his native language as Po-go-nay-ke-shick, must have been one of the first images of this type he created. Whitney's gallery followed closely in the tradition of the ethnographic artists who had been painting the region's Indians since the 1820s. Yet the photographer appears to have been motivated by a desire for commercial reward rather than a wish to create a comprehensive and enduring visual record of Minnesota's Indian inhabitants.

While most nineteenth-century portraits were made for the sitters themselves, photographs of Indians were usually taken for a white commercial market. Portraits of Indians, in other words, were usually commodities rather than keepsakes for their subjects. As a result, these photographs frequently reveal more about the racial preconceptions of whites than the substance of Indian life in the region in the 1850s. For instance, the cultural artifacts featured in Whitney's portraits were supplied by the photographer himself, who posed his subjects with a standard repertoire of pipes, weapons, bags, and necklaces. A master at fashioning images that resonated with white expectations, Whitney conveyed a comfortable exoticism marketable to a national audience that had little personal history with Indians.

PLATE 77

Portraits of Hole-in-the-Day defy the norms of the Indian picture genre. Unlike most Indian subjects, Hole-in-the-Day seemed to be able to assert some kind of control over his photographic images. The Ojibwe leader apparently relished being photographed, posing for at least ten early portraits, several of which he displayed in his own home. Hole-in-the-Day appeared to participate in the staging of these portraits. He was keen to boost his stature as an Indian leader, employing the new technology of photography to cultivate his celebrity status among whites and enhance his leadership profile among his own people. His drive to amass personal wealth and his autocratic tendencies combined to engender bitterness within the community he was trying to lead, resentments that eventually led to his assassination. But he always tried to position himself as a cultural mediator who was neither assimilated nor completely traditional.

In this early daguerreotype, Hole-in-the-Day's American-style coat is accessorized with both peace medals from American government officials and a traditional Indian gun-stock war club. For some reason this image was clumsily altered to show a blade protruding from the club. This type of after-the-fact modification is puzzling because these clubs normally featured blades, which allowed them to function effectively as weapons. In any case, Hole-in-the-Day does appear to have been trying to fashion an ensemble that communicated his determination to use American diplomatic channels and traditional Indian weapons to win the respect of both whites and Indians in mid-nineteenth-century Minnesota.[95]

Plate 78. Dog team from Fort Garry, near present location of West Seventh and Walnut streets, St. Paul, 1858. Minnesota Historical Society.

The urban areas of Minnesota became increasingly enmeshed in the transportation and communication networks of the continental United States while the more rural regions of the territory remained remote through the 1850s. Until the post–Civil War expansion of the state's railroad infrastructure, Minnesotans traveling to the hinterlands during the winter relied on colorful dog sleds like the one pictured here. This sled is shown entering St. Paul, pausing on what is today known as Seventh Street at

PLATE 78

the end of a journey from Pembina. Its drivers are shown in the foreground. An un-identified little boy is also pictured, next to a small bridge spanning one of the many streams that used to trickle from the bluff to the river below.[96] When this picture was taken in 1858, these types of winter sleds were an increasingly exotic novelty to an urban population more accustomed to traveling by steamboat.

Used to transport both cargo and people, dog teams could cover between thirty and forty miles per day and were the only practical way to get between Pembina and St. Paul in the winter. Joseph Rolette played his dogsleds for maximum dramatic effect in January 1852. The jingling bells on his dogs' harnesses drew crowds as he swept into the capital for the start of the territorial legislature. "For the first few days of the session it was hard to tell whether it was the dogs or the honorable members who represented Pembina as the dogs were the first in the legislative halls and the last to leave," remembered one observer. "It was only when the sergeant at arms was ordered to put the dogs out and keep them out, as Pembina was not entitled to double representation, that the two houses were relieved of their presence."[97]

On the bluff behind the dogsled are the first houses built on Summit Avenue. On the far right is the residence of Edward Duffield Neill, who was at this point the pastor of the House of Hope Presbyterian Church. To its left is the Noble family home, which is adjacent to a house built by Henry F. Masterson in 1857. The fourth house in this picture was built by Henry M. Rice, businessman and early senator from Minnesota. The fifth house was newly constructed when this photograph was taken. Henry Neill Paul erected it in 1858, after most other building in the city had come to a halt because of the financial collapse. The Italian villa pictured on the far left side of this photograph still stands today at 312 Summit Avenue, though it has lost the cupola it boasted in these early days of its existence. The house was built by David Stuart, a partner in the Stuart and Cobb lumber business, who died soon after it was completed. The mortgage on the house was foreclosed in 1858, and the property was re-sold three times before the end of the Civil War. The house survived the turmoil of its early years, remaining intact as the isolated bluff developed into the most prestigious thoroughfare in the growing city.[98]

Plate 79. Tallmadge Elwell, Dakota tipis near the frame house of John H. Stevens, Minneapolis, 1852. Minnesota Historical Society.

John H. Stevens followed the urging of his employer — land speculator Franklin Steele, who was hoping to gain control of the water power of St. Anthony Falls — and petitioned the military in 1849 for permission to build a house on land that was still part of the Fort Snelling military reserve. The young veteran of the Mexican-American war offered to ferry passengers across the Mississippi River in exchange for the right to create a small homestead on the west side of the river, where white settlement was still forbidden by the American government. In 1850, Stevens moved into the white frame house that is barely discernible behind the Dakota tipis in this picture; his special arrangement with the military allowed him to stake a claim on the land that would become the center of Minneapolis and avoid being expelled from the Fort Snelling military reserve, a fate that befell earlier squatters. Stevens employed a young English immigrant, John Tapper, to perform the nitty-gritty tasks associated with the ferry service, which was supposed to aid military operations at Fort Snelling; the young land speculator played the role of regular passenger, taking the boat each morning from his new homestead to St. Anthony, where he worked as a bookkeeper for Steele's store in the Jarrett House hotel.

As an outpost of American power on the west side of the river, the Stevens home became a gathering place, hosting church services, court sessions, political meetings, and negotiations between Indians and their American agents. Stevens's closest neighbors were Indians, and he was regularly visited by Ojibwe, Winnebago, and Dakota Indians, whose tipis are pictured here. He later remembered that he would frequently wake in the morning to find that "while we were asleep, the wigwams of either the Sioux, Chippewa or Winnebago, had gone up."[99] Groups of Dakotas camped next to the Stevens house for several weeks in the summer while they patronized the stores of St. Anthony. They bought and sold merchandise, even peddling furs to Stevens himself before crossing the river to buy goods. But the context for these cultural and economic exchanges was transformed soon after Stevens moved into his house; the 1851 Dakota land cession treaties decreed that the west side of the river was no longer Indian country. Settlers began crossing the Mississippi in large numbers, even before the treaties were formally approved or the land opened to homesteaders. The 1855 construction of a suspension bridge strengthened the connections between the west bank of the river and St. Anthony. John Tapper changed occupations, leaving behind his ferry boat to accept the new position of bridge toll collector. Stevens soon decided to leave his homestead as well, selling his forty acres in Minneapolis and moving his family to Glencoe. His house was preserved and later relocated to Minnehaha Park. Its original site became known as Bridge Square, which was seen as the gateway to downtown Minneapolis until the area was flattened by mid-twentieth-century urban renewal.[100]

PLATE 79

PLATE 80

Plate 80. Alexander Hesler, St. Anthony Falls and east side of the river looking from Hennepin Island, 1851. Minnesota Historical Society.

When John H. Stevens established his homestead on the west side of the Mississippi River, the community of St. Anthony had already taken shape on the river's east bank. The row of neat, framed buildings that lined St. Anthony's Main Street in 1851 is visible beyond St. Anthony Falls.

The river scene foregrounded here is unfamiliar to most modern viewers, who know St. Anthony Falls as a sedate stream of water pouring over a concrete curtain constructed by the Army Corps of Engineers. This early image by Alexander Hesler, a pioneering daguerreotyper based in Galena, shows how the rushing water loosened chunks of limestone bedrock, which littered the river and caused the falls to recede upstream. At this point the untamed falls were one of the critical natural features of the region. They had inspired paeans from visitors beginning in the seventeenth century, when Father Louis Hennepin gave them the name they bear today. In 1851, they attracted the attention of Hesler, who decided to create some images of the new territory's natural wonders. Working with the assistance of Joel E. Whitney — who would later become renowned in his own right as a photographer — Hesler made daguerreotype views of St. Anthony Falls and Minnehaha Falls that were used to recruit new settlers and survive today as some of the first photographic images from Minnesota.[101]

St. Anthony Falls were more than a scenic backdrop; they determined the shape of the state's urban development. St. Paul was established below the falls, at the head of navigation on the Mississippi River. Later the town of St. Anthony was situated to take advantage of the hydropower provided by the falls. Journalist and photographer Edward Bromley explained that "the Falls of St. Anthony constituted the nucleus around which everything clustered and was that which caused everything to cluster there. That was the magnet."[102] The U.S. Army built the first mills in the area to supply Fort Snelling in 1821; an extensive milling district took shape around the falls in the mid-nineteenth century. This industrial development made businessmen who were dependent on the waterpower eager to curtail the movement of the volatile falls. Stabilization efforts tamed the magnificent falls, calming the wild waters that had drawn Hesler and so many other visitors to St. Anthony.[103]

Plate 81. Benjamin Franklin Upton, view of Winslow House, Upton Block, and Jarrett House, St. Anthony, 1858. Minnesota Historical Society.

The Winslow House, at the far left of this photograph, overlooked the landscape of St. Anthony. Erected at the height of the 1850s economic boom in Minnesota, this huge hotel opened for business even before its completion in the spring of 1857, when hordes of prospective settlers were overrunning the riverside village. Its capacious ballroom and five-hundred-seat dining room quickly made it the venue of choice for

PLATE 81

stylish balls and other parties. The construction of this stone edifice eased the pressure on the Jarrett House, a three-story frame hotel built in 1856 pictured on the far right of this photograph, which also housed offices for some of the territory's leading entrepreneurs as well as the headquarters of the *St. Anthony Express,* the first newspaper printed west of St. Paul.

The Winslow House was perhaps best known as a destination for Southern tourists who traveled up the Mississippi River in palatial steamers to escape the oppressive summer heat. This clientele turned the hotel into a site of political struggle in 1860; St. Anthony abolitionists brought home national debates about race and freedom when they spirited slave Eliza Winston away from her owners who were vacationing at the Winslow House. This episode helped to end the lucrative tourist trade in St. Anthony, which was soon transformed in many other ways by the start of the Civil War.

The glory days of the Winslow House were short-lived. The hotel was shuttered and its furniture removed in 1861; it remained vacant until 1872, when Macalester College occupied it for a time before it was demolished in 1887. The Upton Block — the building immediately to the left of the Jarrett House in this picture — survived the transformation of St. Anthony from tourist hamlet to manufacturing hub. The brick block housed Moses and Rufus Upton's general store, which sold groceries and sundry hardware and supplies. The building — which received an addition after this photograph was taken — now stands as the oldest commercial building in Minneapolis.[104]

Plate 82. Benjamin Franklin Upton, St. Anthony looking east along Main Street; Hennepin Island at right, 1857. Minnesota Historical Society.

The newly constructed Winslow House provided a scenic overlook for Benjamin Upton, a Maine-born photographer who immediately decided to create overviews of his

PLATE 82

new community after moving to Minnesota.[105] The photographer climbed to the roof of the stone building to take this panoramic view of St. Anthony and Hennepin Island in 1857. In the center of this photograph is the Upton Block, which housed the Upton Brothers' store and provides a visual anchor for modern-day viewers, who can still see this building on the banks of the Mississippi River.[106] The sweep of this image encompasses Minneapolis as well as the more established St. Anthony, which boasted a population of 4,689 when this photograph was taken. The vista includes two bridges. One connected St. Anthony to Hennepin Island; the distant one of the pair spanned the entire river but collapsed in 1859, when spring floods piled an overwhelming number of logs against its supports.[107] The burgeoning industrial district taking shape around St. Anthony Falls is visible on the right side of this image, which shows a growing cluster of mills on Hennepin Island situated to take advantage of the river's water power. This view includes the Farnham and Lovejoy sawmill; the Averill, Secombe & Co. paper mill; Morrison & Prescott's flour mill; and the Upton, Rollins & Co. flour mill. Five years after this image was created, the hulking Winslow House was closed, overshadowed by the district's industrial activity, which had accelerated to meet the demands of the Civil War. English writer Anthony Trollope had been cautioned that he would find the beauty of St. Anthony Falls despoiled by the busy mills. He was somewhat surprised to find the area "extremely picturesque" and asserted that it had been enhanced by the burgeoning industry. In 1862, Trollope found it difficult to imagine the village as a watering hole for Southern gentry. "The interest of the place," Trollope wrote in a comment prescient for the city's future, "is in the saw-mills."[108]

PLATE 83

Plate 83. Benjamin Franklin Upton, panorama of St. Paul looking east from the roof of the courthouse, 1857. Minnesota Historical Society.

Benjamin Franklin Upton climbed to the cupola of the courthouse in St. Paul, at that time situated at Fourth and Wabasha streets, to create this bird's-eye view of the booming city. Exponential population growth over the previous decade had swollen St. Paul to ten thousand souls. One of two cityscapes created by Upton, this scene shows a town more established than the village of St. Anthony. The territorial capital of St. Paul was at the epicenter of the intense real estate speculation that had gripped the region since the signing of the Dakota land cession treaties.[109] The stacks of lumber in the foreground hint at the intense construction activity. Beyond these building materials lies a hodgepodge of businesses and residences; yards offer little more than laundry lines positioned to take advantage of summer breezes.

Reproduced here are two of Upton's nine overlapping images of St. Paul. The scene faces east, with Fourth Street running down the right side of this image. For several years before the summer day captured here, "shops and dwellings were starting out of the ground as if magicians were busy, and all was life, and energy, and hope," according to a description of St. Paul in *Harper's Magazine*. The construction of a "Courthouse, Presbyterian Church, Baldwin School-house, State House, hotels, the new Cathedral, Masonic Hall, theatres, and Odd Fellows' Hall" told the "story of wealth and work" in the bustling community.[110] Soon after Upton clambered down from his scenic overlook, residents of St. Paul found themselves holding properties that had become virtually worthless overnight. All building stopped. A financial panic that began in New York halted almost all economic activity in the territory until the Civil War.[111]

PLATE 84

Plate 84. Robert O. Sweeny, *St. Paul by Moonlight*, 1862. Minnesota Historical Society.

Dayton's Bluff provided the vantage point for this whimsical night view of St. Paul. The town's riverfront is illuminated by a friendly man in the moon, who smiles down on the Wabasha Street Bridge, the lower levee, and the first State Capitol, which is pictured on the far right side of the image. The lighthearted spirit of this drawing stands in stark contrast to the dark context of the time, with the nation embroiled in the Civil War and the state howling for the blood of Indians who had killed hundreds of white settlers.

Artist Robert Ormsby Sweeny could be described as a Renaissance man who had adopted St. Paul as his home in 1852. The levity of the sketch may have reflected his relief at being discharged from the Union Army only a few months earlier, thanks to an injury that left him blind in one eye. He had worked as a pharmacist in the Army, a career he also pursued in St. Paul. While known as a druggist and small business owner, Sweeny excelled as a civic leader, serving as president of the Minnesota Historical Society, founder of the St. Paul Academy of Natural Sciences, and a commissioner of fisheries. Sweeny also remained active as an artist, sketching the urban landscape of St. Paul, the flora of the state, and portraits of Indians.[112]

Sweeny's vista encompasses the main transportation arteries connecting St. Paul to the broader world. The steamboats that plied the lower levee allowed St. Paul to remain the commercial center for the region, situated as it was at the head of navigation on the Mississippi River. Until several years after the Civil War, when the state's railroad infrastructure began to take shape, St. Paul's lower levee was the gateway for people and goods moving through the state. New settler families were deposited on the shelf of land at the foot of the river bluffs, where they were forced to navigate through a sea of "horsemen, truckmen, footmen, workmen of every sort," and a maze of sundry manufactured goods arriving in the region. The scene at this chaotic terminus was what one journalist described as "complete bedlam."[113] A natural ravine provided a channel for a cartway that connected the levee to the business district at the top of the bluffs.

The picturesque Wabasha Street Bridge shown spanning the river was completed in 1859. Designed to ensure the city's continued role as a commercial center, the privately constructed bridge connected St. Paul to the newly opened lands on the west side of the river. Yet the small settlement on the river's west side remained relatively remote from St. Paul proper until the city assumed control over the bridge and stopped charging a toll for passing over the river in 1874.[114]

Not surprisingly, Harriet Bishop found it rough going as a teacher in her multicultural classroom. With only three "American" families in the town, in her first class she found just "two fair childlike faces . . . a shining light . . . among the dark, forbidding group convened within those decaying log walls." To communicate with her charges, she had to rely on a mixed-blood student to translate lessons into French and Dakota. Though in time the contingent of Anglo students increased, after three years Bishop gave up teaching her uncivilized scholars and turned to the more lucrative pursuits of land agent, author, and territorial booster. She continued, however, in her efforts to uplift the community. Along with other respectable ladies of the town, she was active in founding all sorts of civic organizations. She became a pillar of the First Baptist Church and raised funds for a new school as a member of the St. Paul Circle of Industry. Any project for civic improvement or cultural enlightenment found a supporter in Miss Bishop. But her most passionate cause was the battle against alcohol. A founding member of the state's first temperance society, she abhorred the whiskey-soaked state of the general populace. Interestingly, however, in her writing, though she deplored the "pestiferous influence" of drinking in "fashionable life," culpability among whites was due to individual character flaws. But Indian abuse of alcohol, in her estimation, was a racial characteristic, drunkenness a vice ubiquitous among the "savages." As she informed her readers, "a drunken Indian is the most loathsome, fiendish being that ever wore the 'image of his maker.'"[57]

The few Anglo women who preceded Bishop in St. Paul accommodated themselves more easily to the cultural mix of the little town. Martha Bass, whose husband, Jacob, ran the settlement's rudimentary hotel, was the daughter of a Methodist missionary and had spent her youth in frontier Wisconsin; Nancy Irvine and her husband, John, had more than a decade's experience trading in western hamlets, as did Angelina and Henry Jackson. Moreover, all these families were involved either in storekeeping or innkeeping, which relied heavily on the Indian trade and demanded cordial relations with every sort of customer. But, after 1849, the prevailing character of the settlement rapidly began to change. A traveler's account in 1850 noted a class of newcomers "way too numerous for so small a community . . . a host of lawyers, politicians, office-holders and office seekers . . . refugees from other States . . . the character is decidedly Eastern." These fortune seekers were accompanied by wives with no experience in the West. Like Harriet Bishop, they usually carried with them a strong sense of moral superiority and a desire to remake St. Paul in the image of the homes they had left behind. They dedicated themselves to projects of cultural refinement and moral improvement, and the descriptions of Native people that they penned to their relatives in the East often reflected the same derogatory characterizations that colored Bishop's missives.[58]

To be fair, the transition from their ordered existence in the East to life in a rough-and-tumble frontier town must have been a shock for many a bride in

St. Paul. And confrontations that occasionally occurred between Dakotas and Ojibwes in the near vicinity could only have added to their sense of unease.[59] Understandably, they yearned to replicate the familiar rhythm and ways of their former communities. Bent on this task and armed with moral certainty, St. Paul's civic-minded ladies were on a mission to domesticate what they viewed as social disorder. They had no incentive to find common ground with Indians or "half-breeds."

Unfortunately for historians, Native people left a scant record of their perspective on white cultural norms. Thus, cultural bias in the written record and rampant self-justification following the Dakota treaties make it difficult to discern the actual tenor of Indian and white interactions before the Dakotas were forced to cede their lands. However, a few individuals offer perspectives that diverge from those of Harriet Bishop and her like-minded peers. Nineteen-year-old Rebecca Marshall arrived in St. Paul with her widowed mother in 1849, bursting with excitement "like one let out of prison." Joining her older brothers, who had migrated to Minnesota the previous year, Rebecca delighted in the bustle and freedom from strict convention that she found in St. Paul. Unfettered by the biases that distorted the perceptions of many matrons in the community, Rebecca's description of the Indians she met differed sharply from common stereotypes and suggests instead that many Indians were making enormous efforts to adapt themselves to the new social order that was being thrust upon them. As Rebecca recalled in her memoir, the Indians were dignified and "grand looking": "no body of white men could have behaved better." In particular, she remembered an incident on New Year's Day 1850:

> I was spending the holidays with Mr. and Mrs. Edmund Rice in St. Paul; early in the morning of this day a delegation of Sioux Indians from the west side of the village, which was still an Indian reservation, called to pay their respects. They shook hands with us, said in English, "Happy New Year," and then seated themselves on the floor. . . . After staying a short time, they bowed in a very courteous manner and left. During the afternoon several of the territorial officers called; they were gentlemen born and bred, but they had so far forgotten both birth and breeding that they fell far below our savage guests. Mrs. Rice felt so insulted by their behavior that she had what we women call a good cry, when they at last reeled out of her home.[60]

Rebecca Marshall's candid recollections shed a different light on the relative state of "civilization" in St. Paul.

Julia Wood, a well-educated native of New Hampshire, also left positive reminiscences of the Indians and mixed-blood people she came to know. She and her husband, William, an attorney, came to Minnesota Territory in 1854, looking for adventure. They found it in the unsettled region near the Winnebago reservation, some sixty miles north of St. Paul. Homesteading on the site of the future town of Sauk Rapids, William served as a frontier county attorney and Julia carried on her avocation as a writer for various publications. She wrote some years later with great affection and regard about her friends, Sophia Russell and Eliza Sweet, the Anglo-Ojibwe wives of nearby traders, with whom she came to share a lifelong friendship. She also provided appreciative portraits of her Indian neighbors. As she described them, visiting Winnebagos were "fierce looking" but "stately" and Ojibwe women were graceful and modest "dark-eyed damsels." Despite their relative isolation from civilization, Julia assured her readers that neither she nor William ever felt fear when the Indians came to call. Whatever "peculiarities" she observed were due simply to differences in customary etiquette.[61]

But the cultural openness of Julia Wood and Rebecca Marshall was exceptional among newcomers to the territory. In most new Minnesotans' view, race was the ultimate determinant of civilized behavior. Some whites might fall short of the desired etiquette, but no Indians, regardless of their character, could meet the standard of civilization.

Of course, politics fundamentally shaped cultural perceptions. White Minnesotans, intent on taking ownership of Dakota lands, justified the egregious land grab by telling themselves that, despite decades of effort to turn the savages into good Americans, the project had proved hopeless. Native people only absorbed the worst of the white man's vices and none of the virtues. The only way to "save" the Indian was to isolate him far from contact with white society. As the years passed, even that feeble justification was discarded and history was again rewritten. In 1875 historian J. Fletcher Williams blandly stated, "Though the Sioux had received, in good faith, a large sum as a quit-claim for territory *they had no more actual ownership of than the fowls of the air*, they seemed unwilling to give peaceable possession of it to white people." Yet more proof of their savage and unredeemable nature.[62]

The boom times that commenced once the western lands were taken made it easy to forget the relationships between whites and Indians that had existed in earlier times and paint all Indians in stereotypical terms of inferiority and dependency. The moment that word of the treaties became public, a deluge of settlers, speculators, and hustlers flooded the territory, looking to start a business, claim a homestead, or, most commonly, make a fast buck. Optimism and energy crackled in the air; wagons clattered through the streets of St. Paul; roads were graded, lots platted out; hammers and saws kept up a constant racket; and steamboat whistles pierced the din as they chugged around the bend, curious passengers hanging over the rails. Speculative fever was growing by the day. As recounted by a visiting journalist in 1852:

> My ears at every turn are saluted with the everlasting din of land! land! money! speculation! saw mills! land warrants! town lots, &c., &c. . . . Land at breakfast, land at

dinner, land at supper, and until 11 o'clock, land; then land in bed, until their vocal organs are exhausted—then they dream and groan out land, land![63]

The boom grew more manic with each succeeding month. In 1853, 235 steamboats docked at the St. Paul levee and more than fifty businesses advertised their wares in the town's three newspapers. Two years later, the territory's population had grown to more than 53,000, nearly 5,000 in St. Paul alone. Steamers and packet boats queued up at the landing, sometimes depositing up to 600 visitors and immigrants in a single day. In 1856 the town's four principal hotels registered 28,000 guests. With hotels and boardinghouses bursting at the seams, people even took to camping in the streets. Real estate prices skyrocketed, and everyone seemed driven by a "wild, crazy, reckless spirit of speculation." Harriet Bishop was not alone in giving up teaching to get into the land game. In the words of one eyewitness:

> Everybody seemed inoculated with the mania, from the moneyed capitalist to the humble laborer who could merely squat on a quarter section, and hold it for a rise. The buying of real estate, often at the most insane prices, and without regard to the real value, infected all classes, and almost absorbed every other passion and pursuit. . . . Agriculture was neglected, and breadstuffs enough for home consumption were not raised. . . . Farmers, mechanics, laborers even, forsook their occupations to become operators in real estate, and grow suddenly rich, as they supposed.[64]

St. Paul was the most visible beneficiary of the boom, said by travelers to be "the liveliest town on the Mississippi . . . continually full of tourists, speculators, sporting men, and even worse characters, all spending gold as though it was dross." As the territorial capital and terminus of steamboat navigation, the newly incorporated city "fairly hummed with the rush of busy life. Business was never so brisk." Most immigrants stopped over in St. Paul only briefly before moving west in their search for land, but a host of St. Paul merchants stood ready to provision them for the trek.

An insatiable demand for lumber also grew the milling enclaves of St. Anthony and Stillwater into full-fledged, thriving communities. In the hinterland, town sites sprang up by the hundreds. Speculators platted out imagined cities at any propitious (or often inauspicious) locale, then set about hawking lots to eager buyers who snapped them up, often sight unseen. In 1853 the *Minnesota Democrat* reported that "every eligible site for a town on the Mississippi from the Iowa line to St. Anthony is claimed." By 1860, the census recorded nearly four hundred established towns and townships with populations that ranged from a handful of settlers to more than 1,000 in regional centers like Mankato, Hastings, St. Peter, and Red Wing.[65]

Throughout the territory, land had replaced the Indian trade as the primary underpinning of the economy and "agriculture, manufactures, and commerce" were gaining a substantial foothold. The *St. Paul Advertiser* noted in 1856 that one week's business in St. Paul exceeded the $90,000 that the Dakotas received from the government in a year. As historian Bruce White succinctly notes, with this shift in the economy "no one cared when or where the Indians were paid." Indians had simply become a nuisance and most white Minnesotans begrudged their claim to any small piece of their homeland that they still retained.[66]

More Land Hunger

The millions of acres acquired in the Dakota treaties did not sate the appetite for land. With St. Paul a booming entrepôt and St. Anthony churning out dollars in the form of lumber, urban boosters and speculators pushed ceaselessly for the release of the thousands of acres held unnecessarily within the Fort Snelling reserve. The fort itself, they argued, had become an anachronism of no benefit to the burgeoning cities, a "military carbuncle" that stymied metropolitan growth. In particular, would-be industrialists coveted the west side of the Mississippi at St. Anthony Falls. In 1854, thanks to tireless lobbying by Henry Sibley and Henry Rice (who each had a personal as well as a civic stake in the outcome) and fellow Washington insiders, who were poised to snatch up strategic parcels of land, Congress opened all but a small area of the reserve for public sale. Squatters, many of them proxies for well-heeled investors, had already staked out claims on "almost every inch" of the about-to-be-released territory. Prudently, they banded together in claim associations to protect their putative ownership rights and "discourage" competitors from bidding against them at the upcoming land auction, by force if necessary. Thus, when the sale took place, some 4,500 acres in present-day St. Paul and 20,000 acres of the future city of Minneapolis sold for $1.25 per acre, including the priceless sites at St. Anthony Falls—in the midst of one of the most extravagant real estate booms in the nation's history—netting the government the princely sum of approximately $30,000.[67]

Well-positioned capitalists had immediately pounced to secure the waterpower, and with optimistic investors vying for a piece of the action, in 1856 another milling center entered the game. Seemingly overnight, the town of Minneapolis mushroomed on the river's banks, began spewing lumber, and laid the foundation for industrial growth that within decades would overshadow even St. Paul.

Urban land acquisition was indeed a profitable enterprise, but many speculators and entrepreneurs also had their eyes set on the rich timber and mineral resources of the north. Frustratingly, however, all that potential wealth lay in Ojibwe country. Despite the massive Dakota land cession, the entire northern half of present-day Minnesota remained Indian territory. The time had come, progressive Minnesotans agreed, to deal with the remaining "Indian problem."

The Ojibwes were in a stronger negotiating position than the Dakotas had been. The fur trade, though diminished, still provided a source of income for the northern bands. More important, white settlers were gravitating primarily to the river valleys and rich prairie soils south of St. Paul, putting much less pressure on Indian hunting grounds to the north. The Ojibwes traditionally relied on diverse sources of sustenance. In addition to deer and fur-bearing animals that they hunted and trapped for both meat and for trade, their diet included fish, small game, berries, maple sugar, garden produce, and especially wild rice, which was a nutritional staple. The continued availability of this diverse resource base tended to cushion them from the worst extremes of scarcity that repeatedly weakened the eastern Dakotas, who faced competition from whites as well as diminishing resources in the 1840s and 1850s. Observers frequently commented that the Ojibwes were "a much finer appearing body of men than the Sioux," healthier and usually better clad. Even Harriet Bishop grudgingly described them as "less degraded than the neighboring tribes," though "far from civilized."[68]

Maintenance of these traditional lifeways required an extensive territory to adequately support the population in its seasonal rounds of hunting, fishing, and gathering. Ethnohistorian Charles Cleland estimates that each individual required about 8.6 square miles to "provide the food, clothing, shelter, medicine, and other resources needed for survival, given the extraction methods which were in use." In 1850 the Ojibwes had the land they needed, both in unceded territory and in the usufruct rights they retained on lands ceded in 1837 and 1842.[69]

They freely roamed the ceded territory without much complaint from the sparse contingent of settlers, traders, and lumbermen. In 1850, when rumors began to circulate about government plans to remove the Indians from the ceded lands (a ploy to funnel annuity monies to St. Paul), citizens in the Lake Superior region, most of them related to the Indians by birth or marriage, mounted a vigorous protest campaign. They wanted the Indians to remain "on account of the fish and fur trade." Moreover, they insisted that "the most friendly feeling, strengthened by mutual kind offices has at all times, existed between the Indians and ourselves." In the St. Croix valley and along the Rum River northwest of St. Paul, relatively cordial relations also prevailed between whites and Indians, who initiated a lively trade with timber cutters and new settlers, supplying them with much-needed provisions—wild rice, berries, vegetables, maple sugar, and game. Timber cruiser Daniel Stanchfield declared that he found the Ojibwes "more true and honorable than most white men with whom I came in contact on the frontier." In 1850, despite a steady flow of immigrants into Minnesota Territory, only 892 whites lived in ceded Ojibwe territory—just .09 person per square mile. Relationships between whites and Indians there were based on personal acquaintance and mutual benefit.[70]

Nonetheless, political influence, as always, drove Indian policy. Minnesota officeholders and St. Paul entrepreneurs were determined to bring the annuities of the Wisconsin and Lake Superior bands into the economic orbit of the territorial capital and lobbied intensively for removal. In 1850 President Zachary Taylor acquiesced, signing an executive order revoking the usufruct rights granted in the treaties of 1837 and 1842 and ordering removal of the Ojibwes to a new reservation west of the Mississippi. The Indians, of course, objected strenuously. They had been promised the right to stay on the ceded lands for fifty or even one hundred years. To force compliance to the order, Governor Ramsey and newly appointed Ojibwe agent John Watrous concocted an ingenious, and heartless, plan. Agents hired to shepherd the Indians onto the new reserve did not press the removal issue. Instead, they merely notified the Indians that annuities that year would be given out only at a new agency at Sandy Lake, some sixty miles west of La Pointe and an arduous journey of more than three weeks for the Wisconsin bands. Moreover, annuities and supplies would be disbursed only to those who brought their families with them to the agency, ostensibly so the entire band could see if the Sandy Lake region suited them. Finally, with Machiavellian forethought, Ramsey and Watrous scheduled the payment for late October to ensure that the Indians would be unable to return to their Wisconsin villages before winter set in.[71]

By the end of October nearly 4,000 Ojibwes had gathered at Sandy Lake, many exhausted by a cross-country trip of hundreds of miles. But Agent Watrous was nowhere to be found. Instead, he was in St. Louis, waiting for the delayed annuity payments to arrive from Washington. Weeks passed, and still the funds did not appear. Finally, Watrous headed back to Minnesota empty-handed. Meanwhile, all of the annuity provisions had been used up to feed the waiting Indians, some of whom had been at the agency for five or six weeks. Unable to hunt that fall because of the scheduled payment, people had no resources of their own to draw upon. Soon they were reduced to starvation rations, consisting of rotten flour and a bit of pork. Close quarters and inadequate food created a breeding ground for disease. Measles and dysentery swept through the camps and people began dying. By the time Watrous arrived at the agency at the end of November and made a payment that consisted solely of blankets, guns, and other nonedible goods, conditions had become so desperate that even the St. Paul press began to take notice.[72] The *Minnesota Chronicle and Register* published a letter from the "upper country," headed "Dreadful Sufferings of the Indians":

> The Chippewa payment has just come off. A more miserable set of Indians I never saw—most of them half dead for want of food—not less than eighty-five dead at Sandy Lake—and since the payment, some five or six die every night. I cannot describe the distress of this poor people, and should I, it could not be believed, for it is incredible.[73]

The Ojibwes had no recourse but to make a brutal trip home in the dead of winter, scavenging for food along the way. Some 270 people died on the journey.[74]

The 1850 removal effort was a catastrophic failure that caused more than 400 Ojibwe deaths. Governor Ramsey, in Minnesota for just a year, bore the brunt of the responsibility. Through a combination of hubris and inexperience, he had blundered badly, seduced by the cupidity of St. Paul merchants and traders—with catastrophic consequences. However, his coup with the Dakota treaties the following summer restored his prestige and, for white Minnesotans at least, the tragic debacle at Sandy Lake was soon forgotten. The Ojibwes, however, would not so easily forget the searing experience of government duplicity, embodied in Alexander Ramsey. At the last day of the annuity payment Pillager chief Flat Mouth demanded that a letter be transcribed to the governor. "Tell him," Flat Mouth ordered, "I blame him for the children we have lost, for the sickness we have suffered and for the hunger we have endured. The fault rests on his shoulders." He further gave notice that old relationships of trust had been irreparably broken:

> You call us your children, but I do not think we are your children. If we were we should be white. You are not our Father and I think you call us your children only in mockery. The *earth* is our Father and I will never call *you* so. . . . We did not sell the ground to our Great Father. We gave it to him in order that he might follow our example and be liberal to us.[75]

The hard lessons learned at Sandy Lake erased any remaining Ojibwe illusions that the U.S. government would evenhandedly offer justice to Indian people.

Stung by the scandal of Sandy Lake and lacking either settlement pressure or local support to press the removal effort, the government canceled the order in 1851. The day before he left for Minnesota to negotiate the Dakota land cessions, Commissioner of Indian Affairs Luke Lea ordered the suspension, writing that it was not "required by the interests of the citizens or Government of the United States and would in its consequences be disastrous to the Indians."[76]

Just three years later the "interests of the citizens," and those of the Indians as well, had dramatically changed. The pace of in-migration, development, and speculation, and the rapacious land fever it fed, built pressure to take title to the upper country. Settlers overwhelmingly continued to favor the river valleys and plains to the south, but it was timber and mineral rights that treaty proponents were after rather than farmsteads and town site development. Thus, as in earlier Ojibwe treaties, the goal of treaties proposed in the 1850s was not to expel the Indians from the territory but to gain the rights to resource extraction. In 1854, when the Indians gathered at La Pointe for the fall annuity payment, a treaty council convened to persuade the Lake Superior bands[77] to give up the mineral district north and west of the lake, which included the yet un-discovered fabulous iron deposits of the Mesabi and Vermilion ranges.[78]

With memories of Sandy Lake vividly etched in memory, the Ojibwes were. not eager to sell, making any proposed removal out of the question. George Manypenny, the new commissioner of Indian Affairs, acknowledged that the Ojibwes were "very unwilling to relinquish their present residences." To get them to agree to a land cession ("which on account of its great mineral re-sources [was] an object of material importance to obtain"), it would be "neces-sary to permit them all to remain." Thus, the treaty proposed a reservation in-side the ceded territory, accompanied by hunting, fishing, and gathering rights on the lands they relinquished.[79]

The terms of all the Ojibwe treaties, though they extinguished title, prom-ised the Indians continued access to the ceded lands. As historian Rebecca Kugel notes, the Ojibwes generally preferred a path of cooperation and friend-liness with the government but were positioned to insist on favorable terms. They were not about to be bullied or forced. Even in 1854, though Native pop-ulation growth strained their traditional sources of subsistence, the Indians had not been reduced to a state of dependency, nor were they of a single mind. The La Pointe Treaty negotiation nearly collapsed due to dissent among the 4,000 Indians gathered there over whether to part with their lands under any terms. The prospect of annuities and other material assistance no doubt prom-ised a welcome relief from hardships that regularly beset them, but without the inclusion of hunting, fishing, and gathering rights the treaty surely would have failed.[80]

Under the terms of the treaty that was ultimately signed, the proposed res-ervations seemed to have few drawbacks. Though the combined area was less than 300,000 acres for a population of some 4,000 Ojibwes, the reservations served only as a home base, where white intrusion was prohibited. In fact, new reservations located in territory that had been ceded in 1837 and 1842, as well as in the most recent treaty, seemed to add weight to Indian rights to be on the land, free to continue their seasonal migrations as they had in the past. At least this is how it was explained to them at the time. As Fond du Lac chief Naw-gawnab later testified, "In regard to our reservations, at the time of the treaty the Commissioners . . . told us that our reservations were not to confine us all together to live upon them—that we should have the privilege of going out of it whenever we had a mind for hunting purposes."[81]

Evidence makes it clear that this was indeed the government's intention at the time of the treaty. Though for decades Indian policy had centered on turn-ing Indians into farmers, it had been spectacularly unsuccessful among the Ojibwes. Even had they been willing to take up the plow, the dense forests, poor soil, and short growing season of the north made farming an impossible substitute for the hunting, fishing, and gathering that sustained them. Nor could the relatively minuscule reservations provide an adequate resource base to support the population. With settlement of the region seemingly in the far distant future, if ever, treaty negotiators had no qualms in promising the Indians unrestricted access to the ceded lands, while industrious prospectors and engineers concentrated on riches below the soil.[82]

The pinelands presented a more complicated problem. When loggers first appeared in the Mississippi and St. Croix valleys, the Ojibwes had not objected to their activities as long as the Indians were paid for the timber that the loggers cut, either by contract or treaty. However, two decades of lumbering had left a swath of destruction that endangered the Indians' very existence. Clearcutting, road building, and damming of lakes and rivers drove away game and destroyed the forest resources that were essential to the Ojibwe way of life. Logging operations (that seemed to multiply by the day) had a direct negative effect on Indians' standard of living. By the 1850s, the Ojibwes made a "clear connection between selling their land and their growing poverty."[83]

Timber cutting was on its way to becoming the territory's most profitable industry. Lumber mills as far south as Rock Island, Illinois, swallowed as many logs as the pinelands could deliver. And an insatiable demand for finished lumber in rapidly developing Illinois and Iowa, not to mention the breakneck pace of building in St. Paul, St. Anthony, and upstart Minneapolis, kept local mills up and down the St. Croix and Mississippi busy night and day, turning logs into boards. All this accelerated the number and pace of timber operations, both on ceded lands and in illegal forays into Indian territory. In 1854, 140 million feet of logs passed through the St. Croix boom at Stillwater alone. The result was a growing feeling of alarm and resentment among the Ojibwes. In 1852 a heated dispute erupted between the Mille Lacs band and a timber company over a dam built on the Rum River. The dam, which enabled the loggers to float their logs downriver, backed up into Lake Onamia, destroying the Indians' wild rice crop. Mille Lacs chief Nequenebe first protested to the governor: "We shall have no rice crops, and of course starve to death. . . . Why are those people allowed to dam up the river and destroy our fields?" When peaceful protest failed, the Indians repeatedly tore down the dam to protect the rice crop.[84]

The Rum River dispute exemplified the differing understanding of land ownership that set whites and Ojibwes against one another. The dam and the lumbering operation that constructed it were located on territory ceded in 1837. The lumbermen felt they had every right to develop (and deforest) it as they pleased. However, for nearly two decades the Mille Lacs band had made its home inside the ceded territory in the vicinity of Lake Mille Lacs, with the tacit approval of the government. In the Indians' minds, the resources they depended on still belonged to them. Adding fuel to the growing climate of antagonism was an increasing number of angry encounters between Indians and new settlers, especially European immigrants, who had no knowledge of Ojibwe customs. Culturally at odds, both Indians and whites tended to misread one another's overtures. To the Indians, the settlers seemed stingy, rude, and inhospitable. From the settlers' perspective, the Indians were insolent, had no respect for private property, and seemed generally threatening. With such tensions on the rise in the ceded territory and timber companies anxious to expand their operations northward, Minnesota politicians pushed hard for another treaty that would extinguish Indian title to all Minnesota lands.[85]

Leading the charge was Henry Rice, who had succeeded Sibley as territorial delegate in 1853. The La Pointe Treaty was no sooner concluded than he began urging the secretary of the interior to treat with the Mississippi, Pillager, and Winnibigoshish bands for their lands in the heart of Minnesota's white pine forest. Never one to miss an opportunity for profit, Rice was already elbow-deep in timber investments, yet he purported to be motivated by humanitarian concern for his "friends" the Indians, who, he claimed, were "starving as hunters and gatherers." Nonetheless, he was quick to point out that the hard-pressed Ojibwes could be induced to give up their lands at a bargain price. The silver-tongued and savvy Rice soon had Senate approval in hand and proceeded to work closely with Commissioner Manypenny to arrange the stage for a successful treaty council.[86]

Obviously, Rice pointed out, the La Pointe Treaty had proven the folly of convening the bands as a whole. Internal dissent among the Indians and an overabundance of democracy had nearly scuttled those negotiations. Another treaty council along those lines would "be attended with great expense with results not only disadvantageous to the Indians but to the Government." A more prudent course was to "order" a selected delegation of chiefs to Washington as "authorized spokesmen" for their people. Rice identified the Pillager chief Flat Mouth and young Gull Lake Chief Hole-in-the-Day II as key to the success of the plan. Both men were popular and respected leaders. Rice considered them moderates, who were likely to be reasonable negotiators. Accordingly, Manypenny directed his agent in Minnesota to gather up the two chiefs and a small contingent of other like-minded leaders and send them on to Washington. The agent was to inform them that the president wanted to discuss their lands in Minnesota, "their present comfort and advantage and their permanent welfare in the future." With this purposely vague command invitation, the delegation could only guess what proposition was in store. Flat Mouth later declared that he was "sent for to come to Washington . . . or he would not have come."[87]

The city of Washington itself, as Rice well knew, would put the Indians at a disadvantage. The impressive buildings, trappings of wealth, the carriages and railroads—all acted as a reminder of the power of the U.S. government. Furthermore, none of the Indians spoke English, forcing them to rely on translators and the good offices of Rice to represent their position. In a stunning conflict of interest, Rice was allowed to negotiate on behalf of the Indians and even set the price per acre for the purchased lands. Events moved quickly and in a matter of days a treaty was signed, extinguishing title to all the bands' "lands in the Territory of Minnesota or elsewhere." The language of the treaty was so sweeping that Commissioner Manypenny could only estimate how much land had been purchased—somewhere, he guessed, between eleven and fourteen million acres. With the ratification of the Washington Treaty, the only remaining Ojibwe territory in Minnesota was the far northern borderland, home to the Bois Forte, Pembina, and Red Lake bands, who had not been party to the negotiations.[88]

Despite the high-handed and manipulative nature of the treaty council, it would be a mistake to assume that the Ojibwe delegation was simply duped into agreement. Flat Mouth and Hole-in-the-Day, who did most of the negotiating, were "moderate" because they had a clear understanding of the shrinking options that their people faced against the onslaught of Euro-Americans, backed by the power of the U.S. government. They recognized that the degradation of their traditional resources made annuity payments increasingly critical to Ojibwe survival. Moreover, the treaty ensured reservations inside the ceded territory, a permanent legal right to remain in their homeland. This seemed a preferable alternative to the relocations they had seen forced on the Dakotas and Winnebagos. For the Mille Lacs delegation, who resided in already ceded territory, a designated reservation that gave them permanent possession of choice lands on the lake was a welcome protection from avaricious loggers.[89] The treaty signators generally regarded the reservations as protection rather than confinement. As they understood the terms of the treaty, they retained hunting, fishing, and gathering rights throughout the territory, as they had in all previous treaties. The chiefs also saw the reservations as a means to protect their people from unscrupulous and ubiquitous whiskey sellers. Indian leaders had long been as troubled as any Protestant reformer by the destructive effects of alcohol. They looked forward to reservations that would be off-limits to rum peddlers. Even more important, they hoped the new annuities would help their communities toward regaining their self-sufficiency and alleviate the miseries and discouragement that drove people to drink. As one Ojibwe explained, "When we are poor and cold and hungry, men offer firewater to us, and we drink it." Poverty and alcohol abuse, as they well understood, went hand in hand.[90]

The Washington delegation had no illusion that the treaty was a panacea for the ills that beleaguered their people, but they represented a political faction who believed the only way to save their way of life was to selectively adapt Ojibwe traditions to changes that they were powerless to stop. Hole-in-the-Day exemplified this strategy. The young leader had won renown as a war chief, but he was also an astute politician who knew how to parlay with whites. Seemingly the epitome of progressive adaptation, he lived in a well-furnished cabin, operated a farm and a ferry, and impressed the whites he encountered with his "civilized" dress and courtly manners. Even Harriet Bishop, who seldom had a good word for Native people, approved of the young chief, "a brave warrior, with noble impulses of heart, beloved by his people, and respected by whites." Nonetheless, Hole-in-the-Day spoke only Ojibwe, had not converted to Christianity, and was dedicated to preserving the cultural values of his people.[91]

When the chiefs returned home, they faced a deeply divided people. Many Ojibwes greeted news of the treaty with disbelief and anger, especially the warrior chiefs and their followers, who opposed any sale of their ancestral lands. By what right, they protested, did this handpicked delegation speak for all the people? Hole-in-the-Day and even the venerable Flat Mouth were reviled for their part in the transaction, "accused of betraying or sacrificing the interests of [their] nation." Others, who favored the accommodationist tactics of the civil chiefs, agreed that the reservations and annuities were their best hope to stave off otherwise inevitable disaster. Somehow, despite the rancor and disagreements, Hole-in-the-Day managed to retain his leadership position, a testament to his skill at straddling the white and Indian worlds.[92] But as events played out in subsequent years, not even Hole-in-the-Day's considerable political skills were a match for Euro-American expansionism. Neither reservations nor annuities could hold back the forces that impoverished the Indians. Timber cutters denuded the pineries while towns and farmsteads transformed the hardwood forest. The reservations became more prison than fortress. But in the 1850s, as Indian leaders strategized to make the best of an unequal contest for the future, a different, more optimistic outcome could be envisioned.

Completing the Picture

By 1855 land cession treaties had redrawn the contours of Minnesota. In 1849, when the territory was created, all but the small triangle between the Mississippi and St. Croix rivers had been Indian country. Piece by piece, treaties had taken those lands, opening them to settlement and development. Like a nearly finished jigsaw puzzle, the picture of Minnesota as it exists today was almost complete. The far north and the Red River valley had not yet been acquired, but that was not considered an immediate problem. In the midst of the territory's valuable timberland, however, one unceded tract remained, the last missing piece needed to complete the desired picture.

In 1847, when economic viability depended almost solely on the Indian trade, Anglo-Minnesotans had lobbied to bring treaty Indians and their annuities into Minnesota country. Settlers in Wisconsin and the new state of Iowa were anxious to remove any Indians remaining inside their borders. Fortunately, Minnesota traders and politicians were only too happy to make room for displaced treaty Indians in Minnesota country. They were delighted when the government purchased from the Ojibwes about a million acres of mixed forest (just northwest of present-day St. Cloud) to establish reservations for Wisconsin's Menominee tribe and for the Winnebagos, who had been relocated once already from Wisconsin to the government-designated Neutral Ground in Iowa in 1830. In addition to housing the Iowa Winnebagos, the Minnesota reservation at Long Prairie was intended to become home to the numerous members of the tribe who persisted in Wisconsin, despite all efforts to round them up and ship them to the Neutral Ground.[93]

The Menominees never made the move to Minnesota, resisting removal with such vigor that the government finally abandoned the effort. But the Winnebago bands in Iowa did agree to make the trek to the new reservation, persuaded by their trader, Henry Rice, who relocated to Minnesota along with the Indians in 1847. Clearly, Rice's persuasive skills were already well honed, since the Winnebagos, notoriously averse to relocation, trusted his word about the fine quality of the territory offered them and even allowed him to choose the reservation lands that would be their future home. Rice made a tidy sum managing the removal effort and rounding up fugitive bands in Wisconsin, whom he convinced to join their kinsmen at Long Prairie. He also ensured his status among Anglo-Minnesotans by bringing the rich Winnebago annuities into the reach of St. Paul. However, from the first, the Winnebagos were dismayed by the geography of their new home. They had been promised land "suitable to their habits, wants, and wishes." Instead, they complained, the reserve was "overgrown with trees and undergrowth," "fit for nothing but frogs, reptiles, and mosquitoes." They were a prairie people and did not like the dense woods that surrounded them. Why, asked Winnebago chief Big Canoe, should "we be taken from a good country and placed in a bad one?"[94]

It seems apparent that Henry Rice chose the Winnebago reserve with other priorities in mind. Deep in Indian country and hundreds of miles from their ancestral Wisconsin home, where many homesick Winnebagos still yearned to return, the Long Prairie reservation was ideally situated to benefit Rice's trading interests. Distance would discourage the Indians from wandering back to Wisconsin and isolation kept them from the blandishments of competing traders. In 1847 it would have been hard for anyone to imagine that in a few short years the value of the reservation's timber stands would outweigh the worth of Indian annuities or that Rice would find himself working to retake the reservation lands from the Indians.

But by 1855 the calculus had drastically changed. Land and timber drove the region's economy and the Winnebagos were sitting on a newly attractive piece of real estate. The unhappy Indians had begun petitioning to relocate their reservation shortly after arriving at Long Prairie, where their agency was located. The longer they resided there, the less the Indians liked it. Game was scarce and, hemmed in between hostile Ojibwes and Dakotas, they did not dare trespass on the other tribes' hunting grounds. Many discontented Winnebagos simply migrated off the reservation, some finding their way back to Wisconsin to be near relatives who remained there and the "graves of their fathers." Others wandered south or east of the Mississippi, causing consternation among settlers who were beginning to fill up the country. Those who remained

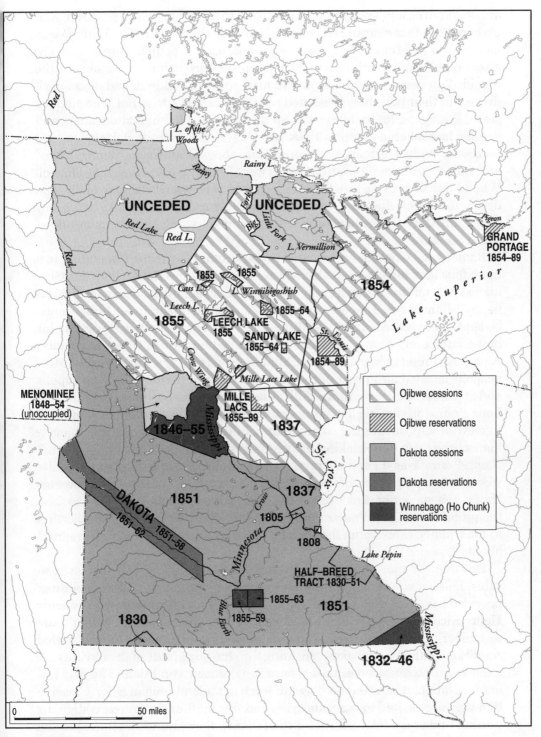

Indian land cessions.

at Long Prairie, aimless and miserable, were easy prey for whiskey sellers, who clustered like flies near the reservation, hawking their wares. The Winnebagos had arrived in Minnesota a proud and independent people. Russell Blakely, a steamboat captain who carried them up the Mississippi, remembered the dignified procession of "two thousand men, women, children, and dogs . . . all dressed in their best, they presented such a picture as I have not seen equaled since." But by the 1850s, after years on the inhospitable reservation, anger and despair had taken a harsh toll. Settlers showered Governor Ramsey and his successor, Willis Gorman, with complaints about Winnebago "depredations" and, indeed, unfriendly confrontations were frequent, often fueled by alcohol. White Minnesotans despised the Winnebagos as the worst example of the lazy, drunken, shiftless Indian, and the governors struggled for years to find a way to deal with the "Winnebago problem" and still keep their annuity money flowing to St. Paul.[95]

Ramsey and Gorman both floated proposals to relocate the reservation to a more felicitous location, but they always met with objections. Governor Gorman stands out for his unstinting efforts to effect a land exchange for the unhappy Winnebagos. He considered that "a promise made to an Indian must be kept"—a novel idea in 1850s Minnesota Territory. Nonetheless, despite his best efforts, every proposal for relocation stalled because of citizen resistance. A proposed reservation near Lake Minnetonka, some ten miles west of Minneapolis, created an uproar of protest meetings and petitions in Minneapolis and St. Anthony. Adding to the difficulties, traders and business interests near Long Prairie, who made a handsome living off the Indians, did not want them to move at all. Nor was the commissioner of Indian Affairs amenable to making a change. No doubt taking the word of Rice, who continued to insist that "Long Prairie was a good country," Commissioner Orlando Brown was quite sure that "only a portion of the more idle and worthless of the tribe" were unhappy. His successor, Luke Lea, was of the same opinion. According to Lea, the problems at Long Prairie derived "less from any well-grounded objection to the country, than from [the Indians'] own reckless disposition and vagrant habits."[96]

However, by 1855 the timbered reservation had significantly increased in value. Lumber was bringing a premium price and the nearby Mississippi River provided easy access to the mills at St. Anthony and Minneapolis. Suddenly Henry Rice, who by now had transferred his attention from the Indian trade to lumbering and land speculation, developed concern about the "unsettled condition" of the Winnebagos, "roaming thro the filled parts of the territory . . . annoying the whites and almost always in a destitute condition." The only humane solution, it now seemed, was to work out a land exchange for a reserve that was more suited to their lifestyle—and free up the current reservation for waiting timber speculators. As for the Indians, they also were attuned to the increased value of the forested reserve. They were as anxious as ever to leave the place behind but also recognized that the timbermen's desire for the land had improved their bargaining position. They could—and did—hold out for a reservation that would enable them to rebuild their community and improve their quality of life. On February 27, 1855, a delegation representing the nineteen Long Prairie bands signed a treaty that exchanged their reservation for a small but fertile tract on the Blue Earth River in southwestern Minnesota— some of the most desirable prairie farmland in the region.[97]

This somewhat startling land exchange indicates the impressive political and economic power that lumber interests wielded at this time. To get hold of Winnebago timberlands, they succeeded in pushing through a treaty that created an Indian reservation in prime farming country—land that had only recently been won away from the Dakota people. The region was rapidly filling up with farmers who, in the words of historian William Folwell, "had no love for 'Injuns,'" but the farmers clearly were no match for the political clout of the lumbermen.[98]

Once established at Blue Earth, the Winnebagos surprised their many detractors by taking up farming with a will. The reservation was too small—only 200,000 acres—to support a lifestyle of hunting and gathering, but the Winnebagos were no strangers to horticulture. Before coming to Minnesota, they had long planted crops as part of their traditional economy. Finally in possession of a place where they believed they could make a home, they had no reluctance to till the land. More fully than any other Minnesota tribe, the Winnebagos adapted their communal lifeways to accommodate Euro-American norms. They cut their hair, adopted European dress, improved the land, and built schools and houses that looked just like those of their white neighbors. Perhaps they were bent on disproving the insulting characterizations that had been heaped upon them. Or maybe, after generations of being forced from one alien reservation to another, they were simply trying to coexist in harmony with their neighbors and hold on to the fine stretch of prairie they could finally call home. Whatever set them on an assimilationist path, the Winnebagos prospered at Blue Earth. According to Indian agent Jonathan Fletcher, problems with alcohol were negligible and the Indians were a model of self-government. For once, it seemed a treaty had truly benefited the Indians as was supposedly intended. But despite the Winnebagos' willingness to conform to the mores of the dominant culture, their white neighbors, most with no experience in Indian country, never fully accepted them as fellow Minnesotans. In less than a decade, when the opportunity arose, whites clamored to remove them from Minnesota altogether, wiping out all the farmer Indians had achieved.[99]

The Winnebago Treaty of 1855 left only the northern reaches of Minnesota to be transferred from Indian possession to the U.S. government and thence into townships, sections, and city lots. And not a moment too soon. Immigrants poured into the territory, axes rang in the woods, sawmills worked day and night to keep up with the demand for lumber. Church congregations and civic organizations set to the task of domesticating the urban frontier. Thousands of acres in the countryside were put to the plow and town sites proliferated like weeds. As Minnesota careened toward statehood, population, progress, and improvements were measured in weeks rather than months or years. Minnesotans had their eye on the future. As far as they were concerned, Indians were fast receding into the colorful but now irrelevant past.

Chapter 9

PLAYING FOR POWER

> Such was the mixed character of the population at the time, that a
> large proportion of the citizens were either by ties of consanguinity
> or trading interest allied to the Indians and their interests, and these
> were known and designated as the "Moccasin Democracy," or "Indian
> Dynasty."
> Captain James Starkey, 1893

Enemies, Alliances, and Political Spoils

The politics that conveyed Minnesota to statehood were a high stakes game.
The territory was bursting with political spoils and riches to be captured, and
"old settlers" vied with newcomers for a place at the head of the line, encouraging bare-knuckle politics with a distinctively local cast. In the early years
of the territory, personal feuds and competing economic interests defined the
political terrain more than party affiliation, and alliances and enmities shifted
frequently as deals were struck or broken. The arguments at heart were about
money and power, but enmeshed at the center of this byzantine political tangle
were notions about race and citizenship. Race, both in the person of Minnesota's Indians and mixed-blood inhabitants and in the heated debate about slavery and black civil rights, came to play an essential role in determining which
political faction would have the upper hand.

On the evening of March 31, 1851, a particularly volatile debate over apportionment and voting rights, with clear racial undertones, nearly devolved into
civic mayhem. A group of armed partisans spent the night on watch outside
the home of Governor Ramsey, intending to confront their political opponents,
who had threatened to burn the governor in effigy. Earlier in the day, Ramsey
had signed a controversial apportionment bill that would enfranchise hundreds of mixed-blood voters. Legislators had nearly come to blows over the

issue, and feelings ran high on the street as well. Disgruntled citizens, who opposed the governor's stance on the matter, were rumored to be planning a fiery protest. According to an eyewitness, the threatened demonstration "aroused the passions of all the Governor's friends to fever heat." Though the effigy burners ultimately failed to appear, tensions between the factions did not abate. Interestingly, nearly all the men involved were self-identified Democrats. Clearly, in Minnesota Territory party affiliation was no guarantee of unity.[1]

[226]

The issue that so inflamed the partisans that March evening was the voting rights of people who lived in the yet unceded Indian country west of the Mississippi, most of them of mixed-blood ancestry. To bring the population up to the territorial threshold of 5,000, every man who, by any stretch of the imagination, could be deemed "non-Indian" had been counted, but when it came to voting, many Anglo pioneers now considered the French-speaking hunters and traders a less desirable constituency. The main problem with these potential voters was political more than racial. Democrats dominated the legislature, holding seventeen of the twenty-five seats. But the party was split into warring factions that supported either Henry Sibley or Henry Rice. Rice, the champion of the entrepreneurial vanguard and already a great benefactor of the budding capital city, had strong urban support, especially among Anglos in St. Paul and St. Anthony. But Sibley had the loyalty of his traders and of nearly all the mixed-blood people. Thus, the voting status of Minnesotans living in Indian country had direct implications for which faction would control the party and the composition of the legislature. Whig journalist John Owens (who had no dog in this fight) observed, "This was purely a political move to shear the Sibley faction of that portion of its strength given it by the Sioux traders and the half-breed vote in the Indian country." The crux of the problem was Pembina. The first territorial census counted 637 inhabitants in and around that settlement of Métis buffalo hunters in the far north, second in population only to St. Paul's 840 residents. When added to Mendota's population of 122 and those in other trading outposts in Indian country, Sibley's fur trade contingent far outweighed Rice's core constituency of Anglo entrepreneurs. St. Anthony was so small that its district had to be gerrymandered to include nearby Little Canada, which was largely French Canadian, to earn a representative in the legislature. When the legislators sat down to work out apportionment after the 1850 census was taken, it seems that "Pembina had shown a larger population than it was supposed to have, and was entitled fully to one councilor and two representatives." Owens wryly observed that "this was where the 'shoes pinched' the worst."[2]

Though the fissure that split the Democrats was clearly about political power—on the surface a simple divide between the old fur trade interests and the economic priorities of newcomers—the division between the two sides had a more complex undertone. After all, Henry Rice, though he was rapidly moving into timber and land speculation, still had a hand in the trade. And Henry

Sibley was no foe of progress. Economic interests undeniably played a powerful role, but a racial undercurrent, though politically inexpedient to vocalize at the time, also funneled people into one camp or the other. The unspoken question, at least for some, was whether French-speaking mixed-blood people had a place in the white man's Minnesota that was being constructed.[3]

As the Anglo population grew in the next few years, racialized rhetoric, though still coded, became less guarded. In debates over the proposed state boundaries in 1857, the character of the trappers and hunters who populated the North came to the fore. One speaker charged that the north country "will never be occupied by any other than a floating population, a population existing one day and extinct the next." Such "do-nothings" would only advance "interests which would forever be a curse to the Territory." Pembina, in particular, came in for harsh assessment. Various orators declared that Pembina had won its legislative seats by fraud and deal making with the fur trade interests; that it should have had no representation at all; and that since it "is willing to be made the pliant tool for anything," it, and the rest of the north country (with its large Métis population), "would hang upon our interest and prosperity like an incubus." The solution proposed was to draw the state's northern boundary to exclude "this northern region [which] will never be settled by a permanent, home abiding population." The attempt to redraw the northern border failed, but the language that framed the debate makes it clear that ideas about race and culture as well as economic priorities were powerful influences.[4]

In 1851, when mixed-blood people were probably a third of the population, such cultural assaults were neither politic nor possible against a people and way of life that still dominated Minnesota Territory's population and economy. Instead Democratic factions were cast as "Furs" versus "Anti-Furs," monopoly interests versus equal opportunity. But no matter how the issues were framed, the contest tended to pit "Moccasin Democrats"—fur trade veterans, many with mixed-blood family members—against Anglo up-and-comers. These newest residents clearly were uneasy about the role of semi-Indian "foreigners" in the political process, and ideas about race almost certainly intensified the apportionment debate. During a recess in the heated session, a supporter of the Rice faction "painted and dressed himself up as a Winnebago Indian" and "took possession" of the Speaker's chair, perhaps acting out a belief that the bill to enfranchise Indian country put Minnesota's future into the hands of uncivilized "half-breeds" who had no rightful place in determining its future. When the bill squeaked through the legislature and Ramsey signed it into law, it sent protestors into the streets with talk of burning the governor in effigy, "the most exciting night that St. Paul had ever witnessed."[5]

As this episode makes clear, in Minnesota's early years political arguments seldom followed the trajectory of traditional party politics. When Governor Ramsey and the other territorial appointees—all Whigs—first arrived in St. Paul in 1849, they encountered a power structure that was overwhelmingly dominated by the men of the fur trade, who, though they bickered among themselves, had long cast their allegiance with the Democratic Party. But, though Democrats in name, they were largely indifferent to national party priorities. Their politics (and differences among themselves) were grounded exclusively in the interests of the Indian trade and their other expanding investments in Minnesota. Most of the territory's citizens were connected in some way with the trade—loyal to Sibley and his lieutenants, and, by extension, Democrats of one stripe or another. Ramsey found himself a lonely Whig in a sea of Democrats. A practical man committed to making his mark in Minnesota, he quickly took the measure of local politics, shed partisan prejudices, and partnered with Sibley to advance their shared ambitions. As for the high-toned Sibley, though his ties were with the Democrats in Washington, he liked to think of himself as above crass politicking, and at home he cast himself, at least at first, as a nonpartisan statesman, a "Jeffersonian Democrat." Thus, he had no qualms about making alliances across party lines to advance the "larger good." Serendipitously, Ramsey's pragmatism and Sibley's loftiness made for an easy alliance between them.[6]

Bipartisan friendship may have elided differences between the nominal heads of the respective parties, but for the rank and file, intraparty factionalism played a larger role in muddling political loyalties, for Whigs as well as Democrats. New immigrants finding their way to Minnesota from New England, New York, and other northern states bolstered the territory's Whig contingent, but the national party was rapidly collapsing, divided by issues of slavery, popular sovereignty, and the cotton trade. "Conscience Whigs," primarily from New England, soon made their voices heard in Minnesota, especially in St. Anthony. But party loyalty was lukewarm at best. The Conscience Whigs charged that business-oriented "Cotton Whigs" (which included the territory's new officials) thought "more of sheep and cotton than of Man." Nor could they embrace the Democracy, deemed the "party of slavery."[7]

Once in Minnesota, however, slavery became less salient an issue for the Conscience Whigs than the general need for moral reform. These new residents considered it their mission to civilize the hard-drinking, rough-and-tumble character of the society they encountered. Many of the fur-trading Democrats seemed scarcely less alien than the Indians. Loren Collins, who arrived in the territory in 1852, recalled his first encounter with trader and future state Supreme Court justice William Flandrau. "Tanned and clad in the garb of the Indian," Flandrau so closely resembled the party of Indians and mixed bloods who accompanied him that Collins "only with difficulty . . . determined which one of the party was the white man." Decades later, Whig journalist John Owens characterized the perceived cultural gap between the "new" Minnesotans and the fur trade fraternity. With careful diplomacy, he excused what he still regarded as the uncivilized behavior of the Democrats: "The charitable and well-disciplined mind could at a glance see the whole cause of their disposition and action." In Owens's estimation, the fur trade veterans, by "the very nature of their trade, which is one of bitter rivalry and factious intrigue from day to day, intensified by their long sojourn away from the refinements of civilization and intercourse with treacherous savages, rendered them more acute to their interests and less trustful of each other than men who work and strive in the daily marts of ordinary business."[8]

Cultural differences aside, in the estimation of the reformers the fur trade Democrats—and the business-minded Whig officials and entrepreneurs who worked with them—wielded entirely too much power in advancing their economic interests at the expense of the new generation of Yankee entrepreneurs. Thus, splintered internally, Minnesota Whigs mustered little organized influence. Until they marched en masse into the newly formed Republican Party in 1855, their numbers swelled by in-migration, individuals tended to vote in a scattered fashion, depending on local issues and personal interests.[9]

[229]

This should have been a boon for the Democrats; however, their internal battles only muddied the political waters further. Minnesota Democrats were largely indifferent to the question of slavery, the central issue on the national stage. Theirs was a purely local contest, pitting the giants of the party, Henry Sibley and Henry Rice, against one another. The apportionment battle in 1851 was only one of many that split the party in the ensuing years. The single constant amid the political ebb and flow was the antipathy between the two party leaders. Occasionally, when circumstances required, they damped the fires of their feud for a season, but as surely as spring turned to fall, it soon flared up again. Journalist John Owens declared that "the personal bitterness that here arose between the two factions was scarcely less than that which existed at the time between the two great Indian tribes whom these rival traders were respectively trading with." Though both fur trade veterans shared similar economic interests, neither spared any effort to thwart the other, even if it meant supporting a candidate from the opposition party. As a result, political contests usually devolved into confusion, pitting one faction of Democrats against the other, with Whigs and Independents attaching themselves to one or the other in ever-changing allegiances. These uncertain and shifting alliances made for rancorous political campaigns in which an "excited and seething madness . . . possessed the people." Describing the electioneering of 1851, editor James Goodhue of the *Minnesota Pioneer* editorialized:

> Never have we before witnessed an election as hotly contested as our election of last Monday. If an empire had been at stake, more zeal, more influence, more active, unscrupulous means and more indefatigable exertions, could not have been called into exercise. Hope, fear, avarice, ambition, personal obligations, money, whiskey, oysters, patronage, contracts, the promise of favors, jealousy, personal prejudice, envy, everything that could be tortured into a motive, has been pressed into the canvass.[10]

At the close of the campaign, when the 1851 legislature convened in Henry Rice's newly constructed brick hotel in St. Paul, the legislators—let alone their constituents—could scarcely sort out enemies from allies. Elected along with warring Rice and Sibley Democrats were Whigs, who counted themselves either Sibley or Rice men; a couple of Independents and a Free Soiler; and one Anglo-Ojibwe, William Warren, who declared himself to be a man "of no politics."[11]

Sibley, away much of the time in Washington, left most of the political ground fighting to his "chief counselor and manager," Joe Brown, described by an admiring political adversary as "one of the shrewdest politicians and most extraordinary men the Northwest has ever produced." Rice, on the other hand, reveled in the slugfest of frontier politics. Both sides relied heavily on the local press to make their case and stoke the political fires. By 1852 four newspapers were churning out daily or weekly editions in St. Paul and, according to the custom of the times, served as unabashed party organs. Owens, who began publishing the *Minnesota Chronicle and Register* in 1849, proudly declared it "thoroughly Whig in politics and . . . regarded as the organ of the National Administration." His chief competitor was James Goodhue's *Minnesota Pioneer,* which after a brief fling at nonpartisanship, had placed itself squarely in the Sibley camp. To counter the *Pioneer,* Rice financially backed another paper, the *Minnesota Democrat,* and also purportedly invested money in the *Chronicle and Register* to buy its editorial slant away from the Whigs. The Whigs in turn launched a new sheet, the *Minnesotian,* which promised a more reliable editorial position.[12]

The papers boiled with vitriol against their political opponents, engaging in slander and libel with abandon. One official was "as unsafe to occupy a public post as a soreheaded dog is to occupy a parlor." Another thrust the "young territory" into the "lower depths of degradation . . . steeped in the foul pool of political corruption." Yet another was "known as a man utterly destitute of moral principle, manly bearing or even physical courage." Looking back, John Owens, who was in the thick of the journalistic mayhem, admitted that "the bitter strife between the papers tended greatly to increase the factious quarrels in the Legislature." As one present-day journalist marvels, it was a wonder "that the courts of the period were not clogged with suits for libel."[13]

In this heated environment, it is not surprising that Minnesota politics took on the character of a blood feud, and politicians and their supporters frequently defended their "honor" with fists as well as words. The papers, party organs all, continually stirred the pot, and no one exceeded James Goodhue at the art of character assassination during his brief but tempestuous career as editor of the *Pioneer*. His pen was finally capped in 1851 when the brother of Judge David Cooper stabbed the colorful editor in retaliation for characterizations of the judge as "'a sot,' 'a brute,' 'an ass,' 'a profligate vagabond,' &c." Before collapsing, Goodhue managed to shoot Cooper twice, leaving both men seriously injured.[14] The public brawl created a brief spate of indignation among the citizens of St. Paul, but soon the presses went back to work in the same vein as before. Joe Brown took over as publisher of the *Pioneer* until a permanent editor could be found, and Henry Sibley provided the funds to keep the paper running. By 1853 St. Paul and St. Anthony had five daily newspapers in publication, each ardently pushing a particular candidate and political agenda.[15]

The Rice faction claimed to be the "true" Democrats, valiantly fighting for the people's interests against the "fur trade monopoly" that supposedly owned Sibley's loyalties (conveniently ignoring Rice's own substantial interests in the trade). Sibley's Democratic dissidents called themselves the People's Party and touted his achievements on behalf of the territory, in contrast to those Democrats "who seek to be elected, not for the advancement of the territory and its interests, but to subserve private ends and selfish purposes." The fractured Whigs, though skeptical about both political powerhouses, lacked the unity—or the numbers—to stand on their own against either.

[231]

With the establishment of Minnesota's Republican Party in 1855, the chaotic nature of state politics began to sort itself out. The economic boom was in full swing and in-migration from the east swelled the ranks of reformers and Yankee entrepreneurs, eager to wrest some of the economic and political spoils from the old guard. These newcomers gravitated naturally into the newly minted Republican Party, which soon exhibited a unity and political muscle that the Whigs had been lacking. Territorial politics began to resemble the national model more closely. With statehood on the foreseeable horizon, Republicans lined up against Democrats to determine who would hold the power to shape the economic and political contours of the soon-to-be state.

A "Peculiar Institution"

Slavery, of course, though largely ignored in Minnesota, was the overriding national issue of the day. The passage of the Kansas-Nebraska Act of 1854 brought the decades-old conflict once again to the point of explosion.[16] Serendipitously, the escalation of the national debate over slavery coincided with and advanced the formation of Minnesota's Republican Party. Despite the fact that slavery had no future as a viable economic system in Minnesota and that fewer than one hundred blacks resided in the territory, politicians in both parties latched onto the "slave question" and correlative issues about the place of African Americans in civil society as the centerpiece of their campaigns to discredit one another and finally cement party unity.

In preterritorial Minnesota, "race" most commonly referred to the difference between white and Indian. But in a world where intermarriage was the accepted custom, racial taxonomy largely was ordered by behavior and self-representation—"civilized" versus "savage"—defined through the lens of culture and custom rather than by skin color or some pseudoscientific biological determination of blood ancestry. Two centuries of intermarriage had created complex genealogies that defied those racial categorizations common in the settled parts of the country. Thus, those who embraced Euro-American ways were considered white and those who favored the lifestyle of Native people were classified as Indian. For example, the Cadotte family, which had begun trading in the Upper Great Lakes in 1670, had intermarried with Indian women for four generations by the 1830s. In ancestry more Indian than white, still Michel Cadotte had no problem securing American citizenship in 1819. As a prosperous and respected trader for the American Fur Company, he was indisputably white by the standards of his world.[17]

Race, as constructed in Minnesota country, put people of African descent in a uniquely liberating position. Prominent trader George Bonga, who was born near Fond du Lac in 1802, was described by an Anglo contemporary as "a man of wealth and consequence . . . a thorough gentleman in both feeling and deportment." He was also the descendant of slaves. In 1782 Bonga's grandparents had come to Michilimackinac as bondspeople, the chattel of a British officer. Freed upon their owner's death, the Bongas remained in the Northwest. Their son Pierre and grandson George both married into the Ojibwe tribe and built reputations as "well known and highly respected" traders. George Bonga was courtly, an astute businessman with polished manners, fluent in French, English, Ojibwe, and several other Indian languages—and a valued member of the trading elite. The Indians, to whom he was kin by both birth and marriage, viewed him simply as another version of European, a "black Frenchman." Among the traders, Bonga's color did not seem to diminish his social status, though they surely recognized him as black—the trader appeared more African than Indian. Nor did Bonga mark himself as racially distinct. As historian William Green observes, he "probably viewed his blackness as incidental." Looking back on his early years in the North without apparent irony, Bonga once famously declared: "Gentlemen, I assure you that John Banfil and myself were the first two white men that ever came into this country." As retold decades later, Bonga's statement was recounted as an amusing anecdote, part of the colorful lore of early Minnesota—testament to the profound changes the 1850s wrought in the meanings ascribed to whiteness.[18]

Most of the Minnesotans who chronicled the state's history had arrived in the territorial years, coming from the East with decidedly different understandings of race. Minnesota, as they proudly noted, was a free state. The practice of slavery had been banned in the articles of the Northwest Ordinance of 1787. However, these self-consciously selective historians glossed over the fact that, despite its prohibition, slavery had not only been tolerated in Minnesota, it had been tacitly supported by the federal government. From the time Fort Snelling was established, officers there commonly relied on slaves as their personal attendants, housekeepers, and nursemaids. To maintain morale and compensate for the hardships of serving on the frontier, the army provided each officer an allowance to keep a servant. Quite often those "servants" were slaves. Officers—even those who came from free states—frequently stopped off at the St. Louis slave markets to purchase bondspeople on the way to their billet in

George Bonga photographed by Charles Alfred Zimmerman around 1870. Courtesy of the Minnesota Historical Society.

the North. Indian agent Lawrence Taliaferro, a patrician Virginia slaveholder, brought numerous slaves into Minnesota country over the seventeen years he served there. Some assisted him at the agency or his home; others he leased to officers at the fort. Apparently Taliaferro managed to ignore the inherent contradiction between Indian rights, which he vigorously championed, and the unfree status of his servants.[19]

[234]   At some point either during or after his tenure in the North, Taliaferro determined to eventually free his slaves—once they were no longer needed to ensure his comfort on the frontier. He also may have eased his conscience by noting that the condition of slavery at Fort Snelling was considerably milder than the way it was experienced in the South. Nearly all slaves were maids or personal attendants, the equivalent of high-status "house slaves" in his native Virginia, attached to masters who treated them with relative benevolence. Indeed, officers, and especially their wives, likely felt more culturally akin to their slaves than to the scruffy enlisted men, let alone Indians, mixed bloods, or even many of the traders, whose ways seemed scarcely more civilized than the "savages." The slaves, much like pianos and tea sets, helped create an island of civility in this alien world. In the 1830s, only six or seven officers at a time were stationed at Fort Snelling. Quite plausibly, in this small circle the mannerly character of black bondspeople was appreciated, and personal relationships between master or mistress and slave may have mitigated the harshest aspects of bondage. Almost always, slaves were delicately referred to as "servants" and only rarely was a slave sold from one master to another, at least as long as the owner remained at Fort Snelling.[20]

Nonetheless, it will not do to romanticize the condition of slaves in Minnesota. Physical punishment was countenanced, as it was for common soldiers, and occasionally could be brutal. Moreover, the military's blatant sanction of slavery cleared the path for civilians to purchase and maintain slaves as well, under conditions that sometimes could be much harsher than those typical at the fort. Though traders generally relied on French Canadian Métis laborers (whose contracts often consigned them to the status of indentured servants), at least a few became slaveholders. Alexis Bailly, for one, purchased at least one slave directly from an officer at Fort Snelling. Another, Sylvanus Lowry, a Kentucky native who amassed a fortune in the Winnebago trade, transported slaves from below the Mason-Dixon line to provide a sheen of southern gentility to his well-appointed home at St. Cloud. Thus, whether as house servants or common laborers, carried into the territory or bought and sold on Minnesota's "free soil," black slaves, though relatively few in number, were an accepted part of the racial mosaic.[21]

One Fort Snelling bondswoman, identified only as Rachael, challenged the extralegal practice of slavery in free territory. Taking her future in her hands, in 1837 she successfully sued for her freedom in a Missouri court. But the court's decision effected no change in the policy of sanctioning slavery at the fort.

Dred Scott, whose quest for freedom became a national cause as it wended its way through the courts in the 1840s and 1850s, also based his case on his residency in free territory—first in Illinois and then in Minnesota, at Fort Snelling, from 1836 to 1840. But Scott waited nearly a decade to sue for freedom for himself, his wife, Harriet, and their daughters, Eliza and Lizzie. Back in the slave state of Missouri in 1846, the Scotts confronted much more daunting difficulties in pressing their case than would have faced them while residing in Minnesota country.[22]

Contemporary commentators and historians alike have long puzzled over why Dred Scott failed to make his bid for freedom years earlier. A close look at Scott's life—and options—at Fort Snelling helps explain his decision and also sheds light on the experience of slavery in the Minnesota borderland. Scott was the first slave purchased by army surgeon John Emerson. In advance of assuming his first post in the Northwest in 1834, Dr. Emerson had probably been advised of the labor shortage on the frontier and the best means to attain a "servant" to accompany him. As part of his preparations then, along with warm clothing and medical supplies, the doctor purchased Scott in St. Louis. The two men remained bound together until Emerson's death in 1843. Emerson, a slaveholder neither by tradition nor temperament, seems to have treated Scott as more of an assistant than slave. And, as Scott could not help but notice, he was better housed, clad, and fed than either enlisted men, fur trade laborers, or certainly the ubiquitous Indians. At Fort Snelling, slaves held a position several rungs up from the "bottom rail." When Scott expressed a desire to marry Agent Taliaferro's slave, Harriet Robinson, both Emerson and Taliaferro blessed the union. Taliaferro himself conducted the ceremony and gave the bride in marriage. The newlyweds set up housekeeping in their own cabin, warmed by a stove procured by Dr. Emerson, who "put his personal prestige and honor on the line in order to obtain a precious and limited commodity, a stove, for Dred and his wife." Meanwhile, enlisted men slept in chilly barracks, four men to a bunk, sixteen to a room.[23]

Of course, none of these relative comforts erased the fact that Dred Scott and his family were not free. However, in the isolation of the north country, their options were limited, and freedom and slavery did not pose a rigid dichotomy. Facing the dangers of the wilderness with neither a woodsman's resources nor skills made flight an untenable choice. Where would they go? Surely not to the savage Indians. Even had they pursued legal manumission, Dred and Harriet Scott would have been left with "nothing but freedom" and a precarious and uncertain future. Not surprisingly, then, they chose the immediate security and limited autonomy provided by Emerson. As legal scholars Lea VanderVelde and Sandhya Subramanian conclude:

> Within Dred's set of choices at that time, remaining with Dr. Emerson, who supported the continuity of Dred's family, represented a willing subordination to one

coercive institution—slavery—in exchange for another range of freedom. Under the protectorate of Dr. Emerson, the Scotts could carve out a sphere of personal and familial independence.[24]

Quite possibly, Emerson, like Taliaferro, promised Scott and his family eventual emancipation. However, with the doctor's unexpected death in 1843 the Scotts' security evaporated. Sale and separation of their family suddenly loomed as an imminent likelihood, and Dred and Harriet put themselves in the hands of the courts.[25]

Despite the atypical contours of slavery at Fort Snelling, slaves had no sure protection against mistreatment. Even those who were well treated must have remained acutely aware that their condition could change at their owner's whim. When officers were transferred, some freed their slaves; others—probably more often—either sold them to incoming officers or put them on the block at St. Louis. The bondswoman Rachael forestalled that eventuality by suing for freedom in the courts, but most slaves, like Dred and Harriet Scott, hoped for the best, relying on their personal relationships with their masters.

A few hardy souls, however, like Joseph Godfrey, escaped to join the Indians. Godfrey was born into slavery in the household of hard-bitten fur trader Alexis Bailly, described as a man with "great vices and also great virtues." Apparently Bailly's wife, Lucy, the mixed-blood daughter of Jean Baptiste Faribault, was equally hard, known for mercilessly whipping the child-servants in her household—black, Indian, and mixed blood alike. According to trader Philander Prescott, whose mixed-blood daughter was in service there, the children "would get from 25 to 50 lashes a day and sometimes more." The outraged Prescott took his daughter away, but neither the slave child nor the "young Sioux girl" who shared his daughter's plight received similar protection. Prescott recalled only that he "would leave the house to get away from the miserable crying of those children when she was cowhiding them." Joseph, as part of a trader's household, was at home among the Dakotas, fluent in their language, and had learned survival skills that were foreign to slaves at the fort. Thus, it is not surprising that he lit out for freedom and was adopted by the Indians.[26]

In preterritorial Minnesota neither whites nor Indians objected to slavery, but they countenanced it as a condition of circumstance rather than of inherent racial inferiority.[27] Thus, Dred Scott was a slave, Joseph Godfrey became an Indian, and George Bonga was considered a white man. Racial categorizations were not set in stone, nor was status determined solely by race. The career of Jim Thompson provides a case in point.

Thompson had already been bought and sold several times by 1827, when he was brought as a slave to Fort Snelling. In the deceptively liberal environment there, he married Marpiyawecasta, a full-blooded Dakota and daughter of respected chief Cloud Man. This union connected him by marriage, at least by the "custom of the country," to Lawrence Taliaferro and Captain Seth Eastman, both of whom fathered children by his wife's sisters. Nonetheless, Jim Thompson was still a slave. When the officer who owned him was transferred to Fort Crawford at Prairie du Chien, Thompson had no choice but to accompany him, leaving his wife behind. Determined to get back to Mary (who had anglicized her name upon her marriage), the enterprising slave seized the opportunity when he met Methodist missionary Alfred Brunson. Brunson, on his way to establish a mission near Fort Snelling, was in search of a Dakota interpreter and Jim Thompson presented himself to the reverend as the perfect candidate for the job. Claiming to be a "good Methodist," as well as fluent in Dakota, he impressed Brunson with his intellect, charm, and apparent piety.[28]

At that time, missionaries may have been the only people on the frontier who were truly uncomfortable with slavery. But dependent on the goodwill of the military, they kept their moral indignation to themselves. In Jim Thompson, Reverend Brunson saw a way to set an abolitionist example and serve his mission's needs as well. Writing to antislavery friends in the East, the minister enthusiastically reported that Thompson had "been converted, had something of the missionary spirit, and was above the average of his race in education and mental ability." His friends soon raised the $1,200 needed to purchase Thompson's freedom "that he might serve in the Methodist church in giving the gospel to the Sioux nation." Thompson, finally a free man, then happily accompanied Brunson to his new mission at Kaposia and reunited with Mary.[29]

Unfortunately, Alfred Brunson may have been the most ill-suited missionary ever to evangelize in the Northwest. Deaf to the customs and culture of the Dakotas and refusing to learn their language, Brunson soon alienated any and all potential converts. Jim Thompson, exercising his rights as a free man, left Kaposia after only a year, possibly discouraged by the missionary's lack of cultural sensitivity. This put Reverend Brunson in a difficult position. Embarrassed to report Thompson's defection in addition to his lack of success in converting the Indians, Brunson wrote home to his supporters that Thompson had "proved unfaithful," though the missionary's daughter later attested that the former slave had served as "a capable and faithful interpreter." As racial prejudices hardened in later years, Thompson's reputation suffered further. Nineteenth-century historian Return Holcombe excoriated Thompson as "a sort of fraud. . . . He was very immoral and liked whiskey and Indian women . . . unintelligent and ineffective." Stephen Riggs, rewriting Thompson's story in 1880, described the fluent Dakota speaker as "a very indifferent interpreter and not a reliable man, [who] was dismissed from the mission before its disbandment." By the twentieth century, a history of Minneapolis referred to Thompson simply as "Nigger Jim."[30]

In reality, Jim Thompson was both reliable and well respected. He and Mary settled in Pig's Eye—soon to be St. Paul—raised a family there, and became valued members of the emerging community. In the fashion of most Pig's

Eye entrepreneurs, Thompson started out briefly as a whiskey seller, but soon was operating the settlement's first ferry service and working as a builder. The only black man in the little town, Thompson apparently was considered a social equal. He helped build the Methodist Episcopal Church with contributions of materials and labor and became a founding member of the Methodist Fellowship. Even more tellingly, in 1841 he served as witness against a white man in a sensational rape trial, a role that would have been unthinkable for a black man in most parts of the country. At the end of Thompson's life, Thomas Newson, who had known him for forty years, summed up his fellow "old settler" as "fully equal both to the white or the Indian when a free man. He had played an important part in the history of our city and state, and during the fifty-seven years that he had trod our soil, I find nothing to mar a well-earned and excellent reputation."[31]

[238]

"Old settler" Thomas Newson's opinion had been shaped by the fluid nature of racial status on the frontier, but the ranks of new Minnesotans who swelled the territory's population in the 1850s most often saw only a black man when they met Jim Thompson—and black most often meant inherently inferior, whether their politics were pro- or anti-slavery. Though the practice of slaveholding fell out of fashion once settlers began streaming into the "free territory" of Minnesota—and was conveniently forgotten in reminiscences of preterritorial days—hardened notions of racial hierarchy became more rather than less rigid. In the days when the territory was forming, when both skilled and unskilled labor was in short supply, Minnesotans had wasted little time worrying about skin color as they worked to transform the rough hamlets they called towns into bona fide commercial and industrial centers. Moreover, the 1849 census counted only forty free people of African descent in the entire territory. Politicians had no incentive to woo this minute population, but neither did their presence excite noticeable bigotry from white neighbors.[32]

In 1850 Minnesota's free black population largely was considered an asset in St. Paul, where nearly all had settled. Most were literate, and like Jim Thompson they contributed needed skills to the little town—as barbers, builders, seamstresses, cooks, and shopkeepers. Culturally, they reinforced the new "Yankee" ethos, much as slaves had done at Fort Snelling. For the most part industrious, churchgoing, family men and women, and native English speakers, St. Paul's black residents made a sharp and favorable contrast to the "lazy" and foreign-seeming French Canadians and mixed-blood people, who, with their traditional way of life disappearing, were rapidly sinking into the laboring underclass. In 1852 the *Pioneer* approvingly described the town's black residents as "a useful class [who] here on the confines of Barbarism do as much to put a civilized aspect upon the face of society as any other class."[33]

Still, along with saw blades, law books, plows, and an entrepreneurial spirit, even in 1849 white Minnesotans who relocated from the East and South carried the baggage of racial prejudice. On a face-to-face, individual basis, they might treat their black neighbors as equals, but ingrained ideas about race trumped personal relationships when it came to establishing political policy. The Organic Act creating Minnesota Territory had limited voting rights in the first election to "free white male inhabitants above the age of twenty-one years," but the territorial legislature was free to revise those restrictions as it saw fit. Tellingly, however, in the first session of the legislature, Benjamin Brunson— Jim Thompson's neighbor, fellow founder of the First Methodist church, and son of the missionary who had purchased Jim's freedom—introduced a bill to permanently limit suffrage to white males. A volatile debate ensued, but it centered on the voting rights of Indians and mixed-blood people, which had vital implications for the control of political power. The "fur power" ultimately succeeded in extending suffrage to "persons of a mixture of white and Indian blood [who] adopted the habits and customs of civilized men." But no one spoke up for the rights of black Minnesotans, who were indisputably civilized, productive members of the community. Historian William Green suggests that legislators, though they bore no ill will toward the African Americans who lived among them, feared that, with the Mississippi a direct conduit from the South, "universal suffrage might attract a flood of blacks to the area"—an unintended consequence that no one desired.[34]

Attempts at racial categorization left many Minnesotans in a state of confusion as they sorted out markers of culture and blood. Nor were they of a single mind when it came to the institution of slavery. However, nearly everyone agreed by 1849 that slavery had no future in Minnesota. A few transplanted southerners, like Sylvanus Lowry, favored the practice and openly kept slaves in their households; others, such as the family of William Marshall, had moved north to get away from its pernicious effects. But the Marshalls' principled stance was an exception. Most Minnesotans opposed slavery for strictly economic reasons, grounded in self-interest. They regarded the South as an undemocratic oligarchy, propped up by its slave economy. If allowed a toehold in Minnesota, slavery would advantage the establishment of a moneyed ruling class and damage the landholding prospects of ordinary citizens. Slavery, they argued, also degraded free labor and would depress the wages of working people. Political pragmatists, especially Democrats like Henry Sibley and Henry Rice, preferred to ignore the issue. They had no desire to quarrel with fellow Democrats in Congress about their right to hold slaves and reasoned that the question was irrelevant to Minnesota, where a slave economy could never flourish. But whether indifferent or actively opposed to the practice of slavery, general opinion, regardless of party, supported the free-state status of Minnesota.[35]

Reform, Rum, and the Politics of Race

Throughout the country, antislavery sentiment primarily derived from political and economic concerns and centered on opposing slavery's *expansion* into new territories rather than supporting any moral imperative to abolish its practice. The rallying cry for free soil and free labor was most often disconnected from concern for the people held in bondage. In fact, by the 1840s most midwestern states had a history of "black codes" on the books, laws designed to discourage black in-migration or restrict civil rights. Attitudes in Minnesota were no exception. In 1854 its territorial legislature considered a bill that would require blacks who intended to settle in the territory to post a bond of $300 to $500 as a guarantee of "good behavior." The proposal was defeated, thanks in large part to the opposition of the mixed-blood delegates from Pembina, whose own indeterminate racial status probably influenced their feelings about the bill.[36]

The bill's defeat so aggravated St. Paul representative John Day that he threatened to "introduce a bill to compel all the negro population" in the territory "to reside in St. Anthony and Minneapolis." Day's ire was aroused by more than an already-blooming intercity rivalry. The town of St. Anthony—bubbling with entrepreneurial schemes and speculative ventures, its mills sawing lumber day and night, with visions of even greater wealth to be made in just-established Minneapolis across the river—was also an unlikely hotbed of radical abolitionism. Consequently, despite their similar economic aspirations, St. Paul and St. Anthony were as unlike as two towns could be.[37]

No one was more surprised at the radical reform character that had overtaken St. Anthony than milling entrepreneur Franklin Steele, the town's first resident and largest landholder. Yet in 1849 Steele had unknowingly set the political and cultural wheels in motion when he recruited lawyer John Wesley North to settle there and serve as his legal counsel. North, a native of New York State, was already a well-known abolitionist and general reformer who spent considerably more time on the abolitionist speaking circuit than on his law practice. As a result, his financial condition was fairly grim, and on a visit to St. Anthony he leaped at Steele's lucrative offer. In a matter of weeks, John and Ann North had set up housekeeping at the falls. As entrepreneurial as any man in the territory, North was soon deep into land speculation and other ventures. But the former New Yorker, unlike most of the acquisitive individualists who were steaming up the river, had a larger vision as well. Unbeknownst to Steele, North dreamed of shaping St. Anthony into a morally upstanding community, populated by only the "right sort" of people—those who valued education and culture and shared his abhorrence for demon rum and the inhumanity of slavery. He envisioned St. Anthony and the future Minneapolis "filled with citizens of such sterling worth that the community would become a political makeweight to . . . the dissolute, ignorant, drunken, Democratic, pro-slavery capital city down the river."[38]

John Wesley North proved to be an unparalleled—and discriminating—promoter. He immediately began penning glowing accounts of St. Anthony's natural beauties and the unlimited opportunities that lay in wait there for enterprising settlers. He placed his missives only in "papers dedicated to abolition, temperance, education, Free Soil, and liberal politics." As inquiries began to pour in, North selectively encouraged only those who seemed to fit his desired profile, assuring them, "Indeed I never knew so young a village, where there was so little vice." In just a year his efforts lured about 1,000 upstanding New Yorkers and New Englanders to Minnesota. A few, debarking at St. Paul, took one look at the bustling, "vice-laden" frontier capital and booked passage on the next boat home; but many made their way to St. Anthony, doubling its population in a year.[39]

At first, Franklin Steele was delighted. His lots were selling like hotcakes, taking some pressure off the always overextended speculator. But soon he realized his town had been taken over by straitlaced reformers who opposed the "Fur Company Democrats" at every turn. Steele, who was Henry Sibley's brother-in-law, friend, and frequent business partner, was incensed at this turn of events. He broke off his association with North, whom he now termed his "eternal enemy." But the damage was done. To St. Anthony's new citizens, intent on making the milling hamlet into an idealized "New England of the West," North was the natural leader to advance their reform agenda throughout the territory. By an overwhelming vote, despite Steele's vigorous opposition, they sent John North to the legislature in 1851.[40]

Initially, the St. Anthony reformers gave little attention to abolitionism. Their days were fully occupied with the twin projects of pursuing financial gain and creating a "whiskey-free, vice-free" community. And, after all, only one African American resided in St. Anthony in 1850. Their reform agenda focused on establishing churches, schools, and temperance campaigns. St. Anthony, they congratulated themselves, was a "dry" town. Toasts were drunk with water on the Fourth of July, in contrast to St. Paul, where it was said that on New Year's Day Governor Ramsey was too drunk to entertain his visitors.[41]

But even in St. Paul, reformers like Harriet Bishop decried the alcoholic haze that hung over the territory. In 1851 the Catholic Temperance Society of St. Paul, led by Bishop Joseph Cretin and the town's respectable French Canadians, joined with Protestant reformers in St. Paul and St. Anthony to push through a referendum prohibiting the manufacture and sale of alcohol in Minnesota. Temperance foes, occupied perhaps with the upcoming Dakota treaties, were caught off guard. The so-called "Maine law" won the voters' approval, and church bells pealed out a victory for the teetotalers. But whiskey selling was an integral part of the economy, and the court quickly and conveniently declared the referendum to be unconstitutional. Harriet Bishop sourly recalled that "on the night of the repeal, a large steamboat bell was mounted upon wheels and attended by scores of miserable human beings, went booming through the streets of the capital, proclaiming death to temperance principles, and loud hurrahs for the movers of repeal." The temperance crusade would never again catch the whiskey faction unawares.[42]

The problem for reform advocates was that they lacked a coherent organizational structure. An assortment of Conscience Whigs, Free Soilers, Liberty Party men, and a few Barnburner Democrats, they were essentially a scattering of political orphans with more or less similar goals.[43] But the passage of the Kansas-Nebraska Act in 1854 transformed the political landscape. Outside the South, nationwide outrage against the act catalyzed the formation of the National Republican Party. A few months later, John North and his fellow radical reformers in St. Anthony met to organize the Republican Party of Minnesota. Because the chief organizers—North, his close friend William Marshall, and Unitarian minister Charles G. Ames—were longtime abolitionists of conscience, the party, from its inception, took a stand to end slavery throughout the United States and its territories. North captured the idealistic zeal of that first meeting with his closing "battle cry:" "Man and Morals first; interest in property, afterwards."[44]

Of course, interest in property was never entirely absent, but the first Minnesota Republican Convention, held in St. Paul in July 1855, bore the indelible stamp of the party's reformist founders. The platform that emerged demanded the abolition of slavery, repeal of the Fugitive Slave Law, and complete prohibition of intoxicating beverages, along with free land and a catalog of other political reforms. As one nineteenth-century historian noted, the party's founding was "governed by a set of men the majority of whom were very radical and might be called purists; they attempted to build a political party upon the lines of a church organization."[45]

It is important to note, however, that despite the party's radical founding principles, most of the disparate opponents of the Democratic power structure who entered the Republican ranks had far more interest in economic issues than reformist—or certainly abolitionist—fervor. Former territorial governor Alexander Ramsey, a Cotton Whig if ever there was one, reluctantly accepted the political reality of the moment and aligned himself with the party, but put off by the radical cast of its platform he "decline[d] the honor" of its nomination as candidate for territorial delegate. Whig-turned-Republican John Phillips Owens described the platform as "in many respects crude and incongruous" due to control of the convention by "the most advanced sentiment of ultra 'abolitionism.'" Decades later, he noted with satisfaction that the party's "sentiment . . . has materially changed since March, 1855."[46]

Indeed, more pragmatic Republicans almost immediately began working to turn the party's focus to economic issues—"railroads, contracts, tariff, cheap labor from immigration, Indian trade, and so on"—rather than strict moral reform. Presbyterian minister Edward Duffield Neill exemplified what would become the dominant character of the party. In 1854 he preached a sermon that identified railroad expansion as "ordained by God." Railroads, he enthusiastically declared, were "agencies in the production of pure and undefiled religion," and Christ was a stationmaster "always in his office." The iron rails would carry God-fearing Protestant immigrants into the territory "to outweigh the heathens, roughs, and nominal Roman Catholics" who presently impeded the establishment of a moral community.[47]

God-fearing or no, a new population already was changing the face of Minnesota. Despite the absence of railroads, new residents were flooding into the territory by the thousands, and even the homogeneous character of the enclave at the falls was eroding. Though Minneapolis and St. Anthony continued to attract mostly old stock Americans who gravitated to the Republican banner, the newcomers tended to have more interest in commerce, land, and railroad expansion than in abolitionism or temperance. By the time the Republican Convention met in July 1855, John Wesley North had become disillusioned with St. Anthony's changing character and decamped for the Cannon River Valley, where he founded the town of Northfield. On the tranquil banks of the Cannon, he hoped to establish the ideal moral community that had eluded him in St. Anthony, which was beginning to bear a disturbing resemblance to dissolute St. Paul. Even a sewing society, supposedly formed to raise funds for the Episcopal Church, had become a source of scandal. According to North's wife, Ann, the members' real purpose seemed to be "to get together once a week, to drink, play cards, and dance all night." The moral tone of the town was definitely slipping.[48]

[243]

Thus, though abolitionism was a centerpiece of the first Republican platform, and William Marshall, a confirmed antislavery man, was nominated as the party's first candidate, Protestant entrepreneurs and farmers already outnumbered the radical reformers. Soon this majority constituency would shift the party's focus to railroad promotion and other avenues of economic growth.

As for the Democrats, engrossed in their internecine feuding, at first they failed to take the Republican threat seriously. In 1855, as usual, they split into Rice and Sibley factions. Sibley himself had temporarily retired from electoral politics; nonetheless, when the party convention nominated Rice once more for territorial delegate, the Sibley camp bolted, convened separately as the People's Party, and nominated David Olmsted to challenge Rice's seat. The well-liked Olmsted, though nominally a Democrat, was at odds with his party on the burning national issue of the day; he had publicly declared slavery "a great moral and political evil" and opposed the doctrine of popular sovereignty, which the Democrats, "decided upholders of the National and Territorial administrations," supported "with the utmost ardor and enthusiasm." John Owens, and probably many of his contemporaries, was convinced that the Sibley Democrats supported Olmsted "merely out of personal hatred for Rice." Minnesota politics were as tangled and confusing as ever.[49]

The prohibition plank in the Republican platform further complicated loyalties, driving voters who were otherwise in sympathy with the Republicans to vote for Olmsted. German immigrants in particular, who were settling in Minnesota in substantial numbers—and who would later form a core of stalwart Republicans—were appalled at the cultural assault on their beloved beer.[50] Thus, the antislavery vote split between Marshall and Olmsted. As a result, the election went to the "pro-slavery" Rice. However, it was whiskey rather than the slavery question that determined the outcome.[51]

Paradoxically, though the rhetoric of race dominated political stumping, Minnesota's small black population encountered very little discrimination through most of the 1850s. When free blacks Ralph and Emily Grey settled in St. Anthony in 1857, where only a handful of African Americans resided, they received a warm welcome from their abolitionist neighbors. Emily recalled with fondness "the good old-time neighborly calls. . . . Civility and kindness seemed to be in the air in those good old pioneer days. You breathed it in with every inhalation of the atmosphere."[52] In St. Anthony, where abolitionism had strong support, such neighborliness might not seem particularly remarkable. More unexpectedly, however, in St. Paul, where political speechifying often deployed rabidly racist rhetoric, black residents experienced little of that animus directed at them as individuals.

In truth, most Democrats fell into the pro-slavery camp by accident of party rather than by strong conviction. For the most part, they simply wished the issue would go away. Minnesotans, regardless of party, were nearly unanimous in deploring the Fugitive Slave Act. They resented federal interference in local matters, with a law that, in the words of minister Henry Nichols, expected Minnesotans to "turn man-hunters & go off like hounds, baying on the track of the fugitive." They had even less tolerance for slave hunters who barged into their communities, "rooting out respectable Negroes from their jobs and families." In 1860 Alexander Ramsey, then governor of the State of Minnesota, offered a $250 reward for apprehension of a slave hunter who had kidnapped an "alleged fugitive slave." Nor did masters in search of errant slaves find much assistance when they debarked at St. Paul. As the northernmost port on the Mississippi River highway, for years St. Paul operated as a stop on the Underground Railway, receiving escapees hidden on the steamboat *Dr. Franklin.* The principal agents of the St. Paul station were reputable and well-liked black barbers William Taylor, David Edwards, and James Highwarden, who sheltered the runaways, then forwarded them on to British territory. Apparently the operation was an open secret that the townsfolk tacitly sanctioned. Taylor was well known on the levee as the man who knew "all about the fugitives that come here," but only rarely did the law rouse itself to inquire about his activities. Taylor's nephew, Joseph Farr, recalled, "I can't tell how many slaves we got away, but we were so industrious that the slave owners gave up bringing their slaves with them, when they came up here, long before the war." It seems that most St. Paulites, nearly all of them Democrats, were no more enamored of slavery than the Republicans, at least on their home ground.[53]

Nonetheless, after 1856, slavery—and the place of African Americans in society—became the most volatile issue in Minnesota, driven more by realpolitik than principle. Pro-slavery Democrat James Buchanan had won the White House and with it the power to bestow or withhold patronage and appropriations to advance Minnesota's development. Consequently, delegate Henry Rice, and most of the territory's Democrats, endorsed the administration's pro-slavery policies with cheerful cynicism. Even the dissident faction, led by Sibley, advocated popular sovereignty, as embodied in the Kansas-Nebraska Act. The Republicans, not surprisingly, were adamantly "anti-Nebraska." But even in that party only the abolitionist core opposed slavery out of moral conviction. The truth was, most Republicans and Democrats alike were far more interested in promoting wealth creation for Minnesota and themselves than embarking on a moral crusade. They shared an agenda for financial and economic growth—land development, road and river improvements, resource extraction, business incorporation, and especially railroad expansion into Minnesota Territory. Leading men of both parties were deep into finance, land, manufacturing, and transportation schemes. They differed not so much in what they wanted to achieve, but rather in who should reap the benefit.[54]

By 1855, however, Minnesota was no longer the entrepreneurial fiefdom of a small cohort of business-minded hustlers. The population had grown from less than 5,000 in 1849 to more than 53,000 in 1855. Two years later it would exceed 153,000. A whole variety of new immigrants now made up the voting constituency—Germans, Irish, and other Europeans, as well as a slew of native-born citizens from all parts of the Union. Politicians had to rely on more than personal relationships and shared business interests to win their allegiance. With this greatly expanded constituency, the staunch loyalty of French-speaking mixed-blood people was no longer enough to keep the Democrats in the majority. Thus, both parties turned to the inflammatory issue of slavery and race as the key mark of difference between them.

Abolitionists carried the banner for the Republicans, excoriating Democrats for countenancing slavery. Fiery newspaper editors like Jane Grey Swisshelm condemned them as "doughfaces and truckling apologists for Southern woman whippers." She also rallied less passionate Republicans to stand up "on Freedom's side, or the Democrats of Northern Minnesota will drive them into the Red Sea of public indignation and drown every sinner of them." Other Republicans used the free-soil economic argument, projecting a scenario where plantations, worked with slave labor, would squeeze out Minnesota's just-planted yeoman farmers. In the vivid prose of St. Anthony's *Minnesota Republican:* "Power will glide into the hands of a few; a system of nabobery will supplant practical democracy; there will be no longer any 'people,' there will remain only the despots and their serfs."[55]

Democrats, for their part, appealed to the basest sort of racist fears and stereotypes, painting their opponents as "'Black Republicans' who were willing that their daughters should marry 'niggers.'" This strategy resonated most with the laboring class, especially the Irish, who in the mid-1850s were the predominant European immigrant group in the territory, most of them residing in

St. Paul. Scorned themselves as low-browed, savage, drunk, and lazy, the Irish in America often found themselves compared to blacks—and not to their advantage. In St. Paul, it must have been particularly galling for the Irish to see well-dressed, property-owning African Americans exchange cordial greetings with the city's most prominent men when they were disparaged and could find only the lowest sorts of work. The one advantage they had was their whiteness, which gave them the right to vote—and they used it to express their resentment.[56]

The racialization of politics was primarily a tool to gain other ends rather than to direct attacks at the small black population, who resided mostly in St. Paul. The effect, nonetheless, was to foster a heightened climate of overt racial prejudice that had real consequences for black Minnesotans. In 1856, in response to complaints, the St. Paul school board began discouraging black children from attending the city's public schools. A year later the board of education formally implemented a policy of segregation. In 1859, the school superintendent removed a student who was "one-quarter black" from the white school he was attending, despite his teacher's protest that he was "no darker than many who were here." In a single decade St. Paul had gone from a multicultural meeting ground, where Harriet Bishop's students had confounded her with their diversity of language and appearance, to a strictly ordered community where segregation of its schools by race was the desirable norm.[57]

While racial fears and prejudices dominated Democratic rhetoric and attracted some voters to the party, other, more immediately pertinent issues also added to their ranks. European immigrants, who by 1856 constituted a substantial part of the population, were suspicious of perceived Republican nativism and anti-Catholicism. The party was dominated by native-born Protestants who made no secret of their belief in Anglo-Saxon superiority, and its press frequently made derogatory reference to Catholics and "ignorant Irishmen." In contrast, the Democratic papers took pains to court the Irish and Catholic vote. In 1855 the *Minnesota Democrat* called for justice to the "Catholic religion" and chastised those (presumably Republican editors) who would "attack some of our best citizens and represent them as criminals of the deepest dye." Republicans looked more favorably on German and Scandinavian immigrants, but the prohibition plank in the party platform put off many German voters. Among the European immigrants, only the small cohort of Scandinavian Protestants, who shared Republican temperance principles and anti-Catholic bias, gravitated in numbers to the party.[58] Unfortunately for the Republicans, as late as 1860, Scandinavians constituted less than 7 percent of Minnesota's population, in contrast to Germans and Irish, who made up more than a quarter of potential voters.[59]

Thus, despite the new coherence of the Democrats' opponents, for the time being at least they maintained the political upper hand. But the Republican Party was rapidly becoming a force to be reckoned with on the national stage, and abolitionism was moving from a fringe movement to a mainstream faction of the party. In Minnesota, where steamboats disgorged hundreds of new residents every week, no one could predict what the turnout would look like for the next election—just when the stakes had never been higher. The 1855 territorial census had tallied a population of 53,000, an increase of more than 100 percent from the year before; without question, Minnesota would surpass the 60,000 residents required for statehood before the year was out. In December 1856, Henry Rice laid the case for statehood before the House of Representatives, introducing a bill that authorized the territory to call a constitutional convention. Illinois senator Stephen Douglas, Minnesota's guardian angel, carried the bill through the Senate, and Minnesota was on the road to statehood.[60]

[247]

Making Minnesota

In 1857, as politicians geared up for the constitutional convention, Minnesota's future had never looked brighter. In two years the territory's population had grown by 150 percent, topping 150,000 residents, and in-migration showed no signs of slowing. Along with the speculators and hustlers who thronged the levee at St. Paul, European immigrants jostled American-born settlers, all eager to snap up farmsteads in the Suland or the fertile prairie immediately north of St. Paul. River towns up and down the St. Croix, Mississippi, and Minnesota rivers were bustling, with Stillwater, Marine, Sauk Rapids, St. Cloud, Red Wing, Winona, St. Peter, and Mankato all awash in metropolitan dreams. Hundreds of farming communities had sprouted from town site prospectuses, and hundreds more existed so far only on paper or in the imagination of the land speculators who promoted them. Though the infant farms as yet produced no measurable agricultural products—indeed, not enough even to feed the burgeoning population of the territory—a robust farm economy was clearly in the making. Meanwhile, timber, furs, and hides flowing from the north stoked the economic engine in the river towns, especially St. Paul, Stillwater, St. Anthony, and Minneapolis. In 1857, 140 million feet of logs passed the St. Croix boom alone; on the Mississippi, eight mills at St. Anthony Falls sawed logs into 12 million feet of lumber. St. Paul, which had grown in population from 4,000 to 11,000 in just two short years, was home to fifty-two lawyers, fourteen bankers, thirteen architects and builders, six newspapers, 158 business houses of various sorts, and thirty-one real estate dealers.[61]

Land fever fueled the boom. Lots in "paper cities" were sold in the East at "exorbitant prices," peddled by land agents like Harriet Bishop, who made numerous trips East with glowing accounts of Minnesota and a pocketbook of deeds for sale. In St. Paul, along with legitimate land brokers, spurious real estate agents, with "no office but the sidewalk, and no capital but a roll of town-site maps, and a package of blank deeds," accosted strangers the moment they stepped off the steamers, vying to sell them their little piece of Minnesota gold. Politicians unashamedly were in the thick of the game. The 1856 legislature approved surveys for nine wagon roads to radiate from the little town of Henderson in the Minnesota River valley. Not coincidentally, the redoubtable Joe Brown was the town's founder and largest landowner. It seemed the entire territory was infused with a "mad, crazy, reckless spirit of speculation." According to eyewitness J. Fletcher Williams, "Farmers, mechanics, laborers even, forsook their occupations to become operators in real estate, and grow suddenly rich, as they supposed."[62]

The land and population boom created a voracious demand for all sorts of goods, services, and institutions. One mill in St. Anthony reported sales in a single day of 20,000 shingles and 25,000 laths, as well as 50,000 board feet of lumber. Everything from groceries to farm equipment, from dress goods to books, flew off merchants' shelves as fast as they could unload them from the steamboats queued up at the St. Paul landing. Builders could almost name their price, and lawyers had an endless supply of clients in need of legal advice. Churches, schools, library associations, and even theaters and lyceums smoothed the rough edges from large and small towns alike, advertising their spiritual and cultural advancement.[63]

Only one persistent problem hindered the unbridled optimism that suffused the dreamers and schemers. All the potential wealth they envisioned was trapped in isolation from access to national markets. From one end of the territory to the other, everyone agreed that Minnesota desperately needed railroads to fulfill its destiny. People from every walk of life were obsessed with railroads as the magic solution to every challenge. The iron horse would free them from the enforced isolation that set in every winter when the rivers froze; it would provide a steady supply of goods and fresh food and create a conduit to markets for all that Minnesota expected to produce. As early as 1854, newspapers were clamoring for railroads. "We must have an outlet," the *St. Anthony Express* had editorialized, "*and an outlet by rail,* and this as speedily as possible, or we are nowhere." Rail connections would turn paper town sites into thriving communities, boost land prices ever higher, and make investors into millionaires in the process. Some seven hundred towns were platted between 1855 and 1857 in the glow of this anticipation. Rail connection also would catapult St. Paul—or Minneapolis/St. Anthony, depending on one's vantage point—into its destiny as the next Chicago.[64]

By 1857 the legislature had granted no fewer than twenty-seven railroad charters. It seems that everyone in the territory with a penny to invest had a hand in at least one railroad flier. Political influence had never been more important. Sibley, Rice, Ramsey, Steele, North, Marshall—indeed, nearly all the political and business elites—had a stake in one proposed line or another and made their leverage felt. One company, chartered in 1854, had already collapsed amid charges of fraud and political corruption. But Minnesotans, gripped by railroad fever, scarcely noticed. A bit of political chicanery could be overlooked in boom-time Minnesota, when everyone expected to get rich.[65]

As Minnesotans went to the polls in the spring of 1857 to choose delegates to the constitutional convention, railroad expansion was the first priority on everyone's mind. Despite all the bright promises and enthusiasm, not a foot of rail had yet been laid in the territory. But statehood, they believed, would get the cars rolling. Statehood would bring federal land grants to encourage investment capital; it would also convey borrowing power for the state itself to invest in the roads. Even more important, with plans for a transcontinental railroad talked of in Washington, statehood would give Minnesotans voting power to lobby for a northern route through their state. Territorial governor Willis Gorman expressed the general sentiment when he declared, "There is no great interest in which Minnesota has so heavy a stake to be won or lost as the Pacific Railroad." Providing that vital connection to international as well as national markets, the transcontinental road will surely "make us one of the wealthiest states in the Union."[66]

[249]

The party in power would shape the direction in which those opportunities would be funneled. And what a wealth of riches there were to be dispensed! Towns and cities to be incorporated, county seats chosen, banks chartered, along with lumbering and manufacturing franchises, all topped off with government patronage—jobs, contracts, and appropriations galore. But the prize that glittered brightest was railroad development and the government land grants that went with it. That was where the real money was to be made. Congress had just granted seven million acres for railroad development in the soon-to-be state. The news had spiked speculative fever to new heights, and a horde of men on the make converged on St. Paul. "Members of Congress; Washington lobbyists; railroad men, and many who wanted to be railroad men; contractors; civil engineers, and people of all classes who had their eye on the main chance of getting rich out of this land grant, were present by the hundreds." In this heated environment, Democrats and Republicans vied for delegates to the all-important constitutional convention.[67]

The parties were indistinguishable on the subject of economic, and especially railroad, development, only differing in who would reap the profits from the endeavor. Thus, to distinguish one party from another—and to determine who would control the convention and its subsequent spoils—Democrats and Republicans concentrated on the issues of slavery and race to woo voters into their respective camps. The campaign for convention delegates was fierce, fraught with "crimination and recrimination" on both sides. The *Pioneer and Democrat* (the two papers had merged in 1855) warned against "Black Republicans," claiming the issue was purely one of "White Supremacy against Negro equality." On the Republican side, the radical reformers who had shaped the party's founding were now outnumbered by business-minded progressives like Alexander Ramsey. But for the moment the antislavery message held sway, covering the Democrats in moral villainy. Ironically though, even as the Republicans condemned Democrats' racism, they also played on racist imagery themselves, portraying their opponents as the party of "Border Ruffians," its constituency riddled with Irish, half-breeds, and uncivilized semisavages who freely traded in the coin of political corruption.[68]

By election day the parties had managed to define themselves, at least in part, by these competing versions of racism, but when the votes were finally tallied, neither argument had proved decisive—though it is instructive to note that of the 108 elected delegates of either party, all but four were old-stock Euro-Americans. The final delegate count split nearly evenly between the parties, leaving the convention majority to rest on the fate of a few contested seats.[69]

With neither side willing to concede a precious delegate, the parties resorted to time-honored political shenanigans. In this contest, the Democrats held a distinct advantage. The sages of the party—Sibley, Rice, Gorman, Rolette, and Brown among them—were old hands at the game of territorial politics. Wisely recognizing that the party no longer had the luxury for internecine feuding, Henry Sibley had emerged from retirement to take on the party chairmanship and conciliate the factions. The former partisans cemented their entente with an understanding that once statehood was achieved they would back Rice for the senate and Sibley for governor, thus ensuring that everyone's interests would be represented.[70]

The majority of the Republicans, on the other hand, were relative newcomers to Minnesota. Few had been in the territory more than two or three years. Moreover, according to veteran journalist John Owens, "most of the Republicans were new men in public life, entirely inexperienced, and strangers to each other." Familiar with legendary tales of Democratic chicanery, they feared—rightly, as events played out—that the wily "Border Ruffians" would steal the convention from them. On July 13, 1857, the day the first session was to convene, a squabble over the rules and assorted "rascality" on both sides resulted in the Democrats convening separately, blithely claiming the Republican gathering to be merely a "meeting of citizens." The two parties carried on separately for weeks, each side hammering out a constitution as though the other did not exist.[71]

Now, irregular tactics were nothing new to Minnesota politics. Over the years, territorial legislators had often employed "creative" methods to get their way. The "Rice Democrats" had absconded with the apportionment bill in 1851 to keep it from being signed; more recently, Democrat Joe Rolette had spirited away a bill that would have moved the territorial capital from St. Paul to St. Peter (where the governor happened to be deep in town site speculation). Once the session adjourned, Rolette jauntily reappeared with the now-dead bill, earning him a hero's standing among grateful St. Paulites. In the most recent election, St. Anthony's register of deeds (a Republican) had disqualified elected Democrats on a specious technicality. To even things out, it was

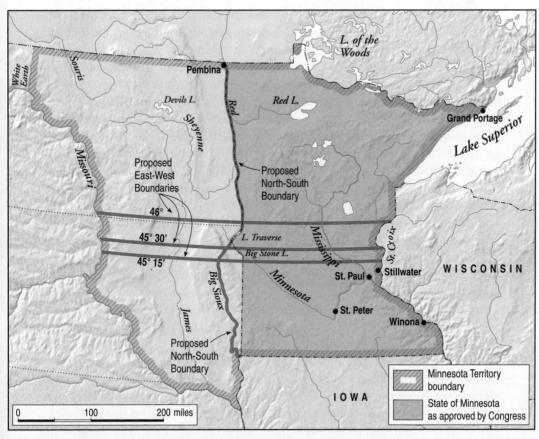

Minnesota Territory and the state boundaries proposed in 1857.

rumored that no election had been held at Pembina, and the delegates supposedly elected there (Democrats, of course) had simply been provided with forged credentials. Legislators also had resorted to fisticuffs more than once to emphasize a debating point. When William Marshall got into a melee with fellow legislator Henry Jackson outside the council chambers in 1849, Marshall was actually praised for his decorum. He had not violated "the dignity and rules of the House by knocking [Jackson] down while the body was in session. He waited for the adjournment before he did it." Apparently not much had changed in the intervening years. During the course of the constitutional convention, now ex-governor Gorman would famously break his cane over an offending Republican delegate's head. Still, no other episode matches the farcical appearance of the "dueling conventions."[72]

With no opposing party to get in the way, delegates took the opportunity to shamelessly promote self-interested schemes. Republican delegates from southern Minnesota, frustrated by the seemingly limitless talent of Democrats to trump their every move, were willing to take extreme measures to wrest political power away from them. Their solution was to propose redrawing the state boundaries laid out in the enabling act, setting the northern boundary at the 46th parallel (about seventy-five miles north of Minneapolis) and extending the western boundary to the Missouri River. The intention, of course, was to eliminate the Democratic stronghold of northern Minnesota and direct resources and political power to Republican counties in the south. However, the

proponents denied that they were driven by "selfish interests" and justified the proposal with arguments that ranged from the foolish to the absurd. According to the "east-west liners," the northern part of the territory contained no resources of value to the state; it simply made sense to "get rid of large tracts of unfertile lands;" moreover, "it is always best to make a State as nearly square as possible." But the argument they emphasized most vigorously was cultural and inherently racist: the suspect character of the "trappers, hunters, miners, and lumbermen" who peopled the north, most notably the mixed-blood "border ruffians" who formed a core element of the Democratic constituency. Few of the southern Minnesotans had ever ventured north of St. Paul, yet they were certain "that they [could] have no sort of feeling in common" with people who were "so politically wicked as to be beyond the pale of redemption."[73]

Veteran party leaders, such as Alexander Ramsey and John Wesley North, blanched at the idea of giving up the pineries, mineral deposits (as yet untapped), the port on Lake Superior, and the rich Red River valley—not to mention some $30 million to $50 million in railroad land grants. Much as they desired Republican ascendancy, the cost in this case was far too high. Delegates from the St. Croix and Mississippi valleys above St. Paul also weighed in on behalf of the lumbermen who were their constituents, if not for the mixed-blood hunters and traders. L. K. Stannard, delegate from Chisago County, asserted with fervor, "I come from a lumbering district, and I cannot sit here and allow gentlemen from any portion of the Territory to say anything which will detract from the character of my constituents. I know they have good heads and noble hearts." Most compellingly, however, with sectional conflict growing more bitter by the day in Congress, and southern congressmen decidedly reluctant to add another free state to the union, they would certainly balk at the admission of a Republican state, which the proposed reconfiguration would almost surely guarantee. Stephen Douglas warned from Washington that meddling with the terms of the enabling act would offer opponents a convenient excuse to delay Minnesota statehood indefinitely. For all these reasons, wiser heads prevailed and the proposal was defeated.[74]

Senator Douglas was so concerned that he traveled to St. Paul to put both parties on notice to stop their wrangling. The bizarre comic-drama of the dueling conventions—simultaneously drafting two different constitutions, as delegates met down the hall from one another in the capitol building—made Minnesotans appear ridiculous and put their cause in jeopardy with Congress. Party leaders had already come to the same conclusion and were craftily nudging their fellows toward points of compromise, most of which centered on the issue of race. Henry Sibley proposed that "white" should be stricken from the qualifications for suffrage, smoothly arguing that the Supreme Court's recent decision in the Dred Scott case had ruled that African Americans were ineligible for citizenship; thus, the point was moot. Quite clearly the Democrats had nothing to gain by excluding the mixed-blood population, who were among the party's most loyal constituents, so the white restriction served no useful purpose. But apparently too many Democrats had come to believe their racist campaign slogans to be swayed by Sibley's logic. Rather than risk a loophole by which blacks could vote, they chose to craft a special exemption for mixed bloods and even included Indians who met stringent "civilization" requirements.[75]

Sibley had assumed that black suffrage was of central importance to the Republicans. But when it came down to drafting their version of the constitution, only a minority of Republicans clung to the principle of equal rights. The abolitionists spoke eloquently on behalf of black Minnesotans, John North arguing, "I know of no principle on which our own rights are based that does not guarantee to every other class of human beings the same rights which we claim for ourselves. . . . The contour of the countenance, the complexion of the face which the Creator has stamped on human beings, does not give one class the right to inflict wrong and injury on another." But the Republican majority showed themselves less enthusiastic about conferring suffrage on African Americans. Freeing southern slaves and accepting blacks as equals in Minnesota were decidedly different propositions. Besides, as one delegate equivocated, he did not think the people were "quite up to the highest mark of principle: the force of prejudice is yet too great among them." It would be more prudent to leave the suffrage question for a later time.[76]

In truth, once the competing constitutions were completed, they were nearly identical in most respects. The delegates, who mingled daily at St. Paul hotels and eating establishments, knew this fact well, which minimized resistance to a compromise solution. Hard-core Republicans, still deeply suspicious of Democratic machinations, were finally won over when the territorial treasurer (a Democrat) announced that only those attending the "legitimate" convention— i.e., the Democratic assemblage—would have their expenses reimbursed, leaving Republican delegates with no way to pay enormous bills they had run up for room and board. With the Democrats holding the ultimate whip hand, the obdurate Republicans capitulated and approved an overture to the Democrats in session down the hall. Since the present state of affairs "have a tendency to injure the reputation of our people—to lessen the confidence of the other States in our integrity, stability and patriotism, and place us in a false position before the world"—they proposed a compromise committee to work out their differences. The Democrats magnanimously agreed, and in short order, on August 28, some six weeks after convening, the two conventions had approved the Democrats' version of the constitution by an overwhelming majority.[77]

The Democrats had conceded nearly nothing. The north-south configuration of the state was intact; mixed-blood voting rights were secure; legislative districts were organized to ensure generous Democratic influence in future representation; and all white men, including "foreigners," would be eligible to vote after residing in the state for a mere six months. The question of black suffrage was forgotten. As the convention came to a close, Democrats must have congratulated themselves that they had ensured party dominance for decades to come. The *Pioneer and Democrat* crowed that the constitution had no hint of "the fanatical dogmas of the Black Republican party." Delegate Amos Coggswell, a staunch Republican from Steele County, expressed his party's general sentiment when he grumbled, "This is a dose that has to go down, and we might as well shut our eyes and open our mouth and take it." No one at the time could have predicted that in less than three years the Democratic Party in Minnesota would be so thoroughly crushed that more than three-quarters of a century would elapse before it recovered.[78]

[254]

Crash!

In all the excitement surrounding the convention and the constitution's ratification, few Minnesotans noticed the failure of the Ohio Life Insurance and Trust Company on August 23 in faraway New York—just five days before the convention delegates finally agreed on the new state's constitution. Never imagining that New York financial problems could affect Minnesota's economic ebullience, they carried on with undiminished speculative fervor. But Ohio Life's collapse set off a rapidly escalating financial panic. Like falling dominoes, the depression flattened one state economy after another. When it reached Minnesota some months later, the consequences were devastating. The speculative bubble that had buoyed the territory's boom burst in spectacular fashion. St. Paulite J. Fletcher Williams vividly recalled the precipitous dive from the heights of prosperity to the depths of disaster:

> To Saint Paul, this pricking of the bubble of speculation was more ruinous and dire in its consequences than perhaps to any other city in the west. Everything had been so inflated and unreal—values purely fictitious, all classes in debt, with but little real wealth, honest industry neglected, and everything speculative and feverish—that the blow fell with ruinous force. Business was paralyzed, real estate actually valueless and unsaleable at any price, and but little good money in circulation. Ruin stared all classes in the face. . . . The banking houses closed their doors—nearly all the mercantile firms suspended. . . . All works of improvement ceased, and general gloom and despondency settled down on the community.[79]

The situation in the rural counties was equally dire. Adding to the sudden financial woes, hordes of grasshoppers had descended on central Minnesota in the summer of 1856, wiping out every growing thing for miles around. The following summer, a second, even more devastating infestation of the insects returned, hatched from eggs left behind in the soil. The voracious locusts devoured everything. One farmer swore that he had left his coat hanging from a fence post while plowing his field and, when he later returned, he found nothing left but the buttons. Livestock died from starvation and blood poisoning caused by bites from the grasshoppers. In the aftermath of this plague, not only did the barely established farmers have nothing to sell, they were literally on the verge of starvation.[80]

It seemed a curse had settled on Minnesota, growing more disastrous by the day. But instead of fostering retrenchment, people clung even more tenaciously to the belief that railroads would save them. Boosters frantically insisted, "If a railroad isn't built, Iowa and Missouri will capture all the emigrants!" Since the eastern investment capital they had depended on to drive the project forward had dried up, the newly elected state legislature determined to put the state's entire credit behind railroad development. With overwhelming support, in April 1858 the legislature floated a $5 million railroad loan bill to prop up four struggling railroad companies. With times so desperate, neither legislators nor voters (who approved the measure by a vote of 25,023 to 6,733) were deterred by the fact that Congress had not yet officially conferred statehood on Minnesota. Thus, when Minnesota came into the Union on May 11, 1858, its economy was reeling, state coffers were already empty, and it had shouldered a gargantuan debt as well. Not surprisingly, no celebration was held to mark the occasion.[81]

The state issued bonds to pay out $2,275,000 in loans to the four railroad companies, taking company bonds as collateral. But the depression continued to spiral downward and all four defaulted on their loan payments within a year, bankrupted before a mile of track was laid. The now worthless railroad bonds were the final straw in the collapse of Minnesota's credit structure. By 1860, nearly every bank in the state and four out of five businesses had failed. Immigration had come to a standstill and St. Paul alone lost 50 percent of its population. Veteran fur trader-turned-banker Theodore Borup, who helplessly watched his considerable fortune evaporate, jumped from a bridge into the Mississippi. Franklin Steele, unable to pay his tax debt, took off in a desperate search for capital. It would take him ten years to recoup his losses. In 1861 Henry Rice bemoaned Minnesota's fall from grace, writing: "One thing I do see is that *all* of the Old settlers in Minnesota are *ruined* hopelessly. I fear Hard times have only just commenced." The boom had turned to a bust of colossal proportions.[82]

Hard times, while sometimes bringing out the best in people, are equally likely to exacerbate resentments and prejudices. Scarcity stoked the fires of anti-Indian sentiment. When the legislature was considering a bill to encourage the killing of gophers and blackbirds, one senator, only partly in jest, had offered an amendment to include extermination of the Dakotas as well. The truth was that Minnesotans, in the throes of unprecedented hardships, bitterly begrudged the annuities and provisions the federal government disbursed to the Indians in accordance with treaty agreements. Why, they reasoned, should such "loafers, thieves, and vagabonds," supposedly too lazy to work for a living, receive "assistance" when hardworking, civilized, white Minnesotans, struck down through no fault of their own, were left to founder? With real estate of any sort unsalable, there was no demand for what little land the Indians still possessed, but in the current circumstances, their very presence in the state seemed an affront.[83]

[256]

Hard times also created a fissure in the Republican ranks over the issue of slavery and black civil rights. When Republican proponents of black enfranchisement raised the issue in the 1860 legislature, they elicited little support, even within their own party. Buried in economic problems, legislators could not be bothered with the political rights of the state's 259 African Americans. Republican Amos Coggswell, formerly a strong "anti-slavery man," "hoped the bill would be indefinitely postponed. It was too late in the session to occupy the time of the members with the nigger question." In the same session, St. Paul Democrat Charles Mackubin introduced a bizarre bill to promote tourism, backed by a petition of 600 residents of St. Paul, St. Anthony, Minneapolis, and Stillwater. Mackubin proposed legalizing slavery in the state between the months of May and October to accommodate "our Southern brethren" who wished to visit Minnesota during "their sickly season." As desperate as they were to bring some revenue into the state, this proposal was too outrageous for most of the legislators to endorse, and the bill resoundingly failed. Nonetheless, everyone understood the economic rationale that lay behind such a seemingly unthinkable proposal.[84]

By the mid-1850s tourism had become a healthy segment of the economy. Wealthy southerners in particular steamed up the river in the summer months to enjoy Minnesota's "healthful" climate and natural amenities. Small hotels and boardinghouses dotted the lakes near St. Paul and Minneapolis. White Bear Lake, some ten miles north of St. Paul, had become a thriving summer resort, with several graciously appointed hotels. St. Anthony, site of the fabled falls, was a premier destination, where the elegant, five-story Winslow House—completed only months before the crash—welcomed visitors in limestone splendor. Of course, the southern visitors traveled with their "customary house servants," as slaves were delicately described, and hotel keepers and merchants wished to assure potential guests that Minnesota, despite its status as a free state and reputation for ignoring the Fugitive Slave Law, would "protect them in their right of possession to their family servants, bond or free." With nearly every other area of commerce and industry in distress and hard money disappeared, tourist dollars were in higher demand than ever. Hotel keepers and newspaper editors urged southerners to "come North, bring their slaves, and enjoy themselves." Visitors had nothing to fear from "the intermeddling propensities of abolition fanatics." The Dred Scott decision assured the legal protection of their property. Moreover, Minnesotans were a "law-abiding people" who would not dream of ignoring the law of the land. The "temporary slavery" bill, though more than even the pragmatic lawmakers could swallow, was merely an extreme attempt to reinforce this ongoing public relations campaign.[85]

St. Anthony abolitionists caused tourism boosters no end of problems, earning them the hearty dislike of both Democrats and the business-minded majority of fellow Republicans. Refusing to discard their principles no matter the economic cost, the abolitionists met arriving steamboats at St. Paul, "booing and hissing southerners who stepped onto the dock with black retainers." Tensions came to a head in 1860, when St. Anthony abolitionists helped Eliza Winston, a slave residing with her owners at the Winslow House, to sue for her freedom. Judge Charles Vandenburgh ruled from the bench in Winston's favor, setting off an explosion of outrage. The abolitionists were reviled and a mob, led by the proprietor of the Winslow House, attacked the homes of William Babbitt and Emily Grey, who had helped Winston win her freedom. The *St. Anthony Falls Evening News* reported that "some *strong, active, enthusiastic, intelligent, high-minded* Republicans talk of lynching those concerned in procuring the poor woman her freedom." Virtuous St. Anthony had never seen such civic disorder. The Democratic press also weighed in from St. Paul. The *Pioneer and Democrat* editorialized, "We don't believe in slavery," but "we don't think it looks well, nor do we believe it right, for us to interfere or coax off these servants, and then raise the 'hue and cry' of Slavery in Minnesota." In short, for most Minnesotans, antislavery principles quickly crumpled when they clashed with economic self-interest.[86]

The aftermath of the Winston event brought the hotel owners' worst fears to fruition. The tourist trade withered and soon the Winslow House was permanently shuttered, adding to the general gloom. Of course, the onset of the Civil War, only six months in the future, would have stoppered the flow of southern visitors in any case. But the immediate consequences of Eliza Winston's quest for freedom included a fractured community, a party internally divided, and most probably a widening resentment against black Minnesotans, whose troublesome presence seemed only to add to the long list of the beleaguered state's problems.[87]

Mired in the depression, it would have been difficult for anyone to foresee how swiftly and radically circumstances were about to change. Soon Minnesotans would find themselves in the midst of two civil wars that would reshape the character of the state. Race would be at the heart of both conflicts. Ironically, one would be a war to save the Union and eventually to abolish slavery; the other, to finalize the right of white Americans to possess and rule all the lands in the place called by the Dakota name Minnesota.

Chapter 10

THE ROADS TO WAR

> We do not live outside, but within, your nation. . . . Why then look
> upon us as a foreign nation? . . . We want to be citizens and to have
> the right to vote. . . . If you grant our request, and you should have a
> fight with any other nation, you can call upon us and we will form a
> portion of your militia. We know how to fight, and will stand by you.
> We want the right of suffrage, the right to vote, to be subject to your
> laws, and we have our hearts set upon it.
> CHIEF HOLE-IN-THE DAY, 1855

> We have plenty of young men who would like no better fun than a
> good Indian hunt.
> *St. Paul Daily Times,* 28 July 1857

On April 12, 1861, Confederate forces fired on Fort Sumter, commencing the long-threatened war between the states. The cannon fire reverberated across the nation, from Charleston Harbor to distant Minnesota. Alexander Ramsey, back in power as Minnesota's governor (elected in the Republican sweep of 1860), happened to be in Washington when news of the attack reached the capital. Anticipating a call for troops, Ramsey seized the opportunity to demonstrate the patriotism of his infant state and hustled off to the Department of War to pledge 1,000 Minnesotans in defense of the Union.[1]

Thus, Minnesota earned distinction as the first state to volunteer troops for the war. However, 1,000 miles to the northwest, far from the unfurling conflict, most Minnesotans had followed growing rumors of secession with only marginal interest. Before war was declared, their attention was fully absorbed by more immediate matters. They were finally beginning to recover from the economic disaster that had overtaken them in 1857. By 1861 prospects had begun to brighten. Two years of good weather had yielded bumper crops of potatoes, corn, wheat, and other grains; in 1860 the state proudly tallied an agricultural and timber export trade of nearly $4 million. Steamboats puffed up the river, once again filled with hopeful new settlers—by 1861 population was topping 200,000 residents—and returned downstream laden with lumber and agricultural surplus. The state's prospects were definitely looking up and boosters were confident that their ambitious railroad dreams would at last be fulfilled.[2]

With development on the upswing, land values rose and speculators and homesteaders once again competed to secure choice acreage and decried the waste of productive land in the hands of "shiftless" Native people. For most Minnesotans, the "Indian problem" was of much more immediate concern than rebellious southerners. Yet the national crisis could not fail to influence the course of local events. Indeed, federal involvement had influenced every step of Minnesota's development. The war's demand for men and resources would make a deep and lasting imprint on the history of the state in unanticipated ways. Most important, it helped precipitate a second civil war that erupted in 1862—this one between white and Indian Minnesotans.

In the grand narrative of the Civil War, the events that rocked Minnesota in 1862—what today is known as the Dakota Conflict—are recalled as no more than a footnote to the national crisis, if remembered at all. But in fact this civil war more profoundly affected the region than the war between the states, marking the final demise of what had once been a multicultural world and the end of possibility for Native people to claim a share in shaping the state's future. For Minnesota, this was its defining civil war.

Combustible Elements

The Dakota Conflict commenced on August 17, 1862, when a few reckless young Wahpeton braves lost their heads and murdered a family of settlers in the small settlement of Acton, some seventy-five miles west of Minneapolis. Within days this isolated incident had escalated into an all-out war. But just as the attack on Fort Sumter was the last in a long series of events that led step-by-step to armed confrontation, the disastrous raid at Acton had been in the making for years. As land fever brought hordes of new settlers into the state, volatile elements combined ever more rapidly toward explosion. Wartime conditions in 1862 precipitated a final set of incidents that set off the Dakota Conflict, but a trail of intentional acts and unintentional consequences had almost inexorably paved the way—marked by the collapse of the traditional fur trade economy, faithless treaty negotiations, and especially by land-hungry settlers who were ignorant of Indian lifeways. In short order between 1849 and 1858, these newcomers overwhelmed the delicate balance that had existed for generations between Indians and Euro-Americans. Without question, before this time, as power shifted increasingly into the hands of white Minnesotans, the quality of Indian-white relations had degraded, but if a single event signaled the first act of the oncoming tragedy, it was a scarcely remembered flare-up on the Minnesota–Iowa border in 1857, dubbed at the time the Spirit Lake massacre.

[260]   The treaties of 1851 notwithstanding, the Dakotas had not unanimously assented to the massive land cessions. The Red Top band of Wahpekutes had refused to participate in treaty making as far back as the Prairie du Chien Treaty of 1830. The band was not represented at Mendota in 1851, nor did they acknowledge any limits to their land rights. They defiantly roamed southwestern Minnesota Territory and northwestern Iowa at their pleasure. Iowa, which had been admitted to the Union in 1846, had removed the Sacs and Fox from their hunting grounds in the northern part of the state, making that region exceptionally attractive to the Wahpekutes now that their traditional enemies had been eliminated from the region. When settlers began trickling in, they found the Red Top band, numbering about 150 lodges, already established as their neighbors. Frustrated white authorities labeled them outlaws and renegades, "a bad lot of vagabonds," but for a number of years the few settlers in this sparsely settled region coexisted with the Indians in relative peace, if not always in harmony.[3]

In the 1850s this was the far edge of the settled frontier. Indian agent Charles Flandrau observed that, though the homesteaders were technically on ceded lands, "they were really in the very heart of Indian country." Settlers grumbled that the Indians stole from them, but whites did their share of thieving as well. Indians frequently complained about dishonest trading practices. At the same time, the settlers and Wahpekutes also shared and traded foodstuffs and goods, and not uncommonly helped one another when in need. And so, a tenuous equilibrium presided, balanced with a shifting mix of goodwill and antagonism.[4]

An unsavory horse thief cum whiskey trader named Henry Lott precipitated the breakdown of this shaky entente. Notorious among both whites and Indians for his unscrupulous ways, in 1848 Lott finally went too far when he stole five ponies from Sintomniduta, chief of the Red Top band. The angry chief and his warriors confronted the horse thief so forcefully that the terrified Lott and his stepson fled headlong to Des Moines, abandoning his wife and the rest of his children to the Indians' anticipated wrath. When Lott returned weeks later with reinforcements, they expected to find the site of a massacre, but instead the cabin was standing and the family unmolested, all safe but for Lott's twelve-year-old son, who had followed his father's tracks and eventually froze to death in the snow.[5]

Lott, who must have appeared both a coward and a fool, soon took up trading with the Indians again, pretending that old disputes were forgotten. But apparently he was merely biding his time to settle the score for his humiliation. The opportunity came in 1853 when, with no trouble expected on the Iowa frontier, the military abandoned Iowa's Fort Dodge, reassigning its troops to Minnesota's Fort Ridgely, near the Lower Sioux Agency (also known as the Redwood Agency) on the Minnesota River. The departure of the troops meant the end of any meaningful law enforcement in the region, giving Lott virtual immunity from apprehension for lawless acts, and that winter he took his revenge. After persuading Sintomniduta to join him on an elk hunt, the trader shot the chief in the back; then he and his stepson returned to Sintomniduta's camp, murdered the chief's mother, wife, and children, stole all the furs the Indians had gathered, and decamped from the region.[6]

It is important to note that the Wahpekutes did not retaliate with violence against their white neighbors, though they quickly identified Lott and his stepson as the culprits. Instead, under the leadership of Inkpaduta, Sintomniduta's kinsman and successor as chief, they applied for justice to the civil authorities at Fort Dodge. An investigation by William Wilson, the peace officer there, quickly put the blame for the crime on Lott. He promised to track down the renegade trader to pay for the crime. Meanwhile, a grand jury indicted Lott in absentia and a coroner's jury was convened. But the prosecutor treated the proceedings as "a farce and a joke," even nailing Sintomniduta's skull (which had been taken as evidence) to a post outside his door.[7]

Even in the wake of this insulting fiasco, the Indians did not turn to violent retribution. Inkpaduta traveled to Fort Ridgely to seek justice from the military authorities there. The officer in charge promised to "look into the matter," but after a brief patrol failed to turn up the murderers, the search was abandoned. Too much time had elapsed to warrant further effort and Lott was never seen again. From the Indians' perspective, it was clear that the white man's legal system had little appetite to redress crimes against Native people. They would have to look for justice elsewhere.[8]

Sintomniduta had maintained relatively friendly relations with white settlers. He sometimes dressed "like a white man" and had sent his children for a time to school in Mankato. Inkpaduta, on the other hand, was committed to retaining the traditional Dakota way of life and thus had long been ill-disposed toward whites. He grudgingly tolerated their presence on what he still considered Indian lands but generally shunned contact with them. As he confided to settler Curtis Lamb, one of his few white friends, he especially despised traders because they sold whiskey to his people. The murder of his relatives understandably increased the chief's bitterness and that of his band. He spoke often of revenge and settlers noted that his attitude became increasingly hostile after Sintomniduta's murder.[9]

Even so, three years passed before simmering resentments came to a boil. Settlers continued to move into the region, creating increased competition for game, and an extraordinarily harsh winter in 1857 put both Indians and settlers in a life-or-death struggle for survival. The weather was brutal, the worst in memory, and food was in short supply among the settlers. The Indians were in even worse straits, people dying from starvation, including Inkpaduta's young granddaughter. To the Indians, it was unforgivable that the settlers refused to share their scarce provisions. Settlers saw it differently, resenting the Indians both for their claims on what were perilously scanty provisions and for competing with them for whatever game could be found. Tensions ran high, and a petty quarrel over a dog between an Indian and a settler ignited festering resentments into a violent confrontation that left a Wahpekute brave beaten nearly to death. The settlers followed up by marching to Inkpaduta's camp and demanding they turn over all their guns and leave the region. Though in hindsight this was clearly a foolhardy move, it demonstrates how little the settlers feared retaliation. Despite later, sensationalized characterizations of "bloodthirsty savages," Dakota violence against whites was rare and, in the few cases on record, it was always a dispute between individuals, never an organized attack. In fact, the Red Top band, before this time, vigorously asserted that they had "never shed white men's blood." Thus, though the settlers in the region knew that the Indians were angry, serene in their sense of mastery, they didn't consider themselves in danger and scoffed at warnings of Indian unrest.[10]

[262]

But they had underestimated the Wahpekutes' fury, born of equal parts insult and desperation. The Indians might have been willing to pack up their camp, but by confiscating their guns, the settlers had not only offended their manhood, they had made the band's survival impossible. If it had ever been in doubt, this incident made clear, as historian Paul Beck points out, "that the whites could care less if Inkpaduta and his band lived or died." Taken by surprise, the Indians were forced to hand over their weapons, but the following day they descended en masse to retrieve them. They did not harm the lone woman they found at the cabin where the guns were stored, but in the days that followed, their retaliation escalated. At first they carried off goods and provisions and slaughtered livestock, as was their custom in expressing displeasure with whites. But each encounter seemed to feed their anger. Soon they were pushing and shoving settlers and briefly held two women captive. After two weeks of such raids, facing no organized opposition, the Indians took their revenge in earnest for all the past injuries they had endured. Along a path that took them north from Iowa's Lake Okoboji and Spirit Lake to the Minnesota settlement of Springfield (now Jackson), twenty miles north of the border, Inkpaduta and his men killed some forty settlers, took four women hostage, and then headed west to safety in Indian country beyond the Big Sioux River.[11]

As news of the rampage spread, the first reaction was disbelief. Citizens in Fort Dodge dismissed the stories as gross exaggerations until terrified settlers began clattering into the town, one after the other, each telling a similar tale. Even in Springfield, directly in the Indians' path, despite rumors of nearby attacks, the local storekeepers sold $80 worth of ammunition to "friendly"

Indians. (A few days later the storekeepers were killed, probably with their own powder.) But once realization set in that the unthinkable had occurred, hysteria swept through the territory, stories of atrocities growing wilder by the day. Refugees from isolated settlements frantically fled to Mankato, St. Peter, and every other town that might offer protection. All across the Suland volunteer companies mustered to track down and "annihilate the savages." Even St. Paul gathered its forces for an expected onslaught after hearing a rumor that "Mankato and St. Peter had been captured and burnt by nine hundred Yankton and Sisseton Sioux." All their worst suspicions about Indian perfidy were confirmed.[12]

Settlers' fears escalated as the military proved entirely incapable of tracking down and punishing the marauders. Troops gamely set out from Fort Ridgely, but as Agent Flandrau disgustedly recalled, "With their leather shoes and their backloads, accompanied by a ponderous army wagon on wheels drawn by six mules," they straggled through trackless drifts in the "utter wilderness . . . about as fit for such a march as an elephant is for a ball room." The truth was that none of the troops posted to Minnesota's frontier were prepared with either equipment or training appropriate for the conditions, let alone for any sort of conflict with the Indians. The army's primary role, as the War Department saw it, was to attend the annuity payments, regulate the whiskey trade, and maintain peace between the Dakotas and Ojibwes, supposedly keeping the Indians in line merely by their impressively marshal appearance. The troops also were meant to reassure prospective settlers that they were in no danger from neighboring "savages." Given the peaceful history between Indians and whites, nearly everyone with real knowledge of conditions in Minnesota assumed this to be true. Thus, the War Department garrisoned its outlying posts, Fort Ridgely in the Minnesota valley and Fort Ripley on the Upper Mississippi near Sauk Rapids, with only a skeleton force, usually no more than a single company of untrained and ill-equipped men. Flandrau shook his head in disbelief at "the imbecility of a military administration, which clothed and equipped its troops exactly in the same manner for duty in the tropical climate of Florida, and the frigid region of Minnesota." The forts themselves had been constructed with no thought of repelling a siege. Not bothering to dig wells, the garrisons depended on the nearby rivers for their water supply, which would require an unprotected and perilous trek if under attack, as soldiers would later discover in 1862.[13]

The failure of the troops to apprehend Inkpaduta suddenly alerted Minnesota's citizens to "the defenceless state of our frontier settlements, everywhere exposed to the incursions of tribes which recent events have shown to be capable of any atrocities."[14] They clamored for more military protection, taking little notice that Indians had gone after Inkpaduta and his men when the army failed and that Indians had recovered the two surviving captives (two others were killed while prisoners), treating them with "utmost kindness" until they could deliver them to white authorities. A band of western Yanktons purchased Abbie Gardner from her captors and treated her as an honored guest until a Sisseton search party arrived to carry her home. Her Indian hosts presented Abbie with "a head dress composed of thirty splendid eagle feathers" as a parting gift and sent her off "loaded with presents" as a sign of their goodwill. And Margaret Marble, rescued by two young Wahpeton brothers, Sounding Heavens and Gray Foot, was delivered to the missionaries "dressed by their mother in the best that the lodge afforded." Flandrau recalled her as "jaunty" in a "squaw costume, very brown cheeks, ear-bobs, short petticoats, trim ankles, and neat moccasins." However, before allowing the former captive to be seen by the public, he made sure she was more appropriately garbed in widow's weeds for "presentation in her role of rescued captive . . . a black statue of woe and grief."[15]

[264]

According to Flandrau, he engineered this transformation in Mrs. Marble's appearance "with her best interest at heart," to win a "generous outburst of sympathy" for the now destitute widow. The plan was successful. As he recalled with satisfaction, "No man could look upon her without opening his heart and purse," and the unfortunate lady left St. Paul with a nest egg of $1,000. But the effect also allowed the public to forget the role of her Indian rescuers. In almost no time, hair-raising tales of the women's captivity made their way across Minnesota, and readers throughout the country eagerly devoured sensational accounts that explained away the rescuers as rare exceptions to their savage race, "far better specimens of intelligent manhood than the average of our Indians." Not coincidentally, it was invariably noted, they also were Christians.[16]

One of the rescuers, Paul Mazakootemane, a Sisseton who was close to the missionaries and had embraced Christianity and a farming lifestyle, was indeed an exception. In a later memoir he explained, "As I now considered myself a white man, my heart was sad for this thing [the killings]." But for most of the Dakotas, cooperation did not necessarily signify sympathy with the settlers' fate. At least some of the Indians assuredly felt the victims had received their just desserts. However, the leaders of the reservation bands rightly feared that they would suffer the consequences of Inkpaduta's rash behavior and felt compelled to differentiate themselves from the perpetrators. Beautiful Voice, one of the rescue party, emphasized to the governor the hardships and danger they had endured to redeem the captives. "It shows," he declared, that "the Wapetons [sic] are good people." Mazakootemane added, "There are good and bad men everywhere. [One] could not point to any nation where all were good." But, he assured his audience, the Sissetons, Wahpetons, and also the Yanktons to the west all desired peace and were not complicit with the outlaw band.[17]

Such reassurances were not enough for the Office of Indian Affairs. With the army and militias clearly unable to deal with the situation—no fewer than three expeditions had returned empty-handed—the commissioner of Indian Affairs, ignoring the Indians' service in recovering the captives, sent word from Washington that all annuity payments must be withheld until the Dakotas themselves tracked down and captured Inkpaduta's band. The Indians, whatever their sympathies, were justifiably incensed. After the recent hard winter, they were deeply in need of goods and provisions. Furthermore, they had no appetite to hunt down their kinsmen for crimes against whites, despite Minnesota superintendant William Cullen's warning that "failure to deliver Inkpaduta and his men meant war with the United States." Unrest simmered on the reservations, and when a party of scouts and soldiers killed Inkpaduta's son, who was visiting relatives at Yellow Medicine, the situation at the Upper Agency, which served the Sisseton and Wahpeton bands, came to a head. "We are on the eve of a general war with these Indians," Major Thomas Sherman frantically wrote to his superiors.[18]

The timely arrival of Little Crow from the Lower Agency averted the brewing crisis. Perhaps more than any other Dakota leader, the Mdewakanton spokesman had succeeded in balancing accommodation and resistance to his advantage. Along with the other seasoned chiefs, he understood the danger that white hostility posed for his people and managed to persuade the bands' councils to undertake an expedition against Inkpaduta. Intentionally, the party of one hundred Indians and mixed bloods included Sissetons, Wahpetons, Wahpekutes, and Mdewakantons, thus demonstrating that all the reservation bands were committed to the effort. When they returned after a ten-day search, they reported to have killed four of Inkpaduta's warriors, though the chief himself remained at large. Perhaps this was true, though the only evidence the party produced of their search were a captured woman and two children who were soon released. Peculiarly, Antoine "Joe" Campbell, the party's mixed-blood interpreter and cousin to Little Crow, admitted that he had not personally seen the bodies. Nonetheless, if newly appointed superintendent Cullen harbored any doubts, he kept them to himself, anxious to distribute the overdue annuities and quell disquiet on the reservations. "I cannot speak too highly of the services of Little Crow," Cullen reported with relief.[19]

After one more fruitless attempt by the military to apprehend Inkpaduta, out of reach on the western plains, the government gave up the chase, annuities were tardily distributed, and life on the reservations superficially returned to normal. However, the events surrounding the incident had profoundly changed relationships between whites and Indians and within the Dakota community itself. Most Dakotas deeply resented the coercion that had forced them to track down their kinsmen. Moreover, they were incensed that the government ignored its legal obligation to pay treaty annuities, placing arbitrary conditions on the payment. The policy was patently unlawful, yet scarcely a soul spoke up on the Indians' behalf. Almost alone, Joe Brown put into print what should have been apparent to all. Writing in the *Henderson Democrat,* he pointed out that the annuities were payment for land that had been purchased, "the sacred obligations of treaty stipulation," and "in no instance should these payments be subjected to any contingency or obligation not prescribed in the treaty providing for the payments." Brown's argument, as usual, served his self-interest as much as the Indians', since he held a raft of Indian credits waiting to be discharged at the annuity payment. Still, his point was legally valid. The government, however, read its legal obligations more loosely and withheld payments at will to exact compliance on issues extraneous to the treaties.[20]

The public was in no mood to parse legal niceties. Feverish anti-Indian sentiment filled the papers, many calling for Indian removal from the territory.

Promoters feared that prospective immigrants would be deterred by tales of bloody uprisings. Current settlers, feeling a new sense of vulnerability, were no longer willing to tolerate Indians as neighbors. Missionary Stephen Riggs reported from Traverse des Sioux with dismay that settlers were "very much prejudiced against the whole Dakota nation" and were pushing to have the "reserve taken off." At the very least, they demanded strict policing of reservation boundaries, drowning out the assurances of formerly influential voices like Joe Brown, Charles Flandrau, and other territorial veterans. Consequently, for the first time the government began to push seriously a policy of containment, insisting that the Dakotas cease their customary hunting migrations in ceded territory and move their villages permanently onto the reservation.[21]

Drawing Boundaries, Breaking Bonds

In this climate of mutual suspicion, it is not surprising that Inkpaduta's brief but deadly raids along the border unleashed hysteria out of all proportion to the threat posed by the renegade band. The raids reached only twenty miles into Minnesota Territory, but they seriously damaged the already eroded relationship between whites and Indians. No more than fifteen warriors were responsible for the murders that took place that winter, members of a band that had long been labeled outlaws by some Dakotas as well as whites. Nonetheless, in the panic that followed, every Indian was suspect and thus endangered. Peaceful parties of innocent Sissetons found themselves chased across the plains, and even the venerable chiefs Sleepy Eyes and Red Iron were threatened and ordered to leave their hunting grounds. Mixed-blood people also came under increased suspicion. When the military expedition pursuing Inkpaduta misread the trail, allowing him to evade capture, many believed that Joe Coursolle and Joseph La Framboise, the party's mixed-blood guides, had intentionally misled the pursuers. Indian agent Flandrau tried to stanch the rumors, declaring that he knew the young men well and would never accuse them of betrayal. He also attempted to stamp out the escalating "suspicion attached to the whole Sioux nation," penning a letter to the *St. Paul Pioneer and Democrat* that assured its readers that only a small band of renegades was responsible for the bloodshed. The annuity Indians who resided in Minnesota had no part in the outbreak. But Flandrau's words were lost in a cacophony of anti-Indian rhetoric.[22]

Journalist John Phillips Owens recalled that "the better informed citizens . . . those who had the coolness to reason the case and compare facts and probabilities, gave no credence whatever to [the] wild reports," but by 1857 newcomers to Minnesota, who drew no distinction between one tribe or band and another, greatly outnumbered those with a history among the Indians. Up to this time leadership in the territory had been dominated by fur trade veterans and other long-established residents of the region—men like Henry Sibley, Henry Rice, Joe Brown, Charles Flandrau, and Alexander Ramsey. The elites of the trading fraternity, as well as the laboring class, had a long history of personal relationships with Native people. Many had Indian wives and had fathered mixed-blood children. Though few of these men hesitated to exploit their friendship with the Indians to their advantage, they also were comfortable living among them. Most believed—some, like Joe Brown, quite fervently—that coexistence between whites and Indians was feasible. Brown repeatedly insisted to all who would listen that the Indian, given opportunity, education, and time, had the "capacity . . . for all the duties and requirements of civilization."[23]

The missionaries who had spent decades with the Indians, especially Stephen Riggs and Thomas Williamson, also remained confident that Indians would eventually embrace Christianity and adapt to white society. Certainly it was problematic that neither the territorial veterans nor the missionaries ever questioned their conviction that Indians must discard their beliefs and traditions—essentially becoming white—to become accepted members of society, but at least they advanced a vision of coexistence rather than banishment or extermination.

When settlers began arriving in earnest in the 1850s, at first they had no choice but to accommodate themselves to the social world they entered. Indians were everywhere in Minnesota and interaction was unavoidable. Even after the treaties technically consigned them to reservation lands, both Dakotas and Ojibwes continued to frequent their old hunting grounds without opposition. Minneapolis pioneer John Stevens explained, "They thought they had a right to be our guests and, as long as they treated us properly, we had no disposition to dispute those thoughts." Other settlers recalled that they often traded food and goods with the Indians to the benefit of both. But for the most part the newcomers were culturally unprepared and unable to forge more intimate bonds of understanding and common humanity. Some, like Harriet Bishop, were appalled that flesh-and-blood Indians were so unlike the "noble savages" of literary renditions. Others viewed them simply as a nuisance that must be endured, much like mosquitoes or frigid winters. But notably, in dozens of old settlers' recollections, few recalled any fear of the Indians. Women who had previously lived in other backcountry settlements seemed to take Indian visitors in stride. Only those ladies fresh from the East, probably primed by tales of Indian butchery, lived in fear of imminent scalping, at least initially.

Recalling her childhood in Minnesota in the early 1850s, Mrs. James Pratt related that her mother, "a timid town-bred woman," lived in constant dread: "The sight of an Indian would nearly throw her into a fit. You can imagine she was having fits most of the time for they were always around."[24]

[268]

Pratt found herself, at age seven, in the position of soothing her mother's fears. But in the context of the times, this peculiar role reversal was not as unlikely as it may seem. Most of the children who came of age in the early settlement period insisted "we were never afraid of the [Indians]." Unbound by adult prejudices or cultural presumptions, they saw the Indians with different eyes. Carrie Stratton related that, while Indian visits at first terrified her mother, seven-year-old Carrie and her siblings thoroughly enjoyed "the novel sight of the Indians in their gay blankets and feathered head dress." Their frequent visits were "always peaceable ones, never committing any misdemeanor." Mary Massolt, living at Taylors Falls at age fourteen, "took a great fancy to the [Indians] and used to spend hours in their camps. They were always so kind and tried so hard to please me." At Minneapolis, friendly Dakotas taught young Edward Conant "how to build, bait and set a trap for small game." To fourteen-year-old Lysander Foster, "the Indians were much like white people. The Sioux boys at their camp at the mouth of Bassett's Creek [near St. Anthony] were always my playfellows. I spent many happy days hunting, fishing, and playing games with them. They were always fair in their play." Scores of similar remembrances described childhood Indian companions with fondness, remarking on their generosity and good nature.[25]

While it would be a mistake to put too much weight on recollections colored by the tricks of memory and nostalgia, still they suggest that in the early years of the territory, between 1849 and 1855, when in-migration advanced at a fairly moderate rate, some slim hope yet remained that a society might emerge with room for both whites and Indians, particularly as a new generation of children with intercultural sensibilities grew to adulthood. However, after 1855, when the land boom and speculative fever took off in earnest, people of all sorts poured into the territory faster than they could be counted, gobbling up acreage more quickly than it could be surveyed. These new Minnesotans had very different attitudes toward sharing the land with Native people. Magazine articles and promotional literature that had lured them westward assured them that "white workers [were] in full possession" of the land and the Indian "race nearly extinct . . . remembered as a curiosity of the past." As *Harper's* magazine piously intoned in 1858, "It is the law of God. The world must be occupied and subdued, and civilized man must occupy and subdue it." Moreover, in case any lingering anxiety about encountering Indians remained, the author assured potential immigrants that a "careful examination of the question has shown that the white man is superior of the red . . . stronger and wilier than the savage." Thus, it was quite a shock to the settlers when they discovered that their neighbors included thousands of vigorous and unbowed Dakotas and Ojibwes. Perturbed by this unwelcome demographic, these farmers and town builders demanded the state keep the troublesome Indians penned in their reservations.[26]

Since the thrust of settlement drove primarily into the fertile prairie lands south and west of St. Paul, the Ojibwes to the north were for the moment somewhat insulated from the growing pressures. Before Minnesota was admitted to the Union, the non-Indian population of the northern half of the future state was still made up largely of fur traders, mixed-blood people, and timbermen, none of whom felt threatened by their Ojibwe neighbors. However, farmsteads and settlements were beginning to take hold in the St. Croix and Mississippi valleys as far north as St. Cloud, and these new Minnesotans regularly complained to the governor about Ojibwe visits to their homesteads that were "far more frequent than pleasant." They begged the governor, without apparent effect, to "remove the Indians and compel them to keep on their reservations." Finally, in the summer of 1857, prodded by the Inkpaduta hysteria, territorial governor Samuel Medary half-heartedly responded. Under pressure from several prominent St. Paul land speculators, who argued that "something must be done or a complete white exodus would take place, and the tide of immigration cease," Medary ordered the newly formed St. Paul Militia Company to ride north and "talk with them [the Indians] about their being on the lands belonging to the white man."[27]

The militia company was in truth primarily a social club. It lacked even the most rudimentary equipment and was composed of young townsmen who had no idea how to handle such a diplomatic expedition. Predictably, their first encounter with a small party of Ojibwe braves turned into a fiasco. The Indians read the ragtag troop's "stern" demeanor as hostile and attempted to flee. The militiamen pursued them; shots were fired on both sides; and young Private Frank Donnelly, as well as several Ojibwe braves, fell casualties to the tragicomic episode. Then the overwrought militiamen, with all thoughts of their diplomatic mission forgotten, somehow managed to take six Indians prisoner and marched them to St. Paul, expecting them to face harsh retribution for their "savage crimes."[28]

For a number of influential Democrats, this was an unexpected and unwelcome turn of events in a key Democratic region. The last thing they wanted was to destabilize their relations with the Ojibwes, which would cause problems for both trading and timbering operations and likely upset their mixed-blood constituents as well. And Democrats ruled St. Paul. Thus, to the militia's dismay, the Democratic press derided the "Cornstalk War" and charges were dismissed against all but one of the Indians. The remaining prisoner, Shagoda, charged with the murder of Private Donnelly, conveniently escaped from house arrest a few days later, probably assisted by the sheriff who held him. To soothe injured Indian feelings, Democratic benefactors treated the other former captives to dinners and parties; Joe Rolette squired them to the theater; and the placated braves journeyed home laden with gifts of blankets, guns, and other tokens of goodwill. Captain James Starkey, who had led the hapless expedition, later recalled the events with disgust, explaining, "Such was the mixed character of the population [of St. Paul] at the time, that a large proportion of the citizens were either by ties of consanguinity or trading interest allied to the Indians and their interests, and these were known and designated as the 'Moccasin Democracy,' or 'Indian Dynasty.'"[29]

[270]

The outcome of the so-called Cornstalk War, especially in the wake of the hysteria wrought by Inkpaduta just a few months earlier, reveals the political and economic calculus that undergirded the cultural transformation overtaking Minnesota. In 1857 the "Moccasin Democracy" retained enough influence in St. Paul to deflect anti-Indian sentiment against the Ojibwes, at least for the moment. But the situation in southwestern Minnesota was quite different. The influx of a new breed of settlers, exploding land values, and an emerging agricultural sector put the Dakotas in a far more perilous position. Still largely a hunting and gathering society, the tribe found itself increasingly under stress. The Indians simply could not survive without free access to lands beyond their skimpy reservations. But new settlers were unfriendly and, worse, were scouring the country of game, driving the Indians to range ever greater distances in their hunt. In addition, homesteaders competed not only for game but also for furs, which they bartered for provisions, breaching what had always been exclusively an Indian prerogative. As historian Rhoda Gilman notes, by the mid-1850s "many a pioneer farmer earned more money trapping muskrat in winter than breaking the stubborn land in summer."[30] Adding fuel to what was already becoming a volatile situation, the winters of 1856 and 1857 were bitterly cold, causing extreme hardship for settlers and Indians alike.

Intercultural contact was now more fraught with misunderstanding than at any time in the past, neither group understanding the other's language or standards of behavior. Euro-American settlers, steeped in the ideology of acquisitive individualism, resented Indians trespassing and hunting on their property, while such a concept of exclusive land rights was incomprehensible, even immoral, to the Indians. New homesteaders often perceived Indian visits as threatening, especially their custom of peering into windows or entering a dwelling without knocking, which was entirely proper etiquette in Dakota and Ojibwe culture. Settlers also were unnerved by the silence of their visitors, which they read as sullenness and hostility, when in fact verbal reticence was merely part of the rhythm of polite Indian conversation.[31]

From the perspective of the Indians, these strangers were interlopers, undeserving of respect. In Dakota and Ojibwe tradition, generosity was a badge of honor. The more one shared his possessions, the greater status he enjoyed. As a matter of common hospitality, Indian visitors expected to be offered food. In the past they had frequently shared game, maple sugar, and wild rice with traders and other whites. Yet this new breed of settlers only grudgingly shared their

PLATE 85

Plate 85. Ojibwe family in front of their home, ca. 1870s. Minnesota Historical Society.

While more insulated than their Dakota neighbors from the onslaught of new settlers in the 1850s, northern Minnesota Ojibwe increasingly crafted a culturally hybrid existence by dint of both necessity and choice. This photograph hints at how one family straddled cultures in the early years of Minnesota statehood. Garbed in Americanized apparel, the family pictured here poses in front of a traditional birch bark house, a type of dwelling preferred by many Ojibwe until the end of the nineteenth century.

New settlers brought changes that upset the delicate racial balance that had governed the region during the first half of the nineteenth century. Land cessions negotiated in 1854 and 1855 left the Ojibwe increasingly impoverished. While they had retained hunting and fishing rights on ceded lands, commercial logging operations transformed the environment in ways that rendered it foreign to its native inhabitants. Clear-cutting drove away game; this practice also eliminated a whole raft of seasonal foods like berries, nuts, and medicinal plants. Depleted forests could no longer provide the raw materials to craft cradleboards, canoes, birch bark houses, and snowshoes, the objects that provided the material underpinning for Ojibwe culture. The Ojibwe were left increasingly dependent on paltry annuities to purchase food and clothing they could no longer extract from traditional sources. As Indians struggled to hold on to traditional subsistence strategies, newcomers worked to intensify commercial logging operations. Both parties came to view each other with misapprehension and suspicion.

While many families preferred to inhabit *wiigiwaam,* like the one pictured here, during the summer months, it would have been increasingly difficult to continue this or any other tradition that distinguished them from the white agrarians who had transformed the region.[115] After the violence of 1862, the Ojibwe faced some of the same hostility that forced the dispossession of the Dakota and Winnebagos. But the effort to remove the Ojibwe to concentrated reservations at Red Lake, Leech Lake, and White Earth was not entirely successful. They were able to resist pressure to abandon their historic communities at Nett Lake, Fond du Lac, Sandy Lake, and Mille Lacs, where they currently maintain reservations.

PLATE 86

Abbie Gardner Taken Captive, March, 1857, Okoboji Lake, Iowa.   Copyright.

Plate 86. *Abbie Gardner Taken Captive, March, 1857, Okoboji Lake, Iowa,* n.d. **Minnesota Historical Society.**

News that a small band of Indians had murdered several groups of settlers living along the Iowa border in March 1857 sent a shock of terror through white communities in Minnesota, which was completely unprepared for any kind of military engagement with the Indian inhabitants of the region. The Inkpaduta incident, or Spirit Lake Massacre as it came to be remembered by whites, was a critical turning point in the state's race relations, setting the stage for the U.S.–Dakota War five years later. The episode seriously undermined the foundations of Minnesota's multiracial society, which was rapidly unraveling as the territory transitioned to American statehood. Ultimately it was Indians who defused the crisis, deflecting more violence and ransoming female captives, including Abigail Gardner, who was held by Inkpaduta's band for four months. But the murders and kidnappings committed by Inkpaduta's small band left white settlers feeling threatened by all Indians and provided justification for the later removal of all Native Americans from the southern part of the state. Inkpaduta's escape from white authorities also emboldened some Indian militants who called for armed resistance to American incursions on Indian lands and sovereignty.

The violence on the state's southern border unleashed virulent hostility to Indians, which found expression in this postcard dramatizing the initial capture of young Abbie Gardner, whose family was the first victims of Inkpaduta's warriors. Gardner herself maintained that the impotent response to Inkpaduta's crimes cleared the way for the U.S.–Dakota War. Twenty-six years after being released from her Indian captors, Gardner returned to St. Paul, where she went to the State Capitol to hold the scalp of Indian leader Little Crow, which was at that point showcased in the state's historical exhibit. Her relief knowing "that he could never again lead his warriors on to murderous deeds" was mixed with a sense of missed opportunities. "Had Inkpaduta's scalp been taken, the Minnesota massacre of 1862 might have been averted," she concluded.[116]

Plate 87. "Miss Gardiner *[sic]* and Her Fearful Adventure," *Ballou's Pictorial,* **August 22, 1857. Minnesota Historical Society.**

Abbie Gardner received a heroine's welcome when she reached St. Paul in June 1857, after spending almost four months as a hostage with Inkpaduta's band. The sixteen-year-old became a state celebrity during her months in captivity, which garnered the attention of Indian agents, military authorities, the territorial governor, and the legislature, which ultimately paid a ransom for her release. When she first returned to white settlement, Gardner was taken aback to find herself besieged by well-wishing crowds and journalists eager to publish the full story of her "fearful adventure" with the "red fiends."[117] Her steamboat docking at St. Paul was greeted by "crowds and deafening shouts from the people." The young orphan was whisked by carriage to one of the city's finest hotels, where she was pampered overnight before being presented to the governor on June 23. This ceremony opened with an exchange of speeches between the state's top officials and her Indian rescuers, who presented the girl with

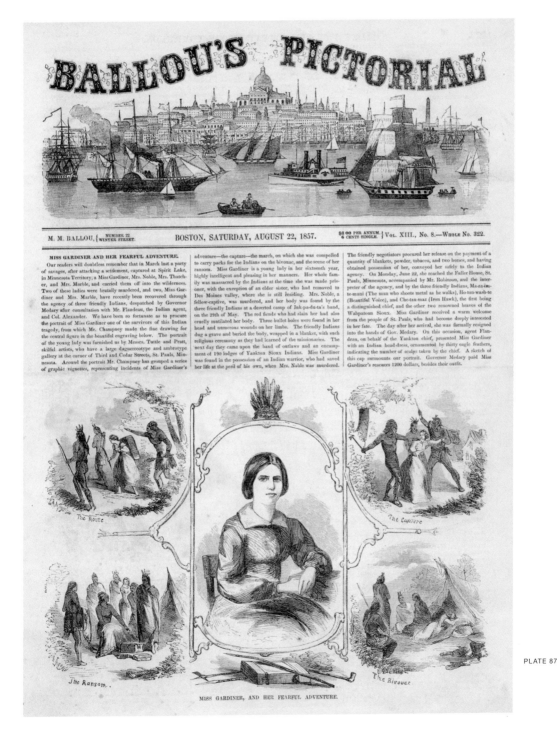

BALLOU'S PICTORIAL

M. M. BALLOU, { NUMBER 22, WINTER STREET. } BOSTON, SATURDAY, AUGUST 22, 1857. { $2 00 PER ANNUM. 6 CENTS SINGLE. } Vol. XIII., No. 8.—Whole No. 322.

MISS GARDINER AND HER FEARFUL ADVENTURE.

Our readers will doubtless remember that in March last a party of savages, after attacking a settlement, captured at Spirit Lake, in Minnesota Territory, a Miss Gardiner, Mrs. Noble, Mrs. Thatcher, and Mrs. Marble, and carried them off into the wilderness. Two of these ladies were brutally murdered, and two, Miss Gardiner and Mrs. Marble, have recently been recovered through the agency of three friendly Indians, despatched by Governor Medary after consultation with Mr. Flandeau, the Indian agent, and Col. Alexander. We have been so fortunate as to procure the portrait of Miss Gardiner one of the survivors of this Indian tragedy, from which Mr. Champney made the fine drawing for the central figure in the beautiful engraving below. The portrait of the young lady was furnished us by Messrs. Tuttle and Pratt, skilful artists, who have a large daguerreotype and ambrotype gallery at the corner of Third and Cedar Streets, St. Pauls, Minnesota. Around the portrait Mr. Champney has grouped a series of graphic vignettes, representing incidents of Miss Gardiner's

adventure—the capture, the march, on which she was compelled to carry packs for the Indians on the bivouac, and the scene of her ransom. Miss Gardiner is a young lady in her sixteenth year, highly intelligent and pleasing in her manners. Her whole family was massacred by the Indians at the time she was made prisoner, with the exception of an elder sister, who had removed to Des Moines valley, where she is still residing. Mrs. Noble, a fellow-captive, was murdered, and her body was found by the three friendly Indians at a deserted camp of Ink-pa-du-ta's band, on the 29th of May. The red fiends who had slain her had also cruelly mutilated her body. Three bullet holes were found in her head and numerous wounds on her limbs. The friendly Indians dug a grave and buried the body, wrapped in a blanket, with such religious ceremony as they had learned of the missionaries. The next day they came upon the band of outlaws and an encampment of 190 lodges of Yankton Sioux Indians. Miss Gardiner was found in the possession of an Indian warrior, who had saved her life at the peril of his own, when Mrs. Noble was murdered.

The friendly negotiators procured her release on the payment of a quantity of blankets, powder, tobacco, and two horses, and having obtained possession of her, conveyed her safely to the Indian agency. On Monday, June 22, she reached the Fuller House, St. Pauls, Minnesota, accompanied by Mr. Robinson, and the interpreter of the agency, and by the three friendly Indians, Ma-za-in-te-mani (The man who shoots metal as he walks), Ho-ton-wash-te (Beautiful Voice), and Che-tan-maz (Iron Hawk), the first being a distinguished chief, and the other two renowned braves of the Walpatooan Sioux. Miss Gardiner received a warm welcome from the people of St. Pauls, who had become deeply interested in her fate. The day after her arrival, she was formally resigned into the hands of Gov. Medary. On this occasion, agent Flandrau, on behalf of the Yankton chief, presented Miss Gardiner with an Indian head-dress, ornamented by thirty eagle feathers, indicating the number of scalps taken by the chief. A sketch of this cap surmounts our portrait. Governor Medary paid Miss Gardiner's rescuers 1200 dollars, besides their outfit.

The Route

The Capture

The Ransom.

The Bivouac.

MISS GARDINER, AND HER FEARFUL ADVENTURE.

PLATE 87

an "Indian war-cap" to demonstrate that she would always enjoy their protection. Abbie recalled that the buckskin headpiece, adorned with thirty-six eagle feathers and trimmed with fur, was "beautiful" when it "was properly adjusted upon the head."[118] This dramatic souvenir proved longer-lasting than the $500 gathered for her by the people of St. Paul and the $30 purse she had received in Shakopee. This nest egg evaporated when the bank holding her deposit failed in the financial collapse that followed her release.[119]

St. Paul daguerreotypers created a portrait of Gardner to sell to a curious public, which was eager to acquire photographic images of contemporary newsmakers. Portraits of her Indian rescuers were also made at the same time. But national publications like *Ballou's Pictorial*, which published this spread to celebrate Gardner's rescue, focused their entire attention on the young woman at the center of the drama, arranging "graphic vignettes" communicating the story of her capture and release around her somber daguerreotype. A drawing of her "war cap" crowned the collage. Indians were posed as "ruthless captors" in these graphic narratives, barbaric foils to what one chronicler called the "afflicted maiden."[120]

Plate 88. Charles DeForest Fredericks, Sisseton-Wahpeton treaty delegation in Washington, D.C., 1858. Minnesota Historical Society.

In the spring of 1858, several groups of Dakota traveled to Washington, D.C., with the understanding that they would have the opportunity to address their grievances over the unfulfilled promises of earlier land cession treaties. But government officials had suggested the journey to facilitate another land cession, in the hope that negotiating an agreement in the faraway nation's capital would isolate these hand-picked elders from the influence of more militant young warriors. Policy makers viewed delegation visits as tools of conquest, arguing that Indians who visited the capital would comprehend the futility of resisting American superior technical and military power. The Dakota representatives from Minnesota were devastated to discover that they had been brought to the capital on false pretenses. After spending more than three months on the East Coast, they returned home having acquiesced to another land cession that halved the size of their reservation along the Minnesota River.

This portrait shows the Sisseton-Wahpeton portion of the delegation, which included a large proportion of so-called farmer Indians, who were more sympathetic to

PLATE 88

the government's proposed system of allotments that would carve the reservation into discrete family farms. These sentiments can be discerned in the delegates' apparel, which is almost entirely Americanized. Red Iron, who was so articulate in protesting the Traverse des Sioux treaty, was the only member of the delegation pictured here in traditional Indian costume. Shown (*left to right*) standing are Joseph Akipa Renville, Scarlet Plume, Red Iron, John Otherday, Paul Mazakootemane, and Charles R. Crawford (interpreter); sitting, Iron Walker, Stumpy Horn, Sweet Corn, and Extended Tail Feathers.

During the winter of 1857–58, thirteen different tribal delegations visited Washington, D.C., to negotiate new treaties with the federal government. All of these delegations posed for portraits like this one, which is credited to Charles DeForest Fredericks. These pictures were not made as souvenirs for their subjects. Photographers like Fredericks and the more well-known Julian Vannerson and Samuel Cohner of James E. McClees Studio set out to create a visual record of the "vanishing race." They touted the importance of creating images that could be used for future historical and scientific study, banking on the fact that they would also be able to market them to a curious public eager for Indian images. Photographs like these had their roots in earlier efforts to produce visual records of Indian life for posterity and commercial exploitation like the gallery of oil paintings envisioned by Thomas McKenney, the first head of the Office of Indian Affairs. By 1857, these earlier schemes had been rendered obsolete by the new technologies of photography, which produced images that were easily reproduced and distributed. McClees later compiled an album of Indian delegation images that he issued for sale in 1858.[121]

Plate 89. Joseph Brown and Little Crow, 1858. Gilcrease Museum.

This portrait of Joe Brown and Little Crow (almost certainly taken by Julian Vannerson and Samuel Cohner of the James E. McClees Studio, Washington, D.C., between March 13 and June 21, 1858) pairs two of the most important protagonists in the struggle over the 1858 land cession negotiations. Brown, who had become Indian agent for the Dakota in 1857 and had kinship ties to the Dakota through his wife Susan, reasoned that reducing the size of the reservation along the Minnesota River would compel the Dakota to abandon traditional subsistence strategies and embrace an agrarian lifestyle. He believed that assimilation was ultimately in the best interest of the Indians he was serving as agent. But his view was also undoubtedly colored by the fact that he stood to gain financially by selling the land released from Indian control. Brown saw a trip to Washington, D.C., as the best way to achieve his twin goals of Indian assimilation and personal enrichment.

The visit to the east was, however, deeply disillusioning for the Indians involved, especially Little Crow. The Dakota leader had been recruited for this delegation because of his track record as a negotiator equally skilled at ap-

PLATE 89

peasing Indians and American policy makers. During the trip to Washington, Little Crow shed his conciliatory demeanor and emerged as a vocal critic of government actions. Little Crow felt humiliated by Washington negotiators, who threatened all the delegates but singled out the leader himself for acting like a "child" when he protested further land concessions. His dignity was undermined at every turn, even by Washington hoteliers. "We thought we would come here and live like white men, and sleep in beds," he complained to Commissioner Charles E. Mix in June 1858, "but we had to sleep on the floor."[122] Government officials enjoyed asserting that no Indian who had seen the nation's capital had dared to resist American power. Little Crow was the first to defy this rule. The duplicity he had experienced in Washington, D.C., made him feel like he had few allies among the Americans. This almost certainly influenced his decision in August 1862 to join the violence so desired by the young warriors in his tribe.[123]

Plate 90. Company D, First Minnesota Regiment, posed at the southeast corner of Nicollet Avenue and First Street, Minneapolis, 1861. Minnesota Historical Society.

A group of men from St. Anthony and Minneapolis organized themselves as the Lincoln Guards and marched to Fort Snelling in the spring of 1861, where they were rechristened Company D of the First Regiment Minnesota Volunteers. This photograph of the men posed in downtown Minneapolis was taken almost one month after they were mustered into the Union Army.

Inspired by the twin calls of patriotism and adventure, men in Minnesota rushed to volunteer after Governor Alexander Ramsey offered a regiment to President Abraham Lincoln. The military of the time bore little resemblance to the modern Army. Volunteers organized themselves into companies according to their own preferences, sorting themselves into units composed entirely of men from their own towns, their own ethnic groups, or their own moral code. In the flurry of patriotic zeal that followed the organization of the First Minnesota regiment in the spring of 1861, each major river town — Stillwater, Wabasha, Hastings, Winona, Faribault, Red Wing, and St. Paul — formed a company that marched into the Union Army.

The English writer Anthony Trollope visited the region soon after this photograph was taken and was horrified to observe the massive deployment of men. "To me it is always a source of sorrow to see a man enlisted," he mourned. Watching new Minnesota recruits change steamboats, the writer bemoaned how "this infant State with its huge territory and scanty population is called upon to send its heart's blood out to the war . . . these men whom I saw entering on their career upon the banks of the Mississippi, many were fathers of families, many were owners of lands, many were educated men capable of high aspirations."[124] The tragic dimensions of the war so evident to Trollope would only become clear to most Americans much later in the war, well after the dreams imagined by Trollope were buried with the soldiers on the conflict's battlefields.

PLATE 90

PLATE 91

Plate 91. Officers of the First Minnesota Regiment in front of the commandant's quarters, 1861. Minnesota Historical Society.

Something of a holiday atmosphere prevailed in the early days of the Civil War when recruits first began arriving at Fort Snelling to be mustered into the Army. A ceremonial presentation of the colors was one of the many events that brought the female relatives of officers to the fort, where they posed for this photograph with the men who had been designated to lead Company D. Women were practically and symbolically central to efforts to build public support for the Union cause. In these early days they demonstrated their enthusiasm for military heroism by organizing elaborate rallies and send-offs for the troops; later they organized drives to raise money and materials necessary to improve conditions for the boys in blue. None of the names of the women pictured here were remembered by later historians, but journalist Edward Bromley identified several men in this photograph. The officer with the flag behind him is Stephen A. Miller, who later became governor of Minnesota. The color bearer is Howard Stansbury.[125]

Once a critical outpost of American power in the old Northwest, Fort Snelling retreated in importance after the land cessions of the 1850s and the declaration of Minnesota statehood. By the time Fort Sumter came under fire in 1861, the military outpost had become so peripheral to military strategy that it had been sold to a private citizen, Franklin Steele, who hoped to develop a "city of Fort Snelling." This plan was scuttled by the collapse of the local real estate market in the financial panic of 1857. The old fort stood empty until the demands of war brought it to life once again, when state officials decided it was the best place to quarter new troops, making it the rendezvous point for Minnesotans enlisted in the Union Army.[126] The men drilled, but the Army did little else to ensure that they were actually prepared for combat. Troops received almost nothing in the way of either uniforms or weapons. Terrible food was the rule. Officers rarely had any military experience; they gained their positions through election by their men, who were most often their friends and neighbors.

The men pictured here were likely enjoying their festive send-off to a war they assumed would be short in duration. They had no way to foresee the horrors they would endure. While the First Minnesota ultimately played a decisive role in the war, its contribution to the Union cause came at enormous cost. Few of the one thousand men who initially enlisted in the First Minnesota survived the war.

NAMES OF MEN DRAFTED

In the Second Congressional District, Minnesota, in the Draft commencing May 28th, 1864, and who have failed to report at these Head-Quarters, and are now Deserters.

WABASHAW COUNTY.

Glasgow.

NAME.	AGE.	OCCUPATION.	BORN.	DESERTED.
Vickolt, Wm. A.	21	Farmer,	Canada,	July 8
Lusk, Wm.	21	Carpenter,	New Brunswick,	July 8
Wabrich, John	21	Farmer,	Germany,	July 11

Greenfield.

Cole, Amos	21	Farmer,	U.S.	July 6
Mahoney, Michael	24	Farmer,	Ireland,	June 19

Highland.

McDonough, Thomas	31	Farmer,	Ireland,	July 6

Hyde Park.

Barnes, James	34	Farmer,	Ireland,	June 11

Minneiska.

Delaney, Thomas	31	Laborer,	Ireland,	Aug. 5
Lamee, John	31	Farmer,	Ireland,	Aug. 5

Mt. Pleasant.

Gilbert, Cyrene	23	Farmer,	Connecticut,	July 12

West Albany.

Purcell, Thomas	24	Farmer,	Ireland,	June 13
McGillion, Michael	55	Farmer,	Ireland,	June 12
McCord, Garrett	50	Saloon Keeper,	Ireland,	June 12
McPike, James	51	Farmer,	Ireland,	June 12
O'Donnell, John	55	Farmer,	Ireland,	June 12
McBride, Alex.	30	Farmer,	Ireland,	July 9
Baxter, Ed. H.	26	Farmer,	England,	Aug. 4
Fox, John	43	Farmer,	Ireland,	Aug. 4

Wautopa.

Dorrigan, Morris	35	Farmer,	Ireland,	Aug. 3
Johnson, Andrew	41	Farmer,	Sweden,	Aug. 3
Daly, Michael	31	Farmer,	Ireland,	June 13
Jones, John	26	Farmer,	Indiana,	Aug. 3
Abbott, Christopher	38	Farmer,	Ireland,	Aug. 3
McCarty, Dennis	31	Farmer,	Ireland,	Aug. 3
Johnson, Andrew	40	Farmer,	Sweden,	Aug. 3

Zumbro.

Dale, John	24	Farmer,	Pennsylvania,	Aug. 4
Hanson, Hiram	50	Farmer,	Maine,	Aug. 4
Adams, Daniel	28	Farmer,	Maine,	Aug. 4

Pell.

Fehan, Patrick	21	Farmer,	Ireland,	July 9

GOODHUE COUNTY.

Leon.

Beverge, Robert	31	Farmer,	New-York,	June 15
Stranahan, D. C.	38	Farmer,	Michigan,	June 14

Warsaw.

Slee, Edward	24	Farmer,	New-York,	June 14
Gossner, John	25	Farmer,	Ireland,	Aug. 3
Tarvinson, Tarnin	40	Farmer,	Norway,	Aug. 3
Gilbertson, Gilbert	36	Farmer,	Norway,	Aug. 3

Belvidere.

Hanson, Ole	31	Farmer,	Norway,	Aug. 2

DAKOTA COUNTY.

Burnsville.

Walsh, William	29	Farmer,	Ireland,	June 11
Foley, Michael	21	Farmer,	Ireland,	June 11
McCarey, John	35	Farmer,	Ireland,	July 7
Kilroy, William	34	Farmer,	Ireland,	Aug. 5
Kennedy, David	37	Farmer,	Ireland,	Aug. 5
Gollersh, Michael		Farmer,	Ireland,	Aug. 5
Colbeck, James	22	Laborer,	Bohemia,	Aug. 5
Walsh, Michael	23	Farmer,	Ireland,	Aug. 5

Eagan.

Quirck, James, jr.	27	Farmer,	Ireland,	June 14
Dorsey, Thomas	26	Farmer,	Ireland,	June 14
Lemay, Flavius	25	Farmer,	Canada,	June 14
Latander, John	29	Farmer,	Germany,	June 10
Kennedy, Michael	21	Farmer,	Ireland,	June 14
Finnerty, Thomas	38	Farmer,	Ireland,	June 14
Laereh, Frank	31	Farmer,	Canada,	Aug. 5
Welch, Morris M.	32	Farmer,	Canada,	Aug. 5
Cloky, Paul	40	Farmer,	Canada,	Aug. 5
Heffernan, Patrick	39	Farmer,	Ireland,	Aug. 5
Haley, William	35	Farmer,	Ireland,	Aug. 5
Maher, John	22	Farmer,	Ireland,	Aug. 5
Dunn, Edward	22	Farmer,	Ireland,	July 11
McDonough, John	35	Farmer,	Ireland,	July 12
Cloky, George	31	Farmer,	Canada,	July 11
Shopelaine, Peter	21	Farmer,	Canada,	July 12
Sullivan, Daniel	35	Farmer,	Ireland,	July 11

Eureka.

Peterson, Andrew	37	Farmer,	Norway,	Aug. 5
Asmondson, Ole	44	Farmer,	Norway,	June 12

Greenvale.

Ryan, Timothy	37	Farmer,	Ireland,	Aug. 5
Shull, Reuben	32	Farmer,	U.S.	Aug. 5
Evenson, Anders	35	Farmer,	Norway,	Aug. 5

Ravenna.

Durkem, John	37	Farmer,	Ireland,	June 9

Rosemont.

Rowe, Michael	24	Farmer,	Ireland,	June 10

West St. Paul.

Ryan, Timothy	22	Deckhand,	Ireland,	June 9
Smith, Charles	35	Laborer,	Ireland,	Aug. 5
Connor, Michael	34	Laborer,	Ireland,	Aug. 5
Beiland, Henry	34	Expressman,	New-York,	Aug. 5

RAMSEY COUNTY.

Mound View.

Armstrong, Michael	22	Farmer,	Ireland,	June 12

White Bear.

Abro, James	29	Farmer,	Canada,	June 13
Bebo, Charles	24	Laborer,	Canada,	Aug. 1
Labor, Antoine	37	Farmer,	Canada,	Aug. 1
Fisk, Van H.	34	Farmer,	Ohio,	Aug. 1
Toro, David	27	Farmer,	Canada,	July 10

New Canada.

Tacket, Charles	34	Farmer,	England,	Aug. 4
McDonald, Barney	38	Laborer,	Ireland,	Aug. 4
McDavitt, Patrick	34	Laborer,	Ireland,	Aug. 4
Lemay, Thomas	27	Farmer,	Canada,	Aug. 4
McCarty, Charles	37	Laborer,	Ireland,	Aug. 4
Rondle, Peter	25	Laborer,	Canada,	Aug. 1
Lochbach, Henry	31	Farmer,	Germany,	Aug. 1

NEW CANADA—(Continued.)

NAME.	AGE.	OCCUPATION.	BORN.	DESERTED.
Haverson, Nels	41	Laborer,	Sweden,	July 11
Lemlin, Francois	21	Farmer,	Canada,	July 9
Demers, Canaday	21	Saloon Keeper,	Canada,	July 9
McDevith, John	29	Laborer,	Ireland,	July 11
Vincent, Theophilus	22	Farmer,	Canada,	July 9

WASHINGTON COUNTY.

Bay Town.

Nelson, Charles L.	28	Teacher,	New-York,	June 13
Eagan, Bernard	29	Laborer,	Ireland,	June 13
Smith, Henry	27	Laborer,	Maine,	June 13

Denmark.

Weigheljohn	27	Farmer,	England,	June 13

MANOMIN COUNTY.

Manomin.

Wheeler, Michael	24	Clerk,	Connecticut,	June 10
Shields, Frederic	27	Laborer,	Ireland,	June 10

HENNEPIN COUNTY.

Bloomington.

Peppin, Peter	35	Farmer,	Canada,	June 12
Breckenridge, Fid.	31	Laborer,	Missouri,	Aug. 5
Peppin, Joseph	30	Blacksmith,	Minnesota,	July 9
Colin, John Baptiste	28	Farmer,	France,	July 9

Corcoran.

O'Laughlin, Patrick	37	Farmer,	Ireland,	June 13
Barrett, Edward	23	Farmer,	Ireland,	June 12
Casey, Patrick	35	Farmer,	Ireland,	Aug. 5
La Crosse, Andrew	38	Farmer,	Ireland,	Aug. 5
Orwell, George	41	Farmer,	Germany,	Aug. 5
Dupont, Joseph	31	Farmer,	Canada,	July 11
Kennedy, John	36	Farmer,	Ireland,	July 11

Maple Grove.

Leller, Peter	36	Farmer,	Bavaria,	July 14

Eden Prairie.

Semon, Fletcher	21	Farmer,	Wisconsin,	June 13

Greenwood.

Yoss, William	41	Farmer,	Germany,	June 12
Rotherford, William	25	Farmer,	Scotland,	June 12
Bigler, Charles	29	Farmer,	Saxony,	June 12
Cochran, James E.				Aug. 5

Crystal Lake.

Bumgardner, Sebastin	29	Farmer,	Germany,	Aug. 5

Medina.

Collins, Cornelius	26	Farmer,	Ireland,	June 13
Courveaux, Joseph	32	Farmer,	Canada,	Aug. 6

Minnetrista.

Deise, Nicholas	41	Farmer,	Germany,	July 8
Ball, Joseph	32	Farmer,	Germany,	July 8

Plymouth.

Buffordling, Peter	50	Farmer,	Germany,	June 11
Boncher, Octave	29	Farmer,	Canada,	June 11
Boylan, Andrew	26	Farmer,	Ireland,	June 13
Bushnell, Byron	35	Farmer,	Maine,	June 11
Burke, Richard	37	Farmer,	Ireland,	July 10
Potvine, Pascal	31	Merchant,	Canada,	July 10
Larzelles, Baptiste	31	Farmer,	Canada,	Aug. 5
Shepherd, George	51	Farmer,	U.S.	Aug. 5
Krats, Ferd.	39	Farmer,	Germany,	Aug. 5
Huot, Eli	36	Farmer,	Canada,	Aug. 6
Basler, Lewis	42	Farmer,	Germany,	Aug. 5

CARVER COUNTY.

Benton.

Engler, Henry	21	Farmer,	Prussia,	June 14
Kongehak, Michael	29	Farmer,	Prussia,	June 15
Nellen, Gerhard	22	Farmer,	Prussia,	June 14
Fowler, Samuel	51	Farmer,	Pennsylvania,	June 15
Urbach, Jacob	56	Farmer,	Germany,	Aug. 6
Huier, Lewis	34	Farmer,	Saxony,	Aug. 6
Springler, John E.	41	Farmer,	Hanover,	Aug. 6
Raschier, Per.	31	Farmer,	Sweden,	Aug. 6
Kongchak, Andrew	23	Farmer,	Prussia,	July 13

Hollywood.

Farley, Patrick	34	Farmer,	Ireland,	June 16
Burns, Michael	34	Farmer,	Ireland,	June 16
Doherty, Charles	45	Farmer,	Ireland,	June 16
Craven, Patrick	38	Farmer,	Ireland,	June 16

San Francisco.

O'Clay, Patrick	27	Farmer,	Ireland,	June 19
Dougherty, Anthony	29	Farmer,	Ireland,	June 19
Brophy, James	30	Farmer,	Ireland,	June 18
Svenson, Peter Julius	29	Farmer,	Sweden,	June 18
Gallegan, Patrick	31	Farmer,	Ireland,	June 16
Cavanaugh, Patrick	31	Farmer,	Ireland,	July 10
Dougherty, John	31	Farmer,	Ireland,	Aug. 3
Lindquist, Andrew	33	Farmer,	Sweden,	Aug. 3
Lynch, Patrick	30	Farmer,	Ireland,	Aug. 3

Watertown.

Higgins, Patrick	31	Farmer,	Maine,	June 16

Camden.

Patterson, John	25	Farmer,	Ireland,	July 15

Chanhassen.

Chase, Charles A.	40	Farmer,	Maine,	July 9
Massen, John	34	Farmer,	Germany,	Aug. 2
Abbott, Herman A.	21	Farmer,	Illinois,	Aug. 2
Richardson, Wm.	36	Farmer,	England,	Aug. 2

Young America.

Ruppretcht, Paul	29	Farmer,	Bavaria,	July 14

Lakotown.

Mattson, George	35	Farmer,	Sweden,	July 10

WRIGHT COUNTY.

Frankfort.

Zohler, William	25	Farmer,	Germany,	June 16
Nellis, John	28	Farmer,	Germany,	June 16
Middlestet, Christian	27	Farmer,	Germany,	June 16
Schnutaler, Anthony	40	Farmer,	Germany,	June 17
Gutzmiller, J.	26	Farmer,	Germany,	June 17
Frei, Hank	47	Farmer,	Germany,	June 17
Kernel, Frank	22	Farmer,	Germany,	Aug. 10
Dudcort, Herman	42	Farmer,	Germany,	Aug. 10
Maas, Mathias	42	Farmer,	Germany,	Aug. 10
Schumaker, John	29	Farmer,	Germany,	Aug. 10

Middleville.

Schatkensbeager, Frank	37	Farmer,	Germany,	June 18
Baker, Aaron	30	Farmer,	U.S.	July 16
Morris, John	55	Farmer,	Virginia,	July 16
Pearson, John F.	25	Farmer,	U.S.	Aug. 8
Lesse, Frank	31	Farmer,	Germany,	Aug. 8

Moser's Prairie.

Lane, Joseph	32	Farmer,	Pennsylvania,	June 17
Wood, Lockley R.	38	Farmer,	Pennsylvania,	June 10
Dustin, Timothy	21	Farmer,	New-York,	Aug. 10

Woodland.

Young, John	29	Farmer,	Ireland,	June 18
Dugan, Michael	29	Farmer,	Ireland,	July 15
Kennedy, Thomas	21	Farmer,	Ireland,	July 15
Porter, Thomas	23	Farmer,	Ireland,	July 15
Bessingham, Thomas	32	Farmer,	Pennsylvania,	July 15
Jordan, Edwin	35	Farmer,	Ireland,	Aug. 10

Maple Lake.

Madigan, James	37	Farmer,	Ireland,	Aug. 13
Deugal, George	40	Farmer,	Switzerland,	Aug. 13
O'Laughlin, James O.	39	Farmer,	Ireland,	Aug. 13
Kiehl, Gottfried	52	Farmer,	Germany,	July 10
Butler, Patrick, jr.	26	Farmer,	Ireland,	July 10

Buffalo.

Berthiume, Zebulon	38	Farmer,	Canada,	June 17

Albion.

O'Laughlin, Thomas	31	Farmer,	Ireland,	June 20
O'Donahue, Michael	29	Farmer,	Ireland,	June 20
Grimes, Com.	27	Farmer,	Minnesota,	Aug. 6

McLEOD COUNTY.

Bergen.

Pryblinta, Angust	38	Farmer,	Germany,	June 14

Winstead.

Corr, John	39	Farmer,	Ireland,	June 13
Corr, Thomas	36	Farmer,	Ireland,	June 13
Corr, Michael	41	Laborer,	Ireland,	July 12
Revert, Joseph	27	Farmer,	Canada,	June 14

Penn.

Lighter, James H.	35	Farmer,	U.S.	July 10

MORRISON COUNTY.

Belle Prairie.

Bastian, Simon	34	Farmer,	Canada,	July 12
LaPoint, John B.	30	Farmer,	Canada,	July 12
Arnoudeau, Alex.	31	Laborer,	Canada,	June 16
Bastian, Baptiste	28	Laborer,	Canada,	June 16

STEARNS COUNTY.

St. Augusta.

Schumaker Engelbert	27	Farmer,	Germany,	June 19
Raeke, Nicholas	37	Farmer,	Germany,	Aug. 5
Letze, Laurus	30	Farmer,	Germany,	Aug. 5
Hanson, Hutter	52	Farmer,	Germany,	Aug. 5
Racery, Michael	47	Farmer,	Germany,	July 15
Brunsch, Henry	37	Farmer,	Germany,	July 15
Krier, J. B.	34	Farmer,	Germany,	July 15

St. Martin.

Barker, Joseph	41	Farmer,	Germany,	Aug. 5
Sanborn, G. N.	28	Farmer,	Germany,	June 17
Nett, Peter	25	Farmer,	Germany,	June 18
Unger, John	38	Farmer,	Germany,	June 15
Allberf, Peter	35	Farmer,	Germany,	July 5
Leonard, William	31	Farmer,	Germany,	July 7
Russell, Lyman	27	Farmer,	Germany,	July 13
Jaught, Wilhelm	35	Farmer,	Germany,	July 13
Leuster, Peter	35	Farmer,	Germany,	July 13

Munson.

Mohn, Mathew	43	Farmer,	Germany,	July 10
Wally, Adam	37	Farmer,	Germany,	Aug. 5
Senegrin, Valentine	34	Farmer,	Germany,	June 14
Even, Nicholas	30	Farmer,	Germany,	June 18
Rothstine, Christian	31	Farmer,	Germany,	June 14
Corty, John	35	Farmer,	Germany,	June 14
Rothstine, John	28	Farmer,	Germany,	Aug. 5
Halfifer, Ernst	24	Farmer,	Germany,	Aug. 6
Myer, John	24	Farmer,	Germany,	Aug. 6
Tometo, John	40	Farmer,	Germany,	Aug. 6

Rockville.

Bower, Peter	27	Farmer,	Germany,	July 15
Lesch, Nicholas	34	Farmer,	Germany,	July 15

Oak.

Schweiters, Bernard	35	Farmer,	Germany,	June 20
Ehlert, John	26	Farmer,	Germany,	June 20
Ulenkott, Herman	40	Farmer,	Germany,	July 15
Ulenkott, John	31	Farmer,	Germany,	July 15
Smetius, Joseph	36	Farmer,	Germany,	July 11
Molli, Joseph	24	Farmer,	Germany,	Aug. 8
Stelling, Gerhard	38	Farmer,	Germany,	Aug. 8
Hewing, Heinrich	41	Farmer,	Germany,	Aug. 8

St. Joseph.

Graham, Thomas	38	Farmer,	Ireland,	Aug. 9
Daniel, Ferdinand	39	Cabinetmaker,	Germany,	July 17
Graham, William	50	Farmer,	Ireland,	Aug. 9
Stanger, Christian	34	Farmer,	Germany,	Aug. 9
Flading, Valentine	41	Farmer,	Germany,	Aug. 9
Kohler, John	38	Blacksmith,	Germany,	Aug. 9
Flanders, Smith	31	Farmer,	Germany,	Aug. 9
Rotter, Frank	30	Farmer,	Germany,	Aug. 17
Theisen, Michael	28	Farmer,	Germany,	Aug. 17
Reimert, Michael	29	Laborer,	Germany,	Aug. 17
Reim, Mathew	40	Farmer,	Germany,	Aug. 17

Verdale.

Nilwinkl, Barnard	37	Farmer,	Germany,	June 18
Hilmer, William	38	Farmer,	Germany,	July 10

Brockway.

Hill, Edward	32	Miller,	U.S.	July 20

Wakefield.

Pick, Nicholas	27	Farmer,	Germany,	Aug. 13
Hennes, Asver	25	Farmer,	Germany,	July 13
Kent, Clement	34	Farmer,	Germany,	Aug. 13
Schnefels, Mathias	21	Farmer,	Germany,	July 14

LAKE COUNTY.

Rattle, James H.	36	Laborer,	U.S.	June 20
McLorens, John	33	Farmer,	Ireland,	Aug. 10
Wieland, Christian	41	Farmer,	Germany,	Aug. 10

CHISAGO COUNTY.

Rushseba.

Berkland, Annis	55	Farmer,	Sweden,	June 11

A REWARD OF THIRTY DOLLARS

Will be paid for the apprehension and delivery of any of the above named Deserters at these Headquarters, or at the Headquarters of any Provost Marshal, except for such as have failed to be notified or are discharged by this Board.

GEO. H. KEITH, *Pro. Mar. and Presl. of Board of Enrollment.*
J. A. THACHER, *Commissioner.*
J. D. WHEELOCK, *Surgeon.*

ST. PAUL PRESS PRINT.

PLATE 92

Plate 92. Newspaper broadside listing men who failed to report for the draft, 1864. Minnesota Historical Society.

Resistance to the Civil War was deepening in 1864, when this newspaper broadside named men who had failed to report for duty in the Union Army. The public was offered thirty dollars for helping to apprehend the listed draft resisters, who were all men without the economic means to hire a substitute. The broadside described the men who had chosen to ignore the call of their draft board by occupation and country of birth; this list shows the resisters to be largely immigrants and farmers, who were probably wary of abandoning a newly homesteaded plot to subject themselves to the miseries of the Union Army.

First instituted by the federal government in 1863, the draft met with deep resistance among many Americans who viewed a military draft as synonymous with European despotism. But the Union Army needed to fill ranks decimated by staggering battlefield casualties. Ever-increasing bounties, or fees paid to those willing to enlist, had failed to fill the federal quota for troops. In Minnesota, the draft went into effect in the spring of 1864, when there were 3,040 men in the state eligible for compulsory military service who did not receive some kind of exemption. Among these men, 272 furnished substitutes and 269 reported for duty (though two of them subsequently deserted). Another 2,497 simply ignored their draft notices.[127] Those who reported for service were mustered immediately after their physical examination, to prevent flight. New recruits were held under guard at Fort Snelling until they were shipped to distant battlefields.

While the reward announced by this broadside may have tempted some Minnesotans to remand neighbors or acquaintances to military authorities, this kind of action carried risks of its own, especially within the German and Irish immigrant communities. Some new arrivals were probably indifferent to the distant and perhaps incomprehensible war. But others harbored a deep aversion to military conscription, which they associated with European tyranny. The Irish in particular developed a reputation for "disloyalty." "For some time the air has been laded with rumors of organized opposition to this enrollment among our Irish population who reside in the lower part of this city," the *St. Paul Pioneer* asserted. "The enrolling officer had avoided this section as dangerous ground."[128] Rounding up unwilling recruits raised the specter of civil unrest in Minnesota, where General Henry Sibley reported that "there will be serious difficulty in some of the counties" in enforcing the draft. Military authorities responded to these concerns by assembling a military force that could be dispatched from Fort Snelling to quell any significant resistance.[129]

Plate 93. Advertisement for "Grand Pleasure Excursion to the Sioux Agency," *St. Paul Pioneer and Democrat*, June 11, 1861. Minnesota Historical Society.

St. Paul had long attracted visitors intent on seeing the "last" of the continent's "vanishing race" of Indians. After the land cession of 1851, however, these types of tourists had to travel beyond the most populous corner of the state to have these encounters. This ad from the *St. Paul Pioneer and Democrat* shows how steamboat operators capitalized on this interest in the region's indigenous inhabitants, turning the annuity payments on the Dakota reservation into a tourist attraction. In 1861 and probably in other years as well, steamboat companies offered an excursion to the Dakota reservation that proved alluring to new settlers as well as foreign tourists. The Thayer family, which had recently settled in Minneapolis, traveled to the reservation to view the Indians annuity payments in a group that included Governor Ramsey, a handful of British travelers, and the well-known abolitionist and writer Henry Thoreau.

When they arrived on the reservation, the St. Paul tour group pooled their money to purchase an ox to be roasted for the hungry Indians, who thanked them by performing a dance. "They were dressed in buckskin shirts, all were painted and wore feathers in their hair," Mary Thayer remembered later. "They began to dance very

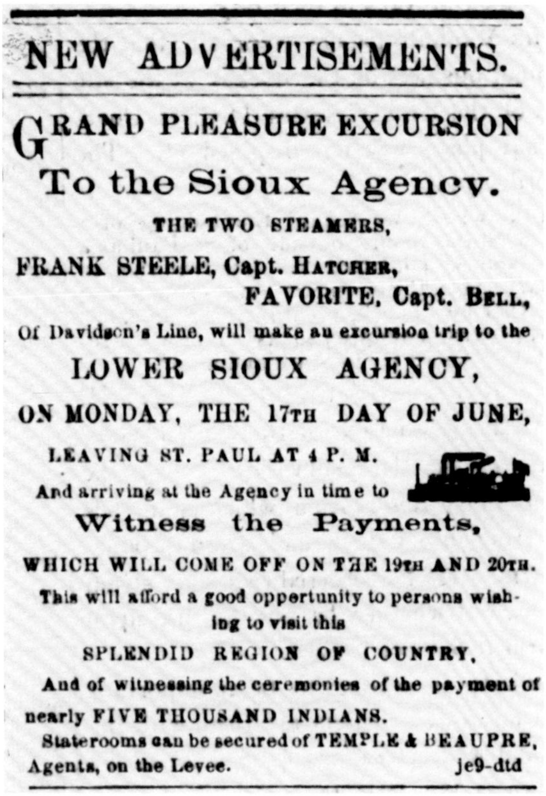

PLATE 93

slowly, moving arms and legs with the music, then faster and faster until they were all in a perfect frenzy, keeping time with the drums, around and around the circle. I have been thankful all my life that I saw that little bit of Indian life, which I never could have seen at any other time."[130]

The Thayers visited the Dakota reservation while one war already raged to the east and south of Minnesota. Like most white Minnesotans, they harbored no foreboding that a second front would open in their newly adopted state. The Thayers were similar to many other newcomers to the region, who had little or no personal experience with Indians and viewed the Dakota as exotic aboriginal curiosities with little relevance to the state's contemporary life. Mary Thayer — who wrote about the excursion as an adult — was a child when she visited the Lower Sioux Agency and perceived no menace in the scene, though she learned later that "the Indians were in a very ugly mood, also that there was great rascality on the part of the Indian agents."[131] Another observer was able to discern the dark rumblings on the reservation in 1861. Sarah Wakefield took up residence as the wife of the newly appointed doctor for the Indian reservation the same month that Thayer visited. The hunger and palpable anger she encountered were unsettling to Wakefield, who also watched the distribution of the annuity payments. She saw how the Indians were surrounded by traders "saying, you owe me so much for flour. Another says you owe me so much for sugar, &c. and the Indian gives it up, never knowing whether it is right or not . . . very seldom a man passes away with his money."[132] Wakefield ended up as a hostage during the U.S.–Dakota War that erupted the next year.

Plate 94. Adrian J. Ebell, Dakota Indians at Dr. Thomas Williamson's home near Yellow Medicine, 1862. Minnesota Historical Society.

This photograph shows a group of Dakota Indians leaving church services at the mission of Dr. Thomas S. Williamson, a Protestant missionary who had worked among the Dakota for close to thirty years. In the summer of 1862, Williamson was operating a Dakota church three miles from the Yellow Medicine Upper Sioux Agency on the Dakota reservation. This church served as the epicenter for a community of Christianized farmer Indians who had given up traditional dress and dwellings. This peaceful scene of Dr. Williamson, his wife Margaret Poage Williamson, and their congregants mingling after church was rendered tragic by its timing. It was recorded on August 17, only one day before the outbreak of the U.S.–Dakota War.

These last moments before the Dakota reservation was bloodied by war and the forced exile of its residents were documented by an almost accidental observer. The photographer was Adrian J. Ebell, a twenty-two-year-old Yale student following in the tradition of ethnographic artists like George Catlin. Ebell had come to Minnesota to document Indian life, accompanied by an assistant, Edwin R. Lawton, a student from the University of Chicago. The men had hoped to photograph the payment of annuities at the Dakota Agency and had been accompanied from St. Paul by two additional tourists: D. Wilson Moore and his wife, a newlywed couple from New Jersey who had

PLATE 94

come to witness the same scene. Their first stop on the reservation was the mission run by Dr. Thomas S. Williamson, where Ebell spent two quiet days chronicling life in the agricultural community before receiving news of the violence. After fleeing the fighting, Ebell ended up at the studio of St. Paul photographer and entrepreneur Joel E. Whitney, who had allowed him to purchase on credit a supply of photographic chemicals before he traveled to the Upper Sioux Agency. Whitney was quick to assist Ebell when he returned to St. Paul, arranging for the processing of his exposed glass plates. Whitney recognized the commercial potential of Ebell's images, and his gallery began peddling these images from the Dakota reservation, portraits of Indian leaders and other prints designed to exploit public fascination with the conflict. This particular image was sold as a carte de visite, a cardboard-mounted photograph that sometimes carried advertising messages on the reverse side.[133]

Plate 95. Adrian J. Ebell, Dakota women and children guarding corn from blackbirds, 1862. Minnesota Historical Society.

Unaware that Dakota warriors had begun to mount a full assault on the Lower Sioux Agency, photographer Adrian J. Ebell spent August 18, 1862, recording the routines of the Dakota agricultural community led by Dr. Thomas Williamson. In this image, Ebell shows women and children perched on a scaffold that allowed them to keep hungry birds from eating their almost-ripened corn. As autumn approached in 1862, everyone in the state was expecting a bumper crop.

Williamson, pictured on the far left side of this image, had pursued an aggressive acculturation program with the Dakota he could attract to his mission. The missionary held out Christianity and agriculture as the only hope for Indian survival, pushing the Dakota not only to plant crops and attend church but also to adopt white farming methods and white dress. A willingness to don trousers, shirts, and coats like the one worn by the little boy in the center of this photograph was seen as a mark of civilization. Whites put enormous importance on the methods Indians used to plant their crops, demanding that corn be cultivated in straight rows and in fields plowed by men rather than in mounds formed by women.[134] Dakota women had always planted corn as part of their subsistence strategy, even increasing their crops with the expansion of the fur trade to sell to traders and soldiers, who did little to produce their own food. But Williamson and other American observers like photographer Ebell were unsettled

PLATE 95

by this Indian division of labor, which accorded women responsibility for the crops. Ebell observed derisively that "we often find the inherent Indian chivalry illustrated in the male members of a family lounging with tomahawks and kinickinick pipes round the fence corners, or by the road-sides, basking in the sunlight, while the squaws are chopping wood, hoeing corn or potatoes, or taking care of the cattle."[135]

Ebell's photograph reveals that Williamson's assault on Dakota values had produced mixed results. Some Dakota had begun to devote more time to farming, but they were using familiar methods that had been passed down through generations of Indian women. In some ways, little had changed since Seth Eastman had recorded women and children protecting Dakota cornfields from predatory birds in the 1840s. The pressure to adopt white ways, however, had opened up new rifts among the Dakota themselves. Ebell observed that "it has been with the greatest difficulty that a few have been persuaded to adopt the dress and habits of the white man. The Indians look upon one of their number who cuts his hair, lays aside his blanket, changes his dress, and goes to work, as having sold his tribal birth-right."[136]

Plate 96. Adrian J. Ebell, People escaping from violence during the U.S.–Dakota War, 1862. Minnesota Historical Society.

This photograph of white refugees fleeing Indian violence is perhaps the most reprinted image from the U.S.–Dakota War. These forlorn-looking settlers, shown huddled together on the prairie of southwestern Minnesota, came to symbolize the travails of the victims of the 1862 violence. Despite the pathos of the photograph's subjects, this familiar image reveals little of the terror experienced by most of the southern Minnesota settlers driven from their homes during those August days. These refugees were cold, hungry, and frightened when photographer Adrian J. Ebell took this photograph. But their flight had been relatively smooth thanks to Dakota friends, who sent word to the missions at sundown on August 18 that nearby whites had been killed by Indians. Missionaries Stephen Riggs and Thomas Williamson took these warnings seriously, gathering their households for a flight to an island in the Minnesota River, where they intended to wait until the danger had passed. After one day, the refugees realized they had to continue traveling east to avoid starvation. Everyone in this party eventually arrived in Henderson unharmed, except for a trader named Orr, who joined them after he had been shot and stabbed. Their fate was very different from that of the German farmers who bore the brunt of the Dakota rage.[137]

The novelty of this image fascinated viewers, who found it both haunting and heart-rending. It serves as an early example of photojournalism, circulating in an era when viewers were accustomed to seeing staged studio portraits and newspapers filled exclusively with text. Photographer Adrian J. Ebell lugged his equipment out onto the Minnesota prairies intending to take pictures of the Dakota for his magic lantern exhibition. He was staying at the mission near the Dakota reservation when the decision to flee was made.[138] Undoubtedly unsettled by his transformation from tourist to refugee, Ebell defied established conventions with this photograph, which showed viewers a "snapshot" from his harrowing journey. By Thursday, August 21, the group had run out of food and decided to chance a rest; they killed an ox from their team and lit a fire that allowed them to dry their wet clothes, roast the meat, and bake bread on sticks over the open fire. This respite allowed Ebell to create this image.[139] The result was a scene with the power to transport viewers to that instant on the prairie, when none of these refugees knew whether they would reach safety. The photograph suspended the refugees at that moment in time, highlighting their fear and vulnerability.

Entrepreneur Joel Whitney was the one who ensured that Ebell's photograph would become an iconic image in Minnesota history. Before embarking on his journey to the Dakota reservation, Ebell had put in Whitney's care the projector for his magic lantern show and his five-octave melodeon, a type of small organ, which he left as collateral for $30 worth of photographic chemicals he got from Whitney on credit.[140] When Ebell reached the safety of St. Paul after his journey across the prairie, he proceeded directly to Whitney's studio where he processed his photographic plates. Whitney recognized the money-making potential of Ebell's work and began printing this photograph in mass quantities. Without crediting Ebell, Whitney affixed the photograph on the cartes de visite he sold to capitalize on the national appetite for pictures relating to the Indian war in Minnesota. The image also circulated widely on stereoscopic cards and postcards.

PLATE 96

PLATE 97

Plate 97. Adrian J. Ebell, Camp Release, 1862. Minnesota Historical Society.

Most of the white captives taken during the fighting of 1862 were freed on September 26 at Camp Release, where they had been gathered together by the Dakota opposed to continuing the war. This antiwar faction had contacted Henry Sibley to inform him of their desire to surrender and offered the white hostages as a sign of their good faith. When Sibley's motley troops entered the Dakota camp, they freed 250 white and mixed-race prisoners, mostly women and children. This moment marked the end of a painful chapter of the war and was seen by white observers as a resounding military and moral victory; one described it as the release of "helpless women and children . . . from the jaws of an earthly hell."[141] These triumphant accounts masked the complexities of the captives' experiences, which differed dramatically.

Photographer Adrian J. Ebell had arrived in the state as a tourist and was transformed first into a refugee and then into a newspaper correspondent by the outbreak of violence. From August to October he provided sustained reportage on the war for the *St. Paul Daily Press*. It was in this capacity that he was present for the emotional emancipation of the white prisoners by Sibley's soldiers. None of the drama described by Ebell is communicated by his photograph, which shows Sibley's soldiers lounging against the artillery, looking away from the camera at an unknown point in the distance. This calm camp scene conveys neither the jubilation nor the relief later remembered by hostages and soldiers alike.

Plate 98. "Indian outrages in the north-west, an American Family murdered by the Sioux Indians, in a grove near New Ulm, Minnesota," *Frank Leslie's Illustrated Newspaper,* **October 25, 1862, 65. Minnesota Historical Society.**

This engraving from *Frank Leslie's Illustrated Newspaper* shows how the national media portrayed the violence in Minnesota as an inexplicable eruption of barbaric sadism that marred an otherwise idyllic landscape. The *New York Times* reported on the violence less than a week after the first murders on the Dakota reservation.

PLATE 98

INDIAN OUTRAGES IN THE NORTH-WEST—AN AMERICAN FAMILY MURDERED BY THE SIOUX INDIANS, IN A GROVE NEAR NEW ULM, MINNESOTA.—FROM A SKETCH BY A CORRESPONDENT.

But "scenes of death and misery" from the still isolated state had to compete with news from the nation's other war for the nation's headlines.[142] Little Crow had not yet retreated west when the Battle of Antietam brought mind-boggling carnage that made September 17, 1862, the bloodiest day of the horrific civil war that divided the nation.

During the fall of 1862, publications like *Harper's Weekly* continued to follow the story from Minnesota's frontier, which fired the imagination of Americans fascinated by frontier violence. The first comprehensive account of the violence published for a national audience was written by Adrian J. Ebell, who had given up his role as war correspondent and returned east. In the last months of 1862 Ebell began transforming his first-person observations into a piece in *Harper's New Monthly Magazine*. "The Indian Massacres and the War of 1862" was published in June 1863, illustrated with a series of engravings by Albert Colgrave, who drew on Ebell's photographs as the basis for his images. Ebell's account was as lurid and sensational as it was detailed, setting the tone for the way the conflict was remembered by generations of white Americans. "I have given but the briefest outline of the late massacre in Minnesota, in which not less than a thousand men, women, and children were indiscriminately murdered and tortured to death, and barbarities of the most hellish magnitude committed," Ebell wrote in his *Harper's* article. "Massacre itself had been mercy if it could have purchased exemption from the revolting circumstances with which it was accompanied; the torture of unborn infants torn from their bleeding mothers, and cast upon their breast; rape and violence of even young girls till death closed the horrid scene of suffering and shame."[143]

Plate 99. "The Attack at New Ulm," *Harper's New Monthly Magazine*, June 1863, 23. Minnesota Historical Society.

The mood of white Minnesotans in the aftermath of the U.S.–Dakota War was powerfully conveyed by this Harper's engraving that illustrated Adrian J. Ebell's first-person narrative of the war. Albert Colgrave's drawing immortalized the murderous fury of New Ulm women who attacked the Dakota men condemned to die for their role in the violence.

THE ATTACK AT NEW ULM.

PLATE 99

After the release of white captives in September 1862, Camp Release was turned into a Dakota prison camp, where a few warriors were tried in a hastily convened military tribunal. The entire entourage was then moved to a site near the former Lower Sioux Agency on the Dakota reservation, where the remaining prisoners were examined and sentenced. Henry Sibley had assured the Indians that only those who had committed murder would be punished. In private, however, he asserted that most of the men were "deeply implicated in the late outrages."[144] The military tribunal agreed with Sibley's assessment and condemned 303 Dakota men to die for their role in the war. These doomed prisoners were chained to wagons, which were then rolled around New Ulm en route to another camp west of Mankato.

Although the prisoners were flanked by mounted soldiers, they were assaulted by German women whom Sibley described as "Dutch she devils." The crowd "showered brickbats and missiles upon the shackled wretches, seriously injuring some fifteen of the latter, and some of the guards." Wielding rocks, butcher knives, pitchforks, clubs, axes, hatchets, pots of scalding water, bricks, table knives, and scissors, they attacked the prisoners, fatally injuring two of the men. These citizens of New Ulm — who had been in the process of reburying their town's dead when the prisoners arrived — had to be driven back from the wagons with a bayonet charge. None of the participants in this mob murder were punished in any meaningful way.[145]

The remaining Dakota from Camp Release — who were deemed innocent of any crimes — were marched in a separate caravan to Fort Snelling. This group of elderly men, women, and children was attacked at Henderson where "men, women, and children, armed with guns, knives, clubs, and stones, rushed upon the Indians as the train was passing by . . . pulling many of the old men and women, and even children from the wagons by the hair of the head and beating them," according to Samuel Brown, the son of the former Indian agent Joseph Brown who was accompanying the marchers. "I saw an enraged white woman rush up to one of the wagons and snatch a nursing babe from its mother's breast and dash it violently upon the ground." The child died a few hours later. Those who survived this trek spent the winter in an internment camp located on the flats below Fort Snelling.[146]

provisions, if at all. The Indians regarded such behavior as shameful, while the settlers decried Indian "begging" as evidence of their inferior character.[32]

American homesteaders had difficulty enough in traversing this unfamiliar cultural terrain. But the problems were compounded for European immigrants, who could converse easily with neither old settlers nor Indians. By 1855 the lure of cheap land in Minnesota had made it a prime destination for trans-Atlantic immigrants, especially those from German-speaking countries.[33] Germans inundated the territory in the 1850s, which marked the peak of German immigration to the United States and coincided with Minnesota's land boom. By 1860 the census counted 18,400 German-born Minnesotans, the largest group of foreign-born residents and fully 10 percent of the young state's population. Hundreds of merchants, artisans, and farmers established themselves in and around St. Paul, adding a new element to the city's cultural diversity. Thousands more flocked to the rich farmland along the Mississippi and especially in the Minnesota River valley, pushing up against the Dakota reservations. Wherever they settled, they tended to establish insular, German-speaking communities. With neither the mentors nor the desire to learn the Dakota language or understand Indian customs, they regarded Native people with deep suspicion.[34]

The Dakotas, on their part, came to have a special antipathy toward their German neighbors, who crowded their hunting and trapping grounds and rejected customary rituals of reciprocity. Though they traded with German storekeepers and farmers, the Indians were certain that the "Dutchmen," whom they called *iasíca*—"bad speakers"—were cheating them. The Germans seemed at least as alien to the Indians as the Indians did to the immigrants. Without the cultural vocabulary to create kinship bonds that had mediated coexistence between whites and Indians in the past, Germans and Dakotas were hopelessly at odds, each group resenting the other's presence. With German homesteads cropping up like weeds on their hunting grounds, as historian Gary Clayton Anderson observes, the Dakotas came to see the Germans as "noticeable symbols of the harm that farming in general was doing to the Sioux." Indeed, the derogatory term *iasíca* soon developed a generic meaning to include all farmers, of whatever ethnicity.[35]

Tensions also began to surface among the Dakotas themselves. In the heightened climate of hostility, a small but growing number of Indians, led by some of the old chiefs, began to accept as inevitable the need to conform to the white man's ways. They donned European-style clothing, cut their hair, took up farming, and, at least nominally, accepted Christianity. Traditionalists, most of them young braves, abhorred what they saw as the surrender of the farmer Indians and the weak-kneed counsel of the old chiefs. They began forming soldiers lodges to challenge the authority of the older generation. Traditionally the soldiers lodge had served as a sort of tribal police, whose role was to enforce collective decisions arrived at in council, but in this permutation it became an oppositional faction. The young warriors also viewed mixed-blood relatives with new suspicion as agents of the hated accommodationism. This intratribal cultural conflict eroded traditional structures of authority and community coherence.[36]

The Inkpaduta incident appreciably exacerbated all these multiple fractures in Minnesota's already crumbling multicultural landscape. Although Inkpaduta was not seen again in Minnesota after he rode off to the plains, his name took on a mythic significance for both whites and Indians. Among terrified whites, he was a symbol of Native savagery and frequently reported to be behind rumored "Indian uprisings" in the making. Indians, who often claimed the elusive chief had reappeared, read his presence quite differently. To many Dakotas, especially young braves, Inkpaduta represented courageous resistance to white domination, an Indian victory in a sea of defeats. As the years passed and tensions spiraled into armed conflict, Inkpaduta's legendary invulnerability grew. He eluded capture, roaming for decades with his band between Dakota Territory and Canada. Some even claimed he participated in the Battle of Little Big Horn in 1876, nearly twenty years after his bloody debut in Iowa. In 1879, Charles Flandrau wrote Inkpaduta's epitaph in an address to the Minnesota Historical Society: "Ink-pa-du-ta is dead, and I am sorry to say, died a natural death, honored by his people as one of the best haters of the whites in the whole Sioux nation."[37]

"More Land Than Required"

By 1856 farmers and speculators were already gazing at the Dakotas' reservation with covetous eyes. The land boom was at its height, statehood was on the horizon, and the Minnesota River valley was prime acreage for producing real estate fortunes as well as wheat or corn. In Washington, Representative Henry Rice was laying the groundwork to reduce the size of the reservations well before the first shot was fired at Lake Okoboji. The Inkpaduta scare serendipitously moved the project forward. "Indian experts" in Minnesota, including Henry Sibley, Joe Brown, Charles Flandrau, and the remaining missionaries, all were convinced that the only way to "contain" and civilize the Indians was to turn them into farmers. By reducing the size of the reservations and dividing them into individual allotments, Indians would simply be unable to sustain their traditional lifestyle. By necessity, then, the feckless hunters would turn into thrifty agriculturalists who would have no reason to roam beyond reservation borders. By 1858, with Minnesotans angrily crying for protection, the Office of Indian Affairs was ready to accede to their demands.[38]

The farming plan seemed to have some potential, particularly after Joe Brown took over as Dakota agent in October 1857. For more than a year before his appointment he had been vociferously campaigning for Indian policy reform. The history of the Office of Indian Affairs in Minnesota was a scandal, riddled with incompetence and fraud. Lawrence Taliaferro, Minnesota's first Indian agent, was also the last to have served with intelligence and honor in the position. Brown was disgusted by the string of agents and superintendents who held their positions by virtue of political connections rather than experience with Indian customs and lifeways—men who did not know "the differences between the habits, manners, customs, and peculiarities of a Sioux Indian and a snapping turtle." Brown, it went without saying, was, at least in his estimation, a far better man for the job. Apparently even many of his political enemies agreed. "From his long experience with Indian habits and customs, and his close acquaintance with the Sioux for many years," wrote Republican journalist John Phillips Owens, Brown was "perhaps the best calculated to do good among them of any agent they had ever had." Historians concur that Brown "possessed a knowledge of the Dakota tribes not surpassed by that of any other man of the time." Immediately upon taking office, with his trademark energy and creativity, he began putting an ambitious "civilization" plan into action.[39]

The idea was certainly not a new one. In the 1820s and 1830s Taliaferro had labored mightily to transform Indian hunters into farmers, and in all the years thereafter, missionaries, Indian agents, politicians, and treaty stipulations had joined to nudge them down an agricultural path. But before 1857, the success of the endeavor had been meager. Missionary Stephen Riggs had gathered about two dozen Christian Indians and mixed bloods at Hazelwood, near the Upper Agency, where they adopted white dress, took up farming, and formed a "republic," declaring themselves a separate, civilized band. A few other Dakotas had begun farming as well, but as long as conditions made it possible, the vast majority of the tribe held fast to their traditional way of life. By 1857, however, with settlers gobbling up their hunting grounds and white antagonism ascendant, even once formidable chiefs like Wabasha, Wakute, and Mankato were coming to believe that survival might require their people to adopt the white man's ways.[40]

Thus, changed circumstances greatly aided Brown in implementing his plan of action. He went to work with a will and within a year had built an impressive record of improvements on the reservation. Using his renowned powers of persuasion, Agent Brown convinced the government to release large sums of money for a massive development project—funds owed from earlier treaties that had been withheld from the Dakotas for years. Brown intended to pay Indians in hard cash for their labor, the money drawn from the agricultural and education funds (ignoring the fact that the funds already belonged collectively to the tribe). Unlike the agents before him, he recognized that modern Indians understood as well as any white man that purchasing power was the key to independence. In the past they had relied on furs to barter for manufactured goods and foodstuffs, but animals were increasingly hard to find, even for the most skilled hunters. The Indians were perennially in debt to their traders and they chafed at their dependence on annuities, which were often late or reduced for various "misbehaviors." Thus, when Brown offered cash payment for farm and construction labor, he was able to persuade a number of men to give it a try.[41]

Joseph R. Brown was no selfless philanthropist. Indeed, personal profit drove every undertaking in his checkered career. His tenure as Indian agent was no exception. He peppered the Office of Indian Affairs with an astonishing number of reimbursement claims for himself and his family and managed to do a bit of trading on the side as well. Out of the profits that he accrued, "Joe the Juggler," as he was nicknamed, eventually built a lavish home for himself at Patterson's Rapids, near the Lower Agency, complete with Persian rugs, imported crystal chandeliers, and a cascading fountain, at a time when Minnesota was only painfully emerging from economic collapse. But, all this aside, he also genuinely believed that his plan would benefit the Indians and enable them to coexist in peace with their neighbors. Kin to the Sissetons by marriage and father to eleven mixed-blood children, he had no animus toward the Dakotas. In his words, "I accepted the office under a fierce conviction, arrived at through a thorough knowledge of the Sioux character, gained by a residence among them and close connection with them for over thirty years, that a proper system, properly carried out, would lead to the civilization of the 'wild and untamable Dakotas.'" In his agile mind, personal profit and benefit to the Indians fit neatly together. Even missionary Thomas Williamson, who generally disapproved of Brown's character, believed that "his sympathies are such that his feelings will incite him to labor for [the Indians'] welfare."[42]

In his first months as agent, Brown made a good beginning, but from the outset he was convinced that communal ownership of Indian land must be replaced by ownership in severalty, which would provide each Indian with an incentive to "improve" his individual homestead. Moreover, the revised treaties of 1851 did not grant the Dakotas permanent right to their lands; rather, they held them "at the president's pleasure" and could be displaced at any time. By 1858 sentiment in Minnesota made removal a real possibility. A judicious land cession, Brown reasoned, would implement and fund his allotment scheme, ensure the Indians legal title to the reserve, which would protect them from arbitrary removal, and coincidentally free up nearly a million acres of prime farmland for investors, including the wily agent himself. Thus, Brown became a key advocate for a new treaty—one that would reduce the Dakota reservations by half, opening all the land northeast of the Minnesota River to settlement.[43]

The Indians were not consulted about their preferences and were outgunned from the outset. Despite Brown's optimism, farmer Indians at this time represented only a small fraction of the Dakota population. Yet, though hunting remained the predominant way of life, Superintendent Cullen confidently informed his superiors in Washington that the Indians had far more land than they needed. Brown and now Minnesota Supreme Court Justice Flandrau strongly concurred—and were already making plans to invest in the rich Minnesota River bottoms the treaty would make available. Other eager speculators also drummed up support for a new treaty. As might be expected, the traders who made their living off Dakota annuities also enthusiastically supported the proposal. As with every past treaty, they expected to profit handsomely, wiping old Indian debts from their books, the totals no doubt padded by some creative accounting. The general public overwhelmingly favored removing the Indians as far from them as possible, and politicians insisted that the treaty was

[275]

Joseph Brown, photographed by Hirsch Brothers around 1853. Courtesy of the Minnesota Historical Society.

absolutely necessary to put an end to allegedly rampant "murders and depredations." Though, in the midst of a disastrous economic depression immigration had come to a halt and land sales were at a near standstill, treaty proponents insisted that, with Minnesota on the verge of statehood, an immediate land cession was urgently needed.[44]

[276]

The problem, of course, was to win Dakota compliance. Clearly, if the negotiations were held locally, an uproar of opposition could be expected. Former agent Flandrau advised Superintendent Cullen to invite a group of the old chiefs to Washington, where they would be "relieved from the influence of their young men" in treaty negotiations. Thus, the plan was hatched to proffer "invitations" to a hand-selected group to "visit" with the president in Washington, where the grandeur of the city would remind the visitors of the government's might. Everyone involved agreed that the well-respected Little Crow, whom whites regarded as a reasonable man, must be a key member of the party.[45]

As Cullen and Brown set about selecting the delegation to represent the bands in Washington, they made no mention of land cession. Instead, they led the Indians to believe that the president wished to "readjust the treaty" to their benefit. The reservation was awash in troubling rumors of forced removal, and the chiefs and headmen were anxious for their "Father in Washington" to confirm their rights to the land. They also saw the trip as an opportunity to reiterate their wish to live in peace with the whites, remind the government of unfulfilled treaty promises, and present a litany of complaints regarding white encroachment on reservation land and abuses of their people. Little Crow especially, made confident by Cullen's praise and appreciation for his assistance during the "Inkpaduta War," carefully compiled a list of unpaid debts and grievances, fully expecting a grateful government to redress the wrongs done to his people. The chiefs were so optimistic that they even agreed to pay their own way to Washington.[46]

Once in the capital city, however, the delegation learned to its dismay that Commissioner of Indian Affairs Charles Mix had no interest in hearing any dissatisfactions they might present. At first, the Indians were treated as foreign dignitaries and Little Crow solemnly informed the commissioner that he had come a great distance and intended, "while in your village, to walk your streets as a proud man." The delegation was feted at a series of receptions, introduced to the cream of Washington society, and squired about the city to see its wonders, including the U.S. Arsenal. But then, once the Indians seemed suitably impressed, Mix got down to business, informing the unsuspecting chiefs and headmen that he wished them to sign away half their remaining lands.[47]

The commissioner, in a strategy of divide and conquer, met separately with the lower and upper reservation bands. Little Crow, as spokesman for the Mdewakantons and Wahpekutes of the Lower Sioux Agency, presented a meticulous accounting of payments still due from the 1837 and 1851 treaties, as well as complaints about misappropriation of funds, settlers who squatted on reservation lands, and abuses of Indian women. To the chief's chagrin, Mix waved these issues aside, wanting only to discuss yet another land cession. When Little Crow persisted, Mix chided him for "talking like a child." He informed the startled Indians that they had no legal right to any of their land, which they occupied only "by the courtesy of their Great Father." When Little Crow protested that "you . . . promised us that we should have this same land forever," Mix whipped out a copy of the amended 1851 treaty, pointing to the pertinent provision, written, of course, in English. A new treaty, he promised, would give the Dakotas permanent right to their remaining lands southwest of the Minnesota River, allotted individually in eighty-acre "farmsteads." In addition, their Father, in his beneficence, would pay them for the ceded land (which, he reminded them, they did not *really* own). If they did not agree, he then threatened, the new state of Minnesota could legally claim the entire reservation, leaving the Indians nothing.[48]

It was painfully clear to Little Crow and his fellow delegates that they had been backed into a corner. Confounded by maps and documents they could not read and facing the alternative of eviction, the delegation had no choice but to surrender. "You gave us a paper," Little Crow sadly admitted to Mix, "and we had it explained, and from that it would seem that the Sioux Indians own nothing! . . . When I saw that paper it made me ashamed. We had, we supposed, made a complete treaty, and we were promised a great many things, horses, cattle, flour, plows, and farming utensils, but now it appears the wind blows it all off and that we got good words and nothing else." Their only small consolation was that payment from this coerced treaty would allow them to clear their debts with the traders and buy provisions that would be needed more than ever on the small strip of land that was left to them.[49]

A similar scenario followed in negotiations with the Sissetons and Wahpetons of the Upper Agency. They put up less resistance, partly because a number of their delegates were farmer Indians, amenable to individual allotments. (Conveniently, the chiefs who would have been most opposed to the treaty had been off on a buffalo hunt when the delegation had been selected.) Still, Shoots-Iron-as-He-Walks protested that they had not yet been paid what was owed them from 1851. Furthermore, he noted, the new treaty would deprive his people of their best timber and allow whiskey sellers close proximity to their villages. Iron Walker also eloquently spoke out for fair treatment, declaring, "We call ourselves American citizens and feel that we are a portion of the American People." Nonetheless, most Sissetons and Wahpetons were buffalo hunters who spent a good part of the year on the western plains, and the reduced reservation would affect them less acutely than those at the Lower Agency. And farmers and hunters alike were anxious to settle their debts with the traders, who remained an essential lifeline for all the bands.[50]

Joe Brown must have been pleased, as everything so far seemed to be going according to plan. However, he had also expected the Indians to profit substantially from the "land sale." Overestimating his influence, he anticipated a sum that, after paying the traders, would still leave plenty to help the Indians transition from hunters to farmers and fund improvements on the reservations. But the Indians, with no negotiating leverage, were bullied into signing treaties with no price set per acre, forced to rely on Mix's word that the Senate would determine a just amount when the agreements were ratified. Agent Brown confidently predicted that they should expect close to $1 million. Anticipating this grand sum, the tribal delegates willingly stipulated that debts to the traders should be subtracted from the payment.[51]

The promises of 1858 proved no more durable than those of earlier treaties, and nearly a year passed before Congress bothered to take up the issue of payment. In his report to the Senate in 1859, an agitated Brown pressed legislators to act, urging fair treatment for "a deeply wronged portion of the human family." He described the ceded land as "some of the best in Minnesota," with twice as much timber as the remaining reservation. Though he reckoned the land was worth at least $5 an acre, given the current lack of buyers in Minnesota he proposed $1 per acre as a fair price—a total of $889,600. This fund, he promised, would provide nearly every Dakota family "a comfortable house within two years and would put them beyond future want." The Committee on Indian Affairs accepted Brown's appraisal as a reasonable valuation, but by the time the bill reached the full Senate, the purchase price had been reduced to a mere thirty cents per acre. Two more years would pass before any monies were appropriated, and when the time for reckoning finally came, Cullen allowed the traders to add debts run up after the treaty to the claims they submitted. In the end, from the pittance of $267,000 the government paid for more than nearly 900,000 acres of prime farmland, the Dakota people received almost nothing.[52]

When news of the land cession reached Minnesota, citizens were jubilant. The *Mankato Independent* pronounced with satisfaction that the chiefs had received "a wholesome impression of the resources and power of the government." Clearly, white mastery had been reaffirmed and the Indians, literally, put in their place. At the Upper and Lower agencies, however, the returning delegation faced a furor of indignation. The chiefs quickly shed the top hats, frock coats, and medals that had been presented to them and tried to calm the people with assurances of a lavish payment for the ceded lands. Still, resentment ran high and young men of the soldiers lodges even talked of assassinating those who had sold half of what remained of their birthright. As the seasons turned with no sign of the promised payment, scorn for the treaty signators, especially Little Crow, greatly diminished their influence in the bands' councils.[53]

Still, with reluctance many Dakotas realized that there was now no going back. In only a matter of months several thousand settlers had moved onto former reservation lands, though Congress had not yet acted on the treaty. The Indians futilely protested as settlers cut the timber and plowed the prairies that had been their hunting grounds. Out of necessity, month by month the ranks of the "Improvement Sioux" began to swell. Brown energetically steamrolled on with his acculturation program, allocating eighty acres to each apprentice farmer, building houses, distributing livestock, and opening schools. "Houses literally sprang up all over the lower reservation," built in large part by Indian labor. Within a year the acreage under cultivation had nearly doubled, yielding bountiful crops of corn and potatoes. The canny agent also rewarded the farmer Indians with gifts of clothing and extra provisions as marks of appreciation and kinship. Those who continued to rely on hunting received nothing but their annuity payment, which amounted to only about $10 per person. By the following year Brown reported that some 700 Dakota men, women, and children, including many of the old chiefs, were living on small family farms not much different from those of the settlers across the river.[54]

[279]

Brown confidently predicted that if he could secure enough livestock and farm equipment, he would soon have another 500 farmers. Superintendent Cullen declared the experiment "an assured success." However, this path of forced acculturation was driving deep rifts within the tribe. Anger was widespread among the traditionalists, disparagingly called "blanket Indians," who were insulted and aggrieved by the agent's discrimination against them. They frequently vented their resentment of the white squatters by killing their farm animals and increasingly tried to intimidate and shame farmer Indians as well. Cullen deducted reparation payments for (sometimes fictive) depredations from the general annuity fund, thus punishing the entire tribe—which only increased tension between the factions. For all his understanding of Dakota ways, as historian Mark Diedrich observes, Brown "saw Dakota culture only as an obstacle to civilization" and was bent on its eradication to "save" the Indians. He seems not to have realized that the more successful he was in breaking up traditional structures, the closer he brought the tribe to social anarchy.[55]

Even among the farmer Indians, only a few who had forged close ties with the missionaries, like Paul Mazakootemane, wholeheartedly discarded their inherited identity. Mazakootemane insisted, "I now considered myself a white man," but even this declaration may have been inspired, at least in part, by the demands of self-preservation. More typical was Mdewakanton chief Big Eagle. Though he joined the farmer band at the Redwood Agency in 1858 and conformed to the norms of dress and behavior that were required of him there, in an interview forty years later the longing for his vanished world was painfully evident:

> The whites were always trying to make the Indians give up their life and live like white men—go to farming, work hard and do as they did—and the Indians did not know how to do that, and did not want to anyway. It seemed too sudden to make such a change. If the Indians had tried to make the whites live like them the whites would have resisted, and it was the same with many Indians. The Indians wanted to

live as they did before the treaty of Traverse des Sioux—go where they pleased and when they pleased; hunt game wherever they could find it, sell their furs to the traders and live as they could.[56]

While some, like Big Eagle, tried to make the best of what they could not change, the pressure to acculturate stiffened resistance among others, especially young men who had not yet been schooled in the limits of possibility. Former missionary Samuel Pond, who had been a serious student of Dakota lifeways, considered that "what was done for them . . . was badly planned and badly executed, and none would wonder that it was a failure and worse than a failure." Indeed, despite statistics that suggested success, acculturation, as implemented by Brown and Cullen, was inherently flawed. Not only were the incentives fundamentally coercive, but the officials followed policies riddled with contradiction. On the one hand, they preached individualism and personal accountability and did all they could to dismantle the collectivism that was central to Dakota culture, eviscerating the traditional authority of the chiefs in the process. On the other, they held the tribe collectively accountable for debts and depredations. The Indians, both farmers and traditionalists, recognized that, whatever their lifestyle, they were held to a different set of rules than the whites they were urged to emulate. Recalling the injustice, Big Eagle observed:

> The Indians had to pay a very large sum of money to the traders for old debts, some of which ran back fifteen years, and many of those who had got the goods were dead and others were not present, and the traders' books had to be received as to the amounts, and the money was taken from the tribe to pay them.[57]

The Dakotas, whether farmers or traditionalists, were a proud people. While officials and politicians applauded the measures "so salutary and beneficial for the future of these savages," multiple injuries, both old and new, kept resentment bubbling beneath the surface of daily life on the reservations. Pressure was building to what would be a tragic explosion.[58]

The Call to War

In the years between 1858 and 1861, as the nation calamitously marched down the road to war, most Minnesotans paid little heed to events on the national stage. Their attention was fully absorbed by local dramas. The railroad debacle, economic collapse, and Indian tensions presented turmoil enough to fill their thoughts. Even the presidential election of 1860 turned primarily on local rather than national concerns. A Republican tide handily won the state for Abraham Lincoln, but the slavery question, though invoked in political stump speeches, was not what propelled Minnesotans into the Republican fold. Rather, it was the issue of federal land policy, which would deeply affect Minnesota's future, that engaged voters' attention. Republicans swept the state elections as well, thanks to widespread indignation at the mismanagement of Minnesota's finances. Both parties had a hand in bankrupting the state, but as the party in power, Governor Henry Sibley and Democratic legislators took the blame. Sibley wisely did not run for reelection and his fellow Democrats took a sound drubbing.[59]

But despite the electorate's single-minded interest in local issues, a handful of ambitious entrepreneurs of both parties had kept a close eye on the currents of national politics. Making the most of political connections, men like Red River agent Norman Kittson, steamboat mogul William Davidson, overland transportation tycoon James Burbank, timber speculator/milling industrialist William Washburn, and politician Henry Rice prospered. While nearly everyone around them was drowning in financial disaster, their fortunes continued to grow. Kittson "enjoyed a government-sponsored monopoly" as supply agent for the Hudson's Bay Company, while the others profited from government contracts for surveying, transportation, mail delivery, and provisioning the Indians. With the profits, they picked up foreclosed land and businesses at rock bottom prices, enriching themselves further. By 1861 those Minnesota entrepreneurs who had weathered the storm were optimistic about returning prosperity and deep into schemes designed to bring wealth to themselves and the region. Henry Rice confidentially observed to Franklin Steele, "One thing I do see is that *all* of the Old settlers in Minnesota are *ruined* hopelessly. I fear Hard times have only just commenced, and yet the people are all crazy." Even at that moment Rice's brother Edmund was in Philadelphia courting investors "for what I don't know."[60]

Hard times notwithstanding, both the state and would-be land barons, often hand in hand, energetically continued to promote immigration as a way out of the economic doldrums. Touting Minnesota's healthful climate and rich soil, the state hired immigration agents, published promotional pamphlets in both English and German, and even established an immigrant aid bureau in New York to capture arriving Europeans. Private individuals also poured energy and money into attracting new homesteaders and, besides promoting their own holdings, encouraged settlement on Dakota lands even before they were ceded in 1858. Politician-cum-town site promoter Ignatius Donnelly, who was elected lieutenant governor in 1859, sagely advised potential settlers on the fine points of squatter rights. As far back as 1857 in his *Emigrant Aid Journal,* he was assuring homesteaders that the government would honor claims staked on reservation lands. "In Minnesota," Donnelly wrote, "there are very populous towns that have been built on some of these reservations, as they are called, and the districts around have been thickly settled, long before any title, save that of the squatter's can be had for the land." In the aftermath of unwelcome publicity surrounding the "Spirit Lake massacre"—and despite locally held fears—newspapers throughout the state took pains to assure prospective settlers that "everything was safe in Minnesota." Jane Grey Swisshelm's *St. Cloud*

Democrat addressed a national audience in 1861: "We beg to assure our Eastern friends once again that there is not the slightest danger to the people of Minnesota from Indians." At the same time she carried on a continuous tirade against the government for failing to protect families from the "starving, thieving savages" who "rob and maltreat the frontier settlements."[61]

[282]

Intent on painting a glowing portrait of Minnesota's opportunities, promoters chose their facts selectively. They failed to mention the destitute condition of most of the state's farmers, still living a hand-to-mouth existence. Nor did they mention that there were "no funds in the treasury and no credit in the state" or that commerce was at a near standstill. Their disingenuous strategy succeeded. By 1860 immigration was picking up; the state's population topped 170,000; nearly 5.5 million bushels of wheat were harvested; and for the first time Minnesota could announce a measurable surplus trade in timber and agricultural products at an estimated value of nearly $4 million.[62]

Just when things were looking up, war was declared, and suddenly Minnesotans riveted their attention on the state of the Union—at least in the towns and cities, where an unprecedented fervor of patriotic nationalism immediately erupted. Ebullient townsmen, in the flush of returning prosperity, rushed to fulfill Governor Ramsey's promise of troops. But the wave of enthusiasm for the war rose from a complicated mix of patriotism, romanticism, and local self-interest. Local elites, like the governor, immediately envisioned a new market for Minnesota goods and services in soon-to-be-let government contracts for provisioning the Union army. Other prominent citizens and ambitious young men leaped at the chance to add a military title to their names, a valued symbol of stature in nineteenth-century America. Ordinary American-born citizens in river towns up and down the Mississippi—Winona, Red Wing, Wabasha, Hastings, Stillwater, and St. Cloud, as well as St. Paul, St. Anthony, and Minneapolis—also quickly embraced the cause. Most were relative newcomers to Minnesota. The war effort brought to mind the patriotic traditions of their hometowns in the East and seemed to bring rough-hewn Minnesota closer to the Yankee ideal on which they sought to model their communities. The ladies responded with special enthusiasm, stepping into the public sphere with patriotic vigor, a role they knew well from their previous lives. Visions of martial glory and adventure danced in young men's heads and girls swooned at the idea of their beaus in uniform. Only a few committed abolitionists took up arms in hopes of ending slavery. In fact, most common soldiers went to war with only vague notions of the issues at stake. Still, they flocked to sign up at festive enlistment rallies, replete with brass bands, high-toned speeches, and cheering citizens. Governor Ramsey, charged by President Lincoln to provide one regiment of 760 men, had to turn more than 500 additional volunteers away. Their services, he informed them, were not needed.[63]

Such enthusiasm would quickly wane as the war dragged on and accounts of battlefield carnage made their way home. But even in the first flush of excitement, what appeared to be wholehearted patriotism derived from complex, primarily local aspirations. First, it must be noted, Lincoln initially called for a mere three-month commitment, and many thought the rebellion would be put down in a matter of weeks rather than months.[64] Historian Richard Moe even proposes that Ramsey may have calculated that the war would be over before troops would be called from far-off Minnesota. Thus, "he could have the distinction of being the first governor to tender troops without actually having to provide them." When, in Ramsey's absence, Lieutenant Governor Ignatius Donnelly issued the call for volunteers, he optimistically stated that enlistments would last three months "unless sooner discharged."[65]

[283]

Despite the short-term commitment, the desire to enlist was far from universal across the state. Of Minnesota's eight organized militia companies, only the St. Paul, St. Anthony, and Stillwater organizations agreed to activate their units for federal service. The rest had been organized in the western counties after the Inkpaduta scare. Settlers there were only just beginning to see faint hints of returning prosperity and militiamen were loath to abandon their farms and businesses even for a few months' time. Moreover, they had joined up to protect their families from Indian attacks, not to fight a distant war hundreds of miles from home.[66]

The city militias were of a different sort. Primarily social and fraternal in character, their ranks were filled with young clerks, professionals, and tradesmen. Almost none of the members had any military training and many did not even own a gun. Still, most of them eagerly volunteered to serve, viewing the romantic allure of military adventure as a welcome antidote to the humdrum routine of ordinary life. Other starry-eyed youths with dreams of battlefield glory quickly vied to fill out newly organized companies. The teenaged teacher of a one-room school outside Minneapolis was so enthusiastic that he shut down the school and immediately set off for Fort Snelling to enlist, along with half his teenage students. In Red Wing, students and professors at Hamline University, the state's foremost institution of higher learning, constituted fully one-fifth of Goodhue County's first company, "pledging their lives, their fortunes and their sacred honor in upholding the stars and stripes against the rebellious assaults now made upon them." And in Minneapolis the St. Charles Hotel temporarily had to close its doors because most of its employees had enlisted.[67]

Numerous farmers signed up as well, though often for more pragmatic reasons. A soldier's monthly pay of $13, though meager, might keep their hard-pressed families afloat. As an added incentive, many communities pledged to provide for local soldiers' families while they were away—a promise that fell by the wayside as the expected brief sojourn stretched into years. Farmers' sons also enthusiastically answered the call, more than happy to trade in dull, backbreaking farm chores for martial adventures in distant places.[68]

Other groups saw the war as an opportunity to claim their American identity. German Minnesotans enlisted in substantial numbers, usually forming exclusively German American companies. At a mass meeting in St. Paul, German volunteers pledged that "the Germanborn citizens of St. Paul, will, till our last breath, remain true to our oaths, and will support the Constitution of the United States." They were joined by ninety German townsmen from New Ulm, who traveled by river to join the company. But given conditions in the countryside, most of the German farmers who enlisted probably were persuaded as least as much by the same financial burdens that plagued their American-born counterparts as by patriotic impulses.[69]

The Irish were noticeably less enthusiastic. Up-and-coming Irishmen signed on with alacrity, seeing military service as a way to secure their place in the American mainstream. But most of Minnesota's Irish were low-paid wage-workers and disinclined to fight in what they called "a rich man's war." As the war dragged on and the draft was instituted, apathy would turn into downright hostility, especially in St. Paul. Enrolling officers avoided the Irish enclaves as "dangerous ground." When they did enter the city's Irish ward of "New Dublin" to register men for the draft, they were flanked by a military escort to quell expected resistance. Even so, according to one of the soldiers, "Some of the pady [sic] women ducked Some of the enrolling officers in dishwater which gave their clothes a verry nice polish." The protesting women were taken off to jail. But that was in 1864, when the state was struggling to fill its quota of recruits. In 1861, with the cream of Minnesota's men queuing up to enlist, Irish laborers were still considered unsuitable prospects.[70]

Other Minnesotans apparently also were deemed "undesirable." Soon after the war began, Ojibwe Chief Hole-in-the-Day, in a letter to the secretary of war, declared himself "deeply impressed with the sentiments of patriotism, and grateful for the aid and protection extended to him and his people." The chief wished "to tender . . . the services of himself and 100 . . . of his headmen and braves to aid in defending the Government and its institutions against the enemies of his country." A few months later Philander Prescott contacted Governor Ramsey from the Lower Sioux Agency with a similar offer: "A large number of the Sioux Indians with whom I have had an intimately personal acquaintance for many years have expressed to me a strong desire to aid the Government . . . in this its hour of peril." They wanted to "tender to you their services in assisting the Government to put down rebellion and treason," asking only "to have for their leader white men who are acquainted with their language and character." Missionary Thomas Williamson reported from the Upper Agency that "some of the 'civilized' Dakotas wanted to aid in the fight, as they had previously been warriors and defeated many enemies."[71]

All such offers were refused and Indians were not among those who marched off to defend the Union in 1861. While it might be expected that white Minnesotans would be reluctant to put arms in the hands of Native people, it may seem more surprising that Indians would volunteer to defend the government that had served them so poorly. Possibly, as whites suspected, it was simply a ploy to gain access to guns and ammunition. But it is equally likely that the war presented an opportunity for the Indians to demonstrate their stature and dignity as men. In their culture, warfare was an essential rite of passage to manhood. To their frustration, white authorities, since first arriving among them, had preached and threatened to keep them from making intertribal war. Perhaps this white man's war would at last acknowledge and value their skill as warriors. As Prescott explained, his Dakota volunteers had "learned that a large number of Indians have been employed by the Southern Confederacy to wage their warfare in Missouri, and they [were] willing and anxious to be lead against them."[72]

It may also have been that, like many of the immigrants who enlisted, these Native volunteers hoped to establish a rightful place for themselves as citizens in the eyes of the nation that had overrun their land. Quite plausibly, as proven allies, they might at last gain the respect and government protection that had been promised so often but denied in practice. Regardless of other accommodations they had made to Euro-American ways—in dress, lifestyle, and religious practice—even farmer Indians continued to face discrimination and coercion. But as warriors the Indians were confident they had no equal. Both the Ojibwes and Dakotas had a history of alliances with the French and British in their colonial wars, which often had worked to their benefit. Perhaps by fighting at the sides of the Americans they could reestablish some negotiating leverage.

Authorities spurned the Indians' overtures, but it might have been wiser to enlist those seasoned fighters, since very few of the Minnesota volunteers had any kind of experience in warfare. The officers were as inexperienced as the men. In the nineteenth-century volunteer army, commanding and field officer commissions were patronage appointments made by each state's governor, usually determined by political and personal ties. Governor Ramsey, to his credit, crossed party lines to appoint former territorial governor and Mexican War veteran Willis Gorman as the first regiment's colonel, since no Republican with military experience could be found. But other than Gorman, only a few officers knew the first thing about training an army. Captains and lieutenants were nearly all military novices, elected by the men of their company. It was a given that the honor of captain would go to the man who had recruited them, usually a middle-class professional with an eye on a military title. Thus the officer corps was made up primarily of lawyers, land developers, politicians, and other civilian elites. It was a common occurrence to see officers drilling the troops with a manual of military tactics in hand.[73]

Adding to the confusion, ammunition was in short supply, firearms were a hodgepodge of outmoded weaponry, and requisitioned uniforms would not arrive for months. Still, to the admiring citizenry, the soldiers "presented a very creditable appearance." The *Stillwater Messenger* reported enthusiastically, "It would be difficult to find a hardier, better natured or a *better looking* set of men, anywhere except in the great northwest." Nearly everyone was certain that the army would easily rout the rebels and the men would be home before the snow began to fly.[74]

The first cohort of volunteers was treated royally. Coachloads of young ladies regularly called at Fort Snelling to watch their heroes drill. Communities feted the soldiers at sumptuous banquets, ladies' organizations sewed and baked in their honor, and citizens showered the regiment with testimonials, and "horse, sword, and flag presentations galore." Morale could not have been higher. But after just a few weeks martial enthusiasm suffered a bit of a setback when President Lincoln issued a proclamation that changed the terms of enlistment from three months to three years. He asked those who had signed up for the shorter term to recommit or be mustered out.[75]

This was quite a shock. As one private recalled, a three-year commitment threw "a decidedly wet blanket over our patriotism." The press poured out passionate appeals to the soldiers' patriotism and pride and officers cajoled and intimidated the men to choose honor over cowardice. Colonel Gorman broke out quantities of beer to buck up those who were wavering. But three years away from home was more than many had bargained for. Three hundred fifty men, more than one-third of the regiment, declined to reenlist. Others later claimed they had been tricked into reenlisting. Some accepted the new terms out of patriotic principle, others because they did not wish to seem cowardly in front of their peers. But most of the youthful recruits were still under the romantic spell of military trappings. They had no desire to give up the seemingly glamorous life of a soldier for their former occupations. And, fortunately for the recruiters, no shortage of eager fellows stood ready to take the place of those who defected. On June 22, a full regiment boarded steamboats that would take them off to war. Nearly the entire population of St. Paul came out to bid them farewell. As they traveled down the Mississippi, at every town "great scenes were enacted" by cheering citizens, with shouts of "Give the traitors hell!" and "God bless you, boys!" echoing off the bluffs. By the account of one soldier, "None of the early organizations was sent southward more enthusiastically than the First Minnesota."[76]

One year later, public sentiment had significantly changed. The war was going badly, with one Union defeat after another. As the names of Minnesota fathers, sons, and brothers began to fill casualty lists, combat quickly lost its attractive veneer. Enlistments declined radically and both the state and local communities were forced to offer cash bounties as inducements to fill the new recruiting quotas imposed on Minnesota. Wives wrote to husbands about difficulties at home and farmsteads falling into disrepair. Mary Partridge, a soldier's wife in Rice County, sorrowfully recalled that in 1862, despite "a promise from the stay-at-homes to take care of the crops and look out for the interests of the family" while her husband served, she experienced "hardships and troubles to which pioneer life could not be compared. I was obliged to see crops lost for lack of help to harvest them; cattle and horses well nigh worthless as there was no sale for them, neither was there male help sufficient to cultivate the farm, which went back to former wildness." News from the front was equally bleak. Soldiers wrote home about shoddy equipment, inedible food, and blankets that fell to pieces in the first rain. Their pay was overdue, officers inept, and battles an unimaginable horror. The reality of war had set in with a vengeance.[77]

Minnesota's Civil War

Other discontents roiled the home front, as relations between whites and Indians reached new levels of antagonism. For years land-hungry politicians, speculators, and settlers had justified their manipulations to acquire Indian lands with pious assertions that they had done all in their power to teach Indians civilized ways. But, they claimed, despite all their efforts, it was now commonly agreed that Indians were uncivilizable savages, stubbornly opposed to "anything approximating towards the manners and customs of white people." Influential missionaries had long asserted that contact with whites had imbued the Indians with none of the white man's virtues and all of his vices. Thus, the argument went, for the Indians' welfare as well as that of the settlers, it was necessary to confine them at remote locales, where they would have minimal contact with white Minnesotans. Traders-turned-politicians, like Henry Sibley and Henry Rice, tirelessly promoted treaty after treaty that supposedly would protect the Indian way of life on inviolable reservations. To survive in this confined existence, government assistance was, of course, essential, paid for by the sale of most of the Indians' tribal lands.[78]

Kintzing Pritchette, a special Indian agent dispatched from Washington in 1857, reported grimly that any hope of absorbing Indians into mainstream society was "a vain dream of impracticable philanthropy." But his conclusion rested more on white hostility than on innate Indian savagery. "One sentiment seemed to inspire almost the entire population," he reported, "and this was the entire annihilation of the Indian race within their borders."[79] Though whites generally persisted in characterizing Indians as mired in a backward-looking, doomed way of life, in fact Native people demonstrated remarkable adaptability to a rapidly changing world. Agent Pritchette could hardly have failed to observe noticeable signs of acculturation among the tribes. The Winnebagos, on their reservation near Mankato, had adopted an agricultural lifestyle, established tidy farmsteads, and donned European-style clothing that nearly mirrored that of their white neighbors. At Hazelwood Station on the Upper Dakota reservation, a community of Christianized Dakotas also had given up traditional dress and dwellings and taken up farming under the tutelage of missionaries Thomas Williamson and Stephen Riggs. Most notably, several important Dakota and Ojibwe chiefs evinced a willingness to blend Indian and white ways, modeling a hybrid lifestyle reminiscent of the middle ground that once flourished in Minnesota.[80]

Young chiefs like Little Crow and Hole-in-the-Day the Younger had shown themselves to be particularly pragmatic leaders, using assimilationist tactics to sustain core traditional values. In treaty negotiations, both men showed a clear understanding of the rules of monetary exchange. Persistently, though unsuccessfully, they presented a precise accounting of payments due them and demanded that the government live up to its treaty obligations. When it became clear that simple claims of justice would not prevail against the overwhelming advantage possessed by the Americans, the chiefs adjusted their strategies in different ways to advance tribal interests.

As early as 1855 the Ojibwe Hole-in-the-Day made the case to the commissioner of Indian Affairs that his people wanted to be accepted as Americans:

> We do not live outside, but within, your nation. . . . Why then look upon us as a foreign nation? . . . . We want to cease to be Indians, and become Americans. We want to be citizens and to have the right to vote. . . . If you grant our request, and you should have a fight with any other nation, you can call upon us and we will form a portion of your militia. We know how to fight, and will stand by you. We want the right of suffrage, the right to vote, to be subject to your laws, and we have our hearts set upon it.[81]

Astutely, he argued that his people needed more money for education, clothes, housing, and farm implements to fulfill their desire to become "civilized."

When the chief's argument failed to win the treaty terms he was seeking, he determined to achieve economic independence for his band through the market. He energetically took up farming and soon he was living "remarkably like a gentleman farmer" and urging his people to follow his example. By 1860 the chief resided in a well-appointed, spacious frame home and had more than one hundred acres under cultivation. He also had established a ferry business and had plans under way for town site development, a model entrepreneur. In 1857 Indian agent David Herriman wrote admiringly that Hole-in-the-Day "was doing more unaided to practically civilize his tribe than has ever been done by white men, backed up though they have been by the influence and money of the government."[82]

Yet, despite his entrepreneurial ventures, Hole-in-the-Day held fast to his Indian identity. His dress was a blend of white and Indian apparel and he wore his hair in traditional braids. He never spoke in English, though he may have understood the language. And though he voiced an "interest" in Christianity, he kept faith with traditional Ojibwe spirituality. Most important to his people, he remained a warrior, leading periodic skirmishes against the Dakotas. In 1860, after one such successful raid, the chief, who had been injured in the fight, returned home to Crow Wing by stagecoach, reportedly carrying the severed head of a Dakota in a gunnysack. A sketch in *Harper's Magazine*

Ojibwe chief Hole-in-the-Day (Po-go-nay-ke-shick) in an 1860 carte de visite published by Whitney's Gallery in St. Paul, one of many photographs of Hole-in-the-Day made by Whitney. Courtesy of the Minnesota Historical Society.

described the paradoxical farmer/warrior as an "anomalous character . . . citizen and savage . . . a civilized barbarian who goes scalp-hunting by stage."[83]

Eastern readers of *Harper's* may not have known what to make of such a "civilized barbarian," but most Minnesotans were less puzzled. Despite his broadcloth jacket and genteel demeanor, Hole-in-the-Day remained indisputably Indian in their eyes and thereby untrustworthy and unacceptable. Daniel Mooers, the mixed-blood son of trader Hazen Mooers, described Hole-in-the-Day as "invariably dressed in the finest broadcloth, always wore handsome leggings and changed his moccasins every day. . . . Not only the neatest man I ever saw, the smartest I ever knew who had no education." A St. Paul paper once described the chief as a man with "a massive brain, a keen, penetrating eye, and a countenance beaming with intelligence." Nonetheless, Hole-in-the-Day was regarded as an aberration rather than an exemplification of Indian ingenuity and intelligence and a savage at heart. Some detractors no doubt coveted Ojibwe land; others simply resented an Indian whose prosperity exceeded their own. Politician Benjamin Brunson probably reflected the general opinion when he grumbled that "no one strutted, or seemed to feel his confidence, more than [Hole-in-the-Day] did."[84]

The long-term effectiveness of Hole-in-the-Day's leadership strategy relied on his ability to straddle two cultures. But sadly, he was a transitional figure in an era when tolerance for cultural fluidity had all but disappeared. In Minnesota, by the eve of the Civil War, the future envisioned for the state had already been reserved exclusively for white Americans. Thus, it should come as no surprise that Hole-in-the-Day's offer of troops for the war effort was declined.

Mdewakanton chief Little Crow similarly sought to bridge the chasm between white and Dakota worlds, but he followed a somewhat different path. He too had observed firsthand the power of the U.S. government. No Indian returned from Washington with illusions remaining that they could force the United States to live up to the letter of its treaties, let alone expel the tide of settlers from Indian country. As Little Crow's biographer notes, "Negotiation and compromise remained the only rational alternatives." Educated by missionaries at Lac qui Parle and later schooled at Kaposia by years of close proximity to St. Paul, Little Crow was familiar with white customs and practices. He willingly engaged in entrepreneurial ventures to advantage his band, trading in furs and whiskey in the manner of white traders. And he advocated education, especially for his children, to enable them to hold their own in the new order that was thrust upon them. However, unlike Hole-in-the-Day, he consistently resisted pressure to turn from hunting and gathering to the life of a farmer. Instead he relied on his charisma, intellect, and diplomacy to broker peaceful coexistence between whites and Dakotas.[85]

For a number of years, Little Crow succeeded. Whites respected his judgment and invariably turned to him in times of tension. His influence with whites then increased his stature among his people. When violence threatened to erupt over the Inkpaduta incident, Little Crow resolved the situation, organizing a party to track down the renegades. When they returned with only a woman and two children to show for their efforts, he convinced the authorities to accept his word that many more of the band had been killed. At least as far as whites were concerned, Little Crow was the premier "spokesman for the Sioux." He was described as "exceedingly gentle and dignified in his deportment," with a face "full of intelligence, his whole bearing was that of a gentleman." He incorporated elements of European dress, especially on his several trips to Washington, where he presented himself in frock coat, gloves, and top hat. On the reservation, he lived in a two-story frame house, drove a stylish buggy, and, though he refused to put his own hand to the plow, his four wives cultivated farm crops on land that government farmers broke for them.[86]

Like Hole-in-the-Day, Little Crow crafted a sort of selective acculturation as a means to preserve what he deemed the essential traditions that sustained tribal values. He refused to cut his hair and modified his dress as circumstances required. He occasionally attended Christian services, which kept him in the good graces of influential missionaries, but remained committed to the religion of his ancestors. He understood English but was never heard to speak it in public. And though he pursued peaceful compromise in disputes with whites, Little Crow prided himself as a warrior against the Ojibwes and proudly brandished scalps taken in battle.[87]

Both men used their considerable political skills to carve a place in the future for their people, balancing adaptation and cultural maintenance. Where they differed was in the path they pursued to secure survival and prosperity. Hole-in-the-Day took the more radical step, urging his people to transform themselves into farmers to achieve economic self-sufficiency; Little Crow put his faith in politics, believing that somehow, by force of his skills as a mediator, he could influence government policy—to secure annuity payments, protect Indian hunting grounds, and thereby ensure the viability of the Dakotas' traditional way of life.[88]

Little Crow and Hole-in-the-Day represent different strategies of accommodation—economic autonomy versus political influence—but both men illustrate a willingness to adapt to the "modern" world that was overtaking Native people. Growing numbers of Indians throughout Minnesota were similarly experimenting with lifestyle changes that would enable them to coexist with the ever-increasing population of white neighbors. Their neighbors, however, harbored no similar desire for coexistence.

Along with white hostility, these cultural brokers also faced internal rifts within the tribes, conflicts between traditionalists and "improvement Indians." In the 1850s the Ojibwes had not yet experienced the full-bore offensive to wrest them from their lands or confine them inside reservation boundaries that would overtake them in the following decades. Thus, the Ojibwes were free to choose either a farming or hunting lifestyle or some combination of both, and

Hole-in-the-Day encountered little organized hostility for his efforts. But the Dakotas were under intensive assault. With each passing year it became more difficult to survive by hunting, forcing increasing numbers of families to turn to farming, however reluctantly. The 1858 treaty that stripped away half the Dakota reservation was a deadly blow to hunters and convinced many that farming was their only remaining option. Not surprisingly, when Little Crow returned from Washington with the coerced treaty, he found himself reviled by many of his people, who had expected their spokesman to resolve existing grievances, not cede the best of what was left of their hunting grounds. Furious young warriors talked of assassination and Joe Brown reported from the Lower Agency that Little Crow and the rest of the treaty delegation "are being accused of having spoken falsely to their young men." According to Mdewakanton chief Big Eagle, "Little Crow was always blamed for the part he took in the sale."[89]

[292]

The treaty cost Little Crow his role as Mdewakanton spokesman. Scorned by his people and bitterly aware that the accommodationist relationships he had so carefully tended with white power brokers had proved valueless, Little Crow became the most traditional of the hereditary chiefs, aligning himself with the young braves who opposed any measure of assimilation. Ironically, the treaty that turned Little Crow into a hard-line traditionalist reduced Indian resistance to change, especially among the Mdewakantons and Wahpekutes on the lower reservation. Even before the treaty was ratified, a deluge of settlers swarmed into the southwestern counties, driving away what game was left, causing widespread hardship among the bands. Thus, by 1860 more than 400 Mdewakantons and Wahpekutes—one-sixth of the tribes—had become farmers, harvesting some 60,000 bushels of corn and 20,000 bushels of potatoes.[90]

Traditionalists, most of them young braves, viewed this with anger and frustration. From time immemorial, Dakota men had proven their manhood as warriors and hunters. In their eyes, farming, which was traditionally women's work, was a mark of shame. Moreover, Agent Joe Brown began to use tribal funds as instruments of cultural change rather than as payments due for ceded lands. He selectively doled out money and goods to reward farmer Indians, in effect punishing those who relied on hunting. Adding to the insult, the agent gave additional "gifts" to those who cut their hair, discarded Indian dress, and lived in the style of white men. The young braves derided those who seemed to give up their traditions so easily. Unlike their elders, they had no conception of the forces aligned against them. They had never seen a railroad or visited Washington. They measured the power of the government only by the skimpy and unimpressive forces garrisoned in Minnesota. Surely, they believed with the naiveté of youth, only lack of courage kept the Dakotas from taking back their lands. Generational discord escalated, deeply undermining the authority of the old chiefs. Community cohesion crumbled. Young braves seethed with contempt and resentment at the "cowardly" farmer Indians, who sold their corn and potatoes to the government instead of sharing it with all those in need. The young men frequently harassed the farmers, killing their livestock and trampling their fields. They also displayed a new hostility toward mixed-blood kin who favored white ways; rather than cultural mediators, the mixed bloods now seemed simply agents of accommodation. And most of all, they harbored a growing hatred for whites, as the source of all the evils that had come upon them.[91]

Catalysts of Disaster

In 1860, while the entire nation knew it stood on the brink of civil war, scarcely a soul imagined that Lincoln's election also would inadvertently strike a match to the tinder of unrest in Minnesota. Wartime circumstances would accelerate the smoldering fire, but ordinary patronage politics ignited the sparks of discontent that would soon become a conflagration.

In the nineteenth century, patronage was the essential lubricant of party politics. It went without saying that a new party in power meant wholesale turnover in government jobs, including the Office of Indian Affairs. As a matter of course, the superintendent and agents in Minnesota—Democrats all—were replaced by Republican loyalists. Unfortunately, nearly anyone who had any familiarity with Indian customs in the state was a Democrat. Admittedly, Superintendent William Cullen, Ojibwe agent David Herriman, and Dakota agent Joe Brown all were guilty of some degree of petty corruption in the management of Indian Affairs in Minnesota. Brown in particular was charged with irregularities by both Indian and missionary critics. Traditionalist Dakotas deeply resented his aggressive acculturation initiatives, and missionary Stephen Riggs wrote a number of letters to the *St. Peter Tribune* excoriating the agent for overexpenditures, nepotism, and various sorts of fraud. Still, while far from ideal, these Democratic officeholders functioned much like urban machine politicians, working for the benefit of the tribes as well as, if not as much as, for themselves. Moreover, they knew how to negotiate according to the etiquette of tribal customs. Joe Brown, despite his failings, had a genuine regard for the Dakotas and understood them as well as any white man in Minnesota. Their Republican replacements would soon prove to be, quite simply, either corrupt, incompetent, or both.[92]

In time-honored fashion, the new Republican administration named party stalwarts to the posts of superintendent and agents without regard for their qualifications for the positions. None of the new officeholders had any experience with Indians. Clark W. Thompson, the new superintendent, was a protégé of Senator Morton Wilkinson. A hard-drinking opportunist, Thompson used his position exclusively to enrich himself and his senatorial patron at Indian expense. Ojibwe agent Lucius C. Walker was equally corrupt. He enthusiastically partnered with Thompson, falsifying annuity rolls, stealing Ojibwe goods and then reselling them to the Indians, and colluding with dishonest traders. Dakota agent Thomas Galbraith also may have lined his pockets a bit at Indian expense (a commonly accepted perk of his position), but his greater sin was ineptitude. A small-town lawyer from the Minnesota River town of Shakopee, he was regarded as a "most pleasant, agreeable, and honorable" young man by his fellow citizens, but Galbraith was far out of his depth on the reservation, as he learned at his first annuity council.[93] Agency carpenter John Nairn, who was present, recounted that Galbraith opened with time-honored poetics about how the Great Father would be pleased "to see the smoke from the wigwam of his red brother ascending and mingling with the smoke from the wigwam of the white man, and he hoped to smoke with them the pipe of peace and so on." But the agent was quickly brought up short by a Dakota spokesman:

> An Indian orator, in reply, would at once launch out into the wrongs of the Indians, scoring, criticizing and condemning the course of the retiring agent and the faithlessness of the government, almost knocking the breath out of his white father by his knowledge of treaty and agency affairs, abolishing and annihilating the preconceived notions of his white father, clipping his soaring wings and landing him on the earth among pork and flour.[94]

With no prior experience in Indian affairs, Galbraith had not expected to have his authority challenged so vigorously and quickly became disillusioned with his new post. He was unable or unwilling to police the traders and government employees who routinely and blatantly cheated the Dakota people. Nor did he have the skills to mediate the increasing tribal conflicts between traditionalists and farmers. Instead, he foolishly pushed Joe Brown's acculturation program even more aggressively. Proclaiming that "the prejudices and habits of the Indian must be eradicated," Galbraith intended to force the Indians to "stay on the reserve and attend to planting." Ignoring the provisions inscribed in the treaties, he withheld food and supplies from those who refused to cut their scalp locks and pick up the plow. In short, Galbraith, though not a villain by any means, was the worst possible agent for this critical moment in time. Lacking Brown's savvy and long acquaintance and regard for the Dakotas, Galbraith's acculturation efforts went tragically awry. His friend, Judge Martin Severance, later painted a damning portrait of the hapless agent: "His excessive use of liquor had brought about a serious impairment of his mental faculties and he was really unfit to hold any official position. Half the time he was out of his head. He had no diplomacy and treated the Indians arrogantly."[95]

Within months complaints about the newly appointed agents flooded into Washington from Indians, missionaries, and the few mixed-blood traders still in the business. A special agent sent to investigate the alleged abuses in 1862 reported to the Indian commissioner, "I have seen proof enough to satisfy the nation & Congress, too, of the fraudulent transactions & robberies committed by the Indian officers." But by that time all attention was focused on the war between the states; Indian problems on the frontier would have to wait. When mixed-blood trader Clement Beaulieu independently began to investigate fraudulent annuity lists on behalf of his Ojibwe kin, Agent Walker revoked his trading license in retaliation.[96]

By 1862, Beaulieu, with his kinship ties to the Ojibwes, was an exception among Indian traders. Most of those who now made their living in the Indian trade were a new breed of merchant with no familial relationship to the Dakota or Ojibwe people. Their sole objective was to wring every cent from the Indians, by fair means or foul, often in collusion with government officials. Adding to the injuries, these men used their power to exploit Indian women. In previous generations marriage between traders and Indian women had bridged cultural differences and established relationships of trust and loyalty, but by the late 1850s exploitation had replaced marriage as common practice. Soldiers and reservation employees, as well as traders, shamelessly used Dakota and Ojibwe women, trading desperately needed food and supplies for sexual favors. Indian spokesmen frequently protested this reprehensible abuse of power, but government officials failed to intervene. This dishonor added fuel to seething Indian resentments. As Mdewakanton chief Big Eagle later recalled, "Many of the whites always seemed to say by their manner when they saw an Indian, 'I am much better than you,' and the Indians did not like this. . . . Then some of the white men abused the Indian women in a certain way and disgraced them and surely there was no excuse for that."[97]

[295]

The reservations were rife with social discord, especially among the lower Dakota bands, hemmed in by scores of new settlers on their former hunting grounds. Unprecedented numbers of German-speaking farmers flocked to the Minnesota River valley in 1861–62, enticed by glowing articles and an array of personal and published letters that extolled the paradisiacal New Germany growing up around the already thriving German town of New Ulm. Hundreds set sail from Europe and whole communities pulled up stakes in Wisconsin, Ohio, and other states to the east to resettle in this new promised land. By the spring of 1862, one settler remembered, "so many people came into the country that we did not know half of our neighbors." As they set about clearing their farmsteads, they had no idea that they were impinging on land that the Dakotas believed had been wrongfully taken from them. Innocently ignorant of both ancient custom and recent history, they unintentionally offended the Indians both by their actions and by their very presence. Assured that the Indians were harmless, the settlers were by turns annoyed, puzzled, or amused by their "colorful" neighbors. Misreading both friendly and hostile Indian overtures, few of the German homesteaders believed they had anything to fear. Some of them did not even own a gun.[98]

In fact, signs of growing hostility were clearly apparent. Farmers frequently found their livestock slaughtered, a signal of Indian anger that would have been understood immediately by old settlers. But officials reassured the farmers that the Indians meant no harm and promised reimbursement for their losses from the annuity fund. Unpleasant confrontations between individual Indians and farmers also became more common. In 1860 Minnie Busse came with her parents and three siblings to Renville County in south-central Minnesota, and it seemed to her that initially the Dakotas were friendly to her family. But by 1862 the little settlement of Sacred Heart had grown to nearly thirty families, and Minnie, though only a child at the time, recognized that "the conduct of our Indian neighbors changed toward us. They became disagreeable and ill-natured. They seldom visited us and when they met us, passed by coldly and sullenly, often without speaking." Still, to most of the Germans, this behavior was puzzling rather than ominous. Lacking the language, cultural tools, or history to understand Indian grievances, they did not recognize the danger brewing.[99]

Agent Galbraith was less sanguine, well aware of multiple sources of unrest. From the first day he arrived on the reservation, he found troubling conditions, amplified by problems caused by the national conflict raging in the South. The first two years of the war went badly, with one defeat after another for Union troops. Disgruntled Democrats, friendly with the Indians, kept them apprised of the army's defeats and warned them that their annuity payments would likely be diverted to support the war effort. Though Galbraith managed to distribute most of the 1861 annuities nearly on time, restitution for settlers' livestock, inflated claims presented by the traders for debts and alleged depredations, and kickbacks to government officials left the Indians with almost nothing. Father Alexander Berghold, a priest from the nearby town of New Ulm, later wrote of the payment at the Redwood Agency, "These bills were shamefully and unmercifully enlarged." Sarah Wakefield, wife of the agency physician, who was present at the Yellow Medicine distribution, offered first-hand testimony of the rampant fraud: "Dakota men did not keep track of what they purchased, so the traders have their own way at the payment . . . cheating [the Indians] very much." The traders generally claimed the Indians owed them exactly the amount they had coming in the annuity payment, and since the Indians had no records, they had no way to contest the charges. However, though the Dakotas kept no written records, they knew that the claims presented were grossly exaggerated and they were furious. Father Berghold later observed, "The Indian is shrewd and wise enough to understand these actions of the civilized man and consequently cannot but hate and despise him and look upon him as a dangerous enemy." Recalling the farce of annuity disbursement, Big Eagle demonstrated that the Indians fully understood the injustice under which they labored: "I know that many white men, when they go to pay their accounts, often think them too large and refuse to pay them, and they go to law about them. . . . The Indians could not go to law, but there was always trouble over their credits." Trouble indeed. In 1861 only the arrival of 130 soldiers with an artillery piece in tow convinced the angry Indians to accept the accounting and disperse to their villages.[100]

Galbraith was in over his head. In his words, from the first day he took office he faced "wrangling, dissatisfaction, and bitter, even threatening complaints on the part of both the upper and lower bands." In 1861 and 1862 the nervous agent often called for troops from Fort Ridgely to shore up his authority. The Indians, he complained, were "restive, turbulent, saucy, insolent, impudent and insulting." However, all the regular troops had been deployed south, replaced by untested Minnesota volunteers. As quickly as the frontier troops shaped up they were sent to the front, replaced by a new contingent of enlistees. Thus, the soldiers who came to Galbraith's aid were a series of green recruits who seemed an unimpressive lot. This contingent of former farm boys and clerks, with neither uniforms nor military bearing, looked a poor substitute for the hard-bitten veterans they replaced.[101]

In the soldiers lodges the young braves counted and recounted insults and injuries they had suffered and assured one another that the United States was not nearly so powerful as the old chiefs claimed. They knew of the defeats the army was suffering in the South, the steady drain of men from Minnesota. And certainly the clumsy young volunteers at Fort Ridgely were no match for the bravery of Dakota warriors. Adding to the unrest, as winter came on the villagers once again experienced severe want. Hunters had to compete with settlers for what little game could be found in the region and an infestation of cutworms the previous summer had destroyed the farmer Indians' promising corn crop. The traders had laid claim to all the annuity funds and by spring, with the nation's resources all funneled into the war, most were refusing to extend further credit, suspecting that annuities would not be paid out the following summer. All this confirmed to the young men that their old chiefs were fools to surrender to white domination.[102]

The traders' suspicions were not without cause. By spring the rumor was that the government, reeling from the costs of war, intended to pay the 1862 annuities in depreciated greenbacks rather than gold. This fueled other rumors that no money at all would be forthcoming. Galbraith shuttled between the Upper and Lower agencies, trying his best to reassure the bands that funds would soon be on their way. Privately, however, he confided his anxiety to Henry Whipple, Minnesota's first Episcopal bishop and a staunch Indian advocate. The agent feared "the Blackest *trick* of Indian Swindles," a new fraud "that must bring a harvest of woe. . . . God only knows what will be the result."[103] Whipple later lay the blame for the ensuing conflict squarely at the government's door for countenancing egregious corruption in the Office of Indian Affairs. In September 1862, the bishop wrote in a published letter:

Citizens, editors, legislators, heads of the departments, and the President alike agree that [the Indian Department] has been characterized by inefficiency and fraud. The nation, knowing this, has winked at it. We have lacked the moral courage to stand up in the fear of God and demand a reform. More than all, *it was not our money*. It was a sacred trust confided to us by helpless men, where common manliness should have blushed for shame at the theft. . . . *Who is guilty of the causes which desolated our border: At whose door is the blood of these innocent victims?* I believe that God will hold the nation guilty.[104]

Had the government lived up to the treaties, Whipple believed, the Indians gradually would have acculturated. He cited Wabasha's explanation for the refusal of the traditionalists to conform to Euro-American norms. The chief told Whipple that "the wild life clings to them like a garment" because the government does not live up to its promises. The people could not believe them and "our hearts are sick." Faithless treaties were indeed serious grievances. After all the claims and expenses were paid, the Dakotas had received almost nothing for the lands they ceded in 1858. But Indian disillusionment was also fueled by repeated indignities suffered by those who *did* attempt to assimilate. The Minnesota constitution had promised citizenship to "civilized" Indians, but when nine farmer Indians, a copy of the Minnesota constitution translated into Dakota in hand, traveled to Mankato to apply for citizenship in 1861, all but one were rejected because they did not speak English. German-speaking farmers and French-speaking mixed bloods were subject to no similar requirement, but the judge ruled that the Dakota language was in itself "barbarous" and thus made the Indians ineligible. According to one of the rejected Indians, "One man made me feel very angry. He said that men with colored skin should never be naturalized—that they could not be made white men. . . . They treat us like dogs and I do not like it." This episode strengthened the traditionalists' argument that it was pointless as well as unmanly to turn away from tribal traditions.[105]

White authorities also made it clear that they had no regard for Indian virtues and talents. In the past Indians had been honored for their wilderness skills, their expertise as hunters and trappers. Now they were urged, even coerced, to abandon these lifeways. Nor were they recognized for their courage as warriors. For more than one hundred years Indians had fought at the side of Europeans in their colonial wars. But when they offered their services to fight with the Americans, they were told "the Great Father already had an abundance of soldiers." Given such repeated evidence of disrespect, it is understandable that many Dakotas, and Ojibwes as well, believed that aspirations for equality were a fanciful dream, whatever course the Indians might pursue.[106]

Most of the hereditary Mdewakanton chiefs, well aware of the forces against them, had come to the conclusion that farming was the only hope left for their people's survival. Many accepted Christianity, at least nominally, in hopes of enlisting the missionaries as protectors and advocates. By the spring of 1862, after another winter of extreme hardship, even Little Crow showed signs of giving in. A pragmatist at heart, he began attending services at the Episcopal mission and started construction of a new brick house. Galbraith reported with satisfaction that the chief finally seemed receptive to becoming "a white man."

But while dire circumstances at home seemed to break down Little Crow's resistance, the young braves read different signals emanating from the national crisis that hardened their resolve to resist.[107]

The vaunted American army was being pummeled in the South. Missionaries reported that Indians closely followed the progress of the war and peppered them with questions. Were northern cities being burned? Had the president been killed or taken prisoner? Perhaps the entire army was as weak as the troops on the frontier seemed to be. The death toll of the war was enormous, and by 1862 the enthusiasm for enlistment had completely evaporated. Recruiters scoured the countryside, and Governor Ramsey, struggling to meet Minnesota's quota, had seemingly overcome his distaste for Indian soldiers. Galbraith, by this time eager for an honorable way to resign his post, was busy recruiting a company of mixed bloods and agency employees as his ticket into the military. Well aware that the government had rejected Indian volunteers only the year before, the Indians read the formation of the Renville Rangers, as they were called, as yet another sign of the army's weakness. According to Big Eagle, "The Indians now thought the whites must be pretty hard up for men to fight the South, or they would not come so far out on the frontier and take half-breeds or anything to help them."[108]

Ojibwe Grievances

Recruiters also ranged into Ojibwe country, but these were primarily whiskey traders, looking to "buy" young men for $50 or $100 to serve as substitutes for reluctant draftees. Missionary John Johnson, an Ottawa Indian also known as En-me-Gah-bowh, related that the recruiters would ply the men with whiskey to get them to sign up, then "as fast as the big Indians are sold they are taken down to Fort Snelling and there are resold to the highest bidder." Ojibwe parents were angry and distressed to see their sons lured away, and Chief Hole-in-the-Day, whose offer of volunteers had been rejected the year before, was incensed at what was essentially human trafficking. He sent word to the Pillager band, "Our Great Father intends to send men and take all the Indians and dress them like soldiers, and send them away to fight in the south, and if we wish to save ourselves, we must rise and fight the whites." Reverend Johnson was convinced that the chief planned to kill "every man, woman, and child" at the agency, then attack Fort Ripley, which was vulnerable since "nearly all the soldiers had been taken away to the South to fight." As events played out, this seems unlikely to have been the plan. More probably, as Hole-in-the-Day's biographer argues, "he had only wanted to scare the whites . . . to prompt government officials to rectify the troubles with [Agent] Walker."[109]

For nearly a year, as chief of the Gull Lake band of Ojibwes, Hole-in-the-Day had been vigorously complaining about the thievery of Lucius Walker. The Ojibwes, like the Dakotas, had a litany of grievances against both their agent and Superintendent Thompson. In fact, in comparison to Walker, Gal-braith seems a model of propriety. In June Hole-in-the-Day had traveled inde-pendently to Washington to demand an investigation of the agent's fraudulent schemes. Indian commissioner William Dole promised to take action. But two months later, though the commissioner was in St. Paul, on his way to negotiate a treaty with the Red Lake and Pembina bands, he had done nothing.[110]

Frustrated and angry, Hole-in-the-Day may have used the recruiting scan-dal to stir up the bands and force the commissioner's attention. If that was the plan, it worked like a charm. On August 18 a terrified Walker sent word to Fort Ripley that warriors were assembling near Gull Lake, threatening to attack the agency. He then immediately abandoned his post. Fleeing pell-mell toward St. Paul, he warned everyone he encountered to run for their lives. By the time he reached the town of Monticello, some forty miles north of Minneapolis, he was so overcome by terror that he committed suicide rather than face the conse-quences of his misdeeds.[111]

Panicked settlers flocked to the protection of Fort Ripley, but the situa-tion was not nearly so dire as Walker portrayed. True, a number of Pillagers at Leech Lake had broken into the storehouses there, taken several white cap-tives, and come south to join the Gull Lake band. And the army's attempts to capture and arrest Hole-in-the-Day had gone comically awry, the inept Fort Ripley force outmarshaled by the chief at every turn. But the Indians did not turn to violence. (The only casualty of the "uprising" was Agent Walker.) What-ever Hole-in-the-Day's intentions may have been, it was clear that the Ojibwe nation was not willing to go to war. Rather, after a bit of hostile posturing, the few hundred braves from Gull and Leech lakes who stood with Hole-in-the-Day agreed to engage in talks with Commissioner Dole—which may have been their goal from the outset. The captives were released and Hole-in-the-Day as-serted that "he did not want war, but only his rights." At the end of an extended parlay, the chief's bold but risky gamble won the day. A state commission that included Governor Ramsey and Henry Rice promised immediate payment of annuities in full and an investigation of the late Lucius Walker's malfeasance. The Ojibwes soon had plenty of beef, flour, and pork and commonly agreed that "Hole-in-the-Day is [a] smart man—the white man could never punish Hole-in-the-Day."[112]

In 1862 the Ojibwes still had some negotiating power. Though technically they had given up much of their land, they continued to range freely across the northern half of Minnesota. Game, fish, and wild rice were abundant and set-tlers relatively sparse. Indisputably, parasitical whiskey traders and corrupt of-ficials wreaked injury on the quality of community life, but the bands' survival was not at risk at this time.[113] Along the Minnesota River, the Dakotas were in much more difficult circumstances.

Chapter 11

CATACLYSM ON THE MINNESOTA

Tell our Great Father that it is hard for him to expect our hearts to be good when he permits men with bad hearts to do us wrong so often. Father, hunt up our money for us; take pity on us for we are very poor and winter is coming.

LITTLE CROW, 1861

Let our present Legislature offer a bounty of $10 for every Sioux scalp, outlaw the tribe and so let the matter rest. It will cost five times that much to exterminate them by the regular modes of warfare and they should be got rid of in the cheapest and quickest manner.

JANE GREY SWISSHELM, *St. Cloud Democrat*, 11 September 1862

Let Them Eat Grass

By the spring of 1862 conditions on the Dakota reservations had deteriorated alarmingly. Both friends and foes agreed that the Indians were in "an extremely destitute condition." After a brutal winter, hunger stalked the villages. Most storekeepers, worried that annuity payments might not be made, were withholding credit, even to the farmer Indians. One or two traders, like mixed-blood David Faribault, honored Dakota traditions of reciprocity and continued to provide credit, but what they could offer was not nearly enough. According to Faribault's wife, Nancy, he "had trusted them [the Indians] for very nearly everything he had, for they were very hard up, and the other stores would not trust them for anything." Dakota agent Thomas Galbraith had tried to help with supplemental rations over the winter, but by spring his storehouses had run low and he spent much of his time away from the reservation. The hungry Indians haunted Fort Ripley and New Ulm, performing traditional "begging dances" in hopes of food or money. Settlers in the surrounding counties complained that Indians were "pests" and "a nuisance." Their begging was bad enough, said the settlers, but the Indians also were competing for game and even killing farmers' cattle and hogs. For the proud Dakotas, all this was humiliation heaped upon humiliation. They were barely hanging on, counting the days until their annuity payments arrived.[1]

The payment was late. June turned into July and then to August and still the payment did not come. Indian needs were far down on the list of priorities in chaotic wartime Washington. Rumors raced among the bands: that the government, pouring all its resources into the war, would try to foist worthless paper money on the tribe rather than gold; that only half the annuity would be paid; or that the money would not come at all. Suspicions seemed confirmed when, in July, Indian superintendent Clark W. Thompson and Galbraith tried to convince the Mdewakanton and Wahpekute chiefs to accept the payment in greenbacks. Despite the officials' assurance that the paper currency was as good as gold, the chiefs did not believe them and "refused to be paid in anything else than that which was properly their due." Frustration and resentment boiled at the Upper and Lower agencies, where the Indians congregated, waiting for the gold to arrive. Despite their obvious need, Galbraith was afraid to hand out what was left of the government provisions—which were under lock and key in his storehouses—in advance of the cash payment.[2]

Desperation fueled anger at the agent and the traders, culminating in what became an infamous exchange at the Redwood Agency between Mdewakanton braves and storekeeper Andrew Myrick. The Indians warned Myrick, who had cut off all credit, "not to cut another stick of wood or to cut our grass." The arrogant Myrick responded, "You will be sorry. After a while you will come to me and beg for meat and flour to keep you and your wives and children from starving, and I will not let you have a thing. *You and your wives and children may starve, or eat grass, or your own filth.*" "Let them eat grass" became a rallying cry in the ensuing conflict, a symbol of all the injustices and humiliations that could no longer be borne.[3]

In early August, a crisis was barely averted at the Upper Agency (Yellow Medicine), where 4,000 starving Sissetons and Wahpetons had gathered. The elderly were dying and children cried from hunger. Settler Sarah Wakefield vividly described the bleak conditions: "Many days these poor creatures subsisted on a tall grass which they find in the marshes, chewing the roots, and eating the wild turnip. . . . I know that many died from starvation or disease. . . . It made my heart ache." Over the preceding months Galbraith had done his best to ameliorate conditions, arguing vainly with the traders to resume sales on credit and meting out what he believed could be spared from agency stores, but there were too many hungry people and not enough provisions. Finally, on August 4, several hundred braves defiantly stormed the storehouse, despite the presence of troops from Fort Ridgely, armed with a pair of howitzers. Violence seemed imminent and Galbraith sent for missionary Stephen Riggs in hopes

PLATE 100

Plate 100. "Interior of Indian Jail," *Harper's New Monthly Magazine*, **June 1863, 23. Minnesota Historical Society.**

The 303 Dakota condemned by the military tribunals spent December 1862 chained to the dirt floor in this unheated log prison in the center of Mankato. The men—who were attired in traditional costumes of breechcloths, leggings, and blankets—spent weeks talking and smoking while they awaited President Abraham Lincoln's decision on their fate. The prisoners had been moved into the log stockade after spending several November weeks in an open field outside of the town. This site was abandoned after it had proven too vulnerable to attacks from local mobs, who had threatened to lynch the prisoners if they were not summarily executed. White citizens had formed secret vigilante organizations dedicated to carrying out the death sentences handed down by the military tribunal. While state officials hectored the White House to provide approval for the executions, newspapers all over the state urged men to take vengeance into their own hands. A crowd of several hundred men answered this call, convening on the outskirts of Camp Lincoln on December 4 to murder the captive Indians. The armed men were only thwarted by the determination of camp commander Colonel Stephen Miller, who threatened to use force against both the mob and local white residents to protect the Dakota men in his care.[147]

Plate 101. President Abraham Lincoln's hand-written order to General Sibley listing thirty-nine men to be executed. December 6, 1862. Minnesota Historical Society.

Two days after the organized attack on Camp Lincoln, President Abraham Lincoln wrote out this order naming thirty-nine men to be hanged in Mankato. The president had deliberated for weeks on the fate of the 303 prisoners condemned to die by the military tribunals that had been convened after the mass surrender at Camp Release. Lincoln penned his directive on Executive Mansion stationery on December 6, after two aides had reviewed the transcripts of the five-man military commission that had handed down scores of hasty sentences determined in perfunctory trials. Judgments were reached after brief statements by the prisoners and a handful of witnesses, some of whom testified in dozens of trials. The proceedings were unencumbered by the strictures of standard legal procedure; none of the accused had the benefit of lawyers or other customary trial rights.

PLATE 101

Executive Mansion,
Washington, December 6th 1862.

Brigadier General H. H. Sibley
St. Paul
Minnesota

Ordered that of the Indians and Half-breeds sentenced to be hanged by the Military Commission composed of Colonel Crooks, Lt Colonel Marshall, Captain Grant, Captain Bailey and Lieutenant Olin, lately sitting in Minnesota, you cause to be executed on Friday the nineteenth day of December instant the following names, towit

"Te-he-hdo-ne-cha" No. 2. by the record
"Tazoo" alias "Plan-doo-ta" No. 4. by the record
"Wy-a-tah-to-wah" No. 5 by the record
"Hinhan-shoon-ko-yag" No. 6 by the record
"Muz-za-bom-a-du" No. 10. by the record
"Wah-pay-du-ta" No. 11. by the record
"Wa-he-hud" No. 12. by the record
"Sna-ma-ni" No. 14. by the record
"Ta-te-mi-ma" No. 15. by the record
"Rda-in-yan-kna" No. 19. by the record
"Do-wan-sa" No. 22. by the record
"Ha-pan" No. 24. by the record

"Shoon-ka-ska" (White Dog) No. 35. by the record
"Toon-kan-e-chah-tay-mane" No. 67. by the record
"E-tay-hoo-tay" No. 68. by the record
"Am-da-cha" No. 69. by the record
"Hay-pee-don or Wamne-omne-ho-ta" No. 70. by the record
"Mahpee-o-ke-na-ji" No. 96. by the record
"Henry Milord" a half breed. No. 115. by the record
"Chaskey-don or Chaskey-etay" No. 121. by the record
"Baptiste Campbell a half breed. No. 138. by the record
"Tah-tah-kay-gay" No. 155. by the record
"Ha-pink-pa" No. 170. by the record
"Hypolite Ango" a half breed. No. 175. by the record
"Na-pay-Shue" No. 178. by the record
"Wa-kan-tan-ka" No. 210. by the record
"Toon-kan-ka-yag-e-na-jin" No. 225. by the record
"Ma-kat-e-na-jin" No. 254. by the record
"Pa-zee-koo-tay-ma-ne" No. 264. by the record
"Ta-tay-hde-don" No. 279. by the record
"Wa-she-choon" or "Toon-kan-shkan-shkan-mane-hay" No. 318. by the record
"A-e-cha-ga" No. 327. by the record
"Ha-tan-in-koo" No. 333. by the record
"Chay-ton-hoon-ka" No. 342. by the record
"Chan-ka-hda" No. 333. by the record

"Hda-hin-hday" No. 373. by the record
"O-ya-tay-a-koo" No. 377. by the record
"May-hoo-way-wa" No. 382. by the record
"Wa-kin-yan-na" No. 383. by the record

The other condemned prisoners you will hold subject to further orders, taking care that they neither escape, nor are subjected to any unlawful violence.

Abraham Lincoln, President of the United States,

Lincoln was disturbed by the large number of death sentences and the irregular context in which they were decided. "Anxious to not act with so much clemency as to encourage another outbreak, on the one hand, nor with so much severity as to be real cruelty, on the other, I caused a careful examination of the trials to be made," Lincoln later wrote to the Senate.[148] His decision to review the evidence for himself ignored demands from Minnesota for the immediate hanging of all the condemned men.[149] The transcripts revealed that there was little evidence of systematic rapes during the violence, belying assertions that "all or nearly all the women who were captured were violated."[150] Lincoln approved the executions of the two men convicted of rape and those linked to particular murders; he commuted the sentences of those who could not be definitely linked to specific crimes. The fate of these men was heavily influenced by Episcopal Bishop Henry Whipple, a lone voice of restraint in Minnesota, who visited Washington to provide the larger context for the violence and assert that "we cannot hang men by the hundreds."[151] Whipple's reasoning ultimately prevailed with the president, who agreed to distinguish between men who had participated in "massacres" versus those who had fought in larger "battles."[152] Acutely aware of the mob mentality that ruled the state at the end of 1862, Lincoln rebuffed claims that a presidential pardon of any of the men "would only lead to riot and blood-shed."[153] His order for execution included the directive that the other prisoners should be held "subject to further orders, taking care that they neither escape, nor are subjected to any unlawful violence."[154]

Plates 102–10. Robert O. Sweeny portraits of condemned men, 1862. Minnesota Historical Society.

The morning of the largest execution in American history, St. Paul artist Robert Sweeny visited the Leach building in Mankato, where he observed and sketched nine of the condemned men and Joseph Godfrey, whose own death sentence had been commuted in recognition of his role as a witness against his fellow prisoners. Sweeny could speak both Dakota and Ojibwe and was greeted warmly by the prisoners, many of whom the artist had known personally for many years.[155] Sweeny had become acquainted with the condemned men during their visits to St. Paul or on his own expeditions around the state, which brought him to Indian communities where he sketched scenes of everyday life. "When irons were struck from their ankles they filed around the room, passing where we stood, and said in the way of farewell, 'How de doo,'" Sweeny remembered

PLATE 102. SHOON KA SKA

PLATE 103. TOON KAN E CHAH TAY MANE

PLATE 104. BAPTISTE CAMPBELL

PLATE 105. MA KAT E NA JIN

in 1886. "As the last Indian left the room we fell in behind the guard, and passed down the dark passage, out into the bright daylight, down between the ranks of armed soldiers, to within a few feet of the gallows."[156]

Sweeny, who later played a leading role in the Minnesota Historical Society, was undoubtedly motivated to visit the jail by a desire to record the execution for posterity. These intimate portraits were not circulated in the contemporary press of the time. The men are named by Sweeny's handwritten scrawl. In the years since the execution, efforts to create a definite and complete list of the men imprisoned in Mankato have been stymied by the poor record keeping of the jailers. Few spoke fluent Dakota and were easily confused by similar sounding Dakota names. Some of the prisoners were known by both Americanized and Dakota names. The military commission

PLATE 106. HYPOLITE ANGE

PLATE 107. WAH PAY DU TA

PLATE 108. WA SHE CHOON NA

PLATE 109. RDE IN YAN KA

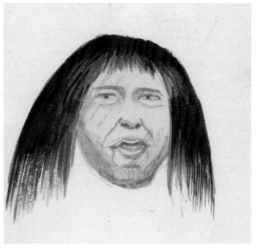

PLATE 110. UNIDENTIFIED

had assigned each man a case number. Stephen Riggs remembered later that "no one could remember which number attached to which person."[157] It mattered little to Riggs and the jailers until Abraham Lincoln ordered Minnesota authorities to separate 39 men from the original 303 originally condemned to die by the military tribunal. At least two men—Chaska and Wa she choon na—were hanged in error after having had their sentences commuted by Lincoln. Protests over the confusion provoked only the short statement that "we all regretted the mistake very much, &c," from Riggs.[158]

Plate 111. W. H. Childs, execution at Mankato, December, 26, 1862. Smithsonian Institution National Anthropological Archives.

This lithograph depicts the largest mass hanging in American history. Ultimately thirty-eight men were hanged in Mankato on the morning of December 26, 1862, since one of the thirty-nine on the president's execution list received a last-minute reprieve from Lincoln. The drawing by W. H. Childs shows a hanging platform surrounded by neat rows of troops and spectators. This orderly scene does little to convey the anticipation and emotion of the moment. Colonel Stephen Miller had decreed martial law in a ten-mile radius of the town, anticipating the arrival of a difficult-to-govern mob. A crowd of four thousand people had waited through the night to witness the execution, filling streets, climbing roofs, and perching on the opposite bank of the Minnesota River to catch a view of the scaffold.

At daybreak on the morning of the hanging, the condemned men began singing a death song, chanting, and painting their faces with streaks of vermilion and ultramarine. They continued singing as their jailers unchained them from the floor and tied their wrists at the front of their bodies and their elbows behind their backs. White

PLATE 111

muslin caps were placed on each man's head. Through all these preparations, Father Augustin Ravoux and Dr. Williamson ministered to the men, praying with those willing to accept their counsel. At ten o'clock the condemned were marched two by two through a line of waiting soldiers to the square scaffold, which had been erected across the street from the jail. The death song grew louder as they climbed the platform and had the nooses fastened around their necks. The men continued chanting, calling to each other, and smoking. The scaffold had been constructed with a single trigger rope that controlled the entire platform. William Duley, who had survived the U.S.–Dakota War but lost three children in the fighting, was given the privilege of cutting the rope with an ax. The platform dropped, the crowd cheered, and twenty minutes later, all the men were pronounced dead.[159]

This rendering of the scene in Mankato was reprinted in local and national publications, including *Frank Leslie's Illustrated Weekly*. Newspapers issued extra editions and special printings of the lithograph to commemorate the historic event. Entrepreneurs like Joel Whitney of St. Paul and the proprietor of the bookstore in St. Cloud also sold copies of the engraving to a public eager to remember this day in Minnesota.[160] As no photographers were allowed at the hanging, this drawing became the sole visual representation of this critical moment, the event that whites came to understand as the end of the war. This iconic visual interpretation of the execution was reproduced in endless popular histories and dramatic retellings of the Dakota Conflict. In the decades that followed it was also emblazoned on commemorative objects—most notably a silver spoon and a beer tray—that were produced to memorialize the execution for Minnesotans still haunted by the bloody summer of 1862.

Plate 112. Joel Emmons Whitney, Cut Nose, 1862. Minnesota Historical Society.

A leader of the Mdewakanton soldiers lodge, which directed much of the violence against white settlers in 1862, Cut Nose was perceived as one of the darkest villains of the U.S.–Dakota War, described by Harriet Bishop as a "wholesale butcherer" and a later historian as a "fiend incarnate."[161] The death of this reviled leader on the scaffold in Mankato was especially welcomed by those who demanded the extermination of all Indians in the state. When the execution was finished, his body was carted to a sandbar on the Minnesota River, where it was dumped into a pit with all the other dead men. When darkness fell, this hastily made grave was disinterred—along with all the others—by local doctors seeking cadavers for medical research.

The band of grave robbers included Dr. William W. Mayo, who founded the Mayo Clinic with his two sons, Will and Charlie. After dissecting Cut Nose with a group of colleagues, the elder Mayo preserved the skeleton of the Indian leader for future use. William Mayo kept the bones in a big iron kettle in his office, where they provided sons Will and Charlie with their earliest lessons in osteology and anatomy. The boys examined the skull and measured the femur while listening to tales about the 1862 war in the Minnesota River valley. Their father had been one of the defenders of New Ulm while their mother waited out the violence with other women and children in Le Sueur. By the 1870s, the skeleton in their father's office had become a remnant from a seemingly distant past for the Mayo brothers, who regarded the life and death of Cut Nose as no more immediate than their favorite Indian tales of James Fenimore Cooper. The skeleton remained with the brothers, who used it for teaching at the Mayo Clinic, until it was eventually repatriated for burial. A piece of the Indian leader's skin that had been tanned and tattooed by a private collector in Chicago was returned to the Lower Sioux community of Morton in 2000.[162]

This portrait of Cut Nose was likely taken before the U.S.–Dakota War. St. Paul entrepreneur Joel Whitney used it to create this carte de visite in 1862 to capitalize on national interest in Minnesota's frontier violence. Cartes de visite were playing-card-sized images that were mounted on stiff backing, precursors of postcards that were purchased to supplement news reports of the time. Whitney began offering cartes de visite in 1860, selling them in his gallery for twenty-eight cents each. Cartes de visite of popular subjects could easily be printed by the hundreds; as many as sixty-four could be printed from one plate onto a single piece of paper, which was then cut apart into individual images.[163] Most cartes de visite were images of prominent individuals or newsmakers of the moment, framed by explanatory text that described the portrait's significance to contemporary events. Since newspapers of the time did not print images, cartes de visite provided visual illustrations of current events.[164] Whitney affixed a caption to each carte de visite that was designed to curry interest in the subject. For this card, Whitney described Cut Nose as the man "who in the massacre of 1862, in Minnesota, murdered 18 women and children and 5 men." By the time he sold his business in 1871, Whitney claimed that he had sold tens of thousands of these mass-produced Indian portraits.

The Dakota Conflict created an explosive demand for this kind of images from Minnesota, and Whitney was well-situated to capitalize on this interest. He profited handsomely by recognizing the American appetite for unsettling images, making mass commodities out of reproductions of the Minnesota execution scene and portraits of the men who met their end on the Mankato scaffold. A "portfolio" of his "Portraits of Sioux Indians connected with the Minnesota Massacre," including this image of Cut Nose, was published in *Frank Leslie's Illustrated Newspaper* on January 31, 1863.[165] This national attention may have helped Whitney market his "photo albums" and cartes de visite, which he promoted in local newspaper advertisements that encouraged St. Paulites to buy albums and cartes de visite for themselves along with examples that they could send to "friends East."[166]

Plate 113. Joel Emmons Whitney, Little Crow, 1862. Minnesota Historical Society.

The vilified Indian leader Little Crow was presented in Americanized attire in this carte de visite, which Joel Whitney marketed as part of his Dakota War series of images.[167] Whitney juxtaposed Little Crow's "citizen's clothing" with a caption describing him as the "Leader of the Indian Massacre of 1862, in Minnesota." This was the last photograph of Little Crow taken before he died, and this carte de visite did more than

WHITNEY,   **CUT NOSE,**   ST. PAUL.

Who in the Massacre of 1862, in Minnesota, murdered 18 Women and Children and 5 Men.

Entered according to Act of Congress, by J. E. Whitney, in the year 1862, in the Clerk's Office of the U. S. District Court for Minnesota.

PLATE 112

WHITNEY,   **LITTLE CROW,**   ST. PAUL.

A Sioux Chief, and Leader of the *Indian Massacre of 1862,* in Minnesota

Entered according to Act of Congress, by J. E. Whitney, in the year 1862, in the Clerk's Office of the U. S. District Court for Minnesota.

PLATE 113

provide a recent image of the notorious Indian leader for a curious public. The combination of image and words provided contemporary viewers familiar with the horrific events of August 1862 a complex story of Indian treachery.

Little Crow posed for this photograph in 1861 at the urging of Governor Alexander Ramsey, who lent the Indian leader his own full dress suit to wear, complete with a high collar shirt and black silk neck tie. Choice of clothing was a powerful indication of cultural sympathies in mid-nineteenth-century Minnesota. Indians who adopted "white" clothing were perceived to be assimilated and sympathetic to the project of "civilizing" the region. This portrait by J. H. Gravenslund, who worked in Whitney's studio, thus presented the leader as a fully assimilated "friendly" Indian.[168]

The violence of the summer of 1862 demonstrated to white Minnesotans that Little Crow had never fully embraced American culture and domination of the region. This portrait reminded viewers that the supposed leader of the Indian war had once presented himself as a friend to whites. He had lived in a house, attended the Episcopal church, visited Washington, and posed for a photographer in white costume. From the perspective of late 1862, this last action was seen as part of Little Crow's efforts to deceive whites, who interpreted the killings on the Minnesota prairie as a sign that the state's Indians never expunged their most savage impulse.

This cautionary tale was perhaps best articulated by the citizens of St. Paul who petitioned President Abraham Lincoln to remove all Indians from the state. "The Indian's nature can no more be trusted than the wolf's," they asserted. "Tame him, cultivate him, strive to Christianize him as you will, and the sight of blood will in an instant call out the savage, wolfish, devilish instincts of the race. It is notorious that among the earliest and most murderous of the Sioux, in perpetuating their late massacre, were many of the 'civilized Indians,' so called, with their hair cut short, wearing white men's clothes, and dwelling in brick houses built for them by the government."[169]

ANPETU-TOKECA (Other Day.)
Who rescued Sixty-two persons from the Indian Massacre at Yellow Medicine, Minnesota, and piloted them safely to Shakopee. Aug. 19th, 1862.

Plate 114. John Emmons Whitney, John Other Day, 1862. Minnesota Historical Society.

Joel Whitney's cartes de visite from the U.S.–Dakota War presented both heroes and villains, telling the entire narrative of the war through a series of images that were framed by explanatory captions. This portrait card celebrated John Other Day, lionized as one of the few Dakota who undertook heroic efforts to save whites during the conflict. Other Day was presented as a Christian Indian who served as a "civilized" foil to villains like Little Crow and Cut Nose. His cultural sympathies are signified by his attire in this portrait, which shows him in entirely Americanized clothing. Whitney's caption narrates that Other Day "rescued Sixty-two persons from the Indian Massacre at Yellow Medicine, Minnesota, and piloted them safely to Shakopee, August 19th, 1862." Other Day appeared in almost every account of the war, his courage at Yellow Medicine overshadowing the myriad acts of other Dakota who also worked to protect white settlers and captives. This public recognition won him a relatively large monetary award from Congress in 1865 but no relief from the relentless pressure to drum all the Dakota out of the state in the decades after 1862.[170]

PLATE 115

Plate 115. Benjamin Franklin Upton, Dakota Indian internment camp below Fort Snelling, 1862–63. Minnesota Historical Society.

Photographer Benjamin Upton's vista of the Dakota internment camp at Fort Snelling presents a seemingly peaceful scene. Smoke curls up from an orderly looking village of Indian tents planted in tight rows, surrounded by a sturdy-looking fence that conveys a facade of security. This almost dreamy image does little to convey the horrors of life for the inhabitants of this camp, which housed women, children, and elderly men over the winter of 1862–63, while the state of Minnesota debated the fate of the Dakota Indians within its boundaries.

After the capture of Camp Release, military authorities refused to allow any Dakota—including those who had worked to protect white settlers during the violence—to return to their homes, for fear they would plot future depredations. After sending male warriors to jail near Mankato, where they awaited execution, the Army marched those Indians deemed innocent of any crimes to this site at the confluence of the Minnesota and the Mississippi Rivers, a place the Dakota viewed as sacred ground. On a strip of land they had visited for games and dances in happier times, these 1,600 "friendly" Indians were subjected to strict supervision and control by an army that viewed their adherence to Dakota culture with deep suspicion. The camp was under constant threat of attacks by white vigilantes, who called for the annihilation of all Indians remaining in the state of Minnesota after 1862. Some residents of the camp managed to escape this environment by joining Henry Sibley's scouting force in western Minnesota; others were allowed to move to Faribault, where they gathered under the protection of Episcopal Bishop Henry Whipple. A few moved to Mendota, where Sibley gave land to a few individuals.

This imprisonment proved fatal for a large percentage of camp inhabitants who remained in the stockade enclosure. The Army's decision to put the Indians on short rations of crackers, flour, and salt pork undoubtedly contributed to their vulnerability. The tents were pitched on a two- to three-acre site, creating dangerously tight quarters. The swampy ground defied efforts to maintain clean and comfortable living quarters. These wet and crowded conditions provided an ideal environment for epidemics, which ravaged the malnourished population of the camp for six months. Hundreds of camp inhabitants, especially children, died of the measles, which swept through St. Paul in the winter of 1862–63. The dead were buried in long trenches by the riverside. By the end of the winter, the camp population stood at 1,318. In May 1863, the surviving inhabitants of the camp were removed to a site of even greater suffering at Crow Creek, in South Dakota.[171]

PLATE 116

Plate 116. Benjamin Franklin Upton, Little Crow's wife and two children at internment camp at Fort Snelling, 1864. Minnesota Historical Society.

Photographer Benjamin Upton did not record the names of the mother and children in this image. He did identify the woman as a "wife of Little Crow," a designation that would have made this portrait into a valuable commodity at a time when public demand was strong for photographs of anyone involved in the U.S.–Dakota War. She may be Saiceyewin or Isabelle Wakeman or Mahkiyahewin, also known as Eva Rice.

For photographers like Upton and Joel Whitney, the Fort Snelling internment camp offered almost endless subjects for the Indian cartes de visite that had proven so profitable. In 1864, Whitney took out an ad in the local press proclaiming "card photographs of Little Crow's son and the Indian prisoners at Fort Snelling on sale at WHITNEY'S GALLERY."[172]

The family pictured here was part of a group of Dakota who surrendered at Pembina in January 1864. They were brought to the camp at Fort Snelling, which had been emptied in the spring of 1863, when its original residents were sent to Crow Creek, South Dakota. In the latter half of 1863, the stockade at Fort Snelling was repopulated as large numbers of once-defiant Dakota began surrendering to the U.S. troops sent to hunt them down. Those first housed in the internment camp at Fort Snelling were friendly noncombatants; many of these later residents of the camp had, in myriad ways, supported the uprising of 1862. They were detained in this camp before being removed from Minnesota. After several months at Fort Snelling, this woman and her children were sent to join the rest of the exiled Dakota at Crow Creek.[173]

The preponderance of women among the prisoners led the photographers to create a unique series of portraits. Photographs of Dakota women are extremely rare. In this portrait, Little Crow's wife wears the same worried expression shared by all camp inhabitants. Their existence was fraught with anxiety and their future more perilous. Dependent women and children had no way of knowing whether they would see their husbands, fathers, or other male relatives again. While disease and malnutrition stalked all camp residents, women were particularly vulnerable to the threat of sexual violence. In November 1862, local newspapers reported that a Dakota woman who had ventured out of the stockade in search of firewood had been raped by a group of Fort Snelling soldiers. Few such incidents received public attention, but women suffered constant harassment from the soldiers stationed at the adjacent fort.[174]

Plate 117. Whitney's Gallery, Dakota tipis in Fort Snelling internment camp, 1862–63. Minnesota Historical Society.

The internment camp at Fort Snelling was surrounded by a wooden stockade that was between twelve and twenty-four feet high. This enclosure made it possible for the military to monitor all the movements of the Indians. It was also justified as a way of protecting the Indians from murderous white vigilantes.[175] But the fence did little to protect residents from photographers and tourists, who were a constant presence in the camp. The confined Indians were allowed no privacy to mourn the death of their children to malnutrition and disease, the absence of their men, and the loss of their homeland. Harriet Bishop described how "visitors daily thronged the enclosure with 'passes' from the post commander."[176] For local white residents like Mary Thayer Hale and her family, the muddy camp on the river flat was a public spectacle in the winter of 1862–63. She peered into the tents and remembered that it was "hard to imagine more wretched looking human beings."[177]

Visits to the internment camp at Fort Snelling followed in the well-established tradition of the ethnotourism enjoyed by visitors to Minnesota since the early nineteenth century. Like the steamboat passengers who alighted at Fort Snelling, the European artists who sketched Indians on the streets of St. Paul, or the group that watched the annuity payments on the Dakota reservation, visitors to the Fort Snelling stockade were intent on observing "authentic" Indians before they "vanished" in the wake of "civilization." Thayer's interest in the Dakota camp was hardly vindictive. She expressed pity rather than fury for the people she saw. "It was not strange that the Indians resented the loss of their lands and hunting grounds, (most people would do the same),"

PLATE 117

TEPEES,
Of the *Sioux Indians*, Minnesota.

she reasoned. But on the "other hand, it was not possible to reserve rich lands for the use of a few roving savages."[178] The internment camp may have presented a sad scene for sympathetic observers like Thayer, but they viewed this pacification of the Indians as an ineluctable aspect of American expansion in the region.

Plate 118. State of Minnesota receipt for payment of $500.00 to Nathan Lamson as a bounty for killing Little Crow, 1864. Minnesota Historical Society.

In February 1864 the state legislature approved this special payment of $500 to Nathan Lamson for killing Little Crow on July 3, 1863, and "thereby rendering great service to the state."[179] When Nathan and Chauncy Lamson shot Little Crow, they did not realize that they were murdering the famous Indian leader. Little Crow, who was accompanied by his son Wowinape, was mortally wounded by the elder Lamson, who shot his victim because he was an Indian rather than a known fugitive. Nathan Lamson was also wounded in the exchange of gunfire; his son Chauncey ran into nearby Hutchinson with news of the conflict and returned with a self-appointed militia, which dragged Little Crow's body into town. The body was identified after the capture of Wowinape near Devil's Lake.

In the aftermath of the bloodshed of 1862 and the resulting exile of the Dakota, the state of Minnesota encouraged white settlers to shoot any Indians they encountered, without waiting to discover their identities or missions. Fresh reports of violence in the summer of 1863 unsettled an already fearful populace. These incidents were interpreted as the precursors of a new massacre by writers like Harriet Bishop, who warned that "everywhere the blood of human beings drenched the soil—everywhere decayed bodies were found—everywhere these nightly depredations were going on!"[180] With few regular troops available to protect the frontier, Adjutant General Oscar Malmros issued a decree on the day after Little Crow's killing that promised cash rewards to volunteers who delivered "scalps" to St. Paul. The initial reward of $25.00 was quickly raised to $75.00 and finally $200. Ultimately the state paid out $150.00 for the murder of four Indians in addition to Little Crow.[181] The Lamsons were singled out for an especially generous award that dwarfed these other payments. Note the image of the "noble Indian" on the receipt.

PLATE 118

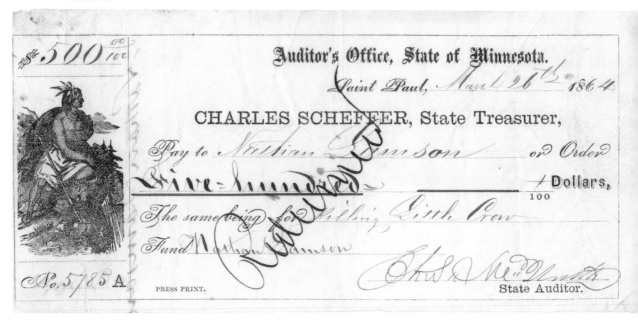

that "something between the lids of the Bible" might defuse the situation. Riggs and Timothy Sheehan, the young lieutenant in charge of the troops, counciled with the Indians and managed to restore calm. Meanwhile, according to Sheehan, Galbraith, apparently unnerved by weeks of unmitigated tension, barricaded himself in his office, "getting drunk and rattled." The lieutenant testified, "The agent never came out at all until the thing was over, and didn't assist me in any way, shape or form." At Sheehan's insistence, Galbraith finally opened the storehouse and handed out what provisions were inside.[4]

Little Crow had rushed to the Upper Agency at the first sign of trouble. Hoping to regain his stature as an effective tribal spokesman, he insisted on equal treatment for the Mdewakantons and Wahpekutes waiting at the Lower Agency. They too were in need of provisions, though conditions at Redwood were not as desperate as at Yellow Medicine. In a thinly veiled warning, he stated, "We have waited a long time. The money is ours, but we can not get it. We have no food, but here are these stores, filled with food. We ask that you, the agent, make some arrangement by which we can get food from the stores, or else we may take our own way to keep ourselves from starving. When men are hungry they help themselves." Everyone present believed that Galbraith had acceded to Little Crow's petition. With the crisis apparently resolved, the Indians dispersed, the troops marched back to their quarters, and Stephen Riggs returned to his mission at Hazelwood, secure that "peace and quiet now reigned at the Yellow Medicine." That evening he penned a reassuring letter to a St. Paul paper. Rumors to the contrary, he wrote, "all is quiet and orderly at the place of the forthcoming payment."[5]

Unaccountably, however, Galbraith reneged on his promise to open the stores at the Lower Agency. Instead he left for Fort Snelling with his newly recruited Renville Rangers, though he had to know that the situation at Redwood was critical. Quite possibly he hoped never to return. To his friend Martin Severance, who saw him in New Ulm that evening, Galbraith seemed "crazy as a loon and had an idea of making himself captain of the company." Clearly, the pressure of his post was taking a toll. Weeks earlier, Superintendent Thompson had written urgently to the commissioner of Indian Affairs, "If the payment is not made very soon, there is but little hope of preventing an outbreak. . . . And there is no knowing where it will end." Employees at the agency also were extremely anxious, sensing trouble in the air. Even officials at New Ulm had become uneasy and petitioned for an increase of troops at Fort Ridgely. Given the state of affairs on the reservation and Galbraith's lack of experience, it would be somewhat understandable if the novice agent was hoping to escape his crushing responsibilities—and not a moment too soon.[6]

The following day, August 17, as the early Sunday morning sun began to warm the valley, no one could have predicted that by nightfall Minnesota would be forever changed. On their scattered farmsteads families gathered together for morning prayer. At the Redwood Agency, farmers, storekeepers, teachers, and missionaries began their usual Sabbath routines of work or worship. Little Crow attended services at the Episcopal chapel at the agency and shook hands with everyone there. Galbraith and his rangers spent the day in New Ulm, "celebrating" before beginning their trek to Fort Snelling. And four young Wahpeton braves from the Rice Creek band were heading for home empty-handed, after scouring the countryside for several days in vain search of a deer or some small game to bring home to their village.

[304]

By afternoon, as they approached a farmhouse near the small settlement of Acton, the hunters were thirsty and discouraged. Accounts vary about what happened next. Some say the men acted on a dare, others that the farmer insulted them and refused them food or water. Whatever precipitated the confrontation, seven white settlers, including a woman and a young girl, soon lay dead in the dooryard. The Indians, realizing suddenly that they had probably signed their death warrants, raced back to Shakopee's village for protection.[7]

Individual attacks on whites were rare but not unknown. In the past, punishment had fallen only on the perpetrators. Even the official outrage over Inkpaduta's infamous raids had been limited to that renegade band. Conceivably, the Acton murders might have been dealt with in a similar fashion. But circumstances had changed greatly since 1857. The rash actions of a few young men ignited a powder keg of anger, disillusionment, and desperation. On that fateful day events had conspired to create what, in today's parlance, could be termed a perfect storm.

The traditionalists who led the soldiers lodges grasped this unpremeditated confrontation as the opportunity they had been waiting for to lead the people into a war against the whites. All night they met in council, strategizing over how to win general support for war. They knew the farmer Indians would oppose an uprising. They needed the stature of a respected chief to rouse the people to fight. Little Crow, the last of the major Mdewakanton chiefs to hold out against acculturation, was the natural choice. Thus, as the first light of dawn began to touch the sky, they marched to his house to demand he lead them in their righteous crusade.[8]

Little Crow had made his reputation as an unparalleled mediator between his people and the whites. As much as any man, he knew that a war against them would be futile. But on that morning his faith in himself was severely battered. After what had seemed a successful negotiation at Yellow Medicine, Galbraith had failed to hand out provisions at the Lower Agency. As a result, Little Crow, who briefly had recovered his stature as spokesman, was again embarrassed. His once thriving village consisted of only about a dozen lodges. And severe want was chipping away at the proud Mdewakanton's resistance to acculturation. The formerly prosperous chief had been reduced to trading his coat for food and only the day before had traded his gun to a settler for a steer. How was he to hunt without a gun? Half-heartedly he warned the excited braves, "The white men are like the locusts when they fly so thick that the whole sky is a snow-storm. You may kill one—two—ten; yes, as many as the leaves in the forest yonder, and their brothers will not miss them." But the young men were in no mood to listen to reason. If Little Crow would not join them, then he was nothing but a coward. This final insult apparently was more than the chief could bear. Fatalistically, he acquiesced, declaring, "You will die like the rabbits when hungry wolves hunt them in the Hard Moon. Taoyat-eduta is not a coward; he will die with you."[9]

And so Minnesota's civil war began.[10] Early on the morning of August 18 Little Crow and the other hostiles swooped down on the Redwood Agency and systematically began killing their enemies. It is important to note, however, that in this first attack the Indians selectively targeted only agency employees, traders, and clerks—those deemed guilty of offenses against the Indians. No women, children, or mixed bloods were killed, suggesting that the offensive had not yet spun out of control. Still, when the attack was over, of the more than eighty people at the agency twenty lay dead, ten were taken captive, and the rest had taken flight in terror.[11]

One of the first to fall at the agency was Andrew Myrick. He was found later, his mouth stuffed with grass, his offense evident to all.[12] But once the violence began, pent-up rage spurred some Indians to spend their fury on any white person in their path. Philander Prescott was gunned down on the riverbank near the agency. The old trader turned government farmer had lived peaceably among the Indians with his Dakota wife and mixed-blood children for more than forty years, a lingering relic of the once thriving borderland culture. In a heartbreaking confrontation, Prescott pled his case to a party of warriors who waylaid him on the road. "I am an old man," he is alleged to have said. "I have lived with you now forty-five years, almost half a century. My wife and children are among you, of your own blood; I have never done you any harm, and have been your true friend in all your troubles; why should you wish to kill me?" The Indians replied, "We would spare your life if we could, but the white man must die; we cannot spare you." Prescott's murder seems to mark the final rupture of the ties that bound Indians and whites in Minnesota for nearly ten generations.[13]

But as war parties fanned out from the agency to attack nearby farmsteads and small settlements, it became apparent that allegiances in this war were not nearly so neatly defined nor ties so precipitously broken. In that first explosion of bloody rage, some of the hostiles rampaged with indiscriminate fury, shooting and hacking to death every white man, woman, and child they encountered. But others made exceptions for people who had kinship ties to the Dakotas either through marriage or reciprocal relationships of respect and friendship. Little Crow himself had warned Prescott in advance of the attack to stay indoors. Had he done so, the old trader might well have survived, as did his wife and children. When the Indians appeared at the home of trader David Faribault, they told him and his wife, Nancy, "We are going to kill all the white people in Minnesota [but] we are not going to hurt you for you have trusted us with goods."[14]

The Faribaults were doubly protected, not only because they honored Dakota customs of generosity but also because both were of mixed-blood heritage.[15] Though in many cases relations between Dakota traditionalists and mixed bloods had frayed nearly to the breaking point, even the most bellicose of the warriors understood that by killing mixed bloods they would make enemies rather than allies of the victims' full-blood kinsmen. Susan Brown, waylaid on the road to Fort Ridgely, used her blood ties to the Sissetons to save herself, her eleven children, and two wagonloads of white settlers. Though she lived in a fine stone mansion and her husband, Joe, was especially hated by the traditionalists for his aggressive acculturation program, Susan Brown's kinship to important Sisseton chiefs shielded the entire party from execution. "Remember what I say," she warned the menacing braves, "if you harm any of these friends of mine, you will have to answer to Scarlet Plume, Ah-kee-pah, and Standing Buffalo and the whole Sisseton and Wahpeton tribe." Though she and her party became nominal captives, they were treated more like honored guests than prisoners until released into the care of her relatives. As further proof that kinship ties had not lost their compelling power, only one mixed blood was killed during the bloody week of raids that left hundreds of bodies strewn across the prairie of southwestern Minnesota.[16]

Though the war cry was to kill all the whites, many Indians found they could not dispassionately ignore previous relationships of trust. At the German settlement of Beaver Creek, a war party brutally murdered everyone but Helen Tarble and her children. Tarble was one of the few Germans to make friends with the Dakotas and learn their language; consequently, even in captivity she was "allowed to do as she pleased." Sarah Wakefield, another friend to the Indians, was taken prisoner but housed at first quite comfortably in Little Crow's home. Throughout the six weeks she spent as a captive, the warrior Chaska and his family vigilantly protected her, often at risk to themselves. Wakefield and Tarble received special treatment because of established friendship with the Dakotas, but a number of women and children without previous ties to the Indians also were taken captive rather than killed. Most of these prisoners understandably lived in terror throughout their ordeal and some suffered brutal treatment, but the undeniable physical hardships they all endured were most often no more than those of their Indian captors. Many of the captives also later recounted numerous acts of kindness. One young German girl, Mary Schwandt, recalled with gratitude that "Mr. Good Thunder" and his wife, Snana, treated her like a daughter. "I want you to know," she wrote in her memoir, "that the little captive German girl you [Snana] so often befriended and shielded from harm loves you still for your kindness and care." Snana remembered Mary with equal affection. She recalled how Mary had been as "dear to me just the same as my own daughter" and how her heart had ached when she bid the girl farewell.[17]

In fact, the majority of the Dakota people never lifted their hand against the whites. The so-called Sioux uprising involved only a fraction of the Dakota nation, probably fewer than 1,000 mostly Mdewakanton braves out of a Dakota population that exceeded 7,000. Perhaps 300 young men of the more than 4,000 Sissetons and Wahpetons came down from the Upper Agency to join in the fighting, but the tribal elders counseled vehemently against participation in what they were sure was a suicidal offensive. Even among the Mdewakantons and Wahpekutes, only a few hundred soldiers willingly went to war. The old chiefs were horrified, knowing well the retribution that would lie ahead. Nor did most of the farmer Indians want to take up arms. A few, like John Other Day, served as scouts for the forces that Henry Sibley would marshal against the Dakotas. Many more, like Paul Mazekootemane, adamantly refused to fight and formed their own soldiers lodge in opposition to the war contingent; others joined in only reluctantly, threatened by the warriors to either fight or die. Many later claimed that, though they were present at the raids and battles, they did not participate in the killing. Throughout the course of the conflict, scores of friendly Indians risked their lives to warn of the impending attacks and protect captives from harm, saving many lives. Nearly everyone at the Upper Agency and Hazelwood escaped, thanks to Indian protectors.[18]

Still, those hot August days and nights were a nightmare of horror for those caught up in the violence. Hundreds of innocent people died in the rampage, estimates ranging between 400 and 1,000 victims. Survivors hid in the woods or crawled on their knees through the tall prairie grasses, quaking at every sound as they struggled toward the relative safety of Fort Ridgely, images of slain husbands, wives, children, and friends burned upon their memory. More children and babies died along the way from thirst and exposure.[19] At first, the Indians had the advantages of surprise and disbelief at the scope of the uprising. When word of the attacks reached Fort Ridgely, Captain John Marsh, in command of the post, set forth with a small party of troops—just forty-six green enlistees along with an interpreter—to quell the trouble at the agency. The captain assured his men that "the sight of the soldiers would cow them as it had so many times before." Hours later, nearly all the men, including the captain, were dead. Fort Ridgely itself, bursting with terrified refugees and only forty remaining inexperienced soldiers to defend them, barely survived an assault two days later. At New Ulm, a war party of between 300 and 600 braves laid siege to the barricaded town. The citizens, under the leadership of Charles Flandrau, managed to repel two separate attacks but at great cost. Twenty-six defenders died and most of the town was reduced to smoking ruins.[20]

The Indians did not press their advantage against the besieged residents of Fort Ridgely and New Ulm. They had achieved their primary objective of

Henry Sibley photographed by Whitney's Gallery in 1862. Courtesy of the Minnesota Historical Society.

driving whites out of their country, as the immediate evacuation of New Ulm made clear. Indian warfare traditionally consisted of brief guerrilla attacks rather than sustained campaigns, which had the benefit of achieving victory at a relatively small cost of lives. Thus, rather than renew the fight to finish off their enemies, the warriors moved off to their camps to celebrate what they considered victory with feasting, dancing, and liquor. Little Crow, however, knew they faced a different sort of enemy, one that would not be satisfied with token revenge. But though he was the nominal leader of the uprising, he had never controlled the strategy or tactics of the war. The soldiers lodge listened to him only when it suited them. He had warned against killing settlers, especially women and children, knowing that the only hope for success would be a negotiated settlement. Now he urged the men to "make war after the manner of white men," but his warnings went unheeded.[21]

Meanwhile, the "white man's army" was gathering its forces. A day after the first attacks, shocking reports from the west had begun pouring into St. Paul. Alexander Ramsey, with neither men nor equipment to draw upon, turned to his old friend Henry Sibley to take command of an expedition against the Indians. Sibley, now fifty-two years old, without a day's experience in the military, reluctantly accepted the governor's commission. The next day he boarded a steamboat to take him up the Minnesota River, loaded with woefully inadequate provisions and ordnance and four companies of raw recruits. As he worriedly described them, "A greener set of men were never got together."[22]

Attempting to train his undisciplined troops en route and commandeering horses and wagons along the way, Sibley led his forces into Fort Ridgely nine days later. Though he confidently promised to drive the savages to the Missouri, privately he feared his nervous soldiers would bolt at the first sight of an Indian. As well they might. It seemed that half the population of the state was in flight. The stories they told were enough to frighten far more hardened soldiers, and the corpses rotting in the hot August sun were a stomach-churning sight. Sibley, who once prized his friendship with the Dakotas, wrote to his wife, "Oh the fiends, the devils in human shape! My heart is hardened against them beyond any touch of mercy."[23]

The Indians chalked up an early victory against Sibley's forces when they ambushed a burial detachment at Birch Coulee, near the Redwood Agency. For thirty-six hours the warriors pinned down the beleaguered party until reinforcements arrived. It was a disaster for the army—thirteen dead and forty-seven wounded, as well as the loss of more than ninety horses. Nonetheless, the eventual arrival of Sibley's eight companies of reinforcements, complete with cannon, must have been a daunting sight. With some 1,600 men now massing against them, the warring Dakotas knew they were outmanned.[24]

Over the next few days the hostile Indians split up into raiding parties that terrorized central Minnesota. They looted and burned the towns of Forest City and Hutchinson. Ignoring the towns' citizens, who had barricaded themselves inside hastily built stockades, the Indians piled wagons high with clothing,

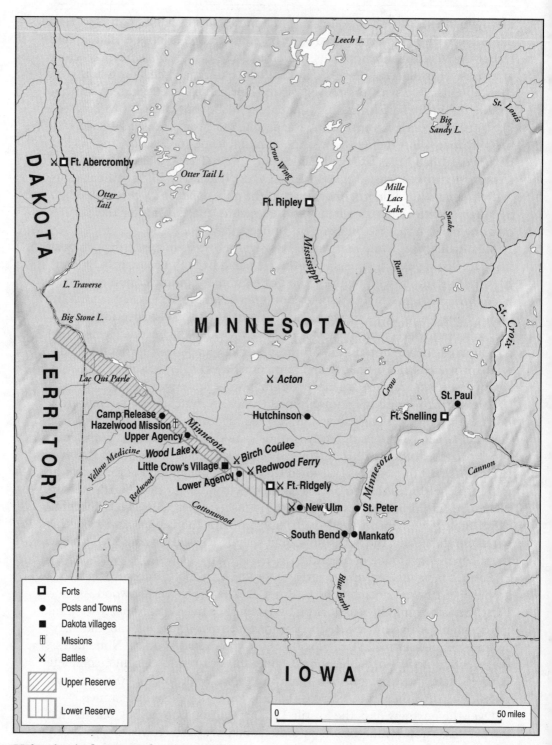

Leech L.

St. Louis

Big Sandy L.

× □ Ft. Abercromby

Otter Tail L.

Crow Wing

Mille Lacs Lake

Otter Tail

Ft. Ripley □

Snake

Mississippi

Rum

L. Traverse

Big Stone L.

St. Croix

M I N N E S O T A

Lac Qui Parle

× *Acton*

Crow

St. Paul

Camp Release ●
Hazelwood Mission ⊞
Upper Agency ●

Hutchinson ●

Ft. Snelling □

Minnesota

Yellow Medicine   Wood Lake ×
Little Crow's Village ■ × Birch Coulee
Redwood   × Redwood Ferry
Lower Agency ●   □ × Ft. Ridgely

Minnesota

Cannon

Cottonwood
× ● New Ulm   ● St. Peter
South Bend ● ● Mankato

Blue Earth

I O W A

	Forts
□	Forts
●	Posts and Towns
■	Dakota villages
⊞	Missions
×	Battles
▨	Upper Reserve
▥	Lower Reserve

0   50 miles

Major sites in the U.S.–Dakota War of 1862.

household goods, and provisions, then torched both towns. The townspeople, peering out from the stockades, helplessly watched their communities go up in flames. This latest foray set off another mass exodus of settlers. In less than a month, the Dakota offensive had almost entirely emptied twenty-four counties of their white population. The warriors could proudly claim they had driven the whites from Indian country and hoped their grateful kinsmen would join with them in finishing the crusade. Though the battles of Fort Ridgely and New Ulm had taken only a few Indian lives, the massing American forces made it apparent that the Dakotas were going to need reinforcements for the next battle. Hoping to recruit additional support for the war effort, the mounted warriors, accompanied by dozens of wagons overflowing with family, prisoners, and plunder began moving west into Sisseton and Wahpeton country. But rather than a hero's welcome, the war caravan met angry opposition from the Wahpetons and Sissetons. In a council with a group of tribal leaders at Hazelwood, the chiefs refused to take part in the war. Standing Buffalo declared that the Mdewakantons had "cut our people's throats." At Red Iron's village, the chief and his men turned their kinsmen away. "You commenced the outbreak, and must do the fighting in your country," they were told. This hostile reception fed a growing unease among the militants. They knew that, victories notwithstanding, the Americans were now on the offensive and, unless the entire Dakota nation stood together, they could not hope to defeat the juggernaut that was tracking them down. As Little Crow had warned at the outset, "Count your fingers all day long and white men with guns in their hands will come faster than you can count."[25]

Through mixed-blood emissaries Joe Campbell and Tom Robertson, Sibley had promised to punish only those who had participated in the massacre of civilians. According to Big Eagle, "I and others understood from the half-breeds that Gen. Sibley would treat with all of us who had only been soldiers and would surrender as prisoners of war, and that only those who had murdered people in cold blood, the settlers and others, would be punished in any way." Many of the soldiers had been reluctant warriors from the outset and, with the odds of success so clearly against them and Sibley's pledge of forgiveness, enthusiasm for continuing the war was waning by the day. A number of Mdewakanton and Wahpekute warriors, including Wabasha and Wakute, took this opportunity to leave the war camp and join the Sissetons and Wahpetons, even penning a secret letter to Sibley offering to assist the American army. Moreover, the peace faction was demanding that the warriors turn over the captives to their care. Little Crow himself tried to persuade them to negotiate an end to the war, but the young men of the soldiers lodge would have no part of it. The chief admitted privately, "I can't do as I would. I wish to make peace. But the young men have been wronged so often and so badly, that they feel as though the choice was between being shot, or being starved to death, and they prefer the first as most honorable." Rather than the hero of his people he longed to be, Little Crow sadly realized that, whatever course he followed, he would be cursed. The peaceful Indians blamed him for bringing destruction down on their heads, but if he wavered in the campaign the war faction would damn him as coward. Fatalistically, the doomed chief soldiered on, declaring that "if he was ever touched by a white man, it would be after he was dead."[26]

For days the two factions argued heatedly over the fate of the captives, until scouts reported on September 22 that Sibley's forces were camped at Wood Lake, just south of the Yellow Medicine Agency. Knowing that the moment of confrontation had arrived, the defiant Mdewakantons and Wahpekutes determined to attack, though they were grossly outnumbered. By this time only a small contingent, perhaps 300 braves, retained any zeal to fight, and they approached the battle with fatalistic stoicism. In the words of Hdainyanka, the son-in-law of Chief Wabasha, "We may regret what has happened but the matter has gone too far to be remedied. We have got to die." The rest of the 700-man war party, dragged unwillingly to the battlefield, simply refused to fight. The so-called battle of Wood Lake thus devolved into little more than a mismatched skirmish between the small Indian attack force and Sibley's 1,600 men. The largely unbloodied American troops, who lost only seven men, declared it a resounding victory. They punctuated their triumph by mutilating and scalping the bodies of the fourteen Indians who fell in combat. As for Little Crow and his men, they knew well this was their last stand. They must finally either surrender or abandon their ancestral woodlands and flee onto the northern plains.[27]

Aftermath

While the hostiles were engaged in fighting, the friendly Indians used the time to transfer nearly all the captives to their camp. Over the next four days, as they impatiently waited for Sibley's forces to arrive, the camp's population steadily grew. By the time the troops marched in, it had become a small city of 150 lodges. Only about 200 warriors followed Little Crow onto the plains, which seemed alien and forbidding to the woodland Mdewakantons and Wahpekutes. Many more, relying on Sibley's word, chose surrender rather than exodus. Mixed-blood prisoner Samuel Brown dryly noted a new spirit of fellowship that sprang up in the camp. "All were friendly to the whites and anxious to shake hands" with Sibley and the others who had so recently been their sworn enemies. One Indian, to emphasize his loyalty, "wrapped the American flag around his body and mounted [his] horse and sat upon him in full view of the troops as they passed by."[28]

Nonetheless, despite promises to the contrary and an initial appearance of forbearance—even allowing the men to keep their weapons—Henry Sibley, under orders from his superior, Major General John Pope, was preparing to exact a full measure of retribution. In recognition for his service in the Indian war, Sibley had just been appointed brigadier general in the U.S. Army and he did not hesitate to use his newly awarded authority. He appointed a five-person military commission, composed entirely of men who had fought against the Dakotas just days earlier, to try suspected hostiles on the spot. As legal scholar Carol Chomsky notes, "It is inconceivable that they came to their task with open minds." Sibley then planned to carry out immediate executions. Better to have orderly hangings where they were, he reasoned, than risk the vigilante justice of an enraged populace if he tried to move the convicted men across the state. Although, he admitted, "perhaps it will be a stretch of my authority . . . necessity must be my justification."[29] He had no doubt that General Pope would approve his actions. The general had recently been reassigned to the Northwest after a resounding defeat at the second battle of Bull Run, and he clearly intended to redeem himself. After failing against the rebels, he would give no quarter to the Indians.[30] Pope had made his instructions clear in a letter, dated September 28:

> The horrible massacres of women and children and the outrageous abuse of female prisoners, still alive, call for punishment beyond human power to inflict. There will be no peace in this region by virtue of treaties and Indian faith. It is my purpose utterly to exterminate the Sioux if I have the power to do so and even if it requires a campaign lasting the whole of next year. Destroy everything belonging to them and force them out to the plains, unless, as I suggest, you can capture them. They are to be treated as maniacs or wild beasts, and by no means a people with whom treaties or compromises can be made.[31]

At first, however, Sibley made only sixteen arrests, the appearance of leniency to lure lingering former hostiles into camp.

At the end of two weeks, when the camp—now christened Camp Release—had swelled to about 2,000 Indians, Sibley sprang the trap. His men surrounded the camp, taking all the Indians into custody, including those who had vigorously opposed the war, saved many whites, and protected the prisoners throughout their ordeal. The soldiers arrested 400 men, clapped them in irons, and soon brought them before what could only be termed a kangaroo court to determine their fate.[32]

The trials moved with rapid-fire efficiency, often lasting no more than five minutes, as many as forty-two cases dispatched in a single day. "Voluntary participation" in the hostilities was the only criterion of guilt, no distinction made between fighting against soldiers versus the murder of civilians or between participation in a battle or a farmstead raid. Former captives and mixed bloods provided some specific evidence of crimes, but most of the defendants were convicted solely on the basis of their own admission that they had ridden with the militants. One defendant was convicted on evidence merely that "he took a few turnips at the Big Woods."[33] Believing Sibley's promise that only the murder of civilians would be punishable, they did not deny their presence at battles in what they thought of as honorable warfare. Most of the prisoners had to rely on interpreters to understand the charges against them. No lawyer represented them, nor were any witnesses admitted in their defense. To the contrary, when Sarah Wakefield vigorously spoke on behalf of Chaska, who had protected her throughout her captivity, she found her own reputation destroyed. As she related, the people at the camp began spreading "horrid abominable reports," claiming "'I was in love,' that 'I was his wife,' that 'I preferred living with him to my husband.'" Despite her protestations—or perhaps because of them—Chaska was sentenced to hang. To Wakefield it was clear that "the Commission was not acting according to justice" and that the outcome of the trials was a foregone conclusion. Sibley's correspondence seems to confirm her assertion. He was quite certain that "most of the women had been repeatedly raped," though no evidence was produced of that fact, and he intended to show the Indians no mercy. Before reviewing any of the trial proceedings, he informed General Pope that he fully expected to approve the results and "hang the villains." In the space of a few weeks, 303 men were sentenced to death and 20 to unspecified terms of imprisonment. Just 69 men were acquitted and only 8 released.[34]

[314]

It may seem out of character that Henry Sibley, who had always been notoriously jealous of his honor and integrity, would have orchestrated such blatantly unjust proceedings. But that very obsession with his reputation may have driven him to fury against the Dakota people whom he had once called friends.[35] Sibley had retired from public office after a brief and inglorious tenure as Minnesota's first governor, with his reputation as "Minnesota's first man" considerably diminished. His election to the office he had so long sought had been tainted by Republican charges of fraud. To make matters worse, he was blamed unfairly for bankrupting the state and was haunted by the unredeemed, worthless railroad bonds that carried his signature.[36] Thus, he may have felt some grim satisfaction when Alexander Ramsey, the popular current governor, turned to the old Moccasin Democrat in the state's hour of crisis. But before he was able to pull his patchwork command into any sort of fighting form, criticism again began to rain down on Colonel Sibley's head.

The expedition had advanced with excruciating slowness, always seemingly a day late to do much good. Sibley was by nature a cautious man and years of experience with the Dakotas had taught him a healthy respect for Indian courage and cleverness. He knew the troops he commanded would be no match in an even fight. The only men he could rely on were a few seasoned fur trade veterans who joined him along the way—Joe Brown, Alexander Faribault, William Forbes, and Jack Frazer, along with a handful of mixed-blood scouts. The rest of the command was a sorry group. The recruits were "green as grass" and the only mounted troops were 300 rambunctious civilian volunteers from Minneapolis and St. Paul, described by an officer at Fort Ridgely as "the scum of creation . . . [who] would not submit to any disaplin." The expedition also suffered from a serious shortage of arms and ammunition. Confronted by bloodcurdling tales of mayhem from the fleeing settlers and with no idea how many Indians might be lying in ambush just ahead, Sibley understand-ably tended to err on the side of caution. Thus, by the time his men reached Fort Ridgely the danger had passed and the Indians had moved on, and when the soldiers marched into New Ulm they found an empty shell and were met by a sad wagon train of refugees departing their burned-out community, head-ing for safety in Mankato.[37]

Rather than take off in immediate pursuit of the Indians, to the consterna-tion of both civilians and his men, Sibley made the decision to assist the refu-gees and bury the dead while he waited for supplies and reinforcements. Joe Coursolle, a mixed-blood scout whose daughters were among those captured, left a vivid account of his frustration:

> We drilled and drilled and drilled while more troops came pouring in. Soon there were two thousand soldiers in the Fort and an almost endless train of wagons haul-ing in supplies. I thought we had enough to lick General Lee but Sibley kept drilling us for two whole weeks!

When the troops finally began to move, Coursolle related:

> We moved like snails. I could have crawled on my stomach and made faster time. Again we cursed Sibley. He was so slow! Every day we started the march in the mid-dle of the foremoon [sic], halted for a noon meal, camped at four o'clock, dug rifle pits and built barricades. Why waste such precious time! We would never catch the Indians dawdling like this![38]

Meanwhile, Minnesotans were screaming for blood. The stark facts of the attacks were horrifying enough, but wild stories of wholesale Indian atrocities proliferated, becoming more gruesome by the day, most of which having only slight basis in fact. Newspapers across the state called for extermination of the entire Dakota nation. In a special session of the legislature, Governor Ramsey vowed, "If any shall escape extinction, the wretched remnant must be driven beyond our borders." Sibley came under relentless fire for his seemingly inef-fectual command. Half the unruly mounted volunteers, itching to "hunt Indi-ans," deserted in disgust, carrying home tales of Sibley's timid leadership. Crit-ics disparaged him every step of the campaign, berating him as incompetent and cowardly, even accusing him and his mixed-blood aides of protecting the Indians. The sheriff of Brown County declared him "a coward and a rascal"; the *Hastings Independent,* a "snail [who] falls back on his authority and as-sumed dignity and refuses to march." After the debacle at Birch Coulee, editor Jane Grey Swisshelm derided him in the *St. Cloud Democrat* as "the State un-dertaker, with his company of grave-diggers."[39]

All this wounded Sibley to the quick. He felt personally betrayed, not only by the ungrateful citizens of Minnesota, but oddly by the Indians themselves. To his mind, he had championed their cause for years, conveniently forgetting his part in impoverishing them and stripping them of their land. Now they repaid his friendship and assistance with savagery, leaving him open to blame for all his earlier "civilizing" efforts. Sibley's anger was palpable. Writing later to Henry Whipple, Minnesota's Episcopal bishop, to justify the trials, he declared, "A great public crime has been committed not by wild Indians who did not know better, but by men who have had advantages . . . by long and intimate intercourse with white men. . . . [They] therefore do not deserve to be judged with the leniency with which entirely wild and ignorant savages might have a claim to be treated." Spurred by his wounded pride, Henry Sibley was ready to hang them all.[40]

Inconveniently, however, before any executions could be carried out, General Pope belatedly realized that death sentences required presidential approval. When Lincoln and his cabinet read Pope's report on the trials and planned executions, they were taken aback, both by the number of men condemned and the irregularity of the proceedings. One cabinet member was "disgusted" by the trials, thought them "discreditable," and went so far as to suggest that the entire episode had been orchestrated to get title to Indian lands. The president ordered a stay of all executions until he personally reviewed the trial transcripts. Sick at heart by the ongoing slaughter in the South, Lincoln had no appetite for mass hangings. He agreed with Commissioner of Indian Affairs William Dole that such actions would be "a stain on the national character." The president also was troubled by a recent meeting with Bishop Whipple, who had eloquently laid out the history of abuses that finally culminated in violence. Lincoln was so moved that he pledged, "If we get through this war, and I live, this Indian system shall be reformed!"[41]

Clergymen were virtually the only voices speaking for the Indians in Minnesota. And most of them raised no more than a timid protest. Dr. Thomas Williamson staunchly stood by the Christian Dakotas, but his missionary son, John, though he stayed with the prisoners throughout their ordeal, admitted, "Such is the state of things that I do not consider it always safe or wise to give my opinion in regard to the treatment of many of these Indians." Stephen Riggs was actively complicit in the trials, assisting the court in translation and sorting through the evidence. In a letter to President Lincoln, he supported the death sentences, despite his "long connection with these Indians, and personal acquaintance with many of them." He was certain that justice required "us to execute the *great majority* of those who have been condemned."[42] Dismayed by Riggs's actions, Thomas Williamson worried that his fellow missionary "had succumbed to the biased atmosphere of the military camp." He wrote to Riggs in indignation:

[I] am satisfied in my own mind from the slight evidence on which these are condemned that there are many others in that prison house who ought not to be there, and that the honor of our government and the welfare of the people of Minnesota, as well as that of the Indians requires a new trial before unprejudiced judges. I doubt whether the whole state of Minnesota can furnish men competent to sit as jurors in their trial. . . . From our governor down to the lowest rabble there is a general belief that all the prisoners are guilty and demand that whether guilty or not they be put to death as a sacrifice to the souls of our murdered fellow citizens.[43]

Later, after widespread calls for genocide evoked criticism in other parts of the country, Riggs began to have second thoughts and admitted some doubts about the conduct of the trials. For even that small concession, he was "roundly condemned." Chastened, he said little more in public, though he wrote privately to the president to express doubts about several convictions. Soothing his conscience, he confided to his son, "I shall not be surprised if new trials

[317]

Reverend Stephen Riggs photographed by Whitney's Gallery in 1862. Courtesy of the Minnesota Historical Society.

are ordered. Our papers and people here talk so much about annihilation and extermination that the people in the East have doubtless thought us crazy."[44]

If not crazy, Minnesotans at the very least were white-hot in their zeal for revenge. As Stephen Riggs learned, anyone who stood even slightly in the way did so at his peril. Only Henry Whipple proved willing to brave the inevitable backlash to publicly raise his voice on behalf of the Dakotas. As a consequence, in the words of one historian, he was the most unpopular man in Minnesota. Since his arrival four years earlier, the bishop had crusaded against the corruption of the Office of Indian Affairs and the injustices suffered by the state's Native population. Following the outbreak, Whipple courageously published an article that sought to tamp down the blood lust that was sweeping across the state. "Who is guilty of the causes which desolated our border?" he asked. "At whose door is the blood of these innocent victims? I believe that God will hold the nation guilty." But people were in no mood to hear the litany of injuries that had driven the Indians to their desperate actions. Some even targeted the bishop with death threats for his words.[45]

When the public learned that Lincoln had stayed the executions, a collective cry of outrage rang throughout the state. "DEATH TO THE BARBARIANS!" bannered the *Stillwater Messenger*. The citizens of St. Paul penned an open letter to the president, accusing the Dakotas of "wanton, unprovoked and fiendish cruelty" and demanding immediate execution. And the *Mankato Weekly Record* warned that the Indians would die "either by order of the President, or by *the will of the people,* who make Presidents." Jane Grey Swisshelm, vitriolic editor of the *St. Cloud Democrat,* urged her readers to be prepared, if the president freed any of the murderers, to "shoot them and be sure they are shot dead, *dead,* DEAD!" Military and civilian authorities joined in the clamor. General Pope had sent the president a series of hysterical accounts of "horrible massacres . . . children nailed alive to trees and houses, women violated and then disemboweled—everything that horrible ingenuity could devise." Now he insisted "the only distinction between the culprits is as to which of them murdered most people or violated most young girls." Senator Morton Wilkinson and Representatives Cyrus Aldrich and William Windom sent a joint letter, filled with more horrific accusations of mutilation and rape "well known to our people." If the executions did not proceed, they predicted, "the outraged people of Minnesota would dispose of these wretches without law . . . if you force the people to it." Ramsey also warned the president that Minnesotans would take matters into their own hands against these "assassins and ravishers of women and girls." Moreover, the state would have no peace until all the Dakotas who were not executed were exiled beyond its borders.[46]

Henry Sibley, as might be expected, felt his honor was at stake in the review of the trials he had overseen. While he privately acknowledged in a letter to Bishop Whipple that some Dakotas had, "with unexampled heroism exposed their own lives and property to destruction while engaged in saving the lives of white men, women, and children," in a printed memorial to President Lincoln he damned the entire race: "Tame [the Indian], cultivate him, strive to Christianize him as you will, and the sight of blood will in an instant call out the savage, wolfish, devilish instincts in his race." Tellingly, he had written to his wife, "I see the press is very much concerned, lest I should prove too tenderhearted." With both his character and competence under scrutiny, Sibley renounced the last vestiges of friendship, respect, and affection he had shared with the Dakotas in his youth.[47]

President Lincoln was caught between intense pressure for vengeance from Minnesota, the undeniable questionable legality of the trials, and opposition to the mass executions that aroused protest from individuals, philanthropists, and religious groups in other parts of the country. A typical editorial in the *Boston Commonwealth* declared the sentences vindictive and diabolical. Lincoln struggled to find a solution that would temper the draconian sentences, yet be severe enough to discourage another outbreak and satisfy the howls from Minnesota. Initially he thought to compromise by planning to execute only those proved guilty of rape—a crime no decent man could excuse. But to his surprise, in the light of all the testimony to the contrary, he discovered "only two of this class were found." With dire predictions of imminent mob violence in Minnesota—Ramsey had telegraphed, "Nothing but the speedy execution of the tried and convicted Sioux Indians will save us, here, from scenes of outrage"—Lincoln then culled from the lists those who had participated in "massacres" rather than "battles" and reluctantly ordered forty Indians, charged with the murder of unarmed civilians, to be hanged.[48]

While awaiting the president's decision, Sibley had been ordered to escort the convicted men to Mankato and send the remaining 1,700 Dakotas in custody—some 250 guiltless full- and mixed-blood men, the rest women, children, and elders—to an internment camp at Fort Snelling until "they can all be removed beyond the limits of the State in the spring." Missionary John Williamson, a steady friend to the Dakotas who had lived among them all his life, remarked, "It is a sad sight to see so many women & children marching off—not knowing whether they will ever see their husbands & fathers again." The journey of these noncombatants to Fort Snelling was a hazardous one. With only 300 soldiers to protect the four-mile-long wagon train along the 150-mile route, Lieutenant Colonel William Marshall, in charge of the caravan, feared attacks from enraged whites, who were beginning to trickle back into the valley. He urged the press to remind citizens along the route that his charges "are not the *guilty Indians* . . . but *friendly Indians, women and children.*"[49]

Marshall took his responsibilities seriously, vowing, "I would risk my life for the protection of these helpless beings, and would feel everlastingly disgraced if any evil befell them while in my charge." Nonetheless, when the caravan entered the town of Henderson, an enraged mob overwhelmed the troops. Samuel Brown, who accompanied the caravan, described the streets "crowded with an angry and excited populace, cursing, shouting and crying":

> Men, women and children armed with guns, knives, clubs and stones, rushed upon the Indians, as the train was passing by, and before the soldiers could interfere and stop them, succeeded in pulling many of the old men and women and even children from the wagons by the hair of the head, and beating them, and otherwise inflicting injury upon the helpless and miserable creatures.[50]

As history has repeatedly demonstrated, war breeds savagery, stripping one's enemy of his humanity. The Dakota war was no exception. Just as Dakota warriors mowed down and mutilated innocent women and children, ordinary white Minnesotans were equally eager to tear guiltless Indians limb from limb and take home their scalps as a prize. In one instance, scalding water was dumped on a cart of old people and children. In another, a Henderson matron rushed up to the wagons, "snatch[ed] a nursing babe from its mother's breast and dash[ed] it violently on the ground." The baby died a few hours later. Samuel Brown, who accompanied the caravan, mused that "uncivilized heathens" and "a *civilized christian* white woman" acted in much the same manner.[51]

Thanks to Marshall's efforts, the pitiable caravan reached Fort Snelling with no further loss of life, though John Williamson recorded a harrowing journey in which, "notwithstanding the guard of soldiers, they [the Indians] received sundry salutations in the form of stones & sticks, to say nothing of the curses which were heaped upon them from doorways & hillsides." The missionary was certain that "had they been in charge of almost any other of our officers . . . they would have been mobbed and many of them killed." Newspapers throughout the state called for "extermination, sure, and terrible . . . the only thing that can give the people of Minnesota satisfaction, or a sense of security." In St. Paul sentiment against the Indians was murderous. After arriving at Fort Snelling, the prisoners first were settled in an open camp on the bottomlands below the fort, but soon they were relocated to a fenced stockade, guarded by soldiers, not to prevent them from escaping but to protect them from the local citizenry. According to Thomas Stewart, a recruit at the fort, "When these Indians had been in camp about two weeks, there were repeated threats that the citizens of St. Paul and Minneapolis were preparing to make a raid and clean out the whole camp." Stewart thought many of the guards would have put up little resistance if such an attack occurred. The Indians spent a miserable winter, wracked by fear for themselves and their loved ones. Nearly 300 died from diseases that swept through the camp. Given the prevailing mood among the soldiers, Private Stewart suspected that not all the deaths were due to natural causes.[52]

Meanwhile, as their families began the trek to their dismal prison at Fort Snelling, the condemned men were readied for transport to Mankato, there to await Lincoln's decision on their fate. As General Sibley loaded some 365 shackled prisoners into wagons, he knew it would be a daunting task to protect them from public retribution along the route, especially since his own men also showed an appetite for revenge. Though he now could rely on the discipline of regular troops, who reinforced the local militia that had composed his initial command, feeling among the men ran high against the Indians. Just days before the departure of the noncombatants, officers had quashed a plot to shell the camp and "kill every living soul in that Indian village," innocent and guilty alike, including women and children. The officers would need to exert close control to ensure that the soldiers took their guard duties seriously. The road to Mankato passed directly through scenes of recent devastation. It was almost inevitable that the sight of the shackled convicts would provoke grief-stricken, infuriated survivors to violence.[53]

Sibley's concerns were well founded. When the wagon train reached New Ulm on the second day of the journey, townspeople there were engaged in the grisly task of removing corpses from shallow temporary graves that had been dug in the streets during the siege. The trauma of identifying the decomposing bodies of friends and loved ones would have been enough to unleash unpremeditated rage. But sources strongly suggest that someone had provided notice that the convoy of convicts was approaching. Sibley wisely chose a route that skirted the town and "strengthened the mounted men on guard," but still the residents rushed to meet the caravan, making a "furious assault" on the prisoners.[54] Eyewitnesses recorded vivid accounts of the attack:

> Hearing that we were passing by, they all rushed forth, men, women and children, armed with clubs, pitchforks, hoes, brickbats, knives and guns, and attacked the prisoners. The women were perfectly furious; they danced around with their aprons full of stones, and cried for an opportunity to get at the prisoners, upon whom they poured the most violent abuse. . . . They were the brutal murderers of their friends.[55]

Using their bayonets, the soldiers drove the mob back, but not before many of the shackled prisoners sustained serious injury. One soldier estimated that "eight out of the ten Indians I was guarding were hurt," some seriously. Two men later died from their injuries.[56] Sibley, incensed at the challenge to military authority, ordered the arrest of some twenty members of the New Ulm militia who had orchestrated the attack, but sensitive to local indignation, he released them a short time later without charges. In his estimation, the women were far more ferocious than the men. "The Dutch she devils!" he commented. "They were fierce as tigresses."[57]

Threats to the prisoners did not diminish once they reached their destination, a prison camp set up near the small settlement of South Bend, just upriver from Mankato. Within a few days, General Sibley departed for St. Paul to take up command of the entire Minnesota district, leaving the prisoners in the charge of Colonel Stephen Miller. Almost immediately rumblings of trouble began. Suspecting that President Lincoln might commute the eagerly awaited executions, men in Mankato, New Ulm, St. Peter, and all the surrounding areas organized vigilante groups to ensure the Indians would not leave Mankato alive. Colonel Miller worriedly wrote Sibley, "I have constant advices of secret meetings here and throughout the country, and a firm and almost universal determination on the part of the citizens to execute the Indians by violence, should the Government much longer postpone [the hangings]."[58]

Miller was no alarmist. Battle hardened by service in the South, he had been called home to Minnesota to serve in the Dakota war. He did not underestimate the threat, nor did he shirk his responsibility. "I know my duty in the premises and shall fearlessly perform it," he promised Sibley, "but the consequences, with the small force at my disposal, must be dreaded." Though he felt little sympathy for the Indians, he was determined to protect their physical safety at all costs. It was an unenviable duty. As frigid November winds and snow whipped the encampment's flimsy tents, soldiers and prisoners alike shivered under shoddy blankets. The colonel fretted that "a few more nights like the last will kill many of [the prisoners], and sicken most of my command." But danger from the elements paled in comparison to the threat of lurking lynch mobs. According to Miller's informants, militia officers and other local officials were behind the plots. Moreover, he wrote Sibley, "It is daily hinted to me that too many of the soldiers participate in this feeling and determination."[59]

Sibley did not brush off Miller's concerns. He repeatedly asked for additional troops and urged Governor Ramsey to discipline the local militiamen who were stirring up the citizenry. But every able-bodied soldier was needed for deployment to the South, and Ramsey, always attuned to the public mood, paid no heed to Sibley's reports of lawless militia activity. Instead, he used the threats of mob violence to pressure Lincoln to proceed with the executions.[60]

Events came to a head on December 4, when Miller received word that a lynch mob was gathering in Mankato. Several hundred men from St. Peter and Traverse des Sioux were in the taverns, "filling up with beer to gain courage" for an assault on the camp. They expected little, if any, resistance from the troops "for many soldiers had friends who had been massacred." But, as one officer later observed, "they didn't know old Col. Miller." He rallied his reluctant troops by vowing "to shoot the first man that refused to shoot [any] citizen that dared to attack us" and sallied forth with a party of cavalry to meet the approaching mob. The vigilantes' Dutch courage proved no match for the steel-spined colonel and they quickly dispersed.[61]

Miller let the men go with no more than a warning, but he knew he had not seen the last of them. He had it on authority that the lynch mob had expected to be joined by a large contingent from New Ulm. Only botched communications had kept them away. The next day Miller ordered the prisoners transferred to a more secure log prison in the center of Mankato. He anticipated no problem getting them into town, "but to get them *out* would require a small

Stephen A. Miller mustered into the service as a lieutenant colonel of the First Minnesota Regiment in 1861. By October 1863 he was a brigadier general and in November was elected governor on the Republican Party ticket. Courtesy of the Minnesota Historical Society.

army." With rumors flying of new planned attacks and no help forthcoming to protect the manacled Indians, Miller used his own funds to hire spies to ferret out any new plots in the making. He also called in a number of Mankato's leading citizens and informed them that if the stockade were attacked, he would not hesitate to "shell and burn a portion of the town."[62]

The colonel's precautions came in the nick of time. On December 6 President Lincoln announced his decision to hang thirty-nine of the prisoners and ordered the rest held until further instructions were received, "taking care that they neither escape nor are subjected to any unlawful violence." This hardly satisfied Minnesotans' hunger for vengeance—not surprising since press reports had wrongly reported that all the condemned men were guilty of murdering civilians. Governor Ramsey tried to allay citizen outrage, assuring them that this was only the first round of executions. And if the president did not follow through, the state courts would see that justice was done. Nonetheless, it is unlikely the governor's promise alone could have held the angry citizens in check. The Mankato town fathers had warned that they could not be held responsible if "the President should pardon or attempt to release the prisoners." But, no doubt thanks to Miller's threats to shell the town, fire on attackers, and even shoot his own men if needed, no further attempt was made to seize the incarcerated Indians. As historian Walt Bachman convincingly argues, Stephen Miller alone kept lynch mobs at bay, who assuredly would have murdered all of the Dakota prisoners.[63]

Throughout this ordeal, the imprisoned Indians existed in bewildered uncertainty. No one informed them what their punishment would be. Some of the convicted men had actively assisted endangered whites and protected captives from harm. Nearly all believed that to act as a warrior was a badge of honor, not a crime. And none admitted to the murder of civilians, though it is almost certain that some were guilty of the crimes, despite their protestations. About twenty men had been convicted on the testimony of fellow participants or survivors, and it is highly unlikely that all the eyewitnesses could have been mistaken. But the most militant Dakotas, those likeliest to have engaged in indiscriminate killing, had not surrendered, choosing instead to defiantly ride northwest onto the plains. As the warrior Wahehna logically pointed out, "If he had believed he had killed a white man he would have fled with Little Crow."[64]

For weeks the convicted Indians waited to learn their fate, chained to the ground, numbed by cold, and helpless to defend themselves from rumored attacks. Under these miserable circumstances, the thirty-nine condemned men may have felt almost relieved when they learned they would die in a few days.[65] At any rate, they accepted the news with outward equanimity. As Stephen Riggs conveyed the president's order in the Dakota language, they showed no sign of fear. A reporter for the *St. Paul Daily Press* noted their cool courage with some astonishment. Riggs went on to inform the prisoners that each "should be privileged to designate the minister of his choice" to make his peace with God. As a man of the cloth, the irony of Riggs's position could hardly have escaped him. He informed the prisoners that regrettably he could not serve as their spiritual adviser because of his official role as government translator, but surely he did not seriously expect the men to entrust their souls to his care when he had been so deeply involved in their interrogation and convictions.[66]

The work of salvation was left to Dr. Thomas Williamson and Father Augustin Ravoux, who had hurried down to Mankato from St. Paul to minister to three condemned mixed-blood Catholics: Baptiste Campbell, Henri Milard, and Hippolyte Auge. None of the condemned full bloods had previously converted to Christianity, but in the days before their execution nearly all submitted to baptism. Rather than experiencing a spiritual epiphany, however, it is probable they hoped to show they were civilized, "good Indians" in a last hope for a reprieve. But whether the conversions were sincere or simply for appearance, when it came to choosing between Reverend Williamson, who had toiled among the Dakotas for nearly thirty years, and Father Ravoux, who had long ago shifted his ministry to white parishioners in St. Paul, they overwhelmingly chose to be baptized by Ravoux as Catholics. Riggs claimed they had been unduly influenced by the Catholic mixed bloods, but it is far more probable that Williamson's lack of success was at heart a judgment on his colleague, Stephen Riggs.[67]

Apparently Riggs's work was not yet done. Over the remaining days he spoke at length with the condemned men, later publishing their testimony in newspapers throughout the state. Designated as "confessions," in fact nearly all the statements were declarations of innocence. Riggs explained this away by asserting that the Indians realized, "and said of their own accord, that so many white people had been killed by the Dakotas that public and general justice required the death of some in return." "And now," Riggs intoned, "guilty or not guilty, may God have mercy upon these poor human creatures, and if it be possible, *save* them in the other world through Jesus Christ, his Son." When not worrying over the Indians' souls, the busy missionary also kept track of any information he gleaned in conversation with them that might prove useful for future prosecutions. He then forwarded a report to Henry Sibley, titled "Revelations Made by the Indians Who Were Executed."[68]

The execution was set for December 26, an unfortunate coda to the celebration of Christ's birth for the newly baptized Christians. On Christmas Eve, while soldiers worked to erect a "great square gallows" in the center of town, the condemned men were allowed to visit with friends and relatives and send messages to distant loved ones. With the sound of hammers ringing in their ears, some of the prisoners were overcome with emotion, but most kept up a cheerful facade, insisting they "expected to go direct to the abode of the Great Spirit and be happy."[69] But not everyone was so resigned. Hdainyanka (Rattling Runner) wrote an angry letter to his father-in-law, Chief Wabasha:

WABASHA: You have deceived me. You told me that if we followed the advice of General Sibley, and gave ourselves up to the whites, all would be well; no innocent man would be injured. I have not killed, wounded or injured a white man, or any white persons. I have not participated in the plunder of their property; and yet to-day I am set apart for execution and must die in a few days while men who are guilty will remain in prison. . . . When my children are grown up, let them know that their father died because he followed the advice of his chief, and without having the blood of a white man to answer to the Great Spirit.

My wife and children are dear to me. Let them not grieve for me. Let them remember that the brave should be prepared to meet death; and I will do as becomes a Dakota.[70]

As becomes a Dakota, the prisoners sang and danced together that evening to prepare for their deaths.

Colonel Miller was making preparations as well. Once the hangings were scheduled, Sibley had dispatched 1,400 additional troops to ensure the executions went off with due decorum. Already humiliated by the president's reversal of most of the trial verdicts, he wanted no breach of order, for which he no doubt would take the blame. But even with such a formidable military presence, Miller was taking no chances. He declared martial law and banned the sale and consumption of alcohol in a ten-mile radius of Mankato. It was a wise precaution. Wagons began swarming into town on Christmas night, overflowing with men, women, and children, eager to see the Indians get what they felt was coming to them. By morning the streets were packed and jammed with spectators—4,000 people, by some estimates. They staked out every possible vantage point, squatting on roofs, hanging out windows, even crowding the bluff across the river from the gallows and a sandbar in the Minnesota River. All waited in breathless anticipation. After all, as the editor of the *St. Peter Tribune* noted, they were about to witness "an event which will always be an important chapter in our history."[71]

In their jail cell, the condemned men calmly prepared for their deaths. As reported in the *St. Paul Daily Press*, "The doomed ones wished it to be known among their friends, and particularly their wives and children, how cheerful and happy they all had died, exhibiting no fear of this dread event." Father Ravoux and Dr. Williamson, who had stayed with the prisoners throughout the night, may have optimistically attributed this to their newfound Christian faith, but the reporter was more skeptical—and probably more accurate. In his estimation, "it appeared not as an evidence of Christian faith, but as a steadfast adherence to [what he called] their heathen superstitions."[72]

The men painted their faces with "streaks of vermilion and aquamarine," shook hands politely with the soldiers and reporters, and waited patiently for the appointed hour. At ten o'clock precisely they formed a procession to the scaffold, walking between columns of soldiers "eagerly and cheerfully, even crowding and jostling each other to be ahead." A local journalist wrote in admiration, "No equal number ever approached the gallows with greater courage, and more perfect determination to prove how little death can be feared." Some of the men even helped adjust the nooses around their necks.[73] Then they commenced to sing a traditional death song, which in Dakota culture exalted the integrity of the person about to die and affirmed the meaning of his existence as an individual and as a member of the tribe.[74] A few moments later drumbeats signaling the execution began. The men grasped one another's hands, calling out their names to each other as the floor of the scaffold dropped with a thud, and thirty-eight bodies suddenly swung lifelessly from the gallows. The rope throttling Rattling Runner snapped and his body fell to the ground. Though his neck was broken, the soldiers strung him up again just to be sure he was dead.[75]

And so concluded the largest mass execution in American history. The crowd was surprisingly subdued. After a moment of hushed silence, they emitted just one, loud, drawn-out cheer in approbation, then quietly began to disperse. Perhaps the unsettling juxtaposition of dignity and horror momentarily damped the celebratory mood. For at least one young woman who was present that day, the memory made a lifelong impression. "[It] was an awful spectacle for a girl of fifteen to witness," Sarah Montgomery wrote many years later. "The scene is as vivid to me now, as it was more than seventy years ago."[76] But many more who lost their homes or friends and family must have felt no regret in seeing Indians—any Indians—pay for their grievous losses. Few of the white victims knew or understood the long history that had led to this moment. They had been caught up in a conflict not of their making, one that touched everyone in the state. White Minnesotans of all ranks and ethnicities—farmers, businessmen, middle-class matrons, laborers—had suffered a collective trauma, their sense of security shattered. As the months ahead would demonstrate, the war against the Indians was by no means over.

Exile

Execution did not end the punishment meted out upon the dead men. After dangling from the scaffold for half an hour, the bodies were cut down and hauled to a shallow mass grave on a sandbar that lay between Mankato's main street and the river. Souvenir hunters stripped them of ornaments and cut off pieces of clothing and locks of hair before covering the corpses with sandy earth. The burial detail might have spared itself the trouble. Before morning nearly all the bodies had been dug up and carted away by local physicians for use as medical cadavers. A Minnesota judge, who saw two of the bodies displayed in a local physician's office, later recalled, "No attempt was made to disguise the fact that these dead bodies had been resurrected for medical purposes." To the contrary, the press treated the disinterment as a joke. Even the *New York Times* joined in, reporting, "The bodies of those buried at Mankato have nearly all been dug up and taken to the dissecting room; among them, 'Cut-Nose,' who is being 'cut up' at Saint Peter."[77]

With the spring thaw of 1863, the river rose to cover the low-lying grave site and whatever remains had not been disinterred washed downstream, leaving no trace of the pitiful Dakota "resting place." But Minnesotans enthusiastically kept the memory of the hangings alive. The mass execution spawned a cottage industry of memorabilia. Newspapers churned out special editions that quickly sold out, chock-full of lurid on-the-spot reporting. Ghoulish souvenirs, from beads to pieces of skin, found a ready market. And lithographs depicting the historic event sold briskly throughout the country. For decades Mankato proudly decked out a variety of items, from souvenir spoons to beer trays, with the macabre scene that became its iconic image.[78]

The terror and fury of war had fully dehumanized Indians in the minds of most Minnesotans. Overwhelming public sentiment made no distinction between murderers and those who were innocent of any wrongdoing: the entire race was guilty of every crime that had been committed. Citizens, journalists, and state officials declared open season on Indians. Inflammatory editor Jane Grey Swisshelm advised, "They should be got rid of in the cheapest and quickest manner." She boasted, "Our people will hunt them, shoot them, set traps for them, put out poisoned bait for them. . . . Every Minnesota man, who has a soul and can get a rifle will go to shooting Indians; and he who hesitates will be black-balled by every Minnesota woman and posted as a coward in every Minnesota home." The *Faribault Central Republican* took aim specifically at the Winnebagos, who had taken no part in the war, warning them that at the first provocation by "the greasy devils," Faribault's citizens would send them to "their happy hunting grounds. . . and there'll be no humbug Military Commissions to try offenders [or] interfere in the matter." They need not have worried. In October General Pope had made his intention clear to "exterminate them all." He had informed Sibley that "all annuity Indians must be notified that hereafter they will not be permitted on any pretext to leave their reservation, that all the soldiers have orders to shoot them wherever they are found, and citizens are authorized to do the same." This applied equally to unoffending Winnebagos as well as Sissetons and Wahpetons who had been out on the plains hunting buffalo and had been nowhere near the war.[79]

With such official carte blanche, citizens organized to effect the removal of all Indians from the state. Towns throughout southern Minnesota formed chapters of the Knights of the Forest, a secret society first established in Mankato. Members included "the most prominent and influential men of Mankato and Blue Earth County." The Knights incorporated all the trappings of a typical fraternal order of the time—secret handshakes, passwords, and rituals—but their single-minded mission was "to use every exertion and influence . . . to cause the removal of all tribes of Indians from the State of Minnesota." The Mankato lodge was particularly keen to expel the Winnebagos, whom they suspected of sympathy with the Dakotas and whose nearby reservation coincidentally encompassed some of the finest farmland in the region. In an open letter to President Lincoln, the *Mankato Weekly Record* went right to the heart of the issue: "Our rich and fertile prairies must either be the abode of thrift, industry and wealth, or the hunting ground of a barbarous and worthless race. Which shall it be, Mr. President?" Convinced that "the future prosperity of Mankato, and indeed of all this region" depended on obtaining the speedy removal of the Winnebagos, the Knights were not content to wait for government action. Members took up guard duty on the outskirts of the reservation, where their pledged "duty was to lie in ambush . . . and shoot any Indian who might be observed outside the lines."[80]

[329]

Thanks to Governor Ramsey and the state legislature, shooting Indians soon could be a profitable as well as satisfying pastime. By summer the state was offering bounties for Dakota scalps. During the spring small groups of former militants, driven from the plains by hunger, had straggled home, desperate to steal some food and horses to keep body and soul together. Predictably, their few chance encounters with whites resulted in bloodshed and reignited widespread panic. "The belief spread far and wide that the Big Woods were full of Indians." Three Indians spotted near Hutchinson led to rumors of a roving band of 300. Half a dozen braves were said to be lurking just outside Minneapolis. Suspicious campfires were reported within twelve miles of St. Paul. The citizenry cried out for protection. But General Sibley, preparing for a massive expedition against Little Crow, had no troops to spare, nor did he think the Dakotas would dare mount a serious attack in Minnesota. Besides, as he reasonably argued, "it was impossible to station a guard at every farmhouse on the border." Citizens must be prepared to defend themselves. Ramsey sent out an envoy to advise people to organize and arm for possible attacks. None of this had a calming effect. In June 1863, after a family was found murdered on the road near the town of Howard Lake, nearly the whole population of Wright and McLeod counties "took to the roads to St. Paul with their live stock and household stuff."[81]

To quell the exodus and respond to public hysteria, the state came up with an ingenious plan at minimal expense to its fiscally strained coffers. Adjutant General Oscar Malmros put out a call for "experienced hunters, scouts or marksmen" to form a corps of elite scouts "to scour the Big Woods for the purpose of exterminating all hostile Sioux." The pay he offered was meager—$1.50 per day. Moreover, the volunteers "will have to arm, equip and subsist themselves at their own expense." However, "a compensation of twenty five dollars will also be given to any body for each scalp of a male Sioux delivered to this office." Apparently this incentive was hard to resist. The sixty-man corps quickly filled its ranks. In addition, anyone who declined to muster into service was invited to act as an "independent scout." These independents would be paid a $75 bounty for each scalp they brought in. Within weeks citizens were out in force, chasing rumored sightings, determined to "kill off the red rascals." But despite these Indian hunters' enthusiasm for the task, few Indians could be found, and they produced only three scalps over the course of the summer. Hoping for better results, the state raised the bounty several times. By fall a scalp was worth $200, but by then most Dakotas had vanished from Minnesota.[82]

Fear and hatred of Indians was a fever that infected nearly every Minnesotan. Yet Lincoln's December reprieve had elicited less public hysteria than expected. The predicted rampage of vigilante justice failed to materialize, probably because Minnesotans were aware that bills to abrogate all the Dakota treaties were already moving through Congress, along with a bill to remove the Winnebagos as well. In the meantime, the pressing problem was what to do with the convicts left in the Mankato jail and their dependents in custody at Fort Snelling. The remaining prisoners, whose fate was still in limbo, spent the rest of that winter chained to the dirt floor of their Mankato prison. Colonel Miller requested permission to supply them with fresh clothing, reporting that their "garments are covered with vermin, very rotten, tattered and filthy." But Sibley, hoping that additional execution orders would soon arrive, was loath to waste his limited resources on men who might shortly hang. He had been ordered to lead an expedition in pursuit of Little Crow's band, and this time he was determined to have adequate arms and provisions. With the ongoing war in the South draining the nation's treasury, Sibley was working with a barebones budget. He warned Miller to make only "*absolutely* necessary" expenditures on food, medicine, or clothing for the unfortunate convicts.[83]

In these grim circumstances, the prisoners became newly receptive to the missionaries' conversion efforts. They had fought to restore traditional Dakota lifeways, but peering through the chinks in their jail walls on execution day, they also had witnessed the price paid by their friends and kinsmen. Clearly, their only hope for deliverance was to embrace "Christian" values, at least in appearance. Father Ravoux had returned to St. Paul, leaving an open field for Dr. Williamson. Within a week of the executions, he was surprised to find the men enthusiastically singing hymns and praying, led by two Christian Sissetons, Robert Hopkins (Chaskaydon) and Peter Big Fire. So many Indians desired religious instruction that Williamson sent for his old friend Gideon Pond to assist him in the work. On a single day in February 1863, they baptized 274 newly minted Presbyterians—far more than they had converted over the past twenty-six years. By April only two prisoners remained unbaptized. To the missionaries, this seemed "a genuine work of the Holy Spirit." After visiting the jail, Stephen Riggs claimed finally to understand "the moral meaning of the outbreak." The Indians had intended it to be "the culmination of their hatred of Christianity. But God . . . had made it result in their submission to him. This," wrote Riggs, "was marvelous in our eyes."[84]

Not everyone was so convinced of the Indians' change of heart. The citizens of Mankato ridiculed the supposed religious conversion. And even Riggs admitted privately that the men were probably as interested in "deliverance from the chain" as from sin. Perhaps so. Certainly, it was true that Christian Indians had influential advocates in Williamson, Riggs, and Bishop Henry Whipple. But no one could deny the sincerity of their concurrent sudden desire for schooling, which had always been the essential second pillar of the missionaries' civilization plan. The prison, according to Riggs, had become "one great school." The men assiduously studied reading and writing, practicing with pens and paper or slates and chalk and poring over copies of Bunyan's *Pilgrim's Progress,* written in Dakota. These exercises may have been yet another desperate demonstration of their willingness to cast off the old ways, but the skills they were developing also had practical value. Writing gave the men a way to communicate with far-off family members. Over the course of the spring, the prisoners sent more than four hundred letters to the camp at Fort Snelling.[85]

Conditions at the fort were nearly as bad as those at Mankato. The biting wind blew off the river, chilling the internees to the bone. Crowded together on the cold, damp bottomland, without adequate food or fuel to warm their tipis, the 1,600 Dakotas confined there had no resistance to outbreaks of mumps, measles, or pneumonia that infected the camp. The elderly and the young were especially vulnerable. More than 200 Dakotas died over the winter, mainly children and old people.[86]

The same religious revivalism and eagerness for schooling that swept through the Mankato prison also burgeoned at Fort Snelling. The many Christian Indians among the internees no doubt influenced the desire for conversion, as did the faithful friendship of John Williamson, who spent the winter among them, "ministering temporally and spiritually to this afflicted people." He recalled with sadness, "The *suspense* was terrible. . . . The ever-present query was, What will become of us, and especially of the men?" Soldiers and visitors cursed and threatened them, and ominous rumors swirled through the camp: all the men were about to be executed, the women and children sold as slaves. Riggs was probably correct when he observed with pious satisfaction, "They laid hold on Christ as their only hope."[87]

In March 1863 the Senate had passed "An Act for the Removal of the Sissetons, Wahpaton, Medawakanton, and Wahpakoota Bands of Sioux or Dakota Indians, and for the Disposition of their Lands in Minnesota and Dakota." All treaties were unilaterally abrogated, all annuities canceled, the funds to be used for reparations to white victims of the late war. The Indians were to be transported to some as yet unnamed destination outside Minnesota. Essentially, the Dakota people were homeless until the president decided how to dispose of them.[88]

Creative schemes abounded. Henry Sibley proposed a reservation near Devil's Lake in present-day North Dakota, surrounded by "a strong cordon of United States troops" to keep them apart from whites. Indian superintendent

Clark W. Thompson wanted to scatter the Indians on farms among the white population, "not more than two families to any county." General Pope thought they should be treated "as the states do lunatics": confine them, feed and clothe them cheaply, deprive them of weapons, and force proper Christian behavior. St. Paul citizen James Taylor proposed that all the Minnesota tribes—Dakotas, Ojibwes, and Winnebagos—be transported to Isle Royale, a rocky island in Lake Superior, "to survive or starve as they could."[89] Agent Thomas Galbraith, who had been roundly criticized for his poor judgment leading up to the war, acknowledged with some disappointment, "Few will contend that the Sioux and all other Indians can be *exterminated* just now." But he advocated a solution that was clearly the next best thing, at least to his mind. He proposed a well-guarded reservation in Dakota Territory, where the Indians would exist in a state of virtual slavery:

> The power of the government must be brought to bear upon them. *They must be whipped, coerced into obedience.* After this is accomplished, few will be left to put upon a reservation; many will be killed; more must perish from famine and exposure, and the more desperate will flee and seek refuge on the plains or in the mountains. . . . A very small reservation should suffice for them.[90]

With no way to speak for themselves and rumors of such pitiless schemes swirling around them, it is no wonder that the prisoners and internees suffered most from an agony of terrible suspense.

Finally in April the waiting was over. Despite intense lobbying from Henry Sibley, Minnesota's congressional delegation, newspaper editors, and assorted other hard-liners, President Lincoln finally declined to order any further executions. Instead he ordered the convicted men to indefinite prison terms at Camp McClellan near Davenport, Iowa. As for the rest of the Dakota people, he approved removal to a reservation on the Missouri River, some eighty miles above Fort Randall in Dakota Territory. Lincoln was assured that Crow Creek, as it was called, was a felicitous site, with "good soil, good timber, and plenty of water."[91]

Eager to be rid of the distasteful duty of protecting Indians from the wrath of their fellow citizens, the military wasted no time preparing to ship them off. The Mankato prisoners were the first to be transported. Flanked by four companies of infantry, they were herded, chained in pairs, onto the steamboat *Favorite* early one April morning, along with fifteen or twenty Dakota women who had cooked and cared for them during their confinement and were to accompany them to their new prison. Though the time of departure was supposed to be secret, many local residents were on hand for a sullen farewell. The *Mankato Weekly Record* editorialized, "All believe they richly deserve hanging," but since that was not to be, "the next best thing was to take them away." Before steaming off to Davenport, the *Favorite* made a quick stop at Fort Snelling, where it dropped off forty-eight men who, though they had been acquitted of

Dakota and Winnebago exile from Minnesota, 1863.

all charges at their trials, had been imprisoned for the duration nonetheless. A company of troops formed a barrier between the steamer and frantic relatives who thronged the shore, searching for a glimpse of their husbands, brothers, and sons. When the boat pushed off again, "a wail of grief went up from hundreds of shrill, wild voices which it was heart-rending to hear." As the *Favorite* churned off downstream, carrying the 329 remaining prisoners away from Minnesota for the last time, the men could only look longingly back as their loved ones on the shore disappeared in the distance.[92]

Two weeks later, the 1,300 Dakotas remaining in custody were crowded like cattle onto two steamboats for the first leg of their journey to Crow Creek. Dusk fell on the river as the second boat pulled away and the Indians began to sing, not the traditional songs of their people but Christian hymns, as if in a final plea for recognition of their humanity. Instead, when they passed St. Paul a crowd gathered on the levee pelted them with rocks and curses. As their sad journey continued down the Mississippi, the exiled Dakotas passed bustling towns that were once the sites of ancestral Mdewakanton villages—Kaposia, Red Wing, Wabasha—where now no trace of the Dakotas remained except in sorrowful memory.[93]

At Hannibal, Missouri, the first boatload of exiles was crammed aboard a train, sixty persons to a freight car, for the next leg of the journey, across the state to St. Joseph, where they met the second boat, the *Florence*, which had traveled up the Missouri to meet them. There, all 1,300 Dakotas were loaded onto the already crowded steamboat for a hot, monthlong, tortuous trip up the Missouri. According to Reverend John Williamson, who accompanied them, "They were crowded like slaves on the boiler and hurricane decks of a single boat, and fed on musty hardtack and briny pork, which they had not half a chance to cook. . . . The mortality was fearful." Illness wracked the wretched passengers, and as the steamboat struggled upriver, it left a trail of makeshift Dakota graves along the riverbank in its wake. Finally, after weeks of misery the surviving human cargo staggered off at Crow Creek, sick and emaciated. Three hundred people died as a result of what Williamson likened to the slaves' "middle passage." He sorrowfully reported that the hills of Crow Creek were soon "covered with graves."[94]

The unfortunate Dakotas soon realized their trials had only begun. Contrary to the description relayed to the president, Crow Creek was a drought-stricken wasteland. Isaac Heard, a devout proponent of extermination, described the reservation with seeming pleasure: "It is a horrible region, filled with the petrified remains of the huge lizards and creeping things of the first days of time. The soil is miserable; rain rarely ever visits it. The game is scarce, and the alkaline waters of the streams and springs are almost certain death." St. Andre D. Balcombe, who had won the dubious honor of serving as agent at Crow Creek, described it as "one wilderness of dry prairie for hundreds of miles around." Despite the forbidding conditions, nearly 600 storekeepers, traders, and various

Plate 119. Newspaper advertisement for "Steven's Great Tableau Paintings Representing the Indian Massacre in Minnesota in 1862." Source unknown.

Joel Whitney was not the only entrepreneur ready to satisfy public demand for details about the violent clash between the Dakota and white settlers in Minnesota. John Stevens, a self-taught sign and house painter who had settled in Rochester in 1853, realized that a panorama that emphasized the sensational elements of the war with the Dakota could likely find a popular audience. Panoramas were nineteenth-century popular entertainment, portable spectacles that dramatized significant historical events or exotic landscapes. Before the Civil War, several popular panoramas describing life along the upper Mississippi River toured in Minnesota; one of these shows may have caught Stevens's fancy and given him the idea of creating a presentation that employed a "liberal use of red paint" to tell the story of the U.S.–Dakota War.

Stevens completed his first *Sioux War Panorama* in 1862, even before the execution of the condemned Dakota in Mankato. The artist crafted his narrative around the accounts of Lavinia Eastlick and her son Merton, one-time Rochester residents who had moved to Lake Shetek immediately before the eruption of violence. Although the Eastlicks survived the attack, they watched four other members of their family and countless neighbors die at the hands of the Indians. It was this experience that Stevens dramatized with his lurid panorama. Scenes from the story were painted on a huge canvas strip that was unrolled during the course of the performance. As the panels moved across the stage, a former riverboat captain, C. E. Sencerbox, waxed eloquent on their meaning. A violinist named "Professor Earl" helped him set the mood for the tragic story.

This advertisement trumpeting the "Great Moral Exhibition of the Age" announced the performance of Stevens's "Indian Massacre" panorama at the St. Paul Opera House in March 1868. The images created by the Rochester sign painter were primitive, demonstrating little mastery of the finer points of composition or human anatomy. His text was equally crude in its emphasis on the "blood-thirstiness of the savages." Audiences in St. Paul may have been accustomed to more sophisticated types of entertainment and showed tepid interest in the show, but his panorama gained an enthusiastic following in small towns across the region. Stevens was himself a masterful promoter, drumming up audiences with an illuminated sleigh, which had translucent

PLATE 119

PLATE 120   PLATE 121

sides painted with scenes from the show. He spent the dark months of winter careening in this contraption through communities in Minnesota, Wisconsin, Iowa, and Illinois where theatrical productions were a novelty; audiences flocked to schoolhouses, town halls, and other local gathering places to view the production touted by Stevens. The original panorama was successful enough to merit the production of later versions in 1868, 1870, and 1872, and the show remained in circulation until at least 1878.

The Stevens panorama reflected the existing preoccupation of white settlers with Indian savagery; it also served to distill the stories of murder and destruction still circulating throughout the state. By articulating the contrast between civilization and savagery and retelling Minnesota's messy civil war as a simple battle between good and evil, it enshrined a version of events that justified the white treatment of Indians that followed. The ongoing war between the U.S. Army and the Lakota to the west provided more urgency to this stage production, which dramatized the importance of American military triumph. Yet viewers continued to find the epic story satisfying so many years after the summer of 1862 because it did more than depict murder and torture and articulate the need for extermination and revenge. The show brought rural neighbors together to celebrate the triumph of American expansion. The panorama ended with a panel that depicted a shower of new babies, the repopulation of the state; viewers could rejoice in the emergence of a new "white" state in the aftermath of the violence.[182]

Plate 120. John Stevens, *Panorama of the Indian Massacre of 1862 and the Black Hills*, scene 12, 1872. Minnesota Historical Society.

This panel juxtaposed the successful industry of white farmers with the murderous destruction of Indians, who were depicted as determined to obliterate any signs of agricultural success. Farming was seen as the noblest calling in mid-nineteenth-century America, which regarded the plow and ax as the tools of civilization. Stevens showed the Dakota attacking farmers while they worked to transform untamed prairie into productive farmland. In scene 12, "the hum of the machine" and the focus required to bring "wealth from golden sheaves" rendered Mr. Gould and his crew of eight "unconscious of danger" as the Indians approached his farm near St. Peter. "Every man was killed and scalped and horribly mangled. From house to house, from farm to farm, these inhuman fiends went torturing, killing and destroying men, women, and children, leaving death and desolation in their tracks," explained Captain C. E. Sencerbox.[183]

Plate 121. John Stevens, *Panorama of the Indian Massacre of 1862 and the Black Hills*, scene 11, 1872. Minnesota Historical Society.

Mrs. Whiznar was absorbed by the milking of her cows as the Dakota approached her farm. She was tomahawked, according to Stevens, by Dakota warriors who also tortured and killed the rest of her family.

Plate 122. John Stevens, *Panorama of the Indian Massacre of 1862 and the Black Hills*, scene 8, 1872. Minnesota Historical Society.

This scene shows the Lake Shetek settlers hiding in a marshy depression, surrounded by hostile Indians. The killing of many of the men forced the women and children to surrender, in the hopes that they would be spared by the Dakota.

Plate 123. John Stevens, *Panorama of the Indian Massacre of 1862 and the Black Hills*, scene 9, 1872. Minnesota Historical Society.

The settlers from Lake Shetek surrendered only to witness the most vulnerable members of their group suffer horrible deaths. Stevens used this panel to communicate some of the most disturbing elements of Lavinia Eastlick's account. The children of William Duley, who would later be selected to cut the rope at the mass hanging of Indians in Mankato, "were shot and fell across each other as represented. Willie Eastlick with his hands and eyes uplifted to heaven, the life's blood streaming from his gaping wounds, is vainly calling on his mother to shield him from the infuriated savages." The woman in the foreground of the picture is Mrs. Ireland, who was shot after resisting being taken prisoner. Her "little innocent babe" is pictured here trying to "obtain its accustomed nourishment from the cold form" of its dead mother.[184]

Plate 124. John Stevens, *Panorama of the Indian Massacre of 1862 and the Black Hills*, scene 17, 1872. Minnesota Historical Society.

Stevens emphasized the Indians' brutal treatment of their prisoners, detailing the killing and torture of women and children. This scene depicts the murder of two captives, Julia Smith and her mother. "One of the redskins claimed the daughter as his slave, another one raised his gun and fired at the mother, at the same time the daughter sprang forward, and the ball pierced her breast before killing her mother," Captain C. E. Sencerbox asserted. "They fell apparently dead, when the Indians took the tomahawks and literally cut them to pieces."[185]

PLATE 124

PLATE 125

Plate 125. John Stevens, *Panorama of the Indian Massacre of 1862 and the Black Hills*, scene 15, 1872. Minnesota Historical Society.

Here an Indian woman is pictured murdering a small child, who Stevens asserted was "sick one day and a little troublesome." This sadistic captor allegedly responded to the child's crying by fetching a "butcher knife" and "commenced at the child's feet and literally cut it up by inches" while the mother was forced to watch. Stevens attributed the story to a Mrs. Cook, who claimed to have witnessed this horror. While many children were killed by the Dakota during the violence, no other account details this kind of torture. Such tales of atrocities against children were paired with dubious accusations of rape to rationalize the exile and extermination of the Dakota. Because they served as powerful justification for American manifest destiny, these stories persisted for years, belying efforts to demonstrate that they were unsupported by the documentary record. This particular scene resurfaced in the 1950s, at the height of the American fascination with cowboys and Indians, in a *Life* magazine series on "How the West Was Won." Selections from this panorama were chosen to illustrate how Indians in Minnesota "scalped" men, "clubbed to death" children, and raped, killed, and captured women in large numbers before they were pacified by the American military.[186]

Plate 126. Anton Gág, Christian Heller, and Alexander Schwendinger, *Attack on the Lower Agency, August 18, 1862*, detail from panorama, 1892–93. Minnesota Historical Society.

Bohemian-born artist Anton Gág did not settle in Minnesota until 1872, ten years after the Dakota burned the Lower Indian Agency on the Dakota reservation (pictured here) and New Ulm. But residents of Gág's new community had kept the details of the violent clash alive, crafting a civic culture fixated on the memory of the Indian attacks, which one local newspaper characterized as the most important event in the history of Minnesota.[187] The town's frequent commemorations of the violence dovetailed with Gág's own interest in the subject. The professionally trained artist soon felt a call to paint what he perceived to be an epic narrative; he yearned to bring to life the heroism of white settlers defending their homes from menacing Indians.[188]

In 1887, Gág began to research the conflict in earnest, interviewing survivors, reading documents at the Minnesota Historical Society, and visiting what is now known as the Lower Sioux Indian Community near Morton to observe and draw Indians.[189] He acquired what he viewed as authentic Indian attire, including headdresses, fringed leggings, and beaded moccasins. Gág convinced his friends and employees to don

PLATE 126

these costumes—which he completed with long black wigs—and reenact the events of 1862 during summer camping trips along Meyer's Creek. Gág sketched and photographed while his compatriots pretended to lie in ambush, scalp settlers, and carry "wounded" combatants to safety.[190] In 1893, these exhaustive studies culminated in an eleven-scene panoramic narration of the U.S.–Dakota War that he completed with the assistance of Christian Heller and Alexander Schwendinger.

Each scene from Gág's panorama is painted on a seven-by-ten-foot surface. This huge scale makes gory details inescapable. In this depiction of the attack on the Lower Sioux Agency, Dakota warriors tomahawk prostrate women, brandish bloody scalps, beat victims with long-barreled rifles, and brutalize pleading children, while the buildings of the reservation burn in the background. Gág's portrayal of Dakota violence hews closely to white assumptions about Indian savagery. Yet this version of the conflict does more than portray incendiary stereotypes because it displays the skill of an accomplished artist with a firm grasp of both composition and the documented chronology of events.

John Stevens's panorama was predominantly a work of showmanship and was commercially successful; Gág's obsessive artistry, by contrast, failed to reap him significant material rewards, although his massive work was met with great enthusiasm in New Ulm, where it was first displayed in 1893. Unlike the Stevens panorama, which was moved by a "crankist" across a stage, Gág's panels were fixed in a circle, and viewers walked around it at their own pace.[191] Gág's huge scroll was exhibited at the 1893 World's Columbian Exposition in Chicago, where historian Frederick Jackson Turner read his famous paper on "The Significance of the Frontier in American History." It was later sold to a Chautauqua company.[192] Gág died in 1908, leaving a large, impoverished family that included his eldest daughter, Wanda, who became a well-known artist of national importance.[193]

Plate 127. Anton Gág, *Attack on New Ulm during the Sioux Outbreak, August 19th–23rd, 1862*, 1904. Minnesota Historical Society.

The planners behind Minnesota's third state capitol, which was completed in 1905, envisioned this new center of civic life as a large canvas on which they could paint the history of the state. They commissioned art that would be instructive as well as

PLATE 127

decorative; paintings, murals, and sculptures were selected to illustrate the state's development from a "wilderness" of untamed prairie to a "civilized" region of well-developed towns. Anton Gág —whose Dakota Conflict panorama had earned him a reputation as a history painter—was one of the artists selected for this task. *Attack on New Ulm* was Gág's contribution to the rich collection of paintings and sculpture for which the building has become so famous.[194]

This painting shows Indians advancing on a farm settlement that is already in flames. Gág's portrayal is relatively sympathetic—he presents the Indians as disciplined warriors rather than bloodthirsty savages—reflecting his mixed emotions about the origins of the conflict.[195] Yet the painting is still premised on a belief in the ideology of manifest destiny and American expansionism; viewers see an unprovoked Indian attack on a peaceful agricultural settlement. The painting currently hangs in a House hearing room at the State Capitol, where it gives visual expression to one of the state's foundational myths.

Plate 128. Francis Davis Millett, *The Signing of the Treaty of Traverse des Sioux*, 1905. Minnesota Historical Society.

This painting, which depicts the signing of the Traverse des Sioux treaty in 1851, hangs in a place of honor in the governor's reception room at the Minnesota State Capitol. Permanently installed in an ornately carved frame, it is flanked by five other monumental works illustrating what capitol planners perceived to be the most glorious events in the history of the young state. Four Civil War battle scenes and a portrayal of Father Louis Hennepin discovering the falls of St. Anthony are ensconced next to Francis Millett's painting in this plush room, which features marble fireplaces, gilded moldings, and white oak paneling.[196]

The scene represents, of course, one of the darkest moments in Minnesota history for Native Americans. Turn-of-the-century capitol planners had little appreciation for this fact when they commissioned Millett to depict what they viewed as a triumphant victory. The well-known artist pulled the details for his painting from the visual

PLATE 128

record left by Frank B. Mayer, the young Baltimore artist who spent the summer of 1851 in the treaty camp at Traverse des Sioux. For years after this event, Mayer had failed in his efforts to win a commission from the Minnesota legislature to turn his own "oil sketch" of the signing into a full-blown history painting.

Millett's detailed work conveys the exultant tone sought by capitol designers, who were less concerned with the type of historical authenticity that Mayer could have provided.[197] Millett gives visual expression to turn-of-the-twentieth-century popular understandings of Indian land cessions in Minnesota. His vista of a peaceful and majestic ceremony, conducted under a waving American flag, provides no hint of coercion or desperation. Two groups appear to be meeting to complete a mutually beneficial agreement. This painting was later used to illustrate a popular history narrative, which asserted that "conditions among both Indians and whites seemed to demand the transfer of land. The white man must have more land and this was the choicest land of all." It was only right, according to this writer that "the race that could not make full use of the land must give way to one that could." This narrative cast the dispossession of Indians as inevitable and ultimately beneficial since "the game had become so scarce as to render it practically impossible for the Indian to make a living in his old way. There was much suffering among them."[198] While the Dakota viewed the signing of the treaty of Traverse des Sioux as a tragic turning point that paved the way for the cataclysm of 1862, Millett cast the agreement in an entirely different light, as the auspicious inauguration of a new era of prosperity.

Plate 129. "Scalp of 'Little Crow,' Leader of Minnesota Indian Massacre, 1862," n.d. Smithsonian Institution National Anthropological Archives.

Dakota leader Little Crow continued to inhabit a powerful place in the imagination of white Minnesotans, even after the executions at Mankato brought an end to the U.S.–Dakota War for many people in the state. Once renowned as a cultural mediator who had consistently advocated white accommodation, Little Crow came to symbolize Indian savagery after the outbreak of violence in August 1862. When he was killed in the summer of 1863, his scalp was taken as a trophy and tanned by the state. Ultimately

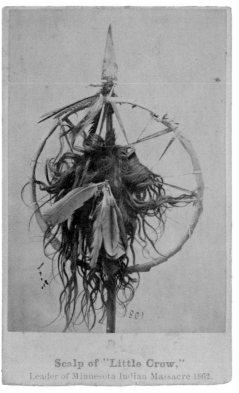

Scalp of "Little Crow,"
Leader of Minnesota Indian Massacre 1862.

PLATE 129

it ended up stretched on a wooden hoop and festooned with feathers at the Minnesota Historical Society, where this image was created by photographer Charles Zimmerman.[199] The hoop was kept on public display there, alongside Little Crow's skull and wrist bones, until 1915.[200]

Zimmerman's photograph served as the basis for both stereoscope cards and postcards like this one, which is currently in the collections of the Smithsonian Institution. This image is deeply offensive to modern eyes and painful for Native American readers in particular. It is included here to illuminate the genocidal rage faced by the Dakota in Minnesota after 1862. The image also demonstrates the depth of the cultural transformation that began when white settlers moved into the state in large numbers. Through the first decades of the nineteenth century, people of diverse racial backgrounds and cultural allegiances had lived and worked together in Minnesota, creating cosmopolitan, extended families that spanned racial, cultural, and linguistic divides. The Americanization of the region brought a racial hierarchy that was hardened by the U.S.–Dakota War, which closed the door forever on this earlier era. In the years that followed, most white Minnesotans viewed Indians exclusively through a racial paradigm that cast them as hostile savages requiring pacification. The decision to create a display trophy out of Little Crow's tanned scalp was a product of this new racial order.

Little Crow's scalp had been displayed at the adjutant general's office until 1868, when it was donated to the state historical society.[201] Most white Minnesotans applauded this acquisition. This kind of trophy, according to Harriet Bishop, provided "a relic of the unparalleled tragedies to which our State has been subjected."[202] The exhibit declared the unequivocal ascendance of American power in the region, providing reassurance to white residents, who saw it as evidence that the savagery of 1862 was safely in the past. For a survivor of the violence like Mary Schwandt, the display in the St. Paul museum left her "feeling a satisfaction" more than thirty years after she had been taken captive by Dakota during the fighting.[203] While white museumgoers would have been appalled by exhibitions of human remains in any other context, the blinders of race allowed them to look on this particular collection of bones and skin with equanimity.

A few Minnesotans could see beyond the racial context of their time, perceiving the historical society's scalp trophy to be an insult to human dignity. The display belied white Minnesotans' claims to be Christian, civilized, or members of a "superior race," in the estimation of Nathaniel West, who avowed that "all that is redeeming in humanity protests against the acquisition; a spectacle which can only feed the temper of a barbarous mind and excite the moral disgust of every man, unblunted by a spirit of revenge."[204] West's call to remove the scalp and the arm bones went unheeded; the historical society expanded its exhibit to include Little Crow's skull in 1895.[205] A few critics would nonetheless continue to condemn the display into the early twentieth century. "Other states have suffered from their Indian wars, but none have thought proper to desecrate their State Capitol with the scalp of a fallen foe," protested Asa Daniels, who served as a doctor on the Dakota reservation until 1861.[206]

Despite these objections, Little Crow's remains were not removed from public view until 1915, when they were placed in a vault at the Minnesota Historical Society. After repeated pleas from Little Crow's descendants and escalating pressure from a Native American community that was embracing fresh political militancy, his bones and scalp were finally interred in a family burial plot in South Dakota in 1971.[207]

Plate 130. Edward S. Ellis, *Indian Jim: A Tale of the Minnesota Massacre* (Cleveland: A. Westbrook, 1908). Children's Literature Research Collection, University of Minnesota.

PLATE 130

The events of the U.S.–Dakota War engaged people across the country fascinated by the question of the frontier conflict with Native Americans. While most Americans were aware of the developments on the northern prairie, only the most dedicated individuals outside the state would have followed all of the newspaper accounts of the violence; fewer still would have had either the time or the resources to devote to the huge literature of histories and autobiographical narratives that emerged to interpret the war in its aftermath. The lessons of this ordeal were more commonly absorbed through more accessible sources, like the 1864 dime novel by Edward S. Ellis (reprinted in 1908 with the fully illustrated color cover featured here) that used the U.S.–Dakota War as the backdrop for its ruminations on the racial character of Indians and the proper course for national Indian policy.

Dime novels were a genre of popular fiction that emerged in 1860, when publisher Beadle & Adams issued its first cheaply printed, paperbound, pamphlet-style novel. These books were universally affordable and enormously popular. Their strict format made them instantly recognizable. They measured four by six inches in size, ran no longer than one hundred pages, and provided stock characters and predictable plots. Like the Stevens panorama, which brought a clear interpretation of the Dakota Conflict to audiences across the Midwest, *Indian Jim* distilled the complexities of the Minnesota war into a story that resonated with a wide-ranging and ever-expanding audience.[208]

Edward S. Ellis probably never visited Minnesota, yet he used actual people and events from the conflict to provide an authority for his narrative, which bolstered popular assumptions about Indian savagery. A steamboat trip up the Minnesota River provided the setting for a debate between two white characters who discussed Native American "racial character." The eastern artist Adolphus Halleck asserted that Indians "as a race, are high souled, brave and chivalrous," and his cousin Marion scoffed that they were "treacherous, merciless, repulsive people, who are no more fit to live than tigers."[209] The plot developed to show Marion's prescience, as they were soon engulfed by the horrors of August 1862. They encountered a landscape littered with the "ghastly, swollen corpses of animals and men, disfigured by all manners of mutilation—infants torn limb from limb, and females so brutally torn and outraged, as to be too revolting for description."[210]

Ellis uses this formulaic frontier romance to insert himself into ongoing debates about national Indian policy, developing his narrative around the premise that the desire to rape white women is what motivated the violence. His characters justify the demands by white Minnesotans for the immediate execution of the 303 Dakota condemned by the military tribunal at Camp Release. One "friendly" Indian warned besieged whites that "Injin after women folks."[211]

This theme is given visual expression by the cover, which pictures an armed Indian dragging a white woman into captivity, even while a "friendly" Indian levels his gun in an effort to stop the abduction. Ellis was one of the most popular and widely read fiction writers of the late nineteenth century. His version of Minnesota's frontier war shaped popular conceptions of Indians—which informed national policies toward Native Americans—for a whole generation of Americans.

PLATE 131

Plate 131. W. Frey, *Die Kämpfe am Minnesota: Eine geschichtliche Erzählung aus den letzten Indianerkriegen* (Mülheim a.d. Ruhr: J. Bagel, 1880s). Minnesota Historical Society.

The story of the U.S.–Dakota War also served as a backdrop for European dime novels, like this one, which identified Minnesota as one of the last sites of frontier danger. *The Battles on the Minnesota: A Historical Narrative from the Last Indian Wars* was a German dime novel from the 1880s that was roughly contemporary with the work of Edward S. Ellis. Wilhelm Frey's work was part of a huge body of "true accounts" featuring Indians that were published between 1875 and 1900 in Germany, where popular fiction set on the American frontier received a particularly warm reception. This fascination may have been inspired, in part, by the massive emigration that brought so many Germans to the northern plains, where they found themselves caught in the violent conflict over American expansion.[212] Germans proved as susceptible as Americans to the romance of the Wild West, thronging to performances of Buffalo Bill's Wild West Show when it toured their country in 1890. The show caused a sensation with its enactments of dime novel plots, displays of exotic animals, and scores of authentic "savage-looking" Indians and helped to create a ready market for popular publications like this one.[213] The cover pictured here shows palm trees in the distance behind the gunslinging white cowboy; this suggests that the narrative inside may have turned more on popular European perceptions than on historical documentation of actual events.

Plate 132. Standard Brewing Company beer tray, n.d. Collection of Jim and Ruth Beaton.

The iconic image of the 1862 Mankato hanging resurfaced on the fortieth anniversary of the U.S.–Dakota War, emblazoned on products created to commemorate the historical milestone. Some companies employed the scene to boost sales, like the cigar makers who affixed it to their packages in 1902. The Standard Brewing Company, a Mankato company founded in 1900, marked the anniversary by issuing this beer tray, which features beer-guzzling soldiers watching the famous hanging. This scenario was fashioned out of fantasy by the brewery's advertising department and has little relation to events on the actual day in 1862, when alcohol sales were banned and the brands of beer pictured did not yet exist.[214] To modern-day viewers, this portrait of jovial soldiers drinking their way through the largest execution in American history seems like a callous trivialization of a horrifying event. But turn-of-the-century

advertisers' usage of the scene reveals more than troubling insensitivity to the tragedies of a violent cataclysm that transformed Minnesota. By illuminating the tenor of
contemporary memories of the Dakota Conflict, it demonstrates how the bloody clash
was recast as an unequivocal American triumph in the decades after the war.

Plate 133. Commemorative silver spoon, n.d. Collection of Nancy Johnson.

The same image of the hanging was also etched on a silver coffee spoon, a commemorative keepsake undoubtedly aimed at a different audience than the beer tray
or cigars. A Mankato jeweler impressed a finely detailed image of the execution onto
the spoon shown here, along with the caption "Hanging 38 Sioux In 1862 Mankato,
Minn." A woman who now lives in Portland, Oregon, inherited what she now calls the
"spoon of atrocities" from her grandmother, who valued the chilling object enough
to make sure it was passed down through her family.[215] The grandmother undoubtedly viewed the spoon—which she might have taken out for guests at formal coffee
klatches—as reassuring rather than macabre. In turn-of-the-century Minnesota, the
execution was seen as the end of a horrendous ordeal. The enormous scaffold came to
signify the end of the dangerous frontier and the dawn of a new era of greater security.

Plate 134. Parade in New Ulm commemorating the fiftieth anniversary of the U.S.–Dakota War, 1912. Minnesota Historical Society.

This photograph shows the parade staged in New Ulm to mark the fiftieth anniversary of the U.S.–Dakota War in Minnesota. The town spent months in preparation for these festivities, which it billed as a celebratory homecoming for past residents and friends of the town. Boulevards and parks were draped with flags and bunting; shop windows received elaborate dressings. In addition to the parade, which featured lavish floats, horse-drawn wagons, and automobiles, the community sponsored pageants and programs. Choirs sang, politicians pontificated, gymnasts leapt and twirled. A peace delegation garbed in ceremonial costumes was received from the Lower Sioux Indian Community, which at the time was known locally as the Morton reservation.[216] Young Wanda Gág saw the anniversary celebration as a chance to improve her family's finances. She crafted clay pipes, cards, badges, bookmarks, bags, and pouches that she decorated with designs she understood to be "Indian" to sell to eager shopkeepers. She even sacrificed the Indian costumes collected by her deceased father to meet the demand for keepsakes generated by the thousands of visitors attracted to New Ulm for the commemoration.[217]

The enthusiasm with which this jubilee was observed shows that the violent events of the U.S.–Dakota War occupied a prominent place in the collective psyche of at least some Minnesotans during the first decades of the twentieth century. But the form and tenor of these commemorations was changing, in concert with shifting American perceptions of Indians. Earlier memorials lionized the heroism of white settlers and championed the triumph of American civilization over Indian savages. By 1910, Minnesotans no longer castigated Indians as the antithesis of civilization; they embraced these "first Americans" as salutary influences on a modern society straining to absorb the transformations wrought by industrialization and immigration. The Minnesotans who invited local Dakota to share in their commemoration of the bloody conflict and who bought Gág's souvenirs in such large numbers were embracing Indians as icons of a new regional identity. The symbolic transformation of Indians from savages into agents of wisdom and peace did little to improve the material conditions of actual Native Americans within the state, however. Both the Dakota and the Ojibwe would continue to suffer the consequences of the systematic dispossession that had been central to the process of incorporating Minnesota into the United States.[218]

PLATE 134

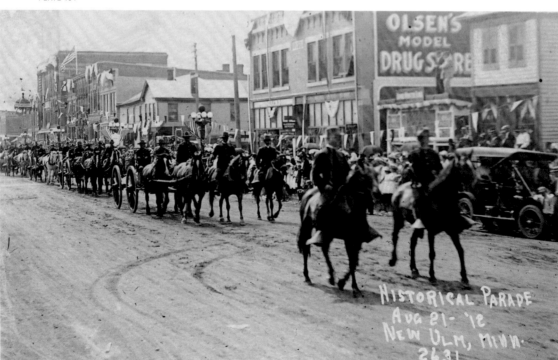

PLATE 135

"OVER WIDE AND RUSHING RIVERS.
IN HIS ARMS HE BORE A MAIDEN."
Henry W. Longfellow.

Hiawatha-Minnehaha Statue, Minnehaha Falls Park, Minneapolis, Minn.

Plate 135. Jakob Fjelde, *Hiawatha and Minnehaha*, 1892, Minnehaha Park, Minneapolis, postcard published ca. 1910. Minnesota Historical Society.

The last decade of the nineteenth century in Minnesota saw the rise of the "white man's Indian," a creative portrait of a spiritual and peace-loving aborigine that found its most developed expression in Longfellow's poem *Hiawatha*. In the popular imagination of the region, this fictional Indian came to eclipse both the "savages" of 1862 and the more complex flesh-and-blood Dakota, Ojibwe, and Winnebagos whose ancestors controlled the north country for hundreds of years. These symbolic Indians carried none of the threat of actual residents of the state, who seemed to vanish from public view in the years after the Civil War, finally fulfilling long-standing predictions that they would "disappear naturally" in the face of "civilization." Both the Dakota and the Winnebagos had been forcibly exiled in the aftermath of the U.S.–Dakota War, which made the existence of the remaining Ojibwe even more precarious.

When *Hiawatha* was published in 1855, it was hailed as "the greatest contribution yet made to the native literature of our country."[219] While it was written in Massachusetts by an author who never visited Minnesota, the poem's narrative fiction was based in part on Mary Eastman's 1849 *Dahcotah*, a romantic collection of Dakota stories she compiled while her husband Seth was stationed at Fort Snelling. Longfellow also borrowed heavily from the Ojibwe legends collected by Indian agent and ethnographer Henry Rowe Schoolcraft, blending them with elements of Iroquois mythology to create his epic story of a composite pan-Indian. *Hiawatha* emerged as a popular as well as critical success, engendering what can only be described as a literary cult that attracted followers from all reaches of the globe.[220]

Longfellow's poem was actually set on the "shores of Gitche Gumee," Lake Superior, in the northern half of the state. But late nineteenth-century Minneapolis leaders overlooked this fact in their eagerness to link their city to this literary phenomenon. City leaders began imprinting their developing urban landscape with names from Longfellow's poem—Hiawatha, Minnehaha, Nokomis—claiming his noble Indians as icons of civic distinctiveness.

In 1889, the city named its newest park after the poem's protagonist. Minnehaha Park became a favorite playground for the city residents; it eventually boasted a picnic area, refractory, and small zoo in close proximity to the famous falls, which had drawn tourists to the site since the 1820s, when they were still known by the more prosaic name Brown's Falls.[221] The development of Minnehaha Park only increased local affection for *Hiawatha*. In tribute, a replica of Longfellow's Cambridge, Massachusetts, home was installed on the grounds. Schoolchildren launched a penny drive to raise the money to bronze the plaster statue that Jakob H. F. Fjelde created in 1893 of Hiawatha carrying Minnehaha "over wide and rushing rivers." In 1912, the figure of the young lovers was placed on the island above Minnehaha Falls. It became a treasured symbol of the growing city, which continued to attract a steady stream of literary pilgrims intent on seeing what they perceived to be the home of Hiawatha and Minnehaha.[222]

Plate 136. *Four American Indian Songs*, harmonized and elaborated by Charles Wakefield Cadman (Boston: White-Smith Music Publishing Company, 1909). Collection of Moira and Leo Harris.

The same kind of fictional Indian immortalized in Hiawatha found musical expression in the work of Charles Wakefield Cadman, an "Indianist" composer who translated the traditional music of the Omaha Indians into a wildly popular group of melodies he called *Four American Indian Songs*. Included among these songs was "From the Land of Sky Blue Waters," a tune rooted in a traditional Omaha courtship melody that became a national best-seller when it was issued in 1909.

This sheet music cover depicts an Omaha man wooing his sweetheart by flute, framed by a rising sun; the illustration shows how Cadman's music satisfied the enormous demand at the beginning of the twentieth century for "Indian romances." Cadman's commercial success provided him with a bully pulpit that he used to expound on his favorite subject: the importance of studying, preserving, and adapting "fast-disappearing" Indian music to make it accessible to popular audiences. He toured the country giving recitals of his compositions, which were accompanied by his "Indian music talk."[223]

While most listeners probably remained indifferent to Cadman's call for ethnographic research, his songs were perceived to be authentic enough to give them educational value. The composer introduced a whole generation of schoolchildren—who were also charged with memorizing Longfellow's *Hiawatha*—to the figure of

PLATE 136

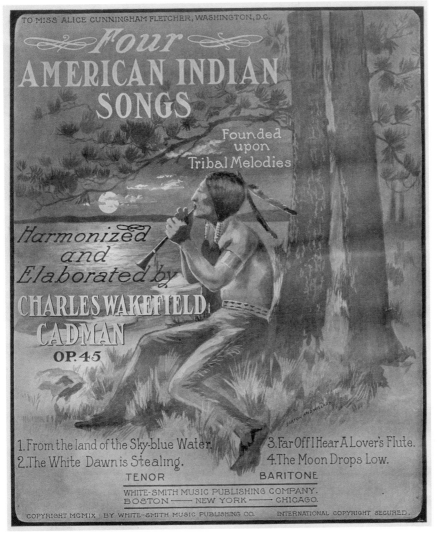

the "noble" Indian. In 1916, Agnes Moore Fryberger, who helped to direct the music curriculum in the Minneapolis public schools, asserted that Cadman's "beautiful songs" were "too refined to sound much like Indian music" but would introduce children to the Indian "legend" on which they are based.[224] These stories would be valuable teaching tools in increasingly diverse urban classrooms, where new immigrants frequently needed additional encouragement to develop "love of country," according to Fryberger.[225]

Cadman's song was written in Pittsburgh after he heard a chant collected by ethnographer Alice C. Fletcher on the Omaha reservation in Nebraska, but Minnesotans claimed "From the Land of Sky Blue Waters" as an anthem for their land of lakes. This meant that it was already familiar in the mid-1950s when the Hamm Brewing Company appropriated it as an advertising jingle that accompanied the antics of a bumbling bear.[226] The Hamm's Bear won a huge following among television viewers in the region, who loved watching him stumble from one disaster to another. The enormous success of this advertising campaign popularized Cadman's melody among a whole new generation of Minnesotans, who no longer associated it with the "noble Indian" it had conjured during the first decades of the twentieth century.

PLATE 137

Plate 137. C. N. Christiansen, "Indian Maiden, Cass Lake, Minn.," ca. 1920. Minnesota Historical Society.

This postcard of a sylvan Indian "maiden" evokes Longfellow's widely popular *Hiawatha*. Bemidji photographer C. N. Christiansen staged the scene of this anonymous Indian woman in a primeval state of nature, where she appears to be uncorrupted by modern influences. Postcards like this one were created for the tourist industry, which played an increasingly important role in Minnesota's economy in the twentieth century. This type of mythic Indian—presented for popular consumption on postcards, in advertising, or in stage shows—was the Native American most accessible to white Minnesotans in the 1920s, when many state residents assumed that nearly all "real" Indians had "disappeared" in the wake of civilization. When this postcard was printed, the fear and violence of 1862 had given way to what one scholar called an "age of Hiawatha."[227] The state's tourist industry enthusiastically embraced this "noble Indian," which it promoted as an icon of Minnesota.

Produced as tourist mementos, postcards served as powerful vehicles for disseminating images. Postcards were more widely available than their predecessors, cartes de visite; they could also be mailed inexpensively anywhere in the country.

Thousands of widely circulated cards featured Ojibwe people from Minnesota, where state boosters had built on the popularity of Buffalo Bill's Wild West Show and Longfellow's Hiawatha to cast resident Indians as tourist attractions capable of satisfying white desires to connect to a mythic past.

Minnesota's "noble Indians" obscured both the state's complicated history of race relations as well as the reality of life for the Native Americans who remained in the state after the exile of the Dakota and the Winnebago. In addition to embodying popular literary fantasies, Indians living in the northern half of the state played practical roles in the state's tourist economy, working as guides, souvenir sellers, and performers in attractions that showcased this manufactured history. The postcards that commemorated these spectacles were labeled with generic captions like "Indian Maiden" or "Indian Chief" that illuminate how Minnesota tourists came to see Indian people in stereotyped terms.[228]

Plate 138. Land O'Lakes sweet cream butter label, 1928–39. Minnesota Historical Society.

As "Indian maidens" and "Indian chiefs" became icons of regional identity, savvy Minnesota marketers seized on these images to distinguish their products. The Minnesota Cooperative Creameries Association rechristened itself Land O' Lakes in 1924 at the suggestion of Ida Foss, who submitted the appellation to the company's naming contest. The cooperative found the trademark that embodied its new identity in 1928, when it adopted a painting that evoked the legend of Hiawatha and Minnehaha, which had a particularly strong following in the cooperative's home city of Minneapolis.[229] The Indian maiden it pictured went on to become synonymous with Minnesota butter.

Earlier advertisers had celebrated the end of "savagery" with their reproductions of the Mankato execution lithograph. By the early twentieth century, this "savage life" had been recast as a romantic narrative to be cherished for its simplicity and appreciation of the natural world. Land O'Lakes adopted its trademark Indian maiden in the hope that buyers would associate its butter with the same qualities of natural simplicity. The Land O'Lakes Indian maiden pictured here is now a brand icon, more familiar to modern viewers than the literary myth it took as its inspiration.[230] While company leaders felt that they were paying homage to the state's Native American heritage with this trademark, their Indian maiden harkens back to an imagined history with little connection to the events that led to the making of modern Minnesota.

PLATE 138

PLATE 139

Plate 139. Minnesota Territorial Centennial Queen Mary Durey with William Littlewolf, Itasca State Park, 1949. Photo by Monroe P. Killy, Minnesota Historical Society.

Minnesota celebrated its territorial centennial in 1949 with a series of historical pageants intended to convey the state's history to a popular audience. These performances—which were shaped more by showmanship than by scholarship— were meant to bolster the state's growing tourist industry instead of providing viewers with challenging historical interpretations. They commemorated the nineteenth-century legends that had come to enshroud the state's more painful history of dispossession, relying on references to the "vanishing race" to gloss over the state's marginalization of its Native Americans.

State pageant director Harold Searls wrote a standard script for these events that borrowed heavily from the imagery of Hiawatha to portray Native Americans in a primeval period "before the white man came." Love songs echoed through villages where Indians "lived in a care-free fashion—hunting, fishing, dancing, singing."[231] Searls's full time job was to coordinate and standardize the performances that drew thousands of spectators; he provided individual counties with advice on music and costumes to accompany his historical narrative. Searls also had direct responsibility for the pageants that were performed in the state's parks, including one held in Itasca State Park on July 2, 1949, which featured performer William Littlewolf, who is shown here posing with Territorial Centennial Queen Mary Durey. This extravaganza featured the "ceremonial dances" of Red Lake reservation members against a backdrop of "canoes, colorful blankets and lighted campfires."[232] The narrative was meant to be celebratory rather than critical of past injustices; Searls suggested ending each pageant with a rousing chorus of "Minnesota, Hail to Thee."[233]

In this photograph, William Littlewolf wears the warbonnet of the Plains Indian, which had been popularized through the Buffalo Bill Wild West Show, western movies, and television portrayals of cowboys and Indians. The traditional woodland

PLATE 140

Ojibwe wardrobe never included the warbonnet, which was completely alien to the indigenous culture of the state, but it became part of the public apparel of the twentieth-century Indian man in Minnesota, who was rarely pictured without this type of spectacular headdress after 1920.[234] This photograph demonstrates the way that mid-twentieth-century Minnesota Indians found their lives increasingly circumscribed by popular stereotypes.

Plate 140. Ralston Crawford, "Standard Service in the Heart of Mankato," n.d. Hirshhorn Museum and Sculpture Garden.

Mankato commemorated the fiftieth anniversary of the U.S.–Dakota War in 1912 by dedicating the 8,500-pound granite monument pictured here. The monument's short epigraph memorialized the largest execution in American history: "Here Were Hanged 38 Sioux Indians, Dec. 26th, 1862." By the time Ralston Crawford shot this photograph in the mid-twentieth century, the imposing marker was completely overshadowed by the manifestations of post–World War II consumer culture. Cars crowded the iron railing that surrounded the monument, which was dwarfed by billboards encouraging passersby to "Enjoy Kato Premium Beer" along with the other offerings of "Baff's Drive In." The dark tone of the memorial struck an increasingly dissonant tone in an era marked by celebrations of Hiawatha-style Indian heritage. The marker became even more problematic in the decades that followed, as the intensifying political militancy of the state's Indians demanded a reconsideration of the U.S.–Dakota War and the mass execution that followed it. In 1971, the monument was unceremoniously removed. Growing public embarrassment about the starkly worded marker converged with a desire to redevelop the downtown block where it stood. The granite block sat in a municipal storage facility until the mid-1990s, when it vanished from city custody. While many Dakota have welcomed the disappearance of what one leader called "that derogatory rock," its covert destruction begs the question of whether Minnesotans will ever reckon publicly with either the violent context of the hanging or the dispossession of the state's Indians that followed.[235]

Plate 141. Headstone marking the grave of Little Crow, Taoyateduta, near Flandreau, South Dakota, 2002. Photograph by Mark Steil, Minnesota Public Radio.

Little Crow survived the violence of 1862 only to be killed the next summer near Hutchinson, Minnesota. He was not buried until 1971, when the increasing political militancy of Indians had begun to shift public perceptions about the legacy of Native American dispossession in Minnesota. Fresh anger about coercive land cessions, broken treaty promises, white violence, and the forced relocation of Dakotas and Winnebagos after the U.S.–Dakota War of 1862 began to destabilize the romantic stereotypes of Indian life that had dominated popular culture in Minnesota during the years surrounding the state's centennial celebrations. This changing context meant that the Minnesota Historical Society was drawing fresh scrutiny for its holdings of human remains. Little Crow's grandson, eighty-eight-year-old Jesse Wakeman, had been pressuring the Minnesota Historical Society to release his grandfather's bones since 1915. This request was granted after fifty-six years when curator Alan Woolworth removed Little Crow's skin and bones from a storage vault in St. Paul and delivered them to South Dakota, where they were placed in a final resting spot chosen by Wakeman.[236] The inscription on the grave marker includes a version, in Dakota and English, of Little Crow's fateful declaration on the eve of the U.S.–Dakota War in August 1862: "You will die like the rabbits when hungry wolves hunt them in the Hard Moon. Taoyateduta is not a coward; he will die with you."

PLATE 141

government employees had trooped to Crow Creek in advance of the Indians, to siphon what profit they could from the meager allocations provided for Dakota subsistence. Indians and missionaries both protested the blatant thievery that was practiced at Crow Creek, to no avail. Episcopal missionary Samuel Hinman wrote with fervor, "The swindle is an awful one because it is now causing so many innocent and helpless people to suffer." According to the testimony of Crow Creek resident Passing Hail, most provisions, clothing, and goods never reached the Indians. He believed the agent traded them away.[95]

Only 176 men were among the 1,318 Dakotas deported from Fort Snelling, and many of those were elderly. Thus, the burden of survival fell primarily on women, who labored heroically to care for their children and parents. Their descendants relate how the women worked the fields and gathered what edible plants they could find. They also "cut and hauled wood to the saw mills, to the boatyard to feed the boilers of the steamships, and to the stoves of the white settlers in the area, for whom they also planted and harvested corn. They cooked and cleaned in the soldiers' mess [and] did their laundry." But despite the women's unstinting labor, survival was impossible by their efforts alone. Unable to grow crops in the parched, sandy soil or to hunt without guns, horses, or permission to leave the reservation, the Indians desperately needed government provisions. But by the time supply trains had traveled the 292 miles from St. Paul to the remote reservation, flour and pork were often spoiled and cattle barely alive. Forced to subsist on condemned meat and flour, the Indians fell prey to malnutrition and illness, with no doctor or medicines to alleviate their suffering. According to Williamson, most of the younger children died in the first year. Conditions were dire. One soldier, on his return from Crow Creek, claimed to have seen women "picking half-digested kernels of grain out of horse manure and boiling them up for soup." Bishop Whipple, who continued his lonely fight on behalf of the Indians, told of respectable women turning to prostitution as the only way to keep their children alive.[96]

Crow Creek was also decreed the new home of Minnesota's Winnebagos. Interestingly, the Winnebago removal order had been enacted in February, a month before the Dakota removal bill became law. With the Dakotas either imprisoned at Mankato, under guard at Fort Snelling, or out of reach on the plains, the Winnebagos—who had taken no part in the war—apparently seemed the more immediate problem. General Pope had insisted throughout the campaign and trials that Winnebagos were coconspirators with Little Crow, and rumors proliferated that they had been seen at various battles or were planning independent attacks, though no credible evidence could be found to support those claims. Nonetheless, Pope ordered the hangings to take place at Mankato, specifically to intimidate the suspect Winnebagos from any thought of rebellion.[97] Mankatoans constantly complained of alleged Winnebago "threats, annoyances and depredations," yet their agent wrote glowingly of their industriousness and efforts at assimilation. The Indians' real crime, as numerous sources make clear, was that their 54,000-acre reservation occupied "nine townships of the most fertile and best watered portion of Blue Earth and Waseca counties"—a fact known as well in Washington as in Minnesota.[98]

The Winnebagos felt the heavy weight of suspicion on them and had frantically tried to demonstrate that they were no friends of the Dakotas. At the height of the war, a group of braves killed a Dakota man who was kin to them by marriage, lest they be tarred with guilt by association. To signal where their loyalties lay, they painted their bodies with the victim's blood and brought his heart, tongue, and scalp to show off in Mankato. Understandably, the gesture proved to have the opposite effect. But a different, more "civilized" show of friendship would probably have been equally futile. Whites were determined the Indians must go and powerful voices in government lobbied for removal. Governor Ramsey vigorously urged "resettlement" as necessary for the peace and prosperity of the state, and Senator Morton Wilkinson led the charge in Washington, couching the "Winnebago problem" in humanitarian terms. "The welfare of the Indians as well as the peace of the whites demand it [removal]," he asserted. Serendipitously, the senator was to benefit quite handsomely from the sale of Winnebago land. Given oversight of reservation land sales, he embarked on a "happy relationship" with the firms that handled the subsequent appraisals and financing.[99]

The Winnebagos did not give up their farms without a struggle. At first they simply refused to leave. The *Mankato Weekly Record* reported that Baptiste LaSallieur, a spokesman for the tribe, protested, "It is a d——n cold country—no water—no wood." He had seen Crow Creek and knew it was "a d——n bad country for Indian." But in May, threats of military force and "a wholesome fear of soldiers" finally emptied the reservation—which was immediately platted into sections and publicized for sale.[100]

The Winnebagos had always been notoriously independent and resistant to relocation, and they proved no more tractable to this forced removal. It took a month of persuasion and coercion to round up 2,000 tribal members for the trip to Crow Creek, and still some recalcitrants scattered to former homes in Iowa and Wisconsin. Many of those who made the trek to the reservation took one look at the barren landscape and began making plans to decamp. In a steady exodus, small groups traveled down the Missouri in canoes made of hollowed cottonwood logs to find refuge with the Omahas in northern Nebraska. Only constant military guard kept more from leaving. In essence, they were treated as prisoners. A walled stockade, christened Fort Thompson, separated them from the Dakotas, howitzers ominously mounted atop its blockhouses. Inside the enclosure, whites enjoyed "fine buildings, comfortably arranged," almost like "a little village." Indians, who were forbidden to enter the fort without a special pass, lived in considerably less comfortable conditions.[101] Shortly after their arrival, a letter from Fort Randall reported:

The Winnebagoes are faring very badly in their new reservation—a desolate wilderness where nothing can be raised any season, this least of all. The dry & parched ground is swept almost constantly by a furious wind, almost equaling in severity the fearful monsoon of the Sahara desert. The children are dying off by the hundreds, and starvation stares the adults in the face.[102]

Still, Superintendent Thompson insisted all was well and the *St. Paul Daily Press* described the reservation as "good enough" for Indians.[103]

Over the next two years, the Winnebagos continued an unauthorized, quiet flight from Crow Creek. Offered a home with the Omahas, most already had relocated to Nebraska by 1865, when the government formally granted them a reservation there. But the Dakotas had nowhere to go. Finally, in 1865 a government commission was established to investigate reservation conditions. Its findings were shocking. In testimony before the commission, Passing Hail described the inhumane situation that prevailed at Crow Creek: physical abuse, rotten food, theft of government blankets and clothing that left the women "crying with cold." "It seemed as though they wanted to kill us," he concluded.

The President gave us some laws, and we have changed ourselves to white men, put on white man's clothes and adopted the white man's ways, and we supposed we would have a piece of ground somewhere where we could live; but no one can live here and live like a white man.[104]

Indeed, there seemed to be no place for Indians in this harsh new world. Coerced to abandon their traditional ways, it was equally impossible to live like white men under these conditions. Agent Balcombe concurred. Unless extinction was the government's plan, he advised, the Indians must be relocated. After visiting Crow Creek and observing firsthand the ongoing "state of semistarvation," the commission acknowledged the inhumane conditions of the reservation and recommended it be closed down. At last, in 1866, after three years in what could only be described as a concentration camp, the displaced Dakotas were moved to a new, more hospitable home near Niobara, Nebraska.[105]

Their tenure at Crow Creek had reduced the Dakotas to a pitiable state. Some 200 additional men had either surrendered or been sent to Crow Creek between 1863 and 1866. Yet by the time they left, the population had diminished to just more than 1,000—900 of them women. Sympathetic witnesses described the people as "wholly indigent, broken-hearted, and without hope in the world." It is a testament to Dakota resilience and resourcefulness that they were able to revive their communities in their Nebraska home. But the sorrows of Crow Creek were not forgotten. Years later, recalling the desolation of those years, John Williamson declared, "The very memory of Crow Creek became horrible to the Santees, who still hush their voices at the mention of the name."[106]

Meanwhile, Minnesota's campaign to expel the Indians had been a grand success. New settlers were eagerly snapping up more than one million acres of prime Winnebago and Dakota lands, and only about 200 Dakota people remained in the state. Exempted from removal because of their service to whites during the war, these "friendly Dakotas" were permitted to return to their former homes. However, they soon discovered that whites would not tolerate Indians as neighbors. With a bounty on Dakota scalps, they found themselves outcasts, in constant danger of assassination. Where were they to go? With all their lands and annuities confiscated and hostile whites a constant threat, self-sufficiency was nearly impossible. Henry Sibley hired some as scouts and allowed their families to live under army protection at Big Stone Lake. He also offered sanctuary at Mendota to a few families. A larger contingent of Christian Indians found a haven at Faribault, where their kinsman, Alexander Faribault, and Bishop Whipple provided much needed work and assistance, over the strenuous objections of many Faribault citizens.[107]

Not even the influence of Alexander Faribault, his city's founder and first citizen, could stanch threats of violence against the wholly innocent Indians. Taopi, a Mdewakanton honored for saving the lives of some 200 women and children, went to Bishop Whipple in despair. "I hear," he said, "that white men say they will kill me. . . . Tell them not to shoot me like a dog, but to send for me to go to the public square, and I will show them how a man can die." Though the threats against him gradually waned, Taopi learned to his sorrow that, as an Indian, he could expect no appreciation for his fidelity, Christian piety, or official letters of commendation. Nor would he be welcomed by his exiled people, who regarded him as a traitor. As he told Whipple, "I shall never have a home until my grave." In fact, most of Minnesota's remaining Dakotas were consigned to impoverished wandering as thanks for opposing the war. Bishop Whipple testified to Taopi's plight: "When I knew him before the outbreak, he had a house and furniture, and stock, and implements of husbandry, and was a well to do farmer. These later years have seen him a poor homeless wanderer." A lone champion of justice for Taopi and the other friendly Indians, Whipple declared, "Their deeds of bravery ought to live forever" in the hearts of a grateful nation. Instead, the government and the people of Minnesota turned their backs.[108]

The Final Act

By 1863 the last remaining tribal lands in Minnesota belonged to the Ojibwes. But officials were hard at work to resolve that troublesome problem. The Ojibwes were not immune from the swell of fear and hatred that broke over the Dakotas and Winnebagos. They knew they were in a precarious position. Certainly the timing of Hole-in-the-Day's saber-rattling threats to force the government's release of provisions to his people had been unfortunate. Though no actual violence occurred, the events at Crow Wing coincided almost exactly with the outbreak of the Dakota war. Conspiracy theories abounded, linking Hole-in-the-Day and Little Crow as partners in a pan-Indian plot to kill all the whites in Minnesota. No one who had any knowledge of the long-standing enmity between the tribes took such an idea seriously, but most Minnesotans drew little distinction between one tribe and another. The politically astute Hole-in-the-Day knew he had a serious problem on his hands. His actions had angered most of the Ojibwes as well as whites. Only the Gull Lake band and a few Pillagers had supported his threatening tactics. Now it was clear that whatever concessions he had won in the short term were clearly not worth almost certain escalated white hostility. Shortly after the Dakota war broke out, a delegation of Ojibwe chiefs and braves visited St. Paul, dressed in their finest regalia, to offer their friendship and services in the war against the Dakotas— an offer that was "tactfully declined." Hole-in-the-Day was not far behind. The chief hustled to the capital city in hopes of repairing both his public image and his damaged relations with Governor Ramsey.[109]

Neither these nor any other expressions of friendship muted the clamor that rose from the St. Croix valley to Duluth to expel the Ojibwes from Minnesota. Even as the newspapers reported clashes between Ojibwes and Dakotas in the border region, they printed suspicions of an alliance between the tribes. Joseph LeMay wrote from Pembina that though the Ojibwes "are nowadays asking nothing of the settlers; that extraordinary courtesy on their part forces us to the belief that they are only waiting for their day of general pillaging, that is soon to come." Timbermen, eager to get hold of valuable reservation timberland, seized the moment and joined voice with fearful settlers who now viewed all Indians as potential murderers. Consequently, even as Sibley and his troops were pursuing the Dakotas, government officials were hatching a plan to move all the Ojibwe bands to remote reservations in the northernmost part of the state. Henry Rice, senator and longtime timber speculator, was the chief architect and proponent of the scheme and Governor Ramsey his enthusiastic collaborator.[110] In October, despite ongoing recruitment responsibilities for the Civil War and pressing concerns regarding traumatized refugees and hostile Dakotas, Ramsey found time to travel to Red Lake to negotiate a land cession with the Red Lake and Pembina bands. The *St. Paul Daily Press* crowed with pleasure over his success:

> Indian title extinguished throughout the entire Red River valley on both sides of the river, except the small & worthless district of impassable swamps & rocky barren which forms the basin of Red Lake. . . . This was readily conceded to the Red Lakers as a perpetual reservation, as it is entirely unfit for the habitation of any other class of beings.[111]

At first most Ojibwes strenuously opposed renegotiation of existing treaties, but their objections were drowned out in the wave of public hostility. Unfounded charges of Ojibwe depredations proliferated, raising the temper against them. As wholesale dispossession of the Dakotas and Winnebagos proceeded, it must have made the Ojibwes painfully aware how little leverage they could exert. Even Hole-in-the-Day, who vigorously opposed an attempted relocation of the Mississippi bands in 1863, was a model of cooperation in treaty negotiations a year later. "If I have ever committed any errors," he pledged, "I wish to correct them, and my young men all feel the same way." As the official spokesman for the bands in Washington, he signed a treaty that would move the Mississippi, Pillager, and Winnibigoshish bands to a new reserve on the northwest shore of Leech Lake, which proved to be a "sterile location," entirely unfit for agriculture.[112]

[340]

In a series of treaties signed between 1863 and 1867, the various Ojibwe bands reluctantly agreed to exchange their remaining lands for concentrated reservations at Red Lake, Leech Lake, White Earth, Nett Lake, Grand Portage, and Fond du Lac on land that held no attraction for white settlers or speculators. Only the 700 members of the Mille Lacs band somehow tenaciously held onto their traditional territory. However, timber poachers and squatters encroached on their lands almost at will. Legal authorities took no notice and the Indians themselves did not dare act against the trespassers, hamstrung by a treaty provision that threatened removal if they should "in any way interfere with or in any manner molest the persons or property of the whites." As for the other bands, by 1870, though the approximately 6,000 tribal members remained within the state's borders, they had relinquished the meadows, forests, and wild rice beds of the lake country for the harsh climate, poor soil, and "immense swamps" of new reservations located hundreds of miles from population centers. As the *St. Paul Daily Press* noted with satisfaction, the isolated nature of the country made it "impassable to travel . . . far outside any route of commerce." Only the White Earth reservation, which had been established in north-central Minnesota through the strenuous advocacy of Bishop Whipple, offered a slight possibility for sustainable lifeways. Thus, at least for the time being, as far as white Minnesotans were concerned, the Ojibwes vanished from public consciousness.[113]

The public obsession with the "Indian problem" seemed abruptly to evaporate once the troublesome Indians were out of Minnesota or consigned to far-distant, isolated reservations. Indian news had filled reams of newsprint while their fate was undetermined, but only rarely did the papers report on conditions at Crow Creek or Red Lake. Most Minnesotans, relieved to be rid of the "red devils," cared little about what became of them in the future. The Dakota war itself was a different matter. The public had a seemingly endless appetite for tales of massacre and bloody mayhem, violated women, and perilous escape. Almost immediately a deluge of first-person accounts and histories appeared and were snapped off newsstands and bookshelves as quickly as they were churned out. All this assured that at least one group of "vanished" Indians would not be forgotten—Little Crow and his soldiers who had fled to the plains.

Over the winter of 1862–63 Little Crow's caravan of about 300 people, including women and children, wandered the plains in a fruitless search for allies. First they trekked to Sisseton and Wahpeton winter camps at Big Stone and Devil's lakes, seeking their kinsmen's assistance in continuing the fight. The chiefs soundly rebuffed Little Crow's appeal. Sisseton chief Standing Buffalo blamed him for starting what was clearly a suicidal war. "You have already made much trouble for my people," he charged. "Go to Canada or where you please, but go away from me and off the lands of my people." The Mdewakantons had no better luck on the Missouri. The Lakota Yanktons and Yanktonais wanted no part of the rebellion, and the Mandans and Arikaras opened fire when Little Crow tried to approach their camps. Truly the Mdewakantons were outcasts.[114]

Finally, Little Crow turned to the British for help, relying on old alliances made in the War of 1812. In May he and his men rode into Manitoba's Fort Garry in an impressive display of false bravado. Displaying British medals and a union jack that had been awarded their grandfathers, the Mdewakanton outlaws professed "peace and friendship" toward the Canadians and undying vengeance against the Americans. Hoping the British would jump at the opportunity to damage their old enemies, Little Crow asked for arms and ammunition to carry on the fight. But Alexander Dallas, governor of the Hudson's Bay Company, had no wish to incite an international incident or disrupt trade relationships by meddling in Indian affairs. He diplomatically informed Little Crow that he must deny the request, offering instead only a few presents and some food. As the disappointed Mdewakantons were leaving, the governor politely asked them not to return.[115]

Little Crow was out of options. By June the Indians were short on food, had no horses, and very little ammunition. Word had come that Henry Sibley was marching an army of more than 3,000 men and numerous artillery pieces up the Red River to hunt down the Dakota soldiers. The prospect of facing this daunting force took the will to fight out of many of the men. Recognizing that their cause was hopeless, some abandoned the war party to stay with the Sissetons and Wahpetons. Others headed to Canada or west to the Missouri, hoping to outrun Sibley's forces. But Little Crow unaccountably elected to return to Minnesota with a small party of eighteen family and close friends. By some accounts, his plan was to steal horses, by others to slaughter as many whites as possible, but Dr. Asa Daniels, who had known the chief well for nearly a decade, rejected those explanations. Daniels believed that, "knowing all had been lost, home, friends, and country, he sought his enemies, expecting, and perhaps seeking, the death that followed." Historian Gary Clayton Anderson concurs in his authoritative biography of Little Crow, writing that the proud chief had seemed to know from the beginning that death was the inevitable outcome of his war against the whites. Surrender certainly was not an option. He had once pledged that no white man would touch him while he was alive. Now he may have intended that his life should end on his terms, not as a condemned convict or a refugee, fleeing from the soldiers, but unbowed in the land of his fathers. It is unlikely that he had any expectation of returning from Minnesota alive. Declaring calmly that he was a dead man, Little Crow began his journey home.[116]

Henry Sibley's orders were quite clear. Little Crow was the main prize he was after. Governor Ramsey had told Sibley in no uncertain terms to make sure the chief was dead. Minnesotans were obsessed with Little Crow, whose very name embodied all the horror of the past summer's war. Throughout the winter the papers had followed the chief's every move, detailing his visits to Pembina and Canada, quoting purported threats to kill all the Americans, and greatly exaggerating the size of his forces. When facts were not available, rumors served just as well. All of this kept citizens in a state of heightened fear, convinced that unless the almost mythical Little Crow were killed, an Indian army of thousands would return and murder them all. General Pope was so determined to apprehend the outlaw Dakotas that—despite dreadful losses in the South and an urgent need for additional troops—he sent *two* expeditions after Little Crow and his warriors. While Sibley's army approached from the east, General Alfred Sully had orders to travel up the Missouri, then cut off retreat from the west. All told, 6,000 troops were deployed to defeat no more than 300 Indians. The irony of the moment is inescapable: as Sibley's juggernaut rolled slowly westward, his most wanted quarry was walking, largely unprotected, almost to the outskirts of St. Paul.[117]

By late June Little Crow's party, traveling on foot, had reached Yellow Medicine, where they split into several groups, hoping to steal horses and food. At least two parties met up with whites, whom they killed before taking their horses. In one particularly brutal raid, they slaughtered a family on the road near Howard Lake. Well informed about the hangings, imprisonment, and deportation of their relatives and friends who had surrendered, the Indians exacted a bloody revenge on the hapless travelers. Days later, their mutilated, decomposing bodies were found on the road. Papers across the state bannered the "horrible and ghastly details" of the murders, reigniting the hysteria of the previous summer. Once again Sibley was excoriated, this time for leaving villages and settlements defenseless while his Brobdingnagian army lurched westward with the excruciating slowness and the "dignified leisure of commissary trains."[118] The *St. Paul Daily Press* editorialized:

> The humiliating fact stares us in the face that after all our vast and elaborate preparations to rid the state of these infernal red devils, our familiar settlements, except some few fortified villages, are almost as defenceless against the peculiar modes of Indian warfare, as if we hadn't a single military guard in the state.[119]

Of course, the truth was far less alarming. But the public had no way of knowing that less than a dozen hostile Mdewakantons, with scarcely any horses, ammunition, or provisions, were the source of their terror.

A few days later the small party broke up, half heading north, the others south. Only Little Crow and his sixteen-year-old son, Wowinape, stayed behind in the Big Woods near Hutchinson. On July 3 as dusk fell, they discovered a raspberry patch and settled in to feast on the fruit. The sweet, juicy taste of the berries must have elicited memories of happier days as it assuaged their hunger. It was a beautiful evening. Suddenly a shot rang out and Little Crow, after a brief exchange of fire, fell, mortally wounded.[120]

[343]

In an ironic twist of fate, amid a massive manhunt to take down the dreaded chief, an unprepossessing farmer and his son became the accidental heroes who slayed Little Crow. Nathan Lamson and his son, Chauncey, out hunting deer, were startled to spy two Indians in the raspberry patch. His head filled with wild tales of bloodthirsty Dakotas prowling everywhere, Nathan took aim at the Indians, probably more out of fear than vengeance. Wounded slightly in the exchange of fire, the elder Lamson collapsed in the grass and his terrified son shot once more before running toward town for help, as fast as his shaking legs could carry him. Neither man had any idea that they had killed the infamous Little Crow.[121]

In fact, it took weeks to ascertain the identity of the slain Dakota. Before leaving his father, Wowinape, who was uninjured, had tenderly placed new moccasins on Little Crow's feet for his journey into the spirit world, folded his arms, and carefully wrapped him in a blanket. But when a party of soldiers and citizens returned with Chauncey to the site of the shooting on the following day, they wasted no time scalping the body, including the ears, before carelessly tossing the corpse into a wagon to haul it off to Hutchinson. The dead Indian quickly became the exciting centerpiece of the town's Independence Day celebration, already in progress. A couple of soldiers insisted to the crowd that the corpse was that of Little Crow, pointing out the distinctive teeth and deformities in the arms caused by old, poorly set breaks. But most people remained unconvinced. It must have seemed impossible that the fearsome chief had met his end in a raspberry patch at the hands of a local farmer. While the argument continued, a few jovial boys stuffed firecrackers into the dead Indian's nostrils and ears and set them off, making identification even more difficult. Offended adults quickly put an end to the repulsive entertainment by dumping the body in a slaughterhouse pit and thinly covering it with dirt. But a cavalry officer soon dug up the remains and severed the head from the body. By this time the corpse scarcely resembled a human being, let alone a particular individual. Debate continued over the identity of the dead Indian for weeks and was finally resolved only in late August, when Sibley's men captured the "half-starved and nearly naked" Wowinape, who confirmed that the Indian killed by the Lamsons was indeed his father.[122]

Sibley must have received the news with mixed emotions. He and his men had turned back toward Minnesota after a brutal summer spent chasing elusive Dakotas across the drought-stricken prairie, where temperatures routinely rose above 100 degrees. The general had little to show for the campaign. His army had engaged in just a few minor skirmishes with hunting parties who were concerned only with protecting their women and children. Perhaps 200 Indians were killed in all. Meanwhile some anonymous farmer had slain Little Crow by happenstance and become the hero of Minnesota. On the other hand, Sibley had lost just half a dozen men and had driven the Indians in a pell-mell flight across the Missouri River. He also had avoided the needless killing of women and children, which probably would have occurred in an all-out battle. Though the war had hardened Sibley's heart toward the Dakotas, his history with them was too long and intimate for him to join the calls for extermination. As his critics charged, perhaps he had too much sympathy for the Indians to carry out the ruthless task he had been assigned. At any rate, he put the best face on the conclusion of the expedition, declaring victory at the Missouri River: "The campaign has been a complete success," he informed his men. "You have marched nearly six hundred miles from St. Paul, and the powerful bands of Dakotas . . . have succumbed to your valor and discipline and sought safety in flight." His weary, sweat-soaked troops, eager to go home, were only too happy to agree.[123]

General Sully did not share Sibley's scruples, nor did he hesitate to slay any and every Indian he came upon. Delayed by low water on the Missouri, by the time his army reached their rendezvous point at Fort Pierre in Dakota Territory, Sibley was already on his way back to Minnesota. Not to be denied a fight, Sully's forces marched on until they scouted out a large Dakota encampment. The general ordered his cavalry to surround the camp, then charge, firing at will. One of the soldiers recalled that only nightfall ended the "bloody work": "Infants, innocent children, women alike shared the fate of their guilty fathers."[124] The newspapers jubilantly reported a grand victory, but young Samuel Brown, writing indignantly from Crow Creek to his father, Joe, painted a different picture:

> I don't think he ought to brag of it at all, because it was what no decent man would have done, he pitched into their camp and just slaughtered them. . . . It is lamentable to hear how those women and children were slaughtered it was a perfect massacre, and now he returns saying that we need fear no more for he has "wiped out all the hostile Indians from Dakota" . . . and the worse of it, they had no hostile intention whatever.[125]

The Dakota war had come full circle, it seems, beginning and ending with the deaths of innocents.

Sully mounted another expedition against the Dakotas the following year, but by then Minnesotans had recovered their equilibrium and were considerably less invested in the outcome, more intent on planning for the future than worrying over bad memories. After four years of bloodshed, they were ready to put both their civil wars behind them. Union forces at last had taken the upper hand in the war against the Confederacy and the end of that bloody contest was finally in sight. The war against the Indians—waged indirectly against the Winnebagos and Ojibwes as well as the Dakotas—was already an indisputable triumph. All trace of the multicultural world of the Upper Mississippi had vanished, along with any visible Indian presence. With prospects ahead unlimited, Minnesotans resolutely put their shoulders to the wheel of progress. If they looked back at all, it was only to fashion a selective memory that shone with benevolence on their brave new world.

[345]

Epilogue

————◆————

PASTS REMEMBERED,
PASTS FORGOTTEN

Thus it was they journeyed homeward;
Thus it was that Hiawatha
To the lodge of old Nokomis
Brought the moonlight, starlight, firelight,
Brought the sunshine of his people,
Minnehaha, Laughing Water,
Handsomest of all the women
In the land of the Dacotahs,
In the land of handsome women.

HENRY WADSWORTH LONGFELLOW, *Song of Hiawatha,* 1855

On a September day in 1915 Jesse Wakeman traveled to St. Paul from his home in Flandrau, South Dakota, to take care of some important family business. Wakeman, the son of Wowinape and grandson of Little Crow, had learned that his grandfather's remains were on exhibit at the Minnesota Historical Society, housed in the new state capitol building. Sure enough, when Wakeman entered the society's rooms, he discovered an artful arrangement of Little Crow's bones, skull, and scalp displayed for public edification. Heartsick at the sight, Wakeman threatened to get a lawyer if the remains were not immediately removed from public view. By the following day the Little Crow exhibit had disappeared to a storeroom, never to be seen by the public again. But another half century would pass before the boxed-up remains received a proper burial.[1]

Jesse Wakeman was not the first to object to the unseemly display. In 1881 the *Minneapolis Tribune* called "the ghastly memorial of ferocious hatred . . . a disgrace to a state professing to be civilized and christian." In his 1889 biography of Henry Sibley, Nathaniel West also vehemently protested "the perpetual exhibition of such relics" as "disgraceful to a 'Christian civilization.'" And Dr.

[346]

Asa Daniels, who had been friends with Little Crow before the conflict of 1862, wrote in 1908, "Other states have suffered their Indian wars, but none have thought it proper to desecrate their State Capitol with the scalp of a fallen foe. Such a spectacle reflects sadly upon the humanity of a Christian people, and all citizens who prize the good name of our state should desire its removal."[2]

Such protests, however, were the exception. In the years immediately following the U.S.–Dakota War, as in most wars, a hunger for revenge overwhelmed more humane impulses toward the defeated enemy. Former captive Mary Schwandt, whose family had been murdered, understandably admitted that she felt a sense of satisfaction at the sight of Little Crow's scalp. But as years went by and survivors of the conflict dwindled, most of the public viewed the "anthropological" exhibit as a harmless curiosity and the "ghastly display" of the chief's remains elicited less rather than more indignation. Daniels puzzled over this, noting that in the immediate aftermath of the war "there was some excuse for our people resorting to the extreme retaliation that was adopted, but the condition no longer exists." How then could "citizens who prize the good name of our state" fail to protest this barbaric "spectacle?"[3]

[347]

In fact, it was that very distance from the tragic summer of 1862 that made Indian bones seem as appropriate for museum display as mastodon tusks or shards of prehistoric pottery. The Dakota conflict was the last act in a cultural transformation that divided the history of "modern" Minnesota from that of the multicultural borderland that had existed for the previous two hundred years. That world, where Indians and whites mingled, intermarried, and accommodated, if not always appreciated, one another's customs, had changed with lightning speed after Minnesota became a territory in 1849. The rapid influx of newcomers, mostly American born, imposed new customs and norms that profoundly changed these long-standing relationships. The Dakota conflict and subsequent Indian removals carved already evident cultural fault lines into an unbridgeable chasm. In the minds of forward-thinking Minnesotans, the borderland and the Indians who inhabited it were relegated to colorful irrelevance, merely the "pre-history" of the North Star State.

In the immediate aftermath of the conflict, such historical amnesia seemed not only unlikely but impossible. The events of 1862 were seared into the memory of those who had experienced the terror and hysteria of the brief uprising. The death toll had been stunning. No one knew with certainty how many settlers had been killed, since record keeping failed to keep up with the steady flow of immigrants who came and went from the region. Some bodies were probably never found, with no one left behind to search for them. Estimates of the dead ranged from 400 to a probably inflated figure of 1,000. But even the lowest estimate made the Dakota conflict the largest mass killing of civilians in American history to that point.[4] White Minnesotans, driven by grief, outrage, and hunger for revenge, applauded the scalping and mutilation of Indian dead by soldiers and civilians, justifying it no doubt as retribution for atrocities perpetrated on white victims. Henry Sibley, who had known and traded with the Dakotas for decades, deplored such barbarous behavior and did his best to keep his soldiers from desecrating the dead, many of whom he had known in life. "God's image should not be thus mistreated and disfigured," he declared. However, in the eyes of most Minnesotans the war had fully dehumanized Indians, evidenced by the scalp bounty offered by the state legislature in 1863. The Minnesota Historical Society also extended "special inducements" for citizens to "scour the Big Woods" for "trophies . . . scalps, bones, and trinkets made out of bones of human beings." Thus, it was not surprising that disinterments and appropriation of body parts as souvenirs raised no murmur of protest from respectable, churchgoing Minnesotans.[5]

Conscious of the historic significance of the events of 1862, the historical society also collected parts of the scaffold and rope used in the mass Mankato hanging as well as the axe used to release the platform. Eventually, individuals who had grabbed up Little Crow's bones and skull as souvenirs turned those over to the society as well. The scalp went directly to the state, exchanged for a generous bounty. Some historically minded state official had then prudently paid $5 to have the scalp tanned to preserve it for posterity, and for several years Adjutant General Oscar Malmros displayed the trophy in his office. By 1868, however, with boosters and state officials bent on promoting Minnesota as a model of progressive development, the scalp was an inappropriate reminder of its all too recent violent past, and Malmros threw it in the trash. A sharp-eyed janitor retrieved the scalp and donated it to the society. In its 1869 annual report, the society announced the acquisition as an "accession of value and interest. . . . It is *tanned* and thus in a measure imperishable, and is certainly a curious memento of that dark period in our State history."[6]

By 1869, for most people, Indian body parts had become curiosities rather than symbols of revenge. For those who had experienced the bloody conflict, the memories remained sharp and anger undiminished—especially in places like New Ulm and Mankato, where children and grandchildren of the victims would tell and retell harrowing accounts of the summer of 1862 for generations. But by 1870 the census revealed that the state's population had grown to nearly 440,000; more than 60 percent of Minnesotans had arrived after the Indians had been banished and only a dwindling minority had firsthand memories of the uprising.[7] The newcomers seldom saw an Indian, and tales of bloody massacre seemed worlds away from the bustling cities and towns and thriving agricultural hinterland of post–Civil War Minnesota, the folklore of a vanished frontier past.

This perfectly suited Minnesota politicians and boosters, who were assiduously courting new residents, both from within the Union and abroad. Hair-raising accounts of Indian savagery were unlikely to attract many immigrants. Well before the conflict had commenced, boosters were working to assuage the fears of potential settlers. In an open letter to "our Eastern friends" in 1861, the

St. Cloud Democrat had assured that there was "not the slightest danger to the people of Minnesota from Indians." The sensational Indian war had been an undeniable setback and Minnesota boosters were eager to portray it as the last act of a vanquished and now vanished people. The historical society's exhibit of Little Crow's remains as "artifacts" affirmed that the trauma of 1862 was indeed part of a now bygone era. In its annual report the society counted the newly acquired scalp among its "collection of Indian relics, stone weapons and remains of the aboriginal tribes." In its original condition the scalp apparently had seemed a bit "raw" for the archaeological cabinet, so before its unveiling for the public it was artfully strung inside a hoop and decorated with feathers and beads to make it less disturbing. The resulting image, which was captured by a local photographer and sold widely throughout the country, spoke not of violence and danger but of the conquest of savagery by civilization, a completed domestication of the frontier—exactly the image boosters desired to convey.[8]

But that safe and civilized image of Minnesota as an Indian-free, domesticated garden of opportunity was challenged for a number of years by a troubling counternarrative of murder and mayhem produced by a raft of entrepreneurs. By the time the hanging of thirty-eight Dakotas took place in Mankato, a profitable cottage industry was already emerging, peddling stories and pictorial representations of the conflict to an eager public. Survivors, journalists, artists, photographers, historians, and independent writers with big imaginations all fed a seemingly insatiable national appetite for bloodcurdling portraits of Indian barbarity, the more gruesome the better. Some histories of the events, though not surprisingly biased against the Indians, maintained at least some modicum of dispassion. But many more reveled in the sensationalism that audiences craved.[9] Literary entrepreneur Harriet Bishop, recently divorced and fallen on hard times, was among the first to rush into print with *Dakota War Whoop*, published in 1863. The author of previous paeans of boosterism, Bishop did Minnesota no favors with her luridly embellished tale of rape and pillage by Indian "fiends incarnate."[10]

Other writers and publishers sought out survivors and former captives for first-person accounts to sell to a national audience. Some survivors, like Lavinia Eastlick, used the stories of their ordeal to help rebuild their shattered lives. Eastlick self-published an account of her sixty-mile flight from her home at Lake Shetek to New Ulm, liberally sprinkling the narrative with apocryphal details of Indian savagery. The work sold so well that she was able to use the money earned from the pamphlet and lectures to establish a new homestead with her two surviving sons.[11]

Artists and photographers also found a ready audience for depictions, real or imagined, of the events of 1862. And Rochester sign painter John Stevens embarked on an ambitious project to create a panorama of the conflict, "unparalleled in sensational dramatic appeal and news value." Panoramas were the nineteenth-century precursor of motion pictures, a series of pictures painted on an enormous canvas that unrolled to give viewers a vicarious visual experience of events. Stevens's panorama depicted "flaming cabins and scorched settlements, the ravaged farmsteads and murdered infants, the suffering, torture, and privation"—largely drawn from harrowing episodes told by Lavinia Eastlick, who served as the painter's muse. Stevens accompanied the visual display with a florid narration that vividly described "the storm of fierce, savage murder, in its most horrid and frightful forms." The panorama was an immediate sensation at opera houses and town halls throughout the Midwest, where audiences eagerly queued to cough up twenty-five cents for admission.[12]

Visual and literary representations of the conflict enthralled a national audience for at least twenty years, providing vicarious thrills to a wage-earning public whose day-to-day lives in industrial America were decidedly lacking in adventure. The West served as the ultimate in escapism, replete with violence but also with romance, a renewed model of American masculinity and the ultimate satisfaction of conquest. It seemed to city dwellers to be the essence of American character, an antidote to the sense of powerlessness that many felt in the face of late-nineteenth-century industrial might.[13] The appetite for "true" accounts and dime novels that chronicled frontier daring, danger, and independence only increased as the century neared its close. This love affair with the West was nowhere more exuberantly evident than in the spectacularly enduring popular appeal of Buffalo Bill Cody and his Wild West Show.[14]

But for Minnesotans, the Wild West, as it referred to them, represented an image problem rather than a site of unfulfilled desire. Tellingly, as early as 1868, when Stevens's panorama came to St. Paul, it played to a nearly empty house. The *St. Paul Daily Press* advertised that "the picture would give new settlers an accurate idea of the massacre," but by 1868 that was the last thing forward-looking Minnesotans desired.[15] Those days were over, as they would have been quick to tell potential immigrants, both American and European. Minnesota was no longer the edge of the civilized world; it was a booming, full-fledged state with railroads (at last), modern conveniences, well-appointed hotels, fledgling industries, prosperous farms, and unlimited opportunity for growth. Indians and all the dangers and hardship they represented had been rendered invisible. Though some 6,000 Ojibwes and a much smaller number of Dakotas (probably fewer than 300) still made their homes in the state, in the progressive narrative of the "new" Minnesota, they had faded into what was already becoming a distant mythologized past.

Minnesota's self-promotion as a fully civilized, booming hub of trade and industry succeeded so well that soon it was no longer perceived as part of the West at all. Still, the national imagination had so thoroughly integrated Indians into its perception of Minnesota that it would have been impossible to erase all trace of them from its image. Reminders of Native people were everywhere, embedded in the very geography in the names of rivers, counties, towns, even of the state itself—Mini Sota Makoce—"the place where the Dakota dwell." Thus, rather than deny the existence of Indians as part of Minnesota's identity or cast them as the dangerous barbarians of pulp fiction, image makers retold their tragic history by embracing an older fiction of the Indian as noble savage, drawing on the romantic, idealized myths long embedded in literature and popular culture. Flesh-and-blood Dakotas, Ojibwes, and Winnebagos, coercively removed to barren prairies or swampy scrubland, were replaced in the telling by noble red men whose inevitable destiny was to vanish silently and harmoniously into the mists of the American past.[16]

[351]

This transformation of a historical clash of cultures into a harmonious heritage had an appeal at least as powerful as the narrative of western conquest, evidenced by the phenomenon of adulation that greeted Henry Wadsworth Longfellow's *Song of Hiawatha*, first published in 1855. In fact, it was the reconstruction of the Indian as a mythical figure that allowed Americans to ignore the human cost implicit in shoot-'em-up depictions of the West. As cultural historian Michael Kammen notes, Longfellow's exercise of literary imagination "assuaged the American conscience" by transforming a shameful history of American Indian relations into a romantic portrayal of "a proud yet primitive people finally giving way to a more accomplished society foredestined to supplant them."[17]

Minnesota's mixed-blood people also "disappeared," though many traveled only a few miles or remained where they had always been. In the wake of the hysteria set off in 1862, Indian ancestry was not only reviled, it was also dangerous. Of those who favored their Euro-American forebears, many chose to invent a selective genealogy that expunged all trace of their Indian roots, often "vanishing in plain sight." They blended into white society, some with more success than others. Suggestively, "French Canadians" radically declined as a percentage of the population of St. Paul in the last decades of the nineteenth century. Some simply anglicized their names to disguise their backgrounds, others migrated to ethnic enclaves like Little Canada and Centerville, just a few miles from the city, where they were not subject to whispers about their suspect bloodline. Some chose to follow their Dakota or Ojibwe kin to reservation communities, embracing their identity as Indians.[18]

For those whose features favored their Indian ancestry, the options were more limited. Though mixed-blood people did not experience forced removal, nonetheless those with identifiable Indian features "became" Indians in the eyes of the majority population and most probably were viewed as social inferiors. Anecdotal evidence reveals that many mixed-blood people eventually migrated from the settled parts of the state to Indian communities in Nebraska, Dakota Territory, or northern Minnesota.[19] Individual motivations no doubt differed, but clearly whether people of mixed ancestry blended into the white population or joined their Indian kin, either by choice or imposition, racial identity was no longer malleable in the new social order. The "people in-between," who had been the linchpin of Euro-American and Indian coexistence, now only muddied the invented narrative of civilization's harmonious triumph over a romantic but primitive and ahistorical world.

This version of western settlement served as a much more useful past for Minnesota as it began to boom in the 1870s. Fortunately for the state's image builders, Longfellow had set *Hiawatha* in Minnesota —based with considerable literary license on Ojibwe traditions gleaned from the journals of Henry Schoolcraft and writings of Mary Eastman. Longfellow's mythological Indians embodied peace rather than war and harked back to the lyric depictions of an "Indian Eden" penned by George Catlin, Joseph Nicollet, and other early travel writers and explorers—unthreatening images of a benevolent people, long gone, that Minnesotans eagerly promoted. Apparently the evocative power of these images trumped the depiction of Minnesota as a wild and dangerous locale in the minds of potential residents. By 1880 the state's population had grown to nearly 800,000 persons; a decade later it had reached 1.3 million.[20]

[352]

Evidence of the early, compelling attraction of this mythic past is revealed in the founding of the town of Pipestone in 1873, near the famous quartzite quarries described by Catlin and others as sacred to the Dakotas. Captivated by Indian legends (constructed by whites) about the region, Iowa druggist Charles Bennett persuaded a group of fellow Iowans to join with him in an unlikely town site development project near the quarries. Located in the far southwest corner of the state, the proposed town would be fewer than a dozen miles from Indian territory, nearly one hundred miles west of New Ulm and forty miles from the nearest rail line, yet Bennett was convinced that the quarries' "mythic past and reputation as a place of peace" would outweigh any practical disadvantages or lingering recollections of 1862. Bennett's gamble paid off. Though founded in the midst of a national economic panic, by 1879 Pipestone was a full-fledged community, with streets named Hiawatha, Longfellow, and Catlin and a local newspaper that vigorously promoted Pipestone's connection to popular Indian legends.[21]

Notably, the first generation of Pipestonians was made up largely of middle-class Protestants from the Northeast and Great Britain, where the romantic myth of the Indian held the strongest sway. Their notions of Native people were derived from literary fancies, and according to historian Sally Southwick, "they sometimes experienced disappointment in their encounters with living tribesmen, whose dress did not always project the kind of image that would attract tourists and meet visitors' expectations." Nonetheless, they wedded their town's identity firmly to Longfellow's romantic Indian saga, enlarging and reinventing the mythological significance of the quarries until, by the twentieth century, the quarries had evolved in promotional literature into a pan-Indian sacred shrine of peace. In 1949 the National Park Service paid homage to this invented past by designating the quarries as "America's original peace shrine." As late as 2007, the highlight of the summer in Pipestone was its annual *Song of Hiawatha* pageant. Ironically, for many years, even as the town used a constructed version of Indian heritage to promote its development, it was simultaneously engaged in ongoing legal disputes with modern-day Yanktons over rights to and preservation of the quarries.[22]

Cities and towns across Minnesota engaged in similar projects to enshrine an imagined Indian heritage as part of their identity.[23] Playing off the Indian names that christened their communities, towns like Winona and Red Wing established pageants that celebrated mostly fabricated legends while they ignored the more painful history of dispossession that underlay their settlement. Minneapolis made the legend of Hiawatha its own in myriad ways, creating the "jewel" of its city park system around Minnehaha Falls in 1889. The rechristened cascade, once more prosaically known as Brown's Falls (after the ubiquitous Joe Brown), was already a tourist magnet, thanks to Longfellow's epic fiction. In years to come, the Hiawatha connection grew into a treasured civic emblem that stamped itself on the city in everything from roadways to Minneapolis-made products. Contributions from local schoolchildren funded a statue of Hiawatha holding Minnehaha in his arms, and other admirers acknowledged the city's debt to its most famous nonresident bard with a statue of Longfellow and a two-thirds-size replica of the poet's home in Cambridge, Massachusetts. Though he had never visited Minnesota, if his spirit journeyed there posthumously, Longfellow would have felt like a most appreciated native son.[24]

From the capital city to the smallest towns, local identity commonly incorporated a transmuted Indian heritage, unmoored from historical events. St. Paul ultimately bested other communities in the sheer size of its monument to an imagined past. In 1936 the city installed a 38-foot-high, 60-ton onyx sculpture of the "Indian God of Peace" in the main concourse of its new city hall and courthouse. But perhaps the most striking example of present-day Minnesota's disassociation with its history is found on a highway between the small towns of Spicer and New London. Located in the lake country of Kandiyohi County, just miles from where Little Crow's warriors struck terror into settlers in 1862, in 2009 visitors and residents can play a round of golf or celebrate special events at the well-appointed, municipally owned Little Crow Country Club. A more historically dissonant memorialization could hardly be imagined.[25]

The Good War

Throughout the waning decades of the nineteenth century, the Dakota Conflict of 1862 was a site of contested memory, sensationalized recollections vying with romantic myth making to situate the place of Indians in Minnesota's past and present. Meanwhile, in the years immediately following General Robert E. Lee's surrender at Appomattox Court House in 1865, the Civil War went largely unmemorialized. Sorrow rather than celebration seemed the order of the day as soldiers straggled home, physically and emotionally scarred by the carnage that had engulfed them. The evidence was all too apparent on the streets of every town—men who returned with missing limbs or, more commonly, with haunted eyes that spoke of the psychological toll the war had taken. What today would be termed post-traumatic stress syndrome in 1865 had no name. Wives and families simply knew that the husbands and sons who marched away had returned as different men. Even worse was the sorrow of those families whose sons did not return at all. In 1865, as the war was grinding to a close, Abraham Brower of Sauk Center wrote a heartrending letter to Minnesota governor Stephen Miller—the former colonel who had protected the Dakota prisoners—asking to serve as a substitute for his recently drafted son. Of his five boys, two had died in service and a third languished somewhere in a Confederate prison camp. His eldest son, a volunteer with the First Minnesota, had returned home "with his constitution partly broken." Twenty-two-year-old Jacob, the last of Brower's adult sons, had already served one term of enlistment in General Sibley's Indian expedition and now had been called up again in a supplementary draft. Brower begged the governor to take him in Jacob's stead, "the only one left of my four boys whose health and strength is left to him." Capturing the sorrows that bore down on countless Minnesota families, Brower concluded his plea, "An aged grandfather of Eighty-five mourns the loss of his grand children the last of his race. A Mother weeps and is not comforted. Brothers look with sorrow upon the vacant places and the father broken hearted most earnestly entreats your influence." When the war ended the following month, families like the Browers no doubt felt a great surge of relief, but their losses were too great and immediate to give way to celebration.[26]

[354]

By war's end Minnesota had raised in excess of twelve regiments, sending more than 24,000 men into battle, the equivalent of one-seventh of the state's 1860 population. Nearly 3,000 lost their lives, more than half to untended wounds or diseases that wracked the camps. At Bull Run and at Gettysburg, Minnesota's pride, the First Minnesota, had suffered the highest percentage of casualties of any northern regiment—nearly 82 percent at Gettysburg alone. Those who returned home were met by a war-weary populace that roused itself with difficulty to cheer their homecoming. The veterans themselves seldom spoke about the days of their service, most quietly returning to civilian life, eager to forget the horrors of war. Though a Minnesota chapter of the veterans group the Grand Army of the Republic (GAR) formed in 1866, for years it struggled to gather enough members to even hold a meeting.[27]

Minnesota's reluctance to memorialize the war was mirrored throughout the nation. The battle-scarred southern states, their world in tatters, were sunk in despair, contemplating the enormity of their defeat. But the victorious North had been traumatized as well by the enormous cost of holding the Union together—more than 360,000 dead and countless more either physically or emotionally damaged. Tellingly, for more than a decade private efforts to raise funds for war memorials or even a tribute to the martyred Lincoln all floundered for lack of support. The only significant commemoration of the war was the establishment of Memorial Day in 1866, promoted by the GAR as a national day of mourning.[28]

By 1880, however, Civil War remembrance was rapidly reviving, not as a means of mourning the dead but as a unifying celebration of American patriotism. In the postwar years, rapid industrialization, unprecedented immigration, increasing impoverishment of common farmers and workers, and accumulation of massive fortunes by a favored few had opened class fissures that threatened to overturn elite control of politics and, by extension, the economic order. Up to this time, the Civil War had been most useful politically as a means to retain Republican control in the North and Democratic rule in the South—what was called "waving the bloody shirt" of sectional loyalties. However, by 1880 the power of wartime antagonisms was diminishing in the face of class grievances and the infusion of masses of new immigrants—more than five million entered the country between 1860 and 1880—for whom sectional loyalties carried no weight. Unlike earlier generations of new arrivals, these immigrants found themselves funneled almost exclusively into low-paying laboring jobs. This exponential growth of an aggrieved working class and growing chasm between the rich and poor had the potential for a radical political realignment.[29] The Civil War became the vehicle to reunify support behind the business interests that dominated the Republican Party in the North and the Democrats in the South, as elites of both parties formed a Whiggish alliance that subsumed party differences to counter populist challenges.[30]

[355]

Beginning in the 1880s and exponentially picking up steam in the 1890s, Civil War commemoration exploded across the American landscape. However, it was a reinvented history of the war that celebrated both sides as equally valorous and honorable. The divisive issue of slavery—and black civil rights—was purged from the rhetoric, replaced by an emphasis on a brotherhood of reconciliation between northern and southern whites. Reunion, in the words of historian Nina Silber, became a way to rearticulate "America's distinctive moral purpose in the late nineteenth century." Confronted with "the troubling fractures and divisions of the Gilded Age . . . the culture of conciliation, along with the accompanying celebration of the South, offered a soothing alternative to this moral dislocation." The war became the emblematic symbol of core national qualities: unity, patriotism, and sacrifice.[31] It also reconfirmed the cultural centrality of Anglo-Americanism, as exemplified in the Civil War generation. Celebrated in a deluge of popular literature, music, and theater and public commemorations and monuments, the Civil War became the iconographic historical moment for late-nineteenth-century Americans, a romance with an invented past that endures to the present day.

In this era Minnesota was the site of a cultural as well as political challenge. Only three years a state when the Civil War began, to most Americans

Minnesota still seemed a foreign outpost on the fringe of the American empire. The Dakota war only enhanced that perception. Moreover, with land still available and with the passage of the Homestead Act of 1862, European immigrants poured into the state in the postwar years. By 1880 roughly 30 percent of the population was foreign born. Even more telling, 71 percent of Minnesotans were either first- or second-generation immigrants.[32] The old stock citizens who had worked so hard to impose their cultural imprint on the infant state and attain recognition as a full-fledged part of the nation had no sooner rid themselves of the Indians than they began to feel overwhelmed by hordes of foreign-speaking Germans and Scandinavians. American-born Minnesotans found themselves in a quandary: they needed and encouraged immigration into the state to develop its economy, but they also were determined to maintain their cultural authority. Civil War memorializations, along with organizations like the Old Settlers Association and the Territorial Pioneers, served to reinforce the privileged place of Anglo-Americans and cement Minnesota's identity as part of the nation.[33] They also functioned as an ideal cultural tool to school new citizens in "appropriate" values and speed their assimilation from "foreigners" to Americans.

In the 1890s the class fissures of the decade before became ever more glaring. An economic collapse in 1893 brought on the worst depression yet experienced in the nation's history. Agricultural prices plummeted and violent strikes erupted throughout the country, including a successful brief but costly railroad strike in St. Paul. Anarchists, socialists, and communists, many of them foreign born, railed against the government. And a populist coalition of workers and farmers seemed on the verge of becoming a major political force. As the 1896 presidential election approached, Republican power brokers sought to stem the populist tide by appropriating the already popularized revisionist memory of the Civil War. Hailing the renewed brotherhood that emerged from the national trauma, they stigmatized political critiques of class inequality as unpatriotic, even treasonous threats to the Union. Minnesota was right in the thick of this cultural/political war.

Hundreds of miles distant from the battlefields where Union men and Rebels had clashed, Minnesota surprisingly became a major player in promoting a reconstructed memory of the Civil War, thanks to railroad mogul James J. Hill, St. Paul's archbishop John Ireland, and thousands of veterans in the Grand Army of the Republic. Hill was the architect of this strategy to hold the Midwest for the Republicans. Alarmed by growing labor militancy and burned in a railroad strike three years earlier, the transportation tycoon vigorously supported Republican presidential candidate William McKinley, using his significant resources to discredit Democratic candidate William Jennings Bryan. One of the key Republican strategies was to accuse the Democrats of fomenting a class war to destroy the Union that valorous veterans had given their all to defend. Republicans lionized the bravery and honor of the Civil

War generation in implicit contrast to the suspect immigrant and radical, unpatriotic Democratic constituency. Hill helped immeasurably to spread that message throughout the Midwest. He used his leverage with Archbishop Ireland, whom he had recently saved from bankruptcy, to encourage the Catholic prelate to issue a ringing denunciation that, among other things, accused Democrats of stirring up a "revolution against the United States." "It is secession," Ireland zealously asserted in his open letter, "the secession of 1861, which our soldiers believed they had consigned to eternal death at Appomattox." As one of the most well-known figures in the American Catholic Church, Ireland created a national sensation with his political pronouncement. A hyperpatriot in his own right, the archbishop no doubt spoke from conviction; however, he might not have publicly attacked the Democrats—the party of most of the country's Catholics—without some vigorous arm twisting from Hill.[34]

As historian Fitzhugh Brundage has observed, "Crafters of memory are eager to erase the origins of the memories they promote."[35] This was certainly true in Minnesota in 1896. Ireland's words received national attention in the media and the Republican National Party distributed 250,000 copies of his letter in pamphlet form, along with the cover story, concocted by Hill, that Ireland had written the letter at the urging of "twenty-seven of the leading citizens of Minnesota . . . representing both political parties."[36]

Hill also enlisted the GAR in his machinations to use war veneration as a political tool. The veterans, universally admired, were reliable constituents of the party of Lincoln, not only because of wartime loyalties but because the Republicans had repeatedly delivered "a remarkably generous array of Federal benefits . . . to the aging Billy Yanks."[37] Serendipitously, the GAR held its national encampment in St. Paul in 1896 and James J. Hill provided free passes to the event on his Great Northern Railway. He also underwrote a barnstorming tour of Union generals that was wildly effective in knitting the Civil War, patriotism, and Republican Party into a seamless case in support of McKinley.[38]

As historian Patrick Kelly notes, all this Civil War ballyhoo was "aimed as much at defining the country's future as memorializing its past." And it worked. McKinley crushed Bryan in the election. In Minnesota, which had been a hotbed of labor unrest and rural populism, McKinley won by 60,000 votes out of 340,000 cast. But the frenzy of patriotic evocations also reified an already growing deification of the Civil War as the defining moment of Minnesota's identity. As the state's official history of the war proclaimed, "History furnishes no parallel to the patriotism and valor of the people of the young state of Minnesota." The state's GAR, along with its Ladies Auxiliary, the Daughters of Veterans, and assorted other organizations, as well as nearly every local community, made commemoration into a virtual civic religion that celebrated Minnesotans as patriots without peer and situated the state firmly in the national firmament. Not surprisingly, the western campaign against the Indians seldom received mention.[39]

The centrality of this moment in Minnesota's collective memory is vividly apparent in the halls of the state capitol building, completed in 1905. Portraits of Civil War heroes look down from the walls and battle flags and memorabilia are prominently displayed. Most notable are the paintings in the governor's elaborately appointed reception room, which were commissioned to illustrate "glorious moments in the history of the state." Of the six massive oils, one portrays Father Hennepin's "discovery" of St. Anthony Falls; one depicts the Treaty of Traverse des Sioux, marking an allegedly orderly transfer of Dakota lands to the United States. The other four are scenes of Civil War battles in which Minnesota regiments participated. Interestingly, a painting titled "Attack on New Ulm during the Sioux Outbreak" by noted New Ulm artist Anton Gág, was also commissioned, perhaps at the urging of those who still considered the Dakota war as *their* defining moment in history. But unlike the oils depicting southern battles, the only public acknowledgment of Minnesota's civil war has always been consigned to an inconspicuous hearing room, outside the general visitor's path.[40]

By the time the state capitol was built and embellished, Minnesotans no longer feared that their prosperous state would be marginalized or viewed as an uncivilized outpost. But they had other reasons to "forget" the violent clashes of 1862 and subsequent expulsion of the Dakotas and Ojibwes from their homeland. Any sustained examination of the Treaty of Traverse des Sioux, wrought with such dignity and ceremony in the painting that graces the governor's reception room, or any of the other treaties that followed, starkly revealed that fraud and bad faith played an equal role with the axe and the plough in making Minnesota. Better, it was thought, to look forward—to celebrate the state's achievements and let the regrettable events of the past stay buried. Thus, the selective memory that survived memorialized a sanitized Civil War in vivid recollection—the emblematic event that made Minnesota truly a part of the nation.

The two hundred years of mingled Indian and European/American history that had gone before dissolved into a fanciful past where jolly voyageurs and noble but doomed savages paddled the rivers in birch bark canoes and tracked the beaver to its lodge—the stuff of summer camp adventures and bedtime tales. And so, for much of the twentieth century, myth rather than history shaped what most Minnesotans knew about the place of Indians in the state's past, vague romantic or cartoonish images concocted from the thin gruel of popular culture—school mascots, community pageants, and ubiquitous logos for Minnesota-made products. At midcentury, an official statewide celebration marked Minnesota's territorial centennial. It was an opportunity to recall an era when fewer than 5,000 Euro-Americans made their home on the edge of what was then nearly all Indian country, a propitious moment to reflect on the world that had existed then. Instead, centennial events focused firmly on what was to come, celebrating with special pride the Treaty of Traverse des Sioux that opened the Suland to settlement by the legions of settlers whose industry and courage made Minnesota "the prosperous state it is today."[41] As for the Indians, though more than 12,000 Ojibwes and Dakotas made their home in Minnesota in 1950,[42] publications and pageants invariably described them as a "vanished" people, replicating a by then familiar story, illustrated succinctly in an earlier popular publication:

> The Sioux was a noble savage, with splendid physique and many fine characteristics. Sioux art and music are today the basis of some of our most beautiful achievements in those lines of culture. He was a born orator, and his speeches show a deep poetical appreciation of nature. He was a good father, for a savage, honest in his dealings and generous to his friends. But he was a savage for all that; he did not and could not make use of the land that he held. He was ignorant and superstitious, cruel, improvident and unprogressive. Where eight thousand of them suffered hardship in making a meager living, today hundreds of thousands of the finest type of men and women live in comfort and make life better for the rest of the world.
>
> The tide of civilization was rolling westward; the Sioux could not adapt himself to it or meet its conditions and he went down under it. The race that could not make full use of the land must give way to one that could. Savagery gave way to civilization and barbarism to Christianity.
>
> It is better so.[43]

In recent decades the scholarly tide has turned. Historians, anthropologists, archaeologists, and geographers have produced a veritable library of work that challenges the popular narrative of Minnesota's past. And public historians, led by the Minnesota Historical Society, have mounted exemplary exhibits that re-create the complex world whose last remnants were swept away by events in the 1860s. Most important, Native people themselves have insisted that their voices be heard, their ancestors honored. Still, despite all these efforts most Minnesotans remain unaware of the rich history that flows beneath their feet, like veins of precious metal. The lived experience of the world as it is creates a sense of inevitability, making it difficult to imagine a radically different ordering of society in the past. The refrains of popular history, once memorized, are familiar and comfortable and not easily displaced.

For decades Little Crow's family members appealed for custody of his remains, without success. Finally in 1971, a climate of heightened cultural sensitivity, along with public pressure by the Native American community, persuaded the Minnesota Historical Society to turn the chief's bones over to his descendants for a proper burial. On a September day, more than one hundred years after the tragic events of the Dakota war, family members gathered in Flandrau, South Dakota, to quietly lay to rest the Mdewakanton chief so celebrated and feared in his day. Eighty-eight-year-old Jesse Wakeman had lived long enough to see his grandfather "buried among his own with only his own at hand."[44]

The public took little notice of the ceremony, yet the somber burial of Little Crow marked a beginning rather than a conclusion, a call too long delayed to excavate the buried past of this place called Minnesota and fully integrate the tragedy as well as the triumphs of how it became the North Star State. Today, some thirty-eight years after Little Crow's burial, that history is still too often obscured by popular misconceptions. The task remains to listen to all the voices that called this land home, to comprehend what was lost as well as what was gained—and at what cost. It is a complicated story and a discomforting one, the history not just of Minnesota but of America itself, and the work to fully come to terms with it has only just begun.

Acknowledgments

In the years spent wrestling with this manuscript, I not infrequently wondered what I had been thinking when I agreed to take on the task. A new history of Minnesota was long overdue. The wealth of scholarship produced in the past forty years demanded a new perspective, a rethinking of the narrative that explained Minnesota's transformation from unsettled forest and prairie to twenty-first-century dynamo. With the state sesquicentennial just around the corner, the Office of the President of the University of Minnesota commissioned this book as the university's gift to the state. And I took up the challenge to rewrite Minnesota history.

The scope of this undertaking pushed publication beyond the 2008 sesquicentennial year, but I am consoled by the knowledge that Theodore Blegen's "centennial" history (the last authoritative history of the state) appeared in 1962, five years after the anniversary it was intended to celebrate. Unfortunately, within a few years Blegen's weighty and significant work began to seem dated and incomplete. Beginning in the 1960s and exploding in the decades following, a new generation of scholarship transformed the historical landscape. Influenced deeply by the new social history, issues of race, class, and gender were central to its analysis of the past. This work shifted emphasis from "Great White Men" to a more diverse, and largely neglected, array of people who shaped history in the uncelebrated course of their daily lives. Still, it could not be denied that a cohort of powerful people (almost all of them men) indelibly stamped historical outcomes. My charge was to integrate the new social history and the politics of power in a narrative that would more fully illuminate the dynamics that shaped Minnesota's past.

I set to work, intending to craft a cohesive narrative that would span some 350 years, incorporating the best current political, social, and economic scholarship to understand how Minnesota came to be the state it is today and situate its place in the nation and the world. The richness and breadth of the sources were daunting, but a far more problematic realization changed the nature of this volume. As I immersed myself in the sources, it became clear that Minnesota had two histories: the familiar story of settlement and development that carries us from the mid-nineteenth century to the present was quite literally built on the ruins of an earlier multicultural society. A chasm, clearly identifiable in the 1860s, divided those two histories. I became convinced that this earlier world, the "north country" of the title, needed and deserved a book in its own right. The book in your hands today is the history of that earlier society, a story only briefly touched upon in other state histories and one that will surprise, perhaps dismay, and (most important, I hope) stimulate questions about the inevitability of the world as we know it today.

My debts are many in the crafting of this work. First, I thank the University of Minnesota and St. Cloud State University, which cosponsored the project by granting me the time for research and writing. Without the support of these institutions this book would not have been possible. I owe thanks to my fellow faculty members in the history department at St. Cloud State; though my absence added to their responsibilities, they generously cheered me on, even as the project seemed to stretch into infinity. I cannot imagine more supportive colleagues.

I am indebted to the advice of Hy Berman and Ann Pflaum, my collaborators in what we came to call the Minnesota History Project. We met regularly throughout the research and writing process, and their good counsel helped guide the direction of the manuscript. The project provided able research assistance from Lisa Blee and from Macalester College student Annie Cullen, who gamely combed hundreds of pages of nineteenth-century newspapers.

Minnesota is fortunate to have what may be the finest historical society in the country. Its library and archives are matchless, a true state treasure. Even more invaluable is its knowledgeable and dedicated staff. I am particularly indebted to Patrick Coleman and Debbie Miller for access to collections, brilliant suggestions, and encouragement throughout the course of this project. I also frequently benefited from participation in monthly research meetings, convened by Debbie, that bring together all sorts of scholars working on Minnesota topics.

Of necessity, because of the many facets and breadth of this history, my analysis relies significantly on the published research of a wide range of scholars. The book's bibliography covers only works cited in the text, a fraction of the articles and books that enriched my understanding of the life and times of the period. Though each of these works had some part in my conception of the whole, a few scholars were so central to my analysis that they must receive individual acknowledgment. First and foremost, William Watts Folwell, whose four-volume history of Minnesota was published in the 1920s, remains the most authoritative source for much of the state's history. His footnotes alone were worth their weight in gold. Among contemporary scholars, the work of Bruce White, Gary Clayton Anderson, and Alan Woolworth was essential for understanding Native American culture. On the fur trade, the scholarship of Rhoda Gilman, Carolyn Gilman, and David Lavender untangled an incredibly complex economic and social matrix. Rhoda Gilman's nuanced biography of Henry Sibley distilled an entire social world through the lens of the man who was arguably the most powerful figure in nineteenth-century Minnesota.

In the course of writing, I encountered incredible generosity from a number of scholars who shared work in progress and documents gleaned from years of archival research. Curtis Dahlin answered several important research questions, and the illuminating work of David Beaulieu and Stephen Osman contributed significantly to my understanding of key events. Walt Bachman not only shared previously undiscovered material he unearthed in the National Archives, he allowed me to read and cite from his book manuscript, "Black Dakota," a pathbreaking new perspective on race in Minnesota. Carrie Zeman, a talented historian and unparalleled researcher, unreservedly shared her work, and I could count on lively conversations with Carrie to give me a fresh perspective on familiar sources.

I was fortunate to have a number of very smart people read and comment on the manuscript as it progressed. Walt Bachman, Jim Stewart, and Carrie Zeman read several chapters and offered invaluable suggestions; William Green and Michael Witgen provided helpful comments on the completed manuscript; my friend and colleague Rob Galler read numerous chapter drafts and spent countless hours in spirited discussion about my conclusions; and Rhoda Gilman and Bruce White read and critiqued every chapter, saving me from errors of fact and interpretation. My debt to them is incalculable.

Throughout this process I was blessed with strong support from the University of Minnesota Press. The director of the Press, Doug Armato, was engaged from beginning to end and endorsed the intellectual framework that evolved. Editorial assistants Andrea Rondoni and Kristian Tvedten chased down illustrations and permissions and attended to dozens of details. My editor, Todd Orjala, was magnificent. His unswerving belief in the project and amazing patience carried me through. He read every chapter, oversaw each element of production, and even found the perfect cover image. His commitment to excellence is apparent on every page.

Finally, I express my profound appreciation for the contributions of Kirsten Delegard. Kirsten and I were colleagues in graduate school, and by some great stroke of luck, just as I was beginning work on this project, she returned to Minnesota and offered to provide research assistance. She gave me so much more. An accomplished historian in her own right, she brought all her talents to bear in her nuanced research; as a colleague fully engaged in the meaning of the story that emerged, she also helped me work through the analytical and interpretive turns that shaped the manuscript. Kirsten and Todd chose the

Acknowledgments

images and maps that appear in the volume, and Kirsten wrote the beautifully interpreted accompanying captions. Her friendship, intelligence, and steadfast support picked me up more times than I can count.

Looking back over the years spent working on this book, I am most grateful for the intellectual and personal relationships that sustained me: all these people contributed to whatever has been achieved. The shortcomings are mine alone. This book is not the last word on Minnesota's early history, but I hope it will be a starting point for new conversations and new research. As the preceding pages reveal, there is much yet to be learned.

[364]

Mary Wingerd
St. Paul, Minnesota
May 2009

Notes

Prologue

1. Marling, *Blue Ribbon*, 211.
2. "Minnesota Centennial Story Rolling on Railway Wheels," Minnesota Statehood Centennial news release, 27 March 1958; "Minnesota Centennial Train" souvenir booklet; both items located in Statehood Centennial Commission Files, Minnesota Historical Society; Bodnar, *Remaking America*, 154–58.
3. Lowenthal, *Heritage Crusade*, 119–22.

1. The Fortunate Land

1. The nomenclature "Sioux" derives from European adoption of the Ottawa name *na-towe-ssiwa*, which literally means "people of an alien tribe" or "enemy." Europeans shortened the name to Sioux. Dakota and Lakota, what the people called themselves, simply meant "the people" or "human beings." Gibbon, *The Sioux*, 2.
2. G. Anderson, *Kinsmen of Another Kind*, 2–3; Blegen, *Minnesota*, 20.
3. Common descriptors, such as tribe, nation, or confederation, are problematic in discussing Native American social and political configurations since they inevitably bring to mind European concepts of social and political organization that were foreign to the Indian worldview. According to Richard White, "Socially and politically, this was a village world. The units called tribes, nations, and confederacies were only loose leagues of villages. . . . Nothing resembling a state existed." White is referring specifically to Algonquian peoples, but his point is equally pertinent in the case of the Dakotas. R. White, *Middle Ground*, 16. See also Albers, "Symbiosis, Merger, and War," 94–132. In using the term "confederation," I do not mean to imply any sort of formal military alliance, but rather a recognition of shared culture, language, and kinship.
4. Gibbon, *The Sioux*, 2–5; Ewers, "Intertribal Warfare as the Precursor of Indian-White Warfare," 407. See also G. Anderson, "Early Dakota Migration," 17–36.
5. Pond, *Dakota Life*, 26–31; G. Anderson, *Kinsmen of Another Kind*, 2–8.
6. Blegen, *Minnesota*, 20; R. White, *Middle Ground*, 11; G. Anderson, *Kinsmen of Another Kind*, 2, 19.
7. A. Taylor, *Divided Ground*, 4–6; Richter, *Ordeal of the Longhouse*, 62–64; Worchester and Schilz, "Spread of Firearms," 104.
8. C. Gilman, *Grand Portage Story*, 24.
9. R. White, *Middle Ground*, 1–11; G. Anderson, *Kinsmen of Another Kind*, 2.
10. R. Gilman, "Fur Trade in the Upper Mississippi Valley," 3–8. Even prehistoric people seem to have had some contact with

far distant regions. Most notably, in 1931 the remains of a fifteen-year-old girl (strangely labeled "Minnesota Man") dating back at least 10,000 years were discovered in Otter Tail County. Among her bones archaeologists found a conch shell ornament that could have come only from the Gulf of Mexico. Blegen, *Minnesota*, 11. For a vivid sense of the thick networks of Native trails and interaction hidden in the seemingly "unpeopled" Southwest, see Cabeza de Vaca, *Adventures in the Unknown Interior of America;* see also G. Anderson, *Kinsmen of Another Kind*, 29.

11. Skinner, *Upper Country*, 3; B. White, "Encounters with Spirits," 381–82.

12. Worchester and Schilz, "Spread of Firearms," 109–10.

13. B. White, "Encounters with Spirits," 381–88.

14. Eccles, *Canadian Frontier*, 12–23.

15. Folwell, *History of Minnesota*, 1:1–6; Blegen, *Minnesota*, 34–36; Eccles, *Canadian Frontier*, 23–34.

16. Podruchny, *Making the Voyageur World*, 22; Folwell, *History of Minnesota*, 1:6–7; Lass, *Minnesota*, 56.

17. Folwell, *History of Minnesota*, 1:7; Eccles, *Canadian Frontier*, 137.

18. J. Peterson, "Many Roads to Red River," 42; Greer, *People of New France*, 78–79; Eccles, *Canadian Frontier*, 68–69.

19. In 1665 a musket and measure of powder traded for eight beaver skins, each valued at more than 100,000 livres. Worcester and Schilz, "Spread of Firearms," 103; G. Anderson, *Kinsmen of Another Kind*, 42.

20. Historians differ regarding the actual course of these expeditions since Radisson's account of the journeys, the only source, is riddled with inaccuracies, exaggerations, and falsehoods. A well-researched account of their journey can be found in B. White, *Grand Portage as a Trading Post*, 27–34. See also Folwell, *History of Minnesota*, 1:7–13; Blegen, *Minnesota*, 36–39; Lass, *Minnesota*, 56–57.

21. For a close analysis of Radisson, see Warkentin, "Discovering Radisson," 75–101.

22. B. White, "Encounters with Spirits," 382–84. On gift-giving, see also B. White, "'Give Us a Little Milk,'" 60–71.

23. As Germaine Warkentin notes, "This instinct for the political infuses every page of Radisson's six narratives." Warkentin, "Discovering Radisson," 80–83; Folwell, *History of Minnesota*, 1:8.

24. Folwell, *History of Minnesota*, 1:8; Blegen, *Minnesota*, 38–39; Warkentin, "Discovering Radisson," 99–101.

25. R. White, *Middle Ground*.

26. Ibid., 50–51.

27. The name "Chippewa" derives from a phonetic distortion of Ojibwe.

28. Bohaker, "*Nindoodemag*," 25–29, 39–40. See also Greenberg and Morrison, "Group Identities in the Boreal Forest," 75–102.

29. To illustrate the confusion that beset Europeans regarding Indian political organization circa 1740, the French explorer La Vérendrye identified sixteen tribes north and west of Lake Superior; Andrew Graham, a Hudson's Bay trader between 1749 and 1775, in an attempt to organize the various tribes that frequented his trading region, came up with no fewer than twenty-nine tribes. Notably, the two lists are entirely different from one another. Greenberg and Morrison, "Group Identities in the Boreal Forest," 78–81, and appendices A and B.

30. M. Meyer, *White Earth Tragedy*, 11–13; Cleland, "Preliminary Report," 19. On clan identities, see Warren, *History of the Ojibway People*, 41–53.

31. Witgen, "Rituals of Possession," 641; M. Meyer, *White Earth Tragedy*, 12–13, 20–28; R. White, *Middle Ground*, 19; Danziger Jr., *Chippewas of Lake Superior*, 26; Warren, *History of the Ojibway People*, 87.

32. Jacques Marquette, quoted in G. Anderson, "Early Dakota Migration," 24.

33. By 1660 the population at Sault Ste. Marie was reported to exceed 1,000. See Treuer, "Ojibwe-Dakota Relations," 91–92.

34. Ibid.; R. White, *Middle Ground*, 147; Danziger Jr., *Chippewas of Lake Superior*, 26–31; M. Meyer, *White Earth Tragedy*, 12–17; Hickerson, *Southwestern Chippewa*, 67; G. Anderson, *Kinsmen of Another Kind*, 31–32; G. Anderson, "Early Dakota Migration," 24.

35. R. White, *Middle Ground*, 15–19;

Warren, *History of the Ojibway People*, 164–65.

36. Buffalohead, "Farmers, Warriors, Traders," 237; B. White, "The Woman Who Married a Beaver," 115; Treuer, "Ojibwe-Dakota Relations," 51–52; Pond, *Dakota Life*, 27–28, 65.

37. B. White, "The Woman Who Married a Beaver," esp. 129–30.

38. On Ojibwe marriage customs, see Densmore, *Chippewa Customs*, 72–73. On Dakota customs, see Pond, *Dakota Life*, 137–40.

39. Richter, *Facing East from Indian Country*, 183; Van Kirk, *Many Tender Ties*, 28–52; Sleeper-Smith, "Women, Kin, and Catholicism," 424; Sleeper-Smith, *Indian Women and French Men*, 3–4.

40. The intendant was the chief civil administrator of the colony, responsible for colonial finances, administration of justice, and all civil matters. Eccles, *Canadian Frontier*, 67.

41. Talon, quoted in Folwell, *History of Minnesota*, 1:16.

42. For a textured analysis of this ceremony, see Witgen, "Rituals of Possession," 639–68. See also Folwell, *History of Minnesota*, 1:17; Blegen, *Minnesota*, 40.

43. As Michael Witgen notes, with their ceremonies and documents, the French tried to impose "the perspective of empire onto places that empire did not reach." Witgen, "Rituals of Possession," 642.

44. Eccles, *Canadian Frontier*, 101, 5.

45. R. White, *Middle Ground*, esp. 94–99; B. White, "'Give Us a Little Milk,'" 60–71; Witgen, "Rituals of Possession," 641, 655, 657–79.

46. Folwell, *History of Minnesota*, 1:18–22; Blegen, *Minnesota*, 41–42.

47. Worchester and Schilz, "Spread of Firearms," 109; G. Anderson, *Kinsmen of Another Kind*, 32. The Crees had good reason to undermine the proceedings since they were at war with the Dakotas and determined to keep firearms out of their hands.

48. Folwell, *History of Minnesota*, 1:22–24; Blegen, *Minnesota*, 46–48; Lass, *Minnesota*, 58.

49. Blegen, *Minnesota*, 46.

50. B. White, "'Give Us a Little Milk,'" 63–64; G. Anderson, *Kinsmen of Another Kind*, 32; R. White, *Middle Ground*, 15–19; R. Gilman, "Fur Trade," 5–6; Treuer, "Ojibwe-Dakota Relations," 99.

51. Eccles, *Canadian Frontier*, 5.

52. R. Gilman, "Reversing the Telescope," 3–17.

53. Folwell, *History of Minnesota*, 1:28–29. For an illuminating reinterpretation of Hennepin's narrative, see B. White, "Encounters with Spirits," esp. 387–88.

54. Folwell and Blegen relate essentially the same facts but their interpretations slightly differ. While Blegen states categorically that the explorers were "captured," Folwell's narrative is less conclusive. He appears puzzled by seeming inconsistencies in the evidence that would have been nearly impossible to reconcile within the parameters of historical thought in the 1920s when he was writing. Blegen, *Minnesota*, 48–50; Folwell, *History of Minnesota*, 1:27–30.

55. R. White, *Middle Ground*, 17–19.

56. None of the standard histories of Minnesota challenge this account, though Blegen alone uncritically relates Du Luth's version of the events. Folwell gives it minimal attention. Lass confines himself to noting that Du Luth "effected the release of the prisoners." Blegen, *Minnesota*, 48–51; Folwell, *History of Minnesota*, 1:30; Lass, *Minnesota*, 58–59.

57. La Salle, quoted in Upham, *Minnesota in Three Centuries*, 1:231.

58. Folwell, *History of Minnesota*, 1:30.

59. Folwell, *History of Minnesota*, 1:31; Blegen, *Minnesota*, 49–50; Lass, *Minnesota*, 60.

60. On the uses of captivity narratives, see Slotkin, *Gunfighter Nation*, esp. 10–16; Burnham, *Captivity and Sentiment*.

61. G. Anderson, *Kinsmen of Another Kind*, 33–35; Folwell, *History of Minnesota*, 1:36–38. On the "immensity of the task" of mediating peace among the warring tribes, see R. White, *Middle Ground*, 34.

62. Folwell, *History of Minnesota*, 1:37–38.

63. Perrot, quoted in R. White, *Middle Ground*, 96.

64. G. Anderson, "Early Dakota Migration," 22; Folwell, *History of Minnesota*, 1:38–39.

65. Eccles, "Fur Trade," 341–43; Folwell, *History of Minnesota*, 1:39.

66. Blegen, *Minnesota*, 52–53; Folwell, *History of Minnesota*, 1:40–41.

67. Blegen, *Minnesota*, 53; G. Anderson, *Kinsmen of Another Kind*, 35–36.

68. No record exists to determine if Le Sueur had taken a Dakota wife, though, as Gary Clayton Anderson suggests, it is likely he did so: "The full nature of Le Sueur's kinship ties . . . never surfaced in the discussion, yet the Dakotas were obviously pointing to a family bond." G. Anderson, *Kinsmen of Another Kind*, 37.

69. Blegen, *Minnesota*, 46; G. Anderson, "Early Dakota Migration," 24.

70. Eccles, *Canadian Frontier*, 5–7, 24, 38; Eccles, "Fur Trade," 345. See also R. White, *Middle Ground*.

71. No mention of the "ore" appears in subsequent official records. Most sources agree that Le Sueur had no illusion that his load of dirt had any mineral value.

2. Cultural Crossroads

1. Nash, "Hidden History of Mestizo America," 947; Adelman and Aron, "From Borderlands to Borders," 814–15, 819.

2. Nash, "Hidden History of Mestizo America"; Adelman and Aron, "From Borderlands to Borders."

3. Witgen, "Rituals of Possession," 646–48; Albers and Kay, "Sharing the Land," 47–91.

4. Eccles, *Canadian Frontier*, 5–7, 132–56; Eccles, "Fur Trade," 348–49; Rich, "Colonial Empire," 318; Adelman and Aron, "From Borderlands to Borders," 819–20.

5. R. White, *Middle Ground*, 119–28; Adelman and Aron, "From Borderlands to Borders," 819–20; Desbarats, "Cost of Early Canada's Native Alliances," 616–17.

6. On the series of French and Indian Wars, see Eccles, *Canadian Frontier*, 132–85.

7. G. Anderson, *Kinsmen of Another Kind*, 39.

8. Eccles, "Fur Trade," 344–45.

9. Eccles, *Canadian Frontier*, 137–47; Desbarats, "Cost of Early Canada's Native Alliances," 610.

10. Nicholas Perrot, quoted in Hickerson, *Southwestern Chippewa*, 66.

11. R. White, *Middle Ground*, 148–50.

12. Eccles, *Canadian Frontier*, 145–47; Lass, *Minnesota*, 62; Eccles, "Fur Trade," 353.

13. Eccles, "Fur Trade," 350.

14. Desbarats, "Cost of Early Canada's Native Alliances," 621; Kellogg, "Fort Beauharnois," 237–40; Blegen, *Minnesota*, 54–55; Eccles, *Canadian Frontier*, 148–49. For an extended treatment of the Fox wars, see R. White, *Middle Ground*, 149–75.

15. Fort Beauharnois was named in honor of Charles de la Boische, Marquis de Beauharnois, the governor general of New France. Commandant of the fort was Réné Boucher, Sieur de la Perriére. The Jesuit missionaries were Michel Guignas and Nicolas de Gonnor. Kellogg, "Fort Beauharnois," 235–37.

16. The fort was occupied on an occasional basis several times over the following decade with little success and permanently abandoned in 1737. Folwell, *History of Minnesota*, 1:46–47; Kellogg, "Fort Beauharnois," 232–46.

17. G. Anderson, *Kinsmen of Another Kind*, 39–40, 46.

18. Desbarats, "Cost of Early Canada's Native Alliances," 610, 620; Greer, *People of New France*, 19; R. White, *Middle Ground*, 121–22; Eccles, "Fur Trade," 347–49.

19. Naval secretary Jean-Frédéric Phélypeaux, Comte de Maurepas, 1731, quoted in Desbarats, "Cost of Early Canada's Native Alliances," 619.

20. R. White, *Middle Ground*, 145.

21. R. White, *Middle Ground*, 182; C. Gilman, *Grand Portage Story*, 37.

22. G. Anderson, *Kinsmen of Another Kind*, 44.

23. C. Gilman, *Grand Portage Story*, 35–36; Treuer, "Ojibwe-Dakota Relations," 111.

24. Blegen, *Minnesota*, 56–57; Treuer, "Ojibwe-Dakota Relations," 111; C. Gilman, *Grand Portage Story*, 36–37. The tribal identity of some of the northern bands is difficult to ascertain since individuals frequently moved back and forth between villages. On Cree-Ojibwes, see B. White, *Grand Portage as a Trading Post*, 38; and Greenberg and

Morrison, "Group Identities in the Boreal Forest," 75–102.

25. Eccles, *Canadian Frontier*, 149; C. Gilman, *Grand Portage Story*, 36–37; Nute, "Posts in the Minnesota Fur-Trading Area," 362.

26. B. White, *Grand Portage as a Trading Post*, 41–42; Treuer, "Ojibwe-Dakota Relations," 111–13; C. Gilman, *Grand Portage Story*, 37.

27. Treuer, "Ojibwe-Dakota Relations," 114–15.

28. The site of the attack is known to this day as Massacre Island. Ibid., 126–27; G. Anderson, *Kinsmen of Another Kind*, 43–44.

29. Treuer, "Ojibwe-Dakota Relations," 123–24, 134–37; G. Anderson, *Kinsmen of Another Kind*, 44–45.

30. C. Gilman, *Grand Portage Story*, 37–38; G. Anderson, *Kinsmen of Another Kind*, 46–47.

31. Hickerson, *Chippewa and Their Neighbors*, 66; C. Gilman, *Grand Portage Story*, 38.

32. Treuer, "Ojibwe-Dakota Relations," 136–39; C. Gilman, *Grand Portage Story*, 38.

33. The standard accounts of the Dakota-Ojibwe wars have relied heavily on William Warren's *History of the Ojibway People*, first published in 1885. Warren, a mixed-blood Ojibwe, drew his evidence from the oral histories of his people, which quite naturally emphasized the bravery and accomplishments of the Ojibwes. No comparable chronicle exists for the Dakota side of the conflict.

34. Treuer, "Ojibwe-Dakota Relations," 142–46.

35. Ibid., 141–47.

36. Treuer, "Ojibwe-Dakota Relations," 146, 153–55. On the contours of Indian warfare, see R. White, *Middle Ground*.

37. Following the Pueblo War in 1680, the western tribes began to have access to horses. By 1700 horses began to appear among the Dakotas.

38. G. Anderson, *Kinsmen of Another Kind*, 46–47; R. White, "Winning of the West," 323; G. Anderson, "Early Dakota Migration," 25–26; Gibbon, *The Sioux*, 53–54.

39. Treuer, "Ojibwe-Dakota Relations," 153–66; Warren, *History of the Ojibway People*, 175–78.

40. G. Anderson, *Kinsmen of Another Kind*, 49–50; Treuer, "Ojibwe-Dakota Relations," 158–60.

41. King George's War and the French and Indian War were actually the American front of larger imperial conflicts between France and England: the War of Austrian Succession (1740–1745) and the Seven Years' War (1754–1763).

42. R. White, *Middle Ground*, 198–211; C. Gilman, *Grand Portage Story*, 42; G. Anderson, *Kinsmen of Another Kind*, 50–51.

43. R. White, *Middle Ground*, esp. ch. 4 and ch. 5; C. Gilman, *Grand Portage Story*, 42.

44. *Dictionary of Canadian Biography*, 3:431–32; G. Anderson, *Kinsmen of Another Kind*, 48–51; Blegen, *Minnesota*, 60–61.

45. Archaeologist Douglas Birk suggests that the Ojibwe chief Marin, a highly respected figure in the early nineteenth century, may have been the mixed-blood son or grandson of Joseph Marin. See Birk, *John Sayer's Snake River Journal*, 24. On Joseph Marin, see *Dictionary of Canadian Biography*.

46. In 1753 Joseph Marin informed the governor-general that he had expended more than 10,000 livres in gifts to forestall an outbreak of hostilities. Eccles, *Canadian Frontier*, 148.

47. G. Anderson, *Kinsmen of Another Kind*, 49–57; C. Gilman, *Grand Portage Story*, 42.

48. J. Brown, *Strangers in Blood*, 3–5, xii.

49. On the phenomenon of partial cultural assimilations, see J. Brown, *Strangers in Blood*, xvi–xvii.

50. Eccles, *Canadian Frontier*, 8, 89–91. French officials used the terms "Indianization" and "Canadianization" interchangeably to describe what they viewed as a troubling transformation. See J. Peterson, "Prelude to Red River," 47.

51. R. White, *Middle Ground*, 68–70; Eccles, *Canadian Frontier*, 91; J. Brown, *Strangers in Blood*, 3–4.

52. J. Brown, *Strangers in Blood*, 5; G. Anderson, *Kinsmen of Another Kind*, 50–51.

53. B. White, "'Give Us a Little Milk,'" 60–71; Eccles, *Canadian Frontier*, 8.

54. Dickason, "From 'One Nation,'" 22–25.

55. Densmore, *Chippewa Customs*, 70–71; R. White, *Middle Ground*, 17–19; Hilger, *Chippewa Families*, 60–62; Albers, "Santee," 766–67; Pond, *Dakota Life*, 137–40.

56. Before the 1790s, 81 percent of male householders at Michilimackinac were married to Indian or Métis women. J. Peterson, "Prelude to Red River," 48–49; Sleeper-Smith, "Women, Kin, and Catholicism," 424–30; Eccles, *Canadian Frontier*, 89–92; Dickason, "From 'One Nation,'" 23.

57. Richter, *Facing East from Indian Country*, 183; Sleeper-Smith, *Indian Women and French Men*, 4–5; B. White, "The Woman Who Married a Beaver," 129–30; J. Peterson, "Prelude to Red River," 55–56. For an analysis that emphasizes the affection between Indian and white marriage partners, see Van Kirk, *Many Tender Ties*.

58. Buffalohead, "Farmers, Warriors, Traders," 236–44; B. White, "The Woman Who Married a Beaver," 119–20, 123–27.

59. Dickason, "From 'One Nation,'" 30–32.

3. Geographies of Dominion

1. R. White, *Middle Ground*, 278, 256–68. Quote from Gage appears on page 256. Dowd, "Wag the Imperial Dog," 60–63.

2. R. White, *Middle Ground*, 258–59. Johnson and Croghan quoted on p. 269.

3. For a full analysis of Pontiac's Rebellion, see R. White, *Middle Ground*, 269–314. See also Dowd, *A Spirited Resistance*, 23–40; and Lavender, *Fist in the Wilderness*, 9.

4. R. White, *Middle Ground*, 308, 315–18. Johnson quoted on p. 315. See also Dowd, *A Spirited Resistance*, 42–45; and McConnell, *A Country Between*.

5. Holton, "Ohio Indians and the Coming of the American Revolution in Virginia," 453–55.

6. Ibid., 453–78. On Washington's land holdings, see "George Washington to His Brother Charles," 98–101.

7. Ferling, *Leap in the Dark*, 30–42; Holton, "Ohio Indians and the Coming of the American Revolution in Virginia," esp. 477–78.

8. Folwell, *History of Minnesota*, 1:53; Gates, "Narrative of Peter Pond," 44, 56.

9. Eccles, *Canadian Frontier*, 184–85; Treuer, "Ojibwe-Dakota Relations," 170; J. Peterson, "Many Roads to Red River," 40–41.

10. Lass, *Minnesota*, 66–67; Folwell, *History of Minnesota*, 1:54–55.

11. Lass, *Minnesota*, 67–69.

12. Gates, "Narrative of Peter Pond," 45.

13. Lass, *Minnesota*, 69–71; Blegen, *Minnesota*, 68–70. Since Carver's sojourn in the Minnesota River valley began in November and ended in April or May, his description of the region is clearly fanciful.

14. Folwell, *History of Minnesota*, 1:64.

15. Treuer, "Ojibwe-Dakota Relations," 173; G. Anderson, *Kinsmen of Another Kind*, 58–59, 61; R. Meyer, *History of the Santee Sioux*, 14.

16. Treuer, "Ojibwe-Dakota Relations," 173; C. Gilman, *Grand Portage Story*, 45–46.

17. C. Gilman, *Grand Portage Story*, 47.

18. Ibid., 51; B. White, "Skilled Game of Exchange," 11.

19. C. Gilman, *Grand Portage Story*, 47; Lavender, *Fist in the Wilderness*, 10.

20. Schenck, "The Cadottes," 189–94; J. Peterson, "Prelude to Red River," 48.

21. J. Brown, *Strangers in Blood*, 44–45; J. Peterson, "Many Roads to Red River," 59–60.

22. R. White, *Middle Ground*, 68–70, 316–17, Croghan quoted on 316; Eccles, *Canadian Frontier*, 91; J. Brown, *Strangers in Blood*, 3–4; J. Peterson, "Many Roads to Red River," 48, 60.

23. R. White, *Middle Ground*, 316–17; Treuer, "Ojibwe-Dakota Relations," 173; J. Brown, *Strangers in Blood*, 82.

24. Treuer, "Ojibwe-Dakota Relations," 166–67.

25. Ibid.; Carver quoted in Anderson, *Kinsmen of Another Kind*, 60.

26. R. Meyer, *History of the Santee Sioux*, 14; Treuer, "Ojibwe-Dakota Relations," 201–2, 147–53.

27. Warren, *History of the Ojibway People*, 219–20.

28. Birk, *John Sayer's Snake River Journal*, 24–25.

29. Ibid., 10; B. White, "Skilled Game of Exchange," 236–37; C. Gilman, *Grand Portage Story*, 52; Gates, "Narrative of Peter Pond," 27–28; Folwell, *History of Minnesota*, 1:64–65.

30. B. White, "Skilled Game of Exchange," 236–38.

31. Ibid., 229–30; Lavender, *Fist in the Wilderness*, 11; R. White, *Middle Ground*, 179–81.

32. Mancall, "Men, Women, and Alcohol," 437; Rorabaugh, *Alcoholic Republic*, 7–10; Birk, *John Sayer's Snake River Journal*, 35.

33. Mancall, "Men, Women, and Alcohol," 430–31, 436; B. White, "'Give Us a Little Milk,'" 66–67; B. White, "Skilled Game of Exchange," 35–36. For a vivid account of a mourning ritual, see Gates, "Narrative of Peter Pond," 35–36.

34. S. Buck, "Story of Grand Portage," 30–31; C. Gilman, *Grand Portage Story*, 52; Lass, *Minnesota*, 72–73.

35. C. Gilman, *Grand Portage Story*, 52–53.

36. Folwell, *History of Minnesota*, 1:64–66; Holton, "Ohio Indians," 469–72; Laub, "British Regulation of Crown Lands in the West," 52–55.

37. Folwell, *History of Minnesota*, 1:64–66; H. Smith, "Church and State in North America," 464–67; Maier, *From Resistance to Revolution*, 225–26, 238.

38. On the penetration of Catholicism, see Sleeper-Smith, "Women, Kin, and Catholicism," 423–41.

39. G. Anderson, *Kinsmen of Another Kind*, 61–63; S. Buck, "Story of Grand Portage," 30–31; C. Gilman, *Grand Portage Story*, 54–55.

40. The following discussion of the smallpox pandemic is deeply indebted to the work of Elizabeth A. Fenn, *Pox Americana*.

41. Inoculation with live smallpox virus was replaced by vaccination, pioneered by Edward Jenner, in the 1790s. Jenner discovered that introduction under the skin of the relatively benign cowpox virus produced immunity to smallpox without the risk of infecting patients with the smallpox virus itself.

42. Fenn, *Pox Americana*, 10–43.

43. Ibid., 62–78.

44. Ibid., 108, 169–73, 182.

45. Ibid., 137–66; Calloway, "Introduction," *Our Hearts Fell to the Ground*, 5–7; C. Gilman, *Grand Portage Story*, 63; Warren, *History of the Ojibway*, 261–62.

46. Fenn, *Pox Americana*, 271; Henry quoted in C. Gilman, *Grand Portage Story*, 63; Treuer, "Ojibwe-Dakota Relations," 210; Warren, *History of the Ojibway People*, 262.

47. C. Gilman, *Grand Portage Story*, 64.

48. Fenn, *Pox Americana*, 275; R. White, "Winning of the West," 325; Sundstrom, "Smallpox Used Them Up," 305–43; G. Anderson, *Kinsmen of Another Kind*, 19, 74.

49. Danziger Jr., *Chippewas of Lake Superior*, 60; C. Gilman, *Grand Portage Story*, 64–65, 71.

50. C. Gilman, *Grand Portage Story*, 65–66; J. Brown, *Strangers in Blood*, 44–47.

51. J. Brown, *Strangers in Blood*, 45–47; C. Gilman, *Grand Portage Story*, 68.

52. Lavender, *Fist in the Wilderness*, 28–29; J. Brown, *Strangers in Blood*, 47.

53. S. Buck, "Story of Grand Portage," 32; Folwell, *History of Minnesota*, 1:67. For a vivid and nuanced portrayal of a Grand Portage rendezvous, see C. Gilman, *Grand Portage Story*, 5–23.

54. C. Gilman, *Grand Portage Story*, 22–23.

55. J. Brown, *Strangers in Blood*, 39–41.

56. Ibid., 38–42; C. Gilman, *Grand Portage Story*, 80–81.

57. Hickerson, *Chippewa and Their Neighbors*, 102; C. Gilman, *Grand Portage Story*, 80–85.

58. C. Gilman, *Grand Portage Story*, 63–64; Birk, *John Sayer's Snake River Journal*, 16.

59. Birk, *John Sayer's Snake River Journal*, 7–11; Sayer journal, Jan.–Feb. 1805; B. White, "Skilled Game of Exchange," Nelson quoted on p. 239.

60. J. Brown, *Strangers in Blood*, 82–90. On Sayer see Birk, *John Sayer's Snake River Journal*, 24–25.

61. C. Gilman, *Grand Portage Story*,

87–88; B. White, "Skilled Game of Exchange," 239.

62. C. Gilman, *Grand Portage Story,* 86–89.

63. Ibid., 54; G. Anderson, *Kinsmen of Another Kind,* 65–66. The most important companies in the Dakota trade were Robert Dickson & Company, the Michilimackinac Company, the Southwest Company, and the Montreal-Michilimackinac Company, none of which survived more than a few years. See Lavender, *Fist in the Wilderness,* 179–80.

64. G. Anderson, *Kinsmen of Another Kind,* 66–68. I use the term "mixed blood" to distinguish individuals of Anglo-Indian cultural heritage from the Métis, whose cultural identity derives from French-Indian unions. The key difference is cultural rather than genealogical. For example, the children of Jean Baptiste Faribault and his Dakota wife fall into the category of mixed blood because their cultural identity is a mixture of Dakota and Anglo-American, though Faribault's ancestry is French.

65. Ibid., 30–31.

66. Prescott, *Recollections of Philander Prescott,* 56.

67. Gates, "Narrative of Peter Pond," 50.

68. Meinig, *Shaping of America,* 1:338–41.

69. Ibid., 324–27; Folwell, *History of Minnesota,* 1:70–72.

70. Meinig, *Shaping of America,* 1:425–26; Folwell, *History of Minnesota,* 1:76–77.

71. Lavender, *Fist in the Wilderness,* 39; Folwell, *History of Minnesota,* 1:71–72; C. Gilman, *Grand Portage Story,* 90–92.

72. Meinig, *Shaping of America,* 2:58–59; Folwell, *History of Minnesota,* 1:77–79, 88.

4. Shifting Ground

1. Pike's expedition traveled by bateau, a flat-bottomed boat that carried both sail and oars, developed by French Canadians for river travel in the interior.

2. Folwell, *History of Minnesota,* 1:90–91; Brueggemann, "Rendezvous at the Riverbend," 4; Lavender, *Fist in the Wilderness,* 44–46.

3. Lavender, *Fist in the Wilderness,* 39–45.

4. Folwell, *History of Minnesota,* 1:91; Brueggemann, "Rendezvous at the Riverbend," 4–5.

5. Meinig, *Shaping of America,* 1:324–25.

6. Folwell, *History of Minnesota,* 1:91; Brueggemann, "Rendezvous at the Riverbend," 6–7; Neill, "Sketch of Joseph Renville," 12–16; Ackermann, "Joseph Renville of Lac Qui Parle," 232–33.

7. Brueggemann, "Rendezvous at the Riverbend," 11. Pike also negotiated permission to build a post at the mouth of the St. Croix River.

8. Treaty with the Sioux, Sept. 23, 1805, reproduced in Folwell, *History of Minnesota,* 1:93; *Expeditions of Zebulon Pike,* quoted in Brueggemann, "Rendezvous at the Riverbend," 12; Pike to Wilkinson, quoted in G. Anderson, *Kinsmen of Another Kind,* 82.

9. Folwell, *History of Minnesota,* 1:92–94.

10. Ibid., 95–97; Lavender, *Fist in the Wilderness,* 70.

11. Lavender, *Fist in the Wilderness,* 70; Blegen, *Minnesota,* 89–90.

12. Pike's journal, quoted in Brueggemann, "Rendezvous at the Riverbend," 14.

13. Lavender, *Fist in the Wilderness,* 70–71; Brueggemann, "Rendezvous at the Riverbend," 14.

14. Congress first passed the Embargo Act in 1807, which forbade all international trade from American ports. In 1809, the embargo was superceded by the Nonintercourse Act, which forbade trade only with England and France.

15. Pratt, "Fur Trade Strategy," 248–49, 253.

16. Horsman, "British Indian Policy in the Northwest," 52–54; Lavender, *Fist in the Wilderness,* 182–83.

17. Lavender, *Fist in the Wilderness,* 183; Pratt, "Fur Trade Strategy," 64; Treuer, "Ojibwe-Dakota Relations," 231–32. In Dakota custom, band chiefs took on dynastic names—such as Wabasha, Red Wing, and Little Crow—that were passed from generation to generation of leaders. In the period under consideration in this volume, Wakinyatanka, also known as Big Thunder (Little Crow III), and Taoyateduta (Little Crow IV) were both important actors in shaping events.

18. Lavender, *Fist in the Wilderness*, 191; Pratt, "Fur Trade Strategy," 251–52. For a full analysis of the war on the settlement frontier, see R. White, *Middle Ground*.

19. Warren, *History of the Ojibway People*, 368–70.

20. Folwell, *History of Minnesota*, 1:100n29–30; Pratt, "Fur Trade Strategy," 254–68; Treuer, "Ojibwe-Dakota Relations," 233; G. Anderson, *Kinsmen of Another Kind*, 87–91.

21. Pratt, "Fur Trade Strategy," 270–71.

22. R. Meyer, *History of the Santee Sioux*, 30.

23. G. Anderson, *Kinsmen of Another Kind*, 94–102.

24. Folwell, *History of Minnesota*, 1:135–37; G. Anderson, *Kinsmen of Another Kind*, 98–99.

25. The soldiers posted to Fort Snelling were members of the Fifth Infantry Regiment. For recruiting efforts in the East and state of the troops—"only half had uniforms and accouterments, the rest made do with civilian dress of varying degrees of serviceability"—see N. Goodman and R. Goodman, *Joseph R. Brown*, 26–29.

26. Blegen, *Minnesota*, 98–99; Lavender, *Fist in the Wilderness*, 279–80.

27. Folwell, *History of Minnesota*, 1:132–33.

28. Lavender, "Some Characteristics of the American Fur Company," 178–87; G. Anderson, *Kinsmen of Another Kind*, 105–6.

29. C. Gilman, *Grand Portage Story*, 103.

30. Galbraith, "British-American Competition in the Border Fur Trade of the 1820s," 242–43.

31. Ibid.; Prescott, *Recollections of Philander Prescott*, 64–66; C. Gilman, *Grand Portage Story*, 104.

32. Prescott, *Recollections of Philander Prescott*, 65; Galbraith, "British-American Competition," 245. According to Anton Treuer, population estimates for this period vary widely, from 30,000 to as many as 180,000. Even the lowest estimate demonstrates a substantial rebound from the smallpox devastation of the 1780s. Treuer, "Ojibwe-Dakota Relations," 235.

33. Lavender, *Fist in the Wilderness*, 415; C. Gilman, *Grand Portage Story*, 104–5.

34. Treuer, "Ojibwe-Dakota Relations," 236–39; Folwell, *History of Minnesota*, 1:150; Hickerson, *Chippewa and Their Neighbors*, 94–95; Pond, *Dakota Life*, 60–61.

35. Treuer, "Ojibwe-Dakota Relations," 254–61; G. Anderson, *Kinsmen of Another Kind*, 131–33.

36. G. Anderson, *Kinsmen of Another Kind*, 131–33. For a full analysis of the environmental and economic factors leading other tribes to dependency, see R. White, *Roots of Dependency*.

37. Hickerson, *Chippewa and Their Neighbors*, 96–98; G. Anderson, *Kinsmen of Another Kind*, 131–33.

38. Little Crow, quoted in Treuer, "Ojibwe-Dakota Relations," 242–43.

39. Ibid., 279; Folwell, *History of Minnesota*, 1:154; Hickerson, *Chippewa and Their Neighbors*, 88–90, 93–98.

40. According to Indian agent Lawrence Taliaferro, between 1820 and 1837 the Dakota did not "shed one drop of American blood." Neill, *History of Minnesota*, 339.

41. Treuer, "Ojibwe-Dakota Relations," 279–82; Folwell, *History of Minnesota*, 1:155–56.

42. Pond, *Dakota Life*, 19–20; N. Goodman and R. Goodman, *Joseph R. Brown*, 126; Kugel, "Of Missionaries and Their Cattle," 227–40; Prescott, *Recollections of Philander Prescott*, 157–60.

43. Prescott, *Recollections of Philander Prescott*, 153n4; G. Anderson, *Kinsmen of Another Kind*, 67, 106.

44. N. Goodman and R. Goodman, *Joseph R. Brown*, 29–34, 42.

45. See C. Gilman, *Where Two Worlds Meet;* also Lavender, *Fist in the Wilderness*, 84–85; N. Goodman and R. Goodman, *Joseph R. Brown*, 96.

46. Folwell, *History of Minnesota*, 1:136–40; Prescott, *Recollections of Philander Prescott*, 29.

47. Adams, "Early Days at Red River Settlement," 95–97; N. Goodman and R. Goodman, *Joseph R. Brown*, 38, 42–44, 55.

48. Adams, "Early Days at Red River Settlement," 98–99.

[374]

49. Ibid.; N. Goodman and R. Goodman, *Joseph R. Brown*, 45–46. On women's role in domesticating the frontier, see Kolodny, *The Land Before Her*. On the influence of white women on fur trade culture, see Van Kirk, *Many Tender Ties*.

50. N. Goodman and R. Goodman, *Joseph R. Brown*, 45–47, 59–62, 111–12. Brown spent little time with Helen after their marriage, leaving her behind at Fort Snelling while he resided at various trading posts. In 1835, after Brown was well established in the trade (and his father-in-law, Robert Dickson, was long dead), he divorced Helen after seven years of their long-distance marriage.

51. Pond, *Dakota Life*, 19–20; R. Gilman, *Henry Hastings Sibley*, 54.

52. R. Gilman, *Henry Hastings Sibley*, 31–32; R. Gilman, "Last Days of the Upper Mississippi Fur Trade," 106–7.

53. Sibley, "Memoir of Hercules L. Dousman," 193; R. Gilman, *Henry Hastings Sibley*, 36–37; Lavender, *Fist in the Wilderness*, 296–97.

54. R. Gilman, *Henry Hastings Sibley*, 3–21.

55. Ibid., 20–38. Under the terms of the contract, American Fur would supply the capital and own a half interest in the business. "The remaining half was divided among Rolette, Dousman, and Sibley on a 5-3-2 basis. The partners would draw no salary, but Dousman was guaranteed $1,500 per year and Sibley $1,200 before any further distribution of profits" (38). If the season did not return a profit, the partners would receive nothing for the year.

56. Folwell, *History of Minnesota*, 1:141–43. A vast literature exists on the ideology of honor and paternalism that southern slaveholders developed to justify their system of human exploitation. See, for example, Wyatt-Brown, *Shaping of Southern Culture*; Genovese, *Roll, Jordan, Roll*.

57. Lavender, *Fist in the Wilderness*, 308, 325–27; Folwell, *History of Minnesota*, 1:141–43; N. Goodman and R. Goodman, *Joseph R. Brown*, 65–67; R. Gilman, *Henry Hastings Sibley*, 39–40.

58. On Frazer, see R. Gilman, *Henry Hastings Sibley*, 69. On Faribault, see Sibley, "Memoir of Jean Baptiste Faribault," 168–79.

59. R. Gilman, *Henry Hastings Sibley*, 38–39, 44; Lavender, *Fist in the Wilderness*, 371–72. Bailly, it should be noted, was well educated and multilingual; nonetheless, by Taliaferro's measure, Bailly's freebooting ways may have revealed the "Indian" part of his heritage.

60. R. Gilman, *Henry Hastings Sibley*, 30–32; R. Gilman, "Last Days of the Upper Mississippi Fur Trade," 103–5.

61. Prescott, *Recollections of Philander Prescott*, 65–66, 58.

62. Ibid.

63. R. Gilman, *Henry Hastings Sibley*, 41–42.

64. N. Goodman and R. Goodman, *Joseph R. Brown*, 113–15.

65. Taliaferro's journal, quoted in Ibid., 117.

66. R. Meyer, *History of the Santee Sioux*, 48–49; G. Anderson, *Kinsmen of Another Kind*, 134–36; N. Goodman and R. Goodman, *Joseph R. Brown*, 93–94; R. Gilman, *Henry Hastings Sibley*, 50. The half-breed tract was a fifteen-mile-wide strip of land along the western shore of Lake Pepin that extended from Red Wing's village approximately thirty-two miles to the Grand Encampment at Wabasha prairie. Neill, *History of Minnesota*, 400.

67. Ibid.

68. Hancock, *Goodhue County*, 119–20.

5. Highway to the North

1. Blegen, *Minnesota*, 112; Blegen, "The 'Fashionable Tour,'" 73; W. Peterson, *Steamboating on the Upper Mississippi*, 90–107, 146–53.

2. Lavender, *Fist in the Wilderness*, 304–7; Keating, *Narrative of the Expedition*, 272–73.

3. Folwell, *History of Minnesota*, 1:101–16. At the time of Schoolcraft's expedition in 1832, the United States and Great Britain were still squabbling over the precise location of the U.S–Canadian border, each side making "extravagant territorial claims." In 1842 the Webster-Ashburton Treaty established the 49th parallel as the rough international

boundary line. Though the revised boundary was considerably more precise than the vague coordinates inscribed at the Treaty of Paris, the exact international boundary, as it crossed land and water, remained a matter of dispute until finally arbitrated in 1872. In Minnesota country, however, the boundary now lay some 110 miles north of Lake Itasca. Thus, the search for the headwaters of the Mississippi had lost some of its political importance. Meinig, *Shaping of America*, 2:123, 125–27.

4. W. Peterson, *Steamboating on the Upper Mississippi*, 152–54.

5. Ibid., 13–14, 90–106.

6. Ibid.; Folwell, *History of Minnesota*, 1:109–11. Beltrami declared Lake Julia (which he named "in honor of a lady not living") near Red Lake as the source of the Mississippi.

7. Folwell, *History of Minnesota*, 1:122–27; E. Bray and M. Bray, *Joseph N. Nicollet*, 4–12. On the shift from land to real estate, see Cronon, *Nature's Metropolis*, 101–2.

8. E. Bray and M. Bray, *Joseph N. Nicollet*, 8, 17–18; Southwick, *Building on a Borrowed Past*, 17–19.

9. Southwick, *Building on a Borrowed Past*, 19–21; Blegen, "The 'Fashionable Tour,'" 73–74; W. Peterson, *Steamboating on the Upper Mississippi*, 248.

10. Blegen, "The 'Fashionable Tour,'" 73–76; W. Peterson, *Steamboating on the Upper Mississippi*, 248–56, 261–62.

11. On passengers, see W. Peterson, *Steamboating on the Upper Mississippi*, 252–61. On St. Anthony Falls, see Kane, *Falls of St. Anthony*, 9–11.

12. Blegen, "The 'Fashionable Tour,'" 74.

13. R. Gilman, *Henry Hastings Sibley*, 62–63; E. Bray and M. Bray, *Joseph N. Nicollet*, 7–8, 10n17, 217–18.

14. R. Gilman, *Henry Hastings Sibley*, 62–63; W. Peterson, *Steamboating on the Upper Mississippi*, 254–55.

15. Berkhofer Jr., *Salvation and the Savage*, 1–2. On foreign missions, see Phillips, *Protestant America and the Pagan World*.

16. Berkhofer Jr., *Salvation and the Savage*, 4–8. Quote from Riggs appears on p. 7 (italics in the original).

17. R. Meyer, *History of the Santee Sioux*, 48–50; Forbes, "Methodist Mission among

the Dakotas," 52; Berkhofer Jr., *Salvation and the Savage*, 7–10.

18. Berkhofer Jr., *Salvation and the Savage*, 1–15; Bowden, *American Indians and Christian Missions*, 168.

19. Forbes, "Methodist Mission among the Dakotas," 53–54.

20. Kugel, "Of Missionaries and Their Cattle," 227–40.

21. Neill, *History of Minnesota*, 422–23.

22. Letter from William Boutwell, quoted in Ibid., 437–38 (italics in the original).

23. Ibid., 438.

24. Uchida, "The Protestant Mission and Native American Response," 154–58. See also the diary of Alexander Huggins, Minnesota Historical Society.

25. Pond, *Dakota Life*, 60–63, 71–72; G. Anderson, "Introduction," in Pond, *Dakota Life*, vii–xi.

26. G. Anderson, "Introduction," xiv, xix–xxi.

27. Ibid., xi–xiii; Diedrich, "A 'Good Man' in a Changing World," 6–9.

28. G. Anderson, "Introduction," xi–xv; Diedrich, "A 'Good Man' in a Changing World," 10–16; R. Meyer, *History of the Santee Sioux*, 48–53. See also "Memorial Notices of Rev. Gideon H. Pond," in *Collections of Minnesota Historical Society*, 3:356–59.

29. Gates, "Lac Qui Parle Indian Mission," 133–51; G. Anderson, "Joseph Renville," 74–76. For mission chronology, see Willand, *Lac Qui Parle*, 279–90.

30. E. Bray and M. Bray, *Joseph N. Nicollet*, 108; R. Gilman, *Henry Hastings Sibley*, 32, 55–56.

31. Ackermann, "Joseph Renville of Lac Qui Parle," 231–32; Berkhofer Jr., *Salvation and the Savage*, 112; Featherstonehaugh, *Canoe Voyage up the Minnay Sotor*, 1:343; Huggins diary, 1 July 1836.

32. G. Anderson, "Joseph Renville," 68–70; Pond, *Dakota Life*, 18–19.

33. Pond, *Dakota Life*, 18–19; R. Gilman, *Henry Hastings Sibley*, 56–59; Neill, "Sketch of Joseph Renville," 201.

34. Riggs, "Protestant Missions in the Northwest," 125–29; Gates, "Lac Qui Parle Indian Mission," 133–37. For a firsthand

account of the journey, see Huggins diary, 23 June–9 July 1836.

35. G. Anderson, "Joseph Renville," 72–74, 78. See Huggins diary for a catalog of activities the missionaries carried on.

36. Gates, "Lac Qui Parle Indian Mission," 139–48; Uchida, "The Protestant Mission and Native American Response," 158–63; Ackermann, "Joseph Renville of Lac Qui Parle," 241–43; G. Anderson, "Joseph Renville," 74–78.

37. Uchida, "The Protestant Mission and Native American Response," 158–63; Gates, "Lac Qui Parle Indian Mission," 148; Ackermann, "Joseph Renville of Lac Qui Parle," 244n31.

38. For a detailed account of Catholic priests in early Minnesota country, see Reardon, *Catholic Church in the Diocese of St. Paul,* 16–30.

39. Sleeper-Smith, "Women, Kin, and Catholicism," 425–28, 432; Neill, *History of Minnesota,* 423.

40. Sleeper-Smith, "Women, Kin, and Catholicism."

41. Kugel, "Of Missionaries and Their Cattle," 238; Reardon, *Catholic Church in the Diocese of St. Paul,* 36–37. It is important to note that while contemporary sources typically used the terms "Indian" or "French" to describe the Catholics of Grand Portage, very likely the vast majority of the Catholics there (as elsewhere) were Métis.

42. Hoffmann, *Church Founders of the Northwest,* 117–26; Reardon, *Catholic Church in the Diocese of St. Paul,* 39–41. An examination of the baptismal records for Loras's visit reveals the web of kinship that connected whites, Indians, and Métis at this time. See Hoffmann, "New Light on Old St. Peter's and Early St. Paul," 32–37.

43. Hoffmann, *Church Founders of the Northwest,* 127–28, 166.

44. Ibid., 137, 160–62, 166–67; Reardon, *Catholic Church in the Diocese of St. Paul,* 41, 51–52.

45. Reardon, *Catholic Church in the Diocese of St. Paul,* 50–52; Forbes, "Methodist Mission among the Dakotas," 50; Hoffmann, *Church Founders of the Northwest,* 160–62.

46. Reardon, *Catholic Church in the Diocese of St. Paul,* 53–54. By comparison, none of the missionaries working among the Ojibwes at Sandy Lake, Lake Pokegama, Leech Lake, or Fond du Lac could report more than "several" conversions. At Pokegama, the most successful Ojibwe mission, Stephen Riggs related that "eight or ten persons were regarded, in the judgment of charity, as christians." At Lac qui Parle in 1837, after two years of effort, only seven Dakotas had accepted Christianity. The first Dakota man was not baptized until 1841. See Riggs, "Protestant Missions in the Northwest," 121–23, 129–30.

47. Ibid., 51–57; Hoffmann, *Church Founders of the Northwest,* 167–70.

6. A World Unraveling

1. Alexander Huggins diary, 11 July 1836.

2. Glueck Jr., *Minnesota and the Manifest Destiny,* 5–6; R. Gilman, C. Gilman, and D. Stultz, *Red River Trails,* 2; Pritchett, *Red River Valley,* 38–46.

3. Pritchett, *Red River Valley,* 27–33.

4. Ibid., 84–87, 78–79, 90, 101–17; R. Gilman, C. Gilman, and D. Stultz, *Red River Trails,* 2.

5. Pritchett, *Red River Valley,* 196; R. Gilman, C. Gilman, and D. Stultz, *Red River Trails,* 2–3.

6. R. Gilman, C. Gilman, and D. Stultz, *Red River Trails,* 2–3; Adams, "Early Days at Red River Settlement," 81–82, 89–96; Pritchett, *Red River Valley,* 224–25; Neill, "Occurrences in and around Fort Snelling," 127; Glueck Jr., *Minnesota and the Manifest Destiny,* 28–30; Folwell, *History of Minnesota,* 1:217n10.

7. Folwell, *History of Minnesota,* 1:214–19; Glueck Jr., *Minnesota and the Manifest Destiny,* 17–18, 28–29; Adams, "Early Days at Red River Settlement," 76–98.

8. Adams, "Early Days at Red River Settlement," 89–93; Folwell, *History of Minnesota,* 1:223.

9. Though Pembina today, located on the west bank of the Red River, is in the state of North Dakota, until 1858 it was part of

[376]

Minnesota Territory and played an important role in territorial politics. Before Stephen Long surveyed the international border there in 1823, no one knew for certain if the settlement was in the United States or Canada.

10. J. Peterson, "Many Roads to Red River," 39; J. Peterson, "Prelude to Red River," 46, 54; Riggs, *Mary and I*, 65.

11. J. Peterson, "Prelude to Red River," 57–58.

12. Ibid., 50–53; J. Peterson, "Many Roads to Red River," 55–58, Long quoted on p. 57.

13. Pritchett, *Red River Valley*, 168, 172; Glueck Jr., *Minnesota and the Manifest Destiny*, 37–39.

14. R. Gilman, C. Gilman, and D. Stultz, *Red River Trails*, 34–35. As noted by Bruce White, to nineteenth-century Euro-Americans only those communities that conformed to a "culturally specific set of beliefs about proper land use and, more generally, what constituted civilization" were considered "legitimate" settlements. B. White, "Power of Whiteness," 180.

15. Pritchett, *Red River Valley*, 83–85, 99–100, 140.

16. R. Gilman, C. Gilman, and D. Stultz, *Red River Trails*, 35; Folwell, *History of Minnesota*, 1:352.

17. R. Gilman, C. Gilman, and D. Stultz, *Red River Trails*, 3; Glueck Jr., *Minnesota and the Manifest Destiny*, 28, 44.

18. R. Gilman, *Henry Hastings Sibley*, 51–52; N. Goodman and R. Goodman, *Joseph R. Brown*, 143n42.

19. A. Larson, *History of the White Pine Industry*, 11–13; N. Goodman and R. Goodman, *Joseph R. Brown*, 139–42.

20. G. Anderson, *Kinsmen of Another Kind*, 144–53; N. Goodman and R. Goodman, *Joseph R. Brown*, 139–45.

21. G. Anderson, *Kinsmen of Another Kind*, 143–45; R. Meyer, *History of the Santee Sioux*, 55–56.

22. G. Anderson, *Kinsmen of Another Kind*, 151–52; Folwell, *History of Minnesota*, 1:159.

23. G. Anderson, *Kinsmen of Another Kind*, 147, 151.

24. R. Gilman, *Henry Hastings Sibley*, 66–67.

25. G. Anderson, *Kinsmen of Another Kind*, 148; N. Goodman and R. Goodman, *Joseph R. Brown*, 115.

26. N. Goodman and R. Goodman, *Joseph R. Brown*, 115. The western Dakotas also were demanding compensation for resources extracted from their land. See Riggs, *Mary and I*, 110, 120, 128.

27. G. Anderson, *Kinsmen of Another Kind*, 148–49; R. Gilman, *Henry Hastings Sibley*, 66; Prucha, *American Indian Treaties*, 220.

28. M. Meyer, *White Earth Tragedy*, 37; Minnesota Historical Society, *Land of the Ojibwe*, 28; Kappler, *Indian Affairs*, 2:491–93.

29. Neill, "Occurrences in and around Fort Snelling," 131–32; Taliaferro, "Auto-biography," 214–16; N. Goodman and R. Goodman, *Joseph R. Brown*, 143–44.

30. Kappler, *Indian Affairs*, 2:491–93. The Ojibwes, alone among the northern tribes, never faced removal to the West. The treaty of 1837 set a precedent by which they managed to preserve rights, and later reservations, in their old territory. See Prucha, *American Indian Treaties*, 196.

31. One Wahpeton chief, Iron Walker, was also a member of the party, but he was not a signator on the treaty.

32. Taliaferro, quoted in N. Goodman and R. Goodman, *Joseph R. Brown*, 143; R. Meyer, *History of the Santee Sioux*, 56–57; G. Anderson, *Kinsmen of Another Kind*, 152–53; R. Gilman, *Henry Hastings Sibley*, 66. The mixed bloods who assisted Taliaferro were interpreters Scott Campbell, Augustin Rocque, and Peter Quinn and traders Duncan Campbell and Alexander Faribault.

33. G. Anderson, *Kinsmen of Another Kind*, 154. For an interpretation that suggests the Dakotas were brought to Washington under false pretenses, see R. Meyer, *History of the Santee Sioux*, 56.

34. G. Anderson, *Kinsmen of Another Kind*, 154–56; Kappler, *Indian Affairs*, 2:493–94.

35. R. Gilman, *Henry Hastings Sibley*,

66; G. Anderson, *Kinsmen of Another Kind*, 154–56.

36. N. Goodman and R. Goodman, *Joseph R. Brown*, 141; Neill, "Occurrences in and around Fort Snelling," 133–34; G. Anderson, *Kinsmen of Another Kind*, 156.

37. R. Meyer, *History of the Santee Sioux*, 58–59; R. Gilman, *Henry Hastings Sibley*, 67–68; G. Anderson, *Kinsmen of Another Kind*, 157–58; W. Peterson, *Steamboating on the Upper Mississippi*, 126–27; A. Larson, *History of the White Pine Industry*, 14–16.

38. G. Anderson, *Kinsmen of Another Kind*, 158.

39. Levi W. Stratton, quoted in W. Peterson, *Steamboating on the Upper Mississippi*, 127–28.

40. R. Gilman, *Henry Hastings Sibley*, 67–68; N. Goodman and R. Goodman, *Joseph R. Brown*, 145, 149–52.

41. Pluth, "Failed Watab Treaty of 1853," 4; Kappler, *Indian Affairs*, 2:345–48; Folwell, *History of Minnesota*, 1:308–9; Prucha, *American Indian Treaties*, 196. The Winnebago homeland comprised most of central and southwestern Wisconsin. The reserve laid out in the 1832 and 1837 treaties was a tract mainly located in northeastern Iowa but included a small triangle in southeastern Minnesota.

42. Kappler, *Indian Affairs*, 2:345–48, 498–500; Pluth, "Failed Watab Treaty of 1853," 4; Prucha, *American Indian Treaties*, 196.

43. Kappler, *Indian Affairs*, 2:345–48, 498–500; R. Gilman, *Henry Hastings Sibley*, 66–68, 73; Taliaferro, "Auto-biography," 231, 252.

44. Taliaferro, "Auto-biography," 228; R. Meyer, *History of the Santee Sioux*, 58–62.

45. Taliaferro, quoted in R. Meyer, *History of the Santee Sioux*, 61–62n30.

46. R. Gilman, "Last Days of the Upper Mississippi Fur Trade," 105.

47. Ibid.

48. B. White, "Power of Whiteness," 184–85; N. Goodman and R. Goodman, *Joseph R. Brown*, 194; R. Gilman, "Last Days of the Upper Mississippi Fur Trade," 113.

49. R. Gilman, *Henry Hastings Sibley*, 56–57; G. Anderson, *Kinsmen of Another Kind*, 140; Pond, *Dakota Life*, 15–17.

50. Lavender, *Fist in the Wilderness*, 418–19; R. Gilman, *Henry Hastings Sibley*, 84–85.

51. R. Gilman, *Henry Hastings Sibley*, 68–73 (italics in the quotation added by the author).

52. Ibid., 79–80; A. Smith, *James Duane Doty*, 256–58; N. Goodman and R. Goodman, *Joseph R. Brown*, 194–95; Hughes, "Treaty of Traverse des Sioux," 101–2.

53. Hughes, "Treaty of Traverse des Sioux," 102, 119–26.

54. Ibid., 102; N. Goodman and R. Goodman, *Joseph R. Brown*, 194–95, 211; R. Gilman, *Henry Hastings Sibley*, 81.

55. N. Goodman and R. Goodman, *Joseph R. Brown*, 201–2; R. Gilman, *Henry Hastings Sibley*, 81–82.

56. G. Anderson, *Kinsmen of Another Kind*, 163–64; R. Gilman, *Henry Hastings Sibley*, 81–82; A. Smith, *James Duane Doty*, 258–59.

57. R. Meyer, *History of the Santee Sioux*, 74; N. Goodman and R. Goodman, *Joseph R. Brown*, 201; A. Smith, *James Duane Doty*, 259.

58. A. Smith, *James Duane Doty*, 259–62; N. Goodman and R. Goodman, *Joseph R. Brown*, 211–13; R. Gilman, *Henry Hastings Sibley*, 82–84; R. Meyer, *History of the Santee Sioux*, 75.

59. James Goodhue, 1851 editorial, quoted in Owens, "Political History of Minnesota," p. 132 note.

60. For nuanced studies of Indian-white marriage in fur trade society, see Van Kirk, *Many Tender Ties;* Sleeper-Smith, *Indian Women and French Men;* and J. Brown, *Strangers in Blood.*

61. A. Woolworth, unpublished biographical notebooks, Minnesota Historical Society.

62. On the central role that intermarriage played in cultural mediation, see Murphy, "Public Mothers," 142–66.

63. Riggs, *Mary and I;* Taliaferro, "Auto-biography," 205.

64. Hewitt, "Beyond the Search for Sisterhood," 2; A. Smith, *James Duane Doty*, 53, 57, 63–64.

65. Prescott, *Recollections of Philander Prescott*, 248–50.

66. According to Brown's biographers, it is

fairly certain that he legalized his marriage to McCoy only to secure the "half-breed" benefits due to the two daughters he fathered in the relationship.

67. Philander Prescott was highly critical of Brown's penchant for divorce on "flimsy excuses." Brown indeed comes off poorly in comparison to Prescott's commitment to Spirit-in-the-Moon; however, the fact that Brown felt it necessary to divorce one wife before taking another is evidence that he considered the marriages to be binding unions. See Prescott, *Recollections of Philander Prescott*, 151. On Dakota marriage customs, see Pond, *Dakota Life*, 137–40.

68. N. Goodman and R. Goodman, *Joseph R. Brown*, 127–30; Wheelock, "Memoir of Joseph R. Brown," 212.

69. R. Gilman, *Henry Hastings Sibley*, 73.

70. Ibid., 61, 75–76, 86–87; Carroll, "'Who Was Jane Lamont?'" 192–93.

71. Riggs, *Mary and I*, 46; Carroll, "'Who Was Jane Lamont?'" 185–89.

72. Mary Taliaferro's cousins were Jane Lamont, daughter of Hushes the Night and deceased trader Daniel Lamont; Nancy Eastman, daughter of Stands Sacred and Major Seth Eastman (later commandant of Fort Snelling); and Elizabeth Williams, whose parents' names are uncertain. See Carroll, "'Who Was Jane Lamont?'" 184, 195n2.

73. Sarah Sibley was enduringly hostile toward her husband's mixed-blood daughter, Helen. When Helen died an untimely death at age 21, her husband wrote to Helen's foster father, "I wonder how Mrs. S. [Sibley] feels—death *ought* to banish all harshness and ill will." Sylvester Sawyer to William Brown, quoted in Carroll, "'Who Was Jane Lamont?'" 193, 196n33; see also R. Gilman, *Henry Hastings Sibley*, 165.

74. Carroll, "'Who Was Jane Lamont?'" 188–89.

75. Taliaferro, "Auto-biography," 205, 249.

76. Taliaferro, "Auto-biography," 230 (italics in the original); Riggs, *Mary and I*, 46.

77. R. Gilman, *Henry Hastings Sibley*, 165; G. Anderson, *Kinsmen of Another Kind*, 144; Green, *A Peculiar Imbalance*, 20.

78. Pond, *Dakota Life*, 137–38; G. Anderson, *Kinsmen of Another Kind*, 244–46.

7. Drawing Boundaries

1. U.S. Census, Crawford County, Wisconsin Territory, July 7, 1840. Pembina was second only to St. Paul in population. In 1849 it was home to 637 inhabitants. Neill, *History of Minnesota*, 505.

2. N. Goodman and R. Goodman, *Joseph R. Brown*, 211–18; Neill, *History of Minnesota*, 450–51.

3. Lavender, *Fist in the Wilderness*, 418–19.

4. R. Gilman, "Northwestern Indian Territory," 21.

5. Kappler, *Indian Affairs*, 2:542–45; Cleland, "The 1842 Treaty of La Pointe," 36–41.

6. Cleland, "The 1842 Treaty of La Pointe," 39; Schenck, *William W. Warren*, 21–22; N. Goodman and R. Goodman, *Joseph R. Brown*, 251.

7. Schenck, *William W. Warren*, 13–16, 20; A. Larson, *History of the White Pine Industry*, 13–14.

8. Schenck, *William W. Warren*, 3–27, 155.

9. The Preemption Act of 1841 allowed squatters to claim up to 160 acres of as yet unsurveyed public lands for $1.25 per acre, provided they "improved" it in some way, such as by erecting a shanty or simply driving a spike into a tree. Before passage of the act, only surveyed public land could technically be claimed, under the provisions of the Northwest Ordinance of 1787. However, in practice, preemption and squatter's rights had been recognized for decades, since government surveyors were simply unable to stay ahead of the demand for western lands. See Meinig, *Shaping of America*, 2:240–45; and Wills, *Boosters, Hustlers, and Speculators*, 13–14.

10. Folwell, *History of Minnesota*, 1:217–19; Ferguson, "Eviction of Squatters from Fort Snelling," 24–26; N. Goodman and R. Goodman, *Joseph R. Brown*, 120–21; Williams, *History of the City of St. Paul*, 66–67.

11. Williams, *History of the City of St. Paul*, 58–61; Neill, "Occurrences in and around Fort Snelling," 136–37; N. Goodman and R. Goodman, *Joseph R. Brown*, 165. Sibley and Stambaugh were particularly dependent on their civilian customers since in 1836 the garrison had been drastically downsized, most of its troops sent off to fight Indian wars

[379]

in other regions. See R. Gilman, *Henry Hastings Sibley*, 51.

12. Williams, *History of the City of St. Paul*, 58–76; Fowell, *History of Minnesota*, 1:217–20.

13. Williams, *History of the City of St. Paul*, 68–70.

14. Folwell, *History of Minnesota*, 1:220–21; Ferguson, "Eviction of Squatters," 29; Williams, *History of the City of St. Paul*, 79–81, 93.

15. Williams, *History of the City of St. Paul*, 77–78, 80, 93. On Steele's claim of the falls, see Folwell, *History of Minnesota*, 1:222, 452–54. Folwell provides several versions of what has become a popular Minnesota legend. See also Kane, *Falls of St. Anthony*, 14. A group of Fort Snelling officers also had combined to take out claims on the St. Croix for a future town site and hired Philander Prescott to live on the claim to hold it for them. The claim eventually became the town of Prescott, Wisconsin. See Prescott, *Recollections of Philander Prescott*, 168.

16. N. Goodman and R. Goodman, *Joseph R. Brown*, 167.

17. Kane, *Falls of St. Anthony*, 11, 30–31; Williams, *History of the City of St. Paul*, 77–79, 95–96. Steele had control of the east bank of the falls and Stambaugh was lobbying, unsuccessfully as it turned out, to buy or lease the government mills on the west side of the river.

18. Williams, *History of the City of St. Paul*, 99–101.

19. Ibid., 64–66, 84–86; Newson, *Pen Pictures of St. Paul, Minnesota*, 6, 15–16. See also Wingerd, *Claiming the City*, 19–20.

20. Williams, *History of the City of St. Paul*, 82, 87, 101–4; Newson, *Pen Pictures of St. Paul, Minnesota*, 16–17, 21, 32; N. Goodman and R. Goodman, *Joseph R. Brown*, 229–30; Wingerd, *Claiming the City*, 20. On French-Indian communities, see J. Peterson, "Many Roads to Red River," 37–71; and J. Peterson, "Prelude to Red River," 41–67.

21. R. Gilman, *Henry Hastings Sibley*, 110–12.

22. Reardon, *Catholic Church in the Diocese of St. Paul*, 42–45; Williams, *History of the City of St. Paul*, 108–15; Newson,

Pen Pictures of St. Paul, Minnesota, 23–25; Wingerd, *Claiming the City*, 24–25.

23. Williams, *History of the City of St. Paul*, 99–139, 143; Newson, *Pen Pictures of St. Paul, Minnesota*, 27–49; R. Gilman, C. Gilman, and D. Stultz, *Red River Trails*, 11; Kane, *Falls of St. Anthony*, 15–16.

24. In the 1830s and 1840s population counts for both the Dakotas and Ojibwes showed a steady, modest growth despite outbreaks of smallpox, cholera, "bilious fever," and whooping cough that most likely came as "hidden cargo" on the steamboats that now frequented Minnesota country. See R. Meyer, *History of the Santee Sioux*, 68–69; and McClurken, et al., *Fish in the Lakes*.

25. Riggs, *Mary and I*, 129, 132; R. Gilman, C. Gilman, and D. Stultz, *Red River Trails*, 8; Glueck Jr., *Minnesota and the Manifest Destiny*, 46–48; R. Gilman, *Henry Hastings Sibley*, 84–85, 92–93.

26. R. Gilman, *Henry Hastings Sibley*, 66–67, 92–93.

27. Glueck Jr., *Minnesota and the Manifest Destiny*, 49–51, 64–65; Pritchett, *Red River Valley*, 255–56.

28. Pritchett, *Red River Valley*, 255–56; Glueck Jr., *Minnesota and the Manifest Destiny*, 68–69.

29. R. Gilman, C. Gilman, and D. Stultz, *Red River Trails*, 12; Pritchett, *Red River Valley*, 255–56; Glueck Jr., *Minnesota and the Manifest Destiny*, 68–69.

30. R. Gilman, "Last Days of the Upper Mississippi Fur Trade," 105; Pritchett, *Red River Valley*, 256; R. Gilman, *Henry Hastings Sibley*, 101.

31. Pluth, "Failed Watab Treaty of 1853," 4–5; B. White, "Power of Whiteness," 185–86; Cleland, "Attempts to Move the Chippewa," 60–63.

32. For a detailed discussion of intertribal hostilities in these decades, see Treuer, "Ojibwe-Dakota Relations," 270–97.

33. Hole-in-the-Day, quoted in Ibid., 295.

34. C. Gilman, "Gens Libres," 175–77.

35. Glueck Jr., *Minnesota and the Manifest Destiny*, 63–64. I am grateful to Rhoda Gilman for clarification on Métis ancestry.

36. N. Goodman and R. Goodman, *Joseph R. Brown*, 232–35.

37. Ibid., 235–38.

38. Ibid., 237–38.

39. Pritchett, *Red River Valley*, 256–59; Glueck Jr., *Minnesota and the Manifest Destiny*, 63–65.

40. R. Gilman, C. Gilman, and D. Stultz, *Red River Trails*, 10–11; R. Gilman, *Henry Hastings Sibley*, 93–96.

41. Though payment for the timber was to be made in weapons and manufactured goods rather than currency, this contract was a benchmark in which Indians were selling resources rather than the results of their labor, a significant shift toward the emerging capitalist view of land and resources. Contract, 13 March 1837, microfilm, roll 1, Henry Sibley Papers, Minnesota Historical Society.

42. A. Larson, *History of the White Pine Industry*, 13; N. Goodman and R. Goodman, *Joseph R. Brown*, 115.

43. Riggs, *Mary and I*, 110, 121, 128.

44. G. Anderson, *Kinsmen of Another Kind*, 153–55.

45. Schenck, *William W. Warren*, 14, 22.

46. According to Little Crow biographer Gary Clayton Anderson, Good Thunder's deathbed advice and the mantle of succession were given to another son, rather than Taoyateduta, who was then living at Lac qui Parle. However, Henry Sibley, who was present at the time, identifies Taoyateduta (whom he would have recognized) as the son at his father's bedside. See R. Gilman, *Henry Hastings Sibley*, 97–98; and G. Anderson, *Little Crow*, 36–45. For contemporary biographical sketches of Dakotas who followed an assimilationist path, see Sibley, "Sketch of John Other Day" and "Narrative of Paul Mazakootemane," 82–90, 99–102.

47. G. Anderson, *Little Crow*, 46–52.

48. Ibid., 43, 52.

49. Mancall, "Men, Women, and Alcohol," 428, 434; Buffalohead, "Farmers, Warriors, Traders," 236–44; Kidwell, "Indian Women as Cultural Mediators," 97–101.

50. The legal status of preterritorial Minnesota was indeed complex. The entire Northwest Territory, which included Minnesota east of the Mississippi River, was organized as a single jurisdiction until Ohio became a state in 1803. At that time the Minnesota lands became part of Indiana Territory until the territory was divided in 1809, which made Minnesota part of the new Illinois Territory. In preparation for Illinois's statehood, Congress created Michigan Territory in 1818 and in 1834 added all previously unorganized parts of the Louisiana Purchase to Michigan—the present states of Iowa, western Minnesota, and the Dakotas. For four brief years, all of Minnesota was theoretically included in a single territorial jurisdiction. Then, when Michigan applied for statehood in 1836, Congress created Wisconsin Territory; two years later, with settlers moving into the Iowa region, Congress divided Wisconsin Territory, creating Iowa Territory out of its western half, which included Minnesota west of the Mississippi. When Iowa applied for statehood in 1846, the lands west of the Mississippi reverted to unorganized Indian territory until Minnesota Territory was established in 1849.

51. Folwell, *History of Minnesota*, 1:233; R. Gilman, "Territorial Imperative," 157.

52. Foner, *Free Soil, Free Labor, Free Men*. See also Freehling, *Road to Disunion*.

53. U.S. Constitution, Article I, Section 2; Foner, *Free Soil, Free Labor, Free Men*, 87–89. See also Freehling, *Road to Disunion*. For statistics, see Roark et al., *American Promise*, 249–50.

54. The Mason-Dixon line was drawn by British surveyors Charles Mason and Jeremiah Dixon in 1763, before the United States was founded. Its original purpose was to legally determine the boundary between the colonies of Maryland and Pennsylvania, but it became the de facto imaginary line that separated free and slave states. For a concise history of the Missouri Compromise, see *American Promise*, 249–52.

55. Meinig, *Shaping of America*, 2:432.

56. Meinig, *Shaping of America*, 2:436–38; N. Goodman and R. Goodman, *Joseph R. Brown*, 249–54; R. Gilman, "Territorial Imperative," 157.

57. Newson, *Pen Pictures of St. Paul, Minnesota*, 55–56; N. Goodman and R. Goodman, *Joseph R. Brown*, 249–54.

58. Folwell, *History of Minnesota*, 1:234–36.

59. Ibid., 236.

60. R. Gilman, *Henry Hastings Sibley*, 103; R. Gilman, "Territorial Imperative," 157–58; N. Goodman and R. Goodman, *Joseph R. Brown*, 250–52.

61. N. Goodman and R. Goodman, *Joseph R. Brown*, 273–74; Folwell, *History of Minnesota*, 1:241.

62. R. Gilman, *Henry Hastings Sibley*, 101–4.

63. Owens, "Political History of Minnesota," 100.

64. R. Gilman, *Henry Hastings Sibley*, 104–5; Folwell, *History of Minnesota*, 1:236–38; N. Goodman and R. Goodman, *Joseph R. Brown*, 274–78; Williams, *History of the City of St. Paul*, 182–83.

65. R. Gilman, *Henry Hastings Sibley*, 104.

66. Ibid., 105; N. Goodman and R. Goodman, *Joseph R. Brown*, 275–78.

67. N. Goodman and R. Goodman, *Joseph R. Brown*, 280–83; B. White, "Power of Whiteness," 281–84; R. Gilman, *Henry Hastings Sibley*, 106; R. Gilman, "Territorial Imperative," 158.

68. Folwell, *History of Minnesota*, 1:242–47; R. Gilman, *Henry Hastings Sibley*, 106–8; R. Gilman, "Territorial Imperative," 157–58; B. White, "White Population Growth in the Minnesota Region," in *Fish in the Lakes*, 153–54. On sectionalism in the 1840s, see Foner, *Free Soil, Free Labor, Free Men*.

69. David Lambert, quoted in Williams, *History of the City of St. Paul*, 206.

70. Williams, *History of the City of St. Paul*, 205; Folwell, *History of Minnesota*, 1:248.

71. The key territorial appointees were Alexander Ramsey of Pennsylvania, governor; Charles. K. Smith of Ohio, secretary; Aaron Goodrich of Tennessee, chief justice; and David Cooper of Pennsylvania and Bradley B. Meeker of Kentucky, associate justices. Minnesota appointees were Joshua L. Taylor (with a claim at present-day Taylors Falls), marshal, and Henry L. Moss of Stillwater, U.S. attorney. Neill, *History of Minnesota*, 502–3; Owens, "Political History of Minnesota," 70. See also Folwell, *History of Minnesota*, vol. 1.

72. Newson, *Pen Pictures of St. Paul, Minnesota*, 105.

73. Williams, *History of the City of St.

Paul*, 207, 224, 228; Folwell, *History of Minnesota*, 1:250–51; Owens, "Political History of Minnesota," 44.

74. Folwell, *History of Minnesota*, 2:248–49; R. Gilman, *Henry Hastings Sibley*, 109.

75. B. White, "Power of Whiteness," 185–86.

76. Ibid., 185; B. White, "Pressure for Removal," 160–71.

77. R. Gilman, *Henry Hastings Sibley*, 112–13. On Sibley's financial woes, see 119.

78. Folwell, *History of Minnesota*, 1:254–55, 266–67; Owens, "Political History of Minnesota," 85.

8. Civilized Pursuits

1. Folwell, *History of Minnesota*, 1:278.

2. Bishop, *Floral Home*, 281–87.

3. Folwell, *History of Minnesota*, 1:273–74.

4. G. Anderson, *Kinsmen of Another Kind*, 179; R. Gilman, *Henry Hastings Sibley*, 117–18; G. Anderson, *Little Crow*, 53–54.

5. Folwell, *History of Minnesota*, 1:272–73; G. Anderson, *Little Crow*, 53–54.

6. G. Anderson, *Kinsmen of Another Kind*, 179–80; G. Anderson, *Little Crow*, 54; R. Meyer, *History of the Santee Sioux*, 76.

7. G. Anderson, *Little Crow*, 54–55; G. Anderson, *Kinsmen of Another Kind*, 183–84.

8. G. Anderson, *Kinsmen of Another Kind*, 183–84; R. Gilman, *Henry Hastings Sibley*, 120.

9. R. Gilman, *Henry Hastings Sibley*, 119; G. Anderson, *Little Crow*, 55.

10. Martin McLeod, quoted in R. Gilman, *Henry Hastings Sibley*, 118; G. Anderson, *Kinsmen of Another Kind*, 182; James Goodhue, dispatches from Traverse des Sioux, in Le Duc, *Minnesota Yearbook for 1852*, 47.

11. R. Gilman, *Henry Hastings Sibley*, 121–22; G. Anderson, *Little Crow*, 57, 59.

12. R. Gilman, *Henry Hastings Sibley*, 122; Folwell, *History of Minnesota*, 1:278n28.

13. Goodhue, dispatches, in Le Duc, *Minnesota Yearbook for 1852*, 25, 24, 29.

14. R. Gilman, *Henry Hastings Sibley*, 122–23; Mayer, *With Pen and Pencil*, 150–63;

Goodhue, dispatches, in Le Duc, *Minnesota Yearbook for 1852*, 40.

15. Goodhue, dispatches, in Le Duc, *Minnesota Yearbook for 1852*, 24–47.

16. Ibid., 46.

17. Ibid.

18. Ibid., 33, 63.

19. Ibid., 52–55; R. Gilman, *Henry Hastings Sibley*, 124.

20. R. Gilman, *Henry Hastings Sibley*, 124; Folwell, *History of Minnesota*, 1:279–80.

21. Goodhue, dispatches, in Le Duc, *Minnesota Yearbook for 1852*, 56–59.

22. Ibid., 65–67; Hughes, "Treaty of Traverse des Sioux," 109–11. Treaty reproduced in Kappler, *Indian Affairs*, 2:588–90.

23. After adjustments were agreed upon by the traders, Sibley collected $66,459 on his claims. For detailed accounts of the traders' paper signing, see *Commission to Investigate the Official Conduct of Alexander Ramsey*, 61. See exhibits A–C for trader paper and claims. See also G. Anderson, *Kinsmen of Another Kind*, 187; and R. Gilman, *Henry Hastings Sibley*, 126–27.

24. Goodhue, dispatches, in Le Duc, *Minnesota Yearbook for 1852*, 69–70; R. Gilman, *Henry Hastings Sibley*, 127.

25. Goodhue, dispatches, in Le Duc, *Minnesota Yearbook for 1852*, 76–78; G. Anderson, *Little Crow*, 61–62.

26. Diedrich, *Little Crow and the Dakota War*, 75; *Minnesota Pioneer*, 14 August 1851.

27. G. Anderson, *Kinsmen of Another Kind*, 188–89; G. Anderson, *Little Crow*, 62–63.

28. Goodhue, dispatches, in Le Duc, *Minnesota Yearbook for 1852*, 81.

29. Kappler, *Indian Affairs*, 2:589, 591; Goodhue, dispatches, in Le Duc, *Minnesota Yearbook for 1852*, 76; G. Anderson, *Kinsmen of Another Kind*, 190. In testimony regarding conduct of the treaties, nearly everyone deposed testified that the Indians were not capable of handling their money nor were they likely to pay their legitimate debts. See *Commission to Investigate the Official Conduct of Alexander Ramsey*, 61.

30. R. Gilman, *Henry Hastings Sibley*, 128–29. For a detailed account of Ramsey's council with the Ojibwes, see Babcock, "With Ramsey to Pembina," 1–10.

31. Folwell, *History of Minnesota*, 1:290–91. Regarding bribery, Hugh Tyler, a political crony of Ramsey, was hired as a lobbyist to work for the treaties. The bill he submitted for his expenses far exceeded what would be a reasonable expectation, yet it was paid by Ramsey without a murmur. Rhoda Gilman judiciously notes that "no record was kept of Tyler's activities, but his expenses were considerable." R. Gilman, *Henry Hastings Sibley*, 131. Hercules Dousman also declared that significant bribes had been paid to senators in Washington. G. Anderson, *Kinsmen of Another Kind*, 197. See also *Commission to Investigate the Official Conduct of Alexander Ramsey*, 287–88.

32. Folwell, *History of Minnesota*, 1:290–92; R. Gilman, *Henry Hastings Sibley*, 131.

33. G. Anderson, *Kinsmen of Another Kind*, 190–91; Folwell, *History of Minnesota*, 1:289–90.

34. G. Anderson, *Kinsmen of Another Kind*, 190–91; R. Gilman, *Henry Hastings Sibley*, 129–30; Folwell, *History of Minnesota*, 1:288–90.

35. R. Gilman, *Henry Hastings Sibley*, 109–12.

36. Ibid., 110–13; G. Anderson, *Kinsmen of Another Kind*, 191; Folwell, *History of Minnesota*, 1:274. Contemporary histories of St. Paul, published in the 1870s and 1880s, offer only brief biographies of Sibley but wax eloquent for pages on the virtues of Henry Rice. See Newson, *Pen Pictures of St. Paul, Minnesota;* and Williams, *History of the City of St. Paul.*

37. Folwell, *History of Minnesota*, 1:291–92.

38. G. Anderson, *Kinsmen of Another Kind*, 192–93.

39. Ibid., 190; R. Gilman, *Henry Hastings Sibley*, 130–31; Diedrich, *Little Crow and the Dakota War*, 77; G. Anderson, *Little Crow*, 65–66.

40. G. Anderson, *Kinsmen of Another Kind*, 190–92.

41. Ibid., 190–94; G. Anderson, *Little Crow*, 66–67; Folwell, *History of Minnesota*, 1:293.

42. R. Gilman, *Henry Hastings Sibley,* 131–32; Folwell, *History of Minnesota,* 1:293–95.

43. The president gave permission for the Indians to occupy the reservation lands for five years only, a fact that was not conveyed to the Indians. G. Anderson, *Kinsmen of Another Kind,* 193–94. See also G. Anderson, *Little Crow,* 66–67.

44. It is not clear how much of the $10,000 Rice actually collected. Dousman subtracted at least $5,000 for a note that he held against Rice. Folwell, *History of Minnesota,* 1:294n60.

45. Goodhue, dispatches, in Le Duc, *Minnesota Yearbook for 1852,* 82–87; G. Anderson, *Little Crow,* 64; G. Anderson, *Kinsmen of Another Kind,* 194–96; R. Gilman, *Henry Hastings Sibley,* 128; *Commission to Investigate the Official Conduct of Alexander Ramsey,* see esp. 129–31 and Franklin Steele testimony, 259–65. Treaty reproduced in Kappler, *Indian Affairs,* 2:591–93.

46. *Commission to Investigate the Official Conduct of Alexander Ramsey,* 131.

47. *Commission to Investigate the Official Conduct of Alexander Ramsey,* see esp. testimony of David Olmsted and Franklin Steele, 139–40 and 255–58; and G. Anderson, *Kinsmen of Another Kind,* 196–98.

48. Riggs, *Mary and I,* 139–40; Carroll, "'This Higgledy-Piggledy Assembly,'" 227–28; R. Gilman, *Henry Hastings Sibley,* 134.

49. Folwell, *History of Minnesota,* 1:462–66. For accusations against Sweetser, see Hercules Dousman, quoted, p. 463n34. See also R. Gilman, *Henry Hastings Sibley,* 132–34.

50. *Commission to Investigate Official Conduct of Alexander Ramsey;* Folwell, *History of Minnesota,* 1:appendix 8, 462–70; R. Gilman, *Henry Hastings Sibley,* 133–34.

51. Witness testimony appears in *Commission to Investigate Official Conduct of Alexander Ramsey.* See, for example, Andrew Robertson, 125–26; Franklin Steele, 261–65; Alexander Faribault, 275; Hercules Dousman, 290–91.

52. Daniel Fisher letter, quoted in Hoffmann, *Church Founders of the Northwest,* 130.

53. Beecher was a prominent figure in the mid-nineteenth-century women's moral reform campaign. The movement drew on and enlarged a new ideal of female moral superiority that enabled women to expand their public role in the name of protecting home and family and move beyond their consignment to the private sphere. See Welter, "Cult of True Womanhood," 151–74; and Carroll Smith-Rosenberg, "Beauty, the Beast, and the Militant Woman," 562–84. On Beecher, see Sklar, *Catherine Beecher.*

54. Bishop, *Floral Home,* 52–54; Morton, "Harriet Bishop, Frontier Teacher," 132–33.

55. Bishop, *Floral Home,* 99, 112.

56. Ibid., 60, 71–72, 268–69.

57. Ibid., 69, 83, 94; Sommerdorf, "No Grass beneath Her Feet," 17–19; Sommerdorf, "Harriet E. Bishop," 321–23.

58. "A Stranger Sketches St. Paul," *Minnesota Pioneer,* 6 February 1850; Williams, *History of the City of St. Paul,* 117, 126, 165; Cathcart, "Sheaf of Remembrances," 539–52.

59. Confrontations between the Indians in and around St. Paul, though not frequent, were clearly unsettling. Nearly every contemporary account of the period records these events as noteworthy recollections. See, for example, Newson, *Pen Pictures of St. Paul, Minnesota,* 395–96; Bishop, *Floral Home,* 275–80; Williams, *History of the City of St. Paul,* 336–38.

60. Cathcart, "Sheaf of Remembrances," 526.

61. M. Lee (aka J. Wood), "Life in the Woods," 16 February, 22 March, 5 April, and 12 April, 1860; and J. Wood, "Book on the Early Days." Sophia Russell and Eliza Sweet, the Anglo-Ojibwe daughters of trader Charles Oakes, were married to traders Jeremiah Russell and George Sweet and were Julia Wood's closest neighbors. www.ojibwe.info/Ojibwe/HTML/people.

62. Williams, *History of the City of St. Paul,* 331 (italics added by the author).

63. *Pittsburgh Token,* quoted in Ibid., 332.

64. Williams, *History of the City of St. Paul,* 342–43, 347, 365, 374–80; Wingerd, *Claiming the City,* 28–29.

65. Williams, *History of the City of St. Paul,* 349–50; Folwell, *History of Minnesota,* 1:362; *Population of the United States in 1860,* 257–60.

66. B. White, "Power of Whiteness," 186.

67. Kane, *Falls of St. Anthony*, 31–36; Folwell, *History of Minnesota*, 1:422–32; Wingerd, *Claiming the City*, 29–32.

68. Cleland, "Preliminary Report," 45–47, 54–59; Cathcart, "Sheaf of Remembrances," 529; Bishop, *Floral Home*, 274.

69. Cleland, "Preliminary Report," 85.

70. Ibid., 65, 47; B. White, "Regional Context of the Removal Order of 1850," 154.

71. B. White, "Regional Context," 160–86.

72. Schenck, *William W. Warren*, 82–97; B. White, "Regional Context," 192–93.

73. *Minnesota Chronicle and Register*, 17 December 1850.

74. Schenck, *William W. Warren*, 93.

75. Flat Mouth letter, reproduced in Schenck, *William W. Warren*, 96–97.

76. B. White, "Regional Context," 172–211; Schenck, *William W. Warren*, 82–97.

77. For the purposes of the treaty, the La Pointe, Ontonagon, L'Anse/Lac Vieux Desert, Grand Portage, Fond du Lac, Lac Court Oreilles, Lac du Flambeau, and Bois Forte bands were designated as the Lake Superior bands. See Cleland, "Preliminary Report," 84.

78. Cleland, "Preliminary Report," 82–83; Folwell, *History of Minnesota*, 1:306–7.

79. Cleland, "Preliminary Report, 82–83.

80. Much of the acrimony was between the Lake Superior and Mississippi bands, who originally were intended to participate in the treaty. The treaty was eventually negotiated only with the Lake Superior bands, who occupied the territory to be ceded. But even within those bands, internal dissent raged between supporters of the civil chiefs, who favored the treaty, and the warrior chiefs, who wanted to sign no further agreements with the U.S. government. Kugel, *To Be the Main Leaders*, 55–58; Cleland, "Preliminary Report," 84.

81. Kappler, *Indian Affairs*, 2:648–52; Cleland, "Preliminary Report," 85–86.

82. Cleland, "Preliminary Report," 85–86.

83. Kugel, *To Be the Main Leaders*, 59.

84. A. Larson, *History of the White Pine Industry*, 24–25; B. White, "Regional Context," 282–83.

85. B. White, "Regional Context," 282–87; Kugel, *To Be the Main Leaders*, 61. On cultural misunderstandings, see B. White, "Indian Visits," 99–111.

86. Cleland, "Preliminary Report," 87, 91.

87. Ibid., 87–88; B. White, "Regional Context," 280; Kugel, *To Be the Main Leaders*, 63.

88. Cleland, "Preliminary Report," 90–93; Kappler, *Indian Affairs*, 2:685–90.

89. The role of the Mille Lacs band in the treaty negotiations is unclear. Rice and Manypenny did not intend for them to be part of the delegation, but Governor Gorman insisted on their participation, most likely in hopes of resolving the ongoing disputes between the band and loggers. Plausibly, Gorman used his influence to secure a reservation for the Mille Lacs band, though no records were kept of the negotiations. See B. White, "Regional Context," 282–89; Cleland, "Preliminary Report," 88–90.

90. Cleland, "Preliminary Report," 82–88; Kugel, *To Be the Main Leaders*, 60–61.

91. Cleland, "Preliminary Report," 91; Kugel, *To Be the Main Leaders*, 69–70; Bishop, *Floral Home*, 274.

92. Kugel, *To Be the Main Leaders*, 63–65.

93. Folwell, *History of Minnesota*, 1:310, 320–21.

94. In 1854 the Menominee won for themselves a small reservation in their native Wisconsin and the Minnesota reserved lands were opened for settlement. Ibid., 310, 318, 320–21; Pluth, "Failed Watab Treaty of 1853," 6–8.

95. Pluth, "Failed Watab Treaty of 1853," 5–6; W. Peterson, *Steamboating on the Upper Mississippi*, 136–37; Folwell, *History of Minnesota*, 1:318–19.

96. Stevens, *Personal Recollections of Minnesota*, 226–27; Pluth, "Failed Watab Treaty of 1853," 6–17.

97. Pluth, "Failed Watab Treaty of 1853," 11, 16–18; Lurie, "Winnebago," 699.

98. Folwell, *History of Minnesota*, 1:319–20.

99. Lurie, "Winnebago," 699–70; Folwell, *History of Minnesota*, 1:319–20; Pluth, "Failed Watab Treaty of 1853," 19.

9. Playing for Power

1. Owens, "Political History of Minnesota," 29.

2. Ibid., 120; Harpole and Nagle,

Minnesota Territorial Census, 1850; Neill, *History of Minnesota,* 504–5; Proclamation of Council Districts, 1849, reproduced in Owens, "Political History of Minnesota," 76–79.

3. For an illuminating analysis of the ideal of "white man's country" that shaped midwestern politics, see Schwalm, "'Overrun with Free Negroes,'" 145–74.

4. *Debates and Proceedings of the Constitutional Convention for the Territory of Minnesota,* 221–29. In fact, the delegates from Pembina County probably were ineligible to participate in the constitutional convention. As the state's boundary was drawn in the enabling act, the town of Pembina (where most of the district's population resided) was on the west bank of the Red River and thus outside the boundary of the future state. Nonetheless, the Democrats, who needed these delegates to achieve a majority in the convention, certified them as bona fide delegates, to the frustration of the Republicans. See Owens, "Political History of Minnesota," 373–75.

5. Folwell, *History of Minnesota,* 1:371; Owens, "Political History of Minnesota," 128–30.

6. Owens, "Political History of Minnesota," 82; R. Gilman, *Henry Hastings Sibley,* 109. Ramsey proved an extraordinarily flexible politician. Though most often he worked with Sibley when his interests warranted it, he had no qualms about partnering with Rice, to Sibley's discomfiture. The admiring Owens described the governor as "keeping his eye on the main chances to advance the material interests of the Territory, knowing that by so doing, aside from its being a matter of duty, further political honors would come soon enough. In so far as Mr. Sibley and his friends worked in this direction, he worked with them." Owens, "Political History of Minnesota," 112.

7. Sewell, *A House Divided,* 28–30.

8. Loren Collins reminiscences in Morris, *Old Rail Fence Corners,* 283; Owens, "Political History of Minnesota," 60–62.

9. Folwell, *History of Minnesota,* 1:375.

10. Owens, "Political History of Minnesota," 104; James Goodhue, *Minnesota*

Pioneer, quoted in Owens, "Political History of Minnesota," 105.

11. Owens, "Political History of Minnesota," 90–91, 108–9.

12. Hage, *Newspapers on the Minnesota Frontier,* 26–35; Owens, "Political History of Minnesota," 69.

13. Hage, *Newspapers on the Minnesota Frontier,* 29–31; Owens, "Political History of Minnesota," 100, 114.

14. Owens, "Political History of Minnesota," 87; Williams, *History of the City of St. Paul,* 285–86; Newson, *Pen Pictures of St. Paul, Minnesota,* 100–102; Hage, *Newspapers on the Minnesota Frontier,* 36. Neither man's wound was immediately fatal, but in a matter of months both men were dead, due to complications from their injuries.

15. R. Gilman, *Henry Hastings Sibley,* 142; Hage, *Newspapers on the Minnesota Frontier,* 39–40, 45. Unfortunately for Sibley, in 1854 his new handpicked editor, Earle Goodrich, shifted the paper's allegiance to Henry Rice. Apparently Rice offered to back the paper more handsomely than Sibley's resources allowed.

16. The Kansas-Nebraska Act overturned the Missouri Compromise of 1820, which had outlawed the expansion of slavery north of the latitude 36°30'. It introduced the doctrine of "Popular Sovereignty," giving the people of the new territories of Kansas and Nebraska the right to determine for themselves if they wished to allow slavery. By the 1850s, the press of western expansion demanded the creation of new territories, but such additions would upset the balance between free and slave states in the Union. Supporters of the act, led by Stephen Douglas, who introduced the bill, expected that Kansas would vote for slavery and Nebraska would not, thereby maintaining the desired balance.

17. Schenck, "The Cadottes," in J. Brown et al., *Fur Trade Revisited,* 189–97.

18. "Black Men in the Fur Trade," *Gopher Historian,* 2–4; Porter, "Negroes and the Fur Trade," 424–25; Porter, "Contacts in Other Parts," 360–63; Green, *Peculiar Imbalance,* 3–4; Flandrau, "Reminiscences of Minnesota," 199.

19. Paymaster's records reveal that between

1832 and 1834, nearly all the officers at the fort had a slave as a servant. Bachman, "Black Dakota," 15. I am grateful to Mr. Bachman for permission to cite from his soon-to-be-published manuscript. See also Green, *Peculiar Imbalance*, 7–10; and Folwell, *History of Minnesota*, 1:143n33.

20. Green, *Peculiar Imbalance*, 9–13. Taliaferro freed all his slaves after resigning his post and retiring to Pennsylvania, asserting in his autobiography that this had been his intention for years. In 1826 he refused to sell his slave, Eliza, to post commandant Joseph Plympton, informing him that he intended to "give her freedom after a limited time." But while in Minnesota country, Taliaferro held onto his slaves, who probably did much to assuage the loneliness and discomfort of his bride, Eliza Dillon, who arrived at the fort in 1828.

21. Taliaferro, "Auto-biography," 235; Bachman, "Joseph Godfrey: Black Dakota," 379; Lehman, "Sylvanus Lowry and Slavery in St. Cloud." On physical punishment, see Bachman, "Black Dakota," 32. For biographical information on Lowry, see Conzen, "Pi-ing the Type," 100–101.

22. My analysis of Dred Scott is greatly indebted to Lea VanderVelde and Sandhya Subramanian, "Mrs. Dred Scott," 1040–1122; see also Green, *Peculiar Imbalance*, 10–11. On the difficulty presented by the Missouri courts, see Vishneski III, "What the Court Decided in Dred Scott v. Sandford," 374–75.

23. VanderVelde and Subramanian, "Mrs. Dred Scott," 1041, 1069–71. It is not clear if Taliaferro sold or gave Harriet to Dr. Emerson upon her marriage to Scott. VanderVelde and Subramanian assert that Taliaferro meant Harriet to be free, but sources, including Taliaferro's autobiography, are vague regarding his intentions. See Taliaferro, "Auto-biography," 235.

24. VanderVelde and Subramanian, "Mrs. Dred Scott," 1069.

25. Ibid., 1071–72.

26. Bachman, "Black Dakota," 8; Prescott, *Recollections of Philander Prescott*, 152. Bachman's research has revealed that at the time of escape Godfrey was serving in the household of Oliver Faribault, Bailly's

brother-in-law. It appears that the two families passed the young slave back and forth between them and also leased his services for some period of time to Henry Sibley. See Bachman, "Black Dakota," 32–37.

27. Many Indian tribes, including the Sioux and Ojibwes, enslaved enemy captives, but it was defeat in battle, not a supposed ethnic or tribal inferiority, that made men and women into slaves. Nor was the condition of slavery generally permanent. Many captives eventually were adopted and married into their captors' tribe—something that would have been unthinkable as slavery was practiced by whites in the American South.

28. Green, *Peculiar Imbalance*, 18–20; Bachman, "Black Dakota," 16–17; Forbes, "Methodist Mission among the Dakotas," 51.

29. Alfred Brunson, quoted in Green, *Peculiar Imbalance*, 19; Riggs, "Protestant Missions in the Northwest," 136; Forbes, "Methodist Mission among the Dakotas," 51–52.

30. Hobart, *History of Methodism in Minnesota*, 22–23; Green, *Peculiar Imbalance*, 19; Forbes, "Methodist Mission among the Dakotas," 51–56; Return Holcombe, quoted in Green, *Peculiar Imbalance*, 22; Riggs, "Protestant Missions in the Northwest," 137; Shutter, *History of Minneapolis*, 1:79.

31. Green, *Peculiar Imbalance*, 26–34; Newson, *Pen Pictures of St. Paul, Minnesota*, 12.

32. Bachman, "Black Dakota," 19–20; D. Taylor, "The Blacks," 73.

33. *Pioneer*, 30 September 1852, quoted in Green, *Peculiar Imbalance*, 51.

34. Green, "Minnesota's Long Road to Black Suffrage," 69–70; Voegeli, "The Northwest and the Race Issue," 237–38; Green, *Peculiar Imbalance*, 41–42, 51–52. The passage of an amendment proposed by St. Paul storekeeper Henry Jackson provides evidence that black disfranchisement was clearly intentional. Jackson clarified the enfranchisement of mixed-blood people as follows: "That nothing in the foregoing act shall be construed as to prevent the voting of all half-breeds, unless they are mixed with African blood." For fears about black migration to the Midwest, see Schwalm, "'Overrun with Free Negroes.'"

35. Lehman, "Sylvanus Lowry"; Cathcart, "Sheaf of Remembrances," 516–17; Foner, *Free Soil*, 58–61; Seeba, "Minnesota, Slavery, and the Coming of the Civil War," 8–9.

36. Foner, *Free Soil,* 59–65; Schwalm, "'Overrun with Free Negroes,'" 151; Dykstra, *Bright Radical Star,* 68–69. By 1840, approximately 93 percent of the free black population in the North lived in states that "completely or practically denied them the right to vote." Green, "Minnesota's Long Road," 71.

37. Green, *Peculiar Imbalance,* 68.

38. Stonehouse, *John Wesley North,* 3–36 (quote appears on p. 36).

39. Ibid., 36–39.

40. Ibid., 27, 52. On the reform spirit in St. Anthony, see Marti, "Puritan Tradition," 1–11.

41. Stonehouse, *John Wesley North,* 39, 47–48, 55; D. Taylor, "The Blacks," 73.

42. Bishop, *Floral Home,* 105–11; Wingerd, *Claiming the City,* 26; Stonehouse, *John Wesley North,* 65–66; Folwell, *History of Minnesota,* 1:264–65.

43. The Liberty Party was founded by northeastern abolitionists. Barnburner Democrats were an antislavery faction of the Democratic Party, so named because they appeared willing to "burn down the barn to get rid of the rats." The Barnburners, though nominally antislavery, also espoused racist principles. Their primary interest was in opposing the extension of slavery—and black migration—beyond the South. See Foner, *Free Soil,* 59–62.

44. Stonehouse, *John Wesley North,* 80–82.

45. "Genesis of the Republican Party in Minnesota," 24–30; Owens, "Political History of Minnesota," 232–39; Stonehouse, *John Wesley North,* 80–83; Return Holcombe, quoted in Stonehouse, *John Wesley North,* 81.

46. Owens, "Political History of Minnesota," 237–39, 243.

47. Stonehouse, *John Wesley North,* 81; Neill, *History of Minnesota,* 597–606.

48. Stonehouse, *John Wesley North,* 66–67.

49. R. Gilman, *Henry Hastings Sibley,* 147–48; Owens, "Political History of Minnesota," 247.

50. The 1860 census counted 18,400 German-born Minnesotans. See Johnson, "The Germans," 158–59.

51. Owens, "Political History of Minnesota," 248–50. The following year, Olmsted moved to the southern Minnesota river town of Winona, declared himself a Republican, and established the *Winona Republican,* which became an influential Republican newspaper.

52. Grey, "Black Community in Territorial St. Anthony," 48–50.

53. Klement, "Abolition Movement in Minnesota," 16; Green, *Peculiar Imbalance,* 64–65; Bachman, "Black Dakota," 49; Swanson, "Joseph Farr Remembers the Underground Railroad," 124–28.

54. R. Gilman, *Henry Hastings Sibley,* 147–48; Folwell, *History of Minnesota,* 378; Wills, *Boosters, Hustlers, and Speculators,* 60–90. See also Stonehouse, *John Wesley North.*

55. Larsen, *Crusader and Feminist,* 42–43; *Minnesota Republican,* 19 October 1854.

56. Folwell, *History of Minnesota,* 1:394; Green, *Peculiar Imbalance,* 67–68. For a nuanced analysis of Irish anti-black sentiment, see Roediger, *Wages of Whiteness,* esp. 133–63.

57. Green, *Peculiar Imbalance,* 69–70; Green, "Race and Segregation," 83–87. St. Paul's school segregation policy ended in 1869 when the state passed a bill that outlawed segregation in Minnesota schools. See Green, "Race and Segregation," 147–49.

58. *Minnesota Democrat,* 12 February 1855. On nativism and anti-Catholicism in the National Republican party, see Oestreicher, "Urban Working-Class Political Behavior," 1261–63. On Minnesota, see Green, "Minnesota's Long Road," 72–73; Green, *Peculiar Imbalance,* 133–34; and Wingerd, *Claiming the City,* 47–48.

59. *U.S. Census, 1860 population.* In a total Minnesota population of 172,000, the 1860 census counted 11,620 Scandinavians (Swedes, Norwegians, and Danes); 26,291 individuals of German or German-mixed birth; and 21,153 Irish-born or of Irish-mixed birth. The Irish total, in particular, underrepresents the number of Irish ethnics in Minnesota, since many second-generation Irish

migrated to the state and are not included in this count.

60. Folwell, *History of Minnesota,* 1:388–93.

61. A. Larson, *History of the White Pine Industry,* 25, 36–37; Wills, *Boosters, Hustlers, and Speculators,* 75–76; Williams, *History of the City of St. Paul,* 370, 379.

62. Sommerdorf, "No Grass beneath Her Feet," 20; Folwell, *History of Minnesota,* 1:379; Williams, *History of the City of St. Paul,* 379–80.

63. A. Larson, *History of the White Pine Industry,* 37; Williams, *History of the City of St. Paul,* 372–78; Wills, *Boosters, Hustlers, and Speculators,* 375–86.

64. Wills, *Boosters, Hustlers, and Speculators,* 86–89; Hofsommer, *Minneapolis and the Age of Railways,* 3–5; Folwell, *History of Minnesota,* 1:362; *St. Anthony Express,* 18 February 1854, quoted in Hofsommer, 3.

65. Wills, *Boosters, Hustlers, and Speculators,* 86–90; Folwell, *History of Minnesota,* 1:378–79. For a full explication of Minnesota's first railroad scandal, see Folwell, *History of Minnesota,* 1:327–50.

66. Folwell, *History of Minnesota,* 1:388–89; Green, "Minnesota's Long Road," 72; Green, *Peculiar Imbalance,* 83–84.

67. R. Gilman, *Henry Hastings Sibley,* 150–52; Folwell, *History of Minnesota,* 1:388–95; Owens, "Political History of Minnesota," 338–39, 351.

68. Folwell, *History of Minnesota,* 1:396; Green, "Minnesota's Long Road," 72; Green, *Peculiar Imbalance,* 83–84; Owens, "Political History of Minnesota," 362; Hall, *H. P. Hall's Observations,* 19.

69. Owens, "Political History of Minnesota," 371–72, 416–17.

70. R. Gilman, *Henry Hastings Sibley,* 151–52.

71. Owens, "Political History of Minnesota," 363–80; Folwell, *History of Minnesota,* 1:397–404.

72. Folwell, *History of Minnesota,* 1:382–87, 398–401; Owens, "Political History of Minnesota," 87, 328–36, 359–63, 373–75; Green, *Peculiar Imbalance,* 86–87.

73. *Debates and Proceedings of the Constitutional Convention for the Territory of*

Minnesota, 221–29; Owens, "Political History of Minnesota," 421–28, 273–74.

74. Owens, "Political History of Minnesota," 420–28; Folwell, *History of Minnesota,* 1:403–9. Southern Minnesota Republicans had tried earlier, during the legislative session, to float a similar "east-west line" proposal. While that failed, they hoped to push the scheme through at the convention, where only Republicans were in attendance. See Owens, "Political History of Minnesota," 268–75.

75. Owens, "Political History of Minnesota," 446–47; Folwell, *History of Minnesota,* 1:412. Notably, it was Joe Brown, veteran of multicultural Minnesota's early days and father to a family of mixed-blood children, who wrote the provision on mixed-blood and Indian suffrage. As the law was enforced, only a handful of Indians were able to meet the citizenship conditions set forth. On the near impossibility of the requirements demanded of Indians for the right to vote, see Green, *Peculiar Imbalance,* 109–13.

76. Green, *Peculiar Imbalance,* 87–89.

77. Folwell, *History of Minnesota,* 1:416–20; Owens, "Political History of Minnesota," 444–49.

78. *Debates and Proceedings of the Constitutional Convention for the Territory of Minnesota;* Green, *Peculiar Imbalance,* 88–89; Folwell, *History of Minnesota,* 1:417–21.

79. Williams, *History of the City of St. Paul,* 380–81; Wills, *Boosters, Hustlers, and Speculators,* 901. For a detailed analysis of the effects of the crash on St. Paul and Minneapolis, see Wingerd, *Claiming the City,* 29–32.

80. Barry, *Jacob's Prairie,* 16–17; Wingerd, "Americanization of Cold Spring," 24–25.

81. *Minnesotian,* 3 March 1857; Folwell, *History of Minnesota,* 2:37–49; Wills, *Boosters, Hustlers, and Speculators,* 90–91.

82. Folwell, *History of Minnesota,* 2:52–53; Williams, *History of the City of St. Paul,* 380–81; Wills, *Boosters, Hustlers, and Speculators,* 94–96; Rice quoted in Wills, *Boosters, Hustlers, and Speculators,* 96.

83. Folwell, *History of Minnesota,* 2:41; Owens, "Political History of Minnesota," 204.

84. Coggswell quoted in Green, *Peculiar*

Imbalance, 94; Owens, "Political History of Minnesota," 562–66.

85. N. Woolworth, *White Bear Lake Story,* 31–32; Green, "Eliza Winston," 108–11.

86. Folwell, *History of Minnesota,* 2:68–70; Green, "Eliza Winston," 114, 107–8, 111–13; *St. Anthony Falls Evening News,* 28 August 1860; *St. Paul Pioneer and Democrat,* 23 August 1860 (both papers quoted in Green, "Eliza Winston").

87. Green, "Eliza Winston," 120.

10. The Roads to War

1. Folwell, *History of Minnesota,* 2:76–77.

2. Governor's Address to the Minnesota Legislature, 9 January 1861; reproduced in Owens, "Political History of Minnesota," 576–82.

3. P. Larson, "New Look at the Elusive Inkpaduta," 25–27; Hughes, "Causes and Results of the Inkpaduta Massacre," 263–64; Flandrau, "Ink-Pa-Du-Ta Massacre of 1857," 387.

4. Beck, *Inkpaduta,* 41–44; Flandrau, "Ink-Pa-Du-Ta Massacre of 1857," 388; P. Larson, "New Look at the Elusive Inkpaduta," 27–28; Hughes, "Causes and Results of the Inkpaduta Massacre," 275.

5. Flandrau, "Ink-Pa-Du-Ta Massacre of 1857," 388; Hughes, "Causes and Results of the Inkpaduta Massacre," 265–66. On Lott's history of misdeeds, see Beck, *Inkpaduta,* 33–34.

6. Hughes, "Causes and Results of the Inkpaduta Massacre," 266–67; P. Larson, "New Look at the Elusive Inkpaduta," 28. Some sources attribute Lott's actions as vengeance for the death of his son and the loss of his wife, who died soon thereafter, "overcome by terror and grief." Others suggest that he acted out of pure avarice, which would have been consistent with his character. Conceivably, Lott also may have harbored a grudge against Sintomniduta for making him appear both a coward and a fool to the party that accompanied him back to his trading post. Most likely, all these motivations contributed to his actions.

7. Hughes, "Causes and Results of the Inkpaduta Massacre," 268–69. Sources disagree about the relationship between Sintomniduta and Inkpaduta. They are frequently cited as brothers; however, Beck makes a persuasive case that the men were kinsmen but not brothers, the confusion arising from the Dakota custom of calling all kinsmen "brother." See Beck, *Inkpaduta,* 31–32.

8. Beck, *Inkpaduta,* 49–50.

9. Ibid., 32, 43–45, 50–51; P. Larson, "New Look at the Elusive Inkpaduta," 27.

10. Beck, *Inkpaduta,* 62–64; Hughes, "Causes and Results of the Inkpaduta Massacre," 269; Folwell, *History of Minnesota,* 2:401n4; P. Larson, "New Look at the Elusive Inkpaduta," 29.

11. Hughes, "Causes and Results of the Inkpaduta Massacre," 268–71, 275–76.

12. P. Larson, "New Look at the Elusive Inkpaduta," 29; Hughes, "Causes and Results of the Inkpaduta Massacre," 275, 278–80.

13. Flandrau, "Ink-Pa-Du-Ta Massacre of 1857," 388, 401; Margaret Hern reminiscence in Morris, *Old Rail Fence Corners,* 149; *Report on Barracks and Hospitals,* 369–72.

14. *St. Paul Pioneer and Democrat,* 1858, quoted in Prucha, "The Settler and the Army," 42; Hughes, "Causes and Results of the Inkpaduta Massacre," 281; Flandrau, "Ink-Pa-Du-Ta Massacre of 1857."

15. Hughes, "Causes and Results of the Inkpaduta Massacre," 281; Flandrau, "Ink-Pa-Du-Ta Massacre of 1857," 398–400.

16. Flandrau, "Ink-Pa-Du-Ta Massacre of 1857," 398; Lee, *History of the Spirit Lake Massacre!,* 36.

17. Mazakootemane, "Narrative of Paul Mazakootemane," 83; G. Anderson, *Little Crow,* 83; Lee, *History of the Spirit Lake Massacre!,* 37–38.

18. Diedrich, *Little Crow and the Dakota War,* 109–11; Folwell, *History of Minnesota,* 2:412; G. Anderson, *Little Crow,* 84. Two Indian agencies were established on the Dakota reservation, which stretched 100 miles along the Minnesota River. The Lower Agency (also known as the Redwood Agency), located where the Redwood River entered the Minnesota, served the Mdewakanton and Wahpekute bands. The Upper Agency (Yellow Medicine), at the conjunction of the Yellow

Medicine and Minnesota rivers, served the Sisseton and Wahpeton bands.

19. G. Anderson, *Little Crow*, 83–87; Folwell, *History of Minnesota*, 2:411–13; Diedrich, *Little Crow*, 109–11.

20. *Henderson Democrat*, 16 July 1857, quoted in Diedrich, *Little Crow*, 113; R. Meyer, *History of the Santee Sioux*, 110; G. Anderson, *Little Crow*, 86–87.

21. P. Larson, "New Look at the Elusive Inkpaduta," 32; Prucha, "Settler and the Army," 46, 51; G. Anderson, *Kinsmen of Another Kind*, 220–21; Riggs, quoted in Diedrich, *Little Crow*, 112.

22. Flandrau, "Ink-Pa-Du-Ta Massacre of 1857," 392; G. Anderson, *Kinsmen of Another Kind*, 217–18.

23. Joseph R. Brown to H. B. Whipple, 20 January 1864, in Return I. Holcombe Papers, box 1.

24. These characterizations are drawn primarily from "old settlers'" recollections collected in Morris, *Old Rail Fence Corners*. See, for example, Mrs. Margaret Snyder, 131; Mrs. Newman Woods, 100; Mrs. Mahlon Black, 30; Mrs. James Pratt, 52; Mrs. C. H. Pettit, 103. Also see John Stevens, quoted in Trimble, *In the Shadow of the City*, 5.

25. Morris, *Old Rail Fence Corners*, see esp. Pratt, 52; Carrie Stratton, 183; Mary Massolt, 134; Lysander Foster, 38. On Edward Conant, see Trimble, *In the Shadow of the City*, 6.

26. "The Upper Mississippi," *Harper's New Monthly Magazine*, 436–38.

27. Starkey, "Reminiscences of Indian Depredations," 262–70; Folwell, *History of Minnesota*, 1:325–26.

28. Starkey, "Reminiscences of Indian Depredations," 267, 270–75.

29. Ibid., 274–77.

30. To suggest the extent of settlers' involvement in trapping, in 1856 St. Paul merchant Joseph Ullmann turned over between $300,000 and $400,000 in raw furs, most of it traded by farmers. Here and above, see R. Gilman, "Last Days of the Upper Mississippi Fur Trade," 130.

31. B. White, "Indian Visits: Stereotypes of Minnesota's Native People."

32. Ibid.; Beck, *Inkpaduta*, 41.

33. The category "German," as it was used in nineteenth-century census records, was not confined only to those who emigrated from modern-day Germany (which did not become a unified nation-state until 1871). People from Luxembourg, Alsace, Austria, Bohemia, Hungary, and other parts of southeastern Europe, as well as the thirty-eight independent German states, were generally deemed German, defined by common language rather than by national origin. Conzen, *Germans in Minnesota*, 4.

34. Ibid., 4–19; Holmquist, *They Chose Minnesota*, 58–59.

35. Calloway, "Historical Encounters across Five Centuries," 59–61; G. Anderson, *Kinsmen of Another Kind*, 240–43. Relatively small numbers of other European immigrant groups also settled the region in this period. To the Indians, however, all settlers who spoke languages other than English or French fell under the rubric "Dutchmen," all equally foreign and unintelligible. According to the 1860 census, Minnesota was home to 8,425 Norwegians and 3,178 Swedes. The state's 12,831 Irish-born residents, second in number to the Germans, tended to gravitate to towns rather than the countryside. We may also assume that the Indians grouped the English-speaking Irish with native-born rather than with other "foreigners." *U.S. Census, 1860 Population*, 255–63.

36. G. Anderson, *Kinsmen of Another Kind*, 12, 213–14, 221–25.

37. P. Larson, "New Look at the Elusive Inkpaduta," 33–35; Flandrau, "Ink-Pa-Du-Ta Massacre of 1857," 407.

38. Folwell, *History of Minnesota*, 2:394; G. Anderson, *Kinsmen of Another Kind*, 226–28.

39. G. Anderson, *Kinsmen of Another Kind*, 223, 227; Owens, "Political History of Minnesota," 147; Folwell, *History of Minnesota*, 2:219. Flandrau, a lawyer by profession, gave up the post of agent when offered a judgeship.

40. Riggs, *Mary and I*, 154–61; G. Anderson, *Little Crow*, 90–92, 108.

41. G. Anderson, *Little Crow*, 107–8.

42. Joseph Brown and Thomas Williamson, quoted in Diedrich, *Little Crow*, 116. For

information on Brown's claims on the Office of Indian Affairs, I am indebted to Carrie Zeman for sharing her as yet unpublished research in the records of the agency. For descriptions of Brown's home, see G. G. Allanson, "G. G. Allanson Writes of Indian Outbreaks," *Traverse County Star,* 12 April 1923; Folwell, *A Visit to Farther-and-Gay Castle,* esp. 125; and Holmquist and Brookins, *Minnesota's Major Historic Sites,* 130–32.

43. Folwell, *History of Minnesota,* 2:393–94; Diedrich, *Little Crow,* 117–18; G. Anderson, *Little Crow,* 91–94.

44. Diedrich, *Little Crow,* 117–18; G. Anderson, *Kinsmen of Another Kind,* 227–28; G. Anderson, *Little Crow,* 92–93; Folwell, *History of Minnesota,* 2:394, 398.

45. G. Anderson, *Little Crow,* 93–94.

46. Ibid.; Diedrich, *Little Crow,* 116–17. In addition to Little Crow, the Mdewakantons were represented by major chiefs Wabasha, Shakopee, Wakute, Mankato, Traveling Hail, and Black Dog, and seven other subchiefs and braves. The Wahpekutes sent Red Legs. The Sisseton and Wahpeton delegation was primarily composed of mission Indians rather than their most influential chiefs.

47. For a detailed account of the Dakotas' tenure in Washington, see Newcombe, "'A Portion of the American People,'" 83–96. Little Crow quoted, p. 86.

48. Folwell, *History of Minnesota,* 2:394–95; G. Anderson, *Little Crow,* 95–103. It is noteworthy that in 1854 Congress had authorized Lincoln to make the reservations permanent, but the president never acted upon the resolution. See G. Anderson, *Kinsmen of Another Kind,* 230.

49. G. Anderson, *Little Crow,* 101–3; Newcombe, "'Portion of the American People,'" 92.

50. Folwell, *History of Minnesota,* 2:394; G. Anderson, *Kinsmen of Another Kind,* 231; G. Anderson, *Little Crow,* 104. Newcombe, "'Portion of the American People,'" 90.

51. Folwell, *History of Minnesota,* 2:396–97.

52. Folwell, *History of Minnesota,* 2:396–400.

53. *Mankato Independent,* 10 July 1858, quoted in Diedrich, *Little Crow,* 126; G. Anderson, *Little Crow,* 106–7.

54. G. Anderson, *Little Crow,* 90, 106–8. The statistics cited in Brown's reports should be viewed with some skepticism, since it was in his interest to count every Indian who even temporarily picked up a plow. Still, the success of his efforts was widely noted by contemporaries.

55. Folwell, *History of Minnesota,* 2:220; G. Anderson, *Little Crow,* 107–12; Diedrich, *Little Crow,* 129.

56. Big Eagle, "Big Eagle's Account," in G. Anderson and A. Woolworth, *Through Dakota Eyes,* 24.

57. Big Eagle, in *Through Dakota Eyes,* 24.

58. Owens, "Political History of Minnesota," 147–48.

59. Ibid., 567–75; Moe, *Last Full Measure,* 13.

60. Wills, *Boosters, Hustlers, and Speculators,* 96–98.

61. *Nininger City Emigrant Aid Journal,* 4 July 1857, 2; Prucha, "The Settler and the Army," 45, 51.

62. Wills, *Boosters, Hustlers, and Speculators,* 95; Owens, "Political History of Minnesota," 472, 576–79.

63. Wills, *Boosters, Hustlers, and Speculators,* 99–109; Moe, *Last Full Measure,* 8–14; I. Bell, *Life of Billy Yank,* 18–21, 37–38; Hicks, "Organization of the Volunteer Army," 363–65. Minnesota's patriotic effusion typified the enthusiastic early support for the war that swept communities in the North. The disillusion that soon followed was also widespread, especially in the Midwest. See Geary, *We Need Men,* 5–6. According to Irvin Bell, throughout the North "the great bulk of volunteers responded to mixed motives, none of which was deeply felt." See I. Bell, *Life of Billy Yank,* 39.

64. It is unlikely that Lincoln believed the war would be won within three months. But only Congress had the authority to raise an army and Congress was not in session when Fort Sumter was attacked. As a stopgap measure until Congress could be convened, the president had the power to activate state militias for a three-month period only. The first wave of volunteers read this as an assurance that the rebellion would be easily put down.

See Hicks, "Organization of the Volunteer Army," 326–27.

65. Moe, *Last Full Measure*, 8–9.

66. Ibid., 9.

67. *St. Paul Pioneer and Democrat*, 20 April 1861; *Winona Daily Republican*, 29 April 1861; I. Bell, *Life of Billy Yank*, 19; Hicks, "Organization of the Volunteer Army," 333, 344–45; Moe, *Last Full Measure*, 11.

68. I. Bell, *Life of Billy Yank*, 37–38.

69. Hicks, "Organization of the Volunteer Army," 345; "German Volunteers," *St. Paul Pioneer and Democrat*, 27 April 1861.

70. Regan, *Irish in Minnesota*, 31; Osman, "They Put Us in the Bull Pen," 1–3. Diary of George W. Doud, quoted on p. 2.

71. I. Bell, *Life of Billy Yank*, 19–20; Moe, *Last Full Measure*, 16; Philander Prescott to Alexander Ramsey, 16 November 1861, Alexander Ramsey Papers; Diedrich, *Little Crow*, 151.

72. Prescott to Ramsey, 16 November 1861.

73. Hicks, "Organization of the Volunteer Army," 348–50; Moe, *Last Full Measure*, 18–20.

74. Moe, *Last Full Measure*, 20–23; Hicks, "Volunteer Army," 355–58.

75. "The Excursion," *Pioneer and Democrat*, 5 May 1861; Folwell, *History of Minnesota*, 2:82; Moe, *Last Full Measure*, 21.

76. Moe, *Last Full Measure*, 23–25, 28–30; Folwell, *History of Minnesota*, 2:82n42; I. Bell, *Life of Billy Yank*, 35.

77. Folwell, *History of Minnesota*, 2:102–3; Geary, *We Need Men*, 12–21; Mary Partridge in Morris, *Old Rail Fence Corners*, 274; Hicks, "Organization of the Volunteer Army," 357–61.

78. Owens, "Political History of Minnesota," 148; G. Anderson, *Kinsmen of Another Kind*, 178–79.

79. Kintzing Pritchette to Indian commissioner James Denver, quoted in R. Meyer, *History of the Santee Sioux*, 101–2.

80. Pluth, "Failed Watab Treaty of 1853," 18–19; Riggs, *Mary and I*, 155–58.

81. Hole-in-the-Day, quoted in Diedrich, *Chiefs Hole-in-the-Day*, 27.

82. Ibid., 27–28.

83. *Harper's New Monthly Magazine*, January 1863.

84. Diedrich, *Chiefs Hole-in-the-Day*, 31, 18–19.

85. G. Anderson, *Little Crow*, 73.

86. Diedrich, *Little Crow*, 109–11; Frank Meyer, quoted in Diedrich, *Little Crow*, 71; G. Anderson, *Little Crow*, 108.

87. G. Anderson, *Little Crow*, 108–9; Diedrich, *Little Crow*, 81–82, 126–27.

88. G. Anderson, *Little Crow*, 108–9.

89. Ibid., 106–7; Big Eagle, in *Through Dakota Eyes*, 23.

90. G. Anderson, *Little Crow*, 109–15; G. Anderson, *Kinsmen of Another Kind*, 232–33.

91. G. Anderson, *Kinsmen of Another Kind*, 256–58; G. Anderson, *Little Crow*, 108–10, 130; R. Meyer, *History of the Santee Sioux*, 107–8; Folwell, *History of Minnesota*, 2:222.

92. For a harsh assessment of Brown and Cullen, see Diedrich, *Little Crow*, 128–43.

93. Diedrich, *Chiefs Hole-in-the-Day*, 32–33; *Shakopee Independent*, 17 November 1855.

94. Nairn, "History of the Sioux Massacre," 2–3.

95. Diedrich, *Little Crow*, 144–48; G. Anderson, *Kinsmen of Another Kind*, 244–48; Martin Severance, quoted in Folwell, *History of Minnesota*, 2:222n15.

96. Diedrich, *Chiefs Hole-in-the-Day*, 32.

97. G. Anderson, *Kinsmen of Another Kind*, 244–46; Big Eagle, in *Through Dakota Eyes*, 24.

98. Conzen, *Germans in Minnesota*, 18–25. For a good representation of German settlers' perspective, see Tolzmann, *German Pioneer Accounts*. Wilhelmina Busse quoted on p. 31. Also see Berghold, *Indians' Revenge*, 50–56.

99. Folwell, *History of Minnesota*, 2:231; "Story of Wilhelmina Busse," in Tolzmann, *German Pioneer Accounts*, 31.

100. G. Anderson, *Kinsmen of Another Kind*, 243–44; Diedrich, *Little Crow*, 148–50; Berghold, *Indians' Revenge*, 63, 70, 80; Wakefield, *Six Weeks in the Sioux Tepees*, 7; Big Eagle, in G. Anderson, *Through Dakota Eyes*, 24.

101. Moe, *Last Full Measure*, 24–27; G. Anderson, *Kinsmen of Another Kind*, 246–48.

102. R. Meyer, *History of Santee Sioux,* 111–12; G. Anderson, *Kinsmen of Another Kind,* 248–49; G. Anderson, *Little Crow,* 114–15; Big Eagle, in *Through Dakota Eyes,* 24–26.

103. G. Anderson, *Kinsmen of Another Kind,* 248–49; Whipple, *Lights and Shadows,* 127.

104. Whipple, *Lights and Shadows,* 126.

105. Diedrich, *Little Crow,* 153; Green, *Peculiar Imbalance,* 108–15.

106. Thomas Williamson, quoted in Diedrich, *Little Crow,* 151.

107. G. Anderson, *Little Crow,* 120–21.

108. Galbraith, *Office of Indian Affairs Report for 1863,* p. 5; G. Anderson, *Kinsmen of Another Kind,* 252; Big Eagle, in *Through Dakota Eyes,* 25–26. I am grateful to Carrie Zeman for sharing her in-depth research on the Renville Rangers.

109. J. Johnson, *En-me-Gah-bowh's Story,* 11–15; Diedrich, *Chiefs Hole-in-the-Day,* 32–33. Even Folwell, no admirer of Hole-in-the-Day, doubts that he intended to start a war. Instead, Folwell characterizes the drama that played out as a form of blackmail perpetrated on the government. See Folwell, *History of Minnesota,* 2:381–82.

110. J. Johnson, *En-me-Gah-bowh's Story,* 27–28; Diedrich, *Chiefs Hole-in-the-Day,* 32–33. Quite plausibly, Hole-in-the-Day had his braves intentionally feed Johnson misinformation about their plans. Johnson was closely allied with whites and the chief could be sure that he would immediately warn them of an impending attack—which he did.

111. Folwell, *History of Minnesota,* 2:374–76; Neill, "History of the Ojibways," 503-4; Diedrich, *Chiefs Hole-in-the-Day,* 34.

112. Folwell, *History of Minnesota,* 2:376–80; Neill, "History of the Ojibways," 503-4; Diedrich, *Chiefs Hole-in-the-Day,* 33–37.

113. Johnson recounts that in the summer of 1863, while traveling from Gull Lake to White Earth, "ducks and geese and deer were very plentiful. My son killed all the ducks and wild geese we needed. My eldest son killed five deer and one bear, and I killed two deer." J. Johnson, *En-me-Gah-bowh's Story,* 39–40.

11. Cataclysm on the Minnesota

1. Diedrich, *Little Crow,* 157, 192–93; Nancy McClure Faribault Huggan in G. Anderson and A. Woolworth, *Through Dakota Eyes,* 80–81; T. S. Williamson to S. B. Treat, 9 January 1862, in American Board of Commissioners for Foreign Missions Papers, Minnesota Historical Society, St. Paul. My thanks to Carrie Zeman for sharing her meticulous research and analysis on Galbraith.

2. Diedrich, *Little Crow,* 157–71, 187; G. Anderson, *Little Crow,* 121–28.

3. Folwell, *History of Minnesota,* 2:232; Diedrich, *Little Crow,* 187; G. Anderson, *Little Crow,* 128 (italics added by the author). Innumerable contemporary accounts of the 1862 war recount some version of Myrick's "Let them eat grass" taunt, as does nearly every historical account.

4. Folwell, *History of Minnesota,* 2:228–31; Wakefield, *Six Weeks in the Sioux Tepees,* 9-10; Diedrich, *Little Crow,* 188–90, Sheehan quoted, p. 190.

5. Diedrich, *Little Crow,* 188–90; Riggs, *Mary and I,* 174–76; Bryant and Murch, *History of the Great Massacre,* 88.

6. Diedrich, *Little Crow,* 194–202; Martin Severance to Thomas Hughes, 7 November 1903, cited in Carrie R. Zeman, "Formation of the Renville Rangers," working paper in Wingerd's possession.

7. For varying accounts of the Acton murders, see Folwell, *History of Minnesota,* 2:239–40; G. Anderson, *Little Crow,* 130; Bryant and Murch, *History of the Great Massacre,* 84–86; R. Meyer, *History of the Santee Sioux,* 114–15; Big Eagle in G. Anderson, *Through Dakota Eyes,* 35–36; D. Buck, *Indian Outbreaks,* 85–90; Berghold, *Indians' Revenge,* 83–87.

8. G. Anderson, *Little Crow,* 130–31.

9. G. Anderson, *Little Crow,* 130–33. For the full text of Little Crow's speech to the braves, see "Taoyateduta Is Not a Coward," 115.

10. Many accounts exist documenting the day-by-day details of the Dakota Conflict, which I will not duplicate here. See, for

example, Folwell, *History of Minnesota,* 2:109–89; Carley, *Sioux Uprising of 1862;* Board of Commissioners, *Minnesota in the Civil and Indian Wars;* Bryant and Murch, *History of the Great Massacre;* Koblas, *Let Them Eat Grass.* For Dakota accounts of the war, see G. Anderson and A. Woolworth, *Through Dakota Eyes.*

11. Diedrich, *Little Crow,* 213–14; G. Anderson, *Little Crow,* 135–36.

12. For an illuminating cultural analysis of this episode, see B. White, "A Mouthful of Grass," 259–67.

13. G. Anderson, *Little Crow,* 136; Stevens, *Personal Recollections of Minnesota,* 364–65.

14. Diedrich, *Little Crow,* 214; Huggan, "Story of Nancy McClure," in *Minnesota Historical Collections,* vol. 6, 450–51.

15. Faribault's son, David Jr., rode with the hostiles during the conflict and his father drove the buggy that carried Little Crow to the battle of Fort Ridgely. David Sr. later claimed he was forced to attend the battle and was not prosecuted, probably because of his long-standing relationship with Henry Sibley. David Jr., however, was tried, convicted, and imprisoned, but later pardoned through Sibley's intervention. The young Faribault also insisted that he was forced to participate in the war, but like many mixed-blood men, he probably was torn by divided loyalties.

16. Huggan, "Story of Nancy McClure," 439–40, 446; "Samuel Brown's Recollections," in *Through Dakota Eyes,* 70–79, 222–25; G. Anderson, *Kinsmen of Another Kind,* 265–66.

17. Tarble, *Story of My Capture;* Calloway, "Historical Encounters across Five Centuries," 61; G. Anderson, *Kinsmen of Another Kind,* 265; Wakefield, *Six Weeks in the Sioux Tepees;* Schwandt, "Story of Mary Schwandt," 471; Snana, "Narration of a Friendly Sioux," 429–30.

18. G. Anderson, *Little Crow,* 145–52; Riggs, *Mary and I,* 176–87; Sibley, "Sketch of John Other Day," in *Collections of the Minnesota Historical Society,* vol. 3, 100–102; Mazekootemane, "Narrative of Paul Mazakootemane," 84–87.

19. Numerous first-person accounts describe the horrors experienced by the fleeing settlers. See, for example, narratives of Helen Carrothers, Justina Krieger, Justina Boelter, Valencia Reynolds, and Mary Worley, all in Bryant and Murch, *History of the Great Massacre.* Since no records exist to document all the new settlers in the region, let alone people passing through, it is difficult to ascertain a definitive death count. Though sources differ, they agree that no fewer than 400 people were killed.

20. See Folwell, *History of Minnesota,* 2:109–46, for a comprehensive account of these events. For a first-person account of the siege of Fort Ridgely, see Margaret Hearn in Morris, *Old Rail Fence Corners,* 143–52.

21. G. Anderson, *Little Crow,* 139–41; Diedrich, *Little Crow,* 222–23.

22. R. Gilman, *Henry Hastings Sibley,* 172–73.

23. Ibid., 174–76.

24. Ibid., 178–79; G. Anderson, *Little Crow,* 154; Folwell, *History of Minnesota,* 2:150–55.

25. G. Anderson, *Little Crow,* 155–56; "Taoyateduta Is Not a Coward," 115.

26. Folwell, *History of Minnesota,* 2:158–63; Big Eagle, "Big Eagle's Account," in G. Anderson, *Through Dakota Eyes,* 235; G. Anderson, *Little Crow,* 156–58. Little Crow quoted in Diedrich, *Little Crow,* 224–25.

27. G. Anderson, *Little Crow,* 158–60; Folwell, *History of Minnesota,* 2:177–83; G. Anderson, *Kinsmen of Another Kind,* 273–75; Hdainyanka, quoted in Chomsky, "United States–Dakota War Trials," 21n44.

28. G. Anderson, *Kinsmen of Another Kind,* 275; Samuel Brown in *Through Dakota Eyes,* 224–25.

29. Chomsky, "United States–Dakota War Trials," 23n58, 55; R. Gilman, *Henry Hastings Sibley,* 184–85. The commission was composed of Lieutenant Colonel William Marshall, Colonel William Crooks, Captain Hiram P. Grant, Captain Hiram S. Bailey, and Lieutenant Rollin C. Olin. Marshall later admitted that "his mind was not in a condition to give the men a fair trial." Chomsky, "United States–Dakota War Trials," 55.

30. Nichols, "The Other Civil War," 6–8.

31. Maj. Gen. John Pope to Sibley, 28 September 1862, quoted in Chomsky, "United States–Dakota War Trials," 23.

32. G. Anderson, *Kinsmen of Another Kind*, 275–76; R. Gilman, *Henry Hastings Sibley*, 183–86; Chomsky, "United States–Dakota War Trials," 22–25. Pope originally ordered Sibley to march the condemned men to Fort Snelling, then rescinded the order. Sibley then moved the camp to the Lower Agency, where much-needed food and supplies were available. See R. Gilman, *Henry Hastings Sibley*, 186.

33. Case 111, cited in Chomsky, "United States–Dakota War Trials," 39n154.

34. Wakefield, *Six Weeks in the Sioux Tepees*, 78; R. Gilman, *Henry Hastings Sibley*, 183. For an extended analysis of the defects of the trials, see Chomsky, "United States–Dakota War Trials," 46–61, 26–28.

35. As Chomsky notes (in "United States–Dakota War Trials," 37n323), Sibley may have believed that the Indians would have a better chance of a fair hearing by the military commission than in state courts, given the white population's overwhelming animus against the Indians. Nonetheless, the trials clearly were a travesty of justice.

36. In 1871 Sibley delivered an impassioned speech before the Minnesota House of Representatives, defending his actions as governor and imploring the legislature to honor the railroad bonds, lest he and his family bear "the intolerable humiliation of being citizens of a repudiating state." Reproduced in Owens, "Political History of Minnesota, Part Second: Early Railroad History," Appendix A, 1–36.

37. R. Gilman, *Henry Hastings Sibley*, 173–76; Folwell, *History of Minnesota*, 2:175; Chomsky, "United States–Dakota War Trials," 19n33.

38. "Joseph Coursolle's Story" in G. Anderson and A. Woolworth, *Through Dakota Eyes*, 239.

39. R. Gilman, *Henry Hastings Sibley*, 178–80, 186; Chomsky, "United States–Dakota War Trials," 20; R. Meyer, *History of the Santee Sioux*, 120; Folwell, *History of Minnesota*, 2:176.

40. Chomsky, "United States–Dakota War Trials," 91–92.

41. Ibid., 29; Bessler, *Legacy of Violence*, 47; Nichols, "The Other Civil War," 8–10; Fisher, *Military Tribunals and Presidential Power*, 52; Whipple, *Lights and Shadows*, 136–37.

42. Glewwe, "Journey of the Prisoners," in Bakeman and Richardson, *Trail of Tears*, 95; Bachman, "Black Dakota," manuscript of forthcoming book, in author's possession, p. 241–42; Nichols, *Lincoln and the Indians*, 103. Riggs has often been cited as the official interpreter at the trials, but this was not the case; rather, he served as an assistant in various ways in preparing cases for trial. I am grateful to attorney and historian Walt Bachman for his expertise in clarifying this and other legal points about the trials and for sharing the manuscript and allowing me to cite from his forthcoming book, "Black Dakota."

43. Williamson to Riggs, 24 November 1862, quoted in Koblas, *Let Them Eat Grass*, vol. 3: *Ashes*, 98.

44. Glewwe, "Journey of the Prisoners," in Bakeman and Richardson, *Trails of Tears*, 93; R. Meyer, *History of the Santee Sioux*, 127; Bachman, "Black Dakota," book manuscript, in Wingerd's possession, 241–43.

45. R. Gilman, *Henry Hastings Sibley*, 190; Whipple, *Lights and Shadows*, 123–30.

46. Chomsky, "United States–Dakota War Trials," 29–30; Nichols, "The Other Civil War," 7–8; Bessler, *Legacy of Violence*, 48–50.

47. Sibley to Whipple, quoted in Whipple, *Lights and Shadows*, 131; Chomsky, "United States–Dakota War Trials," 92; Bessler, *Legacy of Violence*, 49.

48. Folwell, *History of Minnesota*, 2:204–9; Nichols, "The Other Civil War," 9–11; Fisher, *Military Tribunals and Presidential Power*, 53; Hoffert, "Gender and Vigilantism on the Minnesota Frontier," 358; Chomsky, "United States–Dakota War Trials," 32. Two of the condemned men were reprieved before the execution, leaving thirty-eight to hang.

49. *St. Paul Daily Press*, 8 November 1862. For a detailed account of the journey to Fort Snelling, see Bakeman and A. Woolworth, "Family Caravan," 53–78. Pope, quoted, 53; Williamson, 65; Marshall, 62. See also "Sam-

uel Brown's Recollections," in G. Anderson, *Through Dakota Eyes.*

50. Marshall, quoted in Bakeman and A. Woolworth, "Family Caravan," 62; "Samuel Brown's Recollections, in G. Anderson, *Through Dakota Eyes,* 227.

51. R. Gilman, *Henry Hastings Sibley,* 187–88; Samuel Brown, in G. Anderson, *Through Dakota Eyes,* 227–28. See concurring accounts of the Henderson attacks in Bakeman and A. Woolworth, "Family Caravan," 67.

52. R. Meyer, *History of the Santee Sioux,* 124; Williamson quoted in Bakeman and A. Woolworth, "Family Caravan," 70; Stewart, *Thomas R. Stewart Memoirs,* reproduced in part in Ibid., 71–74.

53. Thomas Watts, *Minneapolis Tribune,* 15 July 1925. For a meticulous analysis of the conveyance of prisoners to Mankato, see Glewwe, "Journey of the Prisoners," 79–106. In addition to the 302 condemned men, the convoy included about 65 more men who had either been sentenced to prison or found innocent of charges, as well as 24 women meant to serve as cooks, laundresses, and nurses for the prisoners. At least four women carried nursing infants with them. See Glewwe, 84.

54. Glewwe, "Journey of the Prisoners," 92–99; Sibley quoted, 93.

55. Heard, *History of the Sioux War,* 243.

56. Glewwe, "Journey of the Prisoners," 94; Bachman, "Deaths of Dakota Prisoners," 179–80.

57. R. Gilman, *Henry Hastings Sibley,* 187.

58. Berghold, *Indians' Revenge,* 144; Bachman, "Black Dakota," 221; Miller to Sibley, 21 November 1862, quoted in Bachman, "Colonel Miller's War," 109. Bachman's research has uncovered significant new evidence of widespread, organized plans to murder the prisoners. Most contemporary accounts of these events, not surprisingly, omitted mention of organized vigilantism. Thus, later historians underreported the seriousness of these threats.

59. Bachman, "Colonel Miller's War," 108–10.

60. Ibid., 111–14.

61. Ibid., 110–11.

62. Ibid., 115–16.

63. R. Gilman, *Henry Hastings Sibley,* 189; Bachman, "Black Dakota," 220; R. Meyer, *History of the Santee Sioux,* 128; Bachman, "Colonel Miller's War," 114–18. In 1864 Stephen Miller was elected governor of Minnesota.

64. Heard, *History of the Sioux War,* 281. I am grateful to Walt Bachman for his insights on the merits of the charges against the convicted men.

65. One of the condemned men received a last-minute reprieve, thanks to the impassioned intercession of Jane and Thomas Williamson.

66. Koblas, *Let Them Eat Grass,* 3:105–6; Heard, *History of the Sioux War,* 274–75; Bachman, "Black Dakota," 262–63. Isaac Heard, who served as recorder at the trials, described Riggs as "in effect, the Grand Jury of the court." Heard, *History of the Sioux War,* 251. See also Folwell, *History of Minnesota,* 2:198–99.

67. Father Ravoux baptized thirty-one and administered the sacrament of First Holy Communion to the three mixed bloods. Williamson reported six conversions. Reardon, *Catholic Church in the Diocese of St. Paul,* 129; Riggs, *Mary and I,* 211–12.

68. Riggs, *Mary and I,* 212; Heard, *History of the Sioux War,* 283; Bachman, "Black Dakota," 264–65. The "Confessions" are reproduced in full in Koblas, *Let Them Eat Grass,* 3:110–15.

69. *St. Paul Daily Press,* 28 December 1862; Chomsky, "United States–Dakota War Trials," 34–35.

70. Chomsky, "United States–Dakota War Trials," 35–36.

71. Bessler, *Legacy of Violence,* 59; Koblas, *Let Them Eat Grass,* 3:109; "Execution of the Minnesota Indians," *Harper's Weekly,* 17 January 1863, 39; Bachman, "Black Dakota," 267; Heard, *History of the Sioux War,* 294–95.

72. *St. Paul Daily Press,* 28 December 1862, p. 1; "Execution of the Minnesota Indians," *Harper's Weekly,* 39.

73. *St. Paul Daily Press,* 28 December 1862, p. 1; "Execution of the Minnesota Indians," *Harper's Weekly,* 39; Chomsky, "United States–Dakota War Trials," 36–37; *St. Peter*

[398]

Tribune, 27 December 1862, quoted in Bachman, "Black Dakota," 268.

74. Chomsky, "United States–Dakota War Trials," 36n142. Some sources describe the song as a Christian hymn, sung in the Dakota language. This seems improbable since the men had been baptized only two days earlier and would have been unlikely to have spent their final hours learning hymns.

75. "Execution of the Minnesota Indians," 39; *Daily News*, 1.

76. Bryant and Murch, *History of the Great Massacre*, 478; Sarah Purnell Montgomery, quoted in Koblas, *Let Them Eat Grass*, 3:117.

77. D. Buck, *Indian Outbreaks*, 269–70; Carley, *Dakota War of 1862*, 75; Bachman, "Black Dakota," 269–70, *New York Times* quoted, 270. Multiple sources identify Dr. William Mayo as one of the grave robbers. For many years the skeleton of one of the Indians, said to be Cut Nose, was used for teaching purposes at the Mayo Clinic. See Carley, *Dakota War of 1862*, 75.

78. Bachman, "Black Dakota," 284, 269.

79. Jane Grey Swisshelm, quoted in Hoffert, "Gender and Vigilantism on the Minnesota Frontier," 357, 359; *Faribault Central Republican*, 15 October 1862; Pope to Sibley, quoted in Chomsky, "United States–Dakota War Trials," 25–26n71.

80. *Mankato Semi-Weekly Record*, 4 October 1862; "The Knights of the Forest," *Mankato Review*, 27 April 1886; "John J. Porter, Pioneer, Last of Knights of Forest, Dies," *Mankato Free Press*, 15 January 1929; "Secret Society of the Early Days in Mankato" and "Knights of the Forest," clipping file, Service Organizations folder, Blue Earth County Historical Society, Mankato, Minnesota. I am greatly indebted to Carrie Zeman for alerting me to the existence of this organization and sharing her sources with me. The membership pledge of the Knights of the Forest was, in part, as follows: "I, _____, of my own free will and accord, in the full belief that every Indian should be removed from the State, by the memory of the inhuman cruelties perpetrated upon defenseless citizens, and in the presence of the members of the order here assembled, do most solemnly promise,

without any mental reservation whatever, to use every exertion and influence in my power, to cause the removal of all tribes of Indians from the State of Minnesota. . . . I will protect and defend at every hazard, all members in carrying out the objects of this order."

81. General Order No. 41, printed in *St. Paul Daily Press*, 7 July 1863; Folwell, *History of Minnesota*, 2:288–89; Heard, *History of the Sioux War*, 304–6. Numerous accounts of Indian sightings are noted in Marshall, "Notes on Conditions in 1863," 64–70.

82. General Order No. 41; Folwell, *History of Minnesota*, 2:288–89.

83. Bachman, "Black Dakota," 271–73.

84. Folwell, *History of Minnesota*, 2:249–51; Bachman, "Black Dakota," 280–81; Riggs, *Mary and I*, 214–17.

85. R. Meyer, *History of the Santee Sioux*, 143; Riggs quoted in Bachman, "Black Dakota," 280; Riggs, *Mary and I*, 214, 219; Folwell, *History of Minnesota*, 2:249.

86. Bachman, "Black Dakota, 279–80.

87. Riggs, *Mary and I*, 217–19; Williamson quoted, 217.

88. Chomsky, "United States–Dakota War Trials," 38n150; R. Meyer, *History of the Santee Sioux*, 141.

89. Folwell, *History of Minnesota*, 2:256–58; R. Meyer, *History of the Santee Sioux*, 139–42.

90. T. Galbraith, report to Commissioner of Indian Affairs, quoted in R. Meyer, *History of the Santee Sioux*, 141–42.

91. R. Meyer, *History of the Santee Sioux*, 142, 144; Folwell, *History of Minnesota*, 2:258–59.

92. R. Meyer, *History of the Santee Sioux*, 143–44; Chomsky, "United States–Dakota War Trials," 38n149; Nichols, *Lincoln and the Indians*, 124; Monjeau-Marz, *Dakota Indian Internment at Fort Snelling*, 105–6. After three years' imprisonment, the men were released to join their families, who by this time had been relocated to a reservation near Niobara, Nebraska.

93. Folwell, *History of Minnesota*, 2:259; R. Meyer, *History of the Santee Sioux*, 145; Monjeau-Marz, *Dakota Indian Internment*, 106–7.

94. Folwell, *History of Minnesota*, 2:259; R. Meyer, *History of the Santee Sioux*, 145–46; Riggs, *Mary and I*, 224; Monjeau-Marz, *Dakota Indian Internment*, 108; Hyman, "Survival at Crow Creek," 152–53.

95. Heard, *History of the Sioux War*, 295; R. Meyer, *History of the Santee Sioux*, 147–54; Nichols, *Lincoln and the Indians*, 122, 126; Passing Hail, "Speech to Special Joint Committee on the Condition of the Indian Tribes," in Calloway, *Our Hearts Fell to the Ground*, 100–101.

96. Hyman, "Survival at Crow Creek," 152, 155–59; Virginia Driving Hawk Sneve, quoted in Hyman, "Survival at Crow Creek," 156; R. Meyer, *History of the Santee Sioux*, 146–49.

97. Bachman, "Black Dakota," 268–69. The military commission tried about a dozen Winnebagos, along with the Dakotas, but even by the weak standards applied none were convicted or detained. The *Mankato Weekly Record* accused that "Indian officials and sympathizers" made an unusual effort "to save [Winnebago] necks." Chomsky, "United States–Dakota War Trials," 28n87.

98. *Mankato Review*, 27 April 1886; Nichols, "The Other Civil War," 8. Secretary of the Navy Gideon Welles thought the entire war may have been provoked to seize Winnebago lands, "which white men want and mean to have."

99. Lillian Butler Morehart, in Morris, *Old Rail Fence Corners*, 163; Nichols, *Lincoln and the Indians*, 121–23.

100. *Mankato Weekly Record*, 5 May and 15 May 1863.

101. R. Meyer, *History of the Santee Sioux*, 148; Hyman, "Survival at Crow Creek," 155; Marshall, "Notes on Conditions in 1863," 123.

102. Letter printed in *Winona Republican*, ca. 30 September 1863, copied in Marshall, "Notes on Conditions in 1863," 118.

103. R. Meyer, *History of the Santee Sioux*, 149; *St. Paul Daily Press*, 15 October 1863.

104. Passing Hail, "Speech to Special Joint Committee on the Condition of the Indian Tribes," in Calloway, *Our Hearts Fell to the Ground*, 100–101.

105. R. Meyer, *History of the Santee Sioux*, 150–57.

106. Ibid., 153; Folwell, *History of Minnesota*, 2:437; Williamson, quoted in Riggs, *Mary and I*, 224. Meyer notes a certain irony implicit in Dakota community revival, which required conforming to white economic and cultural norms and came at the expense of the integrity of traditional Dakota culture.

107. Folwell, *History of Minnesota*, 2:263–64; R. Gilman, *Henry Hastings Sibley*, 191; Whipple, *Lights and Shadows*, 134–35.

108. Whipple, *Lights and Shadows*, 134–35, 528–29. For Taopi's account of the 1862 war, see G. Anderson and A. Woolworth, *Through Dakota Eyes*. In 1887, the government established the Sisseton and Devil's Lake reservations in present-day South and North Dakota for those Dakota Indians who had not taken part in the 1862 war. See R. Meyer, *History of the Santee Sioux*, 198–201; and Prucha, *American Indian Treaties*, 276.

109. Diedrich, *Chiefs Hole-in-the-Day*, 39; Cleland, "Treaties of 1863 and 1864," 98; Folwell, *History of Minnesota*, 2:380.

110. Joseph LeMay, letter published in *St. Paul Daily Press*, 28 May 1863. For numerous reports on Ojibwe activities, see *Press* throughout May 1863. Cleland, "Treaties of 1863 and 1864," 99.

111. *St. Paul Daily Press*, 16 October 1863.

112. Cleland, "Treaties of 1863 and 1864," 99–102; Diedrich, *Chiefs Hole-in-the-Day*, 39–40.

113. Cleland, "Treaties of 1863 and 1864," 99–102; Cleland, "Off-Reservation Hunting, Fishing, and Gathering in the Post-Treaty Era," 103; *St. Paul Daily Press*, 16 October 1863.

114. G. Anderson, *Little Crow*, 168–71.

115. Ibid., 173–76: *St. Paul Daily Press*, 23 June 1863.

116. R. Gilman, *Henry Hastings Sibley*, 195; A. Daniels, "Reminiscences of Little Crow," 530. Daniels also doubted that Little Crow had participated in raids against civilians, citing his "superior spirit" and humane treatment of prisoners. See 529. G. Anderson, *Little Crow*, 176–77. For a different

interpretation of Little Crow's motivations, see Diedrich, *Little Crow*.

117. R. Gilman, *Henry Hastings Sibley*, 193–94.

118. Beaulieu, "Fate of Little Crow," Part II, 5–8. I am grateful to Professor Beaulieu for his assistance and permission to cite his work. See also Folwell, *History of Minnesota*, 2:282–83; *St. Paul Daily Press*, 13 June and 7 July 1863. Little Crow made it clear to Governor Dallas at Fort Garry that he was well informed about the punishments that had fallen on his people in Minnesota. See G. Anderson, *Little Crow*, 177–78.

119. *St. Paul Daily Press*, 7 July 1863.

120. G. Anderson, *Little Crow*, 178.

121. Diedrich, *Little Crow*, 247; G. Anderson, *Little Crow*, 178; Folwell, *History of Minnesota*, 2:283.

122. Diedrich, *Little Crow*, 248–49; Beaulieu, "Fate of Little Crow," Part IV, 6–10; Folwell, *History of Minnesota*, 2:283–86; Carley, *Dakota War of 1862*, 84–86.

123. R. Gilman, *Henry Hastings Sibley*, 195–201, Sibley quoted, 200; Carley, *Dakota War of 1862*, 89–90.

124. Folwell, *History of Minnesota*, 2:276–79; Koblas, *Let Them Eat Grass*, 197–205.

125. Samuel Brown, quoted in Carley, *Dakota War of 1862*, 91.

Epilogue

1. "Skull Exhibit Banished," *Minneapolis Journal*, 8 September 1915, p. 11; *St. Paul Pioneer Press*, 7 November 1971, p. 14; Diedrich, *Little Crow and the Dakota War*, 254; G. Anderson, *Little Crow*, 181; Beaulieu, "Fate of Little Crow," 16–17. Sources differ regarding the date that Little Crow's remains were removed from public display, but Minnesota Historical Society records place the date as 1915. See "Year of Reconciliation Raises Questions," 2.

2. Diedrich, *Little Crow*, 253; *Minneapolis Tribune*, 15 March 1881; West, *Ancestry, Life, and Times of Hon. Henry Hastings Sibley*, 333; A. Daniels, "Reminiscences of Little Crow," 530.

3. Schwandt, "Story of Mary Schwandt,"

470; A. Daniels, "Reminiscences of Little Crow," 530.

4. Scholars generally agree that the most accurate count was determined by Marion Satterlee, published in his volume *A Detailed Account of the Massacre by the Dakota Indians of Minnesota in 1862*. Satterlee reported as casualties 77 soldiers, 29 volunteers, and 358 settlers. The death toll of civilians has been exceeded only once, in the attack on the World Trade Center on 9/11.

5. R. Gilman, *Henry Hastings Sibley*, 199; West, *Ancestry, Life and Times*, 333n2.

6. Malmros, *Annual Report of the Adjutant General*, 165; *Annual Report of the Minnesota Historical Society*, 12; skull, arm bones, and scalp of Little Crow listed as items 41, 42, and 338 in Minnesota Historical Society Early Acquisition Records. Acknowledgment of scaffold, axe, and rope in letter from Alexander Ramsey (as president of the Minnesota Historical Society) to "Colonel," 6 June 1863. I am grateful to David Beaulieu and Walt Bachman for copies of these materials. See also Diedrich, *Little Crow*, 253.

7. According to the 1860 census, the state had a population of 172,023; by 1870 it had grown to 439,706, an increase of more than 150 percent. *Twelfth Census of the United States—1900, Census Reports*, vol. 1, Population Part I, 2–3.

8. Prucha, "The Settler and the Army," 51; *Minnesota Historical Society Annual Report*, 11–12; Beaulieu, "Fate of Little Crow," 13; Diedrich, *Little Crow*, 253.

9. Among contemporary histories rushed into print were Heard, *History of the Sioux War;* Bryant and Murch, *History of the Great Massacre*. Bryant and Murch's volume had the additional attraction of including "personal narratives of many who escaped."

10. McConkey, *Dakota War Whoop*.

11. Eastlick, *Personal Narrative of Indian Massacres of 1862*. Though Eastlick portrays herself as a heroic victim, other survivor accounts mention her in much less flattering terms as coldheartedly abandoning anyone who slowed her flight, including her children. (Eastlick's fourteen-year-old son, Merton, carried his infant brother to safety on his own.) At least through the 1880s, she continued

to peddle her pamphlet, with an appendix attached, chronicling her continuing heroic "battle for a living."

12. Heilbron, *Documentary Panorama,* 1–3; J. Bell, "Sioux Panorama and American Mythic History," 279–99; Stevens, script for "Panorama of the Indian Massacre of 1862," p. 1, Stevens Panorama file, Minnesota Historical Society.

13. Seminal works on cultural and social unease in late-nineteenth-century America include Marx, *Machine in the Garden;* Trachtenberg, *Incorporation of America;* and Lears, *No Place of Grace.* For an excellent analysis of the nation's love affair with the West in this era, see Slotkin, *Gunfighter Nation,* 29–62.

14. Buffalo Bill's Wild West Show had an extraordinary run, playing to adoring audiences from 1883 to 1916. Cody was a brilliant entrepreneur who tapped into what had already become a national fascination with the West. See Kasson, *Buffalo Bill's Wild West;* and Slotkin, *Gunfighter Nation,* 63–87.

15. Heilbron, *Documentary Panorama,* 4.

16. On the idealized myth of the Indian, see Deloria, *Playing Indian;* and Trachtenberg, *Shades of Hiawatha.*

17. Kammen, *Mystic Chords of Memory,* 85.

18. For an illuminating study of the hard choices made by one mixed-blood family, see Atkins, *Creating Minnesota,* 61–71. See also Carroll, "Who Was Jane Lamont?" 184–96; and Rubinstein, "The French Canadians and French," 36–50. My research on this subject is in process. Thus, evidence cited here is primarily anecdotal.

19. Atkins, *Creating Minnesota,* 61–71; Carroll, "Who Was Jane Lamont?" 184–96.

20. Southwick, *Building on a Borrowed Past,* 5; *Twelfth Census of the United States,* part I, 2–3.

21. Southwick, *Building on a Borrowed Past,* 32–37.

22. Ibid., 35–37, 40, 97–98, 113.

23. As David Lowenthal notes, history seeks, however imperfectly, to uncover and understand the past, while the invocation of heritage is meant to justify and reaffirm the conditions and values of the present. See Lowenthal, *The Heritage Crusade.*

24. D. C. Smith, *City of Parks,* 43–46.

25. D. Smith, "God of Peace," 17–18.

26. Osman, "The Brower Boys' Civil War," 162–67. Jacob Brower did return to service. Unbeknownst to his father, he had signed on as a seaman aboard the ironclad steamboat USS *Exchange* before his draft notice was served. He returned to Minnesota in August 1865, much to his father's joy.

27. Nziramasanga, "Minnesota: First State to Send Troops," 57; Moe, *Last Full Measure,* 301; Linderman, *Embattled Courage;* Horrigan, "Epilogue," in Kenneth Carley, *Minnesota in the Civil War,* 189–90. The First Minnesota did receive a hero's welcome when its survivors came home but most other state units returned without fanfare.

28. Silber, *Romance of Reunion,* 58–59; Kammen, *Mystic Chords of Memory,* 103; Bodner, *Remaking America,* 28; Savage, *Standing Soldiers, Kneeling Slaves.* The first national monument to the war was sponsored by the Freedmen's Association. Unveiled near the Capitol in Washington, D.C., in 1876, it featured statues of Lincoln and a kneeling slave and celebrated emancipation rather than military valor. See Savage, *Standing Soldiers, Kneeling Slaves,* 114–19.

29. Bodner, *Remaking America,* 28–29; Daniels, *Coming to America,* 124.

30. While the cult of the "Lost Cause" is beyond the scope of this volume, it is important to note that northern Republicans and southern Democrats—the business elites of both regions—had many interests in common, both politically and economically, and were equally invested in inventing a revised narrative of the Civil War that emphasized the valor and honor of both sides. As C. Vann Woodward and David Blight have compellingly noted, reconciliation was good for business. The contested election of 1876 between Rutherford B. Hayes and Samuel Tilden provides a vivid illustration of how northern Republicans and southern Democrats worked together to serve their mutual interests. Deal making in the electoral college that served southern (and northern) business interests threw the election to the Republican Hayes.

See Blight, *Race and Reunion*, 136–39; and Woodward, *Origins of the New South*, 23–43.

31. Silber, *Romance of Reunion*, 94–95, 160.

32. Blegen, *Minnesota: A History*, 307.

33. On settlers' organizations, see Bakeman, "Oldest House in St. Paul," 25–35.

34. Kelly, "Election of 1896," 268–70. On the relationship between Hill and Ireland, see Wingerd, *Claiming the City*, 58–63.

35. Brundage, "No Deed but Memory," in Brundage, *Where These Memories Grow*, 12.

36. Kelly, "Election of 1896," 270.

37. Ibid., 272.

38. Ibid., 276–77.

39. Ibid., 276, 279; Board of Commissioners, *Minnesota in the Civil and Indian Wars*, vol. 1, v; Heck, *Civil War Veteran in Minnesota*, 27.

40. Thompson, *Minnesota's State Capitol*, 66–67; L'Enfant, *The Gág Family*, 51–52. I am grateful to Brian Pease, Minnesota Capitol site manager, for information on the location of the Gág painting.

41. Pamphlet Collection, Minnesota Territorial Centennial, 1949; Statehood Centennial Commission Files, Minnesota Historical Society.

42. Rubenstein and A. Woolworth, "Dakota and Ojibway," in *They Chose Minnesota*, 32.

43. Sperry, *Purchase of an Empire*, 18–19. *Purchase of an Empire* was a commemorative booklet produced by the Hubbard Milling Company to celebrate the treaty of Traverse des Sioux. It was probably distributed as a holiday gift to customers, since the publication date is "Christmas, 1924."

44. *St. Paul Pioneer Press*, 7 November 1971; Diedrich, *Little Crow*, 254.

Plate Captions

1. Berry, *A Boundless Horizon*, 2; Lanegran, *Minnesota on the Map*, 10; Hayes, *Historical Atlas of Canada*, 49–56.

2. Hayes, *Historical Atlas of Canada*, 60.

3. Lanegran, *Minnesota on the Map*, 12–13; Hayes, *Historical Atlas of Canada*, 60–61.

4. Lanegran, *Minnesota on the Map*, 14–15.

5. Ibid., 16–17; Hayes, *Historical Atlas of Canada*, 62–63.

6. Hayes, *Historical Atlas of Canada*, 58–69; C. Gilman, *Where Two Worlds Meet*; Innis, *The Fur Trade in Canada*, 2.

7. Hayes, *Historical Atlas of Canada*, 58–69; C. Gilman, *Where Two Worlds Meet*.

8. Lahontan quoted in Innis, *The Fur Trade in Canada*, 2; Hayes, *Historical Atlas of Canada*, 58–69.

9. C. Gilman, *Where Two Worlds Meet*; Grant, "Revenge of the Paris Hat," 37–44; Crean, "Hats and the Fur Trade."

10. C. Gilman, *Where Two Worlds Meet*; Grant, "Revenge of the Paris Hat"; Crean, "Hats and the Fur Trade."

11. Podruchny, *Making the Voyageur World*.

12. C. Gilman, *Where Two Worlds Meet*; Sayre, *Les Sauvages Américains*, 227.

13. C. Gilman, *Where Two Worlds Meet*.

14. Champlain quoted in Innis, *The Fur Trade in Canada*, 17; Podruchny, *Making the Voyageur World*; C. Gilman, *Where Two Worlds Meet*.

15. Podruchny, *Making the Voyageur World*.

16. Schultze, *Frances Anne Hopkins*; Podruchny, *Making the Voyageur World*.

17. Lanegran, *Minnesota on the Map*, 26.

18. Melish quoted in Short, *Representing the Republic*, 127.

19. Josephy, *The Artist Was a Young Man*; Dippie, *Catlin and His Contemporaries*; MacLeod, "Peter Rindisbacher, Red River Artist"; Morand, "Peter Rindisbacher."

20. D. Anderson, "The Flow of European Trade Goods into the Western Great Lakes Region, 1715–1760"; Peterson and Brown, eds., *The New Peoples*; J. Brown, *Strangers in Blood*; Sleeper-Smith, *Indian Women and French Men*; Devens, *Countering Colonization*.

21. Berry, *A Boundless Horizon*, 11; C. Gilman, *Where Two Worlds Meet*, 86; J. Brown, *Strangers in Blood*; Lansing, "Plains Indian Women and Interracial Marriage in the Upper Missouri Trade, 1804–1868"; Grimes, Feest, and Curran, *Uncommon Legacies*.

22. Podruchny, *Making the Voyageur*

World; Josephy, *The Artist Was a Young Man,* 6; Peterson, "Many Roads to Red River."

23. Josephy, *The Artist Was a Young Man;* Dippie, *Catlin and His Contemporaries.*

24. Josephy, *The Artist Was a Young Man;* Dippie, *Catlin and His Contemporaries.*

25. Jarvis quoted in Feder, *Art of the Eastern Plains Indians,* 11.

26. Brooklyn Museum of Art, "The Nathan Jarvis Collection of Eastern Plains Art"; Grimes, Feest, and Curran, *Uncommon Legacies;* Drinnon, *Facing West.*

27. Indian Agent Thomas Forsyth, quoted in S. Hall, *Fort Snelling,* 9.

28. Leavenworth, quoted in ibid.

29. S. Hall, *Fort Snelling;* Jones, *Citadel in the Wilderness.*

30. Catlin quoted in Dippie, *Catlin and His Contemporaries,* 184–85; Truettner, *The Natural Man Observed;* Catlin, *George Catlin's Souvenir of the North American Indians.*

31. Quoted from the June 28, 1861, *St. Paul Daily Press* in Green, *A Peculiar Imbalance,* 115.

32. George Simpson to Andrew Colvile, May 20, 1822. Quoted in Josephy, *The Artist Was a Young Man,* 30.

33. Josephy, *The Artist Was a Young Man,* 5–6.

34. Lanegran, *Minnesota on the Map,* 41.

35. McKenney quoted in Drinnon, *Facing West,* 176.

36. Dippie, *Catlin and His Contemporaries.*

37. Grimes, Feest, and Curran, *Uncommon Legacies;* B. White, *We Are at Home.*

38. Dippie, *Catlin and His Contemporaries;* B. White, *We Are at Home.*

39. Brooklyn Museum of Art, "The Nathan Jarvis Collection of Eastern Plains Art"; Hanson, "Laced Coats and Leather Jackets."

40. Feder, *Art of the Eastern Plains Indians,* 11.

41. Brooklyn Museum of Art, "The Nathan Jarvis Collection of Eastern Plains Art."

42. B. White, "The Power of Whiteness."

43. Oliphant, *Minnesota and the Far West,* 255.

44. Lanegran, *Minnesota on the Map,* 42–43.

45. Huyda, *Camera in the Interior, 1858;* Kugel, *To Be the Main Leaders of Our People;* B. White, *We Are at Home;* Wilson, "Working the Light."

46. Kugel, *To Be the Main Leaders of Our People;* Johnston, *Eastman Johnson's Lake Superior Indians;* C. Gilman, *The Grand Portage Story;* B. White, *We Are at Home.*

47. Dippie, *Catlin and His Contemporaries;* Boehme, Feest, and Johnston, *Seth Eastman;* McDermott, *Seth Eastman;* A. Woolworth and N. Woolworth, "Eastern Dakota Settlement and Subsistence Patterns prior to 1851."

48. Feest and Kasprycki, *Peoples of the Twilight;* A. Woolworth and N. Woolworth, "Eastern Dakota Settlement and Subsistence Patterns prior to 1851."

49. Dippie, *Catlin and His Contemporaries;* Boehme, Feest, and Johnston, *Seth Eastman;* G. Anderson, *Little Crow.*

50. Eastman, *Dahcotah,* v.

51. Bremer, *The Homes of the New World,* 2:33.

52. Dippie, *Catlin and His Contemporaries;* Boehme, Feest, and Johnston, *Seth Eastman;* A. Woolworth and N. Woolworth, "Eastern Dakota Settlement and Subsistence Patterns prior to 1851."

53. Mason, "A Sweet Small Something"; Boehme, Feest, and Johnston, *Seth Eastman.*

54. Pond quoted in B. White and Wickre, "Before Statehood," 30; Dippie, *Catlin and His Contemporaries;* Boehme, Feest, and Johnston, *Seth Eastman.*

55. Eastman, *Dahcotah,* xvi; Dippie, *Catlin and His Contemporaries;* Boehme, Feest, and Johnston, *Seth Eastman.*

56. Bremer, *The Homes of the New World,* 2:17.

57. Dippie, *Catlin and His Contemporaries;* Boehme, Feest, and Johnston, *Seth Eastman.*

58. Eastman, *Dahcotah,* v; Boehme, Feest, and Johnston, *Seth Eastman.*

59. R. Brown, "The Great Seal of the State of Minnesota."

60. "A Visit to Red River."

61. "The People of the Red River."

62. R. Gilman, C. Gilman, and Stultz, *The Red River Trails,* 86.

63. Hale, *Early Minneapolis*, 6–7.

64. Sweeny quoted in "The People of the Red River."

65. Ramsey, paraphrased in Newson, *Pen Pictures of St. Paul, Minnesota, and Biographical Sketches of Old Settlers*, 105.

66. Lanegran, *Minnesota on the Map*, 44.

67. Mayer quoted in Heilbron, *With Pen and Pencil on the Frontier in 1851*.

68. Mayer quoted in ibid., 149.

69. Mayer quoted in ibid., 152.

70. Mayer quoted in ibid., 160.

71. Mayer quoted in ibid., 159.

72. Mayer quoted in ibid., 228–29.

73. Mayer quoted in ibid., 232.

74. Lanegran, *Minnesota on the Map*, 50–52.

75. "Sketches from Northwestern America and Canada."

76. Folwell, *A History of Minnesota*, 1:362.

77. B. White and Wickre, "Before Statehood."

78. Ibid.

79. Folwell, *A History of Minnesota*, 1:363.

80. B. White and Wickre, "Before Statehood"; "A Primitive Real Estate Office," in Bromley, *Minneapolis Portrait of the Past*.

81. Folwell, *A History of Minnesota*, 1:363.

82. Conzen, *The Germans in Minnesota*, 21; H. Johnson, "The Founding of New Ulm, Minnesota"; Calloway, "Historical Encounters across Five Centuries," 59–60.

83. *St. Paul Minnesota Pioneer*, November 27, 1851, quoted in "Whitney, Joel Emmons," in Palmquist and Kailbourn, *Pioneer Photographers from the Mississippi to the Continental Divide*, 629.

84. Wilson, "Working the Light."

85. "Whitney's Art Depot," *St. Paul Pioneer*, November 29, 1866, quoted in "Whitney, Joel Emmons," in Palmquist and Kailbourn, *Pioneer Photographers from the Mississippi to the Continental Divide*, 631.

86. Minnesota Historical Photo Collectors Group, *Joel E. Whitney*, 1–4; B. White, *We Are at Home*; B. White and Wickre, "Before Statehood"; Heilbron, *The Thirty-Second State*, 97; B. Johnson, *An Enduring Interest*.

87. Seymour, *Sketches of Minnesota, the New England of the West*, and quoted in Williams, *A History of the City of St. Paul*

and of the County of Ramsey, Minnesota, 214–15.

88. Ibid.

89. Neill, "Saint Paul and Its Environs."

90. Ramsey quoted in B. White, "The Power of Whiteness," 31.

91. Feest, "Johann Baptist Wengler"; Feest and Kasprycki, *Peoples of the Twilight*, 220–21; Seymour, *Sketches of Minnesota, the New England of the West*, and quoted in Williams, *A History of the City of St. Paul and of the County of Ramsey, Minnesota*, 214–15.

92. Minnesota Historical Photo Collectors Group, *Joel E. Whitney*.

93. Neill, "Saint Paul and Its Environs"; Andrews, ed., *History of St. Paul, Minnesota*, 67; Williams, *A History of the City of St. Paul and of the County of Ramsey, Minnesota*, 336–38.

94. Seymour, *Sketches of Minnesota, the New England of the West*, and quoted in Williams, *A History of the City of St. Paul and of the County of Ramsey, Minnesota*, 4:214–15.

95. B. White, *We Are at Home*, 33–43.

96. Sandeen, *St. Paul's Historic Summit Avenue*, 1.

97. Murray, "Recollections of Early Territorial Days and Legislation," and quoted in B. White, "The Power of Whiteness," 40; Baker, "History of Transportation in Minnesota"; Robinson, "Early Economic Conditions and the Development of Agriculture in Minnesota."

98. Sandeen, *St. Paul's Historic Summit Avenue*, 1–5.

99. Stevens quoted in Kane, *The Falls of St. Anthony*, 32–33.

100. Bromley, *Minneapolis Album*; B. White and Wickre, "Before Statehood," 10–11; Blegen, *Minnesota*.

101. Le Duc, "Minnesota at the Crystal Palace Exhibition, New York, 1883"; "Whitney, Joel Emmons," in Palmquist and Kailbourn, *Pioneer Photographers from the Mississippi to the Continental Divide*, 629–32; "Minnehaha Falls and Longfellow's *Hiawatha*."

102. Bromley, *Minneapolis Album*.

103. Ibid.; "The Falls of St. Anthony," in B. White and Wickre, "Before Statehood," 6–7; Minnesota Historical Photo Collectors Group, *Joel E. Whitney*.

104. Bromley, *Minneapolis Album;* Heilbron, *The Thirty-second State;* Millett, *AIA Guide to the Twin Cities,* 123; Green, *A Peculiar Imbalance,* 95–100.

105. Wilson, "Working the Light."

106. Millett, *AIA Guide to the Twin Cities,* 123.

107. Bromley, *Minneapolis Album;* Heilbron, *The Thirty-second State.*

108. Trollope, *North America,* 141.

109. B. White and Wickre, "Before Statehood," 16.

110. *Harper's New Monthly Magazine,* March 1858, 446.

111. U.S. Census Office, Report on the Social Statistics of Cities, 2:697, quoted in Reps, *Cities of the Mississippi,* 300.

112. Dunning, "A Sweeny Sampler."

113. *St. Paul Weekly Times,* May 9, 1857, excerpted in B. White and Wickre, "Before Statehood: Transforming Land and Cultures," 22.

114. Hess and Hess, *Wabasha Street Bridge HAER Report.*

115. Kugel, *To Be the Main Leaders of Our People,* 58–59; B. White, *We Are at Home,* 67–77.

116. Gardner-Sharp, *History of the Spirit Lake Massacre and Captivity of Miss Abbie Gardner,* 291.

117. "Miss Gardiner and Her Fearful Adventure."

118. Gardner-Sharp, *History of the Spirit Lake Massacre and Captivity of Miss Abbie Gardner,* 261–62.

119. Ibid., 261–74.

120. Colonel Lee quoted in Gardner-Sharp, *History of the Spirit Lake Massacre and Captivity of Miss Abbie Gardner,* 279.

121. G. Anderson, *Little Crow,* 98; Fleming and Luskey, *The North American Indians in Early Photographs,* 20–23; Sandweiss, "Picturing Indians," 13–38.

122. Viola, *Diplomats in Buckskins,* 127.

123. Ibid., 27–28.

124. Trollope, *North America,* 130–32.

125. "First Regiment Minnesota Volunteers," in Bromley, *Minneapolis Album.*

126. S. Hall, *Fort Snelling;* Hicks, "Raising the Army in 1861."

127. Murdock, *One Million Men,* 6; Carley,

Minnesota in the Civil War, 140–41; Kunz, *Muskets to Missiles,* 72.

128. *St. Paul Pioneer,* July 31, 1863, quoted in Stephen E. Osman, "Fort Snelling and the Civil War," unpublished manuscript, 2007.

129. Murdock, *One Million Men,* 11; H. H. Sibley to Maj. Gen. John Pope, dated May 30, 1864, and Major General John Pope to General H. H. Sibley, dated June 3, 1864, both quoted in Osman, "Fort Snelling and the Civil War."

130. Thayer quoted in Hale, *Early Minneapolis,* 17–19.

131. Ibid.

132. Wakefield quoted in Namias, *White Captives,* 209.

133. A. Woolworth, "Adrian J. Ebell"; Minnesota Historical Photo Collectors Group, *Joel E. Whitney;* Palmquist and Kailbourn, "Whitney, Joel Emmons," in *Pioneer Photographers from the Mississippi to the Continental Divide,* 631.

134. B. White and Wickre, "Before Statehood," 31–33.

135. Ebell, "The Indian Massacres and War of 1862."

136. Ibid.

137. B. White and Wickre, "Before Statehood," 31–33; A. Woolworth, "Adrian J. Ebell."

138. Palmquist and Kailbourn, "Adrian John Ebell," in *Pioneer Photographs from the Mississippi to the Continental Divide,* 227–28.

139. B. White and Wickre, "Before Statehood," 31–33; A. Woolworth, "Adrian J. Ebell."

140. Palmquist and Kailbourn, "Adrian John Ebell," in *Pioneer Photographs from the Mississippi to the Continental Divide,* 227–28.

141. Ebell, "The Indian Massacres and War of 1862," 20; Chomsky, "The United States–Dakota War Trials."

142. Namias, *White Captives,* 230–31.

143. Ebell, "The Indian Massacres and War of 1862," 16.

144. Letter from Col. Henry Sibley to Maj. Gen. John Pope, October 5, 1862, quoted in Chomsky, "The United States–Dakota War Trials," 26.

145. H. H. Sibley to Sarah Sibley, from Camp Lincoln, one and one-half miles from

Mankato, November 12, 1862, quoted in Namias, *White Captives*, 229; Chomsky, "The United States–Dakota War Trials," 30; Bachman, "Black Dakota," 217; Bakeman and Richardson, *Trails of Tears*.

146. G. Anderson and Woolworth, "Samuel J. Brown Recollections," 227; R. Meyer, *History of the Santee Sioux*, 127–28.

147. Bessler, *Legacy of Violence*, 47–59; Chomsky, "The United States–Dakota War Trials"; Bachman, "Black Dakota"; Namias, *White Captives*, 230.

148. "Memorial," 37th Cong., 3d sess., Executive Doc. no. 7 (December 11, 1862), 1.

149. Ibid., 4; Namias, *White Captives*, 231.

150. Quoted in Namias, *White Captives*, 231.

151. Whipple quoted in Bessler, *Legacy of Violence*, 47.

152. Bessler, *Legacy of Violence*, 57; Allen, *And the Wilderness Shall Blossom*, 11–15, 103–9.

153. Lincoln quoted in Namias, *White Captives*, 231.

154. Lincoln quoted in ibid., 230.

155. Robert Sweeny letter, *St. Paul Dispatch*, March 28, 1886.

156. Ibid.

157. Riggs quoted in Bessler, *Legacy of Violence*, 58.

158. Riggs quoted in Namias, *White Captives*, 236–37.

159. Bessler, *Legacy of Violence*, 60–61; Namias, *White Captives*, 233–35; Bachman, "Black Dakota," 267–68; Koblas, *Let Them Eat Grass*, 3:115–22.

160. Fleming and Luskey, *The North American Indians in Early Photographs*, 49.

161. McConkey, *Dakota War Whoop;* Clapesattle, *The Doctors Mayo*, 77–78.

162. Bessler, *Legacy of Violence*, 61; Bachman, "Black Dakota," 269–70; Carley, *The Dakota War of 1862*, 75; Clapesattle, *The Doctors Mayo*, 70–78, 166–67; Haga, "Another Burial for Dakota Leader," 1B.

163. Wilson, "Working the Light," 45.

164. Minnesota Historical Photo Collectors Group, *Joel E. Whitney*, 1–4.

165. Palmquist and Kailbourn, "Whitney, Joel Emmons," in *Pioneer Photographers from the Mississippi to the Continental Divide*, 631.

166. *St. Paul Pioneer*, August 1862–December 1862, quoted in Monjeau-Marz, *The Dakota Indian Internment at Fort Snelling, 1862–1864*, 44.

167. *The Saint Paul Pioneer*, August 1862–December, 1862, quoted in Monjeau-Marz, *The Dakota Indian Internment at Fort Snelling, 1862–1864*, 44.

168. Diedrich, *Little Crow and the Dakota War*, 151.

169. "Memorial," 37th Cong., 3d sess. Executive Doc. no. 7 (December 11, 1862), 5.

170. R. Meyer, *History of the Santee Sioux*, 261.

171. Hyman, "Survival at Crow Creek, 1863–1866," 151; B. White and Wickre, "Before Statehood," 32–33; Monjeau-Marz, *The Dakota Indian Internment at Fort Snelling, 1862–1864*.

172. Ad from the *St. Paul Daily Press*, Tuesday, March 8, 1864, quoted in Monjeau-Marz, *The Dakota Indian Internment at Fort Snelling, 1862–1864*, 123.

173. Monjeau-Marz, *The Dakota Indian Internment at Fort Snelling, 1862–1864*, 116.

174. Ibid., 38–39.

175. Ibid., 40.

176. McConkey, *Dakota War Whoop*, 277.

177. Hale, *Early Minneapolis*, 21.

178. Ibid., 22.

179. Special Laws of Minnesota, 1864, quoted in Beaulieu, *The Fate of Little Crow*, 16.

180. McConkey, *Dakota War Whoop*, 318.

181. Roddis, *The Indian Wars of Minnesota*, 230–31; *Winona Daily Republican*, September 24, 1863.

182. Heilbron, *Documentary Panorama;* Coen, *Painting and Sculpture in Minnesota, 1820–1914*, 27–31; J. Bell, "The Sioux War Panorama and American Mythic History."

183. Stevens, narrative of the *Panorama of the Indian Massacre of 1862 and the Black Hills*.

184. Ibid.

185. Ibid.

186. Ibid.; "Cowboy Days, the Indian Wars, How the West Was Won."

187. L'Enfant, *The Gág Family*, 58.

188. Ibid.

189. Coen, *Painting and Sculpture in Minnesota, 1820–1914,* 74–76; L'Enfant, *The Gág Family,* 51.

190. Scott, *Wanda Gág,* 22–23.

191. Carley, *The Dakota War of 1862,* 13.

192. Trachtenberg, *Shades of Hiawatha,* 47.

193. L'Enfant, *The Gág Family,* 59–60; Scott, *Wanda Gág.*

194. L'Enfant, *The Gág Family,* 51; Coen, *Painting and Sculpture in Minnesota, 1820–1914,* 93.

195. Scott, *Wanda Gág,* 23.

196. Coen, *Painting and Sculpture in Minnesota, 1820–1914,* 99.

197. Dippie, *Catlin and His Contemporaries,* 303.

198. *The Purchase of an Empire.*

199. Minnesota Historical Society, *Annual Report to the Legislature of Minnesota, for the Year 1868,* 12.

200. "Skull Exhibit Banished," *Minneapolis Journal,* September 8, 1915, 11; "Year of Reconciliation Raises Questions," 2.

201. *Annual Report of the Adjutant General to the Legislature of Minnesota, Session of 1864,* 165.

202. McConkey, *Dakota War Whoop,* 319.

203. Schwandt, *The Captivity of Mary Schwandt,* 19.

204. West, *The Ancestry, Life, and Times of Hon. Henry Hastings Sibley,* 333.

205. Beaulieu, *The Fate of Little Crow;* G. Anderson, *Little Crow,* 181. Deep thanks go to David Beaulieu for providing sources on this subject, including copies of the Minnesota Historical Society Museum Collection Accession Books.

206. A. Daniels, "Reminiscences of Little Crow," 530.

207. G. Anderson, *Little Crow,* 181.

208. Ramsey and Derounian-Stodola, "Dime Novels"; Derounian-Stodola, *The War in Words;* Davis, "Edward S. Ellis and the Minnesota Massacre."

209. Ellis, *Indian Jim,* 11.

210. Ibid., 80.

211. Ibid., 65.

212. Feest, "Germany's Indians in a European Perspective."

213. Calloway, "Historical Encounters across Five Centuries," 71; Feest, *Indians and Europe.*

214. Hoverson, *Land of Amber Waters,* 87.

215. "Sioux Spoon," episode 608 of *History Detectives.*

216. Scott, *Wanda Gág,* 99.

217. Ibid.

218. Deloria, *Playing Indian,* 95–127; Trachtenberg, *Shades of Hiawatha.*

219. Trachtenberg, *Shades of Hiawatha,* 53.

220. Ibid., 52.

221. Hallberg, *Minnehaha Creek.*

222. Torbert, *A Century of Art and Architecture in Minnesota,* 40; Coen, *Painting and Sculpture in Minnesota, 1820–1914,* 92.

223. Pisani, *Imagining Native America in Music,* 243–91; Perison, "The 'Indian' Operas of Charles Wakefield Cadman."

224. Fryberger, *Listening Lesson in Music, Graded for School,* 74.

225. Ibid., 152.

226. Harris, "Ho-ho-ho! It Bears Repeating."

227. Trachtenberg, *Shades of Hiawatha,* xxiii.

228. Albers and James, "Tourism and the Changing Photographic Image of the Great Lakes Indians"; Albers and James, "Images and Reality."

229. El-Hai, *Celebrating Tradition, Building the Future.*

230. Harris, "Ho-ho-ho! It Bears Repeating."

231. Searls, "Suggested Outline for Outdoor Centennial Pageantry."

232. Searls, script for radio interview.

233. Searls, "Suggested Outline for Outdoor Centennial Pageantry."

234. Albers and James, "Tourism and the Changing Photographic Image of the Great Lakes Indians"; Albers and James, "Images and Reality."

235. Linehan, "Students Search for Missing Monument."

236. G. Anderson, *Little Crow,* 181.

Bibliography

Ackermann, Gertrude W. "Joseph Renville of Lac Qui Parle." *Minnesota History* 12 (September 1931): 231–46.

Adams, Ann. "Early Days at Red River Settlement and Fort Snelling." With J. Fletcher Williams. In *Collections of the Minnesota Historical Society*, vol. 6. St. Paul: Pioneer Press Company, 1894.

Adelman, Jeremy, and Stephen Aron. "From Borderlands to Borders: Empires, Nation-States, and the Peoples in Between in North American History." *American Historical Review* 104 (June 1999): 814–41.

Albers, Patricia C. "Santee." In *Handbook of North American Indians*, vol. 4. Edited by Raymond J. DeMallie. Washington, D.C.: Smithsonian Institution, 2001.

———. "Symbiosis, Merger, and War: Contrasting Forms of Intertribal Relationship among Historic Plains Indians." In *The Political Economy of North American Indians*. Edited by John Moore. Norman: University of Oklahoma Press, 1993.

Albers, Patricia C., and William R. James. "Images and Reality: Post Cards of Minnesota's Ojibway People, 1900–1980." *Minnesota History* (Summer 1985): 229–40.

———. "Tourism and the Changing Photographic Image of the Great Lakes Indians." *Annals of Tourism Research* 10 (1983): 123–48.

Albers, Patricia, and Jeanne Kay. "Sharing the Land: A Study in American Indian Territoriality." In *A Cultural Geography of North American Indians*. Edited by Thomas Ross and Tyrel Moore. Boulder, Colo.: Westview Press, 1987.

Allen, Anne Beiser. *And the Wilderness Shall Blossom: Henry Benjamin Whipple*. Afton, Minnesota: Afton Historical Society Press, 2008.

Anderson, Dean L. "The Flow of European Trade Goods into the Western Great Lakes Region, 1715–1760." In *The Fur Trade Revisited: Selected Papers of the Sixth North American Fur Trade Conference, Mackinac Island, Michigan, 1991*. East Lansing: Michigan State University Press, 1994.

Anderson, Gary Clayton. "Early Dakota Migration and Intertribal War: A Revision." *Western Historical Quarterly* 11 (January 1980): 17–36.

———. "Joseph Renville and the Ethos of Biculturalism." In *Being and Becoming Indian: Biographical Studies of the North American Frontiers*. Edited by James Clifton. Chicago: Dorsey Press, 1989.

———. *Kinsmen of Another Kind: Dakota-White Relations in the Upper Mississippi Valley, 1650–1862*. Lincoln: University of Nebraska Press, 1984. Reprint with new material, St. Paul: Minnesota Historical Society Press, 1997.

——. *Little Crow: Spokesman for the Sioux.* St. Paul: Minnesota Historical Society Press, 1986.

Anderson, Gary Clayton, and Alan R. Woolworth, ed. *Through Dakota Eyes: Narrative Accounts of the Minnesota Indian War of 1862.* St. Paul: Minnesota Historical Society Press, 1988.

Andres, General C. C., ed. *History of St. Paul, Minnesota.* Syracuse, N.Y.: D. Mason and Co., 1890.

Annual Report of the Adjutant General to the Legislature of Minnesota: Session of 1864. St. Paul: W. R. Marshall, State Printer, 1864.

Annual Report of the Minnesota Historical Society to the Legislature of Minnesota for the Year 1868. St. Paul: Press Printing Company, 1869.

Atkins, Annette. *Creating Minnesota: A History from the Inside Out.* St. Paul: Minnesota Historical Society Press, 2007.

Babcock, Willoughby M. "With Ramsey to Pembina: A Treaty-Making Trip in 1851." *Minnesota History* 38 (March 1962): 1–10.

Bachman, Walt. "Black Dakota." Unpublished manuscript, in the author's possession.

——. "Colonel Miller's War." In Bakeman and Richardson, *Trails of Tears,* 108–22.

——. "Deaths of Dakota Prisoners from the New Ulm Mob Attack." In Bakeman and Richardson, *Trails of Tears,* 179–80.

——. "Joseph Godfrey: Black Dakota." In *Race, Roots, and Relations: Native and African Americans.* Edited by Terry Strauss. Chicago: Albatross Press, 2005.

Bakeman, Mary H. "The Oldest House in St. Paul: A Sesquicentennial Parable." *Minnesota History* 61 (Summer 2008): 25–35.

Bakeman, Mary H., and Antona Richardson. *Trails of Tears: Minnesota's Dakota Indian Exile Begins.* Roseville, Minn.: Prairie Echoes Press, 2008.

Bakeman, Mary H., and Alan R. Woolworth. "The Family Caravan." In Bakeman and Richardson, *Trails of Tears,* 53–78.

Baker, Gen. James H. "History of Transportation in Minnesota." In *Collections of the Minnesota Historical Society,* vol. 9. St. Paul: Minnesota Historical Society, 1901.

Bardon, Richard, and Grace Lee Nute, eds. "George Nelson's Fur Trade Reminiscences, 1802–1803." In *The North Star State: A Minnesota Reader.* St. Paul: Minnesota Historical Society Press, 2002.

Barry, Colman. *Jacobs Prairie: One Hundred Years.* St. Cloud, Minn.: 1954.

Beaulieu, David L. "The Fate of Little Crow, 1863–1970." Privately published, 1970.

Beck, Paul N. *Inkpaduta: Dakota Leader.* Norman: University of Oklahoma Press, 2008.

Bell, Irvin Wiley. *The Life of Billy Yank: The Common Soldier of the Union.* Indianapolis, Ind.: Bobbs-Merrill Company, 1951.

Bell, John. "The Sioux War Panorama and American Mythic History." *Theatre Journal* 48 (1996): 279–99.

Berghold, Alexander. *The Indians' Revenge, or Days of Horror.* San Francisco: P. J. Thomas, 1891.

Berkhofer, Robert F. Jr. *Salvation and the Savage: An Analysis of Protestant Mission and American Indian Response, 1787–1862.* Westport, Conn.: Greenwood Press, 1977.

Berry, Virginia G. *A Boundless Horizon: Visual Records of Exploration and Settlement in the Manitoba Region, 1624–1874.* Winnipeg Art Gallery, September 15–October 30, 1983.

Bessler, John D. *Legacy of Violence: Lynch Mobs and Executions in Minnesota.* Minneapolis: University of Minnesota Press, 2003.

Big Eagle, Jerome. "Big Eagle's Account." In Anderson and Woolworth, *Through Dakota Eyes.*

——. "A Sioux Story of the War." In *Collections of the Minnesota Historical Society,* vol. 6. St. Paul: Pioneer Press Company, 1894.

Birk, Douglas A., ed. *John Sayer's Snake River Journal, 1804–05: A Fur Trade Diary from East Central Minnesota.* Minneapolis: Institute for Minnesota Archaeology, 1989.

Bishop, Harriet E. *Floral Home, or First Years of Minnesota.* Bowie, Md.: Heritage Books, 2002. Originally published 1857.

"Black Men in the Fur Trade with the Indians." *Gopher Historian* 23 (Winter 1968–69): 1–4.

Blegen, Theodore C. "The 'Fashionable Tour'

on the Upper Mississippi." In *Selections from "Minnesota History": A Fiftieth Anniversary Anthology*. Edited by Rhoda R. Gilman and June Drenning Holmquist. St. Paul: Minnesota Historical Society Press, 1965.

——. *Minnesota: A History of the State*, 2nd ed. Minneapolis: University of Minnesota Press, 1975.

Blight, David W. *Race and Reunion: The Civil War in American Memory*. Cambridge, Mass.: Harvard University Press, 2001.

Board of Commissioners. *Minnesota in the Civil and Indian Wars, 1861–1865*. 2 vols. St. Paul: Pioneer Press, 1893. Reprint, St. Paul: Minnesota Historical Society Press, 2005.

Bodnar, John. *Remaking America: Public Memory, Commemoration, and Patriotism in the Twentieth Century*. Princeton, N.J.: Princeton University Press, 1992.

Boehme, Sarah E., Christian F. Feest, and Patricia Condon Johnston. *Seth Eastman: A Portfolio of North American Indians*. Afton, Minn.: Afton Historical Society Press, 1995.

Bohaker, Heidi. "*Nindoodemag:* The Significance of Algonquian Kinship Networks in the Eastern Great Lakes Region, 1600–1701." *William and Mary Quarterly* 63 (January 2006): 23–52.

Bowden, Henry Warner. *American Indians and Christian Missions: Studies in Cultural Conflict*. Chicago: University of Chicago Press, 1981.

Bray, Edmund C., and Martha Coleman Bray, trans. and ed. *Joseph N. Nicollet on the Plains and Prairies*. St. Paul: Minnesota Historical Society Press, 1976.

Bremer, Frederika. *The Homes of the New World: Impressions of America*, 2 vols. New York, N.Y.: Harper and Brothers, 1853.

Bromley, Edward A. *Minneapolis Album: A Photography History of the Early Days in Minneapolis*. Minneapolis, Minn.: Frank L. Thresher, 1890.

——. *Minneapolis Portrait of the Past: A Photographic History of the Early Days in Minneapolis*. Minneapolis, Minn.: Voyageur Press, 1973.

Brooklyn Museum of Art. "The Nathan Jarvis Collection of Eastern Plains Art." Unpublished research pamphlet. New York: Brooklyn Museum of Art, 2002.

Brown, Jennifer S. H. *Strangers in Blood: Fur Trade Company Families in Indian Country*. Vancouver: University of British Columbia Press, 1980. Reprint, Norman: University of Oklahoma Press, 1996.

Brown, Jennifer S. H., and Elizabeth Vibert, ed. *Reading beyond Words: Contexts for Native History*, 2nd ed. Peterborough, Ontario: Broadview, 2003.

Brown, Robert M. "The Great Seal of the State of Minnesota." *Minnesota History* (Autumn 1952): 126–29.

Brown, Samuel. "Samuel Brown's Recollections." In Anderson and Woolworth, *Through Dakota Eyes*.

Brueggemann, Gary. "Rendezvous at the Riverbend: Pike's Seven Days in the Land of Little Crow; The Wilderness That Later Became St. Paul." *Ramsey County History* 40 (Summer 2005): 4–16.

Brundage, W. Fitzhugh. "No Deed but Memory." In *Where These Memories Grow: History, Memory, and Southern Identity*. Edited by W. Fitzhugh Brundage. Chapel Hill: University of North Carolina Press, 2000.

Bryant, Charles S., and Abel B. Murch. *A History of the Great Massacre by the Sioux Indians in Minnesota, including the Personal Narratives of Many Who Escaped*. Cincinnati, Ohio: Rickey and Carroll, 1864.

Buck, Daniel. *Indian Outbreaks*. Minneapolis, Minn.: Ross & Haines, 1965. Originally published 1904.

Buck, Solon J. "The Story of Grand Portage." In *Selections from "Minnesota History": A Fiftieth Anniversary Anthology*. Edited by Rhoda R. Gilman and June Drenning Holmquist. St. Paul: Minnesota Historical Society, 1965.

Buffalohead, Patricia K. "Farmers, Warriors, Traders: A Fresh Look at Ojibway Women." *Minnesota History* 48 (Summer 1983): 236–44.

Burnham, Michelle. *Captivity and*

Sentiment: Cultural Exchange in American Literature, 1682–1861. Hanover, N.H.: University Press of New England, 1997.

Cabeza de Vaca, Nuñez. *Adventures in the Unknown Interior of America*. Translated and edited by Cyclone Covey. Albuquerque: University of New Mexico Press, 1961.

Calloway, Colin G. "Historical Encounters across Five Centuries." In Calloway, Gemünden, and Zantop, *Germans and Indians*.

———. *One Vast Winter Count: The Native-American West before Lewis and Clark*. Lincoln: University of Nebraska Press, 2003.

———, ed. *Our Hearts Fell to the Ground: Plains Indians Views of How the West Was Lost*. Boston, Mass.: Bedford Books of St. Martin's Press, 1996.

Calloway, Colin G., Gerd Gemünden, and Susanne Zantop, eds. *Germans and Indians: Fantasies, Encounters, Projections*. Lincoln and London: University of Nebraska Press, 2002.

Carley, Kenneth. *The Dakota War of 1862: Minnesota's Other Civil War*, 2nd ed. St. Paul: Minnesota Historical Society Press, 1976.

———. *Minnesota in the Civil War: An Illustrated History*, rev. ed. St. Paul: Minnesota Historical Society Press, 2000.

———. *The Sioux Uprising of 1862*. Reprint, St. Paul: Minnesota Historical Society Press, 1976.

Carroll, Jane Lamm. "'This Higgledy-Piggledy Assembly': The McLeods, an Anglo-Dakota Family in Early Minnesota." *Minnesota History* 60 (Summer 2007): 219–33.

———. "'Who Was Jane Lamont?': Anglo-Dakota Daughters in Early Minnesota." *Minnesota History* 59 (Spring 2005): 184–99.

Cathcart, Rebecca Marshall. "A Sheaf of Remembrances." In *Collections of the Minnesota Historical Society*, vol. 15. St. Paul: Minnesota Historical Society, 1915.

Catlin, George. *George Catlin's Souvenir of the North American Indian: A Facsimile of the Original Album*. With an introductory essay and chronology by William H. Truettner. Tulsa, Okla.: Gilcrease Museum, 2003.

Chomsky, Carol. "The United States–Dakota War Trials: A Study in Military Injustice." *Stanford Law Review* 43 (November 1990): 13–98.

Clapesattle, H. B. *The Doctors Mayo*. Minneapolis: University of Minnesota Press, 1941.

Cleland, Charles E. "Attempts to Move the Chippewa." In McClurken, *Fish in the Lakes*.

———. "The 1842 Treaty of La Pointe." In McClurken, *Fish in the Lakes*.

———. "Off-Reservation Hunting, Fishing, and Gathering in the Post-Treaty Era." In McClurken, *Fish in the Lakes*.

———. "Preliminary Report of the Ethnohistorical Basis of the Hunting, Fishing, and Gathering Rights of the Mille Lacs Chippewa." In McClurken, *Fish in the Lakes*.

———. "Treaties of 1863 and 1864." In McClurken, *Fish in the Lakes*.

Coen, Rena Neumann. *Painting and Sculpture in Minnesota, 1820–1914*. Minneapolis: University of Minnesota Press, 1976.

Commission to Investigate the Official Conduct of Alexander Ramsey, 1854. U.S. Documents serial set 699: 61.

Conzen, Kathleen Neils. *Germans in Minnesota*. St. Paul: Minnesota Historical Society Press, 2003.

———. "Pi-ing the Type: Jane Grey Swisshelm and the Contest of Midwestern Regionality." In *The American Midwest: Essays on Regional History*. Edited by Andrew R. L. Cayton and Susan E. Gray. Bloomington: Indiana University Press, 2001.

Coursolle, Joseph. "Joseph Coursolle's Story." In Anderson and Woolworth, *Through Dakota Eyes*.

"Cowboy Days, the Indian Wars, How the West Was Won." *Life* (May 4, 1959): 74–100.

Crean, J. F. "Hats and the Fur Trade." *Canadian Journal of Economics and Political Science/Revue canadienne d'Economique et de Science politique* 28, no. 3 (August 1962): 373–86.

Cronon, William. *Nature's Metropolis: Chicago and the Great West*. New York: W. W. Norton and Company, 1991.

Curran, Mary Lou. *Uncommon Legacies: Native American Art from the Peabody*

[412]

Essex Museum. Seattle and London: University of Washington Press, 2002.

Daniels, Asa W. "Reminiscences of Little Crow." In *Collections of the Minnesota Historical Society,* vol. 12. St. Paul: Minnesota Historical Society, 1908.

Daniels, Roger. *Coming to America: A History of Immigration and Ethnicity in American Life,* 2nd ed. New York: Harper Perennial, 1991.

Danziger, Edmund Jefferson Jr. *The Chippewas of Lake Superior.* Norman: University of Oklahoma Press, 1979.

Davis, Randall C. "Edward S. Ellis and the Minnesota Massacre." Unpublished paper delivered at the American Culture Association Annual Conference, April 10, 1993.

Debates and Proceedings of the Constitutional Convention for the Territory of Minnesota (Republican Convention). St. Paul: George W. Moore, 1858.

Debates and Proceedings of the Minnesota Constitutional Convention (Democratic Convention). St. Paul: Earle S. Goodrich, 1857.

Deloria, Philip J. *Playing Indian.* New Haven, Conn.: Yale University Press, 1998.

Densmore, Frances. *Chippewa Customs.* Washington, D.C.: Smithsonian Institution, Bureau of American Ethnology, *Bulletin 86,* 1929. Reprint, St. Paul: Minnesota Historical Society, 1979.

Derounian-Stodola, Kathryn Zabelle. *The War in Words: Reading the Dakota Conflict through the Captivity Literature.* Lincoln: University of Nebraska Press, 2009.

Desbarats, Catherine M. "The Cost of Early Canada's Native Alliances: Reality and Scarcity's Rhetoric." *William and Mary Quarterly* 52 (October 1995): 609–30.

Devens, Carol. *Countering Colonization: Native American Women and Great Lakes Missions, 1630–1900.* Berkeley: University of California Press, 1992.

Dickason, Olive Patricia. "From 'One Nation' in the Northeast to 'New Nation' in the Northwest: A Look at the Emergence of the Métis." In *The New Peoples: Being and Becoming Métis in North America.* Edited by Jacqueline Peterson and Jennifer S. H. Brown. Winnipeg: University of Manitoba

Press, 1985. Reprint, St. Paul: Minnesota Historical Society Press, 2001.

Dictionary of Canadian Biography, vol. 3. Toronto: University of Toronto Press, 1974.

Diedrich, Mark. *The Chiefs Hole-in-the-Day of the Mississippi Chippewa.* Minneapolis: Coyote Books, 1986.

———. "A 'Good Man' in a Changing World: Cloud Man, the Dakota Leader, and His Life and Times." *Ramsey County History* 36 (Spring 2001): 4–24.

———. *Little Crow and the Dakota War.* Rochester, Minn.: Coyote Books, 2006.

Dippie, Brian W. *Catlin and His Contemporaries: The Politics of Patronage.* Lincoln and London: University of Nebraska Press, 1990.

Dowd, Gregory Evans. *A Spirited Resistance: The North American Indian Struggle for Unity, 1745–1815.* Baltimore, Md.: Johns Hopkins University Press, 1992.

———. "Wag the Imperial Dog: Indians and Overseas Empires in North America, 1650–1776." In *A Companion to American Indian History.* Edited by Philip J. Deloria and Neal Salisbury. Oxford, UK: Blackwell, 2002.

Drinnon, Richard. *Facing West: The Metaphysics of Indian-Hating and Empire-Building.* Minneapolis: University of Minnesota Press, 1980.

Dunning, Mary Nagle. "A Sweeny Sampler." *Minnesota History* (Spring 1968): 29–33.

Dykstra, Robert R. *Bright Radical Star: Black Freedom and White Supremacy on the Hawkeye Frontier.* Cambridge, Mass.: Harvard University Press, 1993.

Eastlick, Lavinia. *A Personal Narrative of Indian Massacres, 1862.* Publisher unknown, 1864.

Eastman, Mary. *Dahcotah: Life and Legends of the Sioux around Fort Snelling.* New York: John Wiley, 1849.

Ebell, Adrian J. "The Indian Massacres and War of 1862." *Harper's New Monthly Magazine* (June 1863): 4.

Eccles, W. J. "A Belated Review of Harold Adams Innis, *The Fur Trade in Canada.*" *Canadian Historical Review* 9, no. 4 (1979): 419–41.

———. *The Canadian Frontier, 1534–1760.*

Rev. ed. Albuquerque: University of New Mexico Press, 1983.

———. "The Fur Trade and Eighteenth-Century Imperialism." *William and Mary Quarterly* 40 (July 1983): 341–62.

El-Hai, Jack. *Celebrating Tradition, Building the Future: Seventy-five Years of Land O'Lakes.* Minneapolis, Minn.: Land O'Lakes, Inc., 1996.

Ellis, Edward S. *Indian Jim.* New York: Beadle and Company, 1864.

Ewers, John C. "Intertribal Warfare as the Precursor of Indian-White Warfare on the Northern Great Plains." *Western Historical Quarterly* 6 (October 1975): 397–410.

"The Execution of the Minnesota Indians." *Harper's Weekly* (17 January 1863): 39.

Featherstonehaugh, George W. *A Canoe Voyage up the Minnay Sotor,* vol. 1. Reprint, St. Paul: Minnesota Historical Society Press, 1970. Originally published 1847.

Feder, Norman. *Art of the Eastern Plains Indians: The Nathan Sturges Jarvis Collection.* Brooklyn, N.Y.: Brooklyn Museum, 1964.

Feest, Christian F. "Germany's Indians in a European Perspective." In Calloway, Gemünden, and Zantop, *Germans and Indians,* 37–38.

———, ed. *Indians and Europe: An Interdisciplinary Collection of Essays.* Aachen: Edition Herodot, Rader Verlag: 1987.

———. "Johann Baptist Wengler: A Portfolio of Drawings, 1850–1851." *European Review of Native American Studies* 1, no. 1 (1988): 43–50.

Feest, Christian F., and Sylvia S. Kasprycki. *Peoples of the Twilight: European Views of Native Minnesota, 1823 to 1862.* Afton, Minn.: Afton Historical Society Press, 1999.

Fenn, Elizabeth A. *Pox Americana: The Great Smallpox Epidemic of 1775–82.* New York: Hill and Wang, 2001.

Ferguson, Eric. "The Eviction of the Squatters from Fort Snelling." *Hennepin History* 59 (Summer 2000): 22–31.

Ferling, John. *A Leap in the Dark: The Struggle to Create the American Republic.* Oxford, UK: Oxford University Press, 2003.

Fisher, Louis. *Military Tribunals and Presidential Power: American Revolution to the War on Terrorism.* Lawrence: University of Kansas Press, 2005.

Flandrau, Charles E. "The Ink-Pa-Du-Ta Massacre of 1857." In *Collections of the Minnesota Historical Society,* vol. 3. St. Paul: Minnesota Historical Society, 1880.

———. "Reminiscences of Minnesota during the Territorial Period." In *Collections of the Minnesota Historical Society,* vol. 9. St. Paul: Minnesota Historical Society, 1901.

Fleming, Paula Richardson, and Judith Luskey. *The North American Indians in Early Photographs.* New York: Harper and Row Publishers, 1986.

Folwell, William Watts. *A History of Minnesota,* 4 vols. St. Paul: Minnesota Historical Society Press, 1921. Reprint, 1956.

———. *A Visit to Farther-and-Gay Castle.* St. Paul: Minnesota Historical Society, 1931.

Foner, Eric. *Free Soil, Free Labor, Free Men: The Ideology of the Republican Party before the Civil War.* New York: Oxford University Press, 1970.

Forbes, Bruce David. "Methodist Mission among the Dakotas: A Case Study of Difficulties." In *Rethinking Methodist History: A Bicentennial Historical Consultation.* Edited by Russell E. Richey and Kenneth E. Rowe. Nashville, Tenn.: United Methodist Publishing House, 1985.

Freehling, William W. *The Road to Disunion: Secessionists at Bay, 1776–1854.* New York: Oxford University Press, 1990.

Fryberger, Agnes Moore. *Listening Lesson in Music, Graded for School.* Boston, Mass.: Silver, Burdett, and Company, 1916.

Galbraith, John S. "British-American Competition in the Border Fur Trade of the 1820s." *Minnesota History* 36 (September 1959): 241–49.

Galbraith, Thomas S. *Office of Indian Affairs Report for 1863.* Records of the Office of Indian Affairs. Washington, D.C.: National Archives and Records Administration.

Gardner-Sharp, Abbie. *History of the Spirit Lake Massacre and Captivity of Miss Abbie Gardner,* 6th ed. Des Moines, Iowa: Kenyon Printing Company, 1910.

Gates, Charles M. "The Lac Qui Parle Indian

Mission." *Minnesota History* 16 (June 1935): 133–51.

——, ed. "The Narrative of Peter Pond." In *Five Fur Traders of the Northwest*. Edited by Charles M. Gates. St. Paul: Minnesota Historical Society, 1965.

Geary, James W. *We Need Men: The Union Draft in the Civil War*. Dekalb: Northern Illinois University Press, 1991.

"Genesis of the Republican Party in Minnesota." *Minnesota History Bulletin* 2 (February 1917): 24–30.

Genovese, Eugene D. *Roll, Jordan, Roll: The World the Slaves Made*. New York: Vintage Books, 1974.

"George Washington to His Brother Charles." *Mississippi Valley Historical Review* 1 (June 1914): 98–101.

Gibbon, Guy. *The Sioux: The Dakota and Lakota Nations*. Malden, Mass.: Blackwell Publishing, 2003.

Gilman, Carolyn. "The Gens Libres." *Minnesota History* 56 (Winter 1998–99): 175–77.

——. *The Grand Portage Story*. St. Paul: Minnesota Historical Society Press, 1992.

——. *Where Two Worlds Meet: The Great Lakes Fur Trade*. St. Paul: Minnesota Historical Society, 1982.

Gilman, Rhoda R. "The Fur Trade in the Upper Mississippi Valley, 1630–1850." *Wisconsin Magazine of History* 58 (Autumn 1974): 3–18.

——. *Henry Hastings Sibley: Divided Heart*. St. Paul: Minnesota Historical Society Press, 2004.

——. "Last Days of the Upper Mississippi Fur Trade." In *People and Pelts: Selected Papers of the Second American Fur Trade Conference*. Edited by Malvina Bolus. Winnipeg: Peguis Publishers, 1972.

——. "A Northwestern Indian Territory: The Last Voice." *Journal of the West* 39 (January 2000): 16–22.

——. "Reversing the Telescope: Louis Hennepin and Three Hundred Years of Historical Perspective." James Ford Bell Lecture No. 18. Minneapolis: University of Minnesota, 1982.

——. "Territorial Imperative: How Minnesota Became the 32nd State." *Minnesota History* 56 (Winter 1998–99): 154–67.

Gilman, Rhoda R., Carolyn Gilman, and Deborah M. Stultz. *The Red River Trails: Oxcart Routes between St. Paul and the Selkirk Settlement, 1820–1870*. St. Paul: Minnesota Historical Society Press, 1979.

Glewwe, Lois A. "The Journey of the Prisoners: Convoy to South Bend." In Bakeman and Richardson, *Trails of Tears*.

Glueck, Alvin C. Jr. *Minnesota and the Manifest Destiny of the Canadian Northwest: A Study in Canadian-American Relations*. Toronto: University of Toronto Press, 1965.

Goodman, Nancy, and Robert Goodman. *Joseph R. Brown: Adventurer on the Minnesota Frontier, 1820–1849*. Rochester, Minn.: Lone Oak Press, 1996.

Grant, Hugh. "Revenge of the Paris Hat: The European Craze for Wearing Headgear Had a Profound Effect on Canadian History." *The Beaver* (December 1988–January 1989): 37–44.

Green, William D. "Eliza Winston and the Politics of Freedom in Minnesota, 1854–60." *Minnesota History* 57 (Fall 2000): 107–22.

——. "Minnesota's Long Road to Black Suffrage, 1849–1868." *Minnesota History* 56 (Summer 1998): 69–84.

——. *A Peculiar Imbalance: The Fall and Rise of Racial Equality in Early Minnesota*. St. Paul: Minnesota Historical Society Press, 2007.

——. "Race and Segregation in St. Paul's Public Schools, 1846–69." *Minnesota History* 55 (Winter 1996–97): 138–49.

Greenberg, Adolph M., and James Morrison. "Group Identities in the Boreal Forest: The Origin of the Northern Ojibwa." *Ethnohistory* 29 (Spring 1982): 75–102.

Greer, Allan. *The People of New France*. Toronto: University of Toronto Press, 1997.

Grey, Emily O. Goodrich. "The Black Community in Territorial St. Anthony: A Memoir." Edited by Patricia C. Harpole. *Minnesota History* 49 (Summer 1984): 42–53.

Grimes, John R., Christian F. Feest, and Mary Lou Curran. *Uncommon Legacies: Native American Art from the Peabody Essex Museum*. Seattle and London: University of Washington Press, 2002.

Haga, Chuck. "Another Burial for Dakota Leader," *Star Tribune*, July 16, 2000, 1B.

Hage, George S. *Newspapers on the Minnesota Frontier, 1849–1860*. St. Paul: Minnesota Historical Society, 1967.

Hale, Mary Thayer. *Early Minneapolis: Personal Reminiscences of Mary Thayer Hale*. Minneapolis: privately printed, 1937.

Hall, H. P. *H. P. Hall's Observations, Being More or Less a History of Political Contests in Minnesota from 1849 to 1904*. St. Paul, Minn.: 1904.

Hall, Steven P. *Fort Snelling: Colossus of the Wilderness*. St. Paul: Minnesota Historical Society Press, 1987.

Hallberg, Jane King. *Minnehaha Creek: Living Waters*. Minneapolis: Cityscapes Publishing Company, 1988.

Hancock, Joseph Woods. *Goodhue County, Minnesota, Past and Present*. Red Wing, Minn.: Red Wing Printing Company, 1893.

Hanson, James A. "Laced Coats and Leather Jackets: The Great Plains Intercultural Clothing Exchange." In *Plains Indian Studies: A Collection of Essays in Honor of John C. Ewers and Waldo R. Wedel*, Smithsonian Contributions to Anthropology, Number 30. Edited by Douglas H. Ubelake and Herman J. Viola, Washington, D.C.: Smithsonian Institution Press, 1982.

Harpole, Patricia C., and Mary D. Nagle, ed. *Minnesota Territorial Census, 1850*. St. Paul: Minnesota Historical Society, 1972.

Harris, Moira F. "Ho-ho-ho! It Bears Repeating—Advertising Characters in the Land of Sky Blue Waters." *Minnesota History* (Spring 2000): 30.

Hayes, Derek. *Historical Atlas of Canada: Canada's History Illustrated with Original Maps*. Seattle: University of Washington Press, 2002.

Heard, Isaac V. D. *History of the Sioux War and Massacres of 1862 and 1863*. New York: Harper & Brothers, 1864.

Heck, Frank H. *The Civil War Veteran in Minnesota Life and Politics*. Oxford, Ohio: Mississippi Valley Press, 1941.

Heilbron, Bertha. *Documentary Panorama: John Stevens and His Sioux War Pictures*. The Folk Arts Foundation of America, undated. Reprinted from *Minnesota History* (March 1949).

——. *The Thirty-second State: A Pictorial History of Minnesota*. St. Paul: Minnesota Historical Society Press, 1958.

——. *With Pen and Pencil on the Frontier in 1851: The Diary and Sketches of Frank Blackwell Mayer*. St. Paul: Minnesota Historical Society Press, 1986.

Hess, Demian J., and Jeffrey A. Hess. *Wabasha Street Bridge HAER Report*. St. Paul, Minnesota, December 1993.

Hewitt, Nancy A. "Beyond the Search for Sisterhood: American Women's History in the 1980s." In *Unequal Sisters: A Multicultural Reader in U.S. Women's History*. Edited by Ellen Carol DuBois and Vicki L. Ruiz. New York: Routledge, 1990.

Hickerson, Harold. *The Chippewa and Their Neighbors: A Study in Ethnohistory*. New York: Holt, Rinehart, and Winston, 1970. Reprint with new material, Prospect Heights, Ill.: Waveland Press, 1988.

——. *The Southwestern Chippewa: An Ethnohistorical Study*. Menasha, Wis.: American Anthropological Association, 1962.

Hicks, John. "The Organization of the Volunteer Army in 1861 with Special Reference to Minnesota." *Minnesota History Bulletin* 2 (February 1918): 324–68.

——. "Raising the Army in 1861." *Minnesota History Bulletin* 2, no. 5 (February 1918): 333.

Hilger, Inez. *Chippewa Families: A Social Study of White Earth Reservation*. Reprint, St. Paul: Minnesota Historical Society Press, 1998.

Hobart, Chauncey. *History of Methodism in Minnesota*. Red Wing, Minn.: Red Wing Printing Company, 1887.

Hoffert, Sylvia D. "Gender and Vigilantism on the Minnesota Frontier: Jane Grey Swisshelm and the U.S.–Dakota Conflict of 1862." *Western Historical Quarterly* 29 (Autumn 1998): 342–62.

Hoffmann, M. M. *The Church Founders of the Northwest: Loras and Cretin and Other Captains of Christ*. Milwaukee, Wis.: Bruce Publishing Company, 1937.

——. "New Light on Old St. Peter's and Early

St. Paul." *Minnesota History* 8 (March 1927): 27–51.

Hofsommer, Don L. *Minneapolis and the Age of Railways.* Minneapolis: University of Minnesota Press, 2005.

Holmquist, June Drenning, ed. *They Chose Minnesota: A Survey of the State's Ethnic Groups.* St. Paul: Minnesota Historical Society Press, 1981.

Holmquist, June D., and Jean A. Brookins. *Minnesota's Major Historic Sites: A Guide.* St. Paul: Minnesota Historical Society, 1967.

Holton, Woody. "The Ohio Indians and the Coming of the American Revolution in Virginia." *Journal of Southern History* 60 (Aug. 1994): 453–78.

Horrigan, Brian. "Epilogue." In Kenneth Carley, *Minnesota in the Civil War.* Revised ed. St. Paul: Minnesota Historical Society Press, 2000.

Horsman, Reginald. "British Indian Policy in the Northwest, 1807–1812." *Mississippi Valley Historical Review* 45 (June 1958): 51–66.

Hoverson, Doug. *Land of Amber Waters: The History of Brewing in Minnesota.* Minneapolis: University of Minnesota Press, 2007.

Huggan, Nancy McClure. "The Story of Nancy McClure: Captivity among the Sioux." In *Collections of the Minnesota Historical Society,* vol. 6. St. Paul, Minn.: Pioneer Press, 1894.

———. "Nancy McClure Faribault Huggan's Account." In Anderson and Woolworth, *Through Dakota Eyes.*

Hughes, Thomas. "Causes and Results of the Inkpaduta Massacre." In *Collections of the Minnesota Historical Society,* vol. 12. St. Paul: Minnesota Historical Society, 1908.

———. "The Treaty of Traverse des Sioux in 1851, under Governor Alexander Ramsey, with Notes of the Former Treaty There, in 1841, under Governor James Doty of Wisconsin." In *Collections of the Minnesota Historical Society,* vol. 10, part I. St. Paul: Minnesota Historical Society, 1905.

Huyda, Richard J. *Camera in the Interior: 1858, H. L. Hime, Photographer, The Assiniboine and Saskatchewan Exploring Expedition.* Toronto: Coach House Press, 1975.

Hyman, Colette A. "Survival at Crow Creek, 1863–1866." *Minnesota History* 61 (Winter 2008–09): 148–61.

Innis, Harold A. *The Fur Trade in Canada: An Introduction to Canadian Economic History.* New Haven, Conn.: Yale University Press, 1930.

Joel E. Whitney: Minnesota's Leading Pioneer Photographer. St. Paul: Minnesota Historical Photo Collectors Group, 2001.

Johnson, Brooks. *An Enduring Interest: The Photographs of Alexander Gardner.* Norfolk, Va.: Chrysler Museum, 1991.

Johnson, Hildegard Binder. "The Founding of New Ulm, Minnesota." *The American-German Review* (June 1946): 8–12.

———. "The Germans." In Holmquist, *They Chose Minnesota.*

Johnson, John. *En-me-Gah-bowh's Story: An Account of the Disturbances of the Chippewa Indians at Gull Lake in 1857 and 1862 and their Removal in 1868.* Minneapolis, Minn.: Woman's Auxiliary, St. Barnabas Hospital, 1904.

Johnston, Patricia Condon. *Eastman Johnson's Lake Superior Indians.* Afton, Minn.: Johnston Publishing, 1983.

Jones, Evan. *Citadel in the Wilderness: The Story of Fort Snelling and the Old Northwest Frontier.* New York: Coward-McCann, Inc., 1966.

Josephy, Alvin M. Jr. *The Artist Was a Young Man: The Life Story of Peter Rindisbacher.* Fort Worth, Tex.: Amon Carter Museum, 1970.

Kammen, Michael. *Mystic Chords of Memory: The Transformation of Tradition in American Culture.* New York: Vintage Books, 1993.

Kane, Lucile M. *The Falls of St. Anthony: The Waterfall That Built Minneapolis.* St. Paul: Minnesota Historical Society Press, 1987. Originally published as *The Waterfall That Built a City,* 1966.

Kappler, Charles J., ed. *Indian Affairs: Laws and Treaties,* vol. 2. Washington, D.C.: Government Printing Office, 1904.

Kasson, Joy S. *Buffalo Bill's Wild West: Celebrity, Memory, and Popular History.* New York: Hill and Wang, 2000.

Keating, William H. *Narrative of the Expedition to the Source of the St. Peter's River, Lake Winnepeek, Lake of the Woods etc. Performed in the Year 1823.* Minneapolis: Ross and Haines, 1959.

Kellogg, Louise Phelps. "Fort Beauharnois." *Minnesota History* 8 (Summer 1927): 232–46.

Kelly, Patrick J. "The Election of 1896 and the Restructuring of Civil War Memory." *Civil War History* 49, no. 3 (2003): 254–80.

Kidwell, Clara Sue. "Indian Women as Creole Mediators." *Ethnohistory* 39 (Spring 1992): 97–101.

Klement, Frank. "The Abolition Movement in Minnesota." *Minnesota History* 32 (March 1951): 15–33.

Koblas, John. *Let Them Eat Grass: The 1862 Sioux Uprising in Minnesota.* 3 vols. St. Cloud, Minn.: North Star Press, 2006, 2008.

Kolodny, Annette. *The Land Before Her: Fantasy and Experience of the American Frontiers, 1630–1860.* Chapel Hill: University of North Carolina Press, 1984.

———. "Rethinking Frontier Literary History as the Stories of First Cultural Contact." *Frontiers: A Journal of Women's Studies* 17 (1996): 14–18.

Kugel, Rebecca. "Of Missionaries and Their Cattle: Ojibwa Perceptions of a Missionary as Evil Shaman." *Ethnohistory* 41 (Spring 1994): 227–44.

———. *To Be the Main Leaders of Our People: A History of Minnesota Ojibwe Politics, 1825–1898.* East Lansing: Michigan State University Press, 1998.

Kunz, Virginia Brainard. *Muskets to Missiles: A Military History of Minnesota.* St. Paul: Minnesota Statehood Centennial Commission, 1958.

Lanegran, David A. *Minnesota on the Map: A Historical Atlas.* With the assistance of Carol L. Urness. St. Paul: Minnesota Historical Society Press, 2008.

Lansing, Michael. "Plains Indian Women and Interracial Marriage in the Upper Missouri Trade, 1804–1868." *Western Historical Quarterly* 31, no. 4 (Winter 2000): 413–33.

Larsen, Arthur J., ed. *Crusader and Feminist: Letters of Jane Grey Swisshelm.* St. Paul: Minnesota Historical Society, 1934.

Larson, Agnes M. *History of the White Pine Industry in Minnesota.* Minneapolis: University of Minnesota Press, 1949.

Larson, Peggy Rodina. "A New Look at the Elusive Inkpaduta." *Minnesota History* 48 (Spring 1982): 24–35.

Lass, William E. *Minnesota: A History*, 2nd ed. New York: W. W. Norton and Company, 1998.

Laub, C. Herbert. "British Regulation of Crown Lands in the West: The Last Phase, 1773–1775." *William and Mary College Quarterly Magazine*, 2nd Ser. 10 (January 1930): 52–55.

Lavender, David. *The Fist in the Wilderness.* Garden City, N.Y.: Doubleday, 1964. Reprint with new material, Lincoln: University of Nebraska Press, 1998.

———. "Some Characteristics of the American Fur Company." *Minnesota History* 40 (Winter 1966): 178–89.

Lears, T. J. Jackson. *No Place of Grace: Antimodernism and the Transformation of American Culture, 1880–1920.* Chicago: University of Chicago Press, 1981.

Le Duc, W. G. *Minnesota Yearbook for 1852.* St. Paul: Minnesota Territory, 1852.

Le Duc, William G. "Minnesota at the Crystal Palace Exhibition, New York, 1883." *Minnesota History Bulletin* 1, no. 7 (August 1916): 351–68.

Lee, Lorenzo Porter. *History of the Spirit Lake Massacre! And of Miss Abigail Gardiner's Three Month's Captivity among the Indians.* New Britain, Conn.: L. P. Lee, 1857.

Lee, Minnie Mary (Wood, Julia A.). "Life in the Woods." Serialized reminiscences in the Sauk Rapids *New Era*, 26 January–19 April 1860.

Lehman, Christopher P. "Sylvanus Lowry and Slavery in St. Cloud," parts I and II. *Crossings* 31 (January and March 2005): 3–8 and 3–12.

L'Enfant, Julie. *The Gág Family: German-Bohemian Artists in America.* Afton, Minn.: Afton Historical Society Press, 2002.

Linderman, Gerald F. *Embattled Courage: The Experience of Combat in the American Civil War.* New York: The Free Press, 1987.

Linehan, Dan. "Students Search for Missing Monument." *Mankato Free Press,* Mankato, Minnesota, 14 May 2006.

Lockwood, James H. "Early Times and Events in Wisconsin." In *Second Annual Report and Collections of the State Historical Society of Wisconsin, for the Year 1855.* Madison, Wis.: Calkins and Proudfit, 1856.

Lowenthal, David. *The Heritage Crusade and the Spoils of History.* Reprint, Cambridge: Cambridge University Press, 2005.

Lurie, Nancy Oestreich. "Winnebago." In *Handbook of North American Indians,* vol. 15. Edited by Bruce D. Trigger. Washington, D.C.: Smithsonian Institution, 1978.

MacLeod, Margaret Arnett. "Peter Rindisbacher, Red River Artist." *The Beaver* (December 1945): 30–36.

Maier, Pauline. *From Resistance to Revolution: Colonial Radicals and the Development of American Opposition to Britain, 1765-1776.* Reprint, New York: W. W. Norton and Company, 1991.

Malmros, Oscar. *Annual Report of the Adjutant General to the Legislature of Minnesota: Session of 1864.* St. Paul, Minnesota, 1863.

Mancall, Peter C. "Men, Women, and Alcohol in Indian Villages in the Great Lakes Region in the Early Republic." *Journal of the Early Republic* 15 (Autumn 1995): 425–48.

Marling, Karal Ann. *Blue Ribbon: A Social and Pictorial History of the Minnesota State Fair.* St. Paul: Minnesota Historical Society Press, 1990.

Marshall, William. "Notes on Conditions in 1863." Handwritten manuscript, Minnesota Historical Society, St. Paul, Minnesota.

Marti, Donald B. "The Puritan Tradition in a 'New England of the West.'" *Minnesota History* 40 (Summer 1966): 1–11.

Marx, Leo. *The Machine in the Garden: Technology and the Pastoral Ideal in America.* New York: Oxford University Press, 1964.

Mason, Carol I. "A Sweet Small Something: Maple Sugaring in the New World." In *The Invented Indian, Cultural Fictions and Government Politics.* Edited by James A. Clifton. New Brunswick and London: Transaction Publishers, 1990.

Mayer, Frank Blackwell. *With Pen and Pencil on the Frontier in 1851.* St. Paul: Minnesota Historical Society Press, 1932.

Mazakootemane, Paul. "Narrative of Paul Mazakootemane." Translated by Rev. S. R. Riggs. In *Collections of the Minnesota Historical Society,* vol. 3. St. Paul: Minnesota Historical Society, 1880: 82–90.

McClurken, James, compiler, with Charles E. Cleland, Thomas Lund, John D. Nichols, Helen Tanner, and Bruce White. *Fish in the Lakes, Wild Rice, and Game in Abundance: Testimony on Behalf of Mille Lacs Ojibwe Hunting and Fishing Rights.* East Lansing: Michigan State University Press, 2000.

McConkey, Harriet E. Bishop. *Dakota War Whoop, or Indian Massacres and War in Minnesota, of 1862–63.* St. Paul, Minn.: published by the author, 1863.

McConnell, Michael N. *A Country Between: The Upper Ohio Valley and Its Peoples, 1724-1774.* Lincoln: University of Nebraska Press, 1992.

McDermott, John Francis. *Seth Eastman: Pictorial Historian of the Indian.* Norman: University of Oklahoma Press, 1961.

Meinig, D. W. *The Shaping of America: A Geographical Perspective on 500 Years of History,* vol. 1, *Atlantic America, 1492-1800.* New Haven, Conn.: Yale University Press, 1986.

——. *The Shaping of America: A Geographical Perspective on 500 Years of History,* vol. 2, *Continental America, 1800-1867.* New Haven, Conn.: Yale University Press, 1993.

"Memorial Notices of Rev. Gideon H. Pond." In *Collections of the Minnesota Historical Society,* vol. 3. St. Paul: Minnesota Historical Society, 1880.

"Memorial to the President of the United

States," 37th Congress, 3rd sess. Executive Doc. No. 7, Dec. 11, 1862.

Meyer, Melissa L. *The White Earth Tragedy: Ethnicity and Dispossession at a Minnesota Anishinaabe Reservation.* Lincoln: University of Nebraska Press, 1994.

Meyer, Roy W. *History of the Santee Sioux: United States Indian Policy on Trial.* Lincoln: University of Nebraska Press, 1967.

Millett, Larry. *AIA Guide to the Twin Cities.* St. Paul: Minnesota Historical Society Press, 2007.

"Minnehaha Falls and Longfellow's *Hiawatha*," *Minnesota History* 8, no. 3 (September 1927): 281–82.

Minnesota Historical Photo Collectors Group. *Joel E. Whitney: Minnesota's Leading Pioneer Photographer.* St. Paul, Minn., 2001.

Minnesota Historical Society. *Land of the Ojibwe.* St. Paul, Minn., 1973.

Minnesota History Bulletin 1, no. 7 (August 1916): 1.

Minnesota in the Civil and Indian Wars, 1861–1865. Reprint, St. Paul: Minnesota Historical Society Press, 2005. Originally published in 1891.

"Miss Gardiner and Her Fearful Adventure." *Ballou's Pictorial* 13, no. 8 (August 22, 1857).

Moe, Richard. *The Last Full Measure: The Life and Death of the First Minnesota Volunteers.* New York: Henry Holt and Co., 1993. Reprint, St. Paul: Minnesota Historical Society Press, 2001.

Monjeau-Marz, Corinne L. *The Dakota Indian Internment at Fort Snelling, 1862–1864.* St. Paul, Minn.: Prairie Smoke Press, 2005.

Morand, Anne. "Peter Rindisbacher: Colonist and Earliest Painter of North American West." *Gilcrease Magazine of American History and Art* 11, no. 1 (January 1989): 22–32.

Morris, Lucy Leavenworth Wilder, ed. *Old Rail Fence Corners: Frontier Tales Told by Minnesota Pioneers.* Reprint, St. Paul: Minnesota Historical Society, 1976.

Morton, Zylpha S. "Harriet Bishop, Frontier Teacher." *Minnesota History* 28 (1947): 132–41.

Murdock, Eugene C. *One Million Men: The Civil War Draft in the North.* Madison: State Historical Society of Wisconsin, 1971.

Murphy, Lucy Eldersveld. *A Gathering of Rivers: Indians, Métis, and Mining in the Western Great Lakes.* Lincoln: University of Nebraska Press, 2000.

——. "Public Mothers: Native American and Métis Women as Creole Mediators in the Nineteenth-Century Midwest." *Journal of Women's History* 14 (Winter 2003): 142–66.

Murray, William P. "Recollections of Early Territorial Days and Legislation." In *Collections of the Minnesota Historical Society,* vol. 12. St. Paul: Minnesota Historical Society, 1908.

Nairn, John. "A History of the Sioux Massacre: The Personal Recollections of the Late John Nairn." Unpublished manuscript, Minnesota Historical Society.

Namias, June. *White Captives: Gender and Ethnicity on the American Frontier.* Chapel Hill: University of North Carolina Press, 1993.

Nash, Gary B. "The Hidden History of Mestizo America." *Journal of American History* 82 (December 1995): 941–64.

Neill, Edward Duffield. *The History of Minnesota from the Earliest French Explorations to the Present Time.* 5th ed. Minneapolis: Minnesota Historical Company, 1883.

——. "History of the Ojibways." In *Collections of the Minnesota Historical Society,* vol. 5. St. Paul: Minnesota Historical Society, 1885.

——. "Occurrences in and around Fort Snelling from 1819 to 1840." In *Collections of the Minnesota Historical Society,* vol. 2. St. Paul: Minnesota Historical Society, 1889.

——. "Saint Paul and Its Environs." *Graham's Magazine* 46, no. 1 (January 1855): 6.

——. "A Sketch of Joseph Renville." In *Collections of the Minnesota Historical Society,* vol. 1. St. Paul: Ramaley, Chaney, and Co., 1872.

Newcombe, Barbara T. "'A Portion of the American People': The Sioux Sign a Treaty

[420]

in Washington in 1858." *Minnesota History* (Fall 1976): 83–96.

Newson, Thomas McLean. *Pen Pictures of St. Paul, Minnesota, and Biographical Sketches of Old Settlers: From the Earliest Settlement of the City, up to and including the Year 1857,* vol. 1. St. Paul, Minn.: Privately published, 1886.

"Next-Door Cultures, New and Old," in White and Wickre, "Before Statehood: Transforming Land and Cultures," *Roots* 20, no. 1 (Fall 1991): 10–11.

Nichols, David A. *Lincoln and the Indians: Civil War Policy and Politics.* Columbia: University of Missouri Press, 1978.

———. "The Other Civil War: Lincoln and the Indians." *Minnesota History* 44 (Spring 1974): 3–15.

Nute, Grace Lee. "Posts in the Minnesota Fur-Trading Area, 1660–1855." *Minnesota History* 11 (December 1930): 353–85.

Nziramasanga, Caiphas T. "Minnesota: First State to Send Troops." *Journal of the West* 14 (January 1975): 42–59.

Oestreicher, Richard. "Urban Working-Class Political Behavior and Theories of American Electoral Politics, 1870–1940." *Journal of American History* 74 (March 1988): 1257–86.

O'Leary, Cecilia Elizabeth. "Blood Brotherhood: The Racialization of Patriotism, 1865–1918." In *Bonds of Affection: Americans Define Their Patriotism.* Edited by John Bodnar. Princeton, N.J.: Princeton University Press, 1996.

Oliphant, Laurence. *Minnesota and the Far West.* London, UK: W. Blackwood and Sons, 1855.

Osman, Stephen E. "The Brower Boys' Civil War." *Minnesota History* 61 (Winter 2008–09): 162–67.

———. "They Put Us in the Bull Pen: The Draft Rendezvous." Unpublished paper, in the author's possession.

Owens, John Phillips. "Political History of Minnesota from 1847 to 1862." Handwritten manuscript, ca. 1870. Minnesota Historical Society, St. Paul, Minnesota.

Palmquist, Peter E., and Thomas R. Kailbourn. *Pioneer Photographers from the Mississippi to the Continental Divide:*

A Biographical Dictionary, 1839–1865. Stanford, Calif. Stanford University Press, 2005.

"The People of the Red River." *Harper's New Monthly Magazine* 18 (January 1859): 169–70.

Perison, Harry D. "The 'Indian' Operas of Charles Wakefield Cadman." *College Music Symposium* 22, no. 2 (Fall 1982): 20–50.

Peterson, Jacqueline. "Many Roads to Red River: Métis Genesis in the Great Lakes Region, 1680–1815." In *The New Peoples: Being and Becoming Métis in North America.* Edited by Jacqueline Peterson and Jennifer S. H. Brown. Winnipeg: University of Manitoba Press, 1985. Reprint, St. Paul: Minnesota Historical Society Press, 2001.

———. "Prelude to Red River: A Social Portrait of the Great Lakes Métis." *Ethnohistory* 25 (Winter 1978): 41–67.

———. "Women Dreaming: The Religiopsychology of Indian-White Marriages and the Rise of a Métis Culture." In *Western Women: Their Land, Their Lives.* Edited by Lillian Schlissel, Vicki L. Ruiz, and Janice Monk. Albuquerque: University of New Mexico Press, 1988.

Peterson, Jacqueline, and Jennifer S. H. Brown, ed. *The New Peoples: Being and Becoming Métis in North America.* Winnipeg: University of Manitoba Press, 1985. Reprint, St. Paul: Minnesota Historical Society, 2001.

Peterson, William J. *Steamboating on the Upper Mississippi.* Iowa City: State Historical Society of Iowa, 1968.

Phillips, Clifton Jackson. *Protestant America and the Pagan World: The First Half Century of the American Board of Commissioners for Foreign Missions, 1810–1860.* Cambridge, Mass.: Harvard University Press, 1969.

Pisani, Michael V. *Imagining Native America in Music.* New Haven, Conn.: Yale University Press, 2005.

Pluth, Edward J. "The Failed Watab Treaty of 1853." *Minnesota History* 57 (Spring 2000): 2–22.

Podruchny, Carolyn. *Making the Voyageur World: Travelers and Traders in the North*

American Fur Trade. Lincoln and London: University of Nebraska Press, 2006.

Pond, Samuel W. *Dakota Life in the Upper Midwest.* St. Paul: Minnesota Historical Society, 1908. Reprint with new material, 1986.

Population of the United States in 1860, Compiled from the Original Returns of the Eighth Census. Washington, D.C.: Government Printing Office, 1864.

Porter, Kenneth. "Contacts in Other Parts." *Journal of Negro History* 17 (July 1932): 359–67.

——. "Negroes and the Fur Trade." *Minnesota History* 15 (December 1934): 421–33.

Pratt, Julius W. "Fur Trade Strategy and the American Left Flank in the War of 1812." *American Historical Review* 40 (January 1935): 246–73.

Prescott, Philander. *The Recollections of Philander Prescott: Frontiersman of the Old Northwest, 1819–1862.* Edited by Donald Dean Parker. Lincoln: University of Nebraska Press, 1966.

Presidential Message, 37th Cong., 3d sess., Executive Doc. no. 7 (December 11, 1862), 1.

Pritchett, John Perry. *The Red River Valley, 1811–1849: A Regional Study.* New York: Carnegie Endowment for International Peace, 1942. Reprint, New York: Russell and Russell, 1970.

Prucha, Francis Paul. *American Indian Treaties: The History of a Political Anomaly.* Berkeley: University of California Press, 1994.

——. "The Settler and the Army in Frontier Minnesota." In *Selections from Minnesota History.* Edited by Rhoda R. Gilman and June Drenning Holmquist. St. Paul: Minnesota Historical Society, 1965, 39–51.

Ramsey, Colin T., and Kathryn Zabelle Derounian-Stodola. "Dime Novels," in *A Companion to American Fiction, 1780–1865,* ed. Shirley Samuels, 262–73. Malden, Mass.: Blackwell Publishing, 2004.

Ray, Arthur J. *Indians in the Fur Trade: Their Role as Trappers, Hunters, and Middlemen in the Lands Southwest of Hudson Bay, 1660–1870.* Toronto: University of Toronto Press, 1974. Reprint 1998.

Reardon, James Michael. *The Catholic Church in the Diocese of St. Paul from Earliest Origin to Centennial Achievement.* St. Paul, Minn.: North Central Publishing Company, 1952.

Regan, Ann. *Irish in Minnesota.* St. Paul: Minnesota Historical Society Press, 2002.

A Report on Barracks and Hospitals: With Descriptions of Military Posts. Washington, D.C.: Government Printing Office, 1870.

Reps, John W. *Cities of the Mississippi: Nineteenth-Century Images of Urban Development.* Columbia and London: University of Missouri Press, 1994.

Rich, E. E. "Colonial Empire." *Economic History Review* 2 (1950): 317–25.

Richter, Daniel K. *Facing East from Indian Country: A Native History of Early America.* Cambridge, Mass.: Harvard University Press, 2001.

——. *The Ordeal of the Longhouse: The Peoples of the Iroquois League in the Era of European Colonization.* Chapel Hill: University of North Carolina Press, 1992.

Riggs, Stephen R. *Mary and I: Forty Years with the Sioux.* Reprint, Minneapolis, Minn.: Ross and Haines, 1969. Originally published 1880.

——. "Protestant Missions in the Northwest." In *Collections of the Minnesota Historical Society,* vol. 6. St. Paul: St. Paul Pioneer Press, 1894.

Roark, James L. et al., ed. *The American Promise: A History of the United States.* Boston: Bedford/St. Martin's, 2000.

Robinson, Edward Van Dyke. "Early Economic Conditions and the Development of Agriculture in Minnesota." *Bulletin of the University of Minnesota, Studies in the Social Sciences,* no. 3 (March 1915): 32.

Roddis, Louis H. *The Indian Wars of Minnesota.* Cedar Rapids, Iowa: Torch Press, 1956.

Roediger, David R. *The Wages of Whiteness: Race and the Making of the American Working Class.* New York: Verso, 1991.

Rorabaugh, W. J. *The Alcoholic Republic: An American Tradition.* New York: Oxford University Press, 1981.

Rubinstein, Mitchell E., and Alan R.

Woolworth. "The Dakota and Ojibway." In Holmquist, *They Chose Minnesota.*

Rubinstein, Sarah P. "The French Canadians and French." In Holmquist, *They Chose Minnesota,* 36–54.

"Saint Paul and Its Environs." *Graham's Magazine* (Philadelphia), 46, no. 1 (January 1855): 3–17.

Sandeen, Ernest R. *St. Paul's Historic Summit Avenue.* Minneapolis: University of Minnesota Press, 2004.

Sandweiss, Martha A. "Picturing Indians: Curtis in Context." In *The Plains Indian Photographs of Edward S. Curtis.* Lincoln and London: University of Nebraska Press, 2001.

Satterlee, Marion. *A Detailed Account of the Massacre by the Dakota Indians of Minnesota in 1862.* Minneapolis, Minn.: Self-published, 1923.

Savage, Kirk. *Standing Soldiers, Kneeling Slaves: Race, War, and Monument in Nineteenth-Century America.* Princeton, N.J.: Princeton University Press, 1997.

Sayre, Gordon Mitchell. *Les Sauvages Américains: Representations of Native Americans in French and English Colonial Literature.* Chapel Hill: University of North Carolina Press, 1997.

Schenck, Theresa M. "The Cadottes: Five Generations of Fur Traders on Lake Superior." In *The Fur Trade Revisited: Selected Papers of the Sixth North American Fur Trade Conference, Mackinac Island, Michigan, 1991.* Edited by Jennifer S. H. Brown, W. J. Eccles, and Donald Heldman. East Lansing: Michigan State University Press, 1994.

——. *William W. Warren: The Life, Letters, and Times of an Ojibwe Leader.* Lincoln: University of Nebraska Press, 2007.

Schultze, Thomas. *Frances Anne Hopkins: Images from Canada.* Manotick, Ontario: Penumbra Press, 2008.

Schwalm, Leslie A. "'Overrun with Free Negroes': Emancipation and Wartime Migration in the Upper Midwest." *Civil War History* 50, no. 2 (2004): 145–74.

Schwandt, Mary. *The Captivity of Mary Schwandt.* Fairfield, Washington: Ye Galleon Press, 1975.

——. "The Story of Mary Schwandt." In *Collections of the Minnesota Historical Society,* vol. 6. St. Paul: Pioneer Press, 1894.

Scott, Alma. *Wanda Gág: The Story of an Artist.* Minneapolis: University of Minnesota Press, 1949.

Seeba, Joseph P. "Minnesota, Slavery, and the Coming of the Civil War." Master's thesis, California State University, Dominguez Hills, 1999.

Sewell, Richard H. *A House Divided: Sectionalism and Civil War, 1848–1865.* Baltimore, Md.: Johns Hopkins University Press, 1988.

Seymour, E. S. *Sketches of Minnesota, the New England of the West.* New York: Harper and Brothers, 1850.

Short, John Rennie. *Representing the Republic: Mapping the United States, 1600–1900.* London: Reaktion, 2001.

Shutter, Marion Daniel. *History of Minneapolis: Gateway to the Northwest,* vol. 1. Chicago: S. J. Clarke Publishing Company, 1923.

Sibley, Henry. "Memoir of Hercules L. Dousman." In *Collections of the Minnesota Historical Society,* vol. 3. St. Paul: Minnesota Historical Society, 1880.

——. "Memoir of Jean Baptiste Faribault." In *Collections of the Minnesota Historical Society,* vol. 3. St. Paul: Minnesota Historical Society, 1880: 168–79.

——. "Sketch of John Other Day." In *Collections of the Minnesota Historical Society,* vol. 3. St. Paul: Minnesota Historical Society, 1880: 99–102.

Silber, Nina. *The Romance of Reunion: Northerners and the South, 1865–1900.* Chapel Hill: University of North Carolina Press, 1993.

"Sioux Spoon." Episode 608 of *History Detectives.* Oregon Public Broadcasting, August 18, 2008.

"Sketches from Northwestern America and Canada: A Portfolio of Water Colors by Franz Holzlhuber." *American Heritage* 16, no. 4 (June 1965): 19–64.

Skinner, Claiborne A. *The Upper Country: French Enterprise in the Colonial Great Lakes.* Baltimore, Md.: Johns Hopkins University Press, 2008.

Sklar, Kathryn Kish. *Catherine Beecher: A Study in American Domesticity*. New Haven, Conn.: Yale University Press, 1973.

"Skull Exhibit Banished." *Minneapolis Journal*, 8 September 1915, p. 11.

Sleeper-Smith, Susan. *Indian Women and French Men: Rethinking Cultural Encounter in the Western Great Lakes*. Amherst: University of Massachusetts Press, 2001.

——. "'An Unpleasant Transaction on This Frontier': Challenging Female Autonomy and Authority at Michilimackinac." *Journal of the Early Republic* 25 (Fall 2005): 417–34.

——. "Women, Kin, and Catholicism: New Perspectives on the Fur Trade." *Ethnohistory* 47 (Spring 2000): 423–52.

Slotkin, Richard. *Gunfighter Nation: The Myth of the Frontier in Twentieth-Century America*. New York: Atheneum, 1992.

Smith, Alice Elizabeth. *James Duane Doty: Frontier Promoter*. Madison: State Historical Society of Wisconsin, 1954.

Smith, Dane. "God of Peace: Milles' Finest Creation in Stone." *Ramsey County History* 17 (1982): 17–18.

Smith, David C. *City of Parks: The Story of Minneapolis Parks*. Minneapolis: Foundation for Minneapolis Parks, 2008.

Smith, Herbert A. "Church and State in North America." *Yale Law Journal* 35 (February 1926): 461–71.

Smith-Rosenberg, Carroll. "Beauty, the Beast, and the Militant Woman: A Case Study of Sex Roles and Social Stress in Jacksonian America." *American Quarterly* 23 (1971): 562–84.

Snana. "Narration of a Friendly Sioux." In *Collections of the Minnesota Historical Society*, vol. 9. St. Paul: Minnesota Historical Society, 1901.

Sommerdorf, Norma. "Harriet E. Bishop: A Doer and and a Mover." *Minnesota History* 55 (Fall 1997): 320–23.

——. "No Grass beneath Her Feet: Harriet Bishop and Her Life in Minnesota." *Ramsey County History* 32 (Summer 1997): 16–21.

Southwick, Sally J. *Building on a Borrowed Past: Place and Identity in Pipestone,*

Minnesota. Athens: Ohio University Press, 2005.

Spangler, Earl. *The Negro in Minnesota*. Minneapolis, Minn.: T. S. Denison & Company, 1961.

Sperry, F. J. *The Purchase of an Empire: The Treaty of Traverse des Sioux with the Sioux Indians on the Minnesota River, July 23, 1851*. Mankato, Minn.: Hubbard Milling Company, 1924.

Starkey, James. "Reminiscences of Indian Depredations in Minnesota." In *Glimpses of the Nation's Struggle*, third series. New York and St. Paul: D. D. Merrill Company, 1893.

Stevens, John. Narrative of the "Panorama of the Indian Massacre of 1862 and the Black Hills." Curator's Notebook, Stevens Panorama. Minnesota Historical Society. St. Paul, Minnesota.

Stevens, John H. *Personal Recollections of Minnesota and Its People, and Early History of Minneapolis*. Minneapolis: Privately published, 1890.

Stewart, Thomas Rice. *Thomas R. Stewart Memoirs*. Reproduced in part in Bakeman and Richardson, *Trails of Tears*.

Stonehouse, Merlin. *John Wesley North and the Reform Frontier*. Minneapolis: University of Minnesota Press, 1965.

Sundstrom, Linea. "Smallpox Used Them Up: Reference to Epidemic Disease in Northern Plains Winter Counts, 1714–1920." *Ethnohistory* 44 (Spring 1997): 305–43.

Swanson, Deborah, ed. "Joseph Farr Remembers the Underground Railroad in St. Paul." *Minnesota History* 57 (Fall 2000): 123–28.

Swisshelm, Jane Grey. *Crusader and Feminist: Letters of Jane Grey Swisshelm*. Edited by Arthur J. Larsen. St. Paul: Minnesota Historical Society, 1934.

Taliaferro, Lawrence. "Auto-biography." In *Collections of the Minnesota Historical Society*, vol. 6. St. Paul: Pioneer Press Company, 1894.

Tanner, Helen Hornbeck. *The Ojibwas*. Bloomington: Indiana University Press, 1976.

"Taoyateduta Is Not a Coward." *Minnesota History* 38 (September 1962): 115.

Tarble, Helen M. *The Story of My Capture*

and Escape during the Minnesota Indian Massacre of 1862. St. Paul, Minn.: Abbott Printing Company, 1904.

Taylor, Alan. *The Divided Ground: Indians, Settlers, and the Northern Borderland of the American Revolution*. New York: Vintage Books, 2006.

Taylor, David Vassar. "The Blacks." In Holmquist, *They Chose Minnesota*.

———. "Pilgrim's Progress: Black St. Paul and the Making of an Urban Ghetto, 1870–1930." Ph.D. diss., University of Minnesota, 1977.

Tester, John R. *Minnesota's Natural Heritage: An Ecological Perspective*. Minneapolis: University of Minnesota Press, 1995.

Thompson, Neil B. *Minnesota's State Capitol: The Art and Politics of a Public Building*. St. Paul: Minnesota Historical Society, 1974.

Tolzmann, Don Heinrich, ed. *German Pioneer Accounts of the Great Sioux Uprising of 1862*. Milford, Ohio: Little Miami Publishing Company, 2002.

Torbert, Donald R. *A Century of Art and Architecture in Minnesota*. Minneapolis: University of Minnesota Press, 1958.

Trachtenberg, Alan. *The Incorporation of America: Culture and Society in the Gilded Age*. New York: Hill and Wang, 1982.

———. *Shades of Hiawatha: Staging Indians, Making Americans, 1880–1930*. New York: Hill and Wang, 2004.

Treuer, Anton Steven. "Ojibwe-Dakota Relations: Diplomacy, War and Social Union, 1679–1862." Master's thesis, University of Minnesota, 1994.

Trimble, Steve. *In the Shadow of the City: A History of the Loring Park Neighborhood*. Minneapolis, Minn.: Minneapolis Community College Foundation, undated.

Trollope, Anthony. *North America*. New York: Harper and Brothers, 1862.

Truettner, William H. *The Natural Man Observed: A Study of Catlin's Indian Gallery*. Washington, D.C.: Smithsonian Institution Press, 1979.

Twelfth Census of the United States—1900. Census Reports, vol. 1, Population Part I, 2–3.

Uchida, Ayako. "The Protestant Mission and Native American Response: The Case of the Dakota Mission, 1835–1862." *Japanese Journal of American Studies* 10 (1999): 153–75.

Upham, Warren. *Minnesota in Three Centuries, 1655–1908*. Mankato: Publishing Society of Minnesota, 1908.

"The Upper Mississippi." *Harper's New Monthly Magazine* 16 (March 1858): 433–54.

VanderVelde, Lea, and Sandhya Subramanian. "Mrs. Dred Scott." *Yale Law Journal* (January 1997): 1033–1122.

Van Kirk, Sylvia. *Many Tender Ties: Women in Fur-Trade Society, 1670–1870*. Norman: University of Oklahoma Press, 1980.

Viola, Herman J. *Diplomats in Buckskins: A History of Indian Delegations in Washington City*. Washington, D.C.: Smithsonian Institution Press, 1981.

Vishneski, John S. III. "What the Court Decided in Dred Scott v. Sandford." *American Journal of Legal History* 32 (October 1988): 373–90.

"A Visit to Red River." *Harper's New Monthly Magazine* 13, no. 73 (June 1856).

Voegeli, Jacque. "The Northwest and the Race Issue, 1861–1862." *Mississippi Valley Historical Review* 50 (September 1963): 235–51.

Wakefield, Sarah F. *Six Weeks in the Sioux Tepees*. Minneapolis: Atlas Print Co., 1863. Reprint, Guilford, Conn.: Globe Pequot Press, 2004.

Wallis, Wilson D. "Beliefs and Tales of the Canadian Dakota." *Journal of American Folklore* 36 (Jan.–Mar. 1923): 36–101.

Warkentin, Germaine. "Discovering Radisson: A Renaissance Adventurer between Two Worlds." In *Reading Beyond Words: Contexts for Native History*, 2nd ed. Edited by Jennifer S. H. Brown and Elizabeth Vibert. Peterborough, Ontario: Broadview, 2003.

Warren, William W. *History of the Ojibway People*. St. Paul: Minnesota Historical Society, 1885. Reprint with new material, St. Paul: Minnesota Historical Society Press, 1984.

Wedel, Mildred Mott. "Le Sueur and the Dakota Sioux." In *Aspects of Upper Great*

Lakes Anthropology: Papers in Honor of Lloyd A. Wilford. Edited by Elden Johnson. St. Paul: Minnesota Historical Society, 1974.

Welter, Barbara. "The Cult of True Womanhood, 1820–1860." *American Quarterly* 18 (1966): 151–74.

West, Nathaniel. *The Ancestry, Life, and Times of Hon. Henry Hastings Sibley*. St. Paul: Pioneer Press Publishing Company, 1889.

Wheelock, Joseph. "Memoir of Joseph R. Brown." In *Collections of the Minnesota Historical Society*, vol. 3. St. Paul: Minnesota Historical Society, 1880.

Whipple, Henry Benjamin. *Lights and Shadows of a Long Episcopate: Being Reminiscences and Recollections of the Right Reverend Henry Benjamin Whipple, Bishop of Minnesota*. New York: Macmillan Company, 1899.

White, Bruce M. "Encounters with Spirits: Ojibwa and Dakota Theories about the French and Their Merchandise." *Ethnohistory* 41 (Summer 1994): 369–405.

———. "'Give Us a Little Milk': The Social and Cultural Meanings of Gift Giving in the Lake Superior Fur Trade." *Minnesota History* 48 (Summer 1982): 60–70.

———. *Grand Portage as a Trading Post: Patterns of Trade at "the Great Carrying Place."* Grand Marais, Minn.: National Park Service, 2005.

———. "Indian Visits: Stereotypes of Minnesota's Native People." *Minnesota History* 53 (Fall 1992): 99–111.

———. "A Mouthful of Grass." In *Ringing in the Wilderness: Selections from the North Country Anvil*. Edited by Rhoda R. Gilman. Duluth, Minn.: Holy Cow Press, 1996: 259–67.

———. "The Power of Whiteness, or The Life and Times of Joseph Rolette Jr." *Minnesota History* 56, no. 4 (Winter 1998): 178–97.

———. "Pressure for Removal." In McClurken, *Fish in the Lakes*, 160–71.

———. "Regional Context of the Removal Order of 1850." In McClurken, *Fish in the Lakes*.

———. "A Skilled Game of Exchange: Ojibway

Fur Trade Protocol." *Minnesota History* 53 (Summer 1987): 229–40.

———. *We Are at Home: Pictures of the Ojibwe People*. St. Paul: Minnesota Historical Society Press, 2007.

———. "White Population Growth in the Minnesota Region." In McClurken, *Fish in the Lakes*.

———. "The Woman Who Married a Beaver: Trade Patterns and Gender Roles in the Ojibwa Fur Trade." *Ethnohistory* 46 (Winter 1999): 109–47.

White, Bruce M., and John Wickre. "Before Statehood: Transforming Land and Cultures." *Roots* 20, no. 1 (Fall 1991): 14.

White, Richard. *The Middle Ground: Indians, Empires, and Republics in the Great Lakes Region, 1650–1815*. Cambridge: Cambridge University Press, 1991.

———. *The Roots of Dependency: Subsistence, Environment, and Social Change among the Choctaws, Pawnees, and Navajos*. Lincoln: University of Nebraska Press, 1983.

———. "The Winning of the West: The Expansion of the Western Sioux in the Eighteenth and Nineteenth Centuries." *Journal of American History* 65 (September 1978): 319–43.

Willand, Jon. *Lac Qui Parle and the Dakota Mission*. Madison, Minn.: Lac Qui Parle County Historical Society, 1964.

Williams, J. Fletcher. *A History of the City of St. Paul to 1875*. St. Paul: Minnesota Historical Society, 1876. Reprint, 1983.

Wills, Jocelyn. *Boosters, Hustlers, and Speculators: Entrepreneurial Culture and the Rise of Minneapolis and St. Paul, 1849–1883*. St. Paul: Minnesota Historical Society Press, 2005.

Wilson, Bonnie G. "Working the Light: Nineteenth-Century Professional Photographers in Minnesota." *Minnesota History* 52, no. 2 (Summer 1990): 42–60.

Wingerd, Mary Lethert. "The Americanization of Cold Spring: Cultural Change in an Ethnic Community." Honors thesis, Macalester College, 1990.

———. *Claiming the City: Politics, Faith, and the Power of Place in St. Paul*. Ithaca, N.Y.: Cornell University Press, 2001.

Witgen, Michael. "The Rituals of Possession:

Native Identity and the Invention of Empire in Seventeenth-Century Western North America." *Ethnohistory* 54 (Fall 2007): 639–68.

Wood, Julia. "Book on the Early Days." Handwritten reminiscence. William H. Wood and Family. Papers. Minnesota Historical Society. St. Paul, Minn.

Woodward, C. Vann. *Origins of the New South, 1877–1913*. Baton Rouge: Louisiana State University Press, 1951. Reprint, 1971.

Woolworth, Alan R. "Adrian J. Ebell, Photographer and Journalist of the Dakota War of 1862." *Minnesota History* (Summer 1994): 87–92.

Woolworth, Alan R., and Nancy L. Woolworth. "Eastern Dakota Settlement and Subsistence Patterns Prior to 1851." *Minnesota Archaeologist* 39, no. 2 (1980): 71–89.

Woolworth, Nancy L. *The White Bear Lake Story*. Publisher unknown, 1968.

Worchester, Donald E., and Thomas F. Schilz. "The Spread of Firearms among the Indians on the Indian-French Frontiers." *American Indian Quarterly* 8 (Spring 1984): 103–15.

Wyatt-Brown, Bertram. *The Shaping of Southern Culture: Honor, Grace, and War, 1760s–1880s*. Chapel Hill: University of North Carolina Press, 2000.

"Year of Reconciliation Raises Questions, Society Responds to Sensitive Cultural Issues." *Minnesota History News* 28 (November–December 1987): 2.

Zeman, Carrie R. "The Formation of the Renville Rangers." Working paper in Wingerd's possession.

[426]

Newspapers

Faribault Central Republican
Mankato Independent
Mankato Weekly Record
Minneapolis Journal
Minneapolis Tribune
Minnesota Pioneer and Democrat
Minnesota Republican
Minnesotian
New Era (Sauk Rapids)
Nininger City Emigrant Aid Journal
St. Anthony Express
St. Cloud Democrat
St. Paul Daily Press
St. Paul Democrat
St. Paul Pioneer and Democrat
St. Paul Pioneer Press
St. Peter Tribune
Shakopee Independent
Stillwater Gazette
Traverse County Star
Winona Republican

Illustration Credits

The University of Minnesota Press gratefully acknowledges the following institutions and individuals who provided permission to reproduce the illustrations in this book.

The illustrations on the following pages are reproduced courtesy of the Minnesota Historical Society (MHS Visual Resources Database negative numbers in parentheses):

Page 94 (83781), page 98 (95363), page 110 (90240), page 119 (97194), page 182 (83849), page 201 (88975), page 206 (64769), page 233 (94486), page 275 (89595), page 289 (63973), page 308 (83378), page 317 (94207), page 323 (88923).

The illustration on page 195 (NL004442) is reproduced courtesy of the Edward E. Ayer Collection, The Newberry Library, Chicago.

Plates 1–3, 5–9, 15, 18, 45, 49, 52, and 54 courtesy of the James Ford Bell Library, University of Minnesota.

Plates 4, 11, 19, 27, 30, 33, 34, 39 (8840), 41, 44, 47 (12701), 55 (49986), 57, 58 (390), 59 (8115), 60, 69, 71 (9177-B), 72 (51515), 73 (34995), 76, 77 (8327), 78 (5787), 79 (583), 80 (821), 81 (7987), 82 (2545-B), 83a (16808), 83b (1815), 84, 85 (82908), 86 (102776), 87,

88 (71401), 90 (96988), 91 (877), 92, 93, 94 (720), 95 (36703), 96 (969), 97 (62949), 98 (11817), 99 (737), 100 (1593), 101–10, 112 (36736), 113 (36715), 114 (35939), 115 (9105-B), 116 (36722), 117 (90850), 118–26, 127 (59027), 128 (3510), 131, 134, 135, 137, 138, and 139 courtesy of the Minnesota Historical Society (MHS Visual Resources Database negative numbers in parentheses).

Plates 10, 12, 13, 14, and 130 courtesy of Archives and Special Collections, University of Minnesota Libraries.

Plates 16 (HBCA 1987/363-C-11A/T72; watercolor) and 21 (HBCA P-116) courtesy of the Hudson's Bay Company Archives, Archives of Manitoba, Hudson's Bay Company Collection, Manitoba Museum.

Plates 17 (1989-401-3; oil), 31 (1988-250-31; watercolor), 32 (1988-250-36; pen and ink over pencil), and 42 (1936-273) courtesy of the Library and Archives of Canada.

Plates 20, 23, and 25 courtesy of the West Point Museum Art Collection, United States Military Academy, West Point, New York.

Plate 22 (G-82-215; watercolor and ink on paper, 8.5 x 10.4 inches) courtesy of the

Winnipeg Art Gallery, acquired with financial assistance from the National Museums of Canada. Photograph by Ernest Mayer, the Winnipeg Art Gallery.

Plate 24 (1964.74; hand-colored lithograph, 9 1/8 x 15 7/16 inches) courtesy of the Amon Carter Museum, Fort Worth, Texas.

Plates 26 (50.67.20a-b) and 38 (50.67.7a) courtesy of the Nathan Sturges Jarvis Collection of Eastern Plains Art, Brooklyn Museum of Art, New York, the Henry L. Batterman Fund and the Frank Sherman Benson Fund.

Plates 28 (0176.2119) and 89 (4326.4756) courtesy of the Gilcrease Museum, Tulsa, Oklahoma.

Plate 29 (1985.66.335) courtesy of the Smithsonian Museum of American Art, Washington, D.C. / Art Resource, New York.

Plate 35 (E25409) courtesy of the Peabody Essex Museum, Salem, Massachusetts.

Plates 36 (08828600), 111 (06585200), and 129 (00627300) courtesy of the National Anthropological Archives, Smithsonian Institution.

Plate 37 (NPG.70.14; oil on canvas, 62.5 x 52.5 x 2.75 inches) courtesy of the National Portrait Gallery, Smithsonian Institution. Gift of May C. Kinney, Ernest C. Kinney, and Bradford Wickes.

Plate 40 (2000.75.1) courtesy of the Minneapolis Institute of Arts. Gift of funds from Duncan and Nivin MacMillan.

Plate 43 (62.181.11) courtesy of the St. Louis County Historical Society, permanent collection, Duluth, Minnesota.

Plates 46, 74, and 75 courtesy of Oberösterreichischen Landesmuseen (Upper Austrian State Museums), Linz, Austria.

Plate 48 (78.29 F; oil on canvas, 37 x 32

inches) courtesy of the Rockwell Museum of Western Art, Corning, New York. Gift of Robert F. Rockwell Jr.

Plates 50 and 51 (watercolor) courtesy of the Seth Eastman, LLC. Photographs courtesy of the Minneapolis Institute of Arts.

Plate 53 (oil on canvas) from the collection of the United States House of Representatives. Photograph courtesy of the Architect of the Capitol.

Plates 56 (55.53.11; lithograph) and 70 (65.39.108; watercolor) courtesy of the collection of Glenbow Museum, Calgary, Canada.

Plates 61 and 63 (watercolor) courtesy of the collection of Goucher College, Baltimore, Maryland.

Plates 62 (NL000334) and 66 (NL000194) courtesy of the Edward E. Ayer Collection, The Newberry Library, Chicago.

Plate 64 courtesy of Museo Civico di Scienze Naturali, Bergamo, Italy.

Plates 65, 67, and 68 courtesy of the Rare Books Division, New York Public Library, Astor, Lenox, and Tilden Foundations.

Plate 132 courtesy of the collection of Jim and Ruth Beaton. Photograph by Robert Fogt.

Plate 133 courtesy of the collection of Nancy Johnson. Photograph by Robert Fogt.

Plate 136 courtesy of the collection of Moira and Leo Harris.

Plate 140 (86.1160) courtesy of the Hirshhorn Museum and Sculpture Garden, Smithsonian Institution, The Joseph H. Hirshhorn Bequest, 1981. Photograph by Lee Stalsworth, Hirshhorn Museum.

Plate 141 courtesy of Minnesota Public Radio News. mpr.org. Photograph by Mark Steil.

Index

*All place names are located in Minnesota
unless otherwise specified.*

abolitionism/abolitionists, 175, 239–45, 247,
253, 257, 282, 388n43

Accault, Michel, 18–20, 367n54, 367n56

acculturation, Indian, xvi, 187, 267, 287, 291,
304–5, 347; Brown's plan for, 273–80, 292,
293, 294, 306; examples of, 172, 173, 265;
resistance to, 272–73, 292–93; strategies
for, 219, 271, 288, 290–91. *See also*
assimilation, Indian; farmer Indians

Acton raid, 259, 304

adoption: by Indians, 13, 19, 22, 32, 56,
387n27

African Americans, 232, 238–39, 244, 246;
laws regarding, 240; segregation of, 246,
388n57; voting rights denied to, 253, 254,
387n34, 387n36. *See also* race; slavery

agriculture. *See* farmer Indians; farming,
white

Aird, James, 70, 145

Aitkin, William, 88, 97, 130, 133, 170

alcohol: attempts to ban, 77–78, 95–96, 184,
207, 241, 242, 243–44, 246; as bargaining
chip, 68, 84, 130, 139, 166, 299; Indians'
consumption of, 68, 138, 158, 183, 218,
222; soldiers' consumption of, 90–91, 95,
158; as trade good, 59, 159, 161, 173, 261

Aldrich, Cyrus, 318

Algonquian Indians, 5, 9, 42, 365n3. *See also*
Ojibwe (Ojibway, Anishinaabeg, Chippewa)
Indians

American Fur Company, 96, 174; bankruptcy
of, 140, 142, 152; Hudson's Bay Company
and, 127, 163; outfits of, 92, 374n55; in
trade wars, 83–85; treaty payments to, 131,
136, 139. *See also* St. Paul Outfit; Western
Outfit

American Revolution, 59–64

Ames, Charles G., 242

ammunition. *See* firearms

Anderson, Gary Clayton, 21, 38, 132, 271,
341–42, 368n68, 381n46

Anglo-Americans, 54, 55, 176, 355, 356,
372n64

Anglo-Canadians, 65, 67, 68. *See also* French
Canadians

Anishinaabeg Indians: origin of name, xv.
See also Ojibwe (Ojibway, Anishinaabeg,
Chippewa) Indians

annuities: delays in payments, 135–36, 188–
89, 193–94, 213–14, 276–77, 297–98, 300–
303; economy based on, 139–41, 166, 181–
83; fraud related to, 133, 138, 169, 197–98,
201, 295–97, 358; Indians' dependence
on, 130, 138–39, 167, 199, 200, 202–3,
218, 274; shifts in payment locations,
140, 166, 212, 213, 219–20, 222; as tribal
income, 171, 188, 194, 288; withholding as
punishment, 204, 264–65, 273, 279, 331.

also Indians: removal of; *and individual reservations and treaties*

respect: Indian code of, 42, 70, 167, 305

Rice, Edmund, 281

Rice, Henry, 201, 239, 255, 281, 386n15; on annuities, 140, 300; as Congressional delegate, 244, 245; Democrats supporting, 198, 226–31, 243–44, 250; as fur trader, xvi, 267; Indian removal efforts, 166, 220, 339; land speculation by, 143, 161, 197–98, 211, 222; partnership with Ramsey, 386n6; prominence in St. Paul, 198, 383n36; rivalry with Sibley, 180, 197–98; role in land cession treaties, 200–201, 217, 272, 287, 385n89; as statehood promoter, 247; as territorial booster, 177, 178, 179; timber speculation by, 153, 222; treaty payments to, 383n44

Richter, Daniel, 14

Riggs, Stephen, 109–10, 237, 266, 293, 317; conversions of Dakotas, 107, 330–31, 376n46; at Dakota Conflict trials, 316–18, 324–25, 396n42, 397n66; on intermarriage, 148, 149; promotes Indian farming, 170, 273, 287; relations with Indians, 267, 302–3; role in land cession treaties, 186, 188, 190, 192, 196, 203

Robert Dickson & Company, 371n63

Robertson, Daniel, 203, 204

Robertson, Tom, 311

Rocque, Augustin, 377n32

Rogers, Robert, 50–51, 52

Rolette, Jane (wife of Joseph, Sr.), 146

Rolette, Joseph, Jr., 124, 269–70; state capital bill, 250

Rolette, Joseph, Sr.: as fur trader, 83, 93, 95, 97–98, 128, 142, 374n55; intermarriage by, 70, 145–46

Rondo (Rondeaux), Joseph, 125, 160

Rum River dispute, 216–17

Rumtown, 159

Running Walker (Dakota leader), 203

Russell, Jeremiah, 384n61

Russell, Sophia, 209, 384n61

Sac Indians: battling white settlement, 82, 89; Dakota peace negotiations with, 99, 134; land cessions by, 137; removal of, 143, 260

Sacred Born (Mdewakanton chief), 22, 30

Sacred Heart (town), 296

Sandy Lake band of Ojibwe, 63, 153

Sandy Lake Indian agency, 78, 213–14, 215

Santee Sioux, 4, 337

Satterlee, Marion, 400n4

Saulters band of Ojibwe, 12–13, 17

Sault Ste. Marie (Michigan), 5, 6, 12–13, 116, 366n33

sawmills, 136, 176, 210, 211, 216

Sayer, John, 58; children of, 57, 68

Sayer, Nancy (Obe-mau-unoqua, Ojibwe, wife of John), 57, 68

scalping/scalps: bounties for, 329–30, 338, 348; exaggerated stories of, 89, 267; by Indians, 30, 291, 336; of Little Crow, 343, 346, 347, 348, 349; by whites, 301, 320, 347–48

Scandinavians. *See* immigrants/immigration: Scandinavian

Schadecker, Barbara Ann, 91, 124–25

Schoolcraft, Henry, 102, 103, 352, 374n3

Schoolcraft, James, 147

Schwandt, Mary, 306–7, 347

Scots-Canadians: in trade wars, 83–85

Scott, Dred, 235–36, 387n23; Supreme Court decision, 253, 256–57

Scott, Harriet Robinson, 235–36, 387n23

Second Great Awakening, 106, 118

segregation, 246, 388n57

Selkirk, Earl of. *See* Douglas, Lord Thomas

settlement/settlers, white: on ceded lands, 100, 196, 199, 202, 278–79; culture of, 150, 377n14; Dakota Conflict and, 311, 348–49; displacement of, 157, 160; effects on fur trade, 97, 123, 131; effects on Indian-white relations, xvi–xvii, 25, 104–5, 259–60, 267–73, 287, 347; expansion of, 99, 104, 144, 281, 338; first, 121; fur trade vs., 60–61, 123, 131, 226–29; hunting hurt by, 199, 267, 270, 273, 279, 292, 295, 297; moratoriums on, 48–49, 59–60, 89, 96, 99, 104, 176; as volunteer soldiers, 282. *See also* immigrants/immigration; squatters; Yankees

Seven Years' War (1754–1763), 369n41. *See also* French and Indian War

Severance, Martin, 294

Seymour, E. S., 151

Shagoda (Ojibwe Indian), 269–70

Shakopee (Mdewakanton chief), 392n46

Mary Lethert Wingerd
is associate professor of history at St. Cloud State University
in St. Cloud, Minnesota. She is the author of *Claiming the
City: Politics, Faith, and the Power of Place in St. Paul.*

Kirsten Delegard
is coeditor of *Women, Families, and Communities* and
author of a forthcoming book on women's politics.